ABSENT VOICES

The Story of Writing Systems in the West

In Memoriam

William Altman

ABSENT VOICES

The Story of Writing Systems in the West

Rochelle Altman

OAK KNOLL PRESS

New Castle, Delaware

2004

First Edition 2004

Published by **Oak Knoll Press**
310 Delaware Street, New Castle, Delaware, USA
Web:http://www.oakknoll.com

ISBN: 1-58456-108-4

Title: Absent Voices
Author: Rochelle Altman
Typographer: R. I. Altman
Publishing Director: J. Lewis von Hoelle

Library of Congress Cataloging-in-Publication Data

Altman, Rochelle.
 Absent voices: the story of writing systems in the West / Rochelle Altman
  p. cm.
 Includes bibliographical references and index.
 ISBN 1-58456-108-4
  1. Writing--History. 2. Written communication--History. I. Title.

P211.A53 2003
411'.09--dc21   2003050627

Excerpts of this book appear in *Psalms from the Paris Psalter: Psalm 23(22)* © 1993; *Beowulf: Diplomatic e-text*, 1994-1995; An Application and a Text: Electronic Research Diplomatic Editions for Computers in the Humanities © 1995; "Writing Systems and Manuscripts" © 1999; "Some Aspects of Older Writing Systems: With Focus on the DSS" © 1999; "Report on the Zoilos Votive Inscription from Tel-Dan" © 2001; "The Writing World of the Dead Sea Scrolls" © 2001; "Report on the James Ossuary," © 2002; "The Size of the Law: Document Dimensions and their Significance in the Imperial Administration," in *Confrontation in Late Antiquity: Imperial Presentation and Regional Adaptation?*, © Orchard Academic Press, 2003; "Report on the Temple Tablet," © 2003.

This work was printed in the United States of America on 60# archival, acid-free paper meeting the requirements of the American Standard for Permanence of Paper for Printed Library Materials.

CONTENTS

ILLUSTRATIONS

Maps

Tables

Plates

Scores

Figures

ACKNOWLEDGEMENTS

This book has been twelve years in the writing and forty-nine years in the making. Thirty-five of those years were spent as an artisan working with, and doing research on, script systems and the history of writing systems; fourteen years were spent in concentrated research on the purely academic side. While this combination may sound somewhat peculiar, as it turned out, both areas—the artisan and the academic—were necessary for a complete understanding of writing systems.

The text itself has gone through sundry incarnations during those twelve years. Originally written as separate scholarly monographs (where the footnotes just about equaled the text), this final version came into being as a result of suggestions made by readers of the scholarly monographs—most of whom appear in sources mentioned in the Bibliography.

After so many years, it may be impossible to name all who have had a hand in this book; nevertheless, there remain more than a few people to whom special thanks are due.

On the artisan side, I wish to acknowledge my debts to Masters Josephine Anderson, Sabrina Engleberg, and J. Cahill. I also want to thank Master Printer Joseph Alkalai who ensured that I could run a press, "just in case."

On the academic side, I must include a long overdue thank you to Dr. Margaret Annan, who many years ago sparked my interest in Old English, and another thank you to Dr. Louis Martin, who thirty years later rekindled that spark.

Particular thanks are due to Marilyn Wurzburger, head of the Department of Special Collections at the Hayden Library on the main campus of Arizona State University. I also wish to express my gratitude to the dedicated, resourceful, and always cheerful staff of the Inter-Library Loan department at the Hayden Library.

Thanks are due to the Trustees of the British Library, London, England; The Master and Fellows of Corpus Christi College, Cambridge, Cambridge, England; the Royal Irish Academy, Dublin, Ireland; the Russian National Library, Saint Petersburg, Russia; and the Syndics of Cambridge University Library, Cambridge, England for permission to include scans from relevant manuscripts.

Among those who read the purely scholarly versions, grateful acknowledgments are due to Dr. Raymond Sherer of Harrisburg, Pennsylvania and Drs. Paul Gottfried and Anthony Matteo of Elizabethtown, Pennsylvania for their encouragement and belief that this complicated subject was worth the time and effort of writing up. I am much obliged to Drs. Robert E. Stevick, Professor Emeritus at the University of Washington; Patrick W. Conner of the University of West Virginia; Robert D. Reynolds of Arizona State University; and Herbert Basser of Queens University, Ontario for their generosity in giving their time in their areas of expertise. Many thanks to Drs. Alan Cooper and Mark Brennan of the Hebrew Union College for help on some knotty philological questions with respect to Biblical Hebrew. Thank you also to Professor John Risseeuw, artist, master calligrapher, and historian of printing at Arizona State University, whose comments were both helpful and amusing.

Dr. Marvin M. Fisher, Professor Emeritus of English Literature, also at Arizona State University, gamely plowed through the first trial "lay" version, for which heroic feat I am eternally grateful.

Somewhere along the line, Timothy Romano, whose innate understanding of poetry is probably unsurpassed, volunteered as reader for this final version. The expansion of overly condensed material and further explanations of what otherwise would have been murky and difficult to grasp are due to his sharp eyes and intelligent comments. Thank you, Tim.

This book, however, would not have been completed without the patience, support, and encouragement of three people in particular. Across ten years, David R. Howlett, Fellow of Corpus Christi College Oxford, read through each version and each chapter of the book as it appeared. Each time he approached the material as if it were new and unfamiliar. Each time his broad and deep knowledge brought forth helpful comments and useful suggestions that could only improve the book. I doubt if it is possible to adequately express my gratitude, but I can at least try: Thank you, David. Needless to say, I bear sole responsibility for any errors that may remain.

If the book be readable, this is due to the efforts of Bette Lee Howland, prize winning author. Her comments and suggestions were always both constructive and to the point. It is impossible to amply thank Bette for taking time away from her own work to act as reader.

My greatest debt is to my husband, William, to whose memory this book is dedicated. Bill was both my severest critic and my greatest supporter. Without him, this book would not even have been begun.

R.I.S.A.

Part One

WORDS

INTRODUCTION

"Why," asks the Mad Hatter, "is a raven like a writing desk?" Because both echo the voice of the speaker! As contradictory as the proposed answer to this riddle may seem, it is a statement of fact.

Writing may have begun with the recording of trade, but its potential for taxation purposes was rapidly perceived. Very early, writing was recognized as a means to spread legal orders and otherwise communicate a spoken word. From the beginning, the main purpose of writing was to record the voice of the speaker—in other words, the writing systems were oral.

Like the raven and the writing desk, the tablet, the scroll, the codex (early book), or other writing allowed the reader to hear the spoken word. Oral writing systems are the concrete reality behind the term "the voice of authority."

This book is about oral writing systems as complex unities. Although there are many publications on written and spoken communications, there are no books that address either oral writing systems or writing systems as systems. Writing systems, however, are systems in the precise dictionary meaning of the word: "A set or assemblage of things connected, associated, or interdependent, so as to form a complex unity; a whole composed of parts in an orderly arrangement according to some scheme or plan." The interconnectedness of a writing system means that when we examine only a script system or a spelling system or a content system, we are creating boxes, separating the parts from the whole. Although it is much easier to examine small pieces, we must remember to put the pieces back into their appropriate places or we lose three quarters of the information.

Writing systems are among the most conservative cultural artifacts in Western society. Their study has a timelessness that lets us understand and apply ancient methods to modern requirements. As an example, the page sizes, layouts, and type faces of modern printed texts are the way they are because of practices initiated more than five-thousand years ago.

All modern Western writing systems are descendants of the Phoenician system. The Phoenicians were a people who lived along what is today the Lebanon coast. A wedge-shaped mark system (**cuneiform**) for recording syllables was developed by the Sumerians and modified by the Akkadians. The Akkadian system was, in turn, modified into a determinate **alphabetic** cuneiform writing system at Ugarit. Cuneiform is a superior method for wet clay, but unsuited for writing on dry surfaces. Southern Phoenicians modified the Ugaritic writing system; other than changing the symbol set, the system retained all the features of the cuneiform model. Designed for dry surface writing, the Phoenician symbol set, selected from among *existing* alphabetic Semitic models, formalized and created the first determinate, purely alphabetic Semitic symbol set.

The oldest written examples are on very small clay tablets—about 1-1/2 to 2 inches long by 3/4 to 1-1/4 inches wide. As technology improved, the size of the writing surfaces grew. Eventually, the connection of a certain size and shape to a specific type of document hardened—first into custom and later into rigid rule. The largest texts were always the formal documents issued by the ruling government.

Although clay is cheap and easy to obtain, it is heavy. Its weight limited the size of a tablet to what one person could conveniently lift. Accordingly, the largest tablets we find are the ancient law codes: 14-15 inches in height by 8-9 inches in width. [1] Because archival clay tablets were baked to harden and preserve them, the edges did not crumble and there was no need to allow for margins. The tablets are entirely covered with writing. [2] By the time material made from the skins of animals began to appear, the relationship of size to content had already become a rule. Skins, however, require a margin to protect the written text. Accordingly, the writing area retained the, by now, rules for size according to the content with the addition of a white space margin. While the size of leather leaves is restricted by the size of the animal (and its skin), even the smallest goat or lamb could be used to produce leaves 14 inches high by 8-1/2 inches wide plus a white space for margins.

Meanwhile, on the African side of the Ancient Near East, the Egyptians were writing on papyrus, a material made from the stalks of a reed-like plant. (The English word "paper" comes from "papyrus.") Papyrus is produced by laying strips of the inner layers of the plant (**pith**), one horizontal layer and one vertical layer, on one another. The height of a papyrus roll was limited by the height of the strips of pith peeled off the inner layers of the plant. A leaf 12 inches high was costly while a leaf 14 inches high was very rare. A papyrus roll 9 inches or more in height was always a luxury item.

Early in the first millennium BCE the Greeks adopted the writing system of the Asian side. When in the fourth century BCE Alexander and his army conquered Egypt, they brought with them the Asian Near Eastern rules governing size. These size rules created a problem because they required that the law codes and government orders be the highest and the largest documents. Papyrus rolls high enough to attain the "correct" 14 inch size were in very short supply. The Greeks solved the problem by rotating the direction of writing ninety-degrees. Greek official documents were 9 to 10 inches high by 14 or more inches wide. In turn, when Rome conquered Egypt from the Ptolemaic Greeks, the Romans adopted the rotation.

The resolution of this document size problem has left the Western world a dual heritage. Religions made heavy use of writing and the battle for religious authority has left its mark. On one side we have the Greco-Roman hierarchies of sizes, scripts, and formats. On the other side we have the North African-Semitic tradition. Both hierarchies occur in various parts of the imperial Roman world.

Public law codes issued in the Asian Near East were written on clay tablets 8-9 inches in width and 14-15 inches in height. The text filled the entire tablet. The transition to writing on animal skins did not change these writing area dimensions; however, now the text was placed within large upper and lower margins. In religious groups following the North African-Semitic (non-Roman) tradition, the writing area of "The Law" (The First Five Books of the Bible) was 14 inches in height. Today we call paper 8-1/2 inches wide by 14 inches high "legal size."

Law codes written in Roman-ruled Egypt were about 11 to 12 inches in height. Because the material, papyrus, restricted the height, in religious groups following the Roman tradition, "The Law" was 12 inches high.

Depending upon the religious persuasion of an area, secular authoritative texts were written on leaves 11 to 12 inches in height to distinguish them from "The Law." Today authoritative but not official texts, reference books such as the *Encyclopedia Britannica* or the *Oxford English Dictionary* (OED), are 11 to 12 inches in height.

In the North African-Semitic tradition, other books of the Bible, the "Writings," such as the Book of Jonah or the collection of Wisdom literature called Proverbs, the poetry of The Song of Songs or the worldly warnings of Ecclesiastes, were 10-1/2 to 11 inches in height. This also has left its mark. Today we write business letters on a paper 8-1/2 by 11 inches—and why not? These, too, are writings, if not of a religious nature.

The formats of our texts are also governed by these two ancient traditions. The reading width in both traditions remained 8 to 9 inches in width. This recurrent dimension of 8 to 9 inches wide is not arbitrary; it is a result of human physiology. Eight to 9 inches is the maximum width for the scanning human eye to process and to comprehend data. While the ancients did not have modern scientific research to confirm this point, they did have pragmatic knowledge. 8 to 9 inches is the width of the reading area of an open scroll. This affected the layout of early books—the codex. It still does today.

In the Alexandrian-Roman tradition, official documents were written in a single, broad column. The more authoritative the document was, the wider the column. One manuscript of Aristotle's *Constitutiones* (Laws of Greece) has columns 7 inches wide. Over on the other side, official documents were written in narrow columns. Among the Dead Sea Scrolls the Pentateuch texts written in the formal Square Script are in this narrow column format. In the Jewish tradition, the reading width of an open scroll is still three narrow columns.

Four columns per open double leaves was the norm for **diplomatic** (multiple editions) texts in late 9th century England. By the twelfth century, four columns were used for authoritative non-religious texts. Until very recently, modern English encyclopedias, such as the *Encyclopaedia Britannica*, were four columns per page. Two-column with central insert was the practice in the Romanized areas of the continent. Modern French encyclopedias, such as *Larousse* use this format to this day.

A modern printed text tells us by its typeface whether its reading matter is serious or frivolous. Back in antiquity, as the cuneiform wedge, the starting wedge produced by the cuneiform wet surface writing technique, was the mark of an authoritative or official script, it was incorporated into all Western official or authoritative script designs. The method for incorporation into the various script designs divides into two distinct branches.

Designs of Branch 1 incorporate the wedge into the starting strokes on the individual graphs and imitates very closely the shape of the wedge-and-thin-line cuneiform graph. Representatives of this branch include Hebrew Square Letter, African half-uncial, and the Insular family of fonts.

In designs of Branch 2, the wedge is added as a finishing stroke. Designs of Branch 2 have two sub-divisions. (1) The scripts and fonts of sub-division One have thick finishing strokes. Representatives of this sub-division include the Aramaic font families and African Rustic Capitals. (2)

Scripts and fonts of sub-division Two have thin finishing strokes with wedges added. Representatives of this sub-division include Roman Capitals and Alexandrian-Roman Greek Biblical Uncials.

Today we call the finishing strokes that imitate the cuneiform wedge in Branch 2 a **serif**. (The serif is the line across the bottom, and the little hook on the top right and crossbar of, for example, 'F'). Modern typefaces (fonts) must have these finishing strokes to carry authority. We call typefaces without these little finishing strokes **sans serif** (without serif). Sans serif fonts suggest "advertising" to the reader, just as they did in the first century CE. Advertisements and graffiti on the walls at Pompeii are sans serif.

On the ballroom floor of human knowledge, it sometimes seems that experts dance to their own beat. Over on one side the papyrologists, who study the Greco-Roman and Egyptian texts, do a fox trot, while the Semiticists, those people who study the ancient Semitic languages, execute a rumba. Off in another corner musicologists, who study the history of music, appear to do a mashed potato, while early biblical scholars waltz to a stately beat. Latin paleographers seem to do a line dance and ignore the Greek and Hebrew scholars who dance to different drums. The five or six souls who study the speaking rhythms of languages hover at the sidelines doing a macarena, while the hard science types appear to prefer a bunny-hop. Across the floor, Carolingian specialists seem to dance a minuet, while the Anglo-Saxonists appear to be doing the Charleston. Each group continues to dance to their own drumbeats.

Many facts presented in this book are so well known in their separate fields that people rarely bother to mention them. If you should ask an expert in one of these areas about them, you will draw in response a surprised "doesn't everybody know that?". The answer is: No. Everybody does *not* know that. This book brings together the "doesn't everybody"'s of many areas along with much information that is new. Technically, this type of drawing together is called "an interdisciplinary study." This is a sixty-four dollar term for presenting the assorted dances to the same beat and sound.

The word "sound" creates an immediate problem. While today we distinguish between sound (aural, of the ear) and speech (oral, of the mouth), in antiquity the distinction was between *voice* (oral), which can be recorded on a page, and *sound* (aural), which cannot. The *sense* or meaning (semantic content) of the words, was only a part of the whole.

Oral writing systems are voice-based (phonetic-based) and inclusive; they record speech along with semantic sense. Modern writing systems are sense-based (semantic-based) and exclusive, except for the informational content, they convey little information to the reader.

Modern music notation (writing) systems are made for the ear. They are sound based (aural based). They convey three elements: the quality of a note, the length of time a note is held, and how loud a note should be when sung or played. Music writing systems, however, contain little or no semantic information.

Phonetic-based writing systems unite *voice* with *sense*. They combine the semantic content of printed text with the aural information of modern musical notation. Their message is presented in ordinary alphabetic and numeric symbols similar to those used on this page. Phonetic-based writing systems use the innate structure of alphanumeric symbol design to encode spoken (**phonological**) patterns. The reader *literally* hears the voice of the absent authors.

The average person cannot tell what makes an *A* an *A* or how we distinguish alphabetic symbols from one another. Nor does he know the rules that govern the design of scripts or the amount of white space (**kerning**) between letters. Not everybody has examined what is involved in the design of a system or how all the components come together so the system will work when someone uses it.

Writing systems are far more inclusive than a "way of recording language by visible marks." [3] These visible marks are graphic symbols, that is, script systems, and only form a part of the whole. Spelling (orthographic) systems are written, but they, too, are only a part. A writing system encompasses the graphic symbols of a given language as well as the method by which these "visible marks" are recorded on stele, tablet, parchment, or paper. It includes the direction of writing—right to left, left to right, vertically, horizontally, diagonally, or **boustrophedon** (back and forth like plowing)—, the permissible limits of white space with regard to comprehension, format conventions, and basis of expression. What is expressed, however, depends upon the purpose of a writing system.

While the necessary components of a writing system have not changed across the millennia, purposes can change. Modern writing systems are semantic-based; their purpose is to convey data. In antiquity, "the voice of authority" was not a metaphor to be tossed about by literary critics, but a concrete, visible reality. For more than four of the five thousand year history of writing, writing systems were phonetic-based; their purpose was to record the voice of absent authority—be it poet, priest, or king.

Accustomed as we are to semantic-based systems, we incorrectly are taught to believe that we can use any script or type style we wish, and it will make no difference. We erroneously assume that the size, format, and script of a text is unimportant and irrelevant.

But semantic-based or no, our modern writing systems use hierarchies of scripts, sizes, and formats to identify a text. We automatically associate size with authority, format with content, and script with a language or a people.

When asked we will say that we have 26 letters in our alphabetic symbol set, which a moment's thought will expose as obviously false. We use a minimum of 52 alphabetic symbols in our familiar English system: 26 Capitals and 26 versions of one of the ancient variant forms—only now we call these variant forms "lowercase letters."

Readers of the modern printed book often accept the unstated assumption that the sole purpose of written letters is to transmit data. They forget to ask an important question: What is the primary purpose of writing?

The purpose of a writing system cannot be taken for granted, for ancient and modern writing systems are not identical either in structure or intent. Writing systems are a continuum and no system is solely semantically or phonetically based; *all* writing systems lie somewhere on the continuum, even the Chinese systems. [4] Nonetheless, there is a distinct difference between a writing system designed primarily to communicate data (semantic-based) and a writing system primarily designed to record speech (phonetic-based).

Semantically oriented systems typically employ typographical visual aids such as bold-face or italic types, or formatting to identify, for example, poetry. Conversely, the natural rise and fall of an utterance in phonetically oriented systems *statistically* tends to separate at semantic units. Nevertheless, there is a major and important difference between their underlying philosophies. Semantic-based writing systems are rooted in data transmission; their primary purpose is to convey information. Phonetic-based writing systems are rooted in oral communication; their primary purpose is to convey a record of a "text" as spoken—with all those factors that serve to identify that specific text as itself and no other (an entity). These factors are: quality (or phone), duration (or length of time), and stress (or volume). Each component of these systems holds meaning.

In phonetic-based systems, the quality, that is, the phonetic value of the symbol is shown by variant forms of the basic symbol. Duration appears on the horizontal plane of a line of writing (the 'x' axis). The letters are clumped together or spaced apart to show how long a sound should be held. Stress, the third component, moves up and down the vertical plane (the 'y' axis). Together, the three components are the equivalent of a visual tape recording—they contain everything besides the actual sound. There remains only one other component—the content, the written message itself.

Writing systems do not happen in a vacuum. Content is important as it contains the message. Content determines the choice of script, the size of a page, and the format. In turn, content is constrained by religious and political affiliations. That is, the data in the written text are influenced by the governing authorities both sacred and secular. They were in antiquity; they still are today. Within any given writing system, be it Eastern or Western, Ancient or Modern, each component holds meaning beyond that of the written word.

It is remarkably common today to separate modern and ancient peoples into "printing" and "manuscript" societies. This distinction implies that modern methods are always better and that there is something primitive and backwards about older ways. This misperception arose in the seventeenth century. The seventeenth-century "enlightened" philosophy was expanded and systemized during the eighteenth and nineteenth centuries. We, in the twenty-first century, are the heirs of these points of view. We embrace their desired standardization, which has its positive aspects, but continue to throw out the baby with the bathwater.

The technical side of these writing systems is actually very simple, easy to explain and to illustrate. Against this, the history, the background material, that is needed to understand and comprehend the use, distribution, and constraints—social, religious, and political—of these systems covers a very broad range of materials and many fields. It is quite a story; it takes some sorting out to tell it.

Modern Western writing and printing followed in the wake of Christianity. Our western dual heritage strikes again. Today's systems are the result of the reintegration of full writing into the impoverished Roman tradition. Our modern lower-case letters come from Akkadian Cuneiform via Ugaritic, Phoenician, and the North African-Semitic tradition. Modern capital letters stem from the Etruscan-Roman-Alexandrian Greek tradition.

Referring to the Roman system as "impoverished" may seem harsh, but it is also true. The inscriptions and scrolls and papyri and codices tell us the story. It is an important story, for it explains why seventeenth-century reformers threw away the ancient writing techniques.

Today's writing systems have been shorn of much that enriched "manuscript societies." It was a much richer reading world. It was a world where Johnny could speak any language, because the writing told him how to say the words. It was a world where a messenger did not need to be a scholar; all he had to do was read the words as written on the page. It was a world where the size and format and script told you the status of the document, the social pecking order. It was a world where you could hear the text and the voice of the absent author.

Our entry into this richer world is through the people who wrote the texts: the scribes. Scribes were human, too. They could be cold or hungry, frightened or annoyed, happy or sad. They lived and breathed, sickened and died. In examining the documents the scribes have left us, we must never forget that these texts were placed there by human hands. Scribes, their training, their peculiarities—and what these tell us about them and their societies—bob in and out of the pages of this book.

Among our cultural artifacts, writing systems are perhaps the most conservative. All of the interdependent components of a writing system are important today. None of them is modern in origin.

Absent Voices: The Story of Writing Systems in the West is divided in two parts. Part I introduces phonetic-based writing systems and how they record the spoken word. Part II concentrates on England from the Medieval through the early modern period (from 650 to 1650). This focus allows us a panoramic view of the codification, dissemination, and slow disintegration of one of the most influential systems in the story of Western writing since antiquity.

Research has much in common with detection. A researcher and a detective find they ask the same questions. How is information encoded into the texts? Where did these techniques originate? How common were phonetic-based systems? When and why were phonetic-based systems replaced? What was lost and what was gained? Why should we re-examine these systems? How can knowledge of these ancient methods benefit modern society?

This book will attempt to answer these questions in a straight-forward and comprehensible manner. Every effort has been made to avoid jargon and to define technical terminology. New concepts and technical or unfamiliar terms are in bold-face type when first mentioned and listed in a glossary as well. Persons, places, and events are situated in context, and quotations from primary sources have been translated into modern English.

The material under discussion is visually oriented. Illustrations are very important in explaining these phonetic-based writing systems to the reader. These ancient handwritten and carved works display an overwhelming amount of information encoded directly into the texts.

Because it is impossible to include thousands of examples within one small book, the examples required careful selection. The criteria for selection are as follows: First, the examples are in the direct line of transmission. Second, they are representative of a given genre. Third, they are in official, formal or complete script systems, and, finally, each has significance within the larger context. Photographs of individual texts directly relevant to the history of the phonetic-based writing system employed in medieval and renaissance England are included in this book. As it is not feasible to gain permissions for photographs of every stele, papyrus, scroll, and codex cited, the majority of the illustrations are calligraphed replicas. (I beg the reader's indulgence. While I have reproduced the examples as closely as possible, I make no claim to have attained the level of professionalism exhibited in the manuscripts.) Readers who wish to study these specimens more thoroughly are referred to generally available facsimile sources.

Citing authorities in a book intended for a lay audience would interrupt the flow of words and has been avoided whenever possible. Many papers and books have been referred to while assembling this work and, while it is impossible to mention everyone, direct cites and references are given in end notes. Similarly, it is impossible within the limitations of a small book to provide sufficient detailed information on all the subjects to satisfy the interested reader. Hence, the inclusion of an extensive bibliography.

We have much to learn from these ancient writing systems, much that can be useful today. We must make the effort to understand them. Compared to these ancient comprehensive writing techniques, modern imitations are, at best, primitive. We have nothing nowadays—not the

International Phonetic Alphabet (**IPA**), nor linear [5] (trees and branches) and nonlinear [6] (layered) systemics, nor component-based analytic techniques, nor alternative pedagogical reading and language learning methods (such as phonics), nor artificial languages (such as Esperanto)—nothing at all that even approaches the comprehensiveness and simplicity that was routine procedure only yesterday.

We can reap many benefits from an understanding of phonetic-based writing systems. The ancient texts contain more than words. Every part of a text written in these systems holds meaning. The scripts and formats and sizes record fierce battles for supremacy. The size of a document tells us the social status of the person who wrote it—a guide to "who's on first." The scrolls, stelae, and manuscripts themselves frequently relate a history appreciably different from the unquestioned "Winner's History" that we read in standard textbooks. The musical notation system gives us back ancient English and Hebrew Psalm song. (A subject that seems of great interest in the English speaking world, as is testified by the more than three hundred attempts to translate the Psalms metrically in the past six hundred years. [7]) There is more. The ancient techniques used in these systems can guide us in new again paths on teaching reading and writing. They are of aid in public speaking. Indeed, these techniques are thoroughly modern and are easy to implement on a computer.

Our modern use of the components of a writing system is completely unconscious; we use them, but we do not know *why* we use them. In antiquity, people knew the meaning and relevance of every component of a writing system.

The modern world has need for a written communication system that contains more than words. The time has come when we must look at the past for our future.

Part One

Words

Chapter One

ABSENT VOICES

"Sticks and stones may break my bones but names will never hurt me!" The child sticks his tongue out at his tormentor in a "so there, take that" gesture—then runs home to mother for comfort. But, if words cannot harm him, why does he invoke the old charm against the power of words? It is not the words written on a page that provokes the use of this charm chant. It is the spoken word, the voiced taunt.

Speech grants one power over the "thing" named. Naming changes the new and feared into something known and manageable. It gives control over the environment. By the act of naming the creatures, Adam exercised power over the animal kingdom (Gen 2:19-20). Words are magic; they create order from chaos (Gen 1). Words destroy; they send armies marching. Words control; they move mountains, sway populations, calm fears.

The power of the spoken word is both exciting and frightening. To speak is to control. To the ancients, speech was as potent a source of power as atomic energy is to us today.

Man is a technological animal. He is always seeking ways to harness the source of power—be it atomic energy, water, or the spoken word. These potent and magic aspects of speech were extremely important when humanity engineered a technology capable of recording the power of speech visually. We call this visual technology "writing."

Writing is a major technological innovation. Then, as now, the primary purpose of writing is to harness the power of speech. Potent power sources must be handled with great care. Today we are more than a little concerned with the design and construction of an atomic power plant. The ancients felt the same way about the technology needed to control the power of words. If man wanted to control this power source, the technique *had* to record the spoken words exactly as they were said. They had to record the **voice** of the speaker.

Today we equate voice with sound; historically a clear distinction was made between voice (which can be written down) and sound (which cannot). Today, it would seem very strange to refer to the voice of a letter; yesterday, this was perfectly normal. Today we assume that "the page's voice" (*voces paginarum*) is a metaphor, yesterday the term was a simple statement of fact. Today, the primary purpose of a writing system is to convey data, yesterday, the primary purpose of writing was to convey a spoken record, the voice and authority of the absent author.

Modern critical theory will tell you that the voice of an author is figurative, a literary metaphor. A literary metaphor is an extension of an immediate metaphor. Words for "things" are immediate metaphors. [1] "Tree" is an immediate metaphor for that "thing" with a trunk and branches. The literary version falls flat on its figurative face if an immediate metaphor does not already exist from which to extend the meaning. For more than four thousand years the "voice of authority" was an immediate metaphor. It referred to a concrete, visible reality.

Ancient and medieval writers speak naturally and simply about voice. They unequivocally tell us that the written text is more than letters on a stele or scroll or parchment leaf.

The ancient Greeks always knew the primary purpose of writing. Aristotle (384-322 BCE) makes a clear distinction between *zoón* ("living," that is, the original, the "figure"), and *eikon* ("icon": image, copy). [2] Aristotle (as did Plato, ca. 427-347 BCE) believed that to be most effective, the image (*eikones*) had to mirror the original. While there can be only one original, if the written word were to retain the power of the spoken word, the voice had to reflect the original. This need to capture the original *voice of authority* as closely as possible explains the purpose behind the ancient writing systems.

Christian writers are very clear about this. To Augustine (354-430), written letters display themselves to the eyes and, apart from themselves, [display] *voices* to the mind. [3] For Isidore of Seville (ca. 560-630), written letters are signs, at the service of memory, which evoke the *voices* of the *absent*. [4] Paraphrasing Isidore, John of Salisbury (ca. 1115-80) writes that letters themselves are figures indicating *voices . . . speaking soundlessly* the *voices* of the *absent*. [5] Ælfric (circa 955-1020) makes it very clear in his *Latin Grammar* [6] that the Old English word "stæf" refers to the pronunciation of the alphabetic symbol, not the graph, and with much the same meaning as "staff" in modern musical notation. Albertus Magnus (circa 1200-80), in his *Commentary on Aristotle's Book of Memory and Recall (De memoria et reminiscentia)*, [7] states that letters stand for *voices* (*voces*). Isidore unequivocally asserts that sound cannot be written. He makes a clear distinction between "voice" (*vox*), which can be written, and "sound" (*sonum*) that cannot. [8] This is a distinction whose importance can hardly be overstated.

Sound varies. Sound refers to the differences among vocalizations of the author's text when read aloud by others. A choir singing in unison produces one auctorial "voice," but vocalizes different "sounds" depending upon whether a singer is a bass, a tenor, an alto, or a soprano. On the other hand, when John of Salisbury states that letters *speak* soundlessly, he is referring to the **invariants** (the unfluctuating portions) of a text. That is, the auctorial content and the relative amplitude, duration, and frequency of the content as "said" by the author—in other words *voice*. These invariants, the relative content, amplitude, duration, and frequency are what is meant by "voice" (*vox*).

Technically stated, *if* a recording is made of two speakers attempting to imitate each other, and *if* the wave forms of both recordings are passed through a **Fourier transform** (a method used to convert wave forms to or from frequency and time domains), and *if* the data is **orthonormalized** (straightened to present relevant data at 90 ^{O} to each other) for mean frequency and amplitude, *then* the wave forms will show nearly identical Fourier coefficients. These coefficients are invariants.

Modern musical notation is an extension of "voice" in this meaning. While the notation indicates the notes to be sung or played, the writing itself does not, and cannot, give us the actual vocalization or instrumentalization, the "sound."

Isidore of Seville was correct: "voice" (*vox*) is constant and can be written. "Sound" (*sono*) is variable and cannot be reproduced in writing, no matter how sophisticated the writing system.

Writing systems, ancient and modern, are highly sophisticated. They are as carefully designed to function as a complete unit as a modern jet airplane. A modern jet is composed of hundreds of sub-systems. For example, there are brake systems and engine systems, wing systems and elevator systems, fuel systems and steering systems, seat placement systems and kitchen facility systems. The placement of each bolt or nut is carefully designed by the system designer and carefully placed (we hope) by the person who performs the design. Each component in a sub-system is designed to function within the sub-system; in turn, each sub-system is designed to function as a self-contained unit within the complete system design. This is also true of a writing system. The components are part of the system design.

There is an important distinction between system design and system performance. They refer to two different domains.

Domain 1 is the **design** of a system and refers to the deliberate construction of a framework within which the listed components function. This deliberate construction is in effect whether the referent is the construction of a modern hot water system, the building of an ark, or the design of a script. Any system design specifies a method of measurement (**mensuration**) for *that* system. The mensural method is an integral part of *that* design. Any change of scale must be applied throughout the system; it cannot be partial.

Domain 2 refers to the **performance** of a system as applied by a plumber, a shipwright, or a scribe. If the system designer specifies 1/4" copper tubing and 1/4" t-joints, but the plumber changes the tubing to 3/8" without changing the t-joint, the tubing will not fit into its appointed place and the system will leak. If the boat design specifications call for a keel and planks thirty cubits in length, but the shipwright uses a twenty cubit keel without changing the thirty cubit planks, the boat will sink. If a scribe uses a pen two minims wide, but a modern scholar uses a centimeter rule to measure the spaces between graphic symbols, the measurements will be meaningless.

These distinctions between design and performance are important to our understanding of writing systems. The structure and components of a writing system are part of the *design*; illustrations of the system as applied by scribes are examples of *performance*.

Each sub-system in a writing system is balanced and designed to work with the others. Unlike the sub-systems of a jet plane, we can list those of a writing system in one short paragraph. These sub-systems are: a finite symbol-set, *prescribed* graphic symbols (script), writing limits, direction of writing, format (format is sometimes called "mis-en-page"; the term is merely French for "layout" or "format"), size, punctuation, comprehension (white space), orthographic, shape, and content systems.

The content is important. Content establishes which script, size, and format system should be used. Content itself is determined by other factors: the current ruling powers, whether sacred or secular. In the phonetic-based writing systems, all the sub-systems *had* to be correct or the document was not the voice of authority.

One term on the list of sub-systems may appear odd; nevertheless, "prescribed" is correct. Scripts are tightly bound to a culture's identity. Scripts were a people's visual statement of independence and identification. We have national flags. Flags are *our* visual statements of identity. We get very upset if a change to this visual identifier should be suggested from within. We fight fiercely when an outside power enforces a change upon us. We consider it a public shame if a foreign flag should fly over our territory. Yesterday, our ancestors fought fiercely to retain their visual cultural identity, their identifying script.

Because writing equaled power and control, we see reforms every time there is a change of power structure. We may even refer to this phenomenon as the "Winner's Standard Operating Procedure." The meaner the origin, the more grandiose the reform. The new ruler must have a better background than any of his subject peoples, so genealogies are created for him. If the new ruling power is a council or city, they write histories to create a background for themselves. The Winners reform the language to meet some nonexistent "ancient" standards. They change the "official" script to a new one. If they cannot create a good background for themselves, they may purposely "archaize," appropriate an older "official" script, as *their* identifying script. The "Winner's" cycle repeats again and again; it has from the very beginnings of recorded history. It is a common way of saying that we, too, have a good background—and a history.

When in the mid 24th century BCE Sargon I conquered Sumer, he created a new official script. The Babylonians replaced the official script and reformed their language—as did the Assyrians, the Persians, the Greeks, and the Romans in their turn.

We will see the same "reform" procedures in use in England, both early and late. Every one of the common Winner's techniques shows up: genealogies, histories, changes in official scripts, and spelling reforms. The British nineteenth century grammar and spelling reforms followed England's rise to power as an Empire. The late twentieth century "Politically Correct" (PC) language reforms are not new or modern at all. They are just another reprise of the change of power dance.

The pages have voices that we can hear—if we listen to them. They tell their own story. Along the way they also write on some of the blank pages of our history. It is quite a tale.

Chapter Two

BEGINNINGS

The caves inspire awe. Looking upwards, we see that the roof of the main cavern at Altimira, Spain is covered with drawings of bison, some wild boars, horses, a hind. Their creators used the curves of the jutting rock face to add depth and bulk. Here and there are some small figures aiming an arrow at a hunted beast. The walls of the Lascaux cave in the Dordogne province of France are equally stunning. The bison are huge, even in comparison to modern man. Their rough curly shoulder manes and delicately curved arching horns are carefully depicted. The period is sometime during the Aurignacian stage of the Paleolithic Age, 28,000-22,000 BCE.

Rounded and realistic sculptures make their appearance during the later part of the Aurignacian, around 22,000. The oldest examples appear to have religious significance. The "venus" head may have been the face of a priestess. By the Magdalenian period, between 15,000-10,000 BCE we find carefully modeled, three-dimensional, and very realistic clay figurines of bison. These beautifully executed, realistic bison are icons, images in the Aristotelian meaning of the word.

Man was learning to use his brain to abstract information from the environment. Drawings and sculptured icons are first levels of abstraction. Both are directly from the "thing." These works record man attempting to control his surroundings.

The paintings in the *main* cavern at Altimira are carefully formed, mostly the works of masters. These wall paintings are forms of sympathetic magic. Precision is necessary if their sympathetic magic is to work. Draw it; then go out and hunt for it. If the "magic" of the imitation ritual worked, the hunter brought home food for his immediate clan. If he were very lucky, he also had horn and bone left over for trade.

Long distance trade dates from about 12,000 BCE. Axe factories and flint mines (dug out with antler horns and as much as twenty feet deep) created an item of trade. The yellow flint of Grand-

Pressigny in France was much in demand. Luxury items such as Mediterranean mussel shells, obsidian from the Greek island of Melos, and the amber of Jutland and East Prussia became the objects of international trade. Such items of trade are found from the fertile crescent to the British Isles.

The four amber roads, so-called because they were used by traders to transport amber, date from this time. One of these amber roads began at the shores of the Adriatic and ran overland through the mountain passes. This road was of importance during the early Christian period as it ran around the perimeter of the Roman Empire. Equally ancient, a salt road begins from the shores of Modern Israel. This road passed through Damascus, Syria, and from thence inland to meet the "Kings' Road" coming up from Yemen. It continued on through Palmyra and beyond. Salt is important to life itself. Man cannot live without salt. Salt was in high demand as an item of trade.

Trade and religion are the two motivating factors behind the invention of writing. Writing, like any technological development, awaited need. Thousands of years passed by until the need for writing came.

The agricultural revolution around 8,000 BCE changed man's lifestyle. Agriculture gave man a fairly dependable food supply. Domestication of animals followed in its wake. Agriculture and husbandry also require a settled lifestyle while waiting for crops to mature or animals to bear young. The change from hunter to farmer was drastic.

Humanity has not changed across the millennia. Man resists change, even when it is to his advantage. He always has. The hunter/warrior/shepherd needs open spaces; the farmer needs enclosures. Some parts of the Bible record truly ancient history for us. The story of Cain (grain—the farmer) and Abel (meat—the hunter/shepherd) tells us that the battle between "the farmer and the cowman" was not exactly peaceful. It also tells us that the relegation of the *peasant* to secondary status is not new.

In the northern climates, the agricultural revolution brought subsistence farming supplemented by some hunting and fishing. The farming settlements typical of the period are small, possibly extended families. Small settlements do not need to record transactions. There is no need for writing when everybody speaks the same language. The trader and his caravan dealt face to face with the peoples. There is no need for writing to record one-on-one sales where pointing and finger counting suffices.

In the Ancient Near East, the longer growing season and the generally fertile soil of the region permitted large cities to arise. Sometime during the fourth millennium BCE, the growth in both complexity and distance of trade created a need for some form of record keeping. Toward the middle of the millennium, this growth in trade fostered a growth in separate cities inhabited by peoples speaking the same language. When enough people separated by distance speak the same language, a means of reproducing that language visually becomes a necessity. The time for a technological innovation had come.

Man already had the capability. After all, he had been practicing visual magic for more than 20,000 years. Words, like paintings and icons, are first-level abstractions. Words are oral images of the "thing." Both visual and oral arts are forms of sympathetic magic; both are attempts to control the environment. When man finally needed writing, the two forms of magic, oral and visual, were combined. They reinforced each other. Because they were "magic," the solution to the problem of visually recording speech needed care and precision.

Two different solutions to the problem of harnessing the tremendous power of speech were designed: the Egyptian and the Sumerian. Neither system was intended only to communicate data.

The two approaches to the problem of visual speech are dissimilar and reflect their ancestry in religion and trade. One is mystic, the other is pragmatic. These differences are perhaps best illustrated in the technology these two societies designed to control flooding.

On the Egyptian side of the Ancient Near East, the Nile River had annual cycles of flood and ebb. The source of the Nile River is high in the mountains more than one thousand miles south of the river mouth. Because the Egyptians could not see the source, they thought of the flooding cycle as magic. The cycle was relatively predictable, but there were times when the annual flood did not occur. (The seven years of famine that Joseph interprets for the Pharaoh provides perhaps the best known instance of the failure of the flooding cycle.) Although the Egyptians deepened the channels opened by the floods as a form of control, they mainly relied on the magic of words, incantations, to guarantee a good flood cycle.

On the Asian side of the Ancient Near East, while the rivers also begin in the mountains, there was one major difference. The inhabitants could see the source and the snow pack. They understood the annual cycles. Their approach was pragmatic. The entire plain between the Euphrates and Tigris rivers was (and is) crisscrossed by irrigation canals.

Egyptian society was mystically oriented and magic was a part of their religion. For the Egyptians, the power of speech was "magic." Once spoken, the words had to be repeated exactly as said the first time, or the magic of the words would not work. There was one and only one way to record the voice of authority.

The Egyptian solution to controlling this potent power source was confinement and constraint. Confinement and control of the technology applied as well to those permitted to learn it. Because the power of the word granted control over the environment (including people), such powerful magic was deemed suitable for only an elite group: priests and kings and their servants—a core of trained scribes. The population as a whole remained illiterate.

The Egyptian hieroglyphic writing system was exceptionally rigid and bound. The result was its complete disappearance early in the Common Era (CE). One remnant of the Egyptian system survives. This remnant did not come directly through them, nor was it very important in the technological development of writing for another three thousand years. This was about the time a small, unimportant clan perched on seven hills in central Italy expanded dramatically to become eventually the Roman Empire.

One small part of our Western dual heritage descends from the Egyptian mystical-magical system by way of Etruria and Rome. In this tradition, writing follows religion. Most of our modern writing systems come from the other side, the one that began on the Asian side of the Ancient Near East. This is the one we call **cuneiform** (nail-head) because the symbols were wedge shaped. In this tradition, writing follows trade.

Unlike the Egyptian religio-mystical bent, the Sumerians, and those following in their wake, were extremely practical. The inhabitants of Mesopotamia established commercial and banking practices, standard weights and measures, written contracts, contract formulas, price and wage fixing, and codified laws. They divided the day into 24 hours, the hour into 60 minutes, the minutes into 60 seconds, and the circle into 360 degrees.

Sumer sat in the midst of a fertile area, the delta where the Euphrates and the Tigris rivers join to enter the Gulf of Persia. It is an area that produces excess food. That is, the agricultural part of the population produces enough food to feed themselves as well as to provide for others. This excess of food is the reason civilization arose in the Ancient Near East. The area is called the fertile crescent for good reason. Enough food was produced by those on the land to allow cities to flourish. It provided leisure time for thought and experimentation. Excess food produces excess goods for trade. Man cannot use his oversize brain for thoughts and experiments when he is trying to fill his belly.

Excess food was unavailable in most northern climates. As late as the eleventh century CE, it took eighteen people on the land to feed one person in the city. Today we are amused at comments in Medieval literature about feeding an oversize person. For us, much of the humor in, for example, the story of *Havelock the Dane* arises when someone offers to keep this "biggest man" alive by supplying his food. We forget that feeding someone that big was a serious problem and not amusing at all. The food situation in the North did not change until the invention of the horse collar. The great Northern cities and civilizations did not, and could not, exist until this invention.

The ease of food production created problems for those who possessed the territory. Abundant food meant wealth. (It still does.) Consequently, the Asian side of the Near East has been fought over for all of recorded history. As conqueror followed conqueror each, in turn, adopted (and adapted) the Sumerian writing system.

Because the new technology allowed the speaker to be physically absent and yet virtually present to deliver orders or guarantee a contract, the capture of the power of the words *as spoken* was vitally important to the Sumerians. Writing had to be very widespread to be effective. These ancient Sumerian, Lagashian, Akkadian, Ugaritic, Phoenician, Moabite, Edomite, pre-Exilic Hebrew, and Babylonian societies were literate in the modern meaning of the word. They have left an enormous number of records for us to read—more than five million tablets. It is a serious mistake to assume that all ancient societies were illiterate and oral.

Except for the very lowest social stratum, these societies considered literacy essential. By law, fathers were required to educate their children to read and to write. There are indications that this practice was already in place by the time of the Akkadian ascendancy under Sargon I in the mid-twenty fourth century BCE. Under Hammurabi (Old Babylon, 18th century BCE), written records were required for all transactions. Everything was recorded, down to the smallest detail of the simplest trade or exchange. [1]

Writing originated in the control of trade; control of trade meant fraud prevention. Nothing had changed when writing became a standard requirement for civilized man. Forgery was a serious problem; hence, many techniques, such as seals and clay envelopes were developed to prevent fraud. Above all, there could be only *one* original, the invariant voice of authority. For this reason, any covenant—vow, oath, marriage contract, treaty, official document, royal letter—had to be in the hand of the author(s). (This is why we still have to sign contracts, tax returns, and so forth, and swear that they are in our own hand.) The great majority of ancient tablets are covenants, hence, holographs. "Copies" were made, to be sure, but what we today refer to as a copy, an exact "Xerox" duplicate, was considered a flagrant forgery. Instead, people wrote what in Biblical Hebrew is called a *mishneh*, that is, an "edition."

One of the effects of public literacy was that many people made their own editions, private copies for personal use, of texts such as laws or literature. To avoid the charge of—and the penalties for—forgery, editions never use either an official script or the script used by an original author.

Editions abound in the Dead Sea Scrolls (DSS) and the Greek and Roman papyri. Among such editions we find changes of lineation, changes in the number of columns, use of near synonyms for a word in the original, and even doodles inserted into the text. Editions are the main reason we find "variants" in ancient texts.

Widespread public literacy has other requirements; it also creates a need for educated and trained people to handle everyday matters. Scribal schools were founded. These schools were the universities of antiquity. Mathematics as a field was born in the scribal schools of Old Babylon. The schools were supported by the reigning government and for the same purpose as our modern universities: trained workers. The modern image of a poor scribe in a monastery or a nineteenth century clerk writing away in a cold room copying page after page is far from reality.

The primary job of a scribe was the equivalent of a modern "administrative assistant." Like a modern secretary-administrative assistant, master scribes held much power. Today, the way to arrange an appointment with the boss is through the secretary. Yesterday, supplicants wrote letters to the scribe of a Governor or ruler. There are many examples of letters to the "Scribe of x Governor" among the papyri. Parents were delighted to hear that a son or daughter had decided to undergo scribal training. If the child succeeded in passing through the rigorous apprenticeship, it guaranteed that their offspring was set for life.

Scribes were highly trained people. A master scribe was the equivalent of a full professor today, with much the same privileges and "perks." The scribe, male or female, not only had to take dictation, but to write form letters. A scribe had to be able to calculate the area of a field (for tax purposes, of course) on the fly; he was the certified public accountant of the age. A scribe had to know legal formulae; he was the notary public of his day. The copying of texts was the lowest of the required skills. Copying was primarily for the apprentice level. It always has been. That is how apprentices learn, by copying.

We can see the copying techniques of apprenticeship at work in the caves of Altimira. The paintings in the main cave are artfully colored and masterfully drawn. Careful shading adds perspective and depth to the depicted creatures. The outlines are drawn with unhesitating sweeps of the drawing instrument. These are the work of masters. However, there are also many small side caves. The walls of these small caves resemble the pages of a modern art student's sketch book. The drawings in these small caves are outlines, not full pictures. They are only in black. They are drawn with charred sticks—the charcoal pencil of the age. The drawings are marked by every sign of the learner. There are hesitation marks, irregular lines, rubbed out areas, and drawings crossing one another. There are even swirls of preparatory motion to "warm up." Some of these drawings are very poorly executed, others show promise, yet others show skill and talent. Most of these drawings are clearly the work of beginners, the scribal apprentices of the Paleolithic age.

Nothing changed when writing appeared on the scene. Scribes, whether Sumerian or Medieval, passed through stages of training. During the medieval period, these were divided into three parts: apprentice, journeyman, and master. The apprentice spent as much as seven years learning the basic skills. These skills ranged from making and preparing the writing surface to laying out a tablet or page, from shaping the writing instrument to learning the graphic symbol sets. Because each writing school had its own formal official and informal everyday symbol sets, the apprentice scribe had to learn the house scripts and fonts.

A Paleolithic master hunt-magic maker had to practice until he could draw without hesitation. A professional scribe had to practice until he could write without hesitation. He had to be able to concentrate on the job at hand, whether copying or taking dictation. While there is a mental connection between a given font and the scribe writing it, this connection is stored in the motor skill area. A working scribe had no time to stop and mentally visualize his font model. This would be the equivalent of a stenotypist telling his boss to stop dictating while he visualized the correct shorthand symbol. A scribe who had to mentally visualize a font model before writing could never pass his journeyman examination; he would always be an apprentice. The scribe's response had to be completely automatic, almost robotic. It had to be so automatic that he or she would associate the feel of a writing instrument with the font or script. Until this response becomes totally automatic, a scribe does not acquire distinguishing trademarks. These trademarks are known as **ideographs**.

Ideographs are systematically formed differences in the way a scribe writes a symbol. It may be as slight as a difference in the twist of the leg of an aleph, or the height of an *s*. It can be as obvious as a tremor in the hand, or the way of writing a *de*. It takes time and practice to acquire these identifying scribal trademarks. Only senior journeymen and masters acquire ideographs. Most of the texts before circa 1200 CE are the works of masters. The master scribes and their ideographs are important; they are our doorway into the past.

We cannot be more precise than to say that sometime in the fourth millennium BCE humans found the technological capability to record speech. There are things we simply cannot know; we lack sufficient information. We do know that writing began in the area of the Euphrates-Tigris delta. We do not know where the Sumerians came from. Their language is unrelated to other groups, nor is it related to the Semitic languages generally found in the area. Still, this is a common phenomenon among the known early peoples. We do not know if the Sumerians were the originators or if an existing icon/token system gave them the idea. We do know that the oldest *textual* material is written in Sumerian. For all practical purposes then, writing began in Sumer at the city of Uruk (Biblical *Erech*).

In 3300 BCE Uruk was one of the three major cities of Sumer. It was a port city situated on the left bank of the Euphrates River. Commerce and trade were a vital part of the economy of the city. Economics is a powerful motivator. The earliest known speech recording system was for trade.

As long as trade is local, the spoken word as assurance suffices. (We still use "oral" contracts. We still speak of "word of honor" or "my word is a guarantee.") When conflicts over a trade arose, the local leader could bring the disputing parties face to face and judge the claims and counterclaims. When trade expands beyond the range of local bounds, some means must be found to record the vocal transactions.

Drawings, icons, and words are immediate abstractions from the original. All writing is a second level abstraction, for writing is an abstraction of an abstraction.

In our modern world, we make the romantic assumption that writing is meant to transmit data; unromantically enough, writing originated in fraud prevention. The oldest known "written" records are clay objects called **tokens**. Unlike the ancient clay icons and wall paintings, the tokens are second level abstractions. They are shaped like the item of trade, but are no longer rounded, realistic representations. The tokens represent the voiced word for the "thing."

The spoken compact was now backed by a concrete visual representation. If one party to a transaction claimed, for example, that he had purchased twenty sheep but received only fifteen, he could show the tokens of promise against sheep received.

While the token system gives a visual means to make speech "audible" beyond the range of hearing, it does not depend upon a language. Tokens suffice as a transaction record as long as people do not speak the same language.

Unfortunately, people being people, someone also could conveniently lose tokens. There was still too much room for theft and chicanery. Something had to be done about this, or trade could not flourish and the government could not get its portion.

By about 3300 impressed clay balls appear. On the outside, we find transaction data such as the number and types of "things" and the personal seals of the parties involved. On the inside, we find tokens corresponding to the same numbers and shapes as those recorded on the exterior. If there arose a dispute, the unbroken ball was brought before a judge. The unbroken ball guaranteed that the transaction was as described; any tampering with the evidence was obvious.

The numbers and seals on the clay balls still do not require knowledge of a language. Further technological advances had to await the arrival of a language widespread enough in use to require further information. This was not long in coming, and tells us something about the rate of expansion of the Sumerian sphere of influence. It seems to have taken approximately 200 years.

By 3100 the clay ball "envelope" had flattened out into tablets. Rather than shape pieces of clay into tokens, a stylus was used to *draw* the shape of the tokens as signs on the tablets. Within a short time, drawing pictures, which is a very slow business, was replaced by incised representational symbols. The writing tool was now a wedge-shaped stylus (thus, cuneiform). The "wedge" end of the tool was poked into the clay and then the sharp edge of the wedge was used to draw straight lines. Wedge and line is a much faster method.

The clay balls had limited data; the tablets contain an array of complex signs. The tokens, and before them the paintings and icons, had represented "things," nouns. The tablets use drawn verbs of action as well. These signs are called **logograms**, that is, abstracted images of, for example, a foot, to represent walking or standing.

A link in the chain of our evidence is missing. Writing historians no longer refer to **pictographs** (simple outline pictures), but call the signs logograms. During the nineteenth and the greater part of the twentieth centuries, scholars assumed writing developed from pictographs. Today we know better. At no point in the history of writing do we find evidence of such a writing system. If such a system had ever existed, we would expect the earliest tablets of Sumer to record this. They do not.

The Sumerian writing system is called a **syllabary**. Each symbol in a syllabary stands for a consonant and a vowel—in other words, one syllable per symbol. The earliest *tablets* show that the Sumerians already used **syllabograms**, (symbols representing the spoken consonant-plus-vowel) rather than logograms.

The syllabograms herald the transition from the purely economic sphere to more general applications. The tokens represented control of the spoken commercial contract both interstate and across language barriers. Syllabograms represented also intrastate control of law and religion.

The drawings of the caves show that man already knew that individual "pictures" could be combined. There are those human archers drawing their bows pointing at bison back in 22,000 BCE. One amusing cave painting from circa 5000 BCE depicts a woman collecting honey—and being stung by the bees for her efforts. We should not be surprised that these early clay tablets also show the Sumerians knew that the syllabograms could be combined (**concatenated**) into clusters to make words. Concatenated syllabograms are still around. Today we call this a rebus: "B + 4" is a syllabogram representing the word "before."

There was one new and major development. The Sumerians found that clustered syllabograms could be combined in many ways to create compound words and to write complex expressions and thoughts.

Neither the cave drawings nor the sculptured icons needed to be ordered. The visual magic in the caves covers surfaces in what can only be called a hodgepodge. They lie at angles to suit the wall surface. The icons are free-standing. The tokens were also free-standing at first. When enclosed within the security ball, they tumbled about as gravity wished. Tablets with their syllabograms and the potential they represented were different. It became obvious that there had to be a way of distinguishing expressions or semantic units from one another. **Limits**, the framework of a writing system, are designed to distinguish semantic units.

Limits follow naturally from the decision to concatenate graphic symbols to create clusters of expressions. Whether written horizontally or vertically and read left-to-right, right-to-left, top-to-bottom, or bottom-to-top, all writing systems assign limits.

Bottom-to-top and boustrophedon writing existed, but disappeared for practical reasons. Writing systems are designed for readability. Boustrophedon reading requires almost a complete double character set. The problems inherent in both bottom-to-top and boustrophedon reading are still pertinent to computer monitor screen rasters. It is more efficient to return an empty line than it is to double the pixel set.

Whether the direction of writing (and reading) is vertical or horizontal, *all* writing systems are essentially **bilinear** (two lines). The outer framework of Western writing systems consists of two horizontal lines: an upper and a lower limit. This structural foundation confines the writing **zone** (the writing area) to two possible formats:

1) a central area with vertical and horizontal movement within the zone,
   or
2) fill the zone entirely.

Bilinear scripts and fonts *fill* the entire space between the upper and lower limits. Because they fill the writing zone, bilinear scripts are tightly constrained on the horizontal plane and cannot move on the vertical plane at all (Figure 2.1).

Because symbols fill the entire space, bilinear limits are necessarily static. The main purpose of a totally bilinear limit system is to confine and constrain the written word. It intentionally "freezes" the words into an unchanging form to preserve the "magic." Consequently, religio-mystical societies choose strictly bilinear limits. The Egyptian system was totally bilinear.

Trilinear (three lines) scripts are written *within* the two limits. They have three positions, **upper limit**, **central space**, and **lower limit**. These scripts have two upper limits. The outer upper limit and the upper edge of the central space. The symbols hang from

Fig. 2.1 The Structured Limits
of Bilinear Scripts

these upper limits, that is, symbols are written from the upper lines downwards. In these scripts, the symbols move both vertically and horizontally within the central zone. The amount of movement within trilinear scripts is forced by the constraints of the central space in proportion to the script design and the upper and lower limits. In turn, these constraints create a central writing zone, an internal area between the upper and lower limits where the bow (the round part of a *p* or *b*) would overlap (Figure 2.2).

Trilinear limit systems are dynamic. Speech itself is dynamic; duration, stress, and phone (quality) change as words are vocalized. The main purpose of trilinear systems is to record speech *as spoken*. Trilinear limits are designed to allow the symbols to move up and down and from side to side within the three limits in imitation of the patterns of speech. Modern writing limits are **quattrolinear** (four lines), which is a refinement of the trilinear limit system.

a) North Semitic
(Monumental and Cursive)

b) Paleo-Hebraic
(Monumental)

c) Phoenician
(Monumental and Cursive)

d) Greek
(Monumental and Cursive)

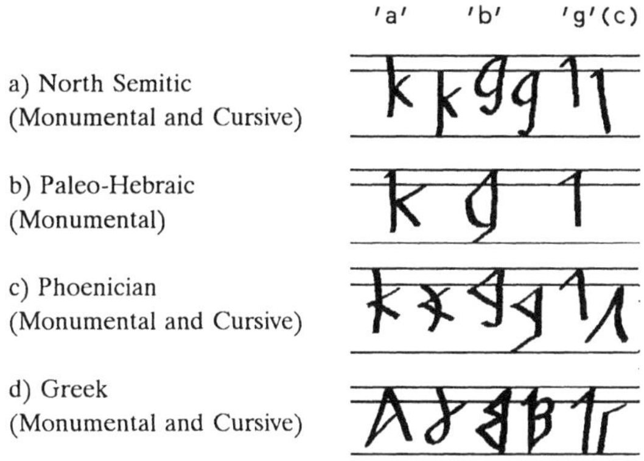

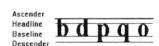

Fig. 2.2 The Structured Limits of Trilinear Scripts

Quattrolinear scripts are written *between* four lines. In palaeographic terms these limit lines are called the **ascender, headline, baseline,** and **descender** (Figure 2.3). Quattrolinear scripts are trilinear scripts moved downward to the former central zone to accommodate ascenders within the horizontal upper and lower limit lines. In these scripts, the ascender line is the former upper limit and the descender the former lower limit of the trilinear systems. The headline is the former upper limit and the baseline the former lower limit of the central writing zone.

Ascender
Headline
Baseline
Descender

b d p q o

Fig. 2.3 The Structured Limits of Quattrolinear Scripts

The Sumerian Cuneiform writing system uses trilinear limits; so do all of its descendants. In all these systems the symbols hang from the top line and move up and down and from side-to-side within the writing zone. They have done so from the very beginning.

Early tablets show cuneiform symbols separated by vertical and horizontal lines (Figure 2.4). Written from left-to-right or right-to-left, the archaic (3300-3100 BCE) form already shows the symbols placed at different heights and grouped by "sound-bites." The vertical lines acted as word dividers, the horizontal ones as sense dividers. These lines are the oldest form of punctuation.

The position and spacing of the symbols are important in reading these oldest tablets. Most of the symbols are in the central space. Higher symbols are stressed. The symbols are already spaced as spoken.

The vertical and horizontal movement, not to mention no fixed direction of writing, proved inadequate. By 2450, cuneiform writing limits and punctuation were stabilized. Each word was encased in its own box (**case**) and arranged from left to right. Inside each case, words were spaced as spoken or "uttered." The right hand margin (incised line) served as a stop (Figure 2.5).

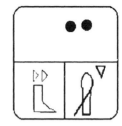

Fig. 2.4 Earliest Cuneiform Limits and Punctuation

Fig. 2.5   Typical Cuneiform Royal Document: Letter from Eannado, King of Lagash (circa 2400 BCE). Upper fifth of clay brick.

The symbols in the letter from Eannado, King of Lagash, hang from the top line. Inside their cases, the symbols are tied together (**ligatured**) as in the upper left hand case on the brick. Two lines on the right hand side of the symbol for "heaven" ($\ast$) purposely cross the tail of the "bird" symbol. In the next case down, the syllables are spaced according to their spoken rhythm. The last syllable has a longer pause than the other two. In the second column, the symbol for mountains ("kur," the three wedges) appears in both the first and fourth cases. In both instances, the symbol is within the central writing zone. This clumping and spacing and vertical movement can be seen throughout the writing on the brick.

The more familiar incised upper and lower limits, appear during the reign of Sargon I (circa 2334-2279 BCE). The texts were now written by **utterance** or **breathings**, that is, the number of words one can say in one breath. The right hand "margin" still served as a stop. Read from left-to-right, the last symbol of a word rested against this margin unless the line ran over. In the last instance, the text was written on the next line at the right margin, which was indented to show continuation. A larger space served as the "begin-new-sentence" marker.

The cuneiform writing system literally records the voice of the speaker. Duration in these ancient systems is indicated by the clumping and spacing of symbols. Syllable symbols will be ligatured or spaced according to the voice pattern. Stress (or volume) is shown by the position of the symbols within the writing limits. Because there is a different graphic symbol for every common syllable, Sumerian syllabaries are only partially phonetic and may or may not indicate quality (phone). Akkadian syllabic cuneiform, however, is completely phonetic, that is, a symbol indicates two phones—a consonant plus a vowel. Phonetic-syllabaries do indicate quality. Complete, systematically designed, and sophisticated graphic symbol systems, that is, scripts, appear by 3000 BCE.

The art of script design has not changed very much across the past five thousand years. It is a highly complex problem requiring years of design and re-design. The process is neither haphazard nor random. The apparently simple letter shapes that we see every day are remarkably subtle. We do not notice the underlying complexity. The fact that today we have computers to draw the various experimental stages for us does not change the nature of the problem.

Scripts are carefully designed finite systems. The problems confronting the ancient designer are the same ones confronting a modern one. The designer must consider an inordinate number of variables. The designer must consider the balance of line weight to space, height to breadth. Above all, a usable font must result in a fusion of the individual letters into a legible working whole. All writing systems employ **frames**, that is, a letter-symbol, or group of symbols, inclusive of its surrounding white space. How much white space does a given symbol require within its frame? How large may a frame be before the text becomes illegible? How do different shapes affect legibility? How far may a symbol be distorted before the letter becomes unrecognizable? What makes an *a* an *a*? What determines *a*-ness?

What makes an alphanumeric symbol that symbol and no other? How do we define *a*-ness? The question is not trivial; it may not even be answerable. The problem has not changed across the millennia. It matters little if we are referring to the most ancient formalized Phoenician *aleph*-plus-vowel or to the most modern computer-generated printed *A*. How can we arrive at an agreement on what constitutes an *a*?

Modern attempts to formulate the exceedingly precise definitions of the parameters necessary for computer-based font systems have shown the complexity of the problem of *a*-ness. Donald E. Knuth is known for his research on the computer font design problem, and for his METAFONT computerized script designer application. [2] He devoted eight years to the development of his font creation system. An underlying principle of his system rests upon what perhaps may be termed a Platonic "*a*-ness," an abstract concept of *a* with a finite number of variables.

Knuth envisioned a fully automated process covering the entire range of font system possibilities; however, in the end, he had to settle for much less than he wanted; there were simply too many variables. There are no rigid set of *A*-defining rules. Nobody can prophesy all *A*'s (Figure 2.6).

Although Roman Square and Rustic Capitals use a triangular form as the essence of *A*, the form need not have a crossbar, a pointed top, or even an opening at the bottom to be recognized as an 'A'. The Rustic form may even have the right-hand leg replaced by a *cephalicus* **neume**. (*Cephalicus*: Greek *kephalikos*, "of or for the head," that is, the head note or tone sounded by the *Precentor* or choir leader. Neumes are the precursors of our modern musical notes.) Uncial script and its descendants use an aleph-*a* (ᔰ) as their **majuscule** (uppercase) form. Later, secretary fonts incorporate a large two-cell form for what we would call a capital letter. The question of *a*-ness cannot be answered at more than a somewhat superficial level.

A-ness appears to reside more in cultural context than in some finite form. It seems to be determined through the recognition of what makes an *a* an *a* by the majority of a given group of users. The perception of a

Fig. 2.6 The Problem of A-ness: What makes an 'A' an 'A'?

graphic symbol as a unique entity is by consensus, context sensitive, and bound within the parameters of a functional font system design.

While a graphic symbol form may be distorted—an *A* may or may not have a **hasta** (cross-bar), may or may not be open at the bottom, may or may not have one long leg, may or may not be solid (filled in), may or may not be square, and so forth—as long as the *A* is within an integrated symbol set design, a reader recognizes the letter as an *A* (Figure 2.7).

A script is composed of a limited number of graphic symbols designed to work together within the constraints of a system design. This holds true whether referring to 24th century cuneiform, 9th century BCE Phoenician, 3rd century BCE Hebrew, 4th century CE monumental Greek, 8th century Official Latin, or modern computer fonts.

Scripts do not simply develop, nor are they merely collections of various available forms. Only when viewed from a distance of millennia can scripts be said to develop. Development implies a continuum; it suggests that one letter form changes here, another there, until finally a totally new script arrives.

Methods develop; scripts do not develop—they mutate. There may be an unfinished quality to random shards, but

Fig. 2.7 Examples of *A* within an integrated symbol set

ancient formal or official inscriptions and tablets display fully formed graphic symbol sets designed to work within their respective writing systems. Ancient cuneiform examples exhibit distinctions between scripts and **fonts**, their mutated descendants (Figure 2.8).

Graphic symbol (a) in Figure 2.8 illustrates the oldest known form, the **syllabogram** (a single syllable graphic symbol). The symbol was drawn on the clay. In illustration (b), the symbols rotate 90° and angularize to suit contemporary writing materials: clay and wedge-stylus. B is a script. Example (c) is a *font*, that is, a mutation of script (b). Example (d) is a new script design, and (e) is a font, a mutation of new script (d).

The fact that scripts mutate rather than develop is a very important distinction. The mutations allow us literally to see history. The scripts and their fonts speak to us; they tell us something about the people who used them.

The delta and plain of the Euphrates and Tigris rivers was inhabited by at least 5000 BCE. The entire area is usually called Mesopotamia. When the Sumerians arrived, they seem to have forced the previous occupants of the delta to move northward. The Empire of Sumer was to the south, the kingdom of Akkad to the north of the Mesopotamian plain.

The Sumerian Empire was situated on the delta at the conjunction of the two rivers. The land of a river delta shifts as the river deposits soil at its mouth. Ur, a great metropolis, sat right on the Persian Gulf. (The modern shoreline in Iraq is approximately sixty miles south of Ur-that-was.) The port was an important factor in the Sumerian economy. A port extends the commercial sphere, and the Sumerian wealth came from commerce and trade.

The Akkadians were a Semitic people. The few skulls known from the area are essentially those of modern Iraqis. Some more perishable genetic traits are notably persistent as well. The sculpture of

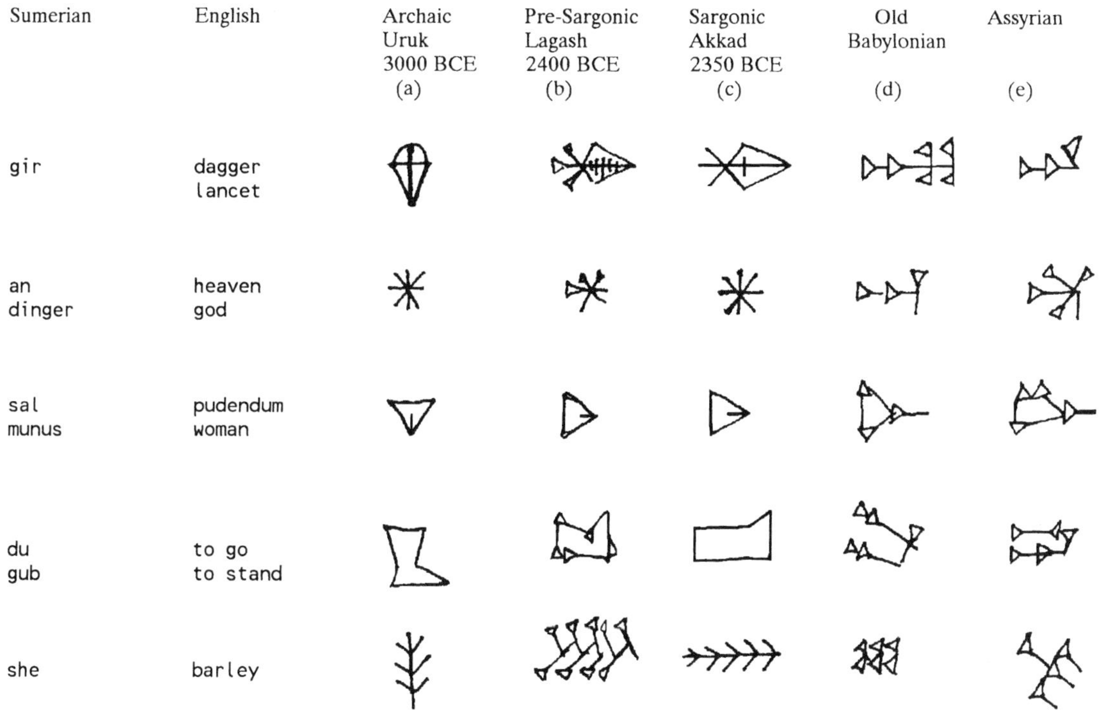

Sumerian	English	Archaic Uruk 3000 BCE (a)	Pre-Sargonic Lagash 2400 BCE (b)	Sargonic Akkad 2350 BCE (c)	Old Babylonian (d)	Assyrian (e)
gir	dagger lancet					
an dinger	heaven god					
sal munus	pudendum woman					
du gub	to go to stand					
she	barley					

Fig. 2.8 Two Cuneiform scripts and their fonts.

Dudu the scribe (circa 2350) would appear to be a realistic portrait. Dudu (the name is cognate to, and a diminutive of, "David") has the same distinctive nose as the modern inhabitants of Baghdad.

Situated north of Sumer, the main cities of the Akkadian kingdom were located higher up along both of the rivers: Akkad was on the Tigris and Babylon on the Euphrates. While the northern kingdom had no lack of excess food or water, the area is landlocked and has no port.

Eventually, the Akkadians conquered (re-conquered?) Sumer. Along with the territory and the port, they adopted the Sumerian writing system. While the scripts make it clear that the Sumerian "national" script was replaced, they also record Akkadian policies. We know from later documents that Sargon I was revered and his reign held up as the example of a good King. The scripts tell us why: Sargon I thought in terms of unification rather than despotism.

Sargon's new script had to be recognized by his Sumerian subjects as "official," yet it also had to have his personal stamp to differentiate his voice from his predecessors'. The result is a mutation of the Sumerian official script. We can see Sargon's approach in font (c).

On the other hand, the Old Babylonians thought in terms of complete control and despotism. They pulled down the "national flag" of Sumer and Akkad and replaced it with their own. The Babylonians designed a completely new official script (d) and official voice. The Assyrians again clearly thought in terms of unification. Their official script is a mutation (e), a font, of the Babylonian official script. While the Old Babylonian and Assyrian conquerors changed the script, they nevertheless continued to use the cuneiform syllabic writing system.

Syllabogramic systems are clumsy; they use a very large number of graphic symbols. A professional, academic scribe around 3000 BCE had to know close to 770 symbols. Writing systems and languages move in the direction of simplification, that is, toward fewer symbols and loss of inflections. The Semitic languages did not need the massive quantity of syllabograms required for Sumerian.

The Akkadians modified the Sumerian symbol set drastically. After Sargon I the system became almost totally phonetic-based. The Post-Sargonic symbol set consisted of a restricted group of monosyllabic signs that included a few common Sumerian logograms (for instance, "king"). Perhaps 100-150 symbols were required for everyday transactions in the Akkadian period. Besides the symbols, the Akkadians used an external subscript marker system to show whether the symbol stood for itself or as a phone in a semantic unit. Sense dividers consisted of spaces. Paragraphs were separated by larger spaces. While Akkadian scribes tried to fit a sentence on one line, if words ran over, they would indent the right-hand margin to show continuation and write the remainder on the next line down.

From about 2350 to approximately 1500 BCE, the Akkadian phonetic syllabary plus Sumerian logograms cuneiform remained the writing system of inter-ethnic diplomacy, local law, and administration. It was in use in most of the Semitic speaking areas.

The Northern Semitic languages separated into North-West, North-Central, and North-East branches. The usual simplification process appears to proceed at a slower pace among the North-East Semitic peoples. A professional "academic" scribe in the Neo-Babylonian Empire (625-538 BCE), the Biblical Babylon, still had to know roughly 600 symbols. The old saying that appearances are deceiving is more than a cliche in this case. The new Babylonian rulers were not direct descendants of the old ones. The superficial conservatism appears to have been archaizing on their part as a tie to the Old Babylonian Empire. Cuneiform was used for "official" legal and religious documents, but not for everyday use. For foreign affairs and commercial transactions, the Neo-Babylonians used the writing system designed and implemented elsewhere.

The Phoenicians arrived in the Mediterranean basin before 3000 BCE. The Kingdom of Ugarit was one of the Phoenician city-states. It was situated on the Mediterranean coast near modern Latakia, Syria. Ugarit (modern Tell Ras Shamra) was the capital city. The site of the city was occupied by Neolithic times (circa 6500 BCE). During the second millennium BCE, Ugarit was a wealthy and influential player in Mediterranean power politics. Among the tablets found in the remains of the Royal Palace at Ugarit we find Akkadian, Hittite, Hurrian, and even some documents written in hieroglyphics. The city sat on a hill between modern Latakia and the Bahluliya plateau. It was surrounded by fertile plains and had a fine harbor (the "White Harbor" of the Greeks, the "Port Blanc" of the Crusaders). Commerce again fostered innovation.

The Sumerians created the means to record speech as spoken. The Akkadians modified the symbol set for the Semitic languages. Ugaritic is a North-West Semitic tongue, an early version of Phoenician. At Ugarit they came up with a momentous refinement. Sometime about 1500 BCE they designed a formalized, determinate, consonantal alphabetic cuneiform writing system.

The Ugaritic writing system combines the graphic syllabic system of cuneiform with the Semitic dry surface consonantal alphabetic symbol set systems used earlier farther to the south. These earlier dry alphabetic systems reduced the cumbersome mass of cuneiform graphs, but were indeterminate, lococentric, and non-transferable. The Ugaritic system reduced this indeterminate mass and formalized them into twenty-two symbols plus variant forms—for a total of twenty-six to thirty graphic symbols. The number of symbols depends upon the level of formality. Official texts are written from left-to-right and use the full thirty symbol set; informal texts and commentaries are written from right-to-left and employ a form of shorthand.

The Ugaritic system design includes yet another major innovation. Their symbol set has variant forms, distinct graphic symbols, for a number of consonant-plus-vowel phones. Among these differentiated graphic symbols we find three distinct graphs of *alep* that record three distinct *a*-phones and two distinct forms of *heh* (*e*-phones). [3] In keeping with their streamlined new design, they also refined the existing punctuation-by-space used in Akkadian cuneiform. Ugaritic texts use a medial (central) point as a word divider and a bar as a sense divider. The point, of course, was a wedge-shaped dot. In systems that used a left to right writing direction, the sense divider looks a great deal like our modern forward slash (/). In systems that used a right to left direction, the sense divider looks like our backwards slash (\). Otherwise, they retained the features of their ancient model. They used trilinear limits; their symbols hang from the top line and move up and down and from side-to-side. The texts are written in breathings. A word may run over onto the next line, because that was the way the words were spoken. This caused no difficulties as their writing system treated the end of a line as the equivalent of a standard *o* space between words. However, Ugaritic was still a cuneiform system with two different symbol-sets. It still required **diacriticals** (external markings) to indicate phones for undistinguished forms, and it employed a recording technique rather useless for dry surfaces. As has already been noted, writing systems move toward simplification. The stage was set for the next development.

Farther down the coast of the Mediterranean in what is today modern Lebanon, some Southern Phoenicians took the Ugaritic alphabetic cuneiform writing system and refined it even further. The Phoenicians created a new script design based upon *existing* Semitic dry-surface models, but retained the determinate Ugaritic symbol-to-phone assignments. They reduced the number of characters to a formalized twenty-two member symbol-set. The result was the first true *determinate* consonantal alphabet. We call this writing system "Phoenician."

The Phoenicians also invented a different way to record the different qualities (phones) of the vowels. Their solution was very simple. Instead of relying on completely different graphic forms or external markings to indicate quality, they designed a script that uses variant forms of a basic graphic symbol shape. Chosen from among the existing Semitic symbol sets, each variant of a basic shape indicated a different phone associated with *that* shape. Now they could encode everything that had been in their cuneiform model in an exceptionally compact form.

Semitic languages use **triliterals**. This means that the roots of words are represented by three consonants. Vowels are not part of the root word. Usually, the form of the word, in context, tells you the correct vowel phone to be pronounced and, therefore, the meaning. The important word in the previous sentence is "usually." Many *cruces* ("crosses," places where the meaning is ambiguous) in the Bible result from not knowing the correct form from context alone. This is a problem for modern scholars; it was not problematic at the time. The Phoenicians and early Hebrews did not know that they were leaving an ambiguous heritage. They thought that their solution was sufficient.

As Ugaritic, Phoenician used three different *a*-phones attached to the consonant *aleph*. In the Phoenician system, a different vowel phone is associated with each of the variant forms. [4] The same is true of *heh* (modern *e*) as well as *vav* (modern *f, u,* or *v*). While it may seem odd that one Semitic form should give different modern letter symbols, the Phoenician, and therefore Hebrew, symbol may be either vocalized (*u*) or consonantal (*v*), voiced (*v*) or unvoiced (*f*). The two remaining vowels of our modern alphabet, *i* and *o*, remain unchanged—but for different reasons. Although a consonant, the Semitic *yod* plus vowel apparently sounded much like the Greek *iota* (jot) and Latin *i*, that is, the modern English long *e* phone. The symbol *o* (*ayin* in the Semitic languages) is the measurement (**mensural**) base for all script design.

Although the art of script design may be complex, the basics are very simple. Proportional scripts (and fonts), bilinear, trilinear, or quattrolinear, are designed relative to the width of the **minim** and the symbol *o*.

The unit of measure is the minim—the width of a vertical stroke—as determined by the width of the writing instrument. In palaeographic circles, the term "minim" sometimes refers only to the upright stroke of an *m* or *n*. However, the minim as the basis of mensuration in these ancient writing systems refers to the width of the upright stroke—whether tall or short.

The writing instrument dictates the width of the *o*. An *o* is the width of a "standard" space. The *o* determines the distance between the baseline and the headline. This may appear complicated, but it is not. These design specifications can be summed up as follows:

> The writing instrument establishes the width of a minim.
> A minim is the width of a vertical stroke.
> The minim is the unit of measurement (scale or method of mensuration).
> The writing instrument establishes the width of the *o*.
> The *o* establishes the width of a standard space.
> The *o* establishes the distance between the baseline and the headline.
> The number of minims per *o* varies with the design, but is usually around three.

Within the ancient writing systems, the width of the minim is the measure for horizontal movement; the height of the *o* (*ayin* in Hebrew and Aramaic fonts) is the measure for vertical movement. Because a written text has a built-in scale, the scribe only has to change the width of his or her pen to change the scale. The writing instrument will determine the distance between headline and baseline when a completed font design is actually performed by a scribe (Figure 2.9).

A 9th century "Scribe's Handbook" states that "the lines should be spaced . . . according to the size of the writing." [5] That is, choose your writing instrument and then draw your writing guidelines.

The standards were set more than five thousand years ago and apply equally well to an inscription on an ancient stele, a Roman Monumental inscription, a tiny fourteenth century book of hours, and a modern printed paperback book. These standards are used by calligraphers to this day and are still the basis of professionally designed proportional scripts, typefaces, and computer fonts. Although there have been attempts across the centuries to vary this basic script design, no-one has yet found anything better for the creation of well balanced, pleasing, and readable fonts. Our modern scripts and fonts are all descendants of the new Phoenician script design.

The Phoenicians could have sat back on their well deserved laurels. Their solution to the phonetic graph symbol problem was ingenious; a major technological advance. The majority of existing Phoenician documents are written in **breathings** (the number of syllables that can be said in one breath) and as a result do not use punctuation; nevertheless, sometime between the fourteenth and tenth centuries BCE, the Phoenicians added further refinements to their punctuation system. They discarded the bar (/) and introduced a three point system: high, medial, and low points. They retained the Ugaritic point as a word divider, but the position of the point had grammatical significance. The high point indicated a clause, that is, a dependent semantic unit. The low point marked the equivalent of our modern semi-colon and the medial point marked closure of both a word and a complete thought.

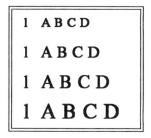

Fig. 2.9 Changing scale by changing minim

Our evidence of this further change comes from texts written in languages other than Phoenician. Figure 2.10 shows a close up of portions of two ninth century BCE stelae written in the Phoenician phonetic-based script and using the new punctuation system.

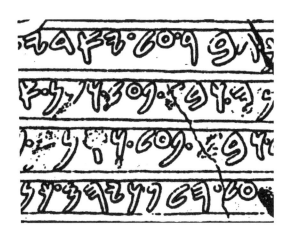 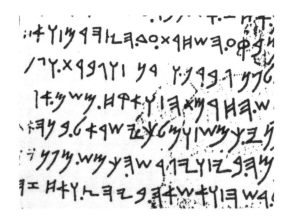

Fig. 2.10   Left: Kilamu, King of Yadi stele. Phoenician Script, high, low, and Medial points.
Right: The Mesha stele. Phoenician script, medial and low points.

The two steles are of interest for more than the text or the writing system. Prior to the seventeenth century CE and the age of "enlightenment," *everything* had significance. Stripes on a garment, the shape and size of a document, the format, the script, a larger letter symbol, everything on a building, tablet, and leaf of papyrus or parchment had meaning. Listen carefully: we can hear their absent voices.

Kilamu, King of Yadi, is wearing a sleeved undertunic with a length of fringed cloth wrapped about him. Each sleeve has four stripes. The cloth is draped so that the fringe creates four more stripes (Figure 2.11). The clothing illustrates a social custom in use today for the same purpose for which it was used in Rome, in the days of the Biblical patriarchs, and in the Sumer of Uruk.

Fig. 2.11 Kilamu, King of Yadi.

The original writing tokens reflected items of importance to the people of Uruk. The majority are food stuffs, but we also find tokens for a bolt of cloth. Among the cuneiform script symbols we find the graph for a "princess." It is a compound word composed of the graph representing a woman resting on top of the graph representing a bolt of cloth. The bolt of cloth has striped bands.

Cloth was very expensive. Only the very wealthy could afford colored cloth; only rulers wore colored stripes. Stripes show the social status of the wearer.

Modern military and police lower ranks wear colored stripes to show their status. Julius Caesar wore the widest stripe in Rome. Caesar's was dyed purple to show that he was a Roman aristocrat. Kilamu's is a 'colored' fringe. The Hebrew word for "stripes" is "passim." Passim necessarily differ in color or texture from the base cloth.

> Genesis 37:3. Now Israel loved Joseph more than all his children, because he was the son of his old age; and he made him a coat of many stripes.
>
> 37:4 And when his brethren saw that their father loved him more than all his brethren, they hated him, and could not speak peaceably unto him.

The story of Joseph is not a simple case of sibling rivalry. There could only be one head of an extended family and only one freeholder of the land. All the rest of the clan members were dependents.

Isaac could not give his blessing to Esau. There could only be one "blessing," the family leadership. When in Gen 27:37 Isaac told Esau: "Behold, I have made him thy lord, and all his brethren have I given to him for servants," the blessing had already been given to Jacob.

Jacob had not been exactly idle all those fourteen years he labored for Laban to gain Rachel as his wife. Joseph had ten older brothers. All were grown men. All of the brothers, maidservants, field hands, shepherds, and every other member of the clan were dependents of Jacob.

While not very happy about it, the ten brothers naturally expected Reuben, the eldest, to succeed Jacob as head of the family. Then Jacob gave Joseph the striped coat. Jacob unequivocally did love him more than the others: he gave young Joseph the stripes of leadership. It was very natural for his older brothers to hate and resent Joseph. Jacob *disinherited* the brothers and publicly declared Joseph his heir.

Young Joseph was touchingly naive and honest. Instead of keeping quiet about his dreams, he told his brothers and his parents. There is more than a hint of maliciousness about the words when the brothers say: "Shalt thou indeed reign over us? or shalt thou indeed have dominion over us?" The brothers sold Joseph into slavery, but the plot backfired. Jacob did not name another heir. And as recorded in the story, all came to pass as Joseph had dreamed. His brothers did bow down before him. Joseph did indeed inherit the clan leadership.

Kilamu's stripes illuminate Joseph's story. The stele of Kilamu, King of Yadi also illustrates the history behind our twentieth century stripes of rank. The stripes are a remnant of a tradition 5000 years old. The Mesha stele tells us another story (Figure 2.12). This is a different type of history. This one is about the shape and size of *The* Law (the Pentateuch).

Law codes fell into two classes: public, that is, placed where all could read them, and archival, that is, for the record. In the Asian Near East tradition, public law codes were inscribed upon monumental steles or upon individual tablets joined together or mounted upon a wall to create a monumental surface. Such public displays had a distinctive shape; the ancient stelae were topped by an arch.

As with so many traditional practices, the story behind the shape of "The" law is both interesting and amusing. Just as the materials themselves play their part in a writing system, the available construction materials ruled architectural features of buildings—both secular and sacred. The shape of "The" law comes from these construction materials.

Lumber was in short supply in the Mesopotamian valley. (This is why the references to the trees of the Lebanon coast in the Bible.) The primary building materials were mud brick, reeds, and plaster made of clay. This lack of wood resulted in two distinctive elements in the architecture of the region: 1) narrow rooms with exceptionally thick walls centered around an open court and 2) the vault or arch.

There were two types of standard religious structures in Mesopotamia: the man-made high place (ziggurat) and the house of god. The house of god building compounds were built on the same plan as the normal house and differed from the homes of the general population only in being far more regularized, more carefully finished, and with a large doorway leading to the central court. From descriptions and from architectural evidence, the large doorway was topped by an arch. (The later architecture of the region, as well as the tunnel-arch roof of early Christian churches, suggests that the roofs of the house of god type buildings were "arched" as well.) [6]

Fig. 2.12 The Mesha Stele.

At first the arch, like the high place, was associated only with religion. The Victory Stele of Naram-Sin (ca. 2371-ca. 2255), [7] is nearly two meters in height and combines the ziggurat of the high place with the arched doorway of the house of god in the form of "clouds."

As we have already noticed, custom hardens into rule rather quickly. The traditional link between shape, size and the authority of "The" law is firmly established by the time of Hammurabi. Hammurabi's law code is written on a stele nearly eight feet in height. In form it is a narrow column slightly wider at the base than at the top and crowned by a high rounded arch. (Figure 2.13) We should note that the shape retains its religious significance wherever it appears; it is a statement that the god of a people stood behind the ruler.

The shape of "The" law is found throughout the North Semitic writing systems. Tablets and stelae of this nature are topped by an arch. Interpretation of the shape on tablet, stele, scroll, and codex varies among the North-East, North-Central, and North-West Semitic peoples and is solely dependent upon the culture.

The shape of the arch can be a fairly tight arc, a stylized "cloud," a wide half-circle, or pointed. The Mesha stele is topped by a wide half-circle arch. The arch on the much later Yehaw-milk stele (ca. 5th-4th centuries BCE) is also the wide half-circle. The shape of the Ptolemaic age Greek-Aramaic stele found at Armazi is a stylized variant of the "cloud" shape we find on the Victory Stele of Naram-Sin. Displaying the conservatism of writing systems, this ancient "cloud" shaped arch is the form used in Syriac gospels [8]

The Western Phoenicians used a pointed "arch" on a narrow rectangular base. The "arch" was either shaped as an integral piece of the stele or cut as a separate piece and placed atop the stele. Examples of this type of pointed arch appear on Phoenician inscriptions from Cyprus (ca. 735 BCE) and Tunisia and show up on the Sinai Peninsula as well.

We can see that Mesha ordered that his stele have the shape of a god-given authority held in common among the North-Semitic peoples. Like the Akkadian Naram-Sin stele, the Mesha stele is a victory stele. The stele is a combination of a broad based version of Hammurabi's stele topped with a wide half-circle arch. The shape itself is a statement that author is backed by his god.

The Greeks picked up this "monumental" public law code practice along with the writing system: the "Decree of Rhodes" states Philip V of Macedon's negotiations in 202/1 BCE. [9] The stele is 94 lines of monumental sculptured capitals. We do not know the size of the twelve tables of Rome, but we can assume that they were large. Certainly, extant Imperial constitutions inscribed in Greek do not contradict this assumption. While many of these Imperial inscriptions have been cut up for other uses (one into 100 paving stones for the Roman agora at Athens) some are almost entire. Hadrian's Epistle to the citizens of Stratonicea Hadrianopolis in 127 CE, [10] totals 92 inches in height by 27 inches in width.

Fig. 2.13 The shape of "The" Law: Hammurabi's stele

There is also little question as to the status of the Mosaic Code under Christianity: Late Antique and Medieval illustrations depict Moses holding enormous, narrow, round-topped tablets longer than his arms—the shape of Hammurabi's stele. *The Law*, the ten commandments, are depicted this way even today.

Writing systems are conservative; continuity of custom long-lived. We might note that the width of the Paleo-Hebraic fragments of Pentateuchal texts found among the Dead Sea Scrolls shows that these texts were taken down from individual wall tablets. We have numerous reasons to believe that those wall tablets were topped with the arch of religious authority we see on the Hammurabi stele.

We find the shape of Mosaic authority in use among early Christian documents. The usual way to present the Gospels and religious calendars is encased in drawn pillared arches—the shape of the Law of Moses. Western church altars, ancient and modern, have round-topped narrow arches encasing the figure of Christ. Wall paintings and stained glass windows show the Patriarchs and the Apostles—encased in the narrow columned round-topped arch of Biblical authority. Norman churches have multilayered round-topped arched entries of which only the outermost is structural. [11] Gothic churches employ the pointed arch structurally. The actual entry arches are round-topped, the shape of the Mosaic code. [12] Look around at the architecture of churches and synagogues even today. Among all the modern squared off shapes, we still see the high round-topped entry doorway outside and round-topped columnar altars inside. It is not at all unusual to see round-topped arch pillared arcades surrounding Roman Catholic churches. Each pillared section copies the arches of the early Gospel illustrations that gained authority from the shape of the Mosaic Law tablets. The oldest synagogues were round-topped domes with courtyard wings. Muslim mosques are built with a central arched dome set off by straight wings to the sides. Stand back a bit and we can see the central shape is that of the tablets on which were written the Mosaic code. [13] Inside modern synagogues, the Torah rests inside wooden round-topped arched niches. All these architectural and graphic features are reflections of the authority granted by the shape of the Law of Moses—and the ancient arch of regnal authority backed by a people's god.

Our modern arched altar and doorway practices date back at least 4500 years. Our modern alphabetic writing practices begin with the Phoenician reforms to the Ugaritic system sometime about the fourteenth century BCE.

The Phoenician phonetic-based writing system was practical, concise, and comprehensive. It was economical of both time and materials. Its small character symbol set was easy to learn and even easier to write. It needed no confusing external markers. Its built-in encoding system was highly suited to recording the voice of the absent authority as a self-contained entity. Within a remarkably short time, the Phoenician comprehensive writing system was adopted throughout most of the Mediterranean basin.

The impact on Western civilization echoes still.

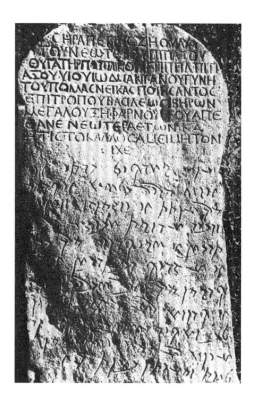

Chapter Three

BORROWINGS

The Mediterranean Sea is essentially an oversized pond. Unlike crossing the Atlantic, navigation is simple. Islands dot the seascape and island hopping is trivially easy. Fierce storms occur, of course, yet sailors are never very far from land and a safe harbor. The longest stretch of sea without sight of land is the straight route from Crete to Egypt—but it is short. There was constant interaction between Mediterranean civilizations.

The Phoenicians were sea people. They were founding trading posts, colonies, in what is modern Spain during the 2nd millennium BCE. They were on Malta by the eleventh century and on Sardinia before the ninth century BCE. They had colonies in South France by the eighth century. Carthage, a Phoenician colony, was founded in the eighth BCE. It was ideally situated for trade on the miniature "horn" of the North African coast located to the west of Egypt. From Carthage to the Iberian peninsula is only a day's sail away. From Carthage to Sicily is a short hop.

The Phoenicians were traders. In fact, their name for themselves "Cana'ani" (of Canaan) means "merchant" or "trader." Various Western societies came into commercial contact with them and their writing system.

The Phoenician writing system was compact, comprehensive, economical, and practical. It recorded the voice of the absent speaker while retaining the speaker's identity. This was accomplished through a variety of sub-systems. These sub-systems consisted of: a twenty-two character plus variant forms symbol set, trilinear limits, a hierarchy of size and format, punctuation, spelling (**orthography**), and content systems. Each sub-system was designed to work together within the complete writing system.

The Phoenician system is the starting point. Their system is the ancestor of modern writing systems from India to Arabia, from Spain to Russia, from Italy to Greece, and, of course, throughout the fertile crescent. During the period from the fourteenth to the ninth century BCE, the majority of the Mediterranean societies adopted the practical Phoenician comprehensive writing system. Each society adapted the writing system to its own needs.

The Etruscans were a people who lived in central and northern Italy. At the height of their power, their territory lay on both sides of the Appenines mountain range. On the Tyrrhenian Sea side of Italy, the territory extended from the River Arno to the bay of Naples, well south of Rome. It included a colony on the Island of Corsica. On the Adriatic side of the Italian "boot," their territory included modern Mantua and Bologna.

The heart of Etruria remains; today we call it Tuscany. The Etruscan area is moderately fertile, but as it does not have the long growing season found in the Near East, it is not nearly as productive of food stuffs. The soil, and climate, of Tuscany itself is better suited to cattle and swine than it is to **corn**. (Corn was the generic name for "grain.")

The Etruscans are somewhat of a mystery. Their language has not as yet been fully deciphered; it is not Indo-European, but appears to be related to the Dravidian group. Nor do we know where the Etruscans came from; they may have come down from Northeastern Asia. Like the Egyptians, Etruscan society had a very strong religio-mystical bias. The majority of their remaining texts are of a religious nature. Many have something to do with divination and omens. Some of the tablets are even formed in the shape of a liver. This last includes marking the various lobes of the liver for interpretation of their portent. This liver-shaped tablet may have been a study guide for learning to be a *haruspex* (one who studies the innards of sacrificial victims for the purpose of divination). [1]

The Etruscans had contact with the Semitic peoples on the Asian side of the fertile crescent—if only commercial. Sometime between the late fifteenth and eleventh centuries BCE, the Etruscans adopted the Phoenician writing system.

When the Etruscans adopted the Phoenician graphic symbols, they either added extensions or rotated the symbols 90 degrees. The oldest Etruscan **Monumentary** script (engraved or incised formal official script used on monuments), for example, is the primary Phoenician "alep" with an extended left-hand leg (Figure 3.1)

Phoenician was written from right-to-left. Formal and official Etruscan texts were written from right-to-left. Some informal handwriting (cursive) examples appear written in boustrophedon. The Etruscans employed the medial point as their primary word divider and a space or paragraph as sense divider. Occasionally, a double point that closely resembles a modern colon (:) appears as an end of phrase marker.

The Etruscans apparently were influenced by the Egyptian approach. They did not retain the trilinear limits; official Etruscan was completely bilinear. Their religious and dedicatory texts use a strictly one-to-one phone symbol system and the symbols are all upper case (**majuscule**). Their mystical bias had far-reaching consequences.

They also had contacts with the Greeks. The rigid and mystically ridden Etruscan civilization appeared to

Greek   Hebrew   Etruscan/Roman

Fig. 3.1 The 3 Phoenician 'Aleps' and their earliest Western descendants.

be gaining some pliancy through this contact, but the Greeks were busily settling the Italian peninsula. They were taking land and moving closer to the Etruscan-held areas. When the Greeks attempted to take over the Bay of Naples, wars broke out. This put a stop to all interchange between the two civilizations. Contact between the Etruscans and Greeks ended in mutual antagonism during the fifth century BCE.

There is little doubt that Etruscan influence on Roman writing systems was very strong. This is not surprising as the Etruscans were the civilized people of Italy and, for a while, Rome was subject to the Etruscans. Early Monumental Latin and Old Roman cursive are directly from the Etruscan symbol set (Figure 3.2).

Like the Etruscan, the official Roman system was also strictly bilinear. They also employed a restricted and very limited symbol set. Although the variant forms appear here and there in Etruscan informal texts, the majority of the Etruscan dialects did not use the Phoenician variant forms in formal texts—*and neither did the Romans.*

This lack of variant forms tells us that, at least before the tenth century BCE, these languages employed a very limited set of phones. The lack of variants also explains the logic behind the Roman language reforms we find at work one thousand years later under Augustus.

By the eighth century BCE, the Etruscans had abandoned the bar as sense divider and used paragraphing and spacing. The Romans retained the older punctuation of word division by medial point and bar as sense divider. Roman punctuation practice did not change until the third century BCE—and it took Greek influence to effect this change.

We know that the Romans borrowed the Etruscan system, their writing limits and graphic symbols tell us that. The oldest examples of Roman writing are written from right-to-left. While examples of Etruscan documents that employ the bar have not as yet turned up, which does not mean that they will not turn up, we know that they must have originally used the more ancient system; examples of punctuation by bar and medial point show up in texts from Rome as late as the first century CE. This tells us that the Romans took their writing system from the Etruscans *before* the Etruscans changed their punctuation system. Because the Greek system uses the later form of Phoenician punctuation, we can also see that the Etruscans borrowed the Phoenician writing system before the Greeks did.

A few Greek symbols appear in the Etruscan symbol

Fig. 3.2

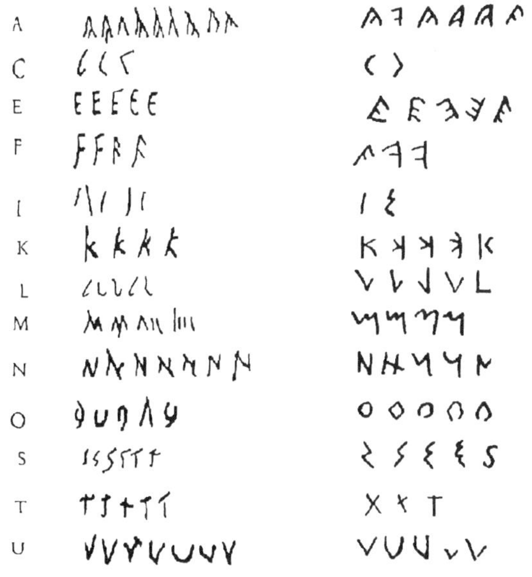

Left:
Examples of Old Roman Cursive scripts from Pompeii (70 CE).

Right:
Northern and Central Etruscan Cursive scripts, circa 8th-5th centuries BCE.

set. Perhaps the use of the double point (:) was under Greek influence, too. These few graphic symbols are the only parts of the Etruscan writing system that came through Greek contacts. The Greeks, after all, arrived on the writing scene several hundred years later than the Etruscans.

The first Greeks (the Achaeans) entered the area around 1900 BCE. The existence of Maltese Neolithic Age motifs on pottery at Bronze Age Crete makes it likely that contact with Semitic peoples occurred back then as the Phoenicians were the shippers of Antiquity, but this must remain in the realm of conjecture. The first *recorded* Greek contact with the Semitic peoples seems to have occurred in the ninth century along the Asiatic coast among the Ionians—the Eastern Greek colonists. The Homeric name for the Ionians is "Yawon(es)." The *w* represents a *digamma* (literally, double-gamma, the name given the graph in the 1st century BCE); the graph is a reflected Phoenician "vav." The phone and symbol fell into disuse by the third century BCE. Like a "vav," a digamma could have been pronounced *v* as in "vest," *f* as in "fest," or *whu* as in "woo"—depending upon locale and dialect. The Hebrew word for Greece is "Yavan"—which is a literal phonetic transcription of "Yawon" with the digamma pronounced *v*. Persian transcribes the name as "Yuana."

The Greeks apparently used the Cretan writing system at first; Cretan Linear B is a Hellenic language. Sometime in the ninth century BCE, however, the Greeks adopted the Phoenician writing system. They took it over wholesale. The **Law of Parsimony** states that a system or organism uses only what is needed—no more. The law of parsimony works in languages and writing systems as much as it does in the hard sciences. Because Greek words contain vowels as part of the root word, they needed vowel symbols. They also had some phones that do not occur in the Semitic languages. As a result, they increased the symbol set but otherwise followed the Phoenician tradition throughout—including variant forms. The Archaic Ionian Greek primary "alpha," for example, is a copy of the third form of Phoenician "alep"—neither reflected nor rotated (Figure 3.1). The oldest Athenian "alpha" is the second Phoenician "alep," as-is. Greek employed the "newer" Phoenician three point punctuation system adding a double point (:). Comments about how letters appear to be "hung" or "suspended" from an invisible top line attest to the fact that the Greeks also retained the trilinear limit system. [2]

Originally, the Greeks wrote right-to-left; boustrophedon writing appears to have been used for incantations and charms. Some early inscriptions also display writing from top-to-bottom, but by the fifth century BCE the direction of writing had settled down to left-to-right. The Greeks even adopted writing by "utterance" or "breathings." Religious texts from the sixth century BCE are found written both by breathings and with punctuation. The use of punctuation depends upon the width of the stele or other writing surface. If the area is large, punctuation by point system is used. If the writing area is narrow, there is no need for punctuation: each line is a separate "breath." Because the text appears to be written in a continuous stream, the modern technical term for this writing technique is *scriptum continuum* (continuous script). This, of course, is not the case at all, but as a technique can easily be misunderstood. If something can be misunderstood or misinterpreted, it will be—and it was.

During the third century BCE, the Romans adopted the Greek model and abandoned their previous practices. They changed from point as word divider and bar as sense divider to a true *scriptum continuum*. Sometimes they wrote by utterance, but more often than not they simply squeezed as many letters onto a line as would fit. If a complete "word" did not fit on the line, they would break it at a syllable. Still, there are always conservative people who refuse to use the new systems. Giessen, Universitaetsbibliothek, Papyrus Ianda 90, which uses the medial point as word divider and bar as sense divider, shows that the older Roman punctuation system was still in use in Rome as late as the first century CE.

When the Romans conquered the surrounding areas on the Italian peninsula, they found a need to write a history, but apparently not to reform their language. (They included the Etruscan "Kings of Rome"; they "forgot" to mention that Rome was a subject kingdom of Etruria at the time.) Later, when the Roman Republic added Greece to their territory, the Romans found their civilized model for the finer arts such as writing, sculpture, and philosophy. Greek became the language of culture. The upper classes spoke Greek. They bought Greek slaves as tutors and writing masters. This infatuation with Greek culture had a profound effect on Roman practices.

With the coming of Empire, Rome promptly initiated all the "Winner's" techniques. Rome had need for a "better" history than any of their subject domains. The Greeks had their Homer, the Israelites had their Bible (The Tanakh), the Egyptians had their God cycles. Virgil's *Aenid* is a Roman-centered imitation of Homer's *Iliad*. They reformed their official voice, and Augustan Roman Capital script came into place. They also very naturally reformed their spelling and grammar. It was the thing to do.

When the Roman reformers reconstructed the "classical" Latin of their ancestors, they apparently assumed that their interpretation of *scriptum continuum* was the "correct" way the ancients wrote. They also insisted that there could be only one phone for each alphabetic graphic symbol.

Latin is classified as **quantitative** language. The quantity (the length of a sound) is an integral part of the language. If the quantity is not correct, these languages become almost incomprehensible. Other languages, such as Hebrew and English, are classified as **stress** languages. In these languages, stress or accent on a sound is important. Stress, putting the accent on the right syllable, is **phonemic**—a part of the phonetic structure of the language. In stress languages, two words that are spelled the same but differ only by stress pattern would be considered two words. For example, the stress patterns of the expression "rehash" vary depending upon whether we are using the verb (rehAsh) or the noun (rEhash). In languages where these distinctions are unimportant, that is, not phonemic, there is no need for vertical movement. It appears that Etruscan ought to be classified as a quantitative language, too. Stress was not phonemic in either official Etruscan or the reconstructed "Classical" Latin. Although the evidence from unofficial texts shows that 'street' Latin was a stress language, the first-century reformers restored their language to a classical state according to some imagined ideal of "pure" ancient Latin.

This reconstructed classical Latin explains why writing in the Official Roman tradition continued to use strictly bilinear limits and no variant forms. The reconstructed Classical Latin was phonetically impoverished and limited. Limited phones means that the Romans did not need the capability to distinguish phones. No stress differentiation means that they did not require the ability to move symbols up and down. Because the reconstructed language was quantitative, Roman writing systems did retain horizontal movement. Even this horizontal durational remnant of the ancient system eventually disappeared in the wake of the late first-century BCE language reformers. The Roman writing tradition remained static and confined until the arrival of Christianity.

In the meantime, the North-West Semitic peoples continued to use the complete comprehensive Phoenician writing system. The North-East Semitic peoples continued to use the older cuneiform system, particularly for official and religious documents.

Sitting right in the fertile area where Sumer once had been, the territory changed hands fairly frequently. The Chaldeans (Neo-Babylonians 625-538 BCE) were conquered by the Achaemenians (Persians 538-332 BCE), who in turn were conquered by Alexander the Great (332-323 BCE). The Seleucid Greeks ruled from 312 to 171 BCE to be conquered in their turn by the Arascids (Parthians 171 BCE-226 CE). The Arascids were replaced by the Sassanids (Persians 226-641 CE), who were still there at the time of the Moslem conquest. The Winner's techniques operated through the centuries. Cyrus the Great, of the Achaemenid dynasties, created a new cuneiform "official" script. (He also created a genealogy.) The Seleucids, of course, favored the Greek writing system among themselves. With such diversity and turmoil there was need for a **koine** (common tongue), if nothing else than for commercial reasons. This commercial tongue was "Aramaic," the language of the Chaldeans.

The North-West Semitic tongues are relatives. All of them are stress languages, Phoenician, Moabite, Hebrew, and Aramean (the language of ninth-eighth centuries BCE Aram), and are very closely related. They are effectively dialects of the same tongue. The differences among them are similar to those dialectic differences between, for example, the American spoken in Maine and that in Boston. Aramaic, that is, Chaldean, a member of the North-Central Semitic tongues, is again a close relative, but somewhat farther away. Here the distinctions are similar to the differences between modern Italian and Spanish.

Moabite and Aramean eventually disappeared. Phoenician resurfaces as Punic and remained an important language along the North African coast. Aramaic had become the language of commerce by the seventh century BCE. A square script Aramaic, a mutation of the ninth-century Phoenician symbol set, was designed during the Neo-Babylonian and Achaemenian periods (circa 625-332 BCE). While the Neo-Babylonians still used cuneiform, they relegated the "official" redesigned cuneiform to monuments and religious texts. Square Aramaic was used for everyday purposes. By the fifth to fourth century BCE, the square Aramaic had become the "official" script of Empire.

All this time, the Hebrew writing system retained the original Phoenician system intact. From around the tenth century through the sixth century BCE, the script systems show small mutations but remain essentially the script of ninth century BCE Phoenician. Today this script is known as Paleo-Hebraic; it is virtually identical with modern Samaritan. During this four hundred year period, the Hebrew culture, like those of the surrounding territories, was literate. We find **ostraca** (pieces of pottery) containing the equivalent of modern "refrigerator notes." Then came the Babylonian exile in 586 BCE.

Not all Judeans were sent into exile; soldiers at Elephantine, country squires, artisans, and tillers of the soil remained unmolested. The people who were carted off were the literate and the educated Judeans, the leaders and intellectuals, the "trouble-makers." There are references in the post-exilic parts of the Bible to "lost books," written books. People carted off in mass cannot take their books with them; particularly not if the books are inscribed on wall tablets or written on heavy leather scrolls. The Judean intellectuals spent more than two generations in exile. It was more than enough time for the people to change their writing habits. Beginning about 538 BCE, when they started to return to their land, the Israelites, henceforth called the Jews, brought the Babylonian Square Aramaic script with them.

The DSS supply ample evidence that the returning exiles rebuilt more than their temple (2nd Temple period). They also set about replacing their lost heritage: their history as given in the books of what we call the Bible.

The Dead Sea scrolls do not come from one time or place. They come from various sources and are an accumulation from across approximately seven hundred years. The greater part of the nearly one thousand hands distinguished thus far are clearly the work of literate people. The earliest of the documents date to the late-sixth century BCE (or perhaps earlier). While the returning Jews adopted and adapted the Square Aramaic script, the scrolls show that they retained the old Phoenician variant forms as well as stress and durational notation.

Today, Torah scrolls are scrupulously copied. No changes are admissible. Although modern scribes do not know why there are "big" and "little" letters, they copy these forms with great care. Because of this care, the ancient stress notation appears in these scrolls to this day.

Although among the scrolls found in the caves near Khirbet Qumran twenty-nine are parts of Deuteronomy, the majority of the scrolls are not texts of the Pentateuch. They mostly consist of treatises on ideal communities, texts on correct behavior and the right way, a fictional account of a future war, exegetical writings, interpretations of the scriptural books, portions of the "lost" books, parts—some very substantial—of other books of the Bible, psalms, non-canonical psalms, hymns, and "housekeeping" records. The copper scroll, for example, is an extensive list of treasures belonging to a community—or somebody.

As we have already noted, there can only be one original: one authoritative and official text. Because what we call "copies," exact duplicates, were considered blatant forgeries, nearly all of the documents found among the DSS are *editions* (Biblical *mishneh*) be they sacred or profane. As nearly all the DSS are editions and not authorized "originals," the majority are written in unofficial, cursive mutations of the formal wedge Square script design used for authoritative texts.

Within the Square Script, we find other evidence of the Babylonian exile. The Babylonian practice was to reserve "antique" forms for the sacred. In many of the DSS, the **tetragrammaton** (YHVH—the four letters that are mistakenly referred to as the "name" of God) is written in what was for many the "antique" Paleo-Hebraic script. The tetragrammaton even appears, here and there, in red colored letters sitting amid the monochrome Square Script symbol set. Apparently borrowed along with the rest of the Phoenician writing system, these DSS traditions record the earliest existing models for Late Antique and Medieval practices when writing religious manuscripts. [3]

The scrolls also give concrete evidence of something else. We know from the texts that there was a great deal of infighting among various Jewish groups. [4] The scrolls herald the fight which was to come in the second century CE between the appeasers and the independents. The scripts tell us that the fight began 500 years earlier. They record the battle.

Unlike 'editions' of Homer, for which no official early texts survive, among the DSS we have fragments of *two* authoritative and "original" texts of the Pentateuch. One such authoritative group of fragments is written in an Authoritative Square Script with incorporated cuneiform wedge; [5] however, we also find fragments of the Pentateuch, "The Law," written in the Paleo-Hebraic script, the Israelite "national flag." These latter scrolls are quite old, [6] but whether they are pre- or post-exilic, they clearly served as a reminder during the "restoration" and "preservation" period of the second-century BCE. When the Hasmonai'im (Maccabees) revolted against Seleucid Greek control, they also issued coins. The writing on most of these coins is in Paleo-Hebraic. The coin-scripts remained in Paleo-Hebraic until after the Bar Kochba revolt against Rome (ended 135 CE). All of these are examples of attempts to assert independence and raise once more the "national flag" of the Hebrew peoples.

"Antique" or not, clearly Paleo-Hebraic was still known, for none of the arguments in the second century CE brought against retention of the ethnic flag even hint that the script was out-dated. One telling argument against Paleo-Hebraic was the fact that the Samaritans had reserved the ancient Hebrew script for themselves. This apparently influenced the academy's decision. The status-quo group won. From this time forth the redesigned Square Aramaic became the "Jewish" Square Letter script.

Two general types of Square Letter occur in the DSS: informal everyday cursive fonts and formal authoritative square fonts. Although the model for the authoritative formal script dates back to at least the late sixth-century BCE and appears in a circa third-century BCE fragment of Exodus, this font is the misleadingly named "Herodian" script.

With Herod, we arrive at the beginning of the Common Era and the advent of Christianity. Until then, the two writing traditions, the mystical-static tradition of Egypt, Etruria, and Rome and the practical-dynamic tradition of Sumer, Akkad, Ugarit, Phoenicia, and Judea had jogged along, if not comfortably, at least side-by-side.

With Christianity, we arrive at the time when the two writing traditions—the North African-Semitic and the Alexandrian Greco-Roman—meet again. This time the meeting is a head-on collision.

Chapter Four

TO SPREAD THE WORD

At the turn of the Common Era, the hand of the Roman Empire lay over a large territory extending from the shores of the Eastern Mediterranean to Britain and Gaul. It was a time of turmoil and upheaval. Rome had a state religion, but permitted their conquered peoples to worship their own Gods—as long as the religion was officially recognized. Men had lost belief in the old polytheistic Roman and Greek Pantheon. At the Eastern edge of the Imperium, one group adhered to monotheism, based upon a covenant made between their forefathers and the one God. Among this group there arose another teacher; after his death, his followers based their teachings upon what they called the new covenant. They were dedicated men. Each brought his own point of view and interpretations to his teacher's words. Each one had his own individual methods of preaching. Each one brought new forms of worship, some partaking of familiar Jewish practices, others unknown and based his concept of his Master's teachings. Yes, they set out to spread the word of their teacher and Master, but their very diversity also set the stage for the bloody religious battles to come.

Papyri, stelae, codices, scrolls, manuscripts—complete or fragmentary—the written remnants of the past tell us a story. They record a battle for religious authority vested in an official script equal to that of the authority granted the Official Script of the Roman Imperium. It was the battle for the right to be *The* Official Source, the Final Authority, the *only* interpreter of *The* Word.

This history is marked with vicious altercations among religious **parties**. Parties, as in our modern political parties, is the term they themselves used. We would do well to keep this point in mind. Coalition parties, with the internal diversity this implies, appear everywhere. They had their compromisers, their conservatives, and their liberals. Each party had their extremists to the far right and left. "Catholic" merely means "universal" and while the Alexandrian factions first made claim to the title in the second century, each party considered themselves to be *The* Catholic Christians. [1] This history also depicts the violent clash between the Semitic and the Hellenized Etrusco-Roman writing traditions.

Our guides through the wilderness of the seemingly disorderly record are the self-defined writing systems. They tell us the story, *if* we are willing to listen. Through them, we can trace the *North African-Semitic* parties, who retained the ancient Phoenician trilinear basis and variant forms; the *Greco-Syrio-Byzantine* parties, who retained movement, but not variant forms; the *Greco-Egyptian* parties, who retained limited movement and variant forms; and the *Alexandrian-Roman* parties, who completely discarded variant forms and the clumping and spacing of the spoken word.

We must bear in mind the origins of the two Bibles, and their means of dissemination. The "Old" Testament, written in Hebrew, was available in a variety of similar, but not identical, Hebrew versions. Translations into other languages were made—first Greek and then various Aramaic versions: the Babylonian recensions and the Syriac ones. Three of the Four Gospels were written either in Hebrew or Western Aramaic and, sometime during the late first century, were translated into Greek.

The divide between Christianities arose from a fundamental disagreement: trinitarianism versus subordinationism. The argument centered around the essence or nature of Jesus. Trinitarians were **homoousians** (same essence); subordinationists were **heteroousians** (different essences). Compromisers ranged from **homooiousians** (similar essence) to **monophysites** (single nature) to **monothelites** (dual nature-single will)—and every possible combination in between.

By the fourth century, for the Alexandrian-Roman trinitarians, the Old Testament was in Greek, *the* LXX. For the subordinationists, the Old Testament was in Hebrew, the New Testament in Greek. In the end, the mainland Rome, Alexandrian Greek, and Constantinople parties followed the trinitarian tradition. Greek scripts and texts, therefore, became the measure for these divisions of early Christianity. In general, the Syrian parties were compromisers, tending towards trinitarianism, but holding to Hebrew via Aramaic as the source of the Syriac Old Testament. Egypt, outside of Alexandria, was aligned either with the North African-Semitic or Monophysite parties. Roman Africa was mixed; while some followed the Alexandrian-Roman parties, most followed the subordinationist traditions.

When in 395 CE the Imperium was divided into Eastern and Western Empires, the official division merely formalized the reality of the political situation. Henceforth, until the Moslem conquest, the **koine** (common tongue) of the Near Eastern Mediterranean was Greek, that of the West and Africa, Latin. In the West, Latin eventually became the language of religion. One important aspect of liturgical language did not change along with the Imperial division: as late as the eighth century, at least half of the Roman liturgy was still in Greek.

A further division among Christian parties arose from governmental attitudes towards literacy as practiced in Semitic and Egypto-Roman areas. On the Asian side of the Near East and in the North African and Carthaginian spheres, public literacy was still encouraged. Although the peasantry might be illiterate, the urbanites ranged from semi-literate to scholars. Jesus, an urbanite himself, clearly was literate in Western Aramaic and Hebrew. As an artisan, he apparently also knew some Greek; enough, at least, to deal with Greek speaking clients. On the other hand, in the Alexandrian Greco-Roman spheres, only the elite was literate; the great majority of the population was not. In this sphere, Christianity had to spread by word of mouth. The fact that Christianity was essentially oral explains the great importance placed upon the Psalter as a means of dissemination. Orality also explains the ease with which so many Winner's techniques could be applied.

The Winner's Standard Operating Procedure is to hide evidence; Winners, after all, write the histories. One standard procedure is to destroy documents written by the opposition or that deviate from the "correct" party line. This process is known as **selective destruction**. Only documents that do not obviously contradict the desired history survive this procedure. More than one work of the Church fathers later was destroyed because it contradicted the chosen history, one example of which is Origen's *Hexapla*.

Origen lived from about 185 to 254. [2] He studied under Clement of Alexandria (circa 150-215), a Church father. These were early years and the history had not yet been settled on. Origen is considered to be the most original and learned of the early Greek Christian writers. He was of the Alexandrian School; but, after a series of disagreements with the Alexandrian authorities, he settled in Caesarea (located on the coast of Modern Israel not far from the modern city of Caesarea). He spent his life writing commentaries and expositions of the entire Bible and working on the Old Greek translations of the Hebrew original; the Old Greek translations are better known as The LXX.

The name, *The* LXX, comes from a legend that the Hebrew Bible was translated into Greek for Ptolemy I of Egypt in 7 years by 70 scholars. The legend is based upon a document known as the *Letter of Aristeas* supposedly contemporaneous with the translation. We now know the legend to be a story made up for political reasons approximately 150 years later by the writer of the letter. Scholars of the Old Greek versions have determined that the Pentateuch was finished early in the 3rd century BCE; but that the other books were translated over a period of more than 100 years. The name, *The* LXX, has stuck; to this day, the Old Greek translations are called *The* LXX. There never was, and there never has been, anything that can be called *The* LXX. This point is very important; it illustrates another of the techniques used by the "Winners" in creating the desired history.

Whether sacred or secular, by calling something *The*, the Winners create an aura of homogeneity and engender an idea of a single, monolithic identity. While the Pentateuch was more or less in its final form by the 6th-5th century BCE, the writings and even the order of the Psalms were in flux. There was no such thing as *The* Hebrew Bible until the 2nd or 3rd centuries CE. There was no such thing as *The* Latin Vulgate until 1546 CE. Nor did Jerome's translations of the Psalms into Latin, known as *The* Romanum, *The* Gallican, and *The* Hebraicum, exist. As a technique, it is still very much alive and well today. There are thousands of modern examples of this *The* technique. One example must suffice. Early translations of the Psalms into the vernacular are commonly compared to *The* Vulgate—and found wanting in accuracy. Obviously, comparing a 7th century translation with a 16th century diplomatic text has little utility. Nevertheless, a doctoral dissertation was written based upon this exact premise as recently as 1985.

For this *The* technique to work, however, there must be no open evidence available that contradicts the aura created by *The*. Many a good intention has gone awry when it runs afoul of *The*, precisely what happened to Origen's *Hexapla*.

The main purpose of the *Hexapla* was to demonstrate the accuracy of *The* LXX, and to provide a solid footing for disputation with the rabbis—for whom the only authority was Hebrew. To this end, Origen designed a new form of presentation for *formal authoritative* texts, and the diplomatic edition, including the apparatus, was born.

The various versions were presented in very narrow parallel columns consisting of, at most, a few words. More often, a column contained a few letters or one Hebrew word (Figure 4.1). The first column was Hebrew (similar to a Masoretic version), followed by Origen's Greek transliteration of the Hebrew. Next came a Greek version by Aquila, which was done under the direction of Akiba ben Josef (circa 69-135 CE), and also subsequently destroyed. Aquila's version was followed by a Greek version attributed to Symmachus (unknown now except through the *Hexapla* and some of Jerome's Latin translations). Number five was Origen's *own* revision of an LXX and the sixth was a version known as the Theodotion (a revision of either an LXX or another Old Greek version). Origen added three more columns for the Psalter, one of which was a Hebrew version found in a jar in the Desert.

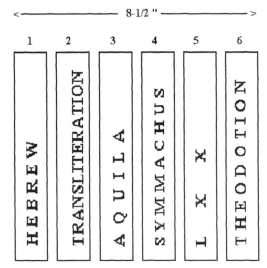

Fig. 4.1 The format of Origen's *Hexapla*

The *Hexapla* may have been intended to create a basis for argument with the Rabbis, but it did not work out that way; it only showed how distant an LXX translation was from an original Hebrew. Although no such thing as "*The* LXX" existed, it became the official text for the Alexandrian-Roman parties. The *Hexapla* definitely threw the accuracy of "*The* LXX" into question and displayed it as just another translation and not as *The* Word. The last known copy of the *Hexapla* disappeared sometime about at the beginning of the 7th century. Today, only fragments of Origen's works remain.

Because of the practice of selective destruction, most of our information about opponents in this deadly battle is conveyed through hostile glimpses. Arius (circa 250-336) in his fight with Athanasius (296-373) survives mainly in Athanasian and other documents written by his opponents. The battle raged over Arius's position that the Godhead cannot be shared. He was heteroousian, and by no means the first to expound this view. (The subordinationist position was first stated by Origen.) Modern researchers are teasing out information about Arius from the fragments of his writings and from some of the more acceptable surviving writings of his associates and followers. Judging from the way he was maligned, he must have been an exceedingly dangerous opponent to the Alexandrian-Roman parties. The data that are turning up present a very different picture from the ones written in the history books. Arius appears to have been a charismatic leader, a logician, a poet, and a persuasive orator.

Selective destruction and this *The* aura are only two of the techniques employed by the Winners. Another technique is to edit the text, particularly if the author is a generally respected Church writer. Origen, for example, wrote many homilies. Only a very small portion of these tracts survive in the original Greek. Rufinus (345-410), an Italian theologian, and Jerome translated Origen's homilies into Latin. As one modern scholar delicately puts it, they tampered with the texts. (Rufinus, at first a friend of Jerome's, later became his opponent. The subject of their dispute was the orthodoxy of Origen.)

Translations, in particular, are susceptible to slanting through editing. At best, translations tell us more about the translator than about the original text. The primary end of Winner's editing is political; nevertheless, the result sometimes can be thoroughly amusing.

The zoology of the Old Greek is more than a little peculiar. We know from other evidence that the translators of the Greek Old Testament were "town mice." In general, translators try to choose a word in the **target language** (here, Greek) that corresponds to the same word in the **source language** (Hebrew). In normal practice, the chosen word in the target language will be used again wherever the source word appears.

The Hebrew term for the desert kite, a member of the family of raptors like the eagle and the hawk, is a *ka'at midbar*. The creature appears in Leviticus 11:18 and Deuteronomy 14:17 on the list of forbidden fowl; it also appears in Psalm 102:7. The Greek translator of Leviticus apparently had no idea what a *ka'at* was; he only knew that it was a bird that frequented barren places. He seems to have been a fairly observant person: Pelicans make their nests on bare, dry rocks near the sea. He therefore decided that a *ka'at* must be a "pelican." The translator tells us that, while he had never been outside of Alexandria, he was familiar with its harbor and its winged inhabitants. He also tells us that there were many large, dry, bare rocks in Alexandria harbor—as well as many pelicans. Unfortunately, his editing of the text to reflect Alexandrian zoology could not be checked by future exegetes. Neither desert kites nor pelicans are available to see and to compare with one another away from the Eastern Mediterranean.

Unlike many of the other Winner's practices, the edit-to-conform technique was very well known, and it could, and did, backfire. Ulfilas (311-383), the bishop to the Goths and a staunch subordinationist, utterly refused to use Latin translations. He stated that all the Latin translators were liars. Ulfilas designed new scripts for his people based upon Greek models: one was a formal liturgical script, the other was a secular version of the formal design. His Gothic translation was from Greek. Even today, editing is still commonly employed to skew data to fit the correct slant. While the edit technique still works, it was too well known at the time and was not the best method to employ to hide differences.

Perhaps the cleverest technique used by the Winners is very simple: how do you hide a tree? By planting it in a forest, of course. Occasionally, though, the Winners miss something and the tree stands alone in a clearing, no longer hidden.

Scholars, understandably, concentrate on the content. There is no question that the content is important; it contains the semantic message. Content, however, also determines: 1) The choice of script, 2) the format, and 3) the size of a document. In turn, these three elements are constrained by political and religious affiliations. The importance of the relationship between these components of a writing system and a given culture cannot be overemphasized. The correct script, format, and size were *required* for the content to be accepted as authoritative or official.

Today, we are taught to believe that no such requirements exist—in spite of the fact that we still associate size with authority, format with content, and script with a people. In our modern semantic-based systems, script, format, and size are seen merely as a background for the content of a printed or written page. Yesterday, the spoken word had supremacy *over* the written word, thus, script, format, and size were as essential to the meaning of a text as the content. Script, format, and size are our three guides through the forest to the trees, these hidden pages of history.

Ancient legalese is very formulaic in character as well as rigid and limited as to types of format permitted. [3] The relationship of the size of a document to its content is as rigid as the formats and formulaic language. Size is dependent upon the social status of the originator, the characteristics of a local pattern, and the content.

As with so much else connected with writing systems, Western formats and sizes began at Sumer. The Sumerians were very methodical: there was a place for everything and everything was in its place. Archaeologists digging at Sumer found the archives nicely organized—by size. Official documents, clay tablets in this case, were stored in baskets. Each basket was carefully indexed as to contents, and the tablets for each type of transaction were all of one size and one format. Size and format depended upon the content of a document.

By the 19th century BCE, in Mesopotamia, written records were required for all transactions. Everything was recorded, down to the smallest detail of the simplest trade or exchange. These documents vary in script, size, and format depending upon content. The largest documents were always *The* Law.

While it would certainly be easier for us if we could simply separate documents by size and format, it is unfortunately not that straightforward. Because each culture adapted the Phoenician writing system to its own needs, it led to a multitude of authoritative and official formats and sizes, each characteristic of a given locale.

The materials themselves are relevant. The weight of the clay tended to limit the height of a document to what could be conveniently lifted by one person. Thus, among authorized documents, the maximum size we find are the ancient law codes: 14-15 inches in height by 8-9 inches in width. When writing transferred to leather sometime around the 8th-7th centuries BCE, margins were added to protect the text; but, the size of the reading area remained the same—14 inches high by 8-1/2 inches wide. Papyrus leaves are limited by the width of the strips of pith. The writing material forced a ninety-degree rotation in order to maintain the "correct" size hierarchy. This simple physical difficulty played an important role in creating a distinction between traditions. By the third century BCE the great diversity among authoritative and official formats and sizes crystallized into two primary streams: North African-Semitic and Greco-Roman.

On one side we find the Semitic descendants of the Phoenician system, which used different official scripts, but retained ancient practices almost intact. In this tradition, authoritative and official texts were written in narrow columns, by utterance, that is, as spoken, and suspended from the upper writing limit. [4] Non-official, yet authoritative, documents were written in broad columns. Law codes were 14 inches in height with a reading area of 8-9 inches in width, *plus* margins. Writings were somewhat shorter, about 11 inches. Secular documents, such as tax receipts, were smaller yet and varied in size depending upon the type of tax. Harking back to Akkad, deeds of sale, for example, were always narrow, approximately 3 to 3-1/2 inches in width, but varied in height depending upon the status of the seller.

On the other side we find a combined Etrusco-Roman-Greek tradition. Greek contact influenced Rome at an early date; but, contact is a two way street. Although Imperial Rome admired and imitated Greek culture, the evidence shows that Romans clung to their ancestral official formats and sizes inherited from the Etruscan tradition. Instead of Greek traditions influencing Roman documentation, with the Roman expansion to the east, official Greek sizes began to conform to Roman standards. This conformation naturally became more rapid after the Greeks lost their dominant position. Eventually, the strictly bilinear Etrusco-Roman official sizes and formats fused with the trilinear Greek authoritative ones. The combined Greco-Roman official documents appear written in broad columns and in *scripto continuo*. Official single sheets were 12 inches high by 14 or more inches wide while official papyrus codices were 12 inches in height by 8-9 inches in width, *including* margins. Writings were 9 to 9-1/2 inches in height. Authoritative, but non-official, texts appear in narrow column format. In this tradition, the size of a tax receipt also depended upon the type of tax and the issuee. (People had to pay for the papyrus in their receipts. A typical low status receipt runs 3 x 5 inches.) Deeds of sale retained the ancient Akkadian practice and appear as very narrow leaves of papyrus.

Because diplomatic editions cast doubt upon the desired *The* aura, such editions were strongly discouraged by the Alexandrian-Roman parties. [5] On the other hand, the North African-Semitic parties encouraged comparative works. In spite of the destruction of the *Hexapla*, Origen cast a long shadow. His condensed triple Psalter version of the *Hexapla* appears to have been copied many times. One well documented and very well known type of diplomatic edition is the three-fold Psalter. These Psalters are arranged in a narrow column format and display Jerome's three translations of the Psalms into Latin: *Gallican* (*Vulgate*), *Romanum*, and *Hebraicum* (so-called because it was translated from Hebrew). When laid flat for reading, these three-fold Psalters imitate Origen's new format for formal authoritative works. (It is no accident that these Psalters appear in areas originally converted by missionaries from the North African-Semitic parties.) Obviously, three versions of the Psalter clearly show that *The* Psalter was open to question. There are too many of these three-fold Psalters to hide them completely. What could be done about this? The answer was simple: fit them into a forest of formats. One example of the format-forest can be seen in later scriptural commentaries. In the Roman tradition, the Biblical text appears written in a central broad column; it is surrounded by the commentary written in narrow columns. The implications of the multi-column format in the three-fold Psalters are hidden. These triple-diplomatic-editions disappear in an apparent welter of columnar formats; the *The* aura of a monolithic Christianity superficially preserved.

One size and format of document appears in both traditions. These texts run about 6 to 8-1/2 inches in height by approximately 5-1/2 in width, or roughly a sheet of modern letterhead paper folded in half horizontally. In size, the resulting folded paper emulates the writing surface of a wax tablet.

Wax tablets were the scratch pads of antiquity; they still were in use as late as the early Renaissance. These tablets were wooden frames with a raised edge that were filled with wax. A stylus was used to scratch notes or trial writings into the wax. Children learned to write by following a template laid over the face of the tablet. When what was written was no longer needed, the wax surface of the tablet could be rubbed clean for use at another time (*tabula rasa*). This size also appears in papyrus and parchment. Because the size indicated erasable material, it eventually became the signal that what was written here was entertainment and not meant to be taken seriously. (It still does; that rip-roaring Western, soppy Romance, or chilling Horror story of a pocketbook is the size of the wax tablets before trimming.)

In Greco-Roman practice, the size of a document within a class depended upon the perception of the social status of the originator. While during the early centuries CE perception of status generally coincided with actual status, these carefully maintained distinctions eroded along with the Roman Empire. In all areas, however, the largest documents were always *The* Law. Under the Imperium, *The* Law was Roman Imperial; under early Christianity, *The* Law was the Pentateuch.

Table 4.1: Some Sizes and Formats of the North African-Semitic and Greco-Roman traditions.

| | North African-Semitic | | Greco-Roman | |
	Height	Column Format	Height	Column Format
Profane Domain				
Official				
The "Law" of the ruling power	14"	Narrow	12"	Broad
Local "Law"	13"	Broad	11"	Narrow
Administration	12"	Broad	10"	Broad
Petitions	10"	Broad	9"	Broad
Literature				
Serious	10"	Broad	8-9"	Narrow
Entertainment	6-8"	Broad	7-8-1/2"	Broad
Sacred Domain	Israelite/Judean		Early Christian	
Authoritative				
Pentateuch	14"	Narrow	7-10"	Narrow
Writings & Prophets	12"	Broad	7-10"	Narrow

The early Christians, however, rejected the Roman scripts, formats, and sizes as "pagan" and, along with Jesus as the messiah, adopted the Judean writing system that we find in documents from the Dead Sea. Christian diversity nevertheless set in with great speed. By around the late fourth to early fifth centuries, when we finally have enough documents to compare against each other, we find that the North African-Semitic parties were adhering to the narrow column format for religious documents and the broad column format for secular documents. On the Alexandrian-Roman side, these parties adopted the Imperial Roman standards along with the broad column format for authoritative, official, and scriptural texts, and used the North African narrow column for authoritative non-scriptural and secular ones. The same two divisions occurred between the hierarchy of sizes. The North African parties stuck to the Semitic size hierarchy while the Alexandrian-Roman groups adopted the Greco-Roman hierarchy of sizes. The most important sizes and formats that can be used in tracing the two traditions appear in Table 4.1.

The table is divided into two domains: Profane and Sacred. There are good reasons for this division. In the Israelite/Judean tradition, the "Law" was the *torah* (*torah* means "instruction" or "rule," not "law") handed down in the Mosaic tradition. The *torat-moshe* (Greek "Pentateuch") was the word of God, hence, above all merely human rules and regulations. In the Israelite and later Judean tradition, the sizes and formats in the profane domain were stepped-down in accordance with the hierarchies of sizes and formats used in the Semitic tradition. There were "official" hierarchies of size and formats in the profane domain, but only "authoritative" documents in the sacred domain. Such authoritative documents were written in an authoritative font, but not the authoritative script. To understand why this restriction, we have to return to Sumer and the origins of writing for a moment.

As we have seen, the written record recorded the voice of authority as spoken; thus, there could only be *one* original of a document, no matter the domain. Because there could be only one original, all covenants *had* to be in the hand of the author(s). Vows and oaths are covenants between a person and his ruler, be it a god or a human; hence, they had to be in the hand of the person making the vow or oath. To this day, covenants must carry the signatures (and the signature on a credit charge slip is a covenant) of the parties involved—and for the very same reason: fraud prevention. There was no such thing as a "copy" in our modern sense of an exact duplicate. Such an exact duplicate was considered a blatant forgery (with penalties to match).

To avoid the charge of forgery, people made a *mishneh*, that is, "an edition." In editions, we find changes of script ("cursive"), changes of format, and changes of size. In some writing systems, such as that used at Ugarit, they would even change the direction of writing.

The one and only original document will be in the correct format for the class of document; the edition will not repeat the format, but use an unofficial or non-authoritative format as prescribed in the hierarchy of formats. The size will be within a range of permissible sizes for the class of document, but will not repeat the size of the original. Cursive fonts, mutations of an official or authoritative script, arise with the need to distinguish between the public and the private domains.

Cursives are never official or authoritative public fonts. They are, by definition, informal, handwriting, and private. Cursive fonts are used to write editions of official documents for archival records; for internal records in a government office, for producing editions of authoritative writings and works of fiction; for the production of profane documents and private correspondence; and, of course, editions of official or authoritative documents for private use. As the majority of the ancient tablets are covenants of one sort or another, thc majority are cursive holographs written by the parties to, for instance, a treaty. (Covenants written on stone were afterwards 'traced' by a stone carver —which gives a different dimension to what is meant by "carved in stone.") Although we do not think about it very much, this division between the one and only original and editions is still in force today. Official and authoritative documents can only be issued by an official or authoritative source—whether one wants a passport or a photocopy of a credit-card statement.

In both traditions—Semitic and Greco-Roman—we find either originals or editions and nothing else. By the late centuries BCE, we find that documents display so many different hands, formats, sizes, and fonts because the majority of the documents are archival editions and/or bookshop editions written by professional scribes, or private editions written by private individuals for their own use. Whether a document is written by a professional or by an amateur, a given edition is never an exact duplicate of the original.

Perhaps this can be best illustrated by an example. When we examine the tablets of the ancient Near East and documents later from the Greco-Roman world we find registers of letters, registers of contracts, registers of loans, but the originals are not where we find the registers. To find the originals we must look elsewhere. The originals show up in the archives amid the ruins of Ugaritic or Hittite palaces; they turn up in papyri from Theadelphia or Arsinoites or Thebes or Oxyrhyncus. Archival editions in "chancery" fonts are found at all the sites; in a few rare cases, we have both the original and the edition.

Wisconsin No. 37, dated 3.11.144 CE and from Theadelphia, is a petition to an assistant of the Imperial Procurator. The lower half of the papyrus includes a letter written by the assistant to his superior pertaining to the petition, and the empty space at the bottom has not been filled in. The document has been folded. Papyrus cracks when folded; any tampering with a document is immediately obvious; the folds serve the same purpose as the clay envelope used with cuneiform tablets. The petition is 11 inches in height by 5.79 in width and written in the different cursive hands of the authors. Wisconsin No. 38 is an edition of this petition: it has no folds, is 5.47 inches in height by 8.62 inches in width, has no blank space, and is written by one hand in a cursive chancery font. Such archival editions are never in the script, format, size, or shape of the original document.

Certainly there are some authorized official texts written by professional scribes among the surviving documents. Official originals and authoritative texts, however, are a minority. The majority of the professionally written texts found in Greco-Roman Egypt and among the DSS are editions written in cursive fonts and not in official or authorized scripts.

Official scripts change each time there is a social upheaval; they are overt and obvious. Formats and sizes are more difficult to hide. This deliberate overlap between the two traditions creates a very good forest within which to hide trees. It leaves us with an impression of massive diversity without order; but, fortunately, this impression is deceptive. What it does mean is a great deal of detective work. First, we must separate the documents by content: secular or sacred, official, authoritative, or unofficial. Next we have to separate the documents by type within each class. Then, we must separate these new piles of documents by size. Next, we have to separate the piles of documents by format. Finally, we must look at the scripts.

Commerce had held the primary role in the distribution and dissemination of writing systems. For nearly 3000 years, scripts had been the national flags of peoples; they signaled ethnic identity. Even under Empires, peoples had their territorial scripts and fonts as flags of ethnic identity. Under the Roman Empire, peoples granted Roman citizenship wrote "official" inscriptions and documents in Latin territorial fonts, but otherwise retained their own "national flags" for local business. With the advent of Christianity, scripts followed religion. Once only the signal of ethnic identity, the scripts now also signal religious party affiliation.

The absoluteness of script-as-authority cannot be stated often enough. Prior to the invention of the printing press, liturgical letter forms had religious significance and their use, shape, and script-model were prescribed, party-affiliated, and obligatory. There exist many examples of the rigidity of script-as-obligation. Biblical scholars need merely look at the script to know the religious affiliation of a group. The Syriac scripts, an offshoot of cursive Aramaic, divide into numerous styles according to party. Syriac texts, translated from Hebrew and Greek originals, were originally written in the authorized script called **Estrangela**. The sub-divisions of the Syriac party were Nestorian, Assyrian, Jacobite, and Melkite. Each of these sub-divisions had their own mutations and fonts of the official Estrangela script. Later, after the Muslim conquest of the area, Syriac texts were written in another official script called **Garshuni**. Transcribed Greek scriptures (rather than translated) are written in two other Syriac sub-divisions: Mandaean and Manichaean. [6] Once a group has chosen an official script, nothing which is not written in that model, to quote the Parsis, "can claim to be considered as part of the sacred literature." It is not coincidental that the two major surviving communities of Parsis use two distinct styles: the older straight "Indian" in India, and the Persian influenced "Iranian" in Iran. Kufic was the official script for the Qur'an until the eleventh century. To this day, Syriac, the Aramaic offshoot, remains the liturgical script of the Kurdish remnants of the Assyrian sub-party.

Paleographers and most historians of script systems scrupulously divide and subdivide the various branches of the descendants of the North-Semitic script systems. Script systems are not only classified by branches, for example, "South Semitic," "Canaanite," "Aramaic," "Non-Semitic Offshoots of the Aramaic Branch," and so on, but by sub-sets *within* each branch. What is often ignored is that the ability to set up these classifications and to divide and subdivide script systems is *because* script equals identity. All these distinctions are already there for us to see.

Because script-equals-affiliation, Semitic paleographers scrupulously retain the distinctions among these scripts. Greek and Latin scripts are also placed into classes and sub-classes. Each of these scripts and fonts have been subject to close scrutiny and individually named. Though fully aware of the enormous variety among them, unlike scholars who deal with Syriac, Hindi, or Muslim documents, the majority of Western Greek and Latin paleographers treat Greek and Latin scripts and fonts as if they were monolithic and homogeneous simply because the documents are written in the local *koine*, the inter-ethnic tongue.

A language of inter-ethnic discourse, however, does not equal identity. The Serbians and the Croatians, for example, speak languages that are mutually comprehensible, but one uses the Cyrillic scripts, the other "Roman"—and one would not be caught dead using the others identifying script. A text printed in English differs substantially from a text printed in French or Spanish. Although all three languages use the "Roman" script families, the difference in script is immediately obvious: English neither uses diacriticals nor chooses the same fonts. Further, without examining the text for spelling differences, we can tell if a book in English was printed in England or in the United States, in Taiwan or in India—from the fonts. Language does not identify a people today, and language does not identify a people in antiquity: script does.

Whether inscribed with a chisel or written with an instrument, the scripts, sizes, and formats of this vast interactive multi-national, multi-lingual Empire, an area of immense religious, cultural, and commercial diversity, reveal that there was no such thing as a "monolithic" Latin or Greek script any more than there was a single hierarchy of sizes or formats. The following is a *very* simplified summary of the salient features of the situation in the Imperium between the first and fifth centuries.

Under the Roman Imperium, technically, the governmental language was Latin. Throughout the Empire, anything being registered under Roman law, such as a manumission, was written in Latin; anything registered under local law, such as a deed of sale, was written in the local governmental language. The script of Rome was the Official Imperial Square Capital (with one short period when Claudius tried to change the official script); African Rustic capitals were elevated to an authorized script for authoritative but not official documents. From the second quarter of the 4th century, the Official Imperial script for Biblical documents was the Greco-Roman Uncial. The format for official Imperial documents was a single broad column written in *scripto continuo*. Each class of official document, however, used the appropriate script, size, and format for its type and its locale. After the fifth century, the languages and hierarchies used in Christian texts and funerary inscriptions reflect the situation under the Imperium.

Rome was Rome: Latin was the official language, while Greek was the language of the aristocracy. By the 4th century, various Gothic and Germanic tongues become important on the Italian mainland, with Lombards to the Northeast, and both Visigoths and Ostragoths scattering to the Northwest and center. These Germanic peoples used their own languages among themselves, but tended to adopt Latin as their official language for pronouncements and inter-ethnic discourse. Their languages necessarily influenced their ideas of Latin. Greek remained the main language of the south. On islands settled by the Phoenicians, such as Malta (eleventh BCE), Sardinia (by the ninth BCE) and Western Sicily (around the tenth BCE), Phoenician remained in local use right alongside Latin. Script, size, and format depended upon locale and who was on first at the time and place.

Rome divided its Mediterranean provinces for a very good reason: the cultures were very different. In Constantinople, Latin was the official language. Many other tongues from different language families were in use; but Greek was the language of local government and commerce with its own hierarchy of Persian-influenced sizes, formats, and styles of scripts.

In post-Roman conquest Judea, Latin may have been the official language, but Western Aramaic was the language of commerce and *koine*, with both Greek and Hebrew in daily use. Unlike many other areas of the Imperium, Latin never became the normal language of inscriptions or inter-ethnic discourse in Judea. Roman coins and Hellenistic ones, issued by the mint at Tyre, show up as legal tender. Size, format, and script depended upon ethnos and content.

During the first and second centuries CE, the governmental languages and scripts of Syria were Greek, Latin, Punic, Syriac, and Aramaic. Palmyra (Tadmor) sat astride three major trade routes. It was the northern terminus for the Kings' Road running up from Yemen. Palmyra was also the eastern terminus for the Ancient Salt road running up from the Mediterranean via Rosh Pina, around the Sea of Galilee, and through Damascus. The Northern road that ran around the edge of the Roman Empire to Northwestern Europe began at Palmyra. At first, Palmyra was staunchly pro-Rome and the inscriptions are in Latin and Palmyrene Aramaic. Latin, as the official language, appears *above* the Palmyrene on the inscriptions. Palmyrene used a branch of the Syriac scripts and fonts as their script system. Then Palmyra rebelled, fairly successfully, at first. It extended its sphere of influence as far south as Egypt, east through Anatolia, and west across the interior of Europe—through what are modern Hungary and Northeast France. Although the rebellion was eventually crushed, there was no return to Latin. The inscriptions from the third century on are in Greek and Palmyrene. [7] The Greek text now appears above the Palmyrene texts. Official Syriac texts are written in narrow columns.

Anatolia, the "hump" of modern Turkey, is very mountainous terrain. The language of government on one side of a mountain frequently was different from the language on the other side. Even in areas where the same language was in use, the dialects differed according to whether a settlement was in the valley or in the mountains. Depending upon the area, during this period we find, among others, Celtic, Greek, Lydian, Hittite, Hurrian, Armenian, Palmyrene, and early Slavic tongues. The governmental languages, scripts, formats, and sizes depended upon what was in use at a municipal level. Latin was the language of the overgovernment; with its hierarchies of scripts, formats, and sizes *adjusted* to local conditions. In some municipalities of Anatolia, legal documents were bigger than the official Roman sizes; accordingly, Rome had to increase the size of their official documents in order to maintain supremacy. With the arrival of Christianity, we find evidence of subordinationists, trinitarians, and compromisers.

In Gaul, Latin was the official language. Gaul covered an extensive territory with Celtic, Germanic, and Semitic language families spoken at various times and places. No texts exist for the Germanic language groups until the sixth century; these few early documents are in Futhark, the ethnic script of the Germanic tribes. The Romance languages did not exist until after the ninth century. A Christian community existed in the area of Lyons by the second century. By the fifth century, Syriac and Hebrew languages and texts are documented from the area near Orleans, France. Their presence is mentioned from the fourth century in this area. Both Syriac and Hebrew used a narrow column format for sacred documents and a broad column for secular documents. Latin texts appear in both Greco-Roman and North African-Semitic formats and sizes. The Latin scripts from the Northwest of France show Syriac influence.

On the African side, Egypt was Egypt. In Egypt, Latin was the "official" language, with its own hierarchies of scripts, formats, and sizes. As usual, any document that would be registered under Roman law, letters to governors, covenants, and legal texts, was in Latin. In Alexandria the governmental language was Greek with Egyptian used in outlying areas. Josephus reports having to translate from Greek into Latin for the Roman Generals. [8] Greek documents use the Egyptian influenced Greek hierarchies of scripts, sizes, and formats. The Egyptian natives spoke Coptic (Egyptian) and still used the Egyptian writing system. Based on Greek symbol sets, the Coptic script makes its first appearance during the late fourth to early fifth centuries.

Africa was two separate provinces under the Imperium. Egypt and Africa. Roman Africa consisted of the Mediterranean coast of Libya, Tunisia, and Algeria. Roman Africa was polyglot. Latin was the language of the overgovernment and of inter-ethnic discourse. As we move west past Egypt along the coast, the main governmental language was Punic. Later it changed to Chadic and then to Berber and then to Arabic. By the early fifth century, the governmental language of Western North Africa was that of the Vandals, a member of the Germanic language group. The governmental language and writing system along most of the African coast was Punic. The language of commerce was primarily Aramaic, except in Alexandria, where it was Greek. The commercial scripts were Greek and Aramaic along with their offshoots. [9]

With the African Christians, though, we find another complication in this already confusing situation. We tend to forget that peoples granted Roman citizenship considered themselves Roman, no matter their origins. Although not effective immediately, eventually Latin, the language of inter-ethnic discourse in the West, became the language of African Christianity. African Christian burial inscriptions are in Latin.

African Christians appear to have had missionary tendencies—and they clearly had the means to travel around: Roman Africa was settled by Western Phoenicians. Writing in the late third-early fourth centuries, Augustine of Hippo (which is located in Modern Tunisia) wrote in Latin. Augustine also was a follower of Mani for a while; this tells us that he read Syriac as well. Mani wrote in the Syriac dialect of Aramaic and was not available in Latin translation. Tertullian, or more exactly, Quintus Septimius Florens Tertullianus (155-220), the first Christian Latin writer and father of liturgical Latin, was born in, and returned to, Neo-Carthage, another Phoencian site. The African Christian writing systems followed either the North African-Semitic or the Alexandrian-Roman tradition depending upon party affiliation.

The situation on the Iberian Peninsula may never be straightened out. Again, Latin was the Official language and required for documents registered under Roman Law. Punic was the language, and Neo-Punic the governmental scripts of the Phoenician-Carthaginian settlements below the Ebro River, and on the Western and Eastern Coasts of Roman Hispania. Sometime during the fourth century BCE, Celts moved into Western Spain and the **Celtiberians**, a mixture of Iberian and Celtic peoples living to the North and West of the River Tagus came into being. These people spoke the now extinct language called Celto-Iberian. A warlike people, they invented the two-edged "Spanish" sword, which was later adopted by the Romans. In addition, we find evidence of two different Hamitic languages, Iberian, and early Basque. By the fourth century, another Germanic language adds to the confusion when the Visigoths took over. Prior to, and during, the Roman occupation, the Peninsular writing systems divided into Eastern and Southern groups. While the language of Iberian Christianity was Latin—Latin was the language used on Christian funerary inscriptions and for their texts—the Christian writing systems divided into North, North-Eastern, Western, and South-Eastern groups. West and Southeast Iberian writing systems followed the North African-Semitic traditions for scripts, sizes and formats; North and Northeast Iberia followed the North African-Roman traditions.

The British Isles present a different pattern. Bronze is an alloy of copper and tin, and major tin deposits are rare. A small deposit, perhaps in Anatolia, was probably the original source for tin at the beginning of the Bronze Age around 3800-3400 BCE. As the wielders of bronze weapons had a decided edge over their opponents, it was only natural that people should search for tin deposits. A small tin lode showed up on Sardinia. A good-size deposit of high grade ore was found on the Iberian Peninsula. This, too, was an insufficient supply for the demand. The only *major* tin deposit of high grade ore in the west of the Eurasian continent was the one in Cornwall. Whoever controlled the Cornish and Iberian tin mines held a near monopoly on an essential ore. Cornish tin was used for bronze and Cornish tin is what permitted the Bronze Age to continue and to spread. The bronze weapons, helmets, shields, and vessels of the ancient Near East, as well as the bronze statues of Classical Greece, used Cornish tin. [10]

Ore is heavy. While the tin could be transported overland, and, back in 2800 BCE undoubtedly was, there are two major problems with land transport from Cornwall to the Eastern Mediterranean. First, the journey takes nearly six months. Second, once the Bronze Age got into full swing about 2200-2000 BCE, even the most ambitious trader could not carry enough ore overland to make the long trip worth his while. By the sea route, however, the trip from the West coast of the Iberian Peninsula took only 2-3 days on the outward voyage and perhaps a week on the return trip. The mass of ore needed to produce, for example, the bronzes of Classical Greece, came by sea.

Seafaring peoples were uncommon in the West; there were, in fact, only three groups who were at home on the sea. The Greeks (and until 1500 BCE the Minoans) rode the sea, but were island-hoppers and always stayed within sight of land. Long-distance sea-traders, people who frequented the open seas, were limited to two groups. The first sea-traders to carry the tin ore from Cornwall seem to have been Iberians from the coastal areas to the North and West of the River Tagus in what is today Portugal. The architecture of stone "beehive" houses found in Ireland resembles the distinctive architecture of those found at Vianna do Castelio and Citaia and are presumed to have been carried to Ireland by these sea-traders. (We will never really know, however, because we cannot say who or what the Iberians were.) Sometime after 1500 BCE, though, another group gained a monopoly on both the Iberian and Cornish ore lodes. The ore was carried by those long-distance seafaring traders, the Phoenicians.

Paintings show square sails in use on the reed cargo-carrier "barges" used on the Nile back in the fourth millenium BCE. Wall paintings of a Battle Fleet at Thera (Santorini) in the Cyclades Islands of Greece make it completely clear that sail on wooden vessels as an auxiliary to oars was in use before the sixteenth century BCE. [11] The name "Phoenician" is Greek; it means "of the Land of Palms." The Phoenician's name for themselves as a people was "Cana'ani," that is "merchant" or "of the Merchants." The Cana'ani used a distinctive, very large, many oared ship, with auxiliary sails for the transport of ore. When laden, the vessel apparently resembled a cross between a *trireme* (three-tiered oared battle ship) and a scow. This type of vessel seems to have been called a "Tarshish."

The older parts of the Pentateuch display an ancient Hebrew habit of identifying a people by a locale or a trait. Upper Egypt is referred to as *tannin* (crocodile), logically enough, as the Upper Nile is crocodile heaven. Lower Egypt is referred to as *rahab* (flat-lands), and the delta of the Nile is indeed very flat. The two Egypts together are referred to by a dual: *Mitzraim* (the two Masri). We find the habit of identification-by-trait in the term *Tarshish*.

If *Tarshish* be a locale, then it is a remarkably mobile location; it moves all over the place. It has been located on various parts of the coast of Lebanon, on the coast of Spain, and on the Red Sea. It turns out that *Tarshish* is not a particular place, but this unusually large and specifically Cana'ani ore-trading vessel. [12] These vessels were so distinctive and so big that, by the eighth century BCE, "Tarshish" was already a cliche for "great size." In other words, "Tarshish" is not a location, but an ancient Biblical way of referring to the sea-faring Cana'ani. It also seems that Herodotus was telling the truth when he wrote that the Phoenicians sailed around the Cape of Africa. After all, they controlled the long-distance trading in the Red Sea, too. The Phoenicians got about quite a bit in those big ore-vessels of theirs; they even left inscriptions in the Azores.

The Phoenicians created settlements (trading posts??) whenever they found a new trading area. Theirs was a commercial empire, not a political one. They were first and foremost merchants; they knew that trade suffers during war. To prosper, trade needs peace; but traders also have to be able to defend themselves when necessary. Although war ships were always stationed at their trading ports, their city-states of Be'erot ("City of Wells": Beirut), Sidon, and Tyre remained primarily major commercial centers; their military center was located at Carthage (*Kyriat Hedesh*, "New City"). They settled on Malta (by the eleventh century BCE), Sardinia (by the ninth century BCE), Provence (by the ninth century BCE), Sicily (by the twelfth century BCE), and the Balearic Islands off the coast of Spain. While written evidence appears between 900 and 700 BCE, sometime around 1500 BCE the Phoenicians also settled parts of *I Shafan* (I Shafan > Isafan > Isfana > Hispania > Espagne [Spain], that is, "Rabbit" or "Coney Island" in Phoenician). For many centuries they traded with the "Far Isles," bringing items such as flax seed and citrus to the Southwest of Britain while bringing back boatloads of tin ore. Contact between the Mediterranean and Southwest Britain began by at least 2500 BCE, if not earlier. The Phoenicians clearly followed their standard practice and created settlements there, too. They carried with them bags of saffron, their favorite spice, on their long-distance trading voyages. As in other Phoenician colonies, such as Marseilles, Cadiz, and Barcelona, the Cornish still use quite a bit of saffron in their cuisine. The early populations of Cornwall and Wales were a mixture of Alpines, Nordics, and Mediterraneans.

The composition of the population in Cornwall and the dates of contact provide a pertinent modern example of the *Edit*-to-conform technique in action. The following entry is from the revised, second edition of *An Encyclopedia of World History: Ancient, Medieval, and Modern, Chronologically Arranged*, (Boston: Houghton-Mifflin, 1948 (1940), page 164. The editor was William L. Langer, Coolidge Professor of History, Harvard University. The list of the sixteen experts from various universities and museums who collaborated on this book includes archaeologists, curators, historians, linguists, and a historical metallurgist from the Massachusetts Institute of Technology.

> Prehistoric Britain. The prehistoric inhabitants of Britain (called *Celts* on the basis of language) were apparently a fusion of Mediterranean, Alpine, and Nordic strains which included a dark Iberian and a light-haired stock. Archaeological evidence points to contacts with the Iberian Peninsula (2500 B.C.) and Egypt (1300 B.C.).

During the nineteenth century, although there were quite a few works published claiming that there had been contact between the Mediterranean and the British Isles, the accepted point of view was that Britain and Ireland were isolated and untouched by contacts with Mediterranean cultures until the arrival of Caesar and his troops. Scientific types dug into the area and found solid evidence that contradicted the nineteenth century establishment view. For a short period during the 1930's and 1940's, it was politically correct to recognize that the British Isles were not isolated and that contacts with the Eastern Mediterranean peoples began back in the third millennium BCE. During the late 1950's, it became the fashion to romanticize the Celtic peoples. All of a sudden, any evidence to the contrary disappeared from the more popular textbooks, encyclopedias, and scholarly works in the humanities. Once again, Britain and Ireland were presented as having been cut off from the outside world until brought into Roman orbit. It was even asserted that Ireland, separated from Britain by only a narrow channel full of islands, had been so isolated that the Romans had not been there.

Although isotopic studies on tin put a dent in the Winner's facade, never underestimate the capacity of the edit technique to mold cultural expectations. Recently, evidence for a Roman presence in Ireland has turned up, much to the surprise of many raised on the romantic idea of Irish isolation.

The entry about the archaeology of Cornwall (under the United Kingdom) in the fifteenth edition of the *Encyclopedia Britannica* is an interesting instance of a modern use of the Edit technique. This is a *signed* article in the "Macropedia." Cornish tin is mentioned in passing and presented as if the Romans could not have known about the ore deposit before Caesar was told about it in Gaul. Contact with the Eastern Mediterranean has been reduced to some amber beads from Cornwall found in Greek graves. The dates are now during the first millennium; the population is now composed only of Nordic strains mixed with earlier unnamed peoples.

As in the past, and as will be in the future, the edit-to-conformers always forget that outside evidence will contradict and expose them. While selective destruction could work during the sixth century on Origen's *Hexapla*, the modern printed data explosion is not so easy to control. There are other fields; in the hard sciences they tend to concentrate on hard data. Geochronologists blithely mention in passing two of *their* "doesn't everybody know that" items: (1) navigation between the British Isles, the Eastern Mediterranean, and the Baltic beginning late in the fourth millennium BCE, and (2) direct contact between Britain and the Red Sea via Egypt during the thirteenth century BCE. Botanists and experts in textiles see flax seed as coming with the Phoenicians and nuclear physicists run isotope analyses on ancient bronze weapons from around the twentieth century BCE and identify the tin as from Iberia and Cornwall.

If we can not trust a signed article in an encyclopedia, what can we do? All we can do is to be alert for contradictions in the presented data. We have to be able to spot those things that suggest a hole; something that is being circumvented or elided. The silence on the missing data can be deafening. In this case, the reader finds two glaring holes. First, the Cornish tin ore, without which the bronze chariots used by the Hittites, for example, could not have been constructed. Second, we have genetics: the well-known presence of small, gracile, dark Cornish, Welsh, and Irish peoples right alongside the tall, robust, fair Celtic stock.

We do not know just when the Celtic peoples arrived in the British Isles, perhaps around 700-600 BCE—perhaps even earlier, about 1000. Although we do not know exactly when they arrived, we do know that the Celts and the Phoenicians got along well—they frequently were allies and Celts from Galatia served as mercenaries on Phoenician war ships. We also know that Celts, Phoenicians, and Iberians intermarried. We should not be surprised that Insular, or Irish Celtic, the best understood of the Celtic tongues, shows the influence of non-Indo-European languages. Neither Iberian nor Punic are Indo-European tongues. [13]

The Punic Wars with Rome are understandable. Between their settlements on Sicily and Sardinia, with easy access to the Italian mainland also from Malta and the Balearic Islands, the Phoenician commercial empire was a serious threat to Rome's ambitions. Cornish tin was one of the main reasons Caesar wanted Britain; it was also one of the reasons Rome garrisoned so many troops on the island. The Romans wanted to protect *their* monopoly on tin ore.

After the First Punic war with Rome, the Phoenicians lost their control of Sardinia with its small tin deposit. After the Second Punic war, they lost their monopoly on tin. Still, we have cause to wonder just when the coasts of Cornwall and Wales became known as smuggler's paradise. There is little doubt that the Phoenicians stayed in contact with Cornwall and Wales from their settlements on the Iberian Peninsula, Sardinia, and on the North African coast. Under the Roman occupation, the inscriptions of Western Britain and Southern Ireland show a mixture of Celtic ethnic writing systems (Ogham) and Official Latin. The Latin scripts used by the British Christians in their texts and on their funerary inscriptions, however, are of the North African-Semitic group.

Similarly, we should not be surprised that Christianity came to Southwest Britain by the sea route. By the second century, Christianity had spread to Phoenician settlements in North Africa and Sardinia, as well as to their cities on the coasts of Spain, for instance, Neo-Carthage (New-New City). Tertullian, whom we have noted as the father of Liturgical Latin, was from Neo-Carthage. He also happened to be one of the leaders of the "heretical" Montanist party. [14]

The Winners techniques were very effective in Southwest Britain and Southeast Ireland. Outside of a few Syrian inscriptions from Britain, we do not possess *direct* written evidence of Semitic tongues on the Islands. Even without the metallurgical, geochronological, and genetic evidence, 3,000 years of contact with the Eastern Mediterranean implies that at least Punic was known, if nothing else, for trade.

To sum up the linguistic picture in the British Isles; Latin was the *koine*, the language of international discourse and Official Government. As the *koine*, Latin was also the language of many early Christians. Brittonic (Welsh, Cornish, and Breton) and Goidelic (Irish, Scots/Irish, and Manx), and assorted Non-Indo-European languages were in use at local levels.

As already stated, the above summary of the general linguistic and writing situation around the Roman Empire is much simplified; many other languages were in use. The picture that emerges is one of a loosely tied together tower of Babel with territorial and national scripts and writing systems employed right alongside the "Official" Roman scripts and systems.

If this immense polyglot mess were not sufficient, each town and village within each language area spoke its own dialects. (The Coptic writing system gives evidence that, although written Coptic was fairly understandable, the Egyptians in the delta had difficulty comprehending the speech of those from the upper Nile.) Further, each school, monastery, or synagogue also used its *own* version of its affiliated hierarchy of scripts, formats, and sizes. If we know nothing else, we do know that there were no monolithic churches, no monolithic writing systems, and certainly no monolithic scripts, either Greek or Latin.

Treating Greek scripts as monolithic has led to a misreading of the early Greek Biblical texts. As good detectives we know that if something looks different, it *is* different. A different script *always* means a different group.

Among the earliest of the Greek Bibles, we find two codices dated to the fourth century. One, the Codex *Sinaiticus*, was until the 19th century at the monastery of Saint Catherine in the Sinai (hence, Sinaiticus). The official story related by Constantine Tischendorf is that he pursuaded the monks of Saint Catherine's to give the codex to Tsar Alexander II of Russia in exchange for protection. This is not the story told by the monks at Saint Catherine. They say that Tischendorf borrowed the codex to "study" it and never returned. In any case, Tischendorf prepared a small edition, based on approximately 43 pages, which was published at Liepzig. He then is said to have given the Codex to the Tsar. The Codex was in Leningrad until 1933 when 347 of its estimated 730 leaves were legally purchased by the British Library (B.L. Additional MS. 43723), where, quite understandably, the manuscript has pride of place. Fragments of 3 more leaves are in Saint Petersburg; another 43 leaves are in the University Library at Leipzig—a suspicious number and suspicious place in light of the "acquisition" version related by the Monks at the Monastery. About a dozen more leaves came to light at St. Catherine's after a fire in 1975. Biblical scholars place the production of the Sinaiticus to Alexandria.

The other early fourth century Greek Bible is the Codex *Vaticanus* (Vatican, MS. Greek 1209). The Vaticanus was a gift. It may have been brought to the Council of Ferrara-Florence in 1438-39 by the delegates from Constantinople. Although its provenance remains the subject of scholarly debate, its place of origin appears to have been Upper Egypt.

While the two codices have much in common, there are some substantial differences. The first major difference between them is their content. Both codices originally contained the texts of the Old and New Testaments. Due to a misreading of the texts by the first editor, for nearly a century it was assumed that the *Vaticanus* included part of the Pseudepigraphic 4 Maccabees. Modern research has shown that the *Vaticanus* never contained anything besides the Old and New Testaments, including the Pauline material. The Sinaiticus, on the other hand, held additional material—including the Epistle of Barnabas, the Shepherd of Hermes, and 4 Maccabees.

We cannot really speak *in general* of a "canon" at this date, for canonical material fluctuated wildly depending upon time and affiliation. On the other hand, both codices are written on vellum, the finest grade of parchment; both are written in Monumental Biblical Book hands. The vellum and the formal book hands places both codices into Class 1 books according to known Ancient standards and price lists found in Roman discussions on book preparation. Class 1 books are authoritative; thus, we already know that we are looking at a difference in what was considered *their* canon by two different groups.

The *Vaticanus* is a square 10.7 by 10.7 inches; when open for reading the format imitates the "landscape" shape and size of a wall inscription under the Ptolemaic hierarchies. [15] The *Siniaticus* is 16.9 by 15 inches; "portrait" in format, it is the size of "The Law" under the African-Semitic hierarchy plus the addition of margins. In proportion to their widths, the *Sinaiticus* is written in four columns per leaf; the *Vaticanus* in three. Both are written in breathings, that is, the number of syllables that can be said in one breath. The two codices also share another fate: both have suffered from later editorializing, such as the addition of punctuation, or the insertion of later "corrections" to bring the text into conformity. The *Sinaiticus* was written by three scribes who clearly were trained at the same *scriptorium*. The *Vaticanus* was "freshened," that is, sometime around the 10th or 11th centuries, another scribe went over the codex overwriting the text letter-by-letter. Freshening usually occurs when the original ink is fading and the text is becoming difficult to read. Because this scribe left one leaf pretty much as it was, we know that, while this scribe added the accent marks, he simply overwrote the original script and did not change the design.

All Greek fonts are related; they are all descendants, mutations, of the same script. The differences are in the details; the second major difference between the codices is their fonts. These two Biblical fonts are totally different designs (Figure 4.2).

The first obvious point of difference between the fonts is that the font of the *Sinaiticus* uses both thick and thin lines, while the font of the *Vaticanus* is **monoline** (one thickness). This difference is a result of the types of pens used to write the texts; the type and cut of a pen is part of a script design. While both scripts are written with reed pens, the pen of the *Sinaiticus* is a chisel-point while that of the *Vaticanus* is a flat-cut nib. A chisel-point nib is cut at a slight angle; when it meets the writing surface, it automatically produces a thick and thin

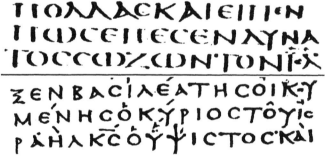

Fig. 4.2   Top: The Font of Codex Sinaiticus (Replica)
            Bottom: The Font of Codex Vaticanus (Replica)

line as the graphs are formed. A flat-cut pen nib meets the writing surface squarely; it will automatically produce a monoline.

We can see the effect of the pen in the form of the graphic-symbols. In the *Sinaiticus*, the uncial-*a* is pointed; in the *Vaticanus*, the form is rounded. Where we see a flattened base on the lobe of the rounded-*a* form, we can also see the hand of the freshener (over-writer). The *O* is also different. In the *Sinaiticus* the symbol has thick and thin strokes; in the *Vaticanus*, the *o* is monoline and flattened.

Second, as already noted, contact is a two-way street. While Rome borrowed much from Greece, Greece borrowed much from Rome. The range of the Roman *imperium* was, to a surprising extent, forced upon the Republic by calls for help from areas as diverse as Macedonia and Illyria. By the late third century BCE, Roman presence in the Hellenic world was well established. By the last quarter of the first century BCE, the Roman model for official scripts was also well established. The Augustan official Roman scripts display thick vertical and thin horizontal strokes, wedge-on-end serifs, tight **kerning** (the amount of overhang intruding upon the frame, or white space, between two letter-symbols), [16] and a narrow *o* base (the mensural base). The Augustan model is the reverse of the third century BCE Square Script models that use thin vertical and thick horizontal strokes, wedge serifs incorporated into the graphs, very tight kerning, and a rounded one-half *o* (ayin) base. In clear contrast, official Classical Greek scripts and fonts show monoline strokes, no serifs, loose kerning, and a wide *o* base.

Greeks borrowed from Rome, to be sure; but borrowing depends upon "who's on first" at a given time. More to the point, the oldest examples of authoritative serifed fonts in the Greek language show up in four documents from Egypt. All four were produced around the second century BCE; all are written in the *koine*; all predate the Official Augustan Roman model; and none of them are Greek fonts. Two of them are fragments of *Deuteronomy*. Deuteronomy was hardly an official text of the Ptolemaic Greek government; it was rather an authoritative text of the Jewish population of Alexandria. That a Greco-Judean authoritative font would have serifs is to be expected: the authoritative Pentateuchal Square Scripts found among the Dead Sea Scrolls incorporate serifs.

One of these Greek fragments of Deuteronomy is dated to the first half of the second century BCE (John Rylands Library, Papyrus III, 458, fragments, Manchester, England). The serifs of this font design follow the Judean practice of incorporated wedge serifs as opposed to the Roman end-wedge serifs. Other than the serifs in the Square Script style, the font follows Greek practices: this font is monoline, the mensural base of this script design is still the wider Greek *o*, the *o* is flattened, and the written text still displays very loose kerning. The other fragment of Deuteronomy (Sociète ègypt de papyrologie, P. Fouad, Inventory 266, Cairo) is normally dated to the middle of the first century BCE on the basis of a "development" towards the "Roman" Model. Scripts, however, do not develop, they mutate; the fragment is probably much earlier. This font design employs the thick horizontal and thin vertical strokes and very rounded *o* (ayin) base of the Authoritative Square Script; further, it has the very tight kerning of the circa third century BCE fragments of Exodus from among the DSS. The serifs on this font, however, are neither the Judean incorporated wedge nor the Roman end-wedge serifs; they are the angled "flip" serifs used in the even earlier Egyptian *Hieratic* models.

These tell-tale Hieratic serifs show up in a third document, a fragment of Homer's *Iliad* (University of California 2390). The Homer document may be safely dated to the middle of the second century BCE as it is part of **cartonage** (a polite way of saying "mummy wrappings") and includes numerous receipts with dates ranging from 144 to 139 BCE. While it would seem that nothing can be more Greek than a copy of Homer, this font is not Greek any more than those of the two Deuteronomy fragments: it is a copy of Homer written for or by an upperclass Egyptian and adapts the Greek symbol-set to a more familiar Hieratic model. The font design includes the distinctive Hieratic "flip" serifs, arched uprights, and "loops" on any graph that has a return stroke (one made without lifting the pen), such as "alpha."

All of our early examples of "Greek" fonts with serifs are from Ptolemaic Egypt, not from Seleucid Syria or mainland Greece. Even the fourth document cited as an example of early Greek serifed fonts is not Greek: it is a school boy's exercise and is written in the Greco-Judean incorporated wedge-serif, thick horizontal, thin vertical script. Language does not identify a group; script does.

Formal serifed Greek fonts only begin to replace the Classical Greek sans-serif fonts following the Roman conquest of Egypt. Further, the Greek font designs retained the old wide *o* base until long after Rome had become a solid presence in the Eastern Mediterranean basin. The change in *o* base does not occur until around the middle of the second century CE. Our oldest example of this new Greek Book font can be seen in a fragment of Hesiod's *Catalog* (Greek poet, lived eighth-century BCE). The font design of the Hesiod fragment incorporates many aspects of the Official Augustan Roman Capitals. It uses a narrower, Roman style *o* base; as a result, its proportions are very different. The graphic symbols are narrower and taller in relation to the *o*, and, to allow for tighter kerning, rounded forms, such as epsilon (*e*) and omicron (little *o*, the mensural base) are much rounder than in older Greek font designs.

Although the serifs on the fragments of Deuteronomy may suggest a Semitic tradition underlying the font of the *Sinaiticus*, upon closer examination, this does not prove to be the case. The designer of the *Sinaiticus* font followed in the footsteps of Sargon I when he borrowed the authority of the Sumerian graph designs to create a **consolidated** official font as *his* voice. [17] The Biblical font of the *Siniaticus* clearly borrows authority from Rome to create a consolidated font as an official voice. The placement of the serifs on Tau, Epsilon, and Sigma (C), and the thin horizontals, thick verticals of the font design follows the Official Augustan Roman model, not the second-century BCE Ptolemaic Greco-Judean one. The kerning between letters is tight; the omicron (o) is very round, as is the epsilon (Є), and the letter-symbols are very narrow and tall in comparison with the *o*.

On the other hand, the font of the *Vaticanus* makes no attempt to unite different factions. This font follows another old practice for borrowing authority: archaization. The design incorporates many features that appear in the oldest existing Greek scripts and fonts. The kerning is large and the *o* is flattened and broad. The epsilon has an almost straight-back. Forms such as the beta (B) and the lambda (/\ ) hark back to the ancient angular carved models. The script of the *Vaticanus* displays deliberate archaization, a return to the authority of Classical Greece.

There were a number of parties who chose Classical Greece as their model. When we think of Classical Greece, we think of Athens and rationality, philosophy, literature, and sculpture; we do not ordinarily pay much attention to the Athenian love of mysticism and mysteries in religion. Their writing limits, however, should remind us of this point. Unlike Ionian or Western Greek writing systems, the Classical Attic writing system used bilinear limits—or rather—as bilinear as could be managed with their symbol set, what Eric Turner refers to as "essentially" bilinear. [18] Both of these early Greek codices use the bilinear limits that were a feature of Attic, Egyptian, and Etrusco-Roman writing systems. This tells us that neither codex was the official text of any of the ultra-conservative subordinationist parties, such as the Anomaeans. The use of a Classical Greek model for the *Vaticanus* means we also can rule out the Montanists, Donatists, or any other groups who were strongly against the Hellenization of Christianity. This anti-Hellenism factor reduces the field somewhat and leaves us with the font of the *Vaticanus* as the official Biblical voice of either the monophysites or one of the Paulist factions among the subordinationist parties.

We have several pieces of evidence that the *Sinaiticus* was produced by affiliates of the Alexandrian-Roman parties. First, dated to the 5th century, another Class 1 book, the Codex *Alexandrinus* (BL Royal I.D. V-Viii), like the *Sinaiticus*, contains material in addition to the Old and New Testaments. Eusebian and Athanasian material was inserted before the Psalms. Now bound in four volumes, the first four books contain the Old Testament, plus the Pseudepigraphic 3 and 4 Maccabees, Psalm 151, and the fourteen liturgical canticles. The Epistles of Clement are appended to the New Testament. According to the table of contents, the Psalms of Solomon were originally part of the Codex, but they have been lost.

This codex uses a much broader two column format rather than the four very narrow ones of the earlier *Sinaiticus*. [19] The text is still written in breathings. New paragraphs are marked by letter-graphs in the white space between columns. The font is a mutation of the Romanized consolidation font of the *Sinaiticus* (Figure 4.3).

When we compare the sizes of these two codices, the *Alexandrinus* tells us that power has shifted from Alexandria to Rome. In the African-Semitic hierarchy, the size of the *Sinaiticus* is the size of "The Law" in the sacred domain; above laws in the profane domain. The *Alexandrinus*, however, has shrunk in size. Written on leaves 12.6 inches in height by 10.4 inches in width, it is now the height and width of Official Imperial documents: the size is a declaration that "The Law" has been subordinated. Control has passed to Rome from Alexandria.

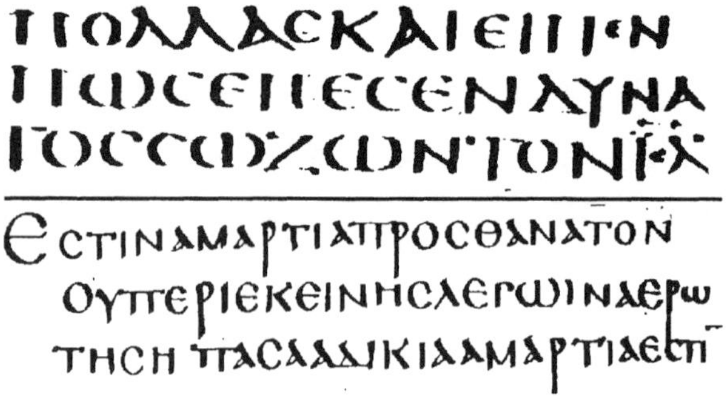

Fig. 4.3 Top: The Font of the *Codex Sinaiticus* (Replica)
Bottom: The Font of *Codex Alexandrinus* (Replica)

In imitating the Imperial hierarchy, the size tells us that the *Alexandrinus* is an Official document. Its status as a Class 1 book tells us that this codex is authoritative. The size also hands us one other piece of information, one that confirms Alexandria as the site of production of the *Sinaiticus*. In view of the declaration of superiority by size, if we look again at the font of the *Sinaiticus*, we can see that it does indeed take authority from Rome; however, the font of the *Sinaiticus* is a consolidation font meant to unite Alexandrian and Roman factions. The font and the inclusion of Athanasian writings and some of the *same* pseudepigraphic material in the *Alexandrinus* strongly suggests that in the *Sinaiticus*, we are seeing the Official identifying script of the Athanasian faction of the Alexandrian-Roman parties.

If the *Vaticanus* was produced in Upper Egypt, its font is the official script of monophysite parties; if it was produced on the Asian side of the Near East, it is the official script of one of the Pauline factions among the subordinationists. While its place of origin is still hotly debated, because scripts identify affiliation, and the same font will be used by all affiliates of a party, paleographic grounds are a very shaky basis to use when trying to pin down provenance. A recent computer analysis of style places the *Vaticanus* in Egypt; though, we cannot be certain. [20]

Nevertheless, we do know what these three codices tell us: In these volumes we are seeing the battle for authority in action. Even if we did not know the later history and the outcome of the battle, the two Romanized fonts in these other two codices, as well as the size of the *Alexandrinus*, tell us a great deal. In other words, the party using the Romanized font *won*.

Because Christianity essentially was passed on orally outside of urban centers, early Greek scriptural documents are scarce. This makes identification of party affiliation very difficult in most cases. This lack of material is not true for Latin texts. If we should need a reminder of how many Latin texts are available, more than 12,000 versions, complete or partial, of Bibles in Latin existed in 1546 when the Council of Trent was called. That 12,000 figure is only a small portion of the known scripturally-related Latin texts.

Unlike the Greek authoritative fonts, we *can* tell affiliation from Latin fonts. As of the last half of the fourth century, all Christian Latin official fonts are descended from one of four and only four scripts: Uncial, African Rustic, Greco-Roman half-uncial, and African half-uncial. Second and third century Latin translations of the Bible can be divided into African and European versions. If we treat Latin scripts and fonts as we treat all other scripts and fonts, by division and sub-divisions, and then place these separate traditions into their historical contexts, along with the formats and sizes, we have a sure guide through the forest to the hidden trees.

Latin scripts, fonts, and symbol sets can be divided into six very distinct groups. There are striking differences among the *Italic* (continental), the Alexandrian *Greco-Italic*, the *Greco-Syriac-Italic* (Byzantine), the *Greco-Persian Italic* (Antiochian), the *North African-Semitic-Italic*, and the *North African-Roman-Italic* scripts, symbol sets, and writing systems. The Iberian group has been included with the North African as the North African scripts incorporate Iberian elements.

The Italic scripts and fonts of these early centuries remain firmly within the Hellenistic influenced Roman tradition. Italic scripts exhibit a restricted symbol set, tend to be square, and are written in *scripto continuo*. It does not matter whether we look at the first century dedication to C. Antonius Rufus erected at Alexandria Troas, [21] or the Public Rustic Capitals of a Pompeiian Election notice, [22] Constantine's Arch from 315, [23] the fourth century manuscript, Vatican, latin 3256, [24] or the fifth century Codex Sangellensis; [25] they all show these unmistakable Italic features. These same features are characteristic of the Italic cursive scripts. Whether we are looking at the formal Roman Cursive of a second century Bill of Sale [26] or the semi-formal cursive scripts inscribed on stone, [27] written on tablets, [28] or as transcribed from wall-graffiti, the cursive forms are square, written continuously, and do not use the ternary base.

Although the Greek scripts and symbols were tenaciously conservative, variant forms begin to make their appearance during the first century CE in formal Greek scripts from *outside* Alexandria. It is not feasible to present photographs of every example: there are numerous papyri from Oxyrhynchus alone (West Bank of the Nile) written in Latin, Greek, demotic Egyptian, Coptic, Hebrew, Syriac, and Arabic. These papyri are dispersed in the collections of a multitude of museums and libraries. Among these documents we find a variety of variant forms, such as the epsilon-*e* (Є), used in contrast with the standard-*e*. [29] A famous fragment of Homer found at Hawara dates to the first half of the second century. The Hawara Homer includes a squared epsilon-*e* to indicate a different phone. [30] While authoritative secular texts remain written in *scripto continuo*, documentary cursive scripts are written with spacing between spoken expressions. [31]

In sharp contrast to the square Italic cursive scripts, the Greco-Italic cursives of these early centuries show the influence of cursive Aramaic scripts in their rounding. The "open-*a*" (ɑ), for example, a normal feature of the Alexandrian Greco-Italic cursive fonts, is a reflected form of one of the *a*'s used in the "Herodian" script from the Dead Sea scrolls. Documents from Fayoum, such as P. Lat. Argent. i, (cira 317-324) in the Bibliothéque nationale et universitaire at Strasbourg, [32] and the draft petition of Flavius Abinnaeus (Papyrus 447, circa 345-6, in the British Library) [33] indicate that by the fourth century, the Alexandrian Greco-Italic cursive font became the everyday script of late Antiquity. [34]

Unlike either the continental Italic or the Alexandrian Greco-Italic writing systems, the Greco-Syriac-Italic, Greco-Persian-Italic, and both of the North African-Italic systems retained the Phoenician writing system in its entirety. Along with the writing system, their graphic symbols exhibit an extensive Latin-language symbol set with variant forms heavily incorporating Greek and Semitic symbols. They all use rounded forms in their official scripts. [35] We find the Greek epsilon-*e* alongside standard-*e*. The Carian (Iberian) short-leg-*r* (ʀ) is used to indicate a different phone from the Italic-*r*, and the round Aramaic-influenced-*m* (ꟽ) is used alongside the Latin straight-*m*. Rounded-*a*'s are influenced by Punic and Syriac symbols.

North African-Roman-Italic and North African-Semitic-Italic systems can only be told apart from their scripts. While both North African systems used the same Phoenician ternary basis and variant forms, the North African-Roman-Italic scripts and fonts are squared; the North African-Semitic are rounded.

The Christian-Semitic systems retained shape-differentiated symbol sets, the point system, phonetic spacing, and writing by phrase. The pre-Christian Greeks dropped the point system, retained writing by breathings, and replaced shape-differentiation by adding new symbols to represent the various phones. By 300 BCE, this lack of form differentiation led to the addition of "accents" to the Greek symbol set. From this time forward, formal Greek symbol sets and writing systems use external notation and reintroduce variant forms under the influence of Biblical models. Etruscan, and as a result the formal Italic writing systems, employ neither variant forms nor stress and durational notation. Only after the spread of Christianity do continental Italic symbol-sets reincorporate some components of the original Phoenician writing system. Towards the end of the first century or the beginning of the second, we find our first small indications of a return to variant forms in Latin texts from *Africa*.

What is probably the oldest example of the reintroduction of variant forms into Latin texts shows up in a fragment of a Papyrus document from the late 1st-early 2nd centuries CE. Number 430, fragment 8, xi.1644 in the papyrus collection at the University of Michigan at Ann Arbor. The fragment shows us two forms of *A* in use (Figure 4.4). The first is a cursive African Rustic-*A*. Because the second one shows a vague resemblance to a form of cursive Rustic *A*, many Latin paleographers consider it a "prototypic" **uncial-*a***.

The uncial *a*'s are very distinctive; they are a script identifier. The uncial and the half-uncial scripts and fonts are important to us for two reasons. First, they are our doorway into the past. The distinctive differences between the Latin uncial schools permit us to trace the various writing systems. Second, our modern lower-case serifed fonts are all descendants of the North African half-uncial; our modern lower-case sans-serif fonts are all descendants of the Greco-Roman half-uncial. Because the uncials and half-uncials are so important, we must examine this script with some care.

Fig. 4.4 The two A's in Mich. PAP. 430.

There are two basic forms of the Latin uncial-*a*: a rounded form (λ) and a pointed one (λ). While the cursive forms of the Rustic capitals *could* have been the model for the uncial script, there are many problems with the claim that the uncial-*A* developed from a Rustic cursive-*A*. One major problem is that, while Latin paleographers note the influence of other territorial scripts and fonts on the Latin graphic sets, nobody thought to look at the Semitic territorial scripts. Another is that, as in all fields, paleographers copy one another; unless something waves a red flag, they do not question received authority. The failure to examine Semitic territorial scripts in what was a Semitic-speaking area is a very big red flag indeed.

Fig. 4.5 Semitic Models (above) for the Uncial-*A*'s (below)

The third difficulty with the idea that the uncials "developed" from Rustic Capitals is simple: scripts do not develop, they mutate. Fourth, there is no such thing as a "proto-typic" script or font. A model must exist for a script or font to mutate *from*. Models for both the distinctive uncial-*a*'s had been available for centuries. The rounded form closely resembles a known coin script *aleph*; the pointed form does not resemble, it *is*, a late formal Phoenician *aleph* (Figure 4.5). The normal practice when copying a symbol design is to rotate or to reflect the Phoenician model depending upon the direction of writing. (The Greek *rho* (P) is identical to the older Phoenician *resh* when written right-to-left and reflected when written left-to-right.) Legs are extended or clipped. In this case, neither model was either turned or reflected, but both models, as in earlier Greek and Etruscan scripts, had their "tails" clipped off. Other than in accordance with a particular script design, the pointed-*a* changed very little across the centuries. At first, the rounded-*a* script designs featured an open-lobe. By the third century, script designs appear with a closed lobe.

The fifth difficulty is equally important: scribes do not *design* scripts, they *learn* them. This means that a complete script design already existed for a scribe to have learned it and to write the forms in a document. Sixth, there is nothing haphazard about these early models. They are not undergoing "development." All examples of early uncial-*a* are obviously designed, and well designed at that, as components of complete script systems.

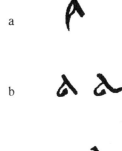

Seventh, while Latin was the official governmental language, Punic, that is, Phoenician, was the primary language in North Africa and Neo-Punic the script. Throughout the empire, Latin scripts were influenced by ethnic ones. We ought to be astonished if these North African Latin scripts and fonts did *not* show the influence of native models.

Finally, although used in *Greek* Biblical fonts by the late second century, uncials were not adopted by mainland Italy until the second quarter of the fourth century, after the conversion of Constantine I. All of our early examples of the uncial-*a* are from *Africa* (Figure 4.6).

Beginning as a book font, by the first century, the African Rustic script had attained the status of an official script for authoritative documents. Most of our early examples are written in Rustic with uncials used to indicate variant phones.

Fig. 4.6 Early Uncial-*a*'s

The fragment known as P.S.I 743, xi.1695 (*Biblioteca Medicea Laurenziana*, Florence, Italy), dates from the second century. Written in

Rustic and Uncial Capitals, the document gives us our earliest example of the pointed uncial-*a*. As the document is only a fragment, we do not have examples of the entire design. This uncial-*a* suggests that the complete script design would have employed heavy and light strokes along with extensions for balance (Figure 4.6a).

Written primarily in African Rustic, the late second-early third-century fragment known as Michigan Papyrus 429, xi.212 illustrates two examples of the open-lobe round uncial-*a* (Figure 4.6b). The entire set was probably a light rounded design that made use of heavy and light strokes. Evidence that the ternary basis was in use shows on the trailer on the second *a* which indicates a held phone; otherwise, the forms are identical.

The third early model is located at Timgad. Dating to the third century, the *Vocontio* stele is a well-known example of the closed-lobe round uncial-*a*. The *Vocontio* displays clear examples of variant forms carved in stone (Figure 4.6c). The uncial forms of this design were quite rounded and show in sharp contrast with the Rustic of the main text. [36]

Except for the use of heavy and light strokes, the design of the last example almost reverts to the original Phoenician aleph (Figure 4.6d). This is from the *Maktar* stele that is dated to the second quarter of the fourth century. The Maktar is carved in Constantine's new official Uncial script.

With Constantine, we come to a new era in Latin scripts. The change in cursive scripts after Constantine was so drastic, that today they are called *Old* Roman Cursive and *New* Roman Cursive. Here we run into one of the problems with the "monolithic" approach to Latin scripts. The "New Roman Cursive script" is neither "New" nor "Roman." The script is a product of the Greco-Syriac-Byzantine school adopted by the Greco-Italic school for writing commercial Latin. The mis-named "New Roman" was the "everyday" script in Alexandria before it was picked up by Rome.

The change in the official script was just as dramatic. Constantine apparently wanted to unify his disparate empire through religion and script. Perhaps Constantine thought he was doing something new and different; but, he was merely repeating history. Back at Akkad, Sargon decided to unify his diverse kingdom through script and religion. [37] Rounded Aramaic forms had already been incorporated into the Greco-Italic scripts. The new Constantine script combined elements from *existing* Latin and Greek models into one new consolidated Imperial Official voice. [38] This is the script we call *uncial*.

The Constantine Uncial is a merger of Italic and Alexandrian Greek square scripts. Although the new official script incorporated some symbols previously borrowed from the African school, there remain sharp distinctions between the symbol sets as well as the scripts. The Greco-Italic forms are still very square, and while rounded at the headline, the upright minims of the *m*, for example, are still perpendicular, lending the symbol a close resemblance to a modern sans-serif type font *m* (m).

The new Uncial symbol set and writing system incorporate writing phrase-by-phrase, as distinct from writing in *scripto continuo*, into its formal and informal texts. The reintegration of a modified point system began during this period, but did not become standard for another century. [39] The writing system is strictly bilinear and follows the rules for the Latin symbol set laid down by the reformers of first-century Rome. There are no variant forms and no evidence of durational and stress notation.

The Imperial uncial script was adopted by the Alexandrian-Roman parties as their official Latin voice. It stayed their official voice for a very long time. The uncial monopoly on Latin liturgical and biblical texts from the fourth through the ninth century is well enough known to be stated by T. Julian

Brown in his article on "Latin-Alphabet Handwriting" in the *Encyclopaedia Britannica*. In the meantime, though, there were other parties involved, and they did not take too kindly to the Alexandrian-Roman uncial script as their official voice.

Latin was the language of officialdom and inter-ethnic discourse. Moving westwards from Egypt, however, the primary languages in North Africa were Punic, Chadic, Hamitic (such as Berber), and, by the fourth century, Vandalic. In other words, a melting pot. Between the first and fourth centuries, the primary scripts along the entire coast were Punic and Latin. The area was a hotbed of Christianities and a fortress for the subordinationist parties. Somewhere along this coast, somebody designed an official Latin voice for the subordinationists. Mutating as it spread among the assorted affiliates, the script travelled very far. Today we call these scripts and fonts African half-uncial: the ancestors of our modern lower-case serifed scripts and fonts.

Rome itself had more Christianities during the fourth and fifth centuries than almost anywhere else. The African half-uncial was in use there, too. Sometime during this period of tumult, somebody came up with a Greco-Roman half-uncial script and the script was given official status. With the acceptance of the Greco-Roman half-uncial as an official script, the North-African "tree" became hidden in the half-uncial forest. Nevertheless, the half-uncial tree still shows itself to the experienced eye.

Professional script designers can tell when a script design has been, in modern parlance, **pirated**. Pirating is a serious problem in the computer age. The design of a script is very time consuming; it took Hermann Zapf seven years to balance his Univers script design. Yet all a pirate has to do is to make small changes to the copyrighted set and the design is considered a new expression. Pirates will, for instance, make an *m* slightly wider, or reduce the serifs on a serifed design. They almost never go through the entire set and change every symbol and the graphic symbols no longer fit together as a complete whole. The pirated set never has the balance and finish of the original design.

E. A. Lowe, a considerable authority on Latin paleography, considered the African School to be very "advanced." He states that "by the year 509/510 African calligraphy had reached a very high level of development, in fact a level not yet attained in the mother land." [40] Whether Lowe realized it or not, he was telling us that the Greco-Roman half-uncial was a pirated design—and indeed it was. Lowe claims the origin of the canonical half-uncial for the African School. He was right. The early uncial and half-uncial scripts and fonts are North African in origin. Lowe was also right that the African half-uncial was at a much higher level of "development." We would expect a script to be of a more "advanced" design in the area where it was created as the official voice. The North African half-uncial and its related cursive mutations are the carefully designed and executed official Biblical script of the subordinationist parties.

In direct opposition to the Alexandrian-Roman factions, the North African-Semitic-Iberian official Biblical writing system retains variant forms and durational and stress notation. It employs rounded as opposed to squared forms, preserves the ancient Phoenician three point punctuation system, and authoritative texts are written phrase-by-phrase in a narrow column format.

We find ourselves with two different half-uncials, one "Official" uncial, and Rustic Capitals. We have overlapping formats and sizes. It all seems very confusing. Nevertheless, it is this diversity within official scripts and writing systems that allows us to categorize them into six primary streams. It also permits us to track and to trace their movements (Map 1).

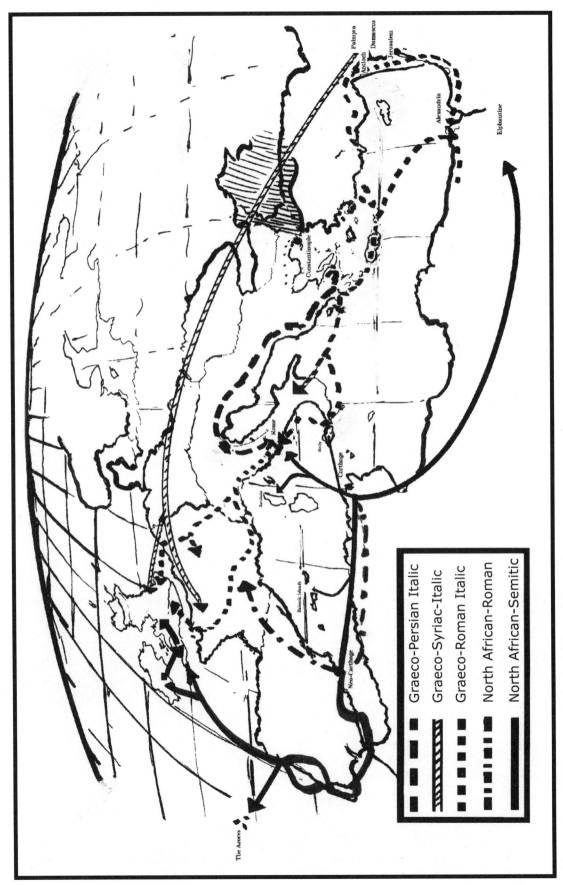

Map 1: The Distribution of the Primary Streams of Italic Writing Systems

The map does not include Continental Italic, one of the original six early streams. After Constantine, Continental Italic was rendered unimportant in the larger world of Western Christianity. In a political move to break away from the authority of the Patriarch at Constantinople, Pope Gregory I (cira 540-604) made an abortive attempt to revive Roman Capitals for monuments and Continental Italic for texts; he did not succeed. Continental-Italic, the old Roman official script system, was not revived as an official script until the Renaissance, nor was this revival under the auspices of religion. Continental Italic returned to its original status as the local voice of the central Italian peninsula. The other five scripts and writing systems are our guides to the distribution of early Christianity.

The Greco-Persian-Italic stream went by way of Greece to Italy sometime between the late-first and third centuries. This Christian Italic script shows a strong Persian influence that dates back to the Greek scripts in use at Antioch during its long period as the capital of the Greek Seleucid Empire. The Benevenetan script is representative of this stream.

The Greco-Syriac-Italic stream went by way of Palmyra close to the area of the Black Sea and across the ancient overland mountain passes via what is modern Hungary to Northeast France. Christianity is reported in the early second century from Northeast France. By the late second century, the records report organized Christian communities at Lyon. [41] The Luxeuil scripts are examples of this Italic stream.

The Greco-Roman-Italic (Alexandrian) stream passed by way of Egypt to Palestine and Greece to Rome, and to parts of England along with Theodore's (602-690) arrival in 668-9. Until Theodore opened his school at Canterbury, only Celtic (Insular) scripts and fonts were used in England. Afterwards, at Roman affiliated monasteries the official book hand was the official Greco-Roman uncial; albeit, in their own distinctive versions. Correspondence scripts from Wearmouth-Jarrow and London are examples of this stream.

The North African systems followed a somewhat different pattern. The main North African stream traveled both east and west along the African coast. It appears among the texts found in upper Egypt and at sites known to have been settled by Phoenicians; it also shows up at Rome. The North African streams interacted with the Iberian stream from a very early date, as both of the North African half-uncial official and cursive scripts include Iberian forms, which appear to date back to the seventh century BCE. [42] Contact between North Africa and Spain was continuous; it never ceased at any point. Sometime during the early centuries of the Common Era, both North African streams, including script, format, and size hierarchies, re-entered Spain. There the stream divided into two main sets: North/North-Eastern, and West/South-Eastern. [43]

The North/North-Eastern North African-*Roman* stream passed through the Pyrenees and into South-Western France. The Monserrat Manuscripts are representative of this stream.

At some point between the first and third centuries, the West/South-Eastern North-African-*Semitic* stream traveled by way of Western Spain to Southwest England. Sometime between the third and fifth centuries, this Western sub-stream entered South-Eastern Ireland.

In England, during the early seventh century, the, by now, North African-Iberian-Brittonic-Goidelic-Italic writing systems and symbol sets were adopted by Anglo-Saxon converts to Christianity. Around the mid-seventh century, the Anglo-Saxons adapted and codified the North African-Brittonic writing system to their language. The new converts were very enthusiastic and Anglo-Saxon missionaries carried their Anglo-Celtic writing system everywhere they went on the Continent. some period between 651 and 731, the age old technique of script-differentiation by language was reincorporated into the Anglo-Saxon writing system. Finally, the system was augmented by the addition of a distinctive and innovative method of musical notation. [44]

History is full of flukes and accidents. Near the end of the seventh century, an Anglo-Roman sub-stream appears on the English scene. The battle for the right to be supreme in England was bleak and bloody. In spite of the grim realities, there are amusing aspects. In one of the greatest ironies of this story, an attempt to hide the North African tree resulted in the establishment of the older North African-Iberian-Brittonic-Goidelic-Anglo-Italic writing system and scripts, better known as the Anglo-Celtic, or Insular, systems, as the most influential systems in the West.

Although any of these Italic writing systems could be followed down the centuries to see behind the facade erected by the Winners, this Anglo-Celtic system is the ancestor of our modern "Latin" writing systems. So, to England we now go.

Part Two

MORE THAN WORDS

Chapter Five

THE BRITISH ISLES

The story of writing in the West is a gigantic jigsaw puzzle 5,000 years deep and two continents wide. When we study writing, we are detectives collecting clues and testimony from concrete evidence in order to place these pieces within their respective positions in the puzzle. Unlike some areas of study, this is a story that is visible for all to see, to touch, to examine, and to affirm for themselves. Writing is a living history that unfolds as we watch. We are there to see it happen as the distant past becomes our current present. We see the story of writing in England acted out before our eyes. As in any good story, we must first set the stage.

In antiquity, commerce held the primary role in the distribution and dissemination of the Phoenician writing system. By the early years of our common era, writing followed the spread of Christianity.

In the beginning, Christianity was an urban religion. The differences between the country mouse and the city mouse were already well established back at Sumer and Akkad. Also well established was the contemptuous attitude of the urbanites towards those who worked the land. During the early centuries CE, Latin was the language of government and the *koine* (common tongue). The Roman upper classes and the elite of urban Alexandria read, wrote, and spoke Greek. These urbanites did not bother to translate the Gospels from Greek into the tongues of the peoples. The only Biblical texts readily available in these early years were Greek and Hebrew "originals." Latin translations began to appear during the mid-second century; these translations may have been done by the Eastern Christian communities at Rome for local use. Mani (cira 215-276), the founder of Manichaeism, believed in translations. Mani's translations were into the Aramaic spoken in Hellenized Syria, that is, Syriac. Not too surprisingly, Mani picked up many followers, among them, for a while, Augustine of Hippo (circa

354-430). Numerous translations into the vernacular and the Western *koine* began to appear. Jerome's three Latin translations of the Psalms date to the late fourth-early fifth centuries.

Christianity arrived in the British Isles very early; earlier than it did in most of the Mediterranean basin itself. We find evidence of its presence well before the battle between the Trinitarians and the Subordinationists got under way in the fourth century back in Alexandria, Egypt. Christian missionaries were in North-East France by the first half of the second century CE. These missionaries appear to have made use of the ancient Salt road that intersected the equally ancient Kings' Road at Damascus. The Kings' Road joined the trader's road that ran around the periphery of the Roman Empire and would appear to have been very useful for adherents of the (then) illegal religion. The Kings' Road began on the sea at Yemen, passed through Damascus and thence through the important trading center of Palmyra (Biblical Tadmor). Palmyrene inscribed markers and stones line the Road all the way from Palmyra to North-East France. [1]

Syriac influence upon the Luxeuil model and other early Frankish fonts is pretty patent. The Syrian scripts used in theological texts **clubbed,** that is, widened, the ascenders. Clubbing in the Luxeuil script approaches the level of "an obsession." [2] Syriac parties were **decatetartos** (fourteenthers); they celebrated Easter on the fourteenth of Nissan, the date of the Jewish Passover (Greek *Pascha*). We can infer that these earliest Gallic Christians were probably affiliates of the Syriac parties. Nor did the Syriac influence disappear. There was still a strong Syriac presence in and about Orleans, France well into the sixth century. Guntram, King of Burgundy, was greeted in Latin, Hebrew, and Syriac upon his entry to Orleans in 585. Syrian Eusebius was appointed Bishop of Paris (591), and Syrian codices show up in Tours and Bordeaux. [3]

Across the English Channel, Christian relics and burial sites dot the British countryside. We find inscriptions, jewelry, coins, and other archaeological evidence on the island. As bishops are only appointed to existing congregations, we have confirmation that the Roman areas of Britain were Christianized long before Constantine I ("the great," 274-337) converted to Christianity in 324. Three British bishops attended the council of Arles in 314.

While Christians apparently came in behind, or along with, Imperial troops, Origen reports Christians in Britain itself during the second century to the north and east of the Roman held area. It seems likely that these Christians were affiliated with the Syriac parties directly across the channel in France and that their scriptural texts were in Syriac. There is little doubt that there were Syrian and compromiser parties in Britain; the presence of "fourteenthers" among the early Anglo-Saxon converts is documented. Evidence of a Syrian presence also comes from the Palmyrene script. Palmyrene, originally the cursive script of the Aramaic-writing population of Seleucid Syria, is found from Egypt to the edges of Western Europe. Palmyrene cursive monumental scripts have been found even in England: a Latin-Palmyrene bilingual inscription resides in the Free Library at South Shields. [4]

Sometime during the late first or early second century, Christianity came to Southwest Britain by sea. This time the missionaries came from North Africa, Sardinia, and Western Spain by way of the old sea route to Britain and Ireland. Evidence of this sea route is supplied by the script and fonts used by this group of Christian parties. Two distinctive features of this script design are the upward **flourish** on the graphs and the incorporation of the cuneiform wedge into the starting strokes of the script design. The fonts show up on Latin inscriptions (such as the specifically Christian burial inscriptions), on tablets, and in early manuscripts. Like the characteristic upward curve ("flourish"), the starting wedge immediately identifies members of this family of fonts. The cuneiform wedge was the mark of an official or authoritative script and dates back to the long reign of cuneiform writing as the official script of inter-ethnic discourse. The Offical script design used in Neo-Babylon imitates the official script of Old Babylonian. In turn, the cuneiform wedge was incorporated into the design of the Authoritative Square Script that we find among the Dead Sea Scrolls. The Square Script cuneiform wedge, in turn, was incorporated into the North African-Semitic-Italic half-uncial script design. The Insular font family is a mutation of the North African-Semitic-Italic script class.

We also have evidence of this North African origin from arguments and outright bloody battles supplied by Bede in his *Historia Ecclesiastica Gentis Anglorum* (The Ecclesiastical History of the Race of Englishmen). These fights make it amply clear that these areas were Christianized by "heretical" North African missionaries.

By the late fourth century, Britain produced its own homegrown heretical Christian party called Pelagianism after its founder Pelagius (cira 360-420).

British Christianity arrived too early to fit into the later desired history. The few Semitic inscriptions are our only piece of *direct* evidence for any knowledge of Semitic languages in the islands. Selective destruction and the Edit technique left the desired picture of limited literacy, some knowledge of Greek and Hebrew, and Christianity arriving only with the Roman mission. The Winners' picture portrayed the existing British Christians as stubborn, selfish, and illiterate barbarians.

Cornwall held the monopoly on tin ore in the West, and had held it for more than 3000 years. The British peoples of Cornwall and Wales were a mixture of Mediterranean (Iberian and Phoenician), Alpine, and Nordic (Celtic) stock. [5] Phoenician and Iberian traders were literate. All of the writing systems in the West are descendants of the new Phoenician writing system and, back in those days, people knew it. Further, the Phoenicians came from societies where it was an obligation laid upon fathers to teach their sons *and* daughters to read and to write. The Celti-Iberians tell us clearly that the Celtic peoples were quick to adopt reading and writing. It would be astonishing if the Celtic peoples of Southwest Britain were *not* literate—and the British Celts were.

The evidence for the notably high cultural level of the British can only be seen through their Latin compositions. The evidence for their generosity and friendliness towards their new neighbors can only be seen through translations into the vernacular by those Anglo-Saxons they converted to Christianity.

We are fortunate that *any* texts written by the Britons survive. The Edit technique was already being applied to their works by the seventh century. Selective destruction took its toll by the late tenth century. Many of the Cornish emigrated to Spain and to Brittany; outside of Christian burial inscriptions in Latin, nothing remains of early Cornish texts. East of the Severn River and to the North of Ireland, all we find are shards and pieces of demolished inscriptions and monuments. Complete steles and monuments carved in the native writing system are found only in Wales and Southern Ireland. Obviously, no manuscripts in the native languages survived. Being in Latin protected more than one British document from destruction, but not, of course, from editing. The Winners could not hide everything; today, *indirect* evidence paints a very different picture.

The Winners' techniques worked for more than 1000 years. One reason the Winners' techniques were so successful and so difficult to see through in the British Isles is very simple: the person reading the material must be fully literate in as many languages as the "ignorant" British were. This little proviso limits the number of people who can do this work to a very small group of scholars.

Punic was indeed known, as were other languages. After all, if someone could read Punic, he could read Hebrew, its sister language, with ease. If there was trade with Egypt, knowledge of Western Aramaic, and later, Greek was essential. During the early period of contact with Egypt, Phoenician and then Aramaic were the traders's *koine*; after Alexander, the literate people of Egypt spoke Greek, not Latin. The Christianities of South-West Britain arrived too early for the scriptures to have been in Roman Latin; their texts were in Greek and Hebrew.

We now have solid evidence that these "ignorant, illiterate, selfish, barbarians" had a vital, brilliant, culture. It was a cosmopolitan, literate culture which, at its height, rivaled that of Classical Greece. They wrote equally well in Standard Classical and Late Literary Latin. They were polyglots who could toss off multilingual puns playing Latin against Greek and Hebrew. [6] Granted Roman citizenship, they considered themselves *Romani*. Being literate in the *koine*, they called themselves *Latini*. Having adopted the new religion, they called themselves *Christani*. Rather than being selfish, they shared their knowledge and religion with their neighbors. [7]

Although we can now firmly assert that it was the British who kept learning alive in Britain, Ireland is a different proposition. There has long been a tradition in Ireland that Christianity came to their Island from Britain. The evidence that is emerging lends some truth to this story, but we will never know. The Winners' trail of destruction removed almost all direct evidence of early interaction between the British and the Irish Celts. Texts inscribed in Inscriptional Old Celtic (IOC) are found on both sides of the Irish Sea. These inscriptions, the only concrete evidence left, are more than a little ambiguous; we cannot know whether the Celtic ethnic writing system was born in Wales or in Ireland.

When we look across the Irish Sea we find archaeological evidence, such as burial sites and coin hoards, that indicate the presence of people who had adopted the culture of Imperial Rome in the first and second centuries CE. The Irish (Welsh?) Celts had their own ethnic script and writing system called **Ogham**. (The name of the Irish system also appears written as Ogam or Og'am. In Old Irish, the *h* is not pronounced, but indicates a softening, that is, **lenition**.) The symbol set of Ogham consists of groups of lines and dots. Although it is sometimes postulated that the Roman writing system influenced Ogham, new research indicates that the Ogham system existed prior to contact with Rome. Ogham-Latin translation tables appear to have been organized only to show the phonetic values of the Ogham symbols in relationship to the Latin symbols. We do not know if some of these Romanized Irish were Christianized, although it would seem unlikely from the evidence of the **bilingual** inscriptions. [8]

Among the hundreds of inscribed stones we find in Latin and Ogham (Figure 5.1) there are more than a few bilingual (or more accurately, bi-ethnos) inscriptions. These are inscriptions with the same text in two languages. Bilinguals were common throughout the Roman Empire. These bilingual texts give us important evidence.

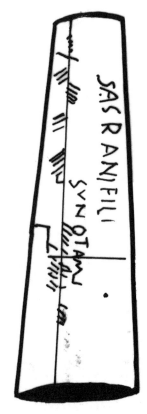

Fig. 5.1 Latin-Ogham bilingual inscription.(Replica based on Photograph

Paleographically, they are always in two ethnic scripts: one for each people. Latin-Greek bilingual *steles* use Latin scripts for the Latin text and Greek scripts for the Greek. The Latin-Palmyrene stele on exhibit at Shields, England has the Latin text in a Latin script and the Palmyrene in the Palmyrene Aramaic one.

Linguistically, these bi- and trilingual inscriptions supply the key to deciphering unknown languages. Bilinguals give us the required **redundancy**, a known source to check upon the unknown. It is impossible to reconstruct the unknown with any degree of accuracy, whether a language or a musical score, without this redundancy.

Socially, bilinguals tell us "who's on first." In ancient practice, the script on top of an inscription or to the right side of a two-column format was the master text. In Greek-Palmyrene doorway inscriptions, Greek runs across the top; the Palmyrene down the sides of the doorframe. The Latin/Ogham bilingual inscriptions display the Latin text in a central position; the Ogham appears on the side or on the bottom.

The scripts themselves give us further data. The Latin portion of these Irish texts are written in pre-Constantine Latin scripts, that is, before the legalization and declaration of Christianity as the official religion of the Imperium. As Christians did not use the "pagan" official Augustan Imperial script, it is unlikely that these inscriptions were the work of Irish Christians.

Whether Christian or not in the early centuries, we do know that by the fourth and fifth centuries, it was the Christian population who kept Latin learning alive in Ireland. There is some scholarly debate as to the exact date of the Christianization of Ireland, but bishops were not missionaries. Bishops were sent out to existing congregations. Palladius (? -431) was sent to be bishop to the Christians of Ireland in 430-31 by Celestine I (Pope from 422-432). This implies that there already had to be a substantial congregation for him to be bishop *to*.

Palladius died en route, which left a convenient hole in the chronology of Irish bishops. In the seventh century, the church at Armagh made use of the hole in its political fight with its rival at Kildare and its arch-enemy, Wilfrid of York. Wilfrid claimed metropolitan authority over Armagh, while Kildare claimed *it* had the authority. In need of a metropolitan authority Armagh did not as yet have, the legend of Patrick was born.

Writings about every Christian leader or martyr are filtered through a literary lens. Our Western dual heritage shows up in the most unexpected places. Although the basic techniques date from antiquity, the versions passed down through the early Christians combined facets of both the Semitic and the Hellenistic traditions. The merged techniques used to described these men and women quickly became stereotyped and turned into a literary genre. We call this genre **Saints' Lives**.

The basic Saints' Life story is always the same. It includes some facts about the person, but more ink is spent reciting the holiness or devoutness of the person in question. Descent from Royal houses or a good background of one sort or another also seems to be a prerequisite. Another part of the technique requires that wondrous miracles be performed by the person or attributed to something the person touched. (There was a brisk business in Saint's relics.) Sometimes, though, we can see past the stereotype and learn something about the person from what slips through–sometimes.

The legend of Patrick (circa 385-461), who is best known as the patron saint of Ireland, incorporates many of the themes of the Saints' Lives genre. He was supposedly the son of a British landowner named Calpurnius. His father was claimed to be a deacon and his grandfather a priest.

They were presumedly wealthy enough to own slaves of both sexes. Patrick's father is said to have been a member of a governing council. Patrick was born, in one version, somewhere near Carlisle, England; in another, at the village of Bannavem; in yet another, he was born in Gaul. Patrick is associated with Germanus of Auxerre (cira 378-448) and is supposed to have studied at the School of Lérins. The legend goes on to have him consecrated as a bishop around 432 by Germanus and then sent to Ireland as Bishop by Pope Celestine in that year. His work during this first period in Ireland is typical of the Saints' Lives genre: he works miracles and he converts everyone in sight. The story then has Patrick visiting Rome in 442, and, getting to the heart of the legend, founding the Church of Armagh in 444. Obviously, if Patrick had metropolitan authority, Armagh also had authority. But the legend asserts that Patrick was in constant conflict with the provincial synod who *questioned* his authority.

If Patrick was the son of a Romano-British official, they could not have been from Carlisle; Carlisle was situated in a military zone, not a villa zone. The family could not have been in Gaul and still have had his father a local Romano-British official in Britain. He probably came from somewhere in the vicinity of the Severn. If Patrick had any official authority whatsoever, a papal or metropolitan card, why did he not claim that authority in response to his critics? The reality is far more interesting and tells us far more about his character than the legend. As hard as it for us to believe today that anyone would undertake such a job on his own initiative, this is exactly what he did. Shorn of later hagiography, stripped of its political purpose, the facts stand out in his *own* words in his *own* letters. In response to his critics, Patrick never named a teacher, never claimed a school, and he never claimed papal backing. Patrick claims that what and who he is comes directly from God. [9]

The Legend of Saint Patrick, with all its political trimmings, shows us another facet of the Winners' (or would-be Winners, in this case) techniques. The creation of an appropriate background is not limited solely to rulers with questionable origins as in Neo-Babylon or in Rome.

Patrick and scholarly disputes aside, it is clear that Ireland was Christianized by the fifth century. As elsewhere, there were multiple Christianities in Ireland; there was no such thing as a unified "Celtic Church." [10]

Patrick, a literate Romano-Briton, was not an isolated and unusual individual in his literacy. The collected volumes of Roman Inscriptions of Britain [11] reveal that Latin literacy was of far greater extent among Romano-Britains than has previously been appreciated. We should not be surprised. What is surprising is to find that modern history books still present the native inhabitants of Britain as primitive and illiterate barbarians.

Britain was a prize in the land sweepstakes. Read the catalogue of resources possessed by the island as given by Bede in Book I, Chapter 1 of his *Historia*.

> The island has good pasturage for cattle and draft animals. It is rich in grain and timber. It has mile after mile of good arable soil, meadows, forests, and vineyards. It has a large variety of land and sea creatures. Britain has reliable water sources, both salt and sweet, as well as hot springs and baths. It is rich in veins of metal: copper, iron, lead, and silver.

Bede does not mention the tin deposit. As whoever held the Cornish tin held a near monopoly on an essential ore, this omission gives us some significant information. We know that the Anglo-Saxons were not in Wales; Bede's description, however, also tells us that the tin mines were still in the hands of the Britons; the Anglo-Saxons did not hold that part of Cornwall at this time. By the ninth century, the English did hold the tin mines. King Ælfred's tin mines were a considerable source of revenue for him. [12] The tin was used for the roofs of many a church and cathedral throughout Southern Europe. (Unalloyed tin cannot be used outdoors in Northern climates; freezing changes its crystalline structure and it disintegrates.) The Cornish tin mines remained an important source of wealth for England until the nineteenth century. We forget that bronze was an important metal for general use and was not replaced by iron until the Bessemer process was invented about 1820.

As important as the Cornish tin ore was, Britain was rich in other trading goods. Further, it was one of the rare exceptions in the Northern climates: it produced enough excess food to support towns, the largest of which held about 14,000 inhabitants. It is easy to understand why Rome garrisoned around 50,000 men on the island to protect these riches. It is also easy to see that the Romano-British leaders and upper classes, expected to rule and to communicate, would be literate.

Recent archaeological evidence indicates that Roman Britain was very heavily populated in the period from 300-350 CE. Aerial surveys are turning up the outlines of hundreds upon hundreds of small communities with their attached farming areas all over the island. Some population estimates range as high as 5,000,000 people. Whatever the exact figure, Britain was not an empty land open for the taking. In the fifth century events occurred that changed this picture.

The Romano-British people had come to depend upon Rome for their military defense. Rome withdrew her last troops sometime between 406-410. The inhabitants of this rich island were attacked from all directions.

While the population decreased under these attacks, this does not account for the apparently massive depopulation that occurred sometime during the mid-sixth century (circa 536). A severe famine (and plague) is recorded by Bede in Book 1, Chapter 14 of his *Historia*, but we simply do not know the causes. Whatever the reasons, the island lay open and practically undefended.

Gildas (496-570), a Romano-British cleric and chronicler, published his *De Excidio Britanniae* (The Destruction of the British) in 540. According to Gildas, the Angles or Saxons were invited over in 452 to defend the country from the Picts in Scotland by an unamed British leader. According to other sources, the name of this leader was Vortigern. "According to" are the operative words for the period from 400-600. We have very little reliable evidence for events. Bede covers this material in Book 1, Chapter 15 of the *Historia*, but his source was Gildas. Still, Gildas was closer to events than we are. There exists a stone in Dyfed (Wales) inscribed in Latin and Ogham. It reads:

MEMORIA VOTEPORIGIS PROTICTORIS

[In memory of Vortipor Protector]

VOTECORIGAS (of Votecorix) is inscribed on the side in k-Celt Ogham, the Celtic writing system. Is this "Vortigern?" The answer is "no." Vortigern lived in what is now Northern England; he is the British leader to whom Gildas alludes in Chapter 23.1 as offering an invitation to the Germanic mercenaries. On the other hand, Gildas mentions five British tyrants in what is now Western Wales. One of these men, named in 31.1, is "Vortipori." As the name in p-Celt is "Voteporigis," we have a concrete check to verify Gildas's report that "Vortipor Protector" existed. This case, however, is unusual. The archaeological record is there, but we have little flesh upon these archaeological bones. Recent research is filling in some blanks, but more is unknown than known.

Whatever caused the decrease in native population, it was not the massacres depicted by Gildas after the arrival of the Angles or Saxons. The countryside was already depopulated. Some areas probably were conquered through bloodshed, but there is no evidence at all for attempted genocide; we find neither mass graves nor mass burial sites. Without doubt, Britons migrated to North-West Spain and across to Brittany, but we now know that the Germanic peoples seemed for the most part to have lived right alongside the native Britons. After recent excavations of burial sites in the midlands, several archaeologists have suggested that, in some areas, the population was roughly equally composed of native Britons and Anglo-Saxons. The continuity in land boundaries and husbandry practices as well as the lack of evidence for reforestation indicates that the majority of Britons stayed on their land. It is possible that so many native Britons had already died or emigrated prior to the coming of the Anglo-Saxons that relatively peaceful coexistence was achievable, but we do not know the particulars. Nor do we know the proportion of Germanic to British among the general population, or very much about daily life. We cannot even say who ruled what and where or when with certainty.

Gildas (and Bede following Gildas) states that all these Germanic invaders were "pagan." This seems highly unlikely, as many of the Germanic tribes had converted to Christianity as early as the third century. Further, at least in the midlands, the native Britons converted their new neighbors. Anglo-Saxon England remains the only place in early Medieval Europe where mass conversions took place without one martyr killed by the hand of "pagans."

Bede describes the arrival of the priest Augustine (later Bishop of Canterbury), who was sent by Pope Gregory I (circa 540-604) in 596 to convert the "pagan" Anglo-Saxons to Christianity. Much to Augustine's dismay, many of the "pagans" were already Christians, and, far worse, of opposing parties. We know that the Germanic "pagans" in the West Midlands were converted to Christianity by their British neighbors well before Augustine's arrival on the scene. We also now know that the Anglo-Norman Cathedral at Canterbury was built upon the foundations of the Anglo-Saxon one. Recent archaeological evidence shows that the Anglo-Saxon cathedral was of the same dimensions as the Norman cathedral and built between the fifth and sixth centuries. [13] A building project this large requires a good size congregation to fund it. Celtic-British Churches were still alive, well, and functioning when the Roman priest arrived. [14] Augustine ran into much resistance and apparently really did not know how to handle these Christians who took the book of Leviticus very seriously. In fact, he was more than a little clumsy in his dealings. [15]

"Pagan" does not really give us much information anyway; it was one of the favorite names to throw about in the slinging matches among opposing Christian parties. We cannot know whether the term "Pagan" refers to subordinationists, fourteenthers, or to polytheists. This particular use of "pagan" in England seems to have originated from the Roman mission at Canterbury. After all, one must establish a reason for being, and setting up an opposing church—particularly if the people you are trying to convert are already converted—can be difficult. In any case, Christian or "pagan," the Angles and other Germanic tribes gained a foothold on the island during the fifth century.

Christianity went hand-in-hand with reading and writing. The Irish Celts had their ethnic flag in Ogham; the Germanic and Gothic tribes had their own identifying ethnic writing systems. One system was created in the 4th century by Ulfilas (circa 311-383), the Bishop to the Gothic tribes. The Gothic writing system is based upon Greek models. The Gothic system was used primarily for sacred texts. It also appears in secular texts in a different font.

The other Germanic writing system is substantially older. Commonly known as Runes, or Runic script, this system was created sometime during the late centuries BCE. The oldest symbol forms are either from an Etruscan or from a Phoenician model. [16] The system also shows Greek influence in some of the graphic forms. The Germanic system is known as Futhark after the first 6 symbols in its symbol set, that is, f, u, thorn, a, r, c (Figure 5.2). The system incorporates variant forms into its symbol set, which tends to point toward a Phoenician model, but the question remains unanswerable.

Their writing system shows us that these tribes had been in the general area somewhere North-East of Etruria and North-West of Mesopotamia for quite a while. The writing system lends truthfulness to what the Germanic peoples themselves passed down orally from generation to generation about their origins. The Lombards-to-be may have been the people referred to by the Etruscans during the fifth century BCE, but again, we do not know. We know nothing substantial about these people before they began invading Roman territory near the end of the second century BCE. Their Runic writing system is our only evidence of their existence in antiquity. On the other hand, we do know that, like other converted peoples, the Anglo-Saxons adopted Christian writing systems in preference to their own "Pagan" one. We also know that, by the sixth century, those Angles living on the Island called themselves "Englisc."

The early sixth century shows us a British landscape crowded with numerous Christian parties all vying for supremacy. When Gregory I sent Augustine the lesser to Britain in the last decade of the sixth century, the Gregorian version of the "Church of Rome" was a latecomer on the religious scene of the island.

The problem is that we cannot say what is meant by the "Church of Rome" at the time. There was no conformity *within* a party, let alone *between* parties. The Lombards, a Germanic clan, based in what is modern Lombardy (Milan and Turin), controlled most of the Italian peninsula. The Lombards remained Subordinationists until the end of the seventh century and had considerable effect on the "church" of Rome. The influential church of Ravenna had its own ideas. The Frankish churches went their own ways as did the various Irish and British churches. At this early date there was no unified church, no official "Roman" liturgy, no official language of religion, and no official writing system, even at Rome.

Writers of textbooks on the History of England have used Bede's *Historia* for our information on these early years. Bede was a very honorable, kindly, and upright man. He never tells lies of commission, but we will find many convenient "white lies" of omission. His book, after all, is on the Roman parties and "the Race of Englishmen." While Bede felt that the Anglo-Irish parties were wrong-headed, he had nothing but admiration for men such as Aidan of Lindisfarne (? -31 August 651). Aidan was held in such respect that changes to tonsure (the monk's haircut) and ritual were delayed until his death. Bede hated and feared the Britons. Today some scholars have changed Bede's title from "Venerable" to "Venomous" because he rejoices at the death of 1200 British monks. If Bede appears so bloodthirsty, it is because these monks are members of hated parties and deadly opponents in a mighty battle for religious supremacy.

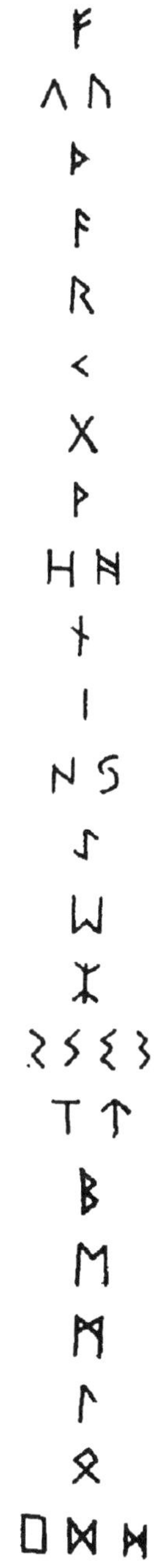

Fig. 5.2
Futhark

Bede tells us his bias out in front. This bias warns us not to treat statements, such as, "all England," as other than applying directly to the allied English and not to the Island as a whole. It was not Bede's fault that nineteenth century scholars did not bother to state his bias. He told us what he was writing.

Bede's repeated emphasis upon the date of Easter and the style of tonsure occurs so many times throughout the *Historia* that we arrive at the point where it passes into meaninglessness. The last occurrence appears in the closing paragraphs of the *Historia* when he sums up the current state of affairs (725-731):

> The Britons, on the whole, have a national odium against the English and hold to their own bad customs against the true Easter of the Catholic Church. (*Historia*, Ch. 23, para. 6)

When Bede states that "all England was brought to Rome," he means that the Roman *date for Easter*, along with the Roman tonsure, was accepted in those areas held by the English. It most definitely was not accepted in those areas held by the Britons.

Bede does **not** mean that all England followed the same rituals: he knew better. Even among those groups that followed the Roman parties, the ritual differed from monastery to monastery, from cathedral school to cathedral school. Bede's own area, the twin monasteries of Wearmouth-Jarrow on the East coast of Northumbria (North of Humber) England, used one set. Over in York, in the center of Northumbria, they used another. As late as 1509/10, before the Reformation and conversion from Roman Catholicism to Protestantism, the Scots used the Sarum (Salisbury) or Lincoln rites and refused to have anything to do with those used at York.

This massive diversity shows up in the writing systems in use during the sixth and early seventh centuries. Each **scriptorium** [writing room] employed the writing system and graphic symbols of its affiliated party; each *scriptorium* also made its own choice as to symbol assignment. Scribes also would write in their own dialects. Texts were passed from one area to another and copied. The result was confusion, a lack of compatibility, and non-transferability. Textual variants and errors appeared with increasing regularity as the Scriptures spread. Sometime during the mid-seventh century, some Anglo-Celtic monks located somewhere in Northumbria decided to do something about this situation. The result was the Anglo-Saxon Comprehensive Writing System. The name of the system *appears* to have been *stæfwritung*.

Originally, Latin borrowed technical terms for the physical act of writing from Greek. The physical act of writing, *caraxare*, was differentiated from the act of composition, *scribere*. While later the term *scribere* included both acts, the earlier Latin term for a scribe was "c(h)araxere" (alpha-symbol writer). The distinctions between the physical and the mental acts of writing are mentioned in Insular Latin texts. [17] *Staef* is the Old English word for an alphabetic symbol; *writung* is the participial form of the verb *writan*, "to write." It is the ancestor of our modern English participle "writing." *Stæfwritung* literally means alpha-symbol writing. *Stæfwritung,* that is, the physical act of writing letters, does not appear in the existing Old English manuscripts. However, a "scribe," *staefwritere*, and "scribes," *staefwriterum*, do appear. *Staefwriterum* shows up as a gloss to *caraceribus*: "scribes." The gloss tells us what a scribe, a physical writer of letters, was called at the time the Anglo-Saxon system was codified. Scholars will undoubtedly complain because the precise form does not appear in the manuscripts; "The Anglo-Saxon Phonetic-Based Comprehensive Writing System" is quite a mouthful. For convenience, we will take our clues from the existing evidence and use *stæfwritung*.

Stæfwritung is a simple, comprehensive, language-independent, and systematic phonetic-based writing system. *Stæfwritung* is elegant in its simplicity. It had to be simple. Western societies followed the Egyptian pattern of elite limited literacy that reinforced the Roman pattern inherited from Etruria. The majority of the populations within the borders of the Old Roman Empire were essentially illiterate and orally based. While most work done on the subject of oral societies is in terms of poetry and folk epics, this oral basis has other and more important implications.

Anglo-Saxon legal terminology constantly stresses the oral aspect of law. A person had to have heard a law publicly proclaimed for him to be held responsible for keeping that law. [18] *Stefn* means "voice." (The only modern remnant of this word is in the phrase "even steven," an even voice.) In Anglo-Saxon legal terminology, a *stefn* is a "summons carried by a mounted person." A *stefn-hyrd* (voice-herd, voice-guardian) is a "regulation" or "direction." The verb *spraecan* means "to speak"; in legal terms, a *spraec* is a "case," "cause," or "claim"—and is mentioned as such in King Æthelstan's (ruled 925-39) 10th-century law code. The *spraec-hus* is the "speech-house" or "council-house," and, descending down the centuries with little change in meaning, the *spraeca* is the "speaker in council" or the "speaker of the house."

The oral basis of Anglo-Saxon law is clear as late as the eleventh century. Wulfstan (d. 1023), Archbishop of York, is best known for his sermons (homilies). While some critics consider his style long-winded and repetitive—even "soporific," we should remember that tastes change. Further, his sermons are meant to be read out loud following the directions as written in the manuscripts. This makes a significant difference.

In Wulfstan we have the model of a rip-roaring, hellfire-and-damnation preacher of the type that was once so popular. *Wulfstan* means "wolf-stone." The most famous of his sermons, "The Sermon of the Wolf to the English" (*Sermo Lupi*: *Lupus*, Latin for Wolf) tears into the populace and blames the people of England and their backsliding for all their current troubles. Wulfstan was an Anglo-Saxon Daniel Webster or Clarence Darrow, a golden-tongued hell-raising orator. We should not wonder at the juxtaposition of two American trial lawyers with this religious leader: Wulfstan was very much a canonist and a legist with a finger in numerous legal pies of both Church and State. In the sacred domain, he wrote the so-called *Canons of Edgar*, a book of canon law aimed at parish clergy. In the secular domain, Wulfstan wrote the legal drafts for King Cnut's Law Code of 1018.

Cnut's code follows the requisite formula of authorization used in all Anglo-Saxon legal documents. Showing its oral basis, the code begins with *and hig gecwaeden* (and they declared). The oral basis of English Common Law is evident to this day. The first procedural action in law is the delivery of a verbal "summons or notice" to obey the "writ." [19] Under English Common Law, the *stefn* is still delivered by a mounted person—the sheriff in his wheeled vehicle.

The implications of an oral society show up everywhere in everyday life. The reciting, chanting, or singing of charms, magical words, has one main purpose: to avoid or void unwholesome influences. Today children chant the charm against rain spoiling their play or, as we have already noted, to prevent names from hurting them. The recitation of charms was not confined to children in Anglo-Saxon England. Most of the Old English charms give directions for stance, ingredients, and so forth.

They include the admonition to *cwet* [say] ("For A Swarm of Bees"), or *cweðe* ("For Loss of Cattle"), or to sing ("For the Water-Elf Disease," that is, chicken pox). The charm "Against a Dwarf" instructs the person who would invoke it first to get seven *lytle* chips of wood and write the names of the Seven Sleepers of Ephesus on them. (The Seven Sleepers may be the origin of the seven dwarfs in Snow White, but, again, we do not know.) The invoker should then say (*cweð*) these names, and finally shall [must] sing (*sceal singan*) the charm three times. ("Sc" is pronounced "sh." *Sceal* is merely "shall" in older dress.)

As anybody familiar with folk medicine will tell us, a charm has to be said correctly, or it will not work. Charms were an important part of the pharmacopeia of a Leech (the medical doctors of the day). Leeches were not known for great scholarly achievements. With the *stæfwritung* system, the Leech merely had to follow the directions as-written in the text. Today pharmacists complain about a doctor's handwriting on a prescription form. Leeches undoubtedly blamed "scribal error" when a charm proved inefficacious.

Merchants were not scholars. It was the rare merchant of the day who enjoyed access to the Seven Liberal Arts, the basis of education during the Medieval period. The town schools taught "readin', writin', and 'rithmetic," the level of literacy necessary for a merchant to conduct business. A semi-literate merchant had to be able to hear the laws governing him as well as understand what he needed to supply. With *stæfwritung*, all he had to do was pronounce the text as written to hear and to comprehend the words.

The Chronicles, the Anglo-Saxon history books, were meant to be read aloud. Charters and grants had to be spoken in front of witnesses before these people signed their attestations. We can see from their handwriting and signatures that many of these witnesses were marginally literate. A royal messenger carrying a summons was more likely to be a fine fighter than an erudite scholar. All of these semi-literate people could be expected to "read," hear, and comprehend this simple writing system.

Stæfwritung is language-independent—a scribe need not know a given language to write down a text. While the phonetic representation may occasionally seem odd, a scribe taking dictation writes what he hears, a scribe will write in his own dialect. **Parsing** (separation into grammatical units) errors are rare in dictated texts. Some of the most peculiar scribal errors in *copied* texts seem to arise from misparsing an unfamiliar language. Likewise, a person need not know a language to reproduce a song, poem, story, sermon, or speech. All the necessary information is recorded, visibly encoded in the text.

This comprehensive system is internally consistent. Texts encoded in the system retain their orientation and qualitative symbol differentiation across copying, independently of script and font styles. Notwithstanding its simplicity, the system is remarkable for its comprehensiveness, for the sheer amount of information it incorporates.

The "Dark Ages" were filled with the light of knowledge. To our sorrow, we lost much of their knowledge during the darkness of the Renaissance and the Age of Enlightenment. The early *Englisc* did not have electricity or the atom bomb, but their understanding of writing systems and the spoken word has yet to be surpassed. Only in the past ten to fifteen years have a handful of researchers begun to examine what was a "doesn't everybody" for the codifiers of the *stæfwritung* system. They knew that words as spoken are ordered segments that follow the **parsing rhythms** of a language.

Parsing rhythms are a critical and inseparable component of speech. They are the basic speech rhythms of a language. Parsing rhythms are what determine the ability of the hearer to parse speech, that is, to separate and distinguish grammatical elements and semantic segments when words are spoken. When visitors ask native speakers to "speak more slowly, please," they are showing unfamiliarity with the parsing rhythms of a language. Sometimes referred to as speech rhythm, tone of voice, or paralanguage, parsing rhythms are actually the music of a language. Like music, these rhythms rise and fall like notes in a melody, change tempo, and increase or decrease in volume. Like music, parsing rhythms reflect what in the fourteenth century Geoffrey Chaucer called the cadences of language.

Spoken language does not separate neatly into the individual **semantic units** of the modern printed page. Semantic units are those segments that contain the sense or meaning of the graphic symbols. Spoken words separate and clump together according to the basic **comprehension units** of a language—which has little connection with reading and writing as expressed in modern semantic units. Comprehension units divide and combine these segments according to the natural rhythms of speech. Semantic units distinguish individual words; but com pre hen sion u ni ts dis tin guish spo ken rhy th ms.

Segments of a spoken language move in all directions through space. Speech, like music, is multidimensional, a **space curve**. Any given sound may recede or advance. It may be short or long; it may be voiced or unvoiced—or even mute, and it has a distinct **quality** (phone). All dimensions in this space curve act independently of each other; that is, they are independent (**orthogonal**) dimensions.

Orthogonal dimensions lie at ninety degrees to one another. This means that any or all dimensions in an orthogonal system may act in concert, in partial conjunction, or individually. No single dimension is dependent upon the others. **Quality** (phone), **quantity** (duration), and **volume** (stress) are orthogonal dimensions. A given sound may be held but not stressed, both held and stressed, not held and stressed, neither held nor stressed, or in some combination of the three dimensions at an intermediary level. In other words, the three orthogonal dimensions represent movement through time and volume or space, as well as quality.

In order to record speech rhythms on a page, we must be able to represent quality, quantity, and volume as spoken. A minimal expression of spoken rhythm is a three dimensional structure. Two dimensional waves may be drawn on a page, but rhythm, a space curve, extends into a third dimension. The human mind can comprehend such three-dimensional concepts, one need only pick up a die to understand the concept "cube," but it cannot visualize them. Accordingly, phonologists and linguists express "nonlinear" relationships in hierarchical "tiers" illustrated by complex trees. A "tier" indicates an hierarchical level on a "tree," that is, syllable, syllable constituent, rhyme constituent, and so on. [20] The Phoenicians and their descendant writing systems had a much simpler solution.

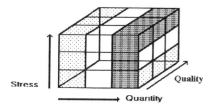

Fig. 5.3 The Geometric Writing Cube

All writing systems descended from Phoenician use the same ternary basis, including *stæfwritung*. These systems use the intrinsically orthogonal properties of a **cube** to show the three dimensions of quality, quantity, and volume. This method preserves the orthogonality of these features yet permits their expression on a two-dimensional surface (Figure 5.3).

Quantity refers to the length of time (duration) a sound is held. Volume refers to the amount of loudness (stress) on a given symbol. Quality refers to the phone. The horizontal and vertical planes of the cube are controlled by the **minuscule** (cursive or "lower case") form of the letter *o* (Figure 5.4).

The three independent components are distributed as follows:

1) *Quantity* is indicated on the **horizontal** base of a cube, with constraints set by the **width** of the letter *o*.
2) *Volume* is presented on the **vertical** plane of a cube within a clearly defined ternary set of vertical levels as defined by the **height** of the letter *o*.
3) *Quality* is indicated by the **shape** of a given letter symbol.

Each letter-symbol has its own **frame**. A frame is a letter-symbol inclusive of its surrounding white space. The distance between frames (kerning) expands or contracts according to the parsing rhythms of the spoken words.

Meant to be easily read by the semi-literate as well as by the scholar, this ternary basis is intuitive and natural: the higher the symbol, the louder the volume of the sound; the wider the symbol or its extensions, the longer the duration of the sound. A person did not really have to know how to read in our modern sense, although the technique made learning to read a simple process. Anyone who had learned only the abc's could read a text aloud *as written*. Once pronounced, a person could hear the spoken words and comprehend the contents. Although the scholar would know the finer distinctions between graphic representations of phones and appreciate the sometimes delicate sound play, the semi-literate could follow the volume and quantity notations without advanced learning.

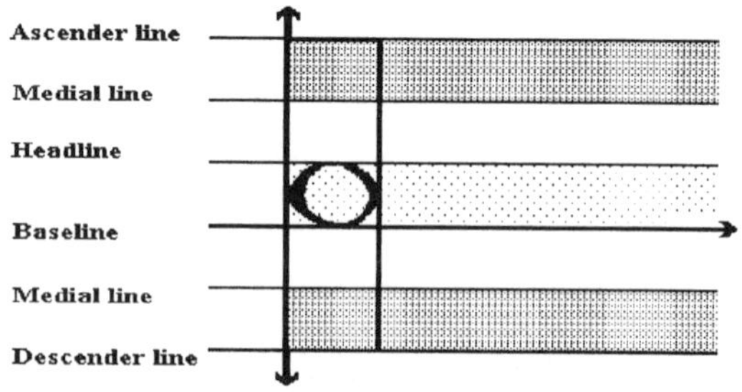

The codification of the Anglo-Saxon writing system had broad consequences. While all Western quattrolinear writing systems used one of the five main streams of phonetic-based systems, *stæfwritung* became the most widely used method of writing in Western Europe. Traces remain to this day. Our modern use of italics (which is merely a different font in the middle of a text) comes directly from this Anglo-Saxon system. The Romance Languages (French, Italian, Spanish) arose when they did from the misapplication of the *stæfwritung* alpha-symbol set—a century after its codification.

Fig. 5.4 The three independent components as written on a page

Our modern Roman lower case type-faces are the descendants of a mutation of an Anglo-Celtic secular font that was elevated to an official script during the late eighth century. Modern musical notation has its roots in the deliberate archaizing of the geometric basis of this system.

Archaizations typically exhibit an attempt to gain power through the emulation of a past authoritative culture. The archaizing of a writing system hides under the term *renovatio* (Modern English "renovation"). Although the first-century reformers of Imperial Rome called it a *renovatio*, the term is both misleading and inaccurate. The term suggests modernization rather than deliberate archaization in an attempt to return to some imagined past ideal. In fact, *renovatio* is merely our old friend, politically motivated standardization, hiding behind a polite alias. Centuries later, when Western reformers latched onto *renovatio*, they followed the precepts set by the first century reformers of Latin. **Classicization** describes exactly what happened as archaization came to the West.

Classicization reflects a given group's perception of Classical Latin precepts at some specific point in history. Classicization and its thinly veiled political purpose occurred, for example, in eighth century Francia and in ninth, tenth, thirteenth, fifteenth, seventeenth, eighteenth, and nineteenth century England. Our modern Western writing systems are the culmination of repeated waves of classicization enforced upon *stæfwritung*.

Classical Latin was an artificial construct. It was the idealized product of what the late antique reformers of Augustan Rome assumed ancient Latin to have been. In this idealized writing system, each symbol represented one phone; variant forms were not permitted. Ligatures (tied symbols) and abbreviations were eliminated. Although assiduously imitated as an ideal again and again down the centuries, Classical Latin was never a living language.

Side-by-side with this artificial frozen ideal, we find texts written in Late Latin that record the language as spoken. These texts follow the ancient Phoenician model. Non-official and informal texts retain horizontal movement: the clumping and spacing of speech rhythms. Ligatured symbols, the record of spoken syllables, occur everywhere. These texts also display variant symbols and, depending upon locale and speech patterns, vertical movement.

The speech of the various Latin-speaking peoples moved farther and farther from the classical ideal. "Correct" Classical Latin also underwent changes in those areas where Latin remained a foreign language. Phones that do not occur in Classical Latin permeate Celtic, Anglo-Celtic, and Anglo-Saxon manuscripts. The Latin language had already undergone a sea-change when Classical Latin was reconstructed in the late eighth century during the first major wave of classicization.

The Rome of Classical Latin stood for paganism; it was un-Christian. While *stæfwritung* is yet another attempt at standardization, its end was not classicization. There is no attempt to borrow the authority of Rome or to freeze language into a magical shell to be read only by the elite few. On the contrary, its intention is to bring order and transferability and to spread literacy along with the Word. Its authorities are the writing systems employed by the Hebrew and Greek testaments as shown in the texts and as transmitted by the early Christian missionaries—whatever their party affiliations. Perhaps this difference in approach explains the durability of the *stæfwritung* system.

Classicization was a long and slow process, one that was resisted fiercely for centuries. Western society has a dual heritage. The two different ancient authorities, the Semitic derived quattrolinear system and the Romano-Egypto bilinear system, clashed again and again. In spite of repeated attempts at classicization and reversion to the authority that was Imperial Rome, the ancient Semitic phonetic-based system, with its authority derived from the two testaments, endured in England for more than 1000 years. By the mid-seventeenth century, the repeated attempts at the classicization of *stæfwritung* finally succeeded.

We take nothing away from the codifiers by pointing out that the Anglo-Saxon achievement does not lie in the invention of the various components of the *stæfwritung* system. The threefold (ternary) basis was designed and implemented in 3300 BCE—back at Sumer. While the Anglo-Saxon Phonetic Alphabet (ASPA) is extremely systematic and clear in its execution, it was drawn from already available graphic phone-symbols. Script-style distinction, another feature of the writing system, originated in antiquity. Another important part of their system, **xenographic** (foreign graph) **exchange,** dates back to the use of Sumerian syllabograms in texts written in Akkadian to signal, among other things, the distinction between the sacred and the profane realms. Their system for indicating a musical key came to England by way of North Africa and dates back to at least Pythagoras (sixth century BCE). The one purely Anglo-Saxon invention, their musical notation system, is based upon another use of xenographic exchange: marking final passages and verses in scriptural texts. Nevertheless, *stæfwritung* is a momentous achievement.

Only after passing through the hands of the Anglo-Saxon codifiers does a rational phonetic-based writing system emerge. Designed as an integrated, precise, and practical tool, *stæfwritung* records everything but the actual sound of a language as spoken. The Anglo-Saxons did not need Isidore of Seville to tell them that sound cannot be recorded on a page but "voice" can be written down. [21] *Stæfwritung* permits the recording and transmitting of a text so that the "voice of the absent" can be heard or reproduced by subsequent readers or performers.

The *stæfwritung* system was not produced at one time. Codification proceeded in stages. The first stage of codification occurred during the mid-seventh century. This stage displays the birth of the Anglo-Saxon Phonetic Alphabet (ASPA). The second stage, script differentiation, occurred sometime during the last quarter of the seventh century and the first quarter of the eighth. The last stage, the invention of the musical notation system, happened sometime between the last quarter of the seventh century, but no later than the mid-eighth century.

The story unrolls before us as we watch codification in process. We observe the creation of the Anglo-Saxon Phonetic Alphabet. We look over their shoulders as the Anglo-Saxons add refinements to their writing system. We follow *stæfwritung* as it assumes its place as the official writing system of empire. We travel in its wake, watching the long, slow, piecemeal disintegration of this once comprehensive writing system. At the end, we hear the ancient voice silenced.

The rest need not be silence; modern society has much to gain from the past. The remainder of this book is devoted to the story of one of the Anglo-Saxons's greatest contributions to Western society: *stæfwritung.*

Chapter Six

MIXED VOICES

When Alice steps out of the looking-glass house into the garden, she finds herself in a most confusing situation. To reach the hill, she must go in the other direction. Everything is most puzzling, yet Alice is handed clues to help her fit the puzzle together. Some, like the view from the hill of the chessboard, are large; others, like the dry biscuits to assuage thirst, are small. When we enter the world of the written word, we find ourselves in a very similar situation. The monstrous jigsaw puzzle known as the story of writing depends upon the fitting of many pieces of evidence into their correct places. Sometimes the clues are the size of elephants and so big that at first we see only the trunk or the tail. At other times, the clues are small and require close attention to tiny details. Our path does not lead through a garden of live flowers; our path begins with the visible voices that speak to us through the pages of the manuscripts.

Most of our early manuscripts are products of a very large number and diverse group of monastic *scriptoria*. The written evidence records a jumble of local and regional graphic symbol sets used within the limits of clearly differentiated official script families. Each party had its own authorized script, and each *scriptorium* used its own version of the affiliated authorized symbol set.

The sphere of influence of a given *scriptorium* appears to remain almost constant at a radius of 20-30 kilometers, whether we examine early neumatic notation, [1] melisma (five or six notes sung to a single syllable) of the post Caroline period, [2] or the decline of a specific monastic *scriptorium*. [3] This means that a person ran into different writing systems and religious practices every time a new sphere of influence was entered. There is little doubt that such diversity led to a confusing state of affairs. We shall never know how many so-called "scribal errors" are a result of the scribe's inability to understand a local symbol set appearing in a borrowed exemplar.

While it may seem somewhat silly to restate the obvious, some facts are worth repetition—lest we overlook a clue. The manuscripts did not occur in a vacuum; they were written for a purpose.

Manuscripts are concrete and visible artifacts of the past. An artifact is necessarily the product of a human hand, here, a scribe. A trained scribe is not an author; he writes what he hears, he copies what he sees. Writing is hard work. A scribe never includes something unless he must, that is, unless a particular format, size, spacing, symbol, or script is required. There is always a reason for a difference in scribal choices; nothing a scribe writes is haphazard or indiscriminate. If something looks different, it *is* different.

Being good detectives, we know that the clues lie in the differences, the evidence of change. If something is different in the written record, we must examine this difference very closely.

The reader of medieval manuscripts confronts numerous differences between one text and another. Among these differences are a large range of scripts and **fonts** (sub-classes or mutations of scripts) that can be very confusing at first sight. Much of this apparent confusion is caused by the different writing systems in use at each *scriptorium*. Still, we have already been given one important clue: scripts are a semaphore for identity.

There are other clues with which to sort out the puzzle. By the seventh century, script as identity had already been extended from its original use as a "national flag." We find official scripts and fonts among this seemingly large and amorphous variety. During the early centuries of the Common Era, official scripts appear in two distinct groups: scripts that identify secular law and those that identify sacred law. Official scripts and fonts are technically called book hands because they appear in the writing of books as opposed to, for instance, letters or accounts. After the spread of Christianity, these book hands may be formal liturgical (sacred authority), formal (secular authority), or informal (just about everything else).

Pontifical fonts are official fonts that are used only for papal correspondence and identify the origin of the correspondent at sight. Chancery fonts, as the name suggests, are those identifying fonts used for internal business by the various official governmental offices. Informal by definition, chancery fonts are rapid, cursive, and minuscule (lower case). They are not intended to be read by outsiders. (The font used by the chancery scribes of the Merovingian Rulers has been said to resemble the "workings of a demented spider.")

Most of our modern names for these scripts and fonts are derived from Latin, leftovers from nineteenth century Latin-oriented scholars. We do not know what the scribes themselves called them. The name "Uncial," for instance, is taken from a reference by Jerome to inch-high letters as *uncialis*. The Uncial script is majuscule, bilinear, and an official post-Christian Imperial script. The half-uncial (*Semi-Uncialis*) scripts incorporate some ascenders and descenders.

The half-uncial scripts are one of our elephant-sized clues. There are two, and only two, half-uncial scripts: Greco-Roman and North African. The bewilderingly large assortment of minuscule fonts are descendants, that is, mutations, of either the Greco-Roman half-uncial or the North-African half-uncial scripts. Which script model was chosen depends upon when and where people received their writing systems.

Our dual Western heritage strikes again. Among the earliest Anglo-Celtic manuscripts, sites using mutations of the Greco-Roman half-uncial script were Christianized by followers of the Alexandrian-Roman affiliated party. Modern paleographers call these fonts Anglo-Saxon. Those sites using mutations of the North-African-Semitic script were originally Christianized by North-African affiliates. The modern terminology for these fonts is Insular.

The twin monasteries at Wearmouth and Jarrow and their affiliates in London use mutations of the pointed Anglo-Saxon minuscule for secular texts and the (then) official Uncial script for sacred texts. The Anglo-Saxon minuscule pointed (pointed *cursiva*) is a mutation (font) of the Greco-Roman half-uncial script. Irish and Anglo-Celtic sites use the Insular half-uncial font for sacred texts and various Insular minuscules for secular texts. The Insular minuscule fonts are mutations of the North-African half-uncial script.

Our earliest Anglo-Celtic documents are in the Insular scripts and fonts. Although these early texts are written in Latin, Anglo-Saxon names and Old English words already appear by the late seventh century. Occasionally, we even know something about the authors who composed and the scribes who wrote the texts.

One of the oldest manuscripts, *The Cathach of St. Columba*, is from the third-quarter of the sixth century. The *Cathach* (a personal Psalter) is said to have originally been taken to, or produced at, Iona, the "Holy Isle," located in the Inner Hebrides off the West coast of Scotland. It is also said that the *Cathach*, inside its sumptuous protective manuscript case, was brought back to Ireland for safety during the Viking invasions of the late eighth century. Tradition attributes its writing to Columba himself. The *Cathach* resides in Dublin at the Royal Irish Academy. The manuscript contains the oldest example of the canonical Irish half-uncial font (Plate 6.1). It is listed in *Codices Latini Antiquiores* (CLA) ii as No. 266.

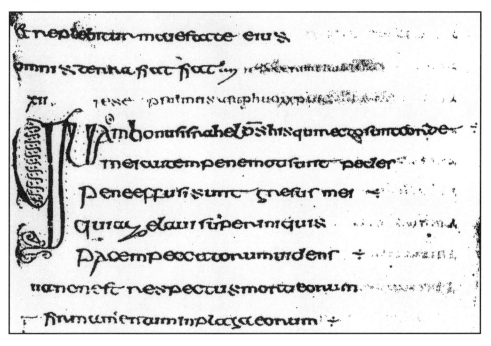

Pl. 6.1 The Cathach of Saint Columba (Courtesy The Royal Irish Academy, Dublin)

Columba's biography was written 100 years after his death by Adamnan, the ninth Abbot of Iona after Columba. Adamnan's biography concentrates on Columba's prophecies, miracles, and visions. It contains embellishments typical of the Saints' Lives genre. However, this is the story as we have it.

Columba was the son of an Irish chief and related to princes in both Ireland and Scotland. Born sometime about 521 in County Donegal, Ireland, he died in 597 at Iona. He founded several monasteries in Ireland. The best known are the ones at Derry, Durrow, and Kells. Columba, in spite of the holiness and saintliness attributed to him, seems to have been more than a little pugnacious. At the very least, he was exceedingly stubborn.

Columba studied under Finnian (died circa 579) in Ulster, and is sometimes referred to as one of his disciples. Finnian, who was reputedly a member of the royal house of Ulster, brought back from a trip to Rome a copy of the second of Jerome's three Latin translations of the Psalter. [4] This was allegedly the first copy of a Latin Psalter in all of Ireland. Columba borrowed the Psalter and made a copy of it. Finnian, apparently outraged that anyone should copy *his* Psalter, demanded that Columba give him the copy. Columba, naturally enough, refused. Copying a Psalter is not a small undertaking. It is more than a little time-consuming—even for an experienced scribe. The dispute gathered force and eventually was put before King Diarmaid who ruled in favor of Finnian.

The next time Columba crossed swords with Diarmaid was more deadly. A kinsman of Columba's, one Curnan of Connaught, sought sanctuary with him. Curnan was slain by Diarmaid's men while under Columba's protection. This slaying erupted into a family feud between Columba's clan and Diarmaid's men. There was a major battle at Cuil Dremne where 3,000 men are said to have been killed. Excommunicated and expelled from Ireland for allegedly causing a war, Columba went to relatives in what is now Scotland. His biographer claims that, filled with remorse (another common feature of the Saints' Lives genre), Columba vowed to convert a like number of pagans to Christianity. He supposedly was accompanied into exile by the requisite twelve disciples and/or relatives in emulation of Christ.

Besides the pugnacity displayed in these two incidents (both times for good cause), Columba must have been a charismatic character and a very persuasive orator. Everywhere he went he converted people to Christianity: first in Ireland, then the Picts in Scotland, the Western Islands, and the Orkneys. He was given the tiny island of Iona for his own. Once on Iona, Columba founded yet another monastery in 563 and remained there until his death. Iona became a center of learning.

Columba shows his stubbornness in other ways. He had his own ideas about the order of liturgy. Also, the Columban church was partly *fourteenther*, that is, if Easter coincided with the fourteenth of Nissan, the evening of Passover, they celebrated that day. But, they did not insist upon the fourteenth of Nissan. Whatever date it fell on, the Columban Easter was on a day different from that of the Roman. In addition, Columban monks wore a different style of tonsure (the monk's haircut). These two points of sometimes violent disagreement appear many times in Bede's *Historia*. Columba also had his own ideas about the correct writing system.

Columba's *Cathach* is fully encoded in the North African-Semitic tradition. Symbols move vertically and horizontally and variant forms indicate distinct phones. There are arguments both for and against the manuscript as an autograph copy. [5] Whether the scribe was Columba or not, he was trained in Columba's writing system and is very competent. Although somewhat confusing, there appears to be some internal consistency in the method of writing.

A title (**titulus**) appears at the beginning of each Psalm. *Titulus* is the technical term for the explanatory remark describing what is occurring and why this psalm is written. As in so many other spheres, *tituli* vary according to party affiliation. [6] The *titulus* to Psalm 73 (72—LXXII, in the Latin text) is written with finer pen in the same font above line 1 of the Psalm. It states: "Jesse Psalm of Asaph." (Here we run into one of the problems with translations. This title is a conflation of the embedded colophon at the end of Hebrew Psalm 72 that translates as "Completed are the Prayers of David, son of Jesse," and the title at the beginning of the next: "a Psalm of Asaph." The words "Amen, Amen," which appear at the end of the previous Psalm, have also been dislocated: they belong to the embedded colophon and are not part of the Psalm text.)

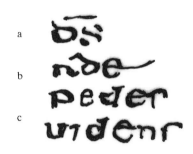

Fig. 6.1 The Cathach of Columba: *d*

The practice of abbreviating the name of God in Christian texts dates back to the Hebrew use of the **tetragrammaton** (YHVH). Greek translations continued the practice, substituting Greek symbols (the Kurios). [7] The abbreviation of the sacred name (*nomina sacra*) became standard in Latin as well and appears as *ds* with the "bar" of omission inserted over the two symbols.

Like all master scribes, the scribe of the Cathach has his own forms, particularly the symbol forms for *d, l, s, a,* and *e*. (As the entire MS is in one hand, we cannot compare the ideographs of this scribe with another one.)

He uses the round-*d* (ꝺ) for the abbreviation of the *nomina sacra*, as we can see in the enlarged illustration in Figure 6.1a. He also uses a round-*d* to show stress and duration, as in the long-limbed round-*d* that appears at the end of line 1 of the Psalm (Figure 6.1b). Both the *d* and the *e* in [co]rde (*corde*—heart) are held sounds. Otherwise, the scribe generally employs straight-backed-*d* as in Figure 6.1c, which shows line 2, pedes (literally, *pedes*—feet; connotatively, to go on foot, take steps) and line 5, uidens (*videns*—seeing, in the sense of "to know" or "to be troubled by").

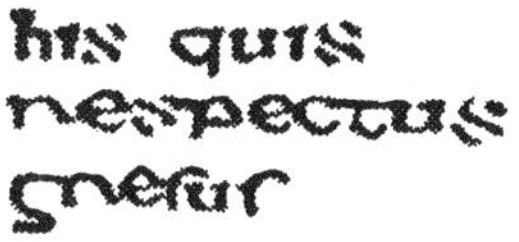

Fig. 6.2 The Cathach of Columba: *s*

Our modern *s* is taken from the Greek symbol "sigma." The technical term for our *s* is sigmoid-*s* (s). The scribe uses the sigmoid form at the end of words, after vowel-pairs (diphthongs) with *i*, after *i* alone (Figure 6.2a) as in his (*his*) and quis (*[ini]quis*), and in the *nomina sacra*.

Whatever patterning is visible is obscured by the use of sigmoid-*s* for both occurrences in respectus (*respectus*—respectful of) as in Figure 6.2b, but long-*s* (ſ) for both in gresus (*gresus*–course, way) as shown in Figure 6.2c. sunt (*sunt*–are) is written twice with long-*s* and once with sigmoid-*s* (Figure 6.3). Quality is altered by environment. There would be a difference between . . .ti sunt (-*ti sunt*) and . . .si sunt (-*si sunt*). Otherwise, the form used is generally long *s* (ſ).

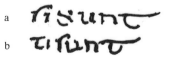

Fig. 6.3 The Cathach of Columba: *sunt*

The scribe also differentiates between clear and dark *l*. Dark *l* occurs when the tongue rolls against the soft palate in the lower jaw.

Clear *l* occurs when a preceding phone forces the tongue to a more horizontal position. If we compare the words "low" and "slow," we can feel and hear the difference between dark and clear *l*. The *l* in "low" is dark: the tongue touches the soft palate. The *s* in "slow" forces the tongue upwards. The *l* in "slow" is clear. Final *l*'s tend to be dark (which is why we double final *l*'s in modern spelling). Both of his forms of *l* are rounded; the dark *l* extends well below the baseline and seems to imitate the rounded shape of the tip of the tongue when forming this phone (Figure 6.4).

Fig.6.4 The Cathach of Columba: *l*: left-dark, right-clear

We can see clear examples of his standard and variant *a* forms in the last line of the previous Psalm. The line reads: omnis cenna flac flac (*omnis terra fiat fiat*–[the] whole earth, let it be done, let it be done). Alpha-*a* (ꝺ) as in *fiat* is his standard form; Latin-*a*, as in *terra* indicates another *a*-phone (Figure 6.5).

Whether written in breathings, as in the *Cathach*, or in comprehension units, Psalms are written phrase-by-phrase. A line normally has a central caesura or pause. A **colon** is the technical term for a one-line phrase, **bicola** for a two-line phrase. This practice of phrase-by-phrase writing dates back to at least the second century BCE in Hebrew. [8] The scribe of the *Cathach* uses a large pointed uncial *a* (ꝺ) if the *a* is in the first expression of a

1

2

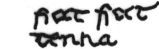

Fig. 6.5 The Cathach of Columba: 1. Alpha-a; 2. Latin-a

colon, as in, Uꝺm (*[Q]uam*–what, surely, verily) or pꝺcem (*Pacem*–peace) as shown in Figure 6.6.[9] These exaggerated forms of *A* display the use of xenographic exchange to indicate the beginning of a verse. The *Cathach*, a Psalter, shows no other signs of musical notation.

There is a large gap in the surviving manuscripts. We must jump from the late sixth century to the late seventh century, where we find another Irish manuscript. *The Bangor Collectarium*, or *Orationale*, is also known as the *Bangor Antiphonale*. An **antiphon** is the technical term for a liturgical chant used in the Roman liturgy. Antiphons are the bits and pieces of Psalms, usually a refrain, set off against prose texts and sung in alternation by two choirs. The manuscript resides in Milan at the Biblioteca Ambrosiana where it has been given the number C. 5.

The Collectarium was written sometime during the Abbacy of Cronan (680-691) at Bangor (or Benchuir) in the North of Ireland, hence its modern name. It was written in a mixture of formal-liturgical and cursive-secular Insular fonts. [10] The hands of the Collectarium show that the scribes learned their trade at different sites.

Our examples are from the work of two scribes; both scribes were clearly professionals. While they use a full range of variant symbols, they do not use the same phone-symbol assignments. The use of symbol forms varies depending upon which scribe writes the text (Figure 6.7).

Fig. 6.6 The Cathach of Columba: *A*

Scribe 1 writes the *nomina sacra* with a straight-*d*; Scribe 2 uses a round-*d*. Scribe 1 uses both round- and straight-*d* while Scribe 2 uses only round-*d*. Scribe 1 uses alpha-*a* as his primary form; Scribe 2 uses Latin-*a*. Scribe 1 prefers the "n" shaped short-*r* (ꞃ), while Scribe 2 prefers the insular short-*r* (ꞃ). Both scribes show duration (quantity) on *m*: Scribe 1 on the left-hand

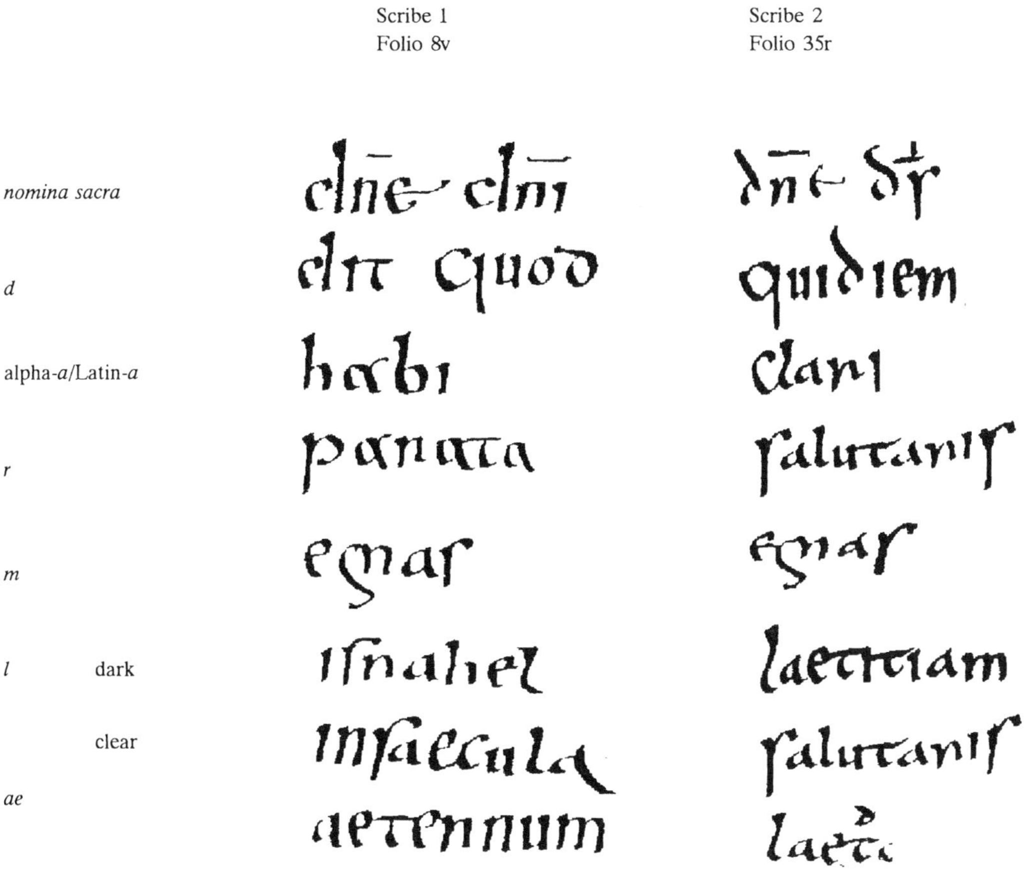

	Scribe 1 Folio 8v	Scribe 2 Folio 35r
nomina sacra		
d		
alpha-*a*/Latin-*a*		
r		
m		
l dark		
clear		
ae		

Fig 6.7 Some symbols of two scribes of the *Bangor Collectarium*

limb, Scribe 2 on both the right- and left-hand limbs. Scribe 1 uses straight-*l* for the clear phone and tailed-*l* for the dark. Scribe 2 uses two rounded forms. Contrary to the precepts of Classical Latin that state the diphthong (two vowels sounded together) *ae* is ligatured because it is sounded as one, neither scribe ligatures *ae*. Both scribes write *ae* as rising diphthongs; the stress is on the *e* not the *a*.

Sometimes the missing pieces in our puzzle can be found in tiny differences or subtle distinctions. We have one small piece of evidence that Scribe 2 was neither Irish nor an Irish scribe trained in England, but an Anglo-Saxon.

Old English has an *a*-phone that does not exist in Latin (or Greek or Hebrew, for that matter): aesc. Unlike Latin *ae*-ligature (ae), *aesc* is not a diphthong composed of two vowels. Aesc is one of the five monophthong (one sound) *a*-phones of the English language. It is not the same phone as Latin *ae*-ligature at all. The graphic symbol for *aesc* is a **monograph** (discrete symbol−Æ), not a **digraph** (composite symbol−a + e). Yet, here, we have a Latin word, *aeternae*, (eternal) written once with the distinctive pointed Anglo-Saxon *a* (ꝺ) and pre-tenth century Anglo-Saxon *e*-merka (ꬲ) in the first syllable and the small-lobed *a*-high *e* Anglo-Saxon *aesc* (ꭡ) in the third syllable (Figure 6.8). One further clue that this scribe was Anglo-Saxon and not Irish can be found in the "ter" of the second syllable. The *e* in "ter" is the high-open *e* and the *r* is the distinctive dipped-arm *r* of the pointed Anglo-Saxon minuscule (Figure 6.8).

Origins of the scribes aside, both scribes of the *Collectarium* use round-lobed uncial *a* (ᴀ). where the scribe of the Cathach employs pointed-lobe uncial *a* (ᴀ). Neither phone-symbol assignment system coincides with the one used in the *Cathach*. Another musical manuscript, the *Collectarium* contains no sign of musical notation.

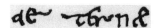

Fig. 6.8 Bangor Collectarium: The Anglo-Saxon font in the word *aeternae*

Official scripts tend toward bilinear limits. Late sixth and early seventh century Irish Insular half-uncial shows its North-African heritage in its inclusion of decided vertical movement within this formal book font. By the end of the seventh or the beginning of the eighth century, this formal book font becomes "officialized." While still encoded using the ternary system, both vertical and horizontal movement are tightly constrained. Ligatured letters are confined to syllables. On the other hand, variant forms indicating different phones appear throughout. We find variant forms of *d, e, g* and *l.* (The rounded, below baseline *l* is the dark *l*.) The use of both short *r* (ꞃ) and uncial *R* (ꞃ) and long (ſ) and sigmoid *s* (ꞅ), in turn, mark their specific phones. The finest example of this new official font appears in the *Lindisfarne Gospels* (Figure 6.9, Top).

This copy of the Gospels was produced at Lindisfarne monastery. Lindisfarne was founded by Aidan (died circa 651), an Irish monk and follower of Columba. Aidan, Bishop of Lindisfarne, was renowned for his learning, his preaching, his kindness to the poor, his holiness, and his dislike of pomp. Under Aidan, Lindisfarne became known as the English Iona and was a major center of learning in the North of England. Located in Northumbria not very far from the twin monasteries of Wearmouth-Jarrow, the Lindisfarne *scriptorium* was influenced by the proximity of the Roman affiliates. If we compare the Official half-uncial used at Lindisfarne with the Official Roman Uncial used at Wearmouth-Jarrow (Figure 6.9, Bottom), we can literally see the battle between the Anglo-Celtic and the Alexandrian-Roman affiliates as depicted in Bede's *Historia*.

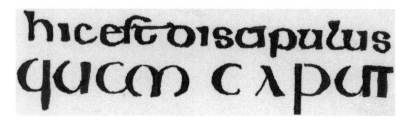

Fig. 6.9 Top: Lindisfarne; bottom: Wearmouth-Jarrow

Manuscript nomenclature can be confusing. The *Schaffhausen Adamnan* is a copy of Adamnan's biography of Columba (*Vita S. Columba*) and resides in the library at Schaffhausen. Adamnan's biography supplies us with what is known of the life of Columba. The Schaffhausen manuscript is not an autograph copy. Dated to about 713, the manuscript is written in both Insular Irish majuscule and minuscule by Dorbbene, another Irish monk. Dorbbene succeeded Adamnan as Abbot of Iona. As Adamnan and Dorbbene are the filters through which we see Columba, it seems logical to know something about these men.

Adamnan, or Adomnán (circa 628-704), appears to have lacked the charismatic character of Columba, nor was he a very persuasive speaker. He also seems to have been easy-going and amenable to outside influences. Adamnan, like Columba, was born in County Donegal, Ireland. Little is known about his family background. At some point he went off to Iona, Columba's main monastery. Adamnan was the 9th abbot of Iona. After his election in 679, Adamnan visited Northumbria and promptly changed his style of tonsure (monk's haircut) and adopted the Northumbrian Roman date for Easter. Back at Iona, he had no success whatsoever in persuading his monks to change as well. He went to Ireland, where he apparently succeeded in converting some areas to Roman practice, but we do not know exactly where he went. Whether it was his failure at his own monastery or something else, Adamnan apparently spent most of his later years in Ireland. He is credited with changing the practices in Ireland with regard to military service for women and in promoting laws protecting children and clergy (*The Law of Adamnan*). [11]

While Adamnan did not succeed in changing the religious practices at Iona, his sojourn in Northumbria influenced writing practices back at the monastery on Iona. We can see some of these influences in his successor, Dorbbene, the tenth Abbot of Iona.

Dorbbene may have followed in the footsteps of Columba, but he does not use the same writing system as used in the *Cathach* or in the *Lindisfarne Gospels*. This time, the teaching went in the other direction. There are English Northumbrian influences in his choice of letter symbols and in the forms of the symbols. This manuscript is not illustrated because, unlike many others, the important points can be reproduced as we read.

Folio 108v of the manuscript includes an early example of a single column in Irish minuscule. The only difference between the lettering of the first and second columns is in size. While Dorbbene distinguishes between high (ℙ) and medial *e* (ð), unlike the scribes of the *Cathach* and *Bangor Collectarium*, he uses only one form of long-*s* (ſ). He also does not differentiate by vertical movement among high (ſ), medial (ſ), and low *s* (ſ). He consistently uses sigmoid-*s* in the names of saints and after *u*. Dorbbene uses a version of the square *a* (ɑ) in both majuscule and minuscule forms and in all positions with one unusual exception. He writes a ligatured *ae* (œ) at a period when the normal way of writing the form is as a vowel pair (ae−two separate letter-symbols). Dorbbene has yet another uncommon habit. He uses an open *a* to write the ligatured form of *ae* in cɑℓum (*caelum*; *cael*−Modern French *ciel*, sky). This ligatured form of open-a + high-e (ɑℙ) is very unusual and does not appear in any other Irish manuscript. [12] This particular form appears only in manuscripts written by Northumbrians from Wearmouth-Jarrow.

Northumbria and Northumbrians played important roles in the history of England and the Christian Church. Northumbria and the city of *Eboracum* (York) were hardly central to Roman Britain; York was so very far away from *Londinium* (London) and the tin mines of Cornwall. The situation was otherwise for the Anglo-Saxon inhabitants of post-Roman Britain. Northumbria was the center of the island with York as its central city.

Northumbria covered far more territory in those days. Modern maps of the island, with their numerous counties, more closely resemble sixth-century Britain than seventh-century England. The island was dotted with small kingdoms. By the early seventh century, the Kingdoms of Elmet, Deira, and Bernicia had already been incorporated into the Northumbrian domain. Northumbrian territory changed as kings died or new alliances were formed. At its height, Northumbria extended along the East coast of the island from north of the Humber to the Forth.

During the mid-seventh century, Lindisfarne and other Anglo-Celtic monasteries were centers of learning. These monasteries used Anglo-Insular scripts and fonts. The twin monasteries of Wearmouth and Jarrow, located on the east coast of Northumbria boasted some impressive ecclesiastical figures, such as Bede (circa 672-735). Their secular documents appear in the late seventh-century Anglo-Saxon fonts. York, an inland city, was a major center of education during the eighth century. Later Northumbrian writers looked back on the reign of Eadberht Eating (737-58) as the golden age of learning. [13] In the mid-eighth century, York Cathedral school reigned supreme. We have an odd bit of evidence to demonstrate for us the internal fighting among affiliates. Just as the rituals at York differed from those used, for example, at Lincoln, York again asserted its independence from other centers: the secular fonts used at York were mutations of Anglo-Insular models. York's position as a major center of learning became of great importance by the late eighth century. In the mid-seventh century, however, the centers of learning were among the Anglo-Celtic monasteries.

Northumbrian Christianity embraced many Irish concepts, as is fully acknowledged by Bede himself. A zeal for sending out missionaries to the continent stands high among these influences. The missionaries took their writing systems with them. We find the unusual open-*a* + high-*e* (ɶ) used by Dorbbene in the name ᚻilɒɶ (Hilda) in the Saints' day entry on the *Willibrord Kalendar*.

With Willibrord (circa 658-739), we have another of the more interesting people of the age. Born in Northumbria, he was educated at Mount Ripon under Wilfrid (634-October 12, 709). We have an odd gap in our information on Willibrord at this point; something is not at all clear.

Ripon was founded by members of the Anglo-Celtic parties. Wilfrid, Willibrord's first teacher, was educated at Lindisfarne and was a follower of the Anglo-Celtic groups. Wilfrid then went to Canterbury, the center of the Roman mission, where he converted to the Roman party. He afterward went to Rome and next spent time in Lyons. Wilfrid came back around 660 and was asked by King Alcfrid of Deira to convert his people to the Roman ritual. The monks at Ripon refused to convert and left en-masse for Melrose. Wilfrid was an arch-enemy of the Anglo-Celtic parties and the victory of the Anglo-Roman party at the Council of Whitby (Strægnalaech – ᚠᛏᚱᚫᚷᚾᚨ lᚨᛂᚳᚻ) in 664 was largely his work. [14] (Wilfrid does not seem to have been the most honest of men; he seemed to operate on the basis that the end justifies the means. Among others of his known subterfuges, he "fudged" the Easter tables that he used to get the Roman date of Easter across at Whitby.) When Willibrord studied at Ripon, Wilfrid had already changed alliances.

It is not peculiar that Willibrord used Anglo-Celtic scripts and fonts; the Anglo-Roman fonts do not appear on the scene until after Theodore, the first Archbishop of Canterbury, opened the Cathedral School at Canterbury about 670. Willibrord learned to write *before* the Anglo-Saxon fonts became the identifying scripts of the Anglo-Roman parties. It is more than a little peculiar, however, that after Willibrord studied under Wilfrid at Ripon for approximately twelve years, he then left for further study in Ireland at Anglo-*Celtic* monasteries. We can sense an underlying conflict, but apparently nothing was written about it to elucidate the situation. We have to leave this part of Willibrord's background with an open and unanswerable question; we simply do not know what happened. Still, it casts a different light on the fact that Wilfrid, supposedly Willbrord's teacher and mentor, is not mentioned in the *Willibrord Kalendar.*

Willibrord embodies the missionary activities of the Irish-influenced English Christians sent out to educate and minister to peoples on the continent. In 690, Willibrord was at Rath Melsigi in County Carlow, Ireland. We are told that Willibrord, along with eleven other monks (that requisite twelve again), set out from Rath Melsigi in 690 as a missionary to Friesland, the northernmost province of today's Netherlands.

Willibrord's life was one of peaks of success and dismal reversals. In 714, he baptized Pepin the Short, the son of Charles Martel and father of Charlemagne (Charles the Great, King of the Franks and founder of the Holy Roman Empire). All Willibrord's successful missionary work was undone when the territory was recaptured in 715. After the conqueror died, Willibrord set out again to convert the "pagans." This time he did so well that he earned the title "The Apostle of the Frisians." Willibrord was made Bishop of Utrecht. He founded Echternach monastery in what is today Luxembourg. Willibrord's influence was so great that, fifty years after his death, Frisians still chose England as the place to send their young to be educated. Showing some resemblances to Columba in his pugnacity, he once destroyed an idol and barely escaped with his life when the priest (naturally enough) attacked him. His end was peaceful; he died at Eternach monastery while on a retreat.

The *Willibrord Kalendar* (Paris, Bibliothèque Nationale MS. Latin 10857) is written in an Insular minuscule liturgical font. Folio 39b has two insertions and a marginal note. The marginal note, written in an insular secular font, is a holograph by Willibrord himself and dated 728 (Plate 6.2).

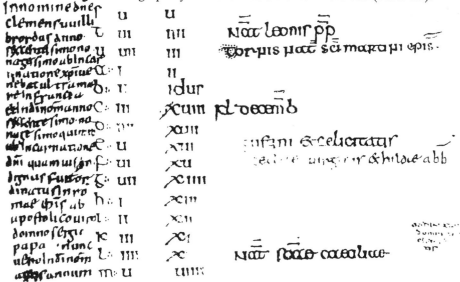

Plate 6. 2 Replica of the central portion of Folio 39b of the *Willibrord Kalendar*

The *Calendar* illustrates the distinctions between formal and informal fonts. Both fonts supply needed information. The formal liturgical font long has been considered the identifying mark of a manuscript as being of Northumbrian origin. The font was in use at Anglo-Celtic *scriptoria* on *both* sides of the Irish channel and can no longer be used to claim Northumbria as a place of origin. Further, we shall never know whether this font was designed in Northumbria or in Ireland. All we can know is that this formal font was used on both sides of the channel by Celtic and Northumbrian scribes trained at Anglo-Celtic centers.

Written in this distinctive Anglo-Celtic formal liturgical font, the calendar itself can be dated very closely. Bound into the manuscript, we find an Easter table for the 19-year cycle beginning in 684. The Easter Table was not continued on the reverse side of the leaf. In other words, the Easter table was outdated by 702 and there was no point in including it along with the Calendar unless it was written on or before 684. This means that the *Willibrord Kalendar* was written in Ireland, for Willibrord and his companions were still in Ireland in 684. [15]

Willibrord's team of missionaries appears to have been a joint venture, for it included members from Wearmouth-Jarrow as well as Anglo-Celtic companions from Ireland. Both insertions have been written with a finer pen in an Anglo-Saxon semi-formal minuscule. One of the insertions appears as an added entry to the calendar itself; the other, triangular in shape, is an expansion on an original entry. The marginal note is written in the Insular secular font that Willibrord learned at Ripon.

Intended for the use of Frisians, the added entry to the calendar lists the feast day of the Anglo-Saxon Saint, Hilda of Whitby. Whitby was one of the coastal monasteries affiliated with the Anglo-Roman parties. Bede devotes Book 4, Chapter 24 of his *Historia* to the life and death of Hilda of Whitby. Illustrative of the Saints' Lives genre, Hilda's story includes a royal background, miracles, and the suffering of the Saint. (From the description, she would appear to have had a painful tumor that eventually killed her.) Inserted opposite "F" on the *Kalendar* we find hιlσιℓ abb (*hildae abb*, with the bar of omission above the *abb*) (Figure 6.10).

Fig. 6.10 Willibrord Kalendar: *Hildae Abbess*

A somewhat rounded pointed-*a* (ɑ) begins the abbreviation for abbess (abb). The letters *ld* (lσ) in the name *hildae* are ligatured. This ligatured *ld* is one of the identifying marks of a scribe trained in an Anglo-Saxon writing school. The aesc in *hildae* is the very distinctive small-lobed ligatured open *a* (ɑℓ) used by the scribes of coastal Northumbrian *scriptoria*. It is also the same type of aesc used by Dorbbene of Iona, when he copied the *Schaffhausen Adamnan* around 713.

The date of the calendar itself only tells us when it was written; it does not tell us when codification occurred. On the other hand, the insertions provide a number of significant clues for us. They tell us that Willibrord's delegation to the Frisians included members trained at the coastal monasteries such as Wearmouth-Jarrow. They also hand us an important clue as to the date of codification of the Anglo-Saxon symbol set. Dorbbene was not an innovator; however, Adamnan was. We know this from his laws and the changes he wished to make at Iona. Codification had to be earlier than 713, but we need more information to narrow down the time-frame. The note in the left-hand margin supplies the missing information. Figure 6.11 (facing) shows an enlargement of the note. Line numbers have been added to aid in locating the cited references.

1 Innominebñes
2 clemenſuuilli
3 brordaſanno.
4 nocteſimonono.yi
5 nageſimoublncar
6 ipnatione xpiue
7 rebatultrumeñ
8 reinfruncta
9 elndinoñannno
10 nocteſimo.no
11 nuſeſimoquinte
12 uincuinutiane
13 dñiquamuiſon.ſ
14 ignurſuctor
15 dinatuſñnro
16 maſthiſub
17 upoſtolicouiroi
18 domnoſctzir
19 papa·ñunc
20 ueholntinoñn
21 ecforannoum

This note is that rarity among surviving medieval texts: a holograph. Written in an Anglo-Celtic secular Insular minuscule, by Willibrord himself, it is in the script—and writing system—he learned back at Ripon before he went to Ireland, and long before he set out for Frisia in 690.

Willibrord's name appears at the end of line 2 (*uuilli*) and continues on line 3 (*brordas*). (The -as at the end of "brord" is a Latin inflectional ending.) The note records the dates of his arrival in Francia (690), his Consecration by pope Clemens (695), and the year of writing (728). [16]

Willibrord uses three *a*'s. His standard *a* form is the Latin round *a* (ɑ), for example, the -*as* in *brordas* (l. 3) and *papa* in line 27. Round-lobe uncial *a* (ᴀ), is used in ᴀnno (*anno*–year) in line 3. His third form, the open-headed aleph-*a* (ɑ), appears in the Greek word ɑpo ſtoli (*Apostles*) in line 25 and the name of the territory, ffᴀnciᴀ (*Francia*) line 8 (Figure 6.12).

Readers sometimes have difficulty distinguishing the aleph-*a* graph from the Latin-*u* graph; however, they are not formed the same way. The aleph-*a* curves toward the right, while the Latin-*u* is upright. We can see the difference between the two graphic symbols on line 23 in [or]ᴅinᴀtu[s] (*ordinatus*, ordination of) (Figure 6.13).

Willibrord distinguishes among high, medial, and low *e* (Figure 6.14). For example, the first *e* in Clﬔenſ (Clemens), is high, the second *e* is medial. The *e* at the end of *nomine*, in line 1, illustrates his low *e* form. He also distinguishes between high and low *s*. In this font design, the symbols are slightly different in shape. The high *s*, as in ſⅿo (lines 4 and 10), has a rounded top; the low *s*, as in Clﬔᴅnſ, is flattened.

The manuscripts have spoken and they tell us what we want to know: where and when codification began. The many pieces of evidence fit into their correct places. This is an exercise that has much in common with a detective story. We know that the whole point about *The Hound of the Baskervilles* is that the hound did not bark. Similarly, we can see from the manuscripts that, prior to the last half of the 7th century, a systematic alphabetic symbol set was not there. On the other hand, we can see from what is there, Willibrord's use of a codified symbol set, that we can pinpoint the time and general place of the first stage of codification.

There is no evidence for the existence of a systematically applied symbol set prior to the codification of *stæfwriting*. Instead, writing systems exhibit the same confusion and

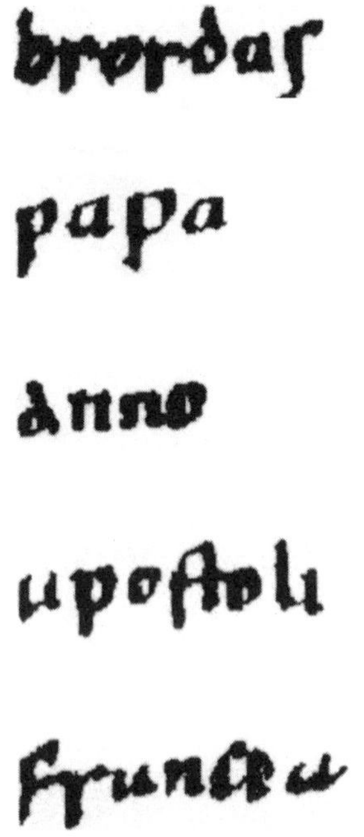

Fig. 6.12 Willibrord Kalendar: Willibrord's three *a*-graphs

Fig. 6.13 Willibrord Kalendar: Willibrord's aleph-*a* and Latin-*u*

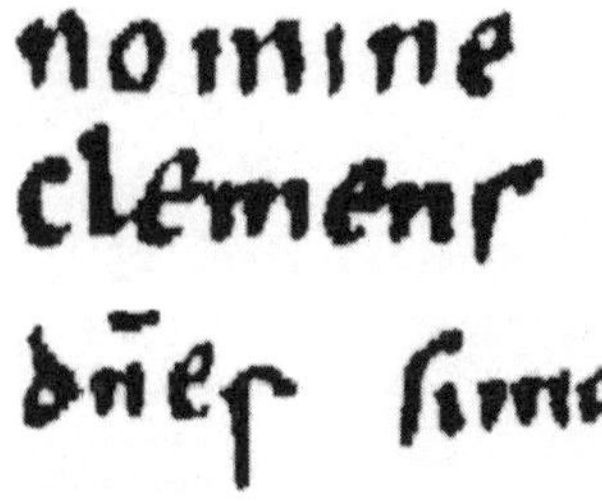

Fig. 6.14 Willibrord Kalendar: Willibrord's *e* and *s* graphs

individuality found in early systems of musical notation where each site searched for its own solutions within the frame of its affiliated parties. [17] Still, it is this lack of system that allows us to track the evidence.

While there seems to be some method at use in Columba's *Cathach*, whatever system used is different from the other systems at work in the *Bangor Collectarium*. Dorbbene, although at Columba's Iona, uses yet another writing method in the *Schaffhausen Adamnan* – and one that displays English Coastal Northumbrian influences.

Born about 658, Willibrord entered school sometime between 665-670. He used the writing system he learned back at Ripon before being sent out on his mission to the Frisians in 690. We now know that the first stage of codification occurred sometime during the first sixty years of the seventh century and before the arrival of Theodore of Canterbury in 668-9. We also know, from the date—and from Willibrord—that *stæfwritung* is a product of an Anglo-Celtic monastery somewhere in Northumbria. In marked contrast to the other early documents, Willibrord's writing system shows the systematic phonetic assignments of the first stage in the codification of *stæfwritung*: the Anglo-Saxon Phonetic Alphabet.

Map 2 Wales, Cornwall, Pictland, The Seven Anglo-Saxon Kingdoms (Heptarchy), The Irish Channel, and Western Ireland in the late 7th-Early 8th Centuries.

Chapter Seven

VISIBLE VOICES

"When *I* use a word," declares Humpty Dumpty, "it means just what I choose it to mean—neither more nor less." The statement leaves Alice sorely puzzled, for it seems to be a proposition for anarchy. With each *scriptorium* deciding on symbol-assignments for itself, the situation in precodification manuscripts seems to echo the anarchy of Humpty's declaration on the meaning of a word. For a people determined to get the Word right, the need for a standardized alphabetic symbol set was both real and urgent. The symbol set had to be logically ordered and methodically applied. It also had to be practical and language-independent. The complete Anglo-Saxon Phonetic Alphabet (ASPA) symbol set is both logical and comprehensive. It had to be; its desired end was a universal alphabet system for Anglo-Saxon England.

What do we mean by the term "alphabet"? Today, most people would say that the term comes from the Greek words for the first two letters of the "Latin" alphabet! [1] Few pause to consider what an alphabet *is*. Is an alphabet simply a "way of recording language by visible marks," [2] or does the term encompass a wider sphere? What precisely is an alphabet?

Although Humpty takes the proposition to an absurd length (as Lewis Carroll intended him to), much confusion could be avoided if we remember the purpose of a word: words mean "neither more nor less" than what they are intended to mean. Likewise, we could avoid much confusion if we remember the primary purpose of alphabetic symbols: alpha-symbols represent neither more nor less than a mnemonic for a given phone. To rephrase David Diringer's comment, each element in a script system corresponds to a specific phone in a given language. [3]

At the most basic level, alphabets are composed of the concrete images of a transduction of a sound. These concrete images—the Phoenician "alep," the Hebrew "aleph," the Greek "alpha," and the modern *a*—are graphic mnemonics, a form of mental shorthand. When the reader sees the symbol, he or she does not think *a*, but associates the sound with the symbol. We call these graphic mnemonics **letters**. Letters, along with digits, spaces, and punctuation marks are, to borrow a term from mathematical logic, part of a given language's symbols. [4]

The number of possible alpha-symbols is infinite. The modern so-called Latin alphabet appears to be a finite set consisting of twenty-six individual letters or symbols. This figure, however, can be shown to be false. There are a minimum of fifty-two symbols: twenty-six lower case and twenty-six upper case. If we examine only the twenty-six lower case symbols, simply by the addition of **bold** face type, we have doubled the original figure to fifty-two lower case symbols. Combining merely these two type styles we arrive at the formula $(a^2 + b^2 + \ldots z^2)(b^2 + c^2 + \ldots z^2)$ and so on. If we now add *italic* type we have 104 individual lower case symbols. The progression is as follows: the symbol *a* can be written either 'a' or '*a*' or '**a**' or '*a*,' that is, a [4]. Now let us add point size modification in the range of from 6 to 30 points or 25 additional factors: there are now 29 possible symbols for *a*. In other words, any alphabet letter can be seen as of the order m^n possible individual symbols. A language set includes punctuation, spaces, and digits, and these symbols also are of the order m^n.

While the number of possible symbols is infinite, alphabets are finite, that is, a limited number of graphic signs. The Sumerian system needed a very large number of symbols. The Akkadian move to a phonetic-based writing system reduced the number needed to express the spoken word. The Phoenician system, following the lead of the Ugaritic one, brought the number down to twenty-two symbols plus five final forms. Our modern English alphabetic system is a finite collection of fifty-two graphic symbols.

In human languages, finite collections (**concatenations**) of a language's symbols are called words; however, phonetic based systems are not written word by word, but utterance by utterance. **Expressions** is a more inclusive statement and makes allowance for the clumping and spacing found in the documents.

Human languages are informal as opposed to the strictly structured and defined formal language used in mathematical logic. Both informal and formal languages contain **variables** as well as **constants**. By definition, a constant is a symbol that keeps the same meaning *across* contexts. A variable, by definition, keeps the same meaning *throughout any one* context. Although the recognition of the symbol as representing the letter *a* remains a constant, *a*-italic is, in fact, a discrete, individual symbol. *A*-italic is a constant by consensus; [5] its appearance in a text is recognized as indicating "foreign word," "book title," or "special meaning." Although written or printed in a variable **symbol-style**, that is, font design, *a*-italic keeps its meaning *across* contexts. While the basic form is a constant, the manifestation of the form in a variety of font-styles is a variable; that is, the constant remains, but varies in a given text according to script-model—square, round, pointed, sans-serif, and so on.

This distinction between variables and constants is the central basis of the **in-text encoding** techniques employed in phonetic-based writing systems. Within these systems, vertical and horizontal movement are variables; symbol forms are phonetic constants.

The phonetic constant assignments in the Irish manuscripts vary from site to site and from local writing system to local writing system. What we see in Willibrord's marginal note is an ordered phonetic constant system. It tells us that the first action of the Anglo-Saxon codifiers was to replace the disorganized, non-transferable alpha-graphic diversity of existing local or regional symbol sets with an ordered, systematically applied, constant graphic symbol set.

The arrangement of the ASPA is exceptionally systematic and methodical. This very methodical arrangement tells us that the codifiers were aware of the origins of both symbols and scriptures. The Anglo-Saxons knew that the scriptures were originally in Hebrew, then translated into Greek and later into Latin. These facts were still common knowledge centuries after codification. The titles of the books of the Pentateuch in the 11th century *Old English Illustrated Hexateuch* are given first in Hebrew, followed by Greek, then Latin, and finally Old English. In the 9th century, King Ælfred (the Great, 849-899) states this clearly in his introductory letter attached to his translation of Pope Gregory the first's *Pastorale Care.* [6]

The passage is given first as written on folios 1v-2r of Bodleian MS Hatton 20. This is followed by a modern standardized transliteration and, finally, by a modern English translation.

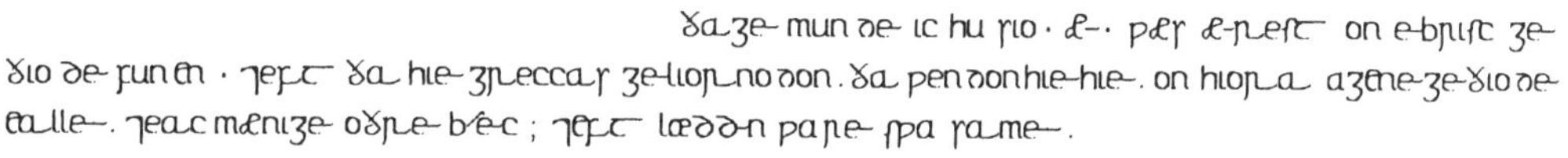

ꝺa ᵹe-mun ꝺe- ic hu ſio · Æ-· pær Æ-ꞃeſꞇ on e-bꞃiſc ᵹe-ꝺio ꝺe- ꝼun en · �;eꝼꞇ ꝺa hie-ᵹꞃeccaꝛ ᵹe-lioꞃ-no ꝺon. ꝺa pen ꝺonhie-hie-. on hioꞃa aᵹene-ᵹe-ꝺio ꝺe-ealle-. �7eac mæniᵹe- oꝺꞃe- bÆc ; 986;eꝼꞇ læꝺꝺn paꞃe- ꞅꝼa ꞃa me-.

ða gemunde ic hu sio .ae. waes aerest on ebrisc geðiode funden. &eft ða hie greccas geliornodon. ða wendon hie hie. on hiora aᵹene ᵹeðiode ealle. &eac maenige oðre bec. &eft laeden ware swa same.

[Then I recalled how .The Law. was first found among the Hebrew people, and afterwards then the Greeks learned it. Then they translated all of it into their own language, and also many other books; and afterwards Latin-dwellers the same.]

If we look at the two passages written in Old English, we see a marked difference between the phonetic-based writing in the manuscript and the semantic-based standardized modern transliteration. The manuscript shows us *stæfwriting* in use. Duration (quantity) appears in the tails on *r*'s and *a*'s and tongues on *e*'s. We see the clumping and spacing of speech as well as the rise and fall of stress. The modern semantic-based rendition gives us the meaning, but strips away all indications of the spoken words as well as eliminating the carefully distinguished phonetic constants. The modern rendition creates semantic boxes sacrificing two-thirds of the content.

Similarly, modern phonological techniques separate phones into tiny individual boxes. This practice gives us phonetic constants, but, except to the initiated, strips away meaning as well as eliminating all traces of the spoken word. There are a
number of problems with the **International Phonetic** f ɔˈ s k ɔˈ ænd s ɛ v n j ir z ɔg o
Alphabet (IPA). The example on the right is written in the IPA.

How many people would recognize the example as the opening word of the Gettysburg Address: "Four score and seven years ago"? [7] The symbol-set of the IPA requires specialized knowledge on the part of the reader. The IPA version gives us the articulated distinctions of the sounds (quality), but no indications as to stress (volume) and quantity (duration). It does not record speech; the script system throws out two-thirds of the data. In terms of technological advances, the IPA is primitive and regressive. The very large symbol set of the IPA could just as well be back in 3000 BCE. While the creation of boxes facilitates the study of individual phones, the IPA system is neither practical nor of general use. A writing system must be readable by other than a specialist to be useful. Sadly enough, the concept of an IPA arose from attempts during the nineteenth century to record Old English.

The Anglo-Saxon codifiers also created boxes, but these are very different from our modern ones. Their boxes are designed to reduce the enormous variety of forms needed to represent speech, yet still provide for the *relative* representation of the spoken word.

The key word is relative. While today's articulative phonologists aim for extreme precision in locating where and how a phone sound is produced and acoustic phonologists think in terms of how the phone sounds, the Anglo-Saxons were concerned with the reproduction of voice, not sound. Sound is relative; voice is bound. The symbols of the ASPA are classified by ranges according to phone class.

Ælfric the Grammarian (*Grammaticus*), an Anglo-Saxon Abbot and pedagogue who lived from around 955 to 1020, states that the Anglo-Saxons classified phones as vowels (*vocales*) and two types of consonants: mute and semi-vowels (*semi-vocales*). [8] The last refers to those in between consonants, liquids such as *l* and *r*, nasals such as *n* and *m*, and sibilants, such as *s* and *z*. Ælfric also tells us that the Anglo-Saxons (as the ancients) were perfectly aware that consonants cannot be sounded without a vowel. (Try to say *b* or *p* without some kind of vowel.)

If the codifiers had required one symbol for each phone, the symbol-set would have rivaled that of ancient Sumer in size. Their solution was simple: they followed the Ugaritic-Phoenician variant form system. The codifiers separated phones into sets, for example, the set of all *a*'s. Each set contained a central form and whatever others were required in variant forms.

The Anglo-Saxons recognized, for example, the distinctions between **palatal** phones, made by the tongue pressing against the palate (the roof of the mouth is the hard palate), and **dental** phones, where the tongue presses against the teeth. They distinguished the difference between **stops** (the air stream is cut off, stopped, by the tongue) and **fricatives** (the tongue relaxes and permits some air to pass, causing friction.) They also understood the difference between **voiced** and **unvoiced** phones.

Although this may sound a bit too technical, there is a little experiment that we can try for ourselves that should make the technical terminology clear. English makes a distinction between voiced and unvoiced *th*. When we place a hand on our throat and pronounce the word "this," the vocal cords vibrate. When the throat vibrates, the phone is voiced. If we now pronounce "thistle," the vocal cords do not vibrate. When the throat does not vibrate, the phone is unvoiced. In both modern words we can also feel that the tongue touches the teeth; therefore, *th* is a dental phone. Finally, we can contrast *t* as in "toy" with *th* as in "this" and "thistle." When we say *t*, the tongue touches the teeth and stops the flow of air; *t* is a dental stop. When we say *th* the tongue relaxes and permits some air to flow across; this makes *th* a fricative. In Modern English, the *th* as in "this" is a voiced dental fricative and the *th* in "thistle" is an unvoiced dental fricative.

Voicing usually is **morphologically determinate**, that is, whether a phone is voiced or not, depends upon the *shape* of the utterance. The codifiers, for example, used only one symbol for *f*. The *f*, for instance, in æfter (after) is preceded by a vowel, but is followed by a consonant; hence the *f* in æfter was unvoiced, that is, pronounced *ph*. When the *f* was **intervocalic** (between vowels), as in heofon or ofer, *f* was voiced, that is, pronounced *v* (heovon, over). As today both voiced and unvoiced *th* are dental phones, we do not distinguish between them orthographically. At the time of codification, however, they also distinguished between palatal *th* and dental *th*; thus, the ASPA has two different symbols to record this distinction.

The codifiers did not classify vowel phones according to their position in the mouth (**oral cavity**) as we do today. In modern vocalic terminology, we refer to, for instance, front vowels. These phones are formed in the front of the oral cavity. Back vowels, obviously enough, are formed towards the back of the oral cavity. Then there are classifications, among others, such as open and closed vowels, as well as high and low vowel phones.

Another little experiment should clarify these terms. When we say *a* as in "father," the mouth is open, the lips relaxed, the sound is produced at the back of the throat, and the tongue is near horizontal. *A* in "father" is, therefore, an open high back vowel. When we say *e* as in "we," the mouth closes, the lips purse, the sound moves forward to the front of the oral cavity, and the tongue curls into the soft palate in the lower jaw. The *e* in "we" is a closed low front vowel. While there are many minute phonetic distinctions made by specialists in the field, these experiments should make it a bit easier to understand modern phonological terminology.

Fig. 7.1 The graphic symbol *a* on the sound continuum

Although the Anglo-Saxons surely would have understood our modern vowel classifications by position, *stæfwritung* uses a very different criterion: clarity. Vowel phones are distinguished by the amount of audible blurring or blending, that is, the proximity or remoteness from **schwa** (the central vowel sound). The chosen symbols represent a sound continuum ranging from clear —> central —> muddy (Figure 7.1). This sound continuum may be illustrated both in 7th century and modern terms. The word "papa" does not appear to have changed very much across the centuries. The first *a* in modern English "papa" is clear, the second *a* is central. Probably the closest equivalent phone to the pre-vowel shift "muddy" *a* would be the modern English short *u* as "aglow."

Latin did not become the official language of Western European liturgy until after the ninth century. During the early centuries of the Common Era, particularly in those areas originally converted by North African or Syriac missionaries, Semitic scripts were the script of the Old Testament and Greek was the script of the New Testament. Latin was the *koine*; the language of inter-ethnic diplomacy and scholarly discourse. The ASPA employs the three major script-models: Latin, Greek, and Hebrew.

The Greek, Latin, and Hebrew languages have different phonetic properties. The codifiers classified symbols by phonetic types according to language. Latin phonotypes, with some schwa, sit right in the middle. Greek phonotypes are quite muddy, with a great deal of schwa. Hebrew phonotypes are quite clear and without schwa; Hebrew's cousin, Aramaic, contains both clear and somewhat muddy phonotypes. Latin forms are the pivot around which other forms rotate, generally in opposing pairs. Latin symbols represent the central and Greek symbols represent muddy, or blurred, sounds. Hebrew forms, with one exception borrowed from Syriac Aramaic, represent the clear. [9]

Some of the elementary sounds, for example, Latin-*i*, Greek-*iota*, and Western Semitic-*yud*-plus-vowel, apparently were so similar as to eliminate the need for an additional graphic symbol. Some of the sounds did not exist in all of the three models. For instance, neither Greek nor Latin have an *aesc* (pronounced "ash"), but Syriac (Aramaic) did. Nor does the relatively rare Latin a-e ligature represent the same phone as the English *aesc*. *Aesc* and *æ* are not the same phone: the former is a monophone and a monograph, the latter a diphthong and a digraph. Other phones occur in OE which did not occur in the three major models, for example, *thorn* and *wyn*, and symbols were taken from Futhark, the common Germanic ethnic script system, to fill the need.

Although we can verify from **Futhorc**, the Anglo-Saxon runic symbol set, that *aesc*, for instance, was a monophthong, the codifiers of the ASPA did *not* use Futhorc for any of their models. The two symbol systems coincide neither in the number and type of vowel phones nor consonants considered necessary to record speech. Perhaps this was because Futhorc was an ethnic symbol set, while the ASPA was intended to be an inter-ethnic symbol system. Whatever the reason, all of the borrowed Germanic symbols in the ASPA are from *Futhark*.

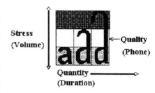

Fig. 7.2 A basic shape and its appearance as stressed (vertical axis)

Rather than create a different symbol to indicate the different levels of stress and duration that may be assigned to each phone, the codifiers assigned a phone to a basic form, but elongated or widened each symbol as necessary. The basic form of an individual symbol is a **constant**, and indicates the *quality* of a given sound. Movement, vertically and horizontally, is a **variable** (Figure 7.2).

The organization of the ASPA is both logical and systematic. This systematic approach to assigning given sounds to the chosen Latin, Semitic, and Greek letter-symbols allows us to determine the phonetic assignments. It must be emphasized that, even when we know that a given form reflects a specific phone, it does not tell us the sound. Sound, as Isidore of Seville stated, cannot be written on a page. [10] We can see from the manuscripts that the Anglo-Saxons rolled or trilled their *r*'s, but we cannot know if this was a rolled-, a trilled-, or a flap-*r*.

The alpha-graphic assignments in Table 1 give only minuscule (lowercase) constants. Majuscule (capital) constants became important later in musical notation. We know that at the time of codification, English vowels followed what today are called continental phones. This means that while today we say *a* (day), *e* (we), *i* (I), and *y* (bye), the Anglo-Saxons said *a* (ma), *e* (day), *i* (we), and *y* (see). Likewise, we know that a *staef*, an alphabetic symbol, was classified as a consonant, vowel, or semi-vowel, but we do not know the Old English terms for phonological distinctions and must rely on modern terminology for these descriptions.

In the following, the symbols of the ASPA are given in their original assignments as of the time of codification, that is, sometime in the first half of the seventh century.

Table 7.1: The Anglo-Saxon Phonetic Alphabet.

	CLEAR	CENTRAL	MUDDY
Monographs			
a	ɑ	ɑ	ɑ
aesc	æ	ℓ	N/A
b		b	
c		c (k)	⊂ (ch)
d		ɔ	
e	e	e	ɛ
f		ſ	
g		3	
h		h / ɦ	
i	N/A	ɩ	
k		k	
l		ɩ	ɩ
m		m, ɱ	
n		n, ⋈	
enʒ		ŋ	
o	N/A	o	
p		p	
q		q	
r	ƨ	ɲ	ʁ
s	ſ / ʃ	ſ	s
t		⊂	
u(v)	ſ	u	ʸ
x		x	
y		y	
z		z	
barred-d		ɣ	
Futhark			
thorn		þ	
wyn		ρ	
Digraphs			
ea		ed	
io		ɩo	

The Anglo-Saxon Phonetic Alphabet

Monographs

a   All Western *a*'s are ultimately derived from the Semitic aleph. While there appear to be many forms of *a*, [11] there are five basic monographic constant forms of this symbol representing five distinct monophones. [12]

ɑ   1. Latin-*a*. This is the central form of the symbol. Whether pointed, square, rounded, or broad and flat-topped, the basic Latin-*a* is a lobe (the rounded portion) set against a minim (the upright stroke). Variations in the basic form (with or without a serif, with or without a "cell," uncial pointed lobe, square top, etc.) follow from the design of a specific font-style and do not affect the quality of the symbol.

ɑ   2. Aleph-*a*. [13] The symbol represents the clear form of *a*. It is a reflected form of the so-called "Herodian" type-2 *a* used in the Dead Sea Scrolls. [14] This is the form which was adopted into the Alexandrian Greco-Italic cursive symbol set around the 1st century BCE. The form appears in the North-African Latin symbol set by the 2nd century CE. Its use in diverse texts throughout Europe indicates that it represented different phones depending upon the local dialect. For example, a superscripted form is used in fourth century Pontifical fonts and a stylized form of the aleph-*a* appears to be the central symbol in seventh century Merovingian fonts. The symbol is included in the Anglo-Saxon formal pointed half-uncial symbol set. This symbol has been referred to as the "cursive *u*-like form." [15] The form indicates a distinct phone, and is not a minuscule version of the horned- or Alpha-*a*.

α   3. Alpha-*a*. This symbol represents the muddy form of *a*. It is a stylized cursive Greek "alpha." The oldest existing examples of the Greek cursive forms date from the Ptolemaic period (3rd century BCE). This form is also referred to as a horned- or double-*c* type *a*. Still another name for the alpha-*a* is the *oc-a*, seemingly produced by running *o* and *c* together. It probably would be preferable to refer to this form as an "alpha-*a*," if nothing else, to preserve its origin.

Æ   4. The small-lobed *aesc* or Semitic-*a* represents the central sound. (Anglo-Saxon Futhorc, the expanded symbol set based upon Germanic Futhark, makes it very clear that *aesc* is a monograph and an *a*-phone.)

    The much reduced *a* + high-*e* form is a monograph, and derives from one of the documented five *a* forms employed in the Palmyrene-Aramaic scripts. The form derived from the ligature of the **vowel pair** (dipthong) *a+e* is a digraph. Bigraph *ae* and monographic Æ are not the same quality. The *ae* ligature represents the coalescence of two sounds; the Æ represents one of the five *a*-sounds found in the Germanic and some Semitic languages, but not in Latin or Greek. This phonetic difference is reflected in the shape of the two symbols. The fundamental distinction in graphic representation between the two forms makes it highly important to distinguish the forms for phonological research.

æ 5. The open-lobed aesc represents the clear phone, that is, without schwa. It is a combination of the Aleph-*a* with the Semitic-aesc.

b   The symbol represents the same phone in all Western scripts and derives from the Semitic *bet*. OE *b* has a straight-back and is full minim length, that is, it runs from the headline to the baseline. The **bow** (the rounded part) begins with a straight stroke rather than a curved stroke (b).

c   There are two forms of *c* in vernacular texts.

c 1. The first *c* is the basic form resembling the Latin letter—except for its straight-back (c). It represents the hard phone: *c* as in "call."

c 2. The second form is angular-*c* (c). The form is taken directly from Futhark where it may originally have represented the soft phone, *c* as in "*ch*icken." [16] We really do not know how this form was originally pronounced. While it certainly represents hard-*c* (as in "cat") in later Futhark texts, the codifiers were rather fussy about the correspondence between symbol and assignment. In the ASPA, the symbol represents the soft phone. Further, although the Futhorc symbol-set includes three different c/k forms, the angular-*c* was thrown out and not used.

        This symbol is one of the forms that tends to support an Etruscan origin for the early Germanic symbol-set. We find both round-*c* and angular-*c* among the earliest North Etruscan symbol-sets in the documents from Sondrio. While this *may* indicate that the angular-*c* was soft and the round-*c* hard in Etruscan, we simply do not know.

        The Western Greeks seem to have distinguished between voiced *c* (*g*) and unvoiced *c* (*k*) using a *gimel* for the voiced (*g*) and a rounded-*gimel* that resembles an open *c* for the unvoiced form (*c*). The displacement of *gimel* (the third letter of Semitic alphabets; *gamma* in Greek) by *c* in modern Western symbol sets seems to derive from Latin via Etruscan.

        Futhark used separate symbols for *g* and *c* (*k*). The angular form occurs most frequently in Old English texts ligatured with epsilon-*e*. Examples of the form may be seen, for instance, in British Library Cotton Vitellius XV.A &cglaf (Ecglafes−of Ecglaf) on folio 141r and secean (secean−to seek) on folio 144v.

d   The symbol is derived from the Semitic *dalet*. Round-*d* (ð) is used in OE texts to represent the palatal stop. The form has an interesting history.

        In early texts, such as the *Cathach of Columba* and the *Bangor Collectarium*, the difference between the straight-backed (d) and rounded forms of *d* (ð) marked the distinction between Latin *deus* and Greek *θeos* (God). Straight-*d* represented the voiced stop and round-*d* the fricative. This distinction accounts for the appearance of round-*d* **medially** (in the middle of words) and finally in manuscripts written prior to the addition of script differentiation to the *stæfwritung* system. We find it used, for example, in the *Épinal Glossary* and in numerous Anglo-Saxon names in various Latin texts. [17] (See also *barred-d*.)

e   The symbol derives from the Semitic *heh*. While there are many forms of this symbol depending upon script or font model, there are only three basic constant forms representing three distinct phones for the letter-symbol *e*: one form from each of the three major alphabet-symbol sets.

e 1. Latin-*e*. This is the central form of the symbol. The symbol appears in Latin cursive scripts from approximately the third century on. Latin-*e* accepts only normal and medial stress notation.

ϵ 2. Semitic-*e*. This form is sometimes referred to as high-*e*. It is one of the Aramaic offshoots, a reflected representation of one of the five forms of Palmyrene-*e*. [18] The evidence shows that scribes were careful to maintain a distinction between the Greek-*e* and Semitic-*e*; these distinctions are most clearly observed in stressed positions. Semitic-*e* accepts only medial and primary stress notation. The symbol is distinct both as to phone and to form; it is not a variant of Greek-*e*.

ε 3. Greek- or epsilon-*e*. Sometimes called an open-*e*, this form is a Greek epsilon. The symbol represents the muddy or blurred form of *e*. The Greek-*e* is a direct importation of an existing second century stylized epsilon. Northumbrian dialects use the Greek-*e* form where West Saxon employs *Æ*, for example, mεʒn and mǽʒən (might). Both ε and *Æ* are monographs representing relatively fine distinctions on the sound continuum. The use of ε in Northumbrian and *Æ* in West Saxon almost certainly represents pronunciational distinctions between dialects rather than phonological sound shifts in the language.

f Uncial-*f*. The form resembles a modern capital *F*—except that the top of the symbol rests at the headline, the crossbar on the baseline, and the minim descends (ϝ).

The symbol *f* derives from the Semitic *waw* (pronounced *vav*). Much confusion arises from the fact that *vav* may be consonantal (*f* or *v*) or vocalic (*w* or *u*) depending upon a speaker's dialect. As a result, the symbol was picked up as *f* in Etruscan (-> Latin), *u/v* in Greek, and *w* in Gothic. The problem of *vav* tends to haunt various symbol-set assignments, and we will see more of this symbol.

g The *g* symbol is a relatively late addition to the Latin symbol-set and represents the voiced-*c* of *gimel/gamma*. Originally, the form was used in both Latin and vernacular texts. After the second stage of codification, *g* (closed-bow) was used in Latin, and ʒ (open-bow) in OE. Either form may have a closed or open-loop tail depending upon script-model. In early Old English, the phone appears to have been a velar-*g*, that is, the "ch" in Scots "loch," only voiced.

h The symbol derives from the Semitic *het*. There are two forms of this symbol used in OE texts. Straight-legged-*h* (h) is used in the body of a text in OE. Round-legged-*h* (h) is normally employed as a majuscule form in vernacular texts to mark begin-new-paragraph, fitt, or line. Medially, round-legged-*h* indicates stress.

i *I* has one basic form representing the central *i*-phone (ɩ). Greek *iota*, Aramaic–Hebrew *iud*, and Latin *i* are so similar in form, that, unless evidence appears to indicate otherwise, the same symbol must have represented a similar sound in all of these languages. The symbol occurs in diverse lengths; these are variables, not constants.

k Greek-*k* or *kappa-k*. The Greek symbol is a reflected form of the early Phoenician *kaph*. The law of parsimony states that a people will only use what is needed in their symbol-set. The symbol was used neither in Classical and Late Latin nor OE. In ancient Latin, *k* represented unvoiced *c* (k) and *c* represented voiced *c* (g). When *g* (voiced *c*) was added to the Latin symbol-set, *k* disappeared from the Latin symbol set except for its use in *Kalend-* (calendar), in some legal abbreviations, and sometimes to spell (K)arthage. In OE, the two forms of *c*, round (C) and angular (ᴄ), represented the hard and soft-*c* phones. *K* represents the same phone as hard-*c*. As such, *k* was unnecessary. In OE, Kappa-*k* was reserved for a special use.

This special use is intended to distinguish between realms or domains. In antiquity, the distinction was between the sacred and the profane. Many modern philosophers and theologians refer to the sacred domain as the "transcendent realm." Yet transcend is not exactly what is meant, as "to transcend" means "to climb beyond or above the *non-physical* world." If we modify the meaning slightly, and restrict "to transcend" to mean only "to reach or to climb beyond the *physical* world," we can have some idea of what this special distinction meant in Antiquity—for this special use is not an invention of the codifiers of the *stæfwritung* system. We must, as usual when examining writing systems, return to Antiquity and to the combined Kingdom of Sumer and Akkad.

When Sargon I reordered the Sumerian symbol set and reduced the cumbersome mass to one hundred graphs to suit the Akkadian language, approximately fifty Sumerian symbols were retained. These Sumerian symbols were used for xenographic exchange, the oldest use of the technique. The purpose of this exchange was to distinguish the transcendent from the mundane realms. The Akkadians, for example, distinguished between grain meant for trade and grain meant for offerings.

Something or someone transcendent is not necessarily a god. It is some thing or person that reaches beyond the physical world; the term can be applied to any being or thing who has attained this beyondness. Of these distinctions Akkadian made between the transcendent realm and the mundane realm, one remained in uninterrupted use from Akkad down to early modern times.

Sumerian had a symbol for "King," Akkadian had phonetic symbols. Akkadian scribes used the Akkadian cuneiform symbols when the reference was mundane. The Sumerian symbol was employed when the reference was transcendent. Hence, a hero or a king in a transcendent role would warrant the use of the Sumerian king symbol in the midst of an Akkadian text.

Writing systems are conservative; in the oldest Hebrew texts, this same distinction appears in the size of the *mem* used in ha*m*elech [the king, mundane] and ha*M*elech [the King/transcendent/God].

Whether Greeks distinguished between realms is an open question. The oversize *Beta* in *Basileus* [king] and *Basileia* [queen] that occurs in Greek texts may also indicate this distinction between the transcendent and the mundane. (This question may be answered someday if scholars examine the original documents in light of distinctions in size between *Beta* and *beta* in context.)

In Roman use we find *Kalend-* used for the correct *calend-* (calendar) in bookkeeping and *k* for *c* abbreviations in legal terminology; these *K* for *c* exchanges normally occur in a context that refers to calendars. The month of June was sacred to Juno and one possiblity is that *kalend-* instead of *calend-* reflects the invocation of Juno. More likely, however, as later Roman Church use tends to indicate (but not prove), this distinction between the *K* and the *c* in *calend-* may have been because the calendar was under the control of the *Pontifax Maximus* [Supreme Pontiff]. Whether an invocation of Juno or a fiat of the *Pontifax Maximus*, this *K/c* use in *calend-* may constitute a transcendent meaning. What the *K* for *C* replacement would mean in Carthage is obscure; still the name is a transcription of Phoenician *Kyriat Hedesh* [New City] into Latin and much depends upon the date of the document. Kappa-*k* also occurs on Latin inscriptions, but may simply be in use to differentiate Greek words from Latin ones; then again, depending upon context, the Kappa-*K* may be invoking the transcendent realm. There is some type of differentiation at work in the Roman use of the *K* and *c* exchange, but it is unclear if this indicates the same transcendent/mundane dichotomy.

While we can never be certain about Roman use, as unlike Greek *Beta/beta* we do not have enough examples to ever know, the situation in Anglo-Saxon England is clear. Kappa-*K* indicated the transcendent realm—whatever the person or object referred to. The *k* for *c* exchange shows up, for example, in references to the Judaeo-Christian God and to other gods; it appears in references to an anointed king as well as to a martyred king. The closed-lobe, or kyrios-*k* (ꝁ) appears during the ninth century, but only came into general use during the Benedictine Reform of the mid-tenth century. During this period, the dichotomy was changed to a trichotomy and kyrios-*k* (ꝁ) was reintroduced to maintain distinctions among the transcendent, the ecclesiastical (that is references to saints, ecclesiastics, church calendars, and so on), and the mundane realms. At the time of codification, however, *cyning* (cyn−ing, that is, of the kin > cyng > cing > king > modern "king") written with a *c* refers to the mundane realm. *Kyning* written with a *k* refers to the transcendent realm.

That the difference in letter symbol reflects the distinction between the transcendent and the mundane is not very surprising. While occasionally embodied in one person in antiquity, the different functions of religion (transcendent) and government (mundane) had already been outlined back at Akkad. In Medieval terms, these functions are better known as the division between Church and State.

Because the kappa-*K* indicates the transcendent realm, its use is not restricted to the masculine gender. During the entire Medieval period, the church is referred to as feminine, the state as masculine. (This gender distinction probably dates back to prehistoric times; statuettes from as far back as 22,000 BCE seem to be of priestesses. In Akkad, religion was the province of women and government the province of men.) One example of this gendered distinction between the mundane and the transcendent appears on folio 117v, lines 5-9 of *Cotton Vitellius A.XV* (Figure 7.3, page 121). The reference occurs in "Alexander's Letter" where six gods (*siehst Ky*[n]/*ing*) of various peoples are being discussed (lines 4-5). The specific reference is in lines 6-9 and refers to two God-threesomes (*tu trio*) of the sun and the moon found [among] the *indisc* (Indian-ish) and *grecisc* (Greek-ish) peoples. The sun threesome is "wæpned *cynnes*" (of weapon kin [masculine]) while the moon threesome is "wif *Kynnes*" (of wife kin [feminine]).

Among the distinctions that were maintained in the forms of the symbol *k*, the most important are the shape and the size. In earlier OE texts, if the reference is to a god, the *K* is always larger than the body text, while if the *k* is used to denote a mundane ruler in a transcendent aspect it may be either somewhat larger or the same size as the body text.

Another distinction used between *cyn-* and *Kyn-* depends upon whether or not the reference is specifically to a God as a word or as a part of a phrase. While *cyning*, for

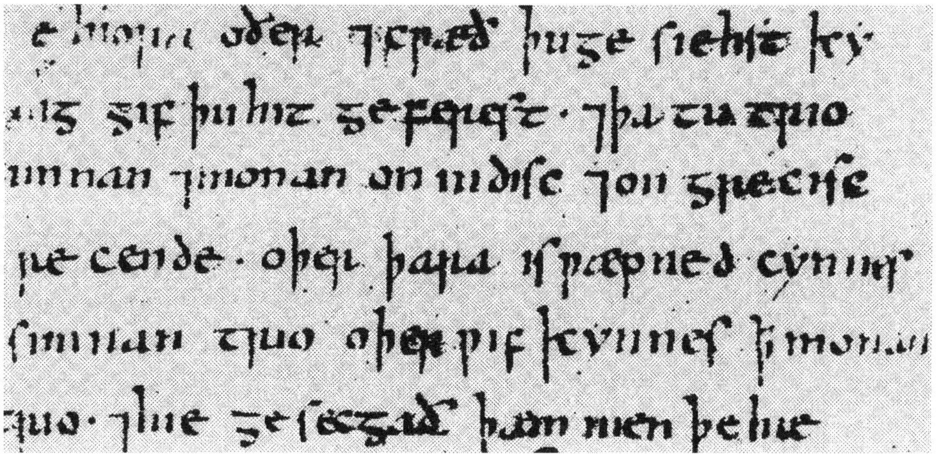

Fig. 7.3 The gender distinction between *K* and *c* in BL CV A.xv, on folio 117v, lines 4-9.

example, may or may not be used as part of a compound word, *Kyning* is always separated from preceding and following expressions. *Kyning* is never written as a compound word. In other words, when the reference is to a God, as the *word* "God," the OE will be spelled *Kyning*, and written by itself. When the reference is a phrase, for example, *wuldor cyning* [Honor/Glory King] or *micla cynincg* [Great King] (*Paris Psalter*, Ps:94.3) the term may be spelled with a *c* as the entire phrase refers to God but the single word (*cyning*) by itself does not.

Similarly, the word "king" may not necessarily refer to a man. How could a masculine noun refer to a feminine "thing"? In modern English, "king" applies to both the masculine gender and sex. Old English was not as restricted. While words had a gender (masculine, feminine, and neuter), the gender was not specifically linked to the physical sex of an object. *Kyning*, as all OE words ending in -ing or -ung, is one of those quasi-participial words that are grammatically **epicene**. That is, they take their gender from the *context*. These words default to masculine gender if nothing indicates otherwise.

The expression *kyning* written with a *k* appears, for example, in Cotton Vitellius A.XV, second manuscript. This manuscript is the *Nowell Codex* and contains the poem, "Beowulf." On folio 144r (old numbering), line 12, we find: Kynınʒ ymb ꝺoꝺe- (*Kyning ymb eode* [literally, King around went everywhere]), a common allusion to the Judaeo-Christian God in Old English texts. Here the phrase occurs amid a lengthy description and discussion of Wealþeow, *ides* [a female intermediary between a people and the transcedent realm, that is, a priestess] *helminga* [of the Helming] and *cwen* [queen] of the Danes by marriage to their king, Hroðgar. Treaty marriages and the role of women as "peace-weavers" are well known. ("Peace-weaver" is a much kinder way of saying a diplomatic marriage for advantage.) As this particular peace-weaver is a priestess among her own people, the point is made that one of the functions of a peace-weaver is the transcendent welfare of her husband's people.

On folio 147r, lines 11-12, we find Kyning /wuldor (Kyning wuldor [Glory or Honor King]), another common Old English way to refer to God. The final occurrence of the distinction between *K* and *c* in this article appears on f. 201v. This leaf is badly damaged by fire and time. Editors have done their best, yet, there is an expression missing in line 15 of f. 201v. When we compare the use of Kyninȝ (Kyning) in line 15 with pyrulocyninȝ (wyruldcyning [worldking]) in line 19 (Figure 7.4), we are left with an unanswerable question.

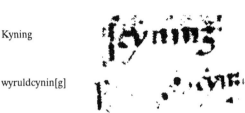

Kyning

wyruldcynin[g]

Fig. 7.4 Folio 201v. The two "kings"

Are the twelve men (apostles?) circling around the burial barrow mourning their king, or is their king being placed in God's hands while they mourn? If the latter, there is a nice distinction implied between the transcedent and the mundane rulers. (Beowulf was the best of mundane kings; but he was not a transcendent King).

l All *l*'s are descendants of the Semitic *lamed* (Greek *lambda*). The symbol has two forms. The two forms are easy to distinguish and the difference has been noted by many paleographers. [19] The distinction between the two forms persisted into the Renaissance.

　ι 1. The symbol is written between the ascender line and the baseline (ι). The form represents a clear-*l* [l].

　ι 2. The symbol is written between the ascender line and the medial position below the baseline (ι). The form represents a dark-*l* [ł].

m *M* derives from Semitic *mem* (Greek *mu*). This symbol has two forms.

　m 1. Minuscule-*m*. The symbol has straight legs.

　ന 2. Uncial-*m* (ന). As all the rounded symbols, the form is influenced by Semitic symbol sets. The form is used in both liturgical and secular texts to mark quantitative differences, and has a role in writing musical notation.

n Our modern *n* derives from the Semitic *nun* (Greek *nu*). There are two forms of this symbol. Both forms are used in both vernacular and Latin texts. Both large and bilinear forms of *n*'s are used to mark "begin phrase."

　n 1. Straight-legged *n*. The same symbol is employed in both Latin and the vernaculars. The apparent dissimilarities are due to script-model.

　ᚻ 2. Uncial-n. This form is used whenever a quantitative difference is to be indicated—both in minuscule and majuscule forms, and is used both medially (inside words) and finally.

ŋ Normally classified as a tailed-*n*, this form represents an **eng** (Greek *nn*) and is a phone distinct from the *n* phone. An African Greco-Semitic form, it is a combination of *n* + *g*, the tail indicates the tail on the symbol *g*. This is the velar (back of the throat, but not guttural) nasal form identified, and used as *eng* under IPA [ŋ]. *Eng* accepts both quantititive and stress distinctions. Quantity is indicated by expansion; stress may be indicated by a lengthening of the tail or an increase in height—depending upon the use at a given *scriptorium*.

o   *O* derives from *ayin* in the Semitic symbol set (Greek *omicron*). The form with a flat-left side (o) is used in OE. [20] The phone originally had the form of a circle (o), even in the Semitic symbol sets.

p   Only one form is used (p). There are very few native words that begin with the letter *p*. The form is a derivative of Semitic *pe*. (*Pe* can also be pronounced *ph*.)

q   *Q* is the Semitic *qoph*. It was taken into archaic Greek as it was written in early Phoenician. There are no native English words that begin with *q*, thus, only one form is used (q).

r   This symbol is derived from Semitic *resh*. Archaic Greek (*Rho*) borrowed the Phoenician form without any changes. With the change from inscription to writing on tablets and papyrus, the symbol acquired its more familiar round bow (*P*). It seems to have acquired its right-hand leg, in a very attenuated form, sometime during the second or first centuries BCE somewhere in North Africa.

There are three basic constant forms of this symbol used in the ASPA; one from each of the three major script-models. The differences among the symbol-forms *may* indicate the amount of trill the symbol received, that is, heavy, average, or light. Alternatively, these differences *may* indicate a perceived distinction among the types of trill or roll: alveolar (trilled), frontal (flap), and velar (rolled) sounds. These distinctions may also refer to both type *and* quantity. Even being relatively certain that the three most common phones for *r* existed, and even which form represents which *r*, does not tell us how the *r* was actually pronounced.

r/ɲ   1. The Latin-*r* (r) and the insular-*r* (ɲ) are actually the same basic form; both are derivations of an earlier Latin-cursive-*r*. The insular-*r* is simply an extended-limb version of the Latin cursive form. The form accepts stress notation. Sometimes the descender is notably curtailed and the form may be confused with *n*, This symbol is the central phone.

2   2. Semitic-*r*. The model for the Semitic 2-shaped-*r* is one of the five Palmyrene *r* symbol forms. Early forms, while definitely 2-shaped, are not as angular as either the Benventan or much later Gothic forms. The form appears both with and without a left-hand minim, particularly when preceded by an o (ор or о2). The symbol may represent either a heavy trill or an alveolar-*r*—or perhaps both.

R   3. Greek short-leg-r is normally used in a subscript position (-eR) as in, for example, the *Épinal Glossary* and the *Bangor Collectarium*. The symbol may represent either a light trill or a frontal-*r*. (See comment above.)

s   *S* derives from the Semitic *Shin/sin*. Greek *sigma* is from *sin*. (Neither Greek nor Latin has a *sh* phone.) The *sh* phone is represented in OE by *sc*. *S* is a sibilant, that is, it "hisses." We cannot know the exact pronunciation of the *s* phones.

There are three basic constant forms of this symbol in the ASPA. Like *a*, *e*, *r*, and *u*, the different shapes are taken from the three major script-models, and designate three distinct phones.

ſ   1. Latin-*s*. This is the central form. It is from an early Latin cursive model. While the form varies according to script-model, the basic shape remains constant. It represents the central phone—whatever that may have been.

ᶘ   2. Semitic- or low-*s*. The form represents the symbol tsade-sofi (final tsadik). It cannot be ascertained whether this *s* came from cursive Hebrew, Punic, or Syriac models, as all the forms represent the symbol tsade-sofi in these alpha-symbol sets. The low-*s may* indicate the sibilant *tz*. The symbol represents a clear phone.

s   3. Greek-*s*. This symbol is called a sigmoid-*s* because it both resembles, and is, a Greek final sigma. While the extremely systematic arrangement indicates that the phone was "muddy," it can not be determined precisely what the Anglo-Saxons considered "muddy."

t   *T* is from Semitic *tof* (Greek *Tau*) and the oldest Phoenician form is *t*. The form of *t* (ᴛ) with a straight-back appears in OE.

u   As we have already seen in our discussion of *f*, the Semitic *vav* is a many faceted symbol fathering *f*, *u*, *v*, *w*, and, as it turns out, *y*. *Y* is the *i*-mutation of vav-upsilon [u > eu > ii/y]. This sometimes leads to confusion.

Fig. 7.5 The Semitic, Latin, and Greek models of the three *u*-phones

    There are three forms of *u* symbols employed in the ASPA symbol-set. Two forms of the symbol frequently have been misclassified as *y*. (Figure 7.5) [21].

u   1. Latin-*u*. This symbol is the central form. The alternate forms of Latin-*u*, a Greek *deuteros* (Ꭹ) and a Latin-*v*, do not represent different phones. *U* and *v* are the same phone. The angular form comes from inscriptions (carved), the rounded form from cursive writing. *Deuteros* means second, as in Deuteronomy (second law, recapitulation), and is used as a musical direction. (The only noticeable change in the Northumbrian secular fonts, across more than three hundred years, was to replace the *u*-form with the *v*-form. Presumably this was to avoid confusion between *u* and aleph-*a*.)

ϝ   2. Semitic-*u*. While sometimes called the "f-form of y," the symbol represents a "shu*ruq*," the Hebrew vocalic-*vav*. The "Interpretation of the Acrostic Letters from Psalm 119 (118)," [22] on folio 6v of the *Vespasian Psalter* marks the difference between the consonantal *vav* [v] and the vocalic *vav* [u]. The name of the form in the explanation of the acrostic is written with a *deuteros*, that is, second form, Ꭹᴁll (vali), not first form, Uᴁll (uali). [23] The symbol represents a clear *u* sound. It may express the *i*-umlaut of the long vowel. [24]

Ꭹ   3. Greek-*u*. This symbol is sometimes referred to as a "horned-y." If something looks different it *is* different. The two phones, *y* and *u* were differentiated among the Ionic and Western Greek speakers by the 4th century BCE.

    The "horned-*u*" is directly from Greek cursive forms in use by the 2nd century CE. In the West Saxon dialect, the symbol is usually written with a very short tail and confined between the head- and baselines. The interlinear translation of the Psalms found in the *Vespasian Psalter* (BL. Cotton Vespasian A.1) is in the Mercian dialect. In this dialect, the form apparently accepted stress and indicated it by an extension of the "tail." Nevertheless, the typical form of the Greek-*u* is confined between the head-

and baselines. The symbol represents a muddy or blurred sound. It *may* express the *i*-umlaut of the short vowel. [25]

x   Latin-*x* derives its form from Etruscan. This form is the same in both Latin and OE (x). It sometimes occurs with an elongated cross-stroke which indicates stress.

γ   Greek-*y* (modern French *i*-Grec; OE grecisca-*y*) is the straight limbed form (γ) and is taken directly from one of the early Phoenician variant forms. (As we have seen, *vav* has four possible phones. It should not be surprising that some Phoenician symbol-sets had four variants forms.)

      Greek-*y* represents the doubled *i*-phone (*ii*), that is, the *i*-mutation of *u*. The doubling of symbols to represent a distinction between phones is common in Greek. Greek-*y* (*ii*) parallels the doubled *o*-form, the *o*-mega (originally written *oo*). This fact explains why the form was, and is, called the Greek-*y* (pronounced *ee*) to distinguish it from the Semitic *vav*, that is, *u*, *v*, *w*, or *f*.

z   One form is used for this symbol (z). Like the *x*, it also occurs with an elongated downstroke indicating stress.

ꝺ   This is the barred- or crossed-*d*. Originally, the straight- and round-*d*'s indicated two distinct phones: the palatal stop (d) and the palatal fricative (ꝺ). When in the next stage of codification straight-*d* was assigned to Latin and round-*d* to OE, barred-*d* was reserved for the vernacular symbol set to represent the palatal fricative.

Futhark

þ   The *thorn* derives from Futhark. Today the *thorn* is said to represent the unvoiced dental fricative (or spirant) and barred-*d* the voiced dental fricative. While comments such as "these two letters, þ and ð, are virtual alternatives in OE writing," are very frequent in Old English textbooks and grammars, [26] the two are used too systematically to accept this assessment unconditionally. Neil R. Ker, a major authority on Anglo-Saxon paleography also has reservations; he notes that *thorn* (þ) is usually used initially and barred-*d* (ð) medially or finally. [27] The manuscripts support Ker's conclusion. For example, written without a space, we find *syððan* (since); written with a space, *syð þan*. Further, much depends upon time and dialect. The barred-*d* started out as a palatal, but over time, seems to have moved forward and become a dental. It seems more likely that the seemingly indiscriminate use of the forms is attributable to scribal dialects as well as the time when a particular manuscript was written.

ƿ   The *wyn* also derives from Futhark. The symbol represents a *w* (double-*u*). Until *wyn* was added to the symbol-set, *w* was represented by either one or two *u*'s. The Futhark form already appears in the *Épinal Glossary*, for example, on folio 6, column d, line 34: norþ pinꝺ (north wind).

c   For angled-*c*, see *c*, above.

Digraphs

There were only two digraphs (diphthongs) at the time of codification. Futhorc, the Anglo-Saxon Runic alphabet that was an expansion of the Germanic Futhark symbol set, appears sometime during the mid-7th century. Futhorc also included two digraphs: *ea* and *io*. (The *aesc* symbol was added around the same time; however, *aesc* is neither a digraph nor a diphthong.) Three other digraphs, *ei, oe* and *oi*, occur in the earliest texts, but had already fallen into disuse as of the time of the codification of the ASPA. These obsolete forms occur primarily in names. Names, in particular, preserve "archaic" or obsolete spellings. These three digraphs probably are remnants of older phonological combinations. The forms are discussed in Campbell under Number 60 (see note 17). Practically all examples of the digraph forms are given in Campbell, Numbers 198-200. Ligatured *a + e* represents the Latin diphthong.

The *ae* ligature is very rare in early texts. If the ligatured form did appear, it was written as two equal height symbols and never stressed. The vowel pair is normally written **in diæresis** (that is, as two separate symbols) in early Latin texts, and most commonly appears assigned to different expressions separated by a space. When the ligatured form was used, it represented the Latin diphthong and was not part of the vernacular symbol set. A somewhat modified ligatured form first appears in OE texts in Font Four of Anglo-Saxon Chronicle A (*Parker Chronicles and Laws*, Corpus Christi College, Cambridge MS 173).

ea The vowel pair occurs in four forms: separated (in diæresis), ligatured either second symbol (eA) or first high (Ea)–depending upon the period, [28] and ligatured–even height (diphthong). The "swallowed" ligature (ɛ̃) where the *e* appears to encompass the *a* is a monophthong. Either member of the vowel pair may be extended, that is, a tongue may be added to the *e*, or a trailer added to the *a*.

ιo The vowel pair very rarely appears ligatured. It most commonly appears as separate symbols of equal height, and appears to be in diæresis. (This may account for its dialectic-connected appearance alongside ɛð in later documents.) When written as what may be called a diphthong, that is, the two forms are connected by a trailer on the *i*, it usually appears as first member high.

These 46 graphs comprise the symbol-set of the Anglo-Saxon Phonetic Alphabet. While the lower case symbol set of the ASPA is larger than our modern English lower case symbol set, it essentially parallels in size the substantially more than 26 lower case alpha-symbols used in modern languages such as German, Spanish, Italian, or French.

The care with which the creators of the ASPA chose their graphic symbols expresses an acute awareness of phonemic nuances on their part. It also displays a thorough knowledge of the origin and distribution of the major language symbol sets. There is little doubt that the assignment of phones was thoroughly methodical. Latin forms are systematically used for central sounds. With the one exception of the Aramaic *aesc*, which like Latin and English has some schwa, Semitic forms are used for clear, and Greek forms for muddy or mixed sounds.

The codifiers brought all their diverse knowledge to the creation of a "universal" alphabetic symbol-set. Sometime shortly after the codification of the ASPA, the Anglo-Saxons added a refinement to their writing system.

Chapter Eight

SEPARATE VOICES

With our twenty-twenty hindsight, we know that script-style differentiation dates back to Sumer and Akkad. From its origins as a sign of ethnic identity, with script and language united, script-differentiation extended to indicate differences by domain, by formality, and by religious affiliation. With the coming of Empires, territorial scripts-by-ethnos within a *koine* were added to the list. Script differentiation-by-domain shows up as part of the Anglo-Celtic writing system used at Rath Melsigi; likewise, script-by-formality and affiliation appear. Documents in Latin, appear written in territorial scripts and fonts that are unmistakably "English"; however, script-by-language, the age-old flag of identity, is utterly *absent* from the earliest vernacular writing. Nevertheless, script-by-language as identity is a very well known and well documented practice of the Anglo-Saxons. Why is it missing from their earliest documents? When was script-by-language added to the *stæfwritung* system? What were the results of this addition? Like practically everything else associated with writing systems, we have to put on our detective hats, pull out our magnifying glasses, and search for beginnings.

The codifiers of the *stæfwritung* system could not help but know all about script-by-language as identity; every writing system descended from the Northwest-Semitic group used it. They were perfectly aware that different peoples used different scripts—and why; their models for the ASPA and their own writing system tell us that. Why, then, is script-by-language missing from Stage 1 of codification? Because the Celtic inhabitants of the Island still thought of themselves as *Romani*; the model for these Anglo-Celtic peoples was the Roman writing system.

In Imperial practice, script differentiation by language was used on formal inscriptions. These bi-ethnic inscriptions are called "bilinguals." On rare occasions, after the elevation of Christianity to the state religion of the Empire, script-by-ethnos was used for the Scriptures. The *Codex Bezae* (Cambridge, University Library, MS II.41) is one of these rare bi-ethnic codices. Every document has a story to tell us, if we will listen to it.

Now missing 128 leaves, the *Bezae* originally contained a facing page Latin and Greek rendition of the Gospels, the Catholic Epistles, and Acts. The Greek text is written in a Greek Biblical Uncial script and the Latin is written in a Latin Biblical Uncial script. The manuscript was produced sometime around the end of the 4th century. Scholars today feel that the evidence points to the important Roman Law school at Berytus (Beirut) as its place of origin because of the strong similarities between the scripts of the *Bezae* and of the law school. The ancient practice of placing the master text to the right side reinforces the evidence of the scripts as to Beirut as the site of origin. The Latin text is to the right, the Greek to the left. In the 4th century, only in a major center of Latin learning would the Latin be placed to the right as the master text.

The number of hands, nine or more scribes made corrections to the text (mainly the Greek) until as late as 700 CE, does not hide the fact that the codex itself was written and formatted by one scribe. The primary scribe has some striking peculiarities: his Latin script is clearly influenced by Greek models, but his Greek script is unlike any other Greek Biblical uncials from around the same period. This Greek script is so different and so carefully mimics the Latin forms that it shouts different party. Which party? We do not know.

When the codex is open for reading, the two languages face each other. Because the pages contain the same contents in each language, the right-hand margins vary and appear "ragged" to modern eyes. This impression is misleading. The pages of the *Bezae* are so carefully designed and balanced, both as to script-styles and as to content, that from a distance we could at first assume that the text is written in one language—except that the **texture** is different.

Writing upon a page makes a repetitive pattern very similar to a repetitive flower pattern on wallpaper or cloth. A font or script in a heavy style gives a very different pattern than one in a light style. The blocks of pattern create a texture on the printed or written pages of a book. When we look at the *Bezae* from a reading distance, we know that the different textures told us the truth. With script-language differentiation, a reader knew what language he or she was reading merely from the texture of the page.

The *Bezae*, nevertheless, is a rare exception to normal Roman practice. In direct contrast with formal and official documents, Latin *texts* differentiated script-by-domain (secular versus sacred), script-by-formality (official versus unofficial), and script-by-affiliation (party or territory), but, except for the occasional codex such as the *Bezae*, documents written in Latin differentiated by territorial scripts, but did *not* differentiate-by-language. They did not need to: for *Romani*, Latin was the language of the West.

Over in Anglo-Celtic England, Latin sacred texts were written in formal liturgical book hands; secular texts in informal minuscules. Willibrord's marginal note is in an informal secular font; the *Calendar* is in a formal liturgical hand. Both fonts on the Calendar are territorial scripts, as is the note about Anglo-Saxon "Hilda abbess." Following the usual practice of their Celtic-*Romani* teachers, the earliest Old English words and names appear in the same font as the Latin text. The texture of the writing gives no clues to a reader as to the languages on the pages. The Anglo-Saxons, however, clearly did not consider themselves *Romani*. Sometime after codification but before 731, the Anglo-Saxon codifiers of *stæfwritung* broke away from the practices of their Celtic mentors and determined to assert their ethnic identity. Script-by-language should be applied to distinguish the *Englisc* from the Romans.

Willibrord's *Calendar* tells us that the ASPA was codified before he went haring off to Frisia in 690. It also tells us that script-by-domain differentiation was applied to distinguish liturgical from secular texts. The *Calendar* does not tell us when Stage 2 of codification occurred; for that we must look elsewhere.

The Anglo-Saxons were missionaries and educators. Manuscripts containing Old English pop up in places all over Western Europe. For example, an eleventh-century collection of Old English religious poetry and homilies resides at the Vercelli Library in Italy and is known as *The Vercelli Book* (Vercelli Biblioteca Capitolare CXVII); no one knows how the book got there. . . or why. Two of the three earliest manuscripts containing Old English are not in England.

The *Épinal Glossary*, Bibliothèque Municipale, MS 72 (Manuscript number 72 in the Municipal Library at Épinal) resides in northeast France. The *Épinal* is an important document in many ways. It gives us our earliest evidence for the use of the ASPA in Old English words. It tells us something about the speed of dissemination of the new writing system; it is our only evidence that codification included spelling reforms. Finally, the *Épinal* gives us our lower time limit on stage 2 in the codification of the *stæfwriting* system.

The leaves of the *Épinal* are divided into many paired columns. Latin words are listed alphabetically and a definition (**gloss**) appears opposite each word (Plate 8.1). The majority of the glosses are in Latin; however, whenever the scribes knew the Old English for something, they translated the term.

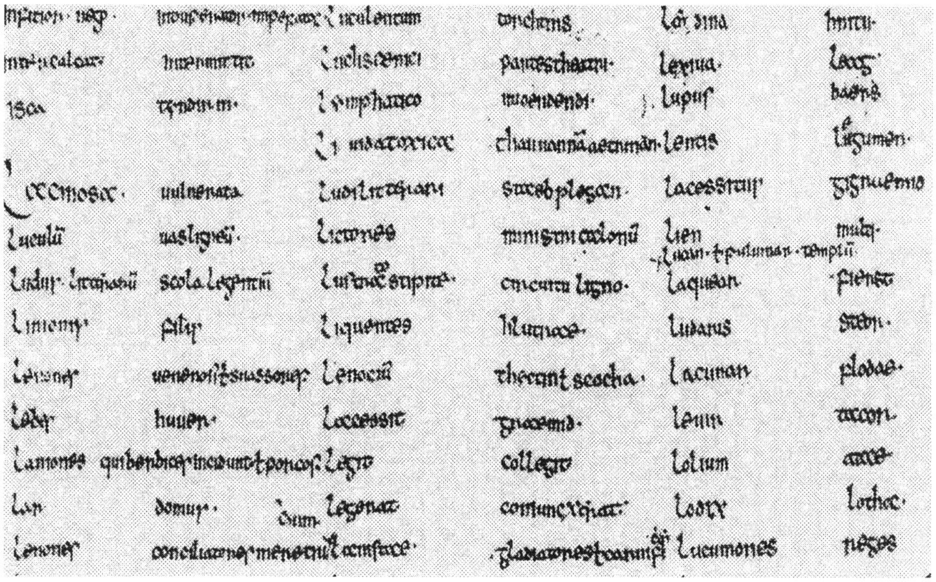

Pl. 8.1. *Épinal Glossary*, fol. 13, columns A-F. lines 5-17.

We know that the scribes were Anglo-Saxons because of the glosses in Old English. The script tells us that they were trained in the Anglo-Celtic school. The text is written in an insular cursive font; the variant forms assigned by the ASPA are written in insular uncials. We also know that most of the scribes were older and that one had been trained fairly recently.

Scribes, in general, lead peaceful and long lives. Their training is such, their responses so automatic, that they find it hard to adjust to changes. As a change to a writing system means a change to identity, scribes can also be very obstinate about innovations to a writing system (as we shall see in some amusing demonstrations of this trait). Even when they are acting under orders to change official script styles, their training interferes. Orders are orders, and they will try to learn the new way, but their products show up as a medley of the new and the old script-styles. A scribe accustomed to writing bookhands will inadvertently use the wrong script-style when writing the vernacular, and *vice versa*. One long-lived scribe can throw a decided monkey-wrench into the dating works. These very facts, however, hand us clues. While all the scribes of the *Épinal* use the same graphic assignments as those we saw in Willibrord's marginal note, only one of them uses the new symbols assigned to Old English.

Although there is some disagreement about the exact date of the manuscript, we can safely place it to no later than 690—and almost certainly much earlier. Page after page of the *Épinal* exhibits the phonetically distinct forms of Stage 1 of *stæfwritung*. Page after page of the *Épinal* also exhibits an intermediate stage between the assignment of the new symbol phones and their adoption into scribal training methods.

The three *a* phones that occur in both Latin and Old English follow the same phonetic distinctions: Latin-*a* central, aleph-*a* clear, and alpha-*a* muddy. All five forms of *a* (ɑ, ɑ, ɑ, Æ, Œ) appear, as well as Latin *ae* and, in *Englisc* words, *ae* alongside the Old English monophthong *Æ*. Archaic combinations of vowels, such as Æɑ (aea) and Æɒ (aeo), also occur.

There are four forms of *r* (ɲ, r, ꝛ, R). The 2–shaped–*r* form after *o* (oꝛ) is considered a characteristic of the twelfth-century "Gothic" fonts, but the symbol already appears in the *Épinal*. We see them in words such as oꝛꞇuꞅ (*ortus*–literally "beginnings," but much depends upon context) and ɲɪꞃᴍɑꞇoꝛ (*firmator*–confirmer [one who confirms], establisher [one who establishes]).

Long and sigmoid-*s* (ꞅ, s), as well as Semitic, Latin, and Greek-*e* (Ƈ, e, ɛ) are used in both languages. Most of the scribes still differentiate between dental stop-*d* (d) and palatal fricative-*d* (ð). We find *thorn* (þ), one of the symbols taken into the *stæfwritung* symbol set from Futhark, in a few Old English words (noɲþ pɪnð–north wind); but *th* is far more common for *thorn* in the Old English portions of the text. *Uu* for *w* is more frequent than *wyn* (w). The forms that represent Old English phones, *wyn*, *thorn*, and barred-*d*, appear only in Old English words, naturally enough, but only in the work of *one* of the scribes. This same scribe also uses the monophthong forms of *aesc* (Æ, Œ), when none of the other scribes do.

The symbol assignments tell us that the ASPA was already codified. But they also tell us that a spelling reform was instituted along with the codification of the ASPA. Some early codices and charters contain Anglo-Saxon and Anglo-British names, but names retain archaic spelling centuries after all else has changed. The *Épinal* gives us ordinary words, not names. The inclusion of archaic forms, such as Æɑ (aea) and Æɒ (aeo), in the hands of most of the scribes, but not all, tell us that new scribes were being trained in a new spelling system. It also shows us that codification of the ASPA was done in two stages: first symbol assignment, then spelling reform. With the exception of names, which retain archaic spelling, these ꬱ (aea) and ꬴ (aeo) combinations do not appear in later documents. We know of later attempts to reform the spelling system; the *Épinal* remains our only evidence for an earlier reformation.

The hand of the one scribe that uses the complete ASPA tells us even more: *the same script is used for both Latin and Old English*. There is no indication at all of script-style distinction by language.

The *Épinal Glossary* confirms that the ASPA was codified before Willibrord left for Frisia. It also tells us that the codifiers were perfectly aware of the limitations and constraints imposed upon scribes by their training as well as the identity crisis imposed by a change to a writing system. Disseminating changes takes time. The system was still so new at the time the *Épinal* was compiled that only new scribes were being trained in the new symbol assignment system. (We will soon see a later example of older scribes undergoing training in the new system—with varying degrees of success.) The *Épinal* also establishes that, although different symbols were being used for the vernacular, script differentiation by language was still not part of the system. Only one of the scribes had been trained in the new system and he did not differentiate by script-style. He did do something else, however; he not only used *wyn, thorn, barred-d*, and *aesc*, this same young scribe is responsible for the **bound form** of the symbol-pair *or* (ᴓ).

Symbols may be **bound** or **free**. When a given group of symbols becomes the normal way to state that particular expression, this is termed a bound form. Bound forms have become "the way x is written" and give no information as to phonological change. On the other hand, if the symbols do not occur in the same order, then they are not another occurrence of a set, but a second and different expression. In the word, "over*ture*," for example, *er* and *re* are different. Both expressions are free, that is, they occur both ligatured and separately. Free expressions give us information as to changing phonology.

If bound forms are useless in terms of tracking phonological changes, they are splendid resources for the writing historian and the paleographer. Ideographs are very important to us—if we are to sort out the evidence. Bound forms are a major source of scribal ideographs. We have run into ideographs before, but their importance cannot be overemphasized—even if scribal training was originally misunderstood.

Although the beginning lies further in the past, the field of modern Western paleography took shape during the 1830's and 1840's. This was a period of intense nationalism and a corresponding renewed interest in ethnic "antiquities." While some of the people interested in these new-again fields were degreed scholars, most were enthusiastic gentlemen amateurs—well-to-do *Victorian* gentlemen amateurs.

The Chinese fad began in the late 18th and reached its height during the 19th century. These pioneering modern Western paleographers knew that, in the Orient, calligraphy was (and always has been) considered the highest form of art. In the Chinese, Japanese, and Arabic traditions, the gentlemanly art of calligraphy has flourished right alongside the working profession of a scribe. In these parts of the world, nobody confuses a calligrapher with a scribe. As usual, if something borrowed can be misunderstood, it will be.

Our Victorian gentlemen amateurs looked at the superbly executed Biblical scripts and fonts in the manuscripts and decided that the writing in the manuscripts was a work of art: calligraphy. (One such book from 1843 goes so far as to refer to the "calligraphic excellence" of a manuscript.) Instead of asking professional scribes how they worked, they asked calligraphers. This was a serious mistake and led to some very peculiar conclusions about the training, abilities, and duties of a professional scribe. [1] There is a very important difference in function between the two professions. Calligraphers call attention to the writing; scribes to what is written.

A calligrapher is a decorative artist. Every item proceeding from the pen of a competent calligrapher is an individual work of art. A calligrapher warms up by practicing the three basic strokes—the vertical line (the minim), the curve (one-half of an *o*), and the horizontal line (the hasta). When asked to use a certain design, a calligrapher either mentally visualizes the script, if he or she knows it, or looks it up in one of the hundreds of books of models available to her or him. If a calligrapher writes 100 invitations, we have 100 separate, unsigned, pieces of artwork. No two invitations will be written automatically and without thought. A calligrapher may develop an identifiable style, but he does not acquire unchanging ideographs.

A scribe is a master craftsman. Professional scribes do acquire ideographs; but only senior journeymen and masters have them. Just as a master carpenter does not have to think about how he holds a saw, the master scribe does not have to think about how he holds a pen or writes a specific script. The script or font has become part of him to the extent that the scribe will write the appropriate script according to the feel of the pen he picks up.

Scribal working conditions frequently were less than ideal. Scribes sometimes worked with cold hands in unheated rooms. Nevertheless, once a scribe has acquired his identifying ideographs he will always write the forms the same way. The professional scribe develops certain ways of writing, for example, ɑſ, Æſ, or ꝭ in Old English and ꝏ, ꝕ, and ꝓ in Latin—all of which are bound forms. *Scribal ideographs are the permanent identification of a given scribe; they do not change.*

Small and subtle differences can be found among any symbols, but bound forms are most revealing of the hand of a specific scribe. Scribal identification can be difficult: scribes were trained to avoid obvious differences. Professional scribes do not call attention to the writing, but to what is written. Master scribes can make a manuscript appear as if only one hand wrote it. One such manuscript is the *Moore Bede*.

The *Moore Bede* (MS Kk.v.16, University Library, Cambridge) is the oldest known text of Bede's *Historia Ecclesiastica*. Because of assorted entries written on the blank verso side of the last leaf, we know that the manuscript was completed before 737. The *Moore*, among other things, tells us when Stage 2 of codification occurred. These "other things" are just as important to our understanding of a manuscript society. The manuscript has quite a tale to tell us.

Even if we did not know that Bede was affiliated with the Roman parties, the format, size and script of the *Moore* would tell us that we are looking at a text authored by a member of this group. The leaves are 29cm (11.69") high by 21.3cm (8.29") wide in accordance with Alexandrian-Roman size practices for authoritative but non-liturgical texts. Similarly, the text is written across the full width of the page as prescribed for non-canonical works of this affiliation. The script is more or less a secular Anglo-Saxon minuscule, the mutation of the Greco-Roman half-uncial used by these groups.

In the nineteenth century, people guessed that the *Moore* was written on the continent, possibly at Echternach, Willibrord's foundation. But Willibrord, affiliated with the Anglo-Celtic factions and still alive at the time the *Moore* was produced, used an insular minuscule as a secular script. The script tells us that the manuscript was written at a site affiliated with the London and Canterbury factions.

The manuscript itself points to Bede's own Wearmouth-Jarrow as the site of origination and to a date sometime around 731.

Wearmouth and Jarrow are known to have had superior *scriptoria*. We would expect a production originating from such a source to appear professional. We would not expect their scribes to call attention to the writing. Bede is known to have had two scribes. The text of the manuscript is written by two scribes.

Both scribes have identifying ideographs and both were Masters. Both scribes give evidence that the transition from Insular minuscule to Anglo-Saxon minuscule is fairly recent.

Scribe 1's angle of attack (the approach stroke when beginning a symbol) is steeper than that of Scribe 2. This steeper angle results in more pointed forms; nevertheless, Scribe 1 still tends to incorporate wedges, particularly on his long-*s* (ſ). The graphs of Scribe 2 are distinctly rounder and he still tends towards the incorporated wedges of Insular fonts, particularly on his 'l', 'm', and 'n'.

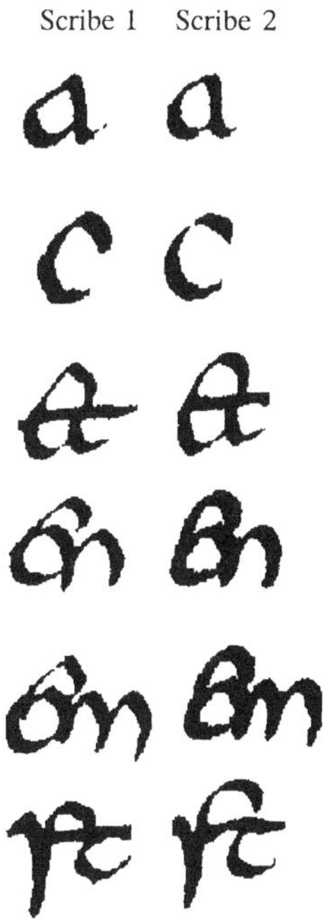

They both form their *a*'s differently. The 'a' of Scribe 1 is semi-pointed; he flattens the lobe to achieve a pointed appearance. The 'a' of Scribe 2 is round. Scribe 1 tends to flatten his *c*'s which also tends to add a pointed appearance. Their *e* graphs are also quite different: Scribe 1's *e* is flattened and pointed while Scribe 2's *e* is rounded. The clearest differences, however, are found in the bound forms: et, en, em, and st (Figure 8.1).

Scribe 1's *e* in ligature are at a steeper angle. He connects his *e*- to the following graph by writing the first stroke of the 'm' or 'n' as a curved continuation of the hasta (cross-stroke) on his *e*. Scribe 2 writes the hasta on his *e*, then runs back over the stroke to drop down to begin the next graph. When we look at the way the two scribes write the bound form *st*, we can see that Scribe 1 writes his long-*s* (ſ) much lower than does Scribe 2. The same two hands and their ideographs appear on every leaf of the manuscript.

So many of the medieval manuscripts are copies, that we are taken by surprise to find an original version of a text. Scholarly opinion places the *Moore Bede* as very close to the original text as written by Bede. It *is* very close. The *Moore Bede* is one of these unusual originals: it is a dictated text.

There are clear and easily visible differences between dictated and copied documents. If we examine documents from the aspect of vertical movement and the intrusiveness of trailers and tongued forms on the horizontal plane, we can see a marked difference between copied and dictated texts. A further obvious difference is in the number of abbreviations. Dictated texts are loaded with abbreviations; copied texts contain relatively few.

Copied (**conformal**) texts are evened out as much as possible without completely removing the horizontal and vertical indicators of speech rhythms. This does not imply that there will be no variants or errors; conformity is governed by levels of *permissible interpretation*. Even among copied texts, however, there are levels of conformity.

The level of conformity is absolute in Class One documents, Liturgical texts and publicly declared laws fall into this class. The text as written is master and no interpretations are permitted.

Scribe 1   Scribe 2

Fig. 8.1 The two hands of the *Moore Bede*.

Class two documents are conformal, but permit additions. Legal formulas must contain not only the correct wording, but, because the words had to be said correctly, they had to retain a higher level of vertical and horizontal movement. This class of document must also permit the inclusion of additions in the form of what is being sold or transferred as well as in the names of witnesses. Many existing charters fall into Class Two.

The third class of copied documents contains our largest group of existing texts. In this class we find that the rhythmic indicators are there, but minimized, and interpretation is left to the performer or reader. These texts are essentially nothing more than general guidelines. Class Three conformal documents are so numerous because they are designed to allow even an indifferent performer or public speaker to deliver a credible performance.

Because there are categories of copied, that is, conformal documents, we must examine the content to see into which category a copied document falls. When we arrive at a later period, we have an abundance of sermons, homilies, and Saints' Lives all of which are class three conformal documents. Both Wulfstan's and Ælfric's texts offer basic guidelines on *how* to say the words. While an experienced speaker knows when to add extra stress or to modify pace, a novice following directions *exactly* could deliver a passable, if uninspired, sermon. A gleeman (minstrel), though, had better supply appropriate dynamics and vary phrasing or he soon will be unemployed.

The notation is clearer in some font styles than in others. Formal book hands are designed to minimize vertical differences. The usual script designer's solution, for example, is to tilt the medial-*e* form (second level on the cube) to allow for ligatures. This technique is used, for instance, in the font of the *Paris Psalter*.

Among the five great poetic codices in Old English, The *Exeter Book*, The *Caedmon Manuscript*, and the *Vercelli Book* are class three copied texts. All three contain instructions indicating appropriate pauses and stressed vowels: interpretation is left to the reader or performer. The *Paris Psalter* is a chorale guide, a Class One conformal document. It gives instructions as to mode, psalm tone, chorus, and first, second, and third singer solo verses; but no allowance for individual interpretation. The *Nowell Codex*, the one that contains the famous "Beowulf" manuscript, is dictated.

Conformal texts are copied from an existing model. Dictated texts are exactly what this implies: a scribe or scribes writing down what is dictated by an author or performer. [2]

The contrasts between copied and dictated texts are striking. Dictated texts have a "busy" look or texture. This "busy" texture is the result of exaggerated movement on the vertical and horizontal planes as well as of the inclusion of many abbreviations. Abbreviations leave marks above (and sometimes below) the symbols, thus adding further "busyness" to the texture of the page.

First, dictated texts are marked by numerous variations in the spacing and clumping of syllables. Second, graph spacing varies greatly, for example, in the vowel pair *ea* we will meet eɑ, eɑ, e-ɑ, ɛɑ, and ɛɑ. A third marker is the large variety in the length of tongues and trailers on vowels, for instance, e, e-, e͝, e-, and on liquids, such as, l and ∟ or ɲ and ɲ∟. Exaggerated extensions at the headline of the symbol *t*, such as ⊂ and ⊏, for instance, are a fourth mark of a dictated text. Fifth, dictated texts display exaggerated vertical movement, such as, ð, ó, ó or ɑ́, ɑ, ɑ. Finally, dictated texts are packed with abbreviations, for example, ǣ, n̄, ȝ̄, on̄, m̄, ᴄ̄. For obvious reasons, scribes taking dictation made heavy use of abbreviations.

The *Moore Bede* exhibits every one of the markers of a dictated text. There are so many abbreviations that a reader would do well to have a crib sheet containing a list of abbreviations alongside him or her while reading the manuscript. The *Moore* has a wide variety in the spacing and clumping of syllables. We find decided variations in the length of tongues, trailers, and headlines. The text exhibits a great deal of vertical movement and there is no sign that the scribes tried to limit movement either horizontally or vertically. On the contrary, the scribes have faithfully recorded for us the author's voice.

Whether we accept Bede as the speaker or not (although the date alone makes anyone else rather unlikely), the person dictating was an experienced lecturer. While he does not slur his speech, he talks fluently and with speed. He tends to roll his *r*'s and hold his *f*'s. He also shows a strong tendency towards emphasis on second syllables in polysyllabic words. He employs the good instructor's use of stress to make a point. He does not fall into that unfortunate entertainer's habit of holding final *e*'s. When he does hold an *e* at the end of a sentence, it is that much more effective for its scarcity. His Latin is not Classical and quantitative; it is qualitative and shows much vertical and horizontal movement. With only 26 exceptions—people and locations written in Old English—throughout the manuscript *a* and *e* are separate vowels, not *ae*-ligature. He said, *a Equip; la Etitiae; Ca edmon; ca elum.*

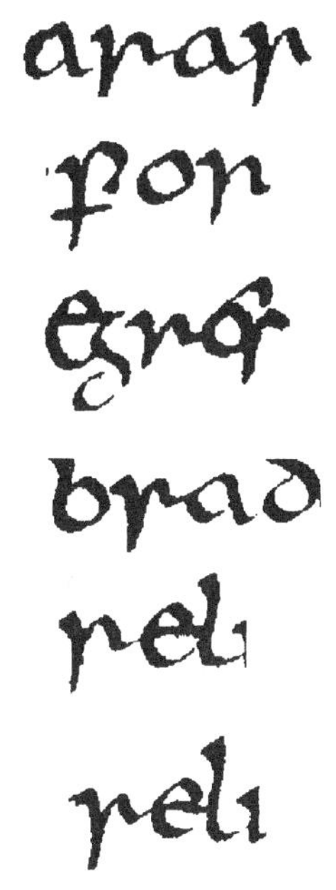

Figure 8.2 shows us a close-up of some examples of his rolled and clipped *r*'s, held *a*'s, stressed *e*'s, and vertical movement. The symbols have been enlarged for ease of examination; none of the examples are complete words and will not be translated. The first symbol cluster in the Figure is the combination *arar*. In the first pair of *ar*'s, the *a* does not have a trailer, but the *r* does; in the second pair, the *a* has a trailer, but the *r* does not. This tells us that the symbols were pronounced *ar_a_r*, (perhaps something along the lines of modern *a-far*?) with the second *r* clipped off. In the second example, *or, r* does not have extensions and therefore is not held. The third, *egres*, is two syllables. There is medial stress on *eg*, the *r* in *res* is held for a short time, and there is primary stress on the *es*. This would be pronounced as *eg r_Es*. In the fourth symbol cluster, *brad*, both the *r* and *a* are held sounds. This cluster would have been pronounced *br_a_d*. The last two examples are from the words *religios*- and *relict*- respectively; one by each scribe. We can see that in both cases, the speaker really rolled his *r*.

Fig. 8.2 *The Moore Bede*: horizontal and vertical movement

In addition to being dictated and one of those rare original texts, the *Moore Bede* tells us when Stage 2 of codification occurred. In this manuscript we find both Stages 1 and 2 of *stæfwriting* used consistently and systematically.

We have already noted that among the shared symbols, that is, symbols common to both Latin and Old English, the script is differentiated by the flat-backs on the Old English graphs. The *Historia* is written in Latin. Throughout the entire manuscript, Anglo-British and Anglo-Saxon names, and *only* Anglo-British and Anglo-Saxon names, are written in a flat-backed pointed Anglo-Saxon minuscule. Latin names are *never* written in the flat-backed script, and, raising all sorts of interesting implications and by-ways to explore, *neither are Irish names*, such as "Aidan" or "Colman."

In figure 8.3, we have examples of the ideographs of the symbol *C* for both scribes. Scribe 1's *C*, as usual, is flatter and more pointed than Scribe 2's. The third example is the British name, *Caedmon* (Cɑeɔmon or Cɑeɔmon or Ceɔmon). The *C* in Caedmon is very straight-backed. This is one of the signs of script-differentiation by language in the *stæfwritung* system.

We have other evidence that the *Moore* was produced after stage 2 of codification. In addition to the straight-backs, the scribes use the small-lobed *aesc* (*Æ*), the angled-*c*, and the Greek-*u* (horned-*u*) in Anglo-Saxon and Anglo-British place names, and *only* in Anglo-Saxon and Anglo-British.

Scribe 2

Scribe 1

Caedmon

Fig. 8.3 *The Moore Bede*: Majuscule *C*

In Chapter 25, for example, Bede relates the story of the Council of Whitby held in 664. (This was the Council where Wilfrid fudged the Easter Tables.) On folio 67A of the manuscript, Bede mentions that the council was actually held at another nearby Northumbrian monastery ruled by Abbess Hilda: *Straegnalaech* (Figure 8.4a). Although difficult to see as other than a smudge, "tr" is set under the *s* in the first cluster of symbols. In this one place name, we can see the straight backs on the *l* and the *h*, the *aesc* in *aEgna*, and the angled-*c* in *ech*. Also on folio 67A, we have two examples of the name *nordan humber* [Northumbria]—one from each scribe (Figure 8.4b). Both examples show the use of the Greek-*u* in "humber." Scribe 1 is more careful than Scribe 2; still, the straight backs on the words in Old English are evident.

A name here and there does not have sufficient mass to create a noticeable texture. This is not the case in our earliest example of an Old English hymn. *Caedmon's Hymn* was a number one pop hit in Anglo-Saxon England. Both the earlier Northumbrian and the later West Saxon versions of it show up 21 times across the centuries either *in situ* in Old English or Latin texts or in the margins of copies of the *Historia*.

The story of Caedmon and his Hymn, as related by Bede, has the quality of a fairy-tale and is as about as true. It is a charming story of a supposedly analphabetic and a-musical herdsman, a "noble savage," who refuses to sing at the evening fires. He has a dream in which he is asked why he does not sing. His answer is that he can't. Told to sing something, anyway, Caedmon comes out with this hymn. Interpreted as a miracle, he turns into a great "natural" poet. Caedmon was at Whitby under Hilda where all sorts of miracles are reputed to have occurred. Bede does not lie; he only tells the tale as it had been passed down. (He also tells with a perfectly straight face of the miracles following in Hilda's wake.)

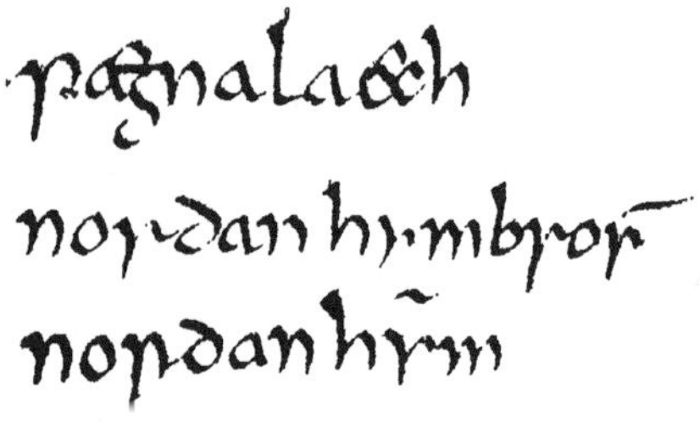

Fig. 8.4 *The Moore Bede*: Old English place names on Folio 67A

Why, then, could scholars unquestioningly accept the impossibility of an exquisite and perfect piece of Hymnody from an a-musical rustic as a true event? In the eighteenth and nineteenth centuries, the concepts of the "noble savage" and the "natural poet" were very much in vogue. Much of the early popularity of Robert Burns was because of his public image as an example of the "natural" untrained poet. (Burns, however, polished and worked over his poetry just like every other good poet does.) Romanticism laid its heavy hand over all the age. People *wanted* to believe in a "natural" poet.

We have to admit that the story of Caedmon antedates these "new" nineteenth century ideas by 1200 years. We also have to admit that the tropes of the natural poet and noble savage show up in many ages. The *Epic of Gilgamesh* contains our oldest example of a "noble savage" (Enkidu) and antedates Caedmon by about 3,000 years. We will never know about Caedmon. Was he, like David, a talented poet who had time to polish his songs while tending his flocks? Did he have perfect pitch and leave the communal songfests because it was painful for him to hear the off-key singing? Did he have a dream telling him that the time had come to sing his song for his abbess? We can never know the truth; but we can see the rapidity with which an event gathers legendary elements. (Modern examples show that five years is more than sufficient time for an event to be smothered in legendary embellishments.) The Caedmon story occurs around 650; Bede was born circa 672. Bede believed in miracles; he also believed in the story of Caedmon.

On folio 91 recto, Bede states unequivocally that the Hymn cannot be translated and he can only give the sense of it. On folio 128 verso, right across the top of the leaf, someone wrote the words of the Hymn down in Old English.

The script is the vernacular version of the Anglo-Saxon minuscule. Apparently (but not certainly) written by Scribe 1 with a finer pen; the backs of the symbols-in-common are straight. He also employs the monophthong *aesc* and differentiates between hard and soft *c*. The *texture* changes immediately upon the completion of the hymn (lines 1-3), although the following ascription and three Latin words with English Glosses on line 4 are written with the same pen and by the same scribe. Line 5 begins a list of Northumbrian Kings ending with Ceolwulf (729-737). The list is written by another scribe at a later date in a larger size; the Latin is in one secular font, the names of the Northumbrian Kings in the straight-backed font used for Old English.

The full text of the Northumbrian Hymn from folio 128v is a follows:

nuſtylun hﬁﬃﬃﬁzan heﬃaﬁﬃﬁucaﬁﬃ uaﬃⱒ mecuⱒﬃﬃ maﬁﬁci ﬁﬃⱒ hiﬃmⱒⱒziⱒⱒanc uﬁicuulⱒuﬃﬃaⱒuﬃ
ſue he-uunⱒﬃazihuaﬁﬃ ﬁⱒﬃyccin ⱒﬃaﬃceliⱒﬁ heaﬁﬃuﬁﬃ ﬃcⱒpﬁﬃⱒa baﬃﬃⱒ hebﬁﬃciihﬃⱒﬃe-
halⱒzﬁﬃﬁﬃ ﬁﬃ chamⱒⱒunzeaﬃⱒmⱒncynnﬁﬃuaﬃⱒ ﬁⱒﬃyccin ﬁﬃcﬁﬁciaⱒﬁ-ﬃﬃumﬃⱒlⱒⱒﬃﬃeaⱒallmﬁciz

Normal practice in the field of Anglo-Saxon Studies is to present all Old English "poetic" works in a system devised during the nineteenth century and as if each genre were the same. Songs may be poems, but poems are not necessarily songs. *Caedmon's Hymn* is a song not poetry; it is a religious hymn and follows the rules of hymnody (which are different from the rules of Psalmody). The following transcription is given per hymnody: verses, refrain, and final.

V1.	nu scylun hergan hefaenricaes uard	metudaes maecti end his modgidanc
V2.	uerc uuldurfadur sue he uundra gihuaes	eci dryctin or astelidae
Refrain	He aerist scop aelda barnum	
	heben til hrofe haleg scepen	
V3.	tha middungeard moncynnaes uard	eci dryctin aefter tiadae
Final	firum foldum frea allmectig	

As Bede pointed out, songs cannot be translated word for word. The following is about as close as we can get today and still retain rhythm, sound, and general sense.

V1.	Now (we) shall praise (the) heavenly kingdom's guard
	(the) mighty carpenter and his mood-thoughts
V2.	Work (of the) Honor* Father, thus his wonders (the)
	Eternal Lord, (the) beginning ordained
Refrain	He first shaped for sons of men** / heaven as a roof, holy shaper
V3.	The middleyard***, mankind's guard,
	Eternal Lord, after established
Final	earth's men, God Almighty.

    *   "Uuldur" (or wuldor) shifted semantically. Originally "honor," as in acclaim, renown, or fame, it was later understood as "Glory" as it appeared to translate Latin *Gloria* (Glory). (It should be noted that the meaning of *gloria* was "acclaim, renown, or fame" in Latin, too, at the time of the early Latin translations of the Bible.)

    **   "aelda barnum" literally means children (barn/bearn—Scots "bairn") of elders (eald—old). That -um indicates a dative (indirect object); we still have remnants of datives around in the pronouns whom, him, them.

    ***   "Middungeard" = Earth.

There are some apparent anomalies in the text and much scholarly ink has been spent on the subject. "Heaven," for example, is written once as *hefaen* and once as *heben*. The *f* in *hefaen* is intervocalic and would have been pronounced *v* (which is why we have modern "heaven"). Depending upon dialect, though, a *v* may or may not have been pronounced as a fricative, which would certainly tend to make it sound very much like a *b*. In fact, in Old Saxon, the word *is* spelled with a *b*. While this point may give us some information about the particular dialect of the scribe who wrote the hymn down, there is a clear metrical reason for the "anomaly." The text as written tells us that the rhythms are not the same. In the first occurrence, the word requires three syllables; in the second it only requires two. The second spelling, *heben*, is merely an archaism and clearly has been used to obtain the required number of syllables to fit the words to the meter. Another example shows up with a single *u* to represent the sound of *w*, for instance, uaɲo (uard [ward/guardian]). This tells us little about the inclusion of *wyn* in the symbol set; we know that *Caedmon's Hymn* was composed about 640-50, that is, before codification of the ASPA. We also know that the hymn was orally transmitted for at least 75 years before it turns up in the *Moore Bede*. The appearance of *u* for *wyn* only tells us that this is the version of the hymn known by the scribe.

Line 4 of the text begins: *primo cantauit caedmon istud carmen* (first sang Caedmon that song). This is followed by three Old English glosses of Latin words: *arula* hearth *destina* feurstud *iugulum* sticung (hearth, fire-stud [prop for a mantel], sticking [pricking]). When there are only single words inserted into the text, place names such as *straEgnalaech* or *nordan humbrorum*, only close examination and attention to detail reveals the differences. We cannot see an obvious change in texture simply by a quick glance; but in these 4 lines we can. The change in the texture of the writing tells us that script-by-language as ethnos differentiation was established before Bede died in 735 (Plate 8.2).

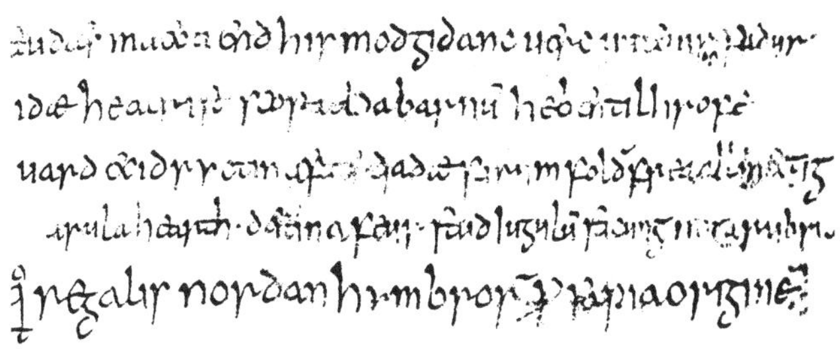

The monograph form of *aesc* that we see in the *Hymn* is the small-lobed aesc (*Æ*) that appears in the Latin text of the *Bangor Collectarium* in the word *aecepnæ* (eternal), on the pages written by an Anglo-Saxon scribe. It is used in the addition to the *Willibrord Calendar* to write the name of the Anglo-Saxon Abbess *hiloæ* (Hilda). We see it used in Old English words written by the same scribe who also uses *barred-d* (ð) to write *th* in the *Épinal Glossary*. The small-lobed *aesc* form is reserved for Old English texts, and only Old English, after stage 2 of codification.

Pl. 8.2 *The Moore Bede*: f. 128v Right hand side. The change in texture between the Old English of *Caedmon's Hymn* and the three Latin words with glosses.

Script differentiation by language and alpha-symbol codification are clearly evident. Instead of diversity, the *Moore Bede* exhibits an extremely regularized and systematic use of symbol forms and script by language differentiation. The texture of the pages shows that the manuscript was dictated; the format shows that the work was authoritative (coming from that source, it would be). Plate 8.3 (p. 140) illustrates the center portion of folio 91 recto, yet the manuscript could be opened at random.

When we turn to another eighth century manuscript from Northumbria, we see scribes in the midst of trying to learn the new writing system. The *Leningrad Bede*, in the Russian National Library at Saint Petersburg (formerly the M. E. Saltykov-Schedrin Public Library at Leningrad, Russia) contains the second oldest copy of the *Historia* (Plate 8.4; p. 141). The manuscript appears to have been written about 746, fifteen years after the *Moore Bede*.

The manuscript has all the marks of a copied text. The *Moore Bede* is written in one column, full of abbreviations, and expressions are written by utterance. The *Leningrad Bede* is written in two columns. The text has been conformed and all but the most common abbreviations have been expanded. Expressions are written as semantic units.

The copied text lacks that "busy" texture we find in the *Moore*, in spite of the fact that all of the scribes use the ternary base. The scarcity of abbreviations, the division into semantic rather than comprehension units, and the reduction of horizontal movement combine to quiet the texture of the pages.

The size, 27cm (10-7/8") by 19cm (7-1/2") and the format tell us that we are still looking at a work produced by parties affiliated with Rome. Bede was a figure of authority before his death; afterwards, his works appear to have been canonized. The canonization of a secular work does not mean the same thing as the canonization of a religious work. It only means that the text in question has been granted status as an authoritative text. These authoritative secular texts are not Class One, no interpretation permitted, documents; they are among the Class Three copied documents. Because these Class Three documents are authoritative but not official, if popular or well known, they make excellent training texts. The *Leningrad Bede* is written in the two-column format of a canonical, authoritative-but-not-sacred book used by these parties; it is also a training text.

uſ eum aeq̄uıſ aſ ar ep̄ ocurc :namq̄ · ıſ ſ enablıſ

p̄ hommon ınſtıtutaıſ canch dıaſ con dıdı crſ ıſ

aducacur · graciſ canchdıaccepcc · unde nıl uınq̄ ·ſ

ruacuıſ poonatuſ raccp̄epocurc · ſed eacc modoſ

nomſ canon reliorıaſ lınguam docebant · ſıcſ docc

r clarıuſq̄ · adconporapueoh oſ ſ acaoaacuſ ſ ſ etuc

ınumalıqnd dıdı ccſ cc · unden nımq̄ ınıunnoc

ıae caıſa docc ſ ecum · ucomnoſ poſ odmon canauſ

ılle ubıadſſ ſnıquaſ e ſ ıbı cehaſ am co ſ nebacſ

ıa cohaſ egreſ ſ ıra dſ uadomuſ ſ hedabacc · qodın

qdamſaccſ ſ ı ccſ relıccadomua ıunıı egreſ ſ uſ ecaa

ıſcoſ quoſ ſ cı cuſcodıa noccerlla ſ pacc delegacuı bı

ıcamon bradedıſ ſ cc ſopoſı · adſ cuaaccıſ dadamſ ſ

ſ alucamſ ac ſ uo appellanſ nomıne · caedmon· ſ

naliquıd · acılle ſ eſ pondoſ ſ neſ cıo ınſ caıſ cantaſ e

euınno egreſ ſ uſ huc ſ eſ ſ ſ rıq cantaſ en pocſ ad ·ſ

ıı cum eo loquebacc · ac cn aıc mıhı cantaſ e habeſ · cc

cantaſ e · ecılle cantalnſ cc · prıncıpıu creacuſ aſ

coſ cſ onſ o · ſcacım ıſ ſ recocorc cantaſ e ın laudem ·

As we have already seen, scribes were trained to minimize differences between hands in order to give a professional one-hand appearance to a finished product. Nevertheless, as we saw with the *Moore Bede*, with all their practice and training, no two scribes write exactly the same. Because no matter how well trained, scribal hands show differences, the ancients developed a procedure to obscure these variations. This procedure is the **staggering technique**. The procedure is indeed ancient. The staggering technique shows up among the Dead Sea Scrolls in authoritative documents and in bookshop products. [3]

The staggering technique is both simple and clever. Whenever a new project was begun, the scribes took turns writing the opening lines. Normally each scribe will write one or one and half lines at the beginning creating an overlap among different hands. After these openers, a scribe writes until his pen runs out of ink or until he has finished his assigned portion or stint. These stints are never too long, at most three to four sentences, nor do the hands always change at the margin. Either long stints or always changing at the margin defeats the purpose for which the technique was invented.

The sole purpose of the procedure is to blur the differences between scribal hands and make these differences less obvious across the entire work. The procedure is effective on cursory inspection, although scribal ideographs give the show away upon careful examination.

There is one other important point about the staggering technique: the procedure is specifically employed with dictated texts. Alerted by the "busy" texture, which tells us that a document probably was dictated, if we find that the document employs the staggering technique, there no longer is any doubt. Any document employing the staggering technique was: a) dictated, b) written by a scribal team, and c) written at a table standing up. The *Moore Bede* uses the staggering technique.

Writing room techniques invented to minimize differences include the scripts and fonts—and even governs the pre-prepared leaves. The appearance of many different fonts of the same family in a codex is in direct violation of the scribal training we see so admirably demonstrated in the *Moore*. There are reasons for such deviations from good practice. Scribes taking dictation and running out of the right type of prepared pens is one possibility; another is when there has been a change in power structure and a new official script has been designated. A third reason for such variety is when scribes are learning a new system. (Yet another reason for such deviation shows up in the early fourteenth century when book production had moved out of the monasteries and into the hands of enterprising commercial scribes. One entrepreneurial scribe was a bit greedy, poor fellow, and bit off more than he could chew. He had to hire other scribes in order to finish the job on time and one of his sub-contractors could not follow directions.)

As good detectives, we know that the information is in the differences. With so many standard techniques carefully designed to blur distinctions, whenever we see a document that violates standard *scriptorium* practices, it means that something unusual is going on. There is decidedly something unusual going on in the *Leningrad Bede*.

There is little doubt that the manuscript was produced at one of the Northumbrian centers. The version of *Caedmon's Hymn* in the *Leningrad Bede* is the Northumbrian one and written down as the scribe knew it—probably humming along as he wrote it across the bottom margin of the leaf. This version of the Hymn differs only slightly from the *Moore* version. The differences are primarily in spelling, which gives us some information about another Northumbrian dialect. In the *Leningrad* we find, for example, *hefen to hrofe* instead of *heben til rofe*. This does not change the meaning of "heaven as a roof." There was no difference between an aspirated-*d* (round-*d*) and an barred-d-*th*, so the fact that in the *Moore* we find *modgiðanc* and in the *Leningrad, modigiðanc* (mood-thoughts) means little. The scribe of the *Leningrad* Hymn uses the open-*aesc* rather than the closed-*aesc* form.

The *Leningrad* is written in *six* different secular more or less Anglo-Saxon minuscules, which seems to point to one of the coastal *scriptoria. Caedmon's Hymn*, however, is written in an *insular* minuscule. It is the only item in the entire codex written in the old Anglo-Celtic affiliated script still used at York. While this could merely mean that the scribe was from Northumbria, the manuscript is a training text. The manuscript had to have been produced at a center where people came for training in the new system. In the mid-eighth century, York would seem the most logical site for such training.

The *Leningrad Bede* shows us scribes in various stages of learning the new writing system. At least six scribes wrote this manuscript; there are four main hands (Scribes 1-4) one very short stint by another scribe (Scribe B) and a "teacher": Scribe A. Scribe A was clearly demonstrating the new system. In the *Leningrad*, the standard scribes-taking-turns staggering procedure is *not* followed.

While both Scribes A and B wrote the opening leaves, Scribe A wrote the entire first leaf. Further, from the way certain symbols are formed, Scribe A apparently wrote the insular text of *Caedmon's Hymn*. Scribe A demonstrated the writing system as well as the format. As this scribe was the teacher, he must have been from the *scriptorium* where the manuscript was produced. He also gives us a sample of the fonts used by the training site. The other scribes were not locals; they all use the same script family but wrote the different font styles used by their own *scriptoria*. The four main scribes did not even *try* to make the book look like a professional, one-hand, copy. One of them, in fact, was not even an Anglo-Saxon.

The scribes clearly were all at least senior journeymen, if not masters. We have already mentioned the fact that it is rather difficult for an older, experienced scribe to learn a new system. Ingrained habit and automatic responses tend to interfere, in spite of his best efforts.

Each scribe wrote continuous sections, which again violates standard *scriptorium* practices for book production. Of the four main scribes, Scribe 1 (Figure 8.5a), who wrote from folio 4b, column a. l. 5 through folio 32 column b, writes a pointed Anglo-Saxon minuscule with Insular features in Anglo-Saxon names. Scribe 2 (Figure 8.5b) took over at folio 33a and continued through folio 63 column b; he writes a rounded minuscule with some distinctive Continental features. Scribe 3 (Figure 8.5c) wrote a very short stint. He began at folio 64, column a and wrote as far as folio 68, column a; his is a round upright Anglo-Saxon minuscule. Scribe 4 (Figure 8.5d) took over at folio 68, column b, and

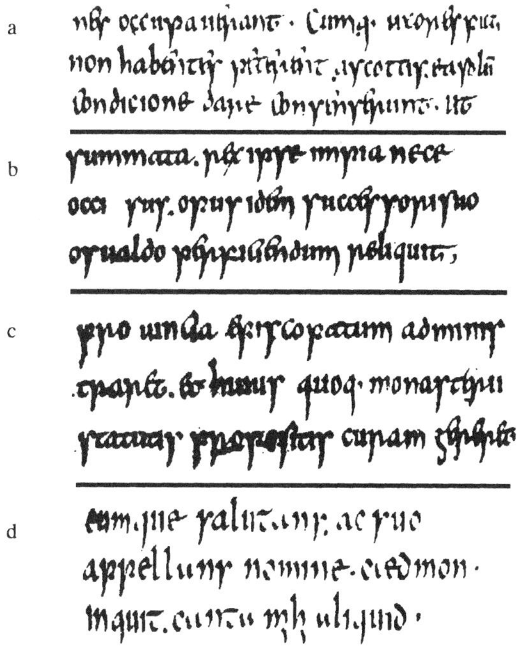

Fig. 8.5 The four main hands of the *Leningrad Bede*.

wrote through to the final leaf at folio 161a. Scribe 4 uses a mixture of both rounded and pointed minuscule.

Scribe 1 is extremely regular in his use of the *stæfwritung* system both in terms of symbol assignments and in script-differentiation. He is careful to distinguish script forms when writing Anglo-Saxon names, but also tends to add the Insular wedge in these cases. He is so proficient, he works with such ease and nonchalance, that it brings a bored student to mind. Sending this scribe off to learn the system was much like a college placement officer putting a graduate of the Eastman School of Music into a Music Theory 101 class.

Scribe 2 appears more or less accustomed to the writing system, but the important words are "more or less." He seems to have been a good pupil and, in general, follows the practices of Scribes A and 1 in his symbol assignments. Like Scribe 1, he uses the aleph-*a* to write the unligatured *a-e*. Scribe 2, however, reverts to his prior training when writing any reference to God: he uses a straight-*d* (d) instead of round-*d* (ð) to write "dominus," "domini," "diuinitatus poteñ / tia_" and in abbreviations of the *nomina sacra*. He also reverts to former habits in his use of a high round-*a* at the beginning of phrases. Yet another indication that Scribe 2 is still struggling with a new writing system shows up when he runs across Anglo-Saxon names. Although he does include the *barred-d* (ð) that became part of the ASPA at least 60 years earlier, he still uses *ae* instead of the aesc (Æ) and round-*d* instead of barred-d in names. He also is unfamiliar with Greek-*u* and angled-*c*; Figure 8.6 shows his attempt to copy the forms. Besides his unfamiliarity with Anglo-Saxon personal and place names, this scribe has one other trait that places him as possibly

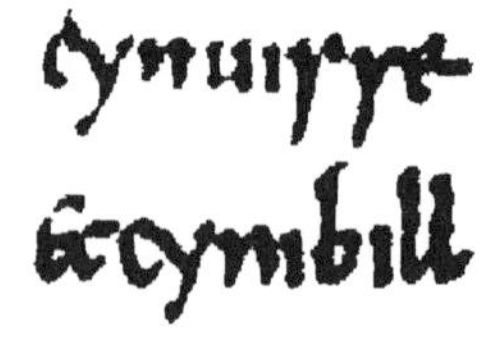

Fig. 8.6
The Leningrad Bede:
Scribe 2's Greek-*u* and
angled-*c*

from Luxeuil or one of its daughter monasteries. Scribe 2 *clubs* his ascenders, particularly on his *l*'s and *b*'s.

When we arrive at Scribe 3, we find a scribe who is having great difficulty adhering to the new standards. He clearly learned his rounded minuscule at another *scriptorium*. He tends towards very long, slender ascenders and descenders. While he follows the same practice as Scribe 2 in the use of straight-*d* for the *nomina sacra* and sacred abbreviations, we already have noticed that this is one of the things that shows Scribe 2 is still adjusting to a new writing system. Scribe 3 takes this particular non-adherence even farther. He mixes up his symbol assignments, sometimes using those of the ASPA, at other times some former learned standard. His stint was so short, that he appears to have given up, or more likely, was removed from the job. After all, a *scriptorium*, is a business office and, whether intended for internal use or for somebody else, the book had been ordered.

The production of a manuscript is both time consuming and costly. Writing is hard work and the materials themselves are expensive. The preparation time is extensive. Even excluding the time involved in preparing the parchment from the skins of the animals, someone had to cut the parchment to size, someone else to prepare and mark the format guidelines on all those parchment leaves and in the correct order, yet another had to prepare the ink, and the scribes also had to prepare all those pens—all this before the first mark was made on a leaf. The *scriptorium* master had to fit the copy into the *scriptorium* work schedule and assign a writing desk where the book was to be written—using up work space. Nobody undertakes the production of a book this size without a work order in hand. The manuscript may have been used as a training exercise, but someone had ordered a copy of Bede's *Historia*. The book still had to be finished.

Scribe 4 took over at folio 68, column b, and wrote the rest of the manuscript—all the way to folio 161a. This scribe's symbols are consistently formed, his lines straight, and he writes rapidly and smoothly. There are good reasons to believe that he was a grumpy old fellow, trained in a different school many years before, and rather averse to learning any of those "new-fangled notions."

Scribes tended to live to ripe old ages. Many a manuscript dating problem arises when an old scribe using archaic or outdated forms shows up. Scribe 4 is an example of such an old and very experienced scribe. The *Leningrad Bede* was written in approximately 746. Like Scribes 1 and 2, Scribe 4 uses an aleph-*a* in his *ae* forms; but, the form is the ligatured *ae* we find used by Dorbbene, the scribe of the *Schaffhausen Adamnan* who died in 713!

Although Scribe 4 is careful to distinguish among the low, medial, and high-*e*'s and the different forms of *s*, this only tells us that he used the ternary base. When we look at *quantity* and *stress*, we find that the symbol-for-symbol correspondence is very high between the *Moore* and *Leningrad Bede*s. When we look at *quality* we find that Scribe 4 is using a totally different symbol assignment set.

Scribe 4's symbol assignments are so different and so clearly precodification, that when we look at the pages, we can almost hear him saying: "You want this book done? Then leave me alone! I'll do it my way or you can get someone else to finish the job!" It almost seems redundant to report that Scribe 4 makes no attempt whatsoever to differentiate script by ethnos.

Scribe 1 of the *Leningrad Bede* uses the new system with consistency and regularity. Scribe 2 uses the system but reverts to another method when writing the *nomina sacra* or references to God. Scribe 3, who wrote only nine sides (fol. 64a-68a), seems to have had more than a little difficulty learning the new system; he retains aspects of an earlier local method in his use of straight-*d* and aleph-*a*. Scribe 4 employs a different phonetic assignment system altogether. His method of distinguishing when and where to use a particular form is so complicated, so varied, and appears to depend upon so many contextual factors, that his portion of the manuscript amply demonstrates the impetus behind the formulation of an "inter-ethnic writing system."

Between them, the *Épinal* and the *Moore Bede*, set the lower and upper limits for us. Stage 2 of codification occurred before 690 when Willibrord went off to Frisia and no later than 731 when Bede dictated his *Historia*. The *Moore Bede* shows that by 731, the first 2 stages of the *stæfwritung* system were fully operative in at least one *scriptorium*.

The circa 746 *Leningrad Bede* gives us some indications as to the speed of the system's acceptance and dispersion. (It also gives us some inside knowledge on scribal training techniques.) Three out of the four main scribes employ the system with varying degrees of expertise. This tells us that, by the mid-8th century, the system is known, used, and accepted—except by Scribe 4 of course—, but not yet mastered or learned by all scribes. The manuscript is written in Anglo-Saxon minuscules; script-by-language is shown in the use of the subtly different flat-backed script and *aesc*, angled-*c*, and Greek-*u* in Anglo-Saxon and British names (but not Irish). Scribe A wrote his opening portion of the manuscript in Anglo-Saxon minuscule; but the Old English version of *Caedmon's Hymn* is written in an insular script. The *Leningrad Bede* gives us our first obvious example of what was to become the norm among the Anglo-Saxon manuscripts: the assertion of ethnic independence and identity through the ancient differentiation of script-by-language.

Script-language differentiation depended upon a carefully ordered symbol set. Once the ASPA was codified, with territorial scripts for Latin and ethnic scripts for English, this one small refinement to the writing system doubled the number of useable symbols without increasing the size of the symbol set. This tiny enhancement made it possible for the reader to distinguish languages at a glance and without fear of conflation. Script-by-language also permitted xenographic exchange (foreign-graph exchange), the use of Script A in a document written in script B. In turn, xenographic exchange enabled the creation of the Anglo-Saxon system of musical notation.

Chapter Nine

INTERMEZZO

"Sing to the Lord a new song": the first line of the Hebrew Psalm 96 became the keynote of the new religion, for was not the new covenant built upon the old? Indeed, this was the point of view of the earliest Church writers—such as Clement of Rome (died circa 99). Early writer after writer stresses that the Psalms should be sung day and night. As Jerome relates of an ideal Christian village, the farm hand sings Alleluia while plowing, the sweating reaper cheers himself with psalms, and the vine dresser sings [songs] of David as he dresses the vines. [1] While many scholars feel that illiteracy was the factor behind this stress on the Psalms as a means of dissemination, orality was only one factor—and a minor one at that. Basil the Great (330-379) specifically writes that spoken maxims and proverbs are not retained by the listeners, but the Psalms are. [2] Ambrose (339-397), Bishop of Milan, declares that song is a type of play, learned effortlessly, and retained with delight. "A psalm joins those with differences," unites foes, and reconciles the offended. [3] Make no mistake: Religious music was recognized as an essential tool for the unification and control of populations as far back as Akkad.

1400 years before King David, 2800 years before Emperor Constantine, we find an attempt to create a state religion that would join peoples, conquerors and conquered alike, under one set of beliefs. The important job of unification through religion was given to a remarkable woman. Her name was Enheduanna. Poetess, priestess, and princess, she was the daughter of Sargon I of Sumer and Akkad. Enheduanna appears to have been a charismatic personality as well. She was appropriately named, for "Hedva" means "joy." She died in 2254 BCE. [4]

Enheduanna was the first in a long line of talented En-priestesses. Her name is known from historical and archaeological records. Her literary style is so distinctive and individual that it can be recognized 1600 years later—even in the midst of the **pseudepigraphy** (works written by others in the name of the known authority) that accrued across the centuries.

Enheduanna also had impressive administrative talents. Enheduanna's measures are our oldest known attempt to standardize religious practices. She worked through music.

Among the existing tablets from Akkad, there is a set that appears to contain a total of 42 religious songs. These are not the oldest known written records of ancient song. As in every other human endeavor, religious music was based upon the work of predecessors; Enheduanna's songs bear some resemblances to hymns from Kesh (2600 BCE). Nevertheless, her talent was so great, her style so individual, that comparing her works to her predecessors is the equivalent of comparing Shakespeare's works to his. Enheduanna wrote quite a few of these songs.

As in manuscripts written 2,500 years later, Akkadian tablets typically had a **colophon**, that is, a paragraph that appears at the end of a work and contains some information, for example, about the scribes, the place of writing, or the authors. Normally a colophon is *not* part of the text—neither back at Akkad nor in a medieval manuscript, as scribal, locational, or auctorial information varies from text to text. These religious songs follow a basic form. While Hymn 42 more or less follows the basic pattern, it nevertheless deviates substantially from the other 41. Suddenly, the deity to whom praise is given shows a change of name and in non-standard form. This is followed by what appears to be a perfectly normal colophon that includes the author, comments upon the work, and the location where it was written. Enheduanna is mentioned by name.

^{d}nisaba zö-mi	Praise Nisaba
lu-dub-KA-kes-da en-he-du7-an-na	The arranger of the tablet [is] Enheduanna
lugal-mu-ni u-tu	My Lord, what has been [here] created
na-me lu nam-mu-un-utu	no one has [before] created.
è-^{d}nisaba erès^{ki}-a	At the house of Nisaba in Eres.

(The superscripted *d* in lines 1 and 8 and the *ki* in line 9 and the subscripted 7 in line 2 are symbol identifiers. That is, they indicate, for instance, whether a symbol is being used phonetically or as itself.)

Nisaba was the patron deity of the scribal arts. It was only natural that the hymn set would have been written at the Akkadian equivalent of a *scriptorium*: "The house of Nisaba" located "in Eres." Nor is this a hymn, as are the other 41, but a closing declaration for the entire collection. "Praise Nisaba" is part of the colophon. In striking contrast to usual practice, the entire colophon became a fixed part of the text. [5]

No longer a variable component, but an integral part of the literary compositions, the entire colophon, including Enheduanna's model for the correct format for the closure of a collection, was copied down the centuries carrying her name with it. The records show that she was known *by name* well into the Neo-Babylonian age. Some additions to her canon may even be pseudepigraphic creations of this late period.

She was an outstandingly talented woman. Her most enduring effects are on the structure of religious song and the organization of written records. The division of psalms into a standard of predominantly **uni-colon** (a line with a central **caesura** [pause]) and **bi-cola** (two lines, each with a caesura) are hers. To this day, religious song in the Western world is written by *cola*.

Enheduanna began the practice of cataloguing songs by first line (**incipits**). Tablets, codices, and books continued to be catalogued and named by first line or words for the next 3,900 years. Even now, except for *Bamidbar* (Numbers), the 5 books of the Pentateuch are called in Hebrew by the first significant word of each one. [6]

There are 22 catalogues of *incipits* among the tablets. In later practice, these *incipits* became the model for the *tituli*. We still use such *tituli* at the beginning of religious songs.

Many of the catalogues show **catch lines** to ensure correct ordering of the canon. **Catch words**, the final word on a page repeated below the main text, were used to order and assemble books until the late nineteenth century CE. This practice instituted by Enheduanna endured more than 4,200 years.

The catalogues are interesting also for their subject matter; Enheduanna formalized the division of religious music into genres. Here we find songs to the gods of battle and to the Zenith of Heaven. We have liturgies to Enlil and to Inanna. There are love (praise) songs of the "normal" type, of the "cover" type; and of the "flute/pipe" type; there are songs of lamentations and of penitence; and there is, of course, that model for the colophon for a collection.

Remnants of her structuring of songs and her organization of books are still visible today in the West. Enheduanna standardized the form of religious music. Her effects on the Psalms of the Psalter are apparent and the effects of the Psalms on Christian liturgy are undeniable. The *tituli*, the line of text that identifies for or to whom the Psalm is written dates back to her organization of the liturgy for her father.

While everybody knew that sound could not be written down, Enheduanna had demonstrated that its visible representations could be organized. There matters stood for at least 2000 years. Although we may simply not recognize it when we see it, if somewhere, sometime, somebody tried to come up with a musical notation system, there is no known evidence before the 2nd century BCE.

In one of the odder quirks of this story, Hebrew writing systems, in general, turned away from their Phoenician origins and shifted to bilinear fixed systems, presumably in imitation of the official Babylonian and Greco-Roman ones. Although the Dead Sea Scrolls make it thoroughly clear that several groups retained the ancient Phoenician system intact, quite a bit of the existing writings come from the **diaspora** (outside the land; literally, lands of dispersion). The shift in writing system was so pervasive that, in Babylon in particular, the purpose of the variant forms and the meaning of the stress notation was forgotten. Mishnaic writings from Babylon record that by the second century CE the Rabbis were already arguing about the meaning of the "big" and "little" letters in the *Torah* (Pentateuch). Forgotten as well was the reason for the embedded collection colophon at the end of Psalm 72.

Even earlier, Greek writing systems had moved in the direction of official bilinear scripts. While the Greeks clung to script-by-ethnos differentiation, they abandoned durational notation in their official scripts. The net result of these changes in the two writing systems had far reaching consequences on their early attempts to write music. Both the Greek and the Hebrew writing systems evolved external notational systems to encode musical information.

Music was an integral part of Greek religion; there are many references to singing accompanying the Eleusinian mysteries. The great plays of Classical Greece with their choruses were written for annual religious festivals. The first known attempts to create a means of writing down melodies shows up around the late 3rd-to-early 2nd century BCE among the Greeks. Having removed durational notation from their writing systems, all early Greek music notations try to incorporate rhythmic indications along with the melody. A fragment of Euripides' *Orestes* (Papyrus Vindobona Greek 2315) uses alphabetic symbols placed above the syllables as melodic and rhythmic notation. Vowels that are sung to more than one note are duplicated. This system occasionally even notes instrumental directions. Clearly, any note system that uses exactly the same symbols as that of the text is bound to confuse rather than clarify. This complete alphabetic system disappeared from Greek manuscripts; nevertheless, it left a legacy. It resurfaces during the eleventh century as part of the bilingual, alphabet-plus-**neumes** (the pre-cursors of modern notes), notation system used in Montpelier MS H. 159, a manuscript of importance in the reconstruction of Gregorian Chant. Among the various notational systems in late medieval and early renaissance periods we find numerous attempts to write down *melodies* using the complete alphabet. The method did not work too well for these later theorists, either.

Apparently there was something in the air around the second century CE. Perhaps the time was ripe for the creation of musical writing systems. From about the early part of the second century we find another papyrus (P. Oxyrhyncus xxv 2436); this one uses numeric rather than alphabetic symbols above the syllables to give melodic and rhythmic notation. In this system, vowels that are sung to more than one note have a hyphen placed under them. Again, traces of this numeric system show up during the late medieval and early renaissance periods in attempts to write down music. While the method may have appealed to later peoples, the Greeks abandoned the numeric method for **chironomic** (or cheironomic) notation. That is: a notation system that graphically reproduces the hand movements of a chorale leader. This notational system records dynamic instructions, but not the melodies.

Accents were added to Greek in the third Century BCE and have fueled arguments among modern scholars as to whether the accents began as rhetorical guides or musical notation. The clashing of pens aside, it is in the second century CE that a musical notation system employing a variety of accents placed above the words appears. This is the oldest evidence of chironomic notation in *Greek* music. Chironomic notation was already in use in Hebrew texts by at least the second century BCE; some of the Dead Sea Scrolls appear to have chironomic symbols. Most of what we know about early Semitic chironomy is from what was written later during the first and second centuries CE. In any case, the resemblance between the simplest Greek and Hebrew chironomic symbols is strong. The entire symbol set, however, differs. In both systems, for instance, the symbol for increase volume is the same and appears as the *tifcha* (\) and the *oXeia* (/) (In Latin, this becomes the *virgule*.) The *merka* (⌒), the symbol for diminuendo, on the other hand, is found only in the Hebrew set.

The Greek chironomic system eventually developed into what moderns call **ektephonic** or ek-phonetic notation. Although the ektephonic notation system began with simple chironomic signs, it became so involved and used so many symbols and signs that it eventually collapsed under its own weight. The ektephonic system disappeared so completely that not until the late nineteenth and early twentieth centuries was it discovered that those puzzling signs on all those Greek texts were, in fact, a system of musical notation.

The old Hebrew chironomic system also underwent changes. The Babylonian system was developed, as the name suggests, in Babylon. The other system was developed by a group centered at the town of Tiberias on the Sea of Galilee and was called, naturally enough, the Tiberian system. Because the meaning of the variant forms was forgotten, the new systems incorporated methods for indicating vowels as well as musical instructions. Unlike the Greek ektephonetic system, however, this Tiberian system is still in use. During the eleventh century CE, the so-called Rashi Square Font (a mutation of the Square Script) was adopted as the standard script. This is a compact font with very little leading between lines. In order to fit between the lines of text, the notation was reduced and a new symbol set created. The new musical notation was placed over, and the vowel notation under, the text. The change in musical symbol set was so drastic, that its relationship with the older chironomic signs was more or less forgotten until early in the twentieth century. [7]

All this time, while the Greek and Hebrew peoples were adopting new writing systems, the early Christians were searching for their own voices. Although they adopted the Phoenician writing system as used in the Hebrew texts, nevertheless, no attempts to record the music of the Psalms can be seen. If the Psalms were so important, then why was nobody interested in finding a way to record the music? The answer is as obvious as it is simple: Jerome tells us why. In the beginning, all translators of the Psalms tried *to fit* the translated *text* to the existing Hebrew *melodies* and rhythms. During these early centuries, nobody ever thought that the music of the Psalms might be forgotten.

Our story is filled with wry events: Because the Greek writing systems, including their alphanumeric musical systems, were considered "pagan," the early Christians adopted as their model the Semitic writing system—variant forms, stress notation, durational indicators, and all; they also adopted the Hebrew chironomic notation. Chironomic notation was thought sufficient to record the necessary information on how to sing the Psalms. This is all well and good, if everyone agreed on how to sing a new song: They, of course, did not.

In one sense, the melodies of the Psalms have never been forgotten; however, the melodies underwent a decided change—a change that depended upon religious party affiliation. Only after the fourth century do we find attempts to record the melodies of the Psalter. Before the fourth century, there was no need to write down the music of the Psalms; after the fourth century, the music of the Psalter became yet another divisive element among Christian parties. As the disagreements between parties heated up, the control of both melodies and words became very important.

The ancients knew that music could be used to control people. They knew this back at Akkad when they used religious song to unite the Sumerian Empire with the Akkadian Kingdom. They knew it when David played his psaltery to soothe King Saul. Nevertheless, not until the Greek philosophers wrote about the power of music do we find any detailed discussions of its control over men. So conscious was Plato (428-348 BCE), the Greek philosopher, of the power of music as a means of control, that he considered music a branch of *ethics*. Plato's desire to regulate music stems from his observations that certain modes (the older arrangements of notes similar to modern scales) excited and unsettled men. His stern approach was to ban all rhythmic and melodic complexities; he said that they led to disorder and depression. His pupil, Aristotle, also recognized the power of music. Unlike Plato, however, Aristotle wanted all modes admitted into the social structure. He believed that happiness and pleasure were positive adjuncts to both individual and state.

Musicologists and musicians, of course, are very much aware of the power of music. In this field, the ability of music to sway emotions is a "doesn't everybody." Elementary textbooks on the theory of music note that **tempo**, the rhythmic flow of music, has a strong tendency to follow a norm. The physiological basis of this norm is reasonably clear. The tempo norm sits more or less around the *average* of the human pulse rate: 84 beats per minute. Music that stays close to this 84 beats per minute seems most natural. Decided deviations from the norm are perceived as fast or slow. Because people are rarely "average," the pulse rate in healthy humans varies from around 70 to 90, deviation from the norm is subjective, that is, it is felt at different points depending upon the individual. Nevertheless, this norm exists and composers use this knowledge all the time.

Towards the end of the second century, what is termed the Hellenization of Christianity began among the Alexandrian-Roman sects. Plato's attitude towards music, as filtered through a Greco-Egypto lens, was adopted by the Alexandrian-Roman parties. The technical term for this Hellenic influx is **Neo-Platonism**. [8] Neo-Platonism influenced many areas, among them, the singing of the Psalms. In keeping with the tenets of Neo-Platonism, the Alexandrian-Roman affiliates kept the old melodies, but they *reduced* the tempo. Further, these groups changed the translation order: instead of the *text* being fitted to the *music*, the *music* was now fitted to the *text*.

Source languages are the language being translated from; **target** languages are the languages being translated into. Unless the parsing rhythms of both source and target languages are very similar, the translated texts have a hard time fitting themselves to the source melodies. While both Greek and Hebrew, for example, are stress languages they use very different parsing rhythms. Parsing rhythms reflect the average length of a word in a given language. Greek words are substantially longer than the Hebrew words being translated. The effort to fit the Old Greek to the Hebrew melodies resulted in some very contorted Greek. Although a Semitic tongue and a stress language, Syriac (North-Eastern Aramaic cousin) has parsing rhythms that are very different from Hebrew; here, too, strange things happened to the language of the translated songs. When we move away from stress languages into quantitative ones, such as Latin, the differences in the parsing rhythms create many problems. All the older Latin versions, *Vetus* [Old], *Gallican* (later *Vulgate*), and *Romanum*, [9] were translated from Greek. The effort to fit the Old Greek translations to the existing melodies had already distorted the rhythms. Even when the text of the source language occasionally stretches syllables out across notes, squeezing longer words into music intended for shorter ones results in **trilling**. "Trilling" also was a problem with parts of Latin translations. While Latin, like Greek, contains many polysyllabic words, which resulted in trilling, on the average, Latin words are shorter than the Greek they were translating. The new Latin text must be stretched out across a series of notes to match the *Greek* text. With the recognition of Christianity as the state religion of the officially Latin-speaking Empire, the difficulties with Latin translations also promoted the adoption of reduced tempi in accord with Neo-Platonism.

The Neo-Platonic model served more than one purpose. It is much easier to fit longer words to a slower tempo. Slower tempi means the elimination of the "trilling" effect; it also cultivates sedateness and mysticism. The use of reduced tempi, incidentally, also hides the obvious "foreignness" of the Greek and Latin texts when sung to Hebrew melodies.

Neo-Platonism was clearly not accepted by all Christianities. Our old acquaintance, Tertullian, that eloquent first writer of Church Latin, showed increasing hostility to Platonism and worldliness in the church. His most famous enjoinder against the Hellenizations creeping into the new religion was: What has Athens to do with Jerusalem?

Some of the North African-Semitic affiliates as well as the Antiochian-Roman groups took Tertullian's admonition to heart. They continued to follow the older translation tradition of fitting the text to the music. They also insisted upon making their own translations. Among these groups were

Montanists, Donatists, Arians, Eusebians, and Anomeans; the last was the ultra conservative branch of the subordinationist affiliates. Another name for the Anomeans, who took the book of Leviticus most seriously, was "the Judaizers."

The earliest clearly Christian texts are written in Greek; Latin Christian texts appear only in the late second to early third centuries. Along with other Greek writing techniques and terminology, the Romans had adopted the Greek chironomic notation. In Roman practice, sometimes the chironomic signs were used for rhetorical purposes and sometimes they showed up as musical notation. As the signs originate in directions to increase volume, or to stress a sound, or to hold a syllable, they may be used for either purpose with equal success. This situation does not help resolve the scholar's burning question: which came first, music or rhetoric? The point is immaterial: The fact is that "pagan" Latin writers also adopted chironomic notation.

Whether Christian Latin writers used the Greek or the Hebrew chironomic system was totally affiliation dependent. Neumes developed from the combined Greco-Syriac chironomic notation systems. As the names of the neumes show, [10] the earliest of the Alexandrian-Roman Latin neumes come directly from the early Greek chironomic signs. The North African-Semitic groups stuck to Hebrew chironomy.

The process of Hellenization, though, left other legacies. During the late antique and early medieval periods there were many attempts to coordinate the planets, the constellations, and planetary conjunctions with musical modes. This practice has long been attributed to Pythagoras, but turns out to have been used first at Old Babylon. Nevertheless, it was the Pythagorean writings that carried the idea of a *musica mundana*, a mathematical harmony between all creation, to the West.

In Alexandria of the second century CE, Claudius Ptolomaeus, better known as Ptolemy the astronomer and geographer, wrote his *Almagest*. (He called his book *The Mathematical Collection*, which turned into *The Great Astronomer*, and, in Arabic of the ninth century CE, Al Magest, hence, *Almagest*.) In this work, Ptolemy presents his geocentric theory of the cosmos and how to coordinate music with celestial bodies: the *Harmonia Mundi* (Harmony of the World). He coordinated the twelve signs of the Zodiac with a twelve-tone musical scale. (Modern Western music uses the twelve-tone scale).

Influenced by Egyptian mythology and the early Judaeo-Christian idea of the cosmic canon, the Pythagorean-Ptolemic cosmogony became basic tenets of the Christian groups, among these were numbered the Gnostic parties. The Coptic church was one of the latter group. (Coptic merely means "Egyptian." The Greeks had a great deal of difficulty with initial consonants in foreign languages. For example, *Giblos* became *Biblos*, although how *Tadmor* became *Palmyra* is a bit more obscure. Except for the initial consonant, the Greeks generally managed to get the rest of the name right. In any case, the name for the area was transcribed in Akkadian as "Hikuptah," which may have been what the people who lived on the site of pre-unification Memphis (Hi = the; the Kufta??) called themselves or the name of one of their kings. As the *k*-phone is a **gutteral** (in the throat), which in some Semitic dialects may be pronounced as a deep gulp, "HiKuftah," perhaps pronounced "iGupta" or "iKhupta," turned into "Aigypta" in Greek. The inhabitants of the country as a whole called themselves *Masri*.)

Under the Greeks, and even more so under the Romans, the natives of Egypt were an underclass supplying labor and services, very low down on the social scale. Textual evidence indicates that there were different law codes for different strata of a given population under the Roman Imperial administration. Under the Greeks there apparently were two distinct codes in Egypt: one territorial and one for Egyptian nationals. With the arrival of the Romans and re-codification of these law codes, Rome added another set of national codes, this time for the Greeks. Further, the Romans differentiated among types of Roman citizens as well. [11]

In the late-fourth century, the Copts adopted the Greek alphabetic symbols and writing system. During this period, somewhere west of Alexandria, a member of the Coptic church designed an involved color-coded musical notation system to graphically describe Ptolemy's theory of celestial coordination.

The manuscript is written in Coptic of the Sahidic dialect, which places it in the fifth century CE. The process of turning the skin of an animal into a parchment is not a skill that can be learned only from watching. Nor is it possible to learn how to lay out a page without training. The document has all the marks of an attempt to imitate the practices of the elite Greek groups by a member of the "lower" classes. This manuscript was prepared and written by someone who learned by observation and not by training.

The text, in an inexpert and uneven hand, is written in red and brown inks on very poorly prepared parchment. The animal skin was not properly dried, stretched, or scraped and the leaves have cracked and turned a deep brown from the residues. The edges show the "scalloping" that results when the animal skin has been pinned unevenly for drying. Even cracked and darkened as this manuscript is, it is easy to see that the margins lack the well known and well established correct proportions of margin-to-text area that we see in professionally prepared manuscripts.

Originally there were six leaves containing a key to the notational system and two hymns. Fortunately, photographs of all six leaves were taken for expert examination *before* five of the leaves were sold to a private collector. Once manuscript leaves "go private," they are rarely available for further study; in fact, it frequently is impossible to trace their whereabouts. Leaf 1, the most important of the six, is in the Special Collections archives at the Hayden Library of Arizona State University. Plate 9.1 (page 155, facing) displays a photograph of Leaf 1. The leaf is so dark, that in spite of a number of attempts by the custodian to obtain a clear photograph from the leaf itself, Plate 9.1 shows the photograph of the leaf used for expert evaluation; this is the best that could be done.

The word "key" appears on the left side over the vertical double-column of colored circles. Below the column is the word "foundation." In the top center we find the phrase: *symphonia pneumadikos* (spiritual music). Written just above the first line of horizontal circles we find the Coptic word for "begin." At the very bottom, below the last horizontal line of circles is the Coptic word for "the end."

Table 9.1: The color coding of the Coptic Manuscript

Color	Key
Yellow	C
Dark Brown	D
Ultramarine	E
Green	F
Black	G
Red	A
Light Blue	B
Pink	C#
Red- Brown	D#
Tan	F#
Orange	G#
Gray	A#

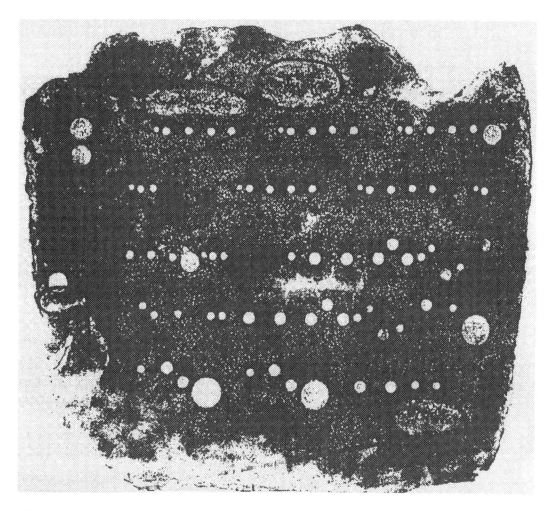

Pl. 9.1   Leaf 1 of the Coptic colored-coded *Harmonia Mundi* musical notation system, shown at 0.62 times actual size. (Courtesy of Special Collections, Hayden Library, Arizona State University.)

Both Ptolemy's cosmic harmony and 12 real tones are expressed in these color-coded circles. The two vertical columns on the far left contain twelve colors. The experts who examined this manuscript used our modern 12-tone scale to determine whether this was a valid notational system. Thus, the seven circles in the left hand column represent the diatonic scale, the white keys on a piano (C, D, E, F, G, A, B). Those in the right column (5 circles) express the chromatic steps, the black keys on a piano (C sharp, D sharp, F sharp, G sharp, A sharp). Together the two columns present a 12-tone scale *and* the 12 signs of the Zodiac. The distribution of the colors is shown in Table 9.1 (page 154, facing) using the order of the group designated as *key*.

The larger portion of the leaf is covered by circles of colors written out horizontally. While only the lightest and brightest circles are clear in the photograph, nevertheless, we can see that these circles vary in size and vertical placement on a line. Although now available for study only from a photograph, at the very top of Leaf 5 the Coptic word *time* is written next to a group of uncolored circles. The duration, that is, the length of time a note is held, is shown by the size of each circle. Color and size contain the complete melodic notation. This color-coded system contains all the information necessary to sing, for example, the music of the Coptic Hymn to Saint John the Baptist written on the leaves.

Unfortunately, although this color-coded method is a very complete notational system, it is also very clumsy. For one thing, it is exceedingly wasteful of space on the leaves. For another, a scribe would need to have a good sized palette of colors on hand. For obvious reasons, this color-coding system never became popular as a professional musical notational system. [12]

While relatively late, this particular attempt to graphically represent the *Harmonia Mundi* gives us pieces of important information. As the Copts were emulators of existing traditions, this document shows us that *color* was already in use as a form of musical notation. We know that colored inks were already used on both sides of the Ancient Near East. While much work has been done on the use of red inks as part of the punctuation system in Assyrian, Ugaritic, and Egyptian texts, [13] nothing has yet been done on the use of colored inks as possible musical notation prior to late Medieval copies of Boethius (ca. 475-524) and the use of a color notation. Yet color is used in early Christian texts and shows up as early as the Dead Sea Scrolls in the Hebrew tradition. It would appear that when the ancients referred to the colors of music, this was meant as literally as the voice of a page (*voces paginarium*). In passing, we should note that when musical staff lines first appear, they are drawn in color; yellow or gold represents "C." [14]

All of these various attempts to record music were known by the sixth century. Because each church and each synagogue used their own *individual* notational methods, there was, in fact, a plethora of different methods available. We find four Greek systems: complete alphabet, numerical, simple chironomic, and ektephonic (with variants depending upon locale) and three chironomic systems: Hebrew, Roman and Syriac—again all with variants. There were also an inordinate number of *different* neumatic notation systems. While script-affiliation governed the extent to which a font could mutate and still be an affiliated script, individual interpretation governed the neumes. Finally, we have an early example of a color-coded system.

Although this color-coded notational system was discarded for the graphic representation of either notes or duration, the concept of color coding the *key* or *Psalm tone* remained. No later than the mid-eighth century, color-coding the Psalm tone was made an integral part of the *stæfwritung* musical notation system.

Chapter Ten

TO SING A NEW SONG

From the texts of the early Church writers, we get the impression that everybody wanted to sing a new song; it also is very clear that they could not agree on how to sing it. Already a bone of contention by the second century, with arguments ranging from extremists, who did not want the Psalms sung out loud, to belligerent bickering about whether the Psalms should be accompanied or not, the correct words, and the correct way to sing the Psalms, was a bitterly disputed point among religious parties. Although between the second and fifth centuries almost every church writer refers to the singing of the Psalms, the written evidence appears in small bits and pieces. We find a comment here on tempo; a reference there on order; another over there on which Psalms should be sung in the morning and which at night; almost everywhere we find arguments on soloist and congregational singing. Countering the declaration that the Psalms should be sung all the time, when plowing, when travelling, and when rowing, we find references, sometimes snide, to congregational singing, responsive singing, and antiphonal singing. What these distinctions meant are speculative and must be inferred from much later developments. Nowhere do we have any examples of *how* the Psalms were actually sung . . . or do we? We do. With all the arguments, with all the opposing positions, even a little forethought demanded that the Psalms be recorded.

What is recorded, however, depends upon purpose. If we are like the Anglo-Saxons who created *stæfwritung*, we ponder over the most difficult part of system design: what precisely do we want the system to *do*? There is no need to worry about recording the rhythms, because the rhythms are already recorded in the text. As it seems inconceivable that anybody might forget the melodies of the Psalms, we conclude that the tunes do not need to be written down. The decision is reached that what is needed is a notational system containing all the essential information on *how* to sing a new song. The system needs something that will record the Psalm formula (mode) and the Psalm tone, the number of singers and which one sings which solos, and when the "singing heap" or congregation [1] should join in.

The notational system, of course, must not interfere with the text. Now, we examine all previous attempts to record music, take the best methods of the lot, and adapt them to the vernacular. Finally, we throw it all into the pot, add a healthy portion of our own ingenuity, stir well, and out comes a system of musical notation that records all the necessary information on *how* to sing a new song. If this seems a somewhat irreverent way to refer to a truly innovative technique, there is a decided resemblance to a rich stew in the components of the musical notation system designed around *stæfwritung.*

The *stæfwritung* musical notation system combines the Greek full-alphabet method, not as a melodic notation, but to indicate responsive singing. It uses an Eastern Mediterranean color-coding technique to set the Psalm tone. The codifiers certainly used neumes, but not to record melody; they replaced the left-hand leg of the symbol *A* with variant forms of the **cephalicus** (*Kephalikos*—Greek, "of or for the head") neume to specify the number and order of lead singers. Script-differentiation requires two sets of chironomic notation; thus, both the Greco-Syriac-Roman and the North African-Semitic chironomic notations are used to indicate special dynamics: one system for Latin, another for Old English. They adopt the Greek idea of alphabetic symbols as numbers to indicate whether a Psalm formula is in first or second mode. Finally, they put the notational system in the most obvious place they could think of: right where chorale leaders could use it. The technique is referred to as **in-text encoding** because their musical notation system appears as *part* of the text.

It should be clear by now that all of these components depend upon the consistent and strict use of script differentiation by ethnos. Xenographic exchange is the basis of the entire notational system: everything else follows. Xenographic exchange, the oldest known form of writing enhancement, dates back to Akkad. At Akkad, xenographic exchange was used sparingly. Employed to distinguish the transcendent from the mundane, script exchange was confined to one word, or, at most, an idiomatic phrase. As we follow the script exchange technique down through the centuries, we find that nobody, nobody at all, ever varied its limits. These narrow and specialized limits were still in force when we arrive at the second century BCE and the Dead Sea Scrolls. Sitting there among the cursive Square Script, we find the Tetragrammaton written in Paleo-Hebraic. Nothing has changed when Christianity comes on the scene; the early Christian texts in Greek and Syriac confine xenographic exchange to a few words. Although Latin Christian texts do use script exchange, they confine the technique to the sacred name and the word *Amen* at the end of a Psalm or prayer.

The codifiers of *stæfwritung* saw that xenographic exchange could be used for far more than separating the transcendent from the mundane. Their outstanding innovation was the use of this technique throughout their writing system. A strict use of script differentiation permitted them to identify language at a glance and to use "italics" to indicate foreign words. It also placed xenographic exchange at the service of religious music.

Religious song has one unusual characteristic that is lacking in all other written records: continuity. From Enheduanna to David, from David to the Dead Sea, from the Dead Sea to Alexandria and to Antioch and thence to North Africa, from North Africa to Spain, Ireland, and Britain, and throughout the Western world, right on through recorded history until today, the written record is there for us to see. Thus, we must pay particular attention to the musical manuscripts.

By musical manuscripts, we include much more than late medieval and early renaissance texts studded with neumes. Most musicologists and music historians begin with melismata and neumes, and ignore any manuscript that does not contain neumatic notation. As good detectives, we know that everything has beginnings. Lest we miss an important clue, our scope is much wider. Under the heading of musical manuscripts we include Antiphonaries, such as the *Bangor Collectarium*; Liturgies, such as Saint Gall manuscripts 339 (*The Cantatorium*) and 359; Hymns, from such as those found among the Dead Sea Scrolls to *Caedmon's Hymn* to the thirteenth-century *Canterbury Hymn*; and, of course, the Psalters—*all* the Psalters—from Q11ps (the large Psalm scroll found in Cave 11 near the Dead Sea) to Columba's *Cathach* to the triple Psalters found around the periphery of the Old Roman Empire to the fourteen Old English versions of the Psalms.

We shall not, of course, examine every one of these manuscripts. We have already looked closely at some, for instance, the *Bangor Collectarium*, the *Cathach* of Columba, and *Caedmon's Hymn*; also many of the documents have previously been mentioned in passing. While the *stæfwritung* musical notation system shows up across all Western Europe, only a few manuscripts require special attention: one of the fourteen Old English Psalters and the two early ninth-century manuscripts from Saint Gall. We shall examine the fourteenth Psalter very carefully, from its format to its size, to its types of translations, and in this Psalter we shall find the complete *stæfwritung* musical notation system in use.

The Old English Psalters are an odd group under the best of circumstances. Sorting out the story told by the Psalters is difficult enough without the added burden of a lack of knowledge of the languages that, besides Latin, were known by the Celtic peoples, and passed on by them to their new converts, the Anglo-Saxons: Hebrew, Greek, and probably Syriac. The story told by the manuscripts and the *stæfwritung* musical notation system is much stranger—and far more interesting—than the Winner's desired history. In addition, it answers the question of what responsive, congregational, and antiphonal singing meant—at least to these people. It also sheds light on a vexing problem: Why should someone as tolerant and kindly as Bede hate the Christian Britons?

The English have a long tradition of insisting upon translations of the Pentateuch, the Gospels, and the Psalter into the vernacular. More than 300 attempts to translate the Psalms into metrical English show up between the fourteenth and nineteenth centuries, an average of one every two and a half years. Wycliffe's late fourteenth-century translation of the Bible into English was not a new idea even then. Preceding Wycliffe by more than half a century, Richard Rolle of Hampole (died 1340) translated the Psalter, with his own peculiar commentaries, into English. (Copies of Wycliffe Bibles are more common; while rarer, 20 of Rolle's Psalters survive. Most of these 20 Psalters were used as family Bibles until well into the sixteenth century. [2]) With the notable exception of Anglo-Saxon England, early translations of the Psalms into the vernacular are unknown from *Western* Europe.

We know that there were already many Christianities in England when the Roman mission headed by Augustine the lesser arrived. Thus, it was to be expected that there were also different traditions of Psalm translations. In actuality, there are three different traditions in England. In view of the fact that Christianity came to Cornwall and Wales from Punic-speaking Spain and North Africa, we are not amazed that of these three translation traditions, two are Latin based, that is, secondary research sources, and one is Hebrew based, in other words, a primary research source for Biblical studies. [3]

These Psalters follow the Old Greek pattern of Psalm numeration. Very early, in some versions of the Psalter, Psalms 9 and 10 were collapsed into one; hence, in some traditions, the Psalms are offset by one. References to Psalms are normally written using the Hebrew Masoretic (Masora merely means "traditional") number first, with the offset number second as in, for example, Ps 33(32).

Not all these fourteen Psalters are complete; not all of them are translations; some are said to be merely glosses—which may or may not be the case. One of the fourteen Psalters is a five-component diplomatic edition with commentaries that was produced about 1170 and is known as the *Eadwine Psalter* after the scribe who wrote it. The *Eadwine* is of special interest as it combines all three traditions—along with the provocative information that Jerome's three Latin versions were sung to different rhythms. The *Eadwine* is trilingual and includes an Anglo-Norman as well as an Old English version, the other thirteen Psalters are bilingual: Latin and Old English.

One tradition is represented by six recensions of what *may* be glosses (not translations) on Jerome's Latin *Gallican* (later called the *Vulgate*). This entire group is late, after the Benedictine reform; all written during and following the heavy-handed political movement to create a conformal Romano-English church. All six were written between 975 and 1075 and all are related. Reform or no, these six Psalters contain limited musical notation written into the Latin text. The use of the Greek full alphabet and the *A-cephalicus* neume parts of the *stæfwritung* notational system to indicate responsive singing can be seen—even on the badly burnt leaves of the *Vitellius* Psalter (BL. MS Cotton Vitellius E. xviii).

The other Latin tradition is older. The *Gallican* versions may or may not be glosses, but based in Jerome's *Romanum*, this tradition is clearly translation. From the evidence of the *Eadwine*, where the Old English is written between the lines of the *Romanum*, the *Gallican* never really replaced it. Also represented by six recensions, this translation tradition, however, has two different transmission paths. Path one contains five related, later translations; Path two contains one isolate. The isolate is known as the *Vespasian Psalter* (BL. MS Cotton Vespasian A1). Written and translated into the Mercian dialect, the *Vespasian* was produced around 825; it is the second oldest translation into Old English. The fourteenth Psalter, *The Paris Psalter* (B.N. MS. Fonds Latin 8824), another isolate, is the oldest. [4]

Our *copy* of the Psalms of the *Paris Psalter* is relatively late; we can date it with confidence to during or after 899, but there is no agreement on how *much* after. (The copy has been dated from as early as 899 to as late as 1030.) A copy, unlike an original, presupposes an existing text from which it is made. There is, therefore, an important distinction between *copy* and *text*. Perhaps this concept can be made clearer by example. Homer's epics were written in the ninth century BCE, hence, the *text* dates from the ninth century BCE. The first *copy*, a fragment, was written approximately in the second century BCE; nobody would ever think of maintaining that Homer's works date from the second century BCE because the *copy* is so much later. While not as great a time span exists between text and copy, the majority of the *text* of the Psalms of the *Paris Psalter* is older than the *copy* by a substantial 200 to 250 years.

The *text* of the Psalter demonstrates unequivocally that it dates from the mid-seventh century—at the very latest. We have neither time nor space to spend upon linguistic or orthographic analysis; nor do we need to. The evidence of the antiquity of the text is written in the manuscript itself. There are many examples, but one will suffice. Alistair Campbell, musing upon the development of some grammatical forms, proposed that, in pre-historic (before written records) Old English, these forms must have been differentiated in some way. He was correct; they were differentiated. Figure 10.1 shows the "pre-

Fig. 10.1
The "pre-Historic" genitive endings of *heora*. F. 18v-19r of the *Paris Psalter*: Caroline, Insular, and aleph-*a*

historic" differentiation among the endings of the genitive (possessive) form of *heora* on folios 18v and 19r of the *Paris Psalter*.

Psalters are Class 1 documents, that is, to be sung as written, no interpretation permitted. The *Paris Psalter* is a Class 1 document, and illustrates one reason for the prescription: every line of text is written sung phrase by sung phrase. The manuscript is in excellent condition, and nearly complete. Only 14 out of the original 200 leaves are missing; they were cut out sometime after the fourteenth century for their illuminations. [5] The writing is extremely clear and legible and easy to read. The Psalter is also a prime example of *scriptorium* training. The execution is so professional, that, like the *Moore Bede*, we can distinguish the number of scribes only from their ideographs and idiosyncrasies: there were three.

The three scribes were told to copy exactly, and two of them did. The scribes were so competent that we can distinguish the hands of Scribes 2 and 3 only by the way they wrote their *e*-merkas. Scribe 2 used a straight-tailed form (℮-) and Scribe 3 a curved *e*-merka (℮). Among the most obvious ideographs with which we may distinguish between Scribes 1 and 2 is their *g*. Scribe 1 uses a wider form than Scribe 2. Of these three scribes, only Scribe 1 had some difficulty following orders. We can see at the top of folio 1 verso where he had to "erase" (scrape the surface) two words and put them on the next line down. (A ghost of the two erased words can be seen on the first line.) He also squeezed the text to the left hand side of a column. We can readily imagine the *scriptorium* master coming around to check on how the work was progressing and saying, "No, No, No! It has to be written line for line, as is!" After correcting his mistake in placing text on the wrong line, Scribe 1 tried to follow orders. He apparently could not. Although he very carefully copied every graph form in the original, he kept squeezing the text towards the left. He was taken off the job in the middle of folio 32. The rest of the manuscript is the work of Scribes 2 and 3. Scribe 2, whose name, Wulfwinus, appears in the colophon was apparently in charge of the project. All corrections and insertions, including one leaf (folio 7), are in his hand.

Xenographic exchange and the variant forms of the ASPA appear throughout this carefully executed manuscript. When we let the manuscript speak for itself, it gives us other examples of such "pre-historic" Old English. Most of the Psalm texts of *The Paris Psalter* dates to the seventh century. Like Jerome's *Hebraicum*, it is a translation directly from the Hebrew.

The difference in the source language of the translation is not the only dissimilarity; *The Paris Psalter* is distinguished from the other thirteen in many ways. First of all, it is a Precentor's Psalter—a chorale guide, intended like the Saint Gall manuscripts, for from one to three singers. As we can expect in a chorale guide, it uses the full *stæfwritung* musical notation system. All the other Psalters use only parts of the notation system. All fourteen, including the *Eadwine*, indicate responsive singing, but the six from the Post-Reform *Gallican* tradition do not use other parts of the system. All six from the *Romanum* tradition, including the *Vespasian*, also include psalm tone, mode, and chironomic signs.

A further difference between the *Paris Psalter* and the other thirteen lies in its size. Twelve of these manuscripts are big, heavy, books intended to be placed on an altar, lectern, or stand. The thirteenth, the *Eadwine*, is both (please excuse the jingle) an altar Psalter and a very large, deluxe, illustrated, research and study guide. In strong contrast, the *Paris Psalter* is a portable Psalter. It is a long, narrow, **holster book**, that is, a book meant to fit into a pouch or sack for ease of transport. 52.6 centimeters high (about 22 inches), when open for use the double leaves are approximately 7-1/2 inches across (Figure 10.2). [6] (To get an idea of the shape of the Psalter, take two pieces of standard letterhead paper; overlapping them slightly, tape them together lengthwise and then fold them in half, long side to long side. The result will approximate the size of the *Psalter*. Now, opening it out enough to see the inside surface, hold the folded paper up as if to sing from what is written on it. We have a chorale guide such as those illustrated on thousands of Christmas cards.)

Yet another difference is that, in all the other Psalters, the Old English is written interlinearly. In the *Paris Psalter*, the two translations are written side by side in narrow parallel columns, a format reminiscent of Origen's *Hexapla*.

The *Paris Psalter* has other peculiarities that distinguish it from all the rest. Not only is the translation into Old English from Hebrew, but the Latin text is more than a little divergent. The original Latin text, in fact, is different enough that, back in the early 1800's, the first editor of the Psalter, Benjamin Thorpe, "fudged" the Latin to bring it into line with *The Vulgate*. The original Latin texts are so distinctive that we can trace the Psalter's whereabouts through them. During the early fourteenth century, the *Paris Psalter* was in Hampole with Richard Rolle being used as one of the texts to make his translation of the Psalms into "modern" English. While Rolle is supposed to have used only the Great Latin Bible, Psalm 96(95) gives the show away. [7] The Latin text of Rolle's Psalm 96(95) is word for word the distinctive Latin text of the *Paris Psalter*. [8]

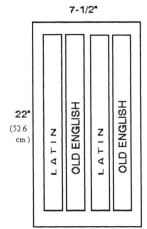

Fig. 10.2 The format and size of the *Paris Psalter*

The reason the Latin text is so different from those of the other thirteen translations is that the original Latin text is a new translation, from scratch, of a variant Old Greek Psalter. The Old English translation is just as distinctive and individual. Hebrew sources were available in both vowel marked (*kere*—as spoken) and consonantal (*ktiv*—as written) versions. By the second century CE, there were a number of places where the *kere* differed from the *ktiv*. We know that the Psalter's Old English text is a translation from a consonantal Hebrew source because it does not have known *kere*'s. We know that it was a variant source text because the translations supply lines of text that fit semantically and rhythmically, but are missing in the Masoretic text and are unknown from Latin or Greek sources. The Old English translations of the *Paris Psalter* are probably the finest translation of the Psalms into a vernacular in existence. Of all translations, it has perhaps the best right to be called "accurate."

What is meant by accuracy in translation is, to be sure, a difficult question. For some, accuracy resides in translating the denotative meaning of a word from the source language into the closest equivalent word in the target language. One major problem with the denotative approach to translation is that words in different languages rarely have even an approximate one-to-one mapping to each other and always carry with themselves their secondary meanings, their semantic baggage. Thus a given word in language A, rarely is synonymous to an "equivalent" word in language B; there are very few word for word equivalents between languages.

The lack of equivalency between languages often leads to the need for an entire sentence to translate a word from the source language into the target language. While this does not cause serious problems with prose translations, sentence-for-word equivalents create great difficulties with verse translations. The King James Version of Psalm 23, for example, translates *yarbitzeni* as "He maketh me to lie down." As *yarbitzeni* is a **causative** (cause or make a person or an abstraction to do something), [9] the KJV is correct in so far as "maketh me" goes, but is misleading as it translates only *part* of the verb. The early Hebrews were pastoral; sheep were an important part of their economy. When something is of enough importance, the vocabulary of a language will reflect it. In this case, Hebrew makes a distinction between human and animal to refer to the act of lying down. The verb *lirbotz* (root רבץ [R-B-Tz]), does not mean to lie down like a person, *lishkav* (root שכב-[Sh-C-B]), but to lie/crouch down like a lamb—with all four legs tucked under the body. Although in Hebrew the distinction is clear and an integral part of the extended metaphor in this Psalm, a translator writing verse cannot write "He causes me to lie/crouch down like a lamb with all four feet tucked under me."

This distinction in meaning between "to lie down like a human" and "to lie down like a lamb" would seem to be difficult enough for a translator to handle; however, there is another problem. Very early, *R-B-Tz* acquired a secondary meaning; "to flow towards one." This latter meaning extended still further to become "to cause to be fed/watered." While it has been suggested that the multivocality of *rovetz* derives from the directions on feeding animals in *Tosefta Bavli* (Mishnaic writings from Babylon), **coherence strategies** (binding techniques) employed in the Psalm make it quite clear that these extended meanings already existed in the Biblical period. The Psalmist could have written *yarbitz oti* (causes me to settle or crouch down like a lamb), or *yarbitz li* (causes to flow to me). He did neither; the choice of words is intentional and meant to convey both senses. Hence, an accurate translation would read: "He causes me to lie down like a lamb with all four feet tucked under me and causes me to be watered/fed." The sheer length of an accurate translation (which is clearly not one to one) distorts the structure of the verse; it also does not fit into the melody.

As everybody was working from more or less the same original, variations among translations depend upon the interpretation of the source language by the translator, and upon his own knowledge of the *target* language. (Many of the more peculiar translations stem from a lack of command of the target language on the part of the translator.) Denotative translations have much in common, a fact that often leads to the conflation of sources when tracing the lineage of Psalter texts. Understandably, the vast majority of early translations of the Psalms are denotative.

Jerome tried three times to translate the Psalms into Latin accurately. His translations are denotative, that is, he chose a word from among denotative possibilities. Jerome, however, was aware that words do not translate one-to-one and carry different cultural connotations. Hence, he also used variants (*variatio*), that is, words with somewhat different connotations chosen from among the denotative possibilities in an attempt to convey the literal sense. His first attempt was based upon existing translations from Greek (*Romanum*). Dissatisfied, Jerome made his second attempt, a fresh translation directly from Old Greek (*Gallican*). Still dissatisfied, when Jerome retired to Bethlehem, he produced yet another translation, this time directly from Hebrew (*Hebraicum*) with the help of Paula (347-404) and her women.

Considering the difficulties of translation from a terse stress language, Hebrew, into a polysyllabic quantitative language, Latin, Jerome did tolerably well. Nevertheless, we cannot really call any of his translations "accurate." Poetry and song cannot be translated based solely on denotations. Many of the Psalms are among the densest poems/songs ever written; much of the meaning rests in the connotations. All too frequently, metaphors depend upon this multivocality.

In addition, in Hebrew prose, verse, and song, as in other languages, sound is typically linked to, and reinforces, sense. Good compositions use many techniques to create redundancy, that is, repetition. The sound-to-sense link is a redundancy creating technique and an additional mnemonic aid. Many of the early translations exhibit attempts to imitate the sound-sense linking patterns. These attempts often lead to the choice of a biased word from among the denotative, almost equivalent, words in the target language. In Jerome's *Gallican*, for instance, line 1 of Psalm 23 reads: D*ominus* r*egit m*e for *A*d*onai* r*o'*i, "The Lord rules/governs me," instead of "My Lord shepherds me." While the sound is carried across, more or less, the multiple senses of the word "shepherd" are lost: A shepherd does *not* rule or govern, he cares for, guides, and provides. Jerome was perfectly aware of the bias: In his *Hebraicum*, he abandoned any attempt to carry through the sound-sense linking pattern. He translated *ro'i* as *pascit me*—shepherds me.

Because of this density, connotative meanings are normally the subject of exegetical treatment; connotative translations are notably rare. In a connotative translation, the translator attempts to include the multiple senses of a word. As we can see from an accurate translation of רבץ [lie down like a lamb with all four legs tucked under *and* watered/fed me], this results in lines that forcibly remind us of the limerick that ends: "He tries to put as many words into a line as ever he possibly can." To moderns, it seems impossible to sing such lines, and such connotative translations are normally classified as "prose" rather than as poetry or song. Connotative translations show up among the early *Targumim* (translations into Aramaic). We also have an example, or rather, a partial example, of such an inclusive "prose" translation in the *Paris Psalter*.

One of the most obvious peculiarities of this *Psalter* is its schizophrenia; it has a split personality. The English Psalms 51 through 150 are called the "metrical psalms," because they are very regular and quite "metrical." The first 50 psalms are called "The Prose Psalms." In other words, the first 50 Psalms are a connotative translation, or, to be more precise, *parts* of these first 50 Psalms are a connotative translation.

Once, all these Psalms were metrical. Pieces of the missing first 50 "metrical" psalms turn up in a manuscript from the last quarter of the *tenth* century: MS Junius 121. Along the lines of "you just can't keep a good song down," right in the midst of the *Romanum* version used in the *twelfth*-century *Eadwine Psalter*, we find stretches of Psalms from the *Paris Psalter*. Eadwine called himself the "prince of scribes," and we can probably take him at his word. Because the *Eadwine Psalter* is a diplomatic edition and a study text, Eadwine was careful to use a different script and a different color ink for the pieces taken from the *Paris Psalter*. The Old English translations from the *Romanum* texts are written in a golden-brown ink; the translations from the *Paris Psalter* insertions are in black.

We really should not say that these first 50 metrical Psalms are missing. Quite a large proportion of the "Prose" Psalms still contain portions of these metrical Psalms; the originals peek out from between the "prose," connotative expansions. We just have to get past the sections that were revised by Ælfred the Great in 899 to see them. Revision is exactly what happened to the first 50 psalms of the *Paris Psalter*—and it was Ælfred's doing. Why did he revise them? King Ælfred was only doing what he considered his job as the shepherd of his people.

In the Ancient Near East, a king, or a clan leader for that matter, was considered the shepherd of his people; they were *his* flock. A good shepherd/king provided shelter, food, clothing, guidance, entertainment, and protection: It was in the job description. The best shepherd/king provided the best of everything. This ancient convention is the reason for much of the "shepherd" imagery in both the Hebrew and Greek bibles. Ælfred clearly knew about this ancient tradition. He took his job as the shepherd of his people very seriously indeed.

We know quite a bit about Ælfred, both from Asser's biography and from his own writings. Among the things Ælfred felt it necessary for him as a good shepherd to provide were education and religious guidance. The educational aspect is very easy to understand; learning in both the vernacular and in the *koine*, Latin, had practically disappeared under the Danish attacks of the ninth century. Records of history wanted, and were supplied by translations of Bede's *Historia Ecclesiastica* and Orosius's history. Religious guidance needs a bit of explanation. Two of the titles on his list of books to be translated were Gregory's *Pastoral Care* and the Psalms. With two translations of the Psalms already available, the question arises why Ælfred should want yet another translation? The answer is rather endearing in the light it casts on the king as a man. So few English were left who could read and write that Ælfred brought in anybody who claimed he knew how. Would-be royal scribes came from every part of the Island. From the scripts, we know that his royal *scriptorium* included people from every Christian party. He could not help but know; it would appear that this diversity disturbed him. Ælfred had seen the Pope as a child; he was more or less of the Roman affiliation and he wanted that his flock be united and turned to Rome, too. Being a good shepherd, though, he tried to use persuasion rather than force.

We have descriptions of how Ælfred worked. He had knowledgeable helpers; men like Asser from Saint David's in Wales. While his helpers would translate and explain things, Ælfred would do the actual translation into Old English. Ælfred was well aware of the problems of denotative translation. He expressed this clearly when he stated that:

þa boc wendan on englisc þe is genemed on læden pastoralis and on englisc hierde-boc hwilum word be worde hwilum andgit of andgiete." [10]

[This book (is) translated into English, that is named in Latin, *Pastoralis*, and in English, Shepherd's-Book, word by word, where possible, otherwise sense by sense.]

Ælfred's command of the vocabulary of the target language, Old English, was superb. His understanding of how far he could push a musical phrase was outstanding. Further, as his works show, Ælfred had been well trained in the correct methods of composition. In spite of these definite advantages, he was no poet; he was not all that good at prose either. "Sense by sense" dominates the Ælfredian works. He was pedantic and precise. He apparently wished that everything be explained in detail, no matter how obvious. He went off into long explanations and explications. Sad to relate in light of his ambitious re-education program, none of Ælfred's works are, in modern parlance, a "good read." The limerick ending describes the Ælfredian voice with a great deal of accuracy. He definitely fits "as many words into a line as ever he possibly can." His voice is so easy to recognize that we can spot his work anywhere it shows up. [11] Ælfred's explicatory voice is strongly evident in these first 50 Psalms.

Why did Ælfred choose the translation from Hebrew instead of the one from a *Romanum*? These 50 Psalms tell us why. Ælfred did what Aldhelm, the renowned *Englisc* poet, had done before him and what others, such as Ælfric, did after him. One of the approved techniques, suggested by some church used, because there is little utility in writing new words to songs if they are not well known among the general population.

We have a number of indications, besides Ælfred's choice, that these particular Psalms *were* popular; that they were very well known and sung among the general population. This translation had already existed for at least 250 years by Ælfred's day. These Psalms were so well known that, in spite of the Benedictine Reform, parts of these Psalms still show up in Junius 121 during the last quarter of the tenth century. They clearly were still known 500 years after translation, for entire Psalms appear in the *Eadwine Psalter*. The language of the Psalms of the *Paris Psalter* was no longer fully understood when Rolle made his new translation into Modern, fourteenth-century, English 700 years after their original translation.

Ælfred, as we have already seen, was a good King and he believed in the powers of persuasion. What better way to gently turn his people away from one church to another than through giving them new words to sing to their songs? So, this is exactly what Ælfred did.

There is no question whatsoever that Ælfred wanted his new psalms to be sung. From Psalm 1 right on through to Psalm 150, the *Paris Psalter* is fully encoded in the *stæfwritung* musical notation system.

The *stæfwritung* system is extremely logical. Psalms are sung according to specific rules. Under these rules we need to know, the melodic formula (later termed mode), psalm tone (starting note), and final (ending note). We need information as to precentor, second, and third singer solos and when the "singende heap" joined in. We need to know stanza repeats; how many beats to a given note, and the length of a musical phrase. All of this information is encoded right in the text.

The Psalm tone is shown by the color of the first letter; for instance, gold or yellow indicates, in modern notation, the key of C or a-minor. (A-minor is the relative minor of the key of C-Major; the natural minor scale is identical to the old Aeolian mode.)

Some of the chironomic notation symbols appear *over* the text, for example, the tifcha/oxeia/virga (´). This symbol imitates the motion of a hand as it rises at an angle and indicates rising stress or volume. Those chironomic symbols that could be incorporated into the graphic symbols appear *in* the text. The *e-merka* (ẻ), for instance, incorporates the chironomic symbol that imitates a hand cupped around an ear and moving slowly away. The extended tongue on an *e* indicates that the note should be held for the number of beats shown by the length of the tail while slowly reducing volume. The number of beats a sound is held is shown by the length of the tongue on an *e*, a trailer on an *l* or *r*, an extended headstroke on a *t*, or an internal expansion in an *S* or an *N* (Figure 10.3).

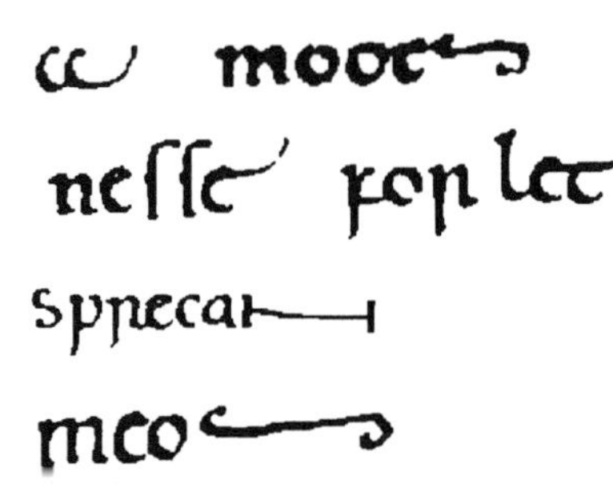

Responsive singing is indicated within the body of a Psalm by xenographic exchange on the first letter of a verse. A Latin-*D* in the Old English text and an Old English majuscule round-*d* in the Latin text designates a soloist verse (Figure 10.4b). The next majuscule symbol employing xenographic exchange indicates a return to congregational singing or responses (Figure 10.4a).

Much of the information is written in the *titulus*, the introductory comment at the beginning of most Psalms stating for

Fig. 10.3 *Stæfwritung*: Directions for held notes

whom, or by whom, or for what purpose the song is written. The Psalm formula, for instance, is shown in the *titulus*, logically enough, by the form of the letter *V* in the word *Vox* (voice). Latin *V* indicates first formula (or mode); �, Greek *deuteros*, or second, indicates 2nd formula (or mode). The number of the soloists and which ones are given by the form of the *cephalicus* neume written as the left hand leg of the Rustic-*A* (Figure 10.5). We can see how the word *Ecclesia* [assembly] uses the common Latin variant spelling, *æcclesia*, to allow the inclusion of the necessary information. Psalm 96(95) is to be sung in 2nd formula with solos by the 1st singer. Psalm 97(96) is to be sung in 1st formula, solos by 2nd singer.

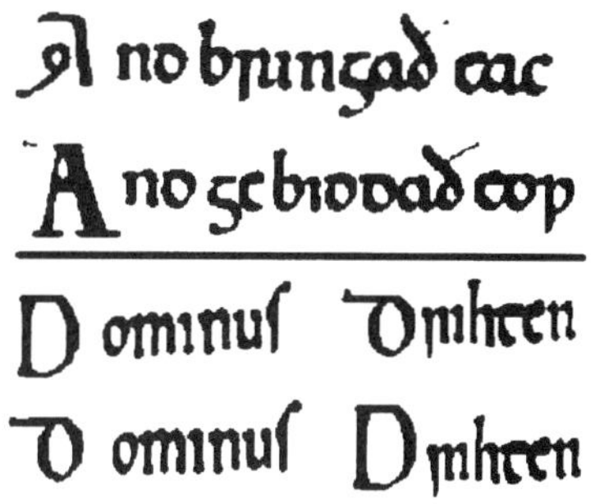

Fig. 10.4 *Stæfwritung*: Xenographic Exchange directions for Responsive singing

All early Psalters—Latin, Greek, Hebrew, Aramaic, and the Old English Psalms of the *Paris Psalter*—are written sung-phrase by sung-phrase. Whatever the language, Psalm texts must *never* be emended. Although it is perfectly permissible to organize one of these Old English Psalms by verse for analytic purposes, the text *must* be returned to its original state else we cannot reconstruct the music, or see how the musical notation system worked. Above all else, whether then or now, we must have the first verse of a Psalm in order to sing it. The first verse sets the melodic formula.

Ælfred seems to have been warned that he should not change the first verse of a Psalm if he wanted his people to sing it. In some cases he listened to this shrewd advice; in others he clearly did not heed the warning. We obviously cannot examine every Psalm, but must limit ourselves to one Ælfredian revised Psalm and the first two verses from a typical representative of the original metrical Psalms. We will also take a quick look at two verses of another Psalm where Ælfred ignored the warning and rewrote the first verse.

The question may arise as to why we need analyze a Psalm at all in order to reconstruct it. The answer is: it has everything to do with it. Analysis supplies necessary redundancy.

One serious problem faced by the reconstructors of the Gregorian Chant is a lack of redundancy. With only one language to work with, Latin, there is no convenient way to verify their reconstruction as to accuracy, a fact that has led to much dispute.

Fig. 10.5 *Stæfwritung*: Formula and Singer Directions Psalms 96(95) and 97(96)

What wants is redundancy: a bilingual key, a second language as a check. It should be noted that the difficulties in reconstructing the music for Latin apply equally to the reconstruction of any early music, including Hebrew: a lack of redundancy—music, linguistic, and graphic. Because the Old English of the *Paris Psalter* is a translation from Hebrew, we have the necessary redundancy for *both* languages. In order to have our bilingual check, though, we must first run a semantic analysis on both texts.

Everybody picks on Psalm 23(22) because it is short, which is an advantage. Although it bears clear evidence of Ælfred's connotative voice, he changed neither the first colon nor the final. Given the redundancy supplied by this Psalter, the music can be reconstructed; the Psalm can still be sung.

Its length, however, is only one of our reasons. Perhaps it seems foolish to try to vindicate someone 1100 years after his death, but nobody has a good word to say for what Ælfred did to Psalm 23(22). There is no question that his revised Psalm is poor poetry. Ælfred's additions have either irritated or amused every person who has ever looked at the Psalms of the *Paris Psalter*. The most frequent complaint is that they are "inaccurate," followed by the comment that they are "unnecessary." The use of the causative "set" (make to sit) in parallel with "fed" to translate both meanings of *yarbitzeni* is considered "inaccurate." The use of *swyðe* (very) twice in the Psalm falls into the "unnecessary" class. As we have seen, "accuracy" lies in a thoroughly nebulous realm; whether something is "necessary" depends upon one's purpose. Ælfred's purpose was to gently turn his people to another affiliation; as to accuracy, the readers will have to decide for themselves.

Although Ælfred rewrote parts of Psalm 23(22), it still has its head, and can be reconstructed. First, though, we need our bilingual check. In order to have our check, we need to find out what the Psalm actually says. While interesting in their own ways, commentaries are useless to us. [12] We have to know what is actually written, not someone's theological interpretation of the words, but what the words actually mean—else we cannot reconstruct the music of the Psalm. This is more of a problem than it might appear to be.

Psalm 23 is written in an highly sophisticated, rhetorically dense, and tightly constructed double envelope pattern. Multilayered and multivocal, the Psalm displays an intricately linked, back-and-forth series of plays on words and sounds, and interplay between surface and secondary domains. The 23rd is one of the Davidic Psalms and demonstrates his distinctive voice. His voice is so distinctive and individual, that the Davidic psalms can easily be distinguished from all the other Psalms. This one Psalm amply illustrates his voice and explains why David was revered as one of the great poets of antiquity.

When examining works of a great master, we must be careful that we do not conflate **conceptual domains** with **metaphorical categories**. The two structures are different in both intent and form. A conceptual domain refers to the sphere or image that carries the idea of a work, whether written or oral. Metaphorical categories refer to the class, or family, of a metaphor.

The Hebrew of Psalm 23 is completely clear: there is *one* sustained metaphorical category—God, the Shepherd. There are *two* conceptual domains. The concept that lamb stands for child is ancient, and in this Psalm the first or surface domain (A) is entirely the viewpoint of a lamb; the second (B) is that of a mischievous child.

The Psalm is packed with what are called **metaphoric triggers**, 30 of them in just 11 lines. Metaphoric triggers are words that signal a change of conceptual domain. [13] Here they function in both conceptual domains because both lambs and children are curious, prone to get themselves into dangerous situations, and in need of guidance and loving care.

The lines refer back and forth to each other throughout the Psalm. Lines 2 through 5 present a general basic list of the needs of a lamb; line 6—the center or pivot of the Psalm—marks a change from needs to benefits. Lines 7-11 present a list of benefits accrued from having such a good shepherd. Line 7 mirrors lines 3 and 5, and line 8 mirrors lines 2 and 5. Line 9 echoes line 3, line 10 echoes line 4, and line 11 iterates lines 2, 3 and 6, and then sums up the result of having the good shepherd of line 1. At the same time, the psalmist plays against secondary meanings, as in line 3 (*mei* waters —against line 2 *R-V-Tz*—cause to flow towards). In addition, there is a change of person: Line 1 speaks *of* the Lord. In lines 2 through 5, the speaker is talking *about* his Lord; in lines 6 through 10, the speaker is talking *to* his Lord. In line 11, the speaker once again reverts to the third person and speaks *of* his Lord. The Psalm comes full circle and attains closure with line 11—and the completion of its external envelope pattern.

Oddly enough, the only early commentator who recognized what this Psalm is about was Athanasius. (If one has read much of Athanasius's writings, it *is* odd.) Athanasius said that this is a "Psalm of boasting in the Lord." Play and levity are not the same thing; playfulness and seriousness do not negate each other. One can be in dead earnest and still be playful. David ben Jesse appears to have had a well developed **agonal** sense, a playful approach to serious contest. [14] His playful touch shows up in even the most somber of his works, such as Psalm 51:7. Blood stains are not easy to remove. Praying for forgiveness, he does not ask that he be "washed clean," he asks that he be *scrubbed* clean; drubbed, beaten against the rocks, like linens, or trodden on, stamped into fuller's earth, like woolens. In Psalm 23, he has given his agonal sense full rein. Athanasius is correct: This is a "Psalm of Boasting in the Lord": Every benefit is the very best possible, as we could expect from the very best shepherd. The speaker is a little boy sticking his tongue out and saying, "Nyah! Nyah! My shepherd is better than your shepherd." The "sunny little Psalm," nevertheless, is grimly serious; the consequences of having a bad shepherd are dire.

Another major problem is the translation barrier created by the undeniably beautiful version of Psalm 23 found in the King James Version. As lovely as it is, when it comes to accuracy, Ælfred and the original translator of the *Paris Psalter* did a far better job. The KJV, for example, translates *naot déshé* as "green pastures," a well known and well loved image. While there certainly is greenery, unfortunately, there is nary a pasture in sight. Although there does exist a nearly one-to-one correspondence between Hebrew *mar'eh* and English *pasture*, this is not what the Psalmist said. If he had wanted to say *bemar'ot* (on pastures), he would have. Instead, he chose *benaot déshé*.

As already noted, the more important something is within a given society, the more that culture will overdifferentiate, create words to fill vocabulary gaps and to describe that necessary "something." Biblical Hebrew distinguishes between two major categories of greenery as distinct from trees or bushes: *ésev* means taller greenery, for example, grasses and vetch, while *déshé* indicates low growing greenery, ground-cover, such as clover. The distinction is important enough to be specifically stated in Genesis 1:11, on the third day of creation. *Déshé*, then, is a specific *type* of greenery.

Next, the Psalmist chose the plural of *naé* (pleasantness or pleasance or pleasure or niceness) to modify this specific type of greenery. *Naé* appears once as *bena'ot* (Ps 23:3) and a total of eleven times throughout the Hebrew Bible. The Hebrew word *midbar* means "a waste," that is, any place unsuitable for grazing sheep. A *midbar* is not necessarily a desert; it may be rocky, swampy, or sandy. *Naé* appears five times either as *na'ot midbar* (waste) or *na'ot hamidbar* (of the waste). In context, the references are to "beauty spot in the waste"—, in other words, an oasis (Jeremiah 9:9, Jeremiah 23:10, Joel 1:19, 1:20, and 1:22, Ps. 65:13). From a lamb's point of view, a good shepherd could not provide better fodder; the *na'ot déshé* are mountain oases, a delectable banquet table of lush green clover. Perhaps the closest Modern English translation of *na'ot déshé* would be "pleasances of clover" or "pleasures of greenery." No known version in Greek or Latin translates either the complete meaning or the imagery. Ælfred's translation uses *swyðe good feoh land* [very good cattle land], for *na'ot déshé* and picks up both the image and the meaning of the words as the very best, the world's most beautiful, animal feeding grounds.

Some of the triggers function in both domains; while some are domain dependent. Trigger I, for instance, *yeshovev*, can mean "return to an original state," "refresh," "calm down," or "restore" (all very early extensions from "return to an original state"). The Psalmist makes use of *all* four meanings. "Return to an original state" is inherent in Domain A, the lamb; "calm down" is inherent in Domain B, the naughty child; while "restore" and "refresh" are in both A and B.

Similarly, the ancient "good-bad" formula, begins with a reverse order trigger (P) in line 5 as "bad/ill (KJV "evil") and links both alliteratively and semantically with the trigger (U) in line 8, a description of the bad/ill/evil. The formula is completed with trigger Y, "good," in line 10: the closure of the internal envelope pattern.

We need to know what the words of the original Hebrew mean in order to have our necessary redundancy. We need a semantic cross-check on the Old English Psalm to reconstruct the Psalm. We shall also, incidentally, check on the accuracy of the Old English translation. This leads us to one more problem: this time not with the Hebrew, but with the Old English.

Back in the nineteenth century, when Anglo-Saxon studies emerged as a discipline among enthusiastic hobbyists, the existence of true glossaries, such as the *Épinal* and Ælfric's Latin Grammar and Glossary, resulted in the assumption that, unless a word showed a clear line of descent from Old to Modern English or could be traced through cognates in related languages, everything had to be a gloss to a Latin word. As a result, there are quite a few "ghost" words in the dictionaries, as well as misunderstandings and mistranslations. It was also not at all uncommon for people to pick up a later meaning of a Latin word. We have more than a few examples of this last type of error. One fairly spectacular example of this type of misreading of Latin led to the word *draco* being translated as "dragon." *Draco*, however, was picked up directly from the Old Greek *dracon*, where it meant either a "water serpent" or a "bright-eyed serpent." It did not mean a "dragon" in Latin either, but a "serpent." All the illuminated Psalters show a serpent, but this was ignored or seen as ignorance on the part of the Anglo-Saxons. Because these nineteenth century workers translated the Hebrew word for "crocodile," (*tannin*) as a "dragon," "dragon" is the meaning that made it into both Hebrew-English and Anglo-Saxon dictionaries.

The translator of the Psalms of the *Paris Psalter* clearly knew that the word *tannin* meant an intelligent and dangerous water creature. He also obviously knew that a serpent, *draco*, was not a good translation; he used *oracon*, the orca, the killer whale. There are no crocodiles in the waters around Britain, but an orca is an intelligent and dangerous water creature. Under the circumstances, *oracon* is a much better translation of *tannin*. Obviously, as it was not a "dragon," the translation was considered erroneous. This type of "error" occurs with frequency throughout the Old English Psalter translations, not only in the *Paris Psalter*. As a result, we have to look at each problematic word in context as used in quotations. Hence, neither the Hebrew nor the Old English of Psalm 23(22) has been translated as a "translation." Instead two tables have been prepared.

Table 10.1 on page 172 gives the Old English text by verse. This is followed by a multivocal denotative translation of the Old English; multiple meanings of a word are shown in descending order of "accuracy." Two Old English words have not been translated as they have no modern equivalents. In both cases, the Old English words are very accurate translations. Their meanings are self evident and, except for using modern spelling, they have been included unchanged. The last column gives a transliterated Hebrew version. The Hebrew has been transliterated to preserve the sound play.

Triggers have been assigned alphabetic numeration and marked in the Hebrew text; where the Old English picks up a trigger, the alphabetic marker appears in the Old English as well.

A concise explanation of the triggers with their multiple meanings, is given on page 173 in Table 10.2. The technical term for this type of table is a **Componential Analysis Matrix**. Such matrices are used by professional translators as the base from which to write a translation. The First column gives the Trigger by alphanumeric "number." The next column gives the transliterated Hebrew in italic-face type. This is followed by columns giving the denotative and connotative meanings and lists them by domain as either intrinsic <i> or selective <s>. Links to other triggers are underlined; the beginning and ending of each envelope is also given.

This is a do-it-yourself translation project. Table 10.2 will permit readers to try and write their own translation of this Psalm and see if they can come up with a more accurate translation than that found in Psalm 23(22) of the *Paris Psalter*. To be fair, it should be pointed out that the Hebrew word for "mercy" is *rachamim*, not *hésed. Rachamim* carries with it sympathy for the one afflicted; *hésed* carries the intent to do someone good irrespective of his condition. Similarly, *tzédek* does not mean "righteous," but someone well versed in the ways of *hésed*, rightness, correctness. Nor are the paths/ways of rightness "straight"; they are "strait," narrow and difficult to follow. Unlike Ælfred, who knew about sheep and shepherding, modern urbanites are unlikely to know why a shepherd carries both a branch (stick/twig/rod/cudgel) and a shepherd's crook (staff). The branch is used as a weapon against animals who prey on sheep; the hook on a crook is used to catch a straying lamb around the neck and pull it back to safety, as well as being something to lean on.

Sound patterning is not required. While the original translator tried to match sound patterning whenever possible, Ælfred did not. Remember, though, the new words must fit into the musical phrases, and, while an occasional grace note is permissible, gross changes are not allowed.

Good or bad translation aside, the Psalm was still meant to be sung. As has been noted, the first verse is critical to reconstruction: the first verse gives us the correct melodic formula. We have our semantic bilingual as a check and all the directions are in the manuscript. All we need now is the Psalm formula.

As we can see from the instructions to sing the Psalms day and night, the original melodies could be sung by anybody. The melodies had to be simple and easy to remember, as is necessary when music is used as a mnemonic device. To be used as working and travelling songs, they had to have had lively and catchy tunes. The new Neo-Platonic chants required trained singers. We would find it most difficult to get any work done at a reasonable rate, let alone sow or reap or row, to the their slow, intricate, and stately melodies. Nor are the slowed chants particularly regular or rhythmic.

We can tell from the rhythms encoded into the text that we are not dealing with any of the Neo-Platonic slowed chants. We also have to remember that this is a translation directly from Hebrew. Roughly 95 years ago, Abraham Idelsohn, a musicologist and cantor, collected as many examples of the musical formulæ as he could find. Although we do not have all the Psalm formulæ, many of the Hebrew Psalm melodies are available in the Idelsohn archives at the Hebrew University of Jerusalem. [15]

Still, just to muddle things even further, what if the source melodies are quite similar, but depend upon where and when a translator hears them? This happens to be the case; there are three different primary branches of melodies for the Psalms. All three use the same basic melodic motifs;

Table 10.1 Psalm 23(22): Possible translations into Modern English

Old English	Modern English (possibilities)	Hebrew
Drihten me [A] raEt [B]	The Lord me guides/counsels/ advises/provides for	Adonai [A] ro'i [B]
ne byð me	nor/no/not will be/is me	lo èchsar [C]
nanes godes wan [C]	of none of good want/lack	
⌐ he me geset [E]	and he me caused to be sat/placed/put	bena'ot dèshè [D]
on swyðe good feoh land [D] .	in/on very good cattle land	yarbitzéni [E]
Ānd fedde me [E]	and fed me	
bewaEtera staðum [F]	by/on/over the banks of waters	al mei menuchot [F]
and min mod [H]	and my spirit/mood/heart/mind	yenahaléni [G] nafshi [H]
gehwyrfde [I]	turned/turned around/revolved/reversed	yeshovev [I]
of unrotnesse on gefean	from unrightness to joy/gladness/ happiness/pleasure	
he me gelaEdde [J] ofer	He me lead over	yenachèni [J]
þa wegas [K] rihtwisnesse [L]	the ways (of) rightwiseness/uprightness/ correctness/rightness/straightness	b'ma'agalei [K] tzèdek [L]
for his naman [M] .	for his name "	l'ma'an shemo [M]
þeah ic nu gange	Though I now go/walk/wander	gam ki élékh
on midde	in middle/mid/amid/amidst	be gai
þa sceade deaðes [N]	the shadow of death	tzal mavet [N]
ne ondræde ic me [O] nan yfel [P]	not dread I me no evil	lo ira [O] r'a [P]
for þa(m) þu	for/because you	ki ata
byst mid me drihten [Q]	will be/are with me Lord.	'imadi [Q]
þin gyrd	Thine twig/stick/branch	shivetekha
and þin staEf [R]	and thine staff/[shepherd's] crook	omishantekha [R]
me afrefredon [S]	me cheered/comforted/consoled/supported	hema yenachamuni [S]
þ(aEt) is þin þreaung [R]	that is thine threat/reproach/reproof/ reprimand/warning/censure	
and eft þin frefrung [S]	and aft[er] thy comfort/solace/consolation	
þu gegearwodest beforan me	You readied/prepared/set up before me	ta'arokh lefanai
swiðe bradne beod [T]	(a) very broad table	shulchan [T]
wiþ þara willan	against the will (of)	neged
þe me hatedon [U] .	those who me hated/afflicted ·	tzorerai [U]
þu gesmyredest me	You smeared/spread me	déshanta
mid ele min heafod [V]	with oil my head	be shemen roshi [V]
drihten hu maEre þin folc nu is	Lord how splendid thine folk now is	cosi reva'ya [W]
aElce daEge hit symblað · [W, X]	every day they feast "	
And folgie me nu [Z]	And follows/pursues me now	akh [X] tov ve hèsed [Y]
þin mildheortnes [Y]	Thine mild-heartedness	yirdefuni [Z]
ealle dagas mines lifes [AA]	all (the) days (of) my life	kol yeme chayai [AA]
þæt ic maEge wunian [AB]	That I may dwell/abide/live	ushavti [AB]
on þinum huse [AC]	in thine house	be bèit Adonai [AC]
swiðe lange tiid [AD]	very long time	le orèkh
oð lange ylde [AD]	until long age	yamim. [AD]

Table 10.2 Psalm 23: Componential Analysis

<i> intrinsic
< > selective

Alpha No. / Trigger	Possible Translation Denotative/Connotative	Domain <A> <B>
A *Adonai*	The Lord	<i> <i>
Trigger AC		
B. *Ro'i*	(my) Shepherd(s me)/	<i> <s>
	Guardian (Guards)/	<s> <i>
Trigger AD	Protector/Provider	<i> <i>
C. *lo èchsar*		
Trigger W	Lack nothing/want not/ have everything	<i> <i>
D. *na'ot dèshè*	places of pleasantness, covered with low greenery	<i> <s>
Triggers T, AC	Mountain Oases	<s> <i>
Open Internal envelope-pattern		
E. *yarbitzéni*	cause to lie down, legs tucked under; feeds	<i> <s>
	Causes to set/settle down;	
Trigger F	- " - to flow towards one	<s> <i>
F. *mei menuchot*	water of rest/relaxation/ refrehment/ease	<i> <i>
	abundance of clear	
Triggers E, T	drinking water	<s> <i>
G. *yenahaléni*	leads	<i> <i>
	guides/conducts	<s> <i>
Trigger J	oversees	<i> <s>
H. *nafshi*	me; that which makes me, me; myself; an entity; an individual	<i> <i>
I. *yeshovev*	return to original state	<i> <i>
Trigger AB	refresh	<i> <i>
	restore	<i> <s>
Play on	calm down	<s> <i>
shovav ->	naughty child	<s> <i>
J. *yenachèni*	lead/guide/teach/intruct	<i> <i>
Trigger Q		
K. *b'ma'agalei*	twisting paths/winding ways/ Circuitous paths	<s> <i>
Trigger N	mountain paths/trails	<i> <s>
L. *tzèdek*	right way/upright	<i> <s>
Trigger Y	correct thing to do	<s> <i>
M. *L'ma'an shemo*	For the sake/honor of His name	<i> <i>
	My Shepherd is better than yours	<i> <s>
	My Daddy is Bigger than yours	<s> <i>
Triggers A, B, AC		
N *gam ki élékh b'gei tzal-mavet*	Though I should wander in canyons/crevices/ ravines of death in the shadows	<i> <s>
	Wander off the right path and get into	
Trigger K	dangerous situations	<s> <i>
O. *lo ira*	That I shall dread not	<i> <i>
P. *r'a*	disorder/ill (vs. good)	<i> <i>
	wildness/troubling	
Triggers U, R, ; Open reverse Good-Ill formula		

Alpha No. / Trigger	Possible Translation Denotative/Connotative	Domain <A> <B>
Q. *Ki ata 'imadi*	Because You stand by me	<i> <i>
Triggers	You are armor at my side/	<s> <i>
O, P,	Because you are with me	<i> <i>
R. *shivetekha umishantekha*		
Triggers	cudgel and crook	<i> <s>
O, P, U	stick and staff	<s> <i>
hema yenachamuni	they comfort me/" a hurt	<s> <i>
	they console me/"for ill	<i> <s>
Trigger F (*menuchot*), I (*yeshovev*)		
T. *ta'arokh lefanai*	you place before my face	<s> <i>
	you spread before my face	<i> <s>
shulchan	a feasting/banquet table	<s> <i>
	an oasis of green clover	<i> <s>
The *na'ot dèshè* of Trigger D		
U. *tzorerai*	those who press upon one/ ill-wisher/afflicters	<s> <i>
	prey upon innocents	<i> <i>
	natural enemies/predators	<i> <s>
Ill of Triggers O, P; plus mirror sound link (*ira ra*)		
Trigger R, part 1: *shivetekha*.		
V. *déshanta beshemen rashi*	smear my head with oil	<s> <i>
	rub my head with oil (scabs)	<i> <s>
W. *cosi reva'ya*	my drinking vessel/cup/horn/tankard/ etc., is filled to the brim	<s> <i>
	my watering-hole is filled - "	<i> <s>
Closure of internal envelope pattern: D through V.		
X. *akh*	Wonderful/Great/Terrific	<i> <i>
	Boy! Do I have it good.	<s> <i>
Y. *tov vehésed*	Good and impartial kindness/	
	Good and "mildheartedness"	<i> <i>
Closure of the Good/Ill formula Triggers P,U.		
Z. *yirdefuni*	follow/pursue me	<s> <i>
	chase/run after me	<i> <s>
Trigger R, part 2: *mishantekha*		
AA *kol yeme chai'yai*	all the days of my life	<i> <i>
Trigger AD		
AB. *ushavti*	And I may sit/may return	<i> <i>
Link back to *shovev/shovav*: Trigger I.		
AC. *be-bèit Adonai*	in the home/house/dwelling of the Lord	<s> <i>
Trigger A	in the oases of the Lord	<i> <s>
AD. *le-orakh yamim*	for a long time	<i> <s>
	until old age	<s> <i>
Trigger B: Closure of external envelope pattern		

nevertheless, they are different. One of the branches, the North African, became what we call today the Sephardic melodies; another became today's European or Ashkenazic ones. The last branch, with quarter tones not found in European or Sephardic music, is called the Yemenite branch; this one underlies the Byzantine chants.

Developments or trends in native hymns and folksongs are indicative. These songs were not sung to the Yemenite branch, or we would find quarter-tone music in English folk songs today. Although folk themes—birth, death, love, marriage, faithfulness, harvest, work, and so forth—are found in every culture, melodic patterns are highly localized. In some areas of Eastern Europe, for example, the performer is expected to improvise upon the basic melodic line in a manner very similar to a personalized cadenza within a classical violin concerto. In Western Europe, however, melodies are the most static part of a folk song. English folk melodies, in particular, display an extreme conservatism. We could almost go so far as to say that, in the English tradition, a good melody goes a long way; it is used again and again. Even though the words to an English folk melody may undergo complete change, [16] the melody tends to constrain what can or cannot be sung in one musical phrase. People seem to accept that the words can change, but the tunes you know are *the* correct ones. When you sing a well known folk song, more often than not, somebody will say that you are singing it wrong: it should be sung *this* way. Clearly, quarter-tones are not used in English song.

The question then becomes which of the other two branches was used for these Psalms. There is one distinctive peculiarity in English rhythms; while a beat of 3 + 2 may be used for variety, the rhythms are essentially variants of a 3/8 beat. The tendency for English to maintain a three times x/8 rhythm is so marked, that it renders Latin hymns that were written in England instantly recognizable. One such hymn, *Excelsus innumine/Benedictus Dominus*, a double motet using voice exchange, may be found in an anonymous late 13th Century English manuscript. [17] The beat is 3/8.

The Ashkenazic branch was tested, but the rhythms of this branch did not suit the rhythms encoded into the text. Considering where and when Christianity, and the Psalms, first came to Britain, it might have seemed logical to test the melodies of the Sephardic branch, first. Instead, this branch was tested last, and proved a rhythmic match.

We have the melodic formula for Psalm 23(22). This Psalm is traditionally sung to the same formula as "The Song of Songs." Now we need the Psalm tone. In most of the Psalter, the Psalm tone is marked in the first letter of the Latin text; the mode is indicated in the *titulus*. In the Ælfredian part, the Psalm tone is marked in both Old English and Latin in the first word of the texts. This Psalm does not have a *titulus*; both mode and psalm tone are given in the first word of the Ælfredian introduction to the Psalm: *dauid* (David). The *d* is gold (yellow), that is, *C* (a-minor), second formula/mode.

Because Ælfred was the type of man to wear both braces and a belt, just in case someone reading only the Latin should not look at the introduction written only in Old English, the Psalm tone is repeated in the first word of the Latin text, *Dominus*, "Lord." The *d* is a large, Roman Capital *D* covered with gold.

Once we have the melodic formula and the Psalm tone, and after both texts have undergone semantic analysis to establish the basis for redundancy, we can reconstruct the music of the Psalm.

The reconstruction is done in the following order. First the Sephardic Hebrew melodic phrase is written down; then solo, harp, and chorus notation are marked from the directions in the manuscript.

Next, because the Old English carries the rhythmic directions, the Old English text is entered first—according to the instructions in the Psalter. Finally, the transliterated Hebrew is recorded as a control on the semantic sense in both languages.

We have two extra pieces of reconstruction help in Psalm 23(22). First, the original translator tried to maintain the sound-sense links; this gives additional aid in verifying our semantic check. Second, the chironomic signs we see in the Old English are placed to semantically mirror the chironomic signs in the Hebrew. Where the Old English is one-word to one-word (e.g. *ræt* / *ro'i*; *heafod* / *roshi*), the chironomic symbol is over the same word in both languages. Where the translation requires more than one word (e.g. *swyðe good feoh land* / *na'ot dêshê*), the chironomic signs are over the Old English words that carry the sense in the Hebrew.

The reconstructed Psalm is on page 176. For obvious reasons, the printed version gives the Hebrew text first. The double equals sign (==) indicates a word that is not broken in the text but has been separated to accommodate modern musical notation; otherwise the accompanying Old English text is *as written*: clumping (e.g. *forþampu*), spacing (e.g. *rot nesse*), and line breaks (e.g. *de/ aðes*). While lines regularly separate into bicola and tricola, bicola predominate. The Old English also tells us where and what type of responsive singing was used in the Hebrew song. In both languages, the pattern of stressed-unstressed syllables is also dominant. There is a strong, but not rigid, tendency to group beats in 3's. The normal beat is brisk; more or less the length of an 1/8 th note at a moderato or allegro tempo. The rhythm is remarkably regular and metrical; it is the prevalent English variant of 3 times x/8.

Psalm 23(22) presented us with a typical Davidic Psalm along with an Ælfredized translation. Although it gives us priceless information as to the manner of responsive singing on the Hebrew side, it does not help too much on the Anglo-Saxon side. This Psalm is not representative of the usual practice of singing the Psalms. Ælfred's changes added what can only be called a melismata at the end of Verse 2 and a typical Ælfredian "as many words into a line as ever he possibly can" at the end of Verse 7. The Ælfredized portion, from *And fedde* in Verse 2 through *symblath* at the end of Verse 7, is marked for solo; the first and the last two verses are congregational.

According to the instructions in the manuscript, Psalm 23(22) conforms to normal practice in only one respect; throughout the Psalter, the first and last verses of a Psalm were sung congregationally. Apart from this one practice, however, the Ælfredized Psalm differs substantially from the norm; the majority of the Psalms were sung in an antiphonal verse form of responsive singing. This means that a soloist would sing a complete verse, then the congregation would respond by singing a full verse.

The instructions encoded into the text give us the information that the standard practice was to sing the psalm tone to set the correct key, then the melodic range of the psalm, apparently played on a harp, was given. This harp cue was normally repeated between verses, perhaps to try and keep the "singing heap" on key.

Psalm 96(95) is one of the "metrical" psalms. In Psalm 96(95), after the psalm tone and harp cues are given, the first verse is sung congregationally. Verse 1 is a standard bicola. The 2nd verse is a variant, a tricola, and sung as a solo. Thereafter, all standard bicola verses are sung congregationally; solos are sung on the variant verses. The psalm is sung in the antiphonal verse responsive manner: bicola congregationally; tricola solo, bicola congregationally, and so on, down to the end, which is sung

congregationally. Except for some spelling and a few exchanges of words, the "metrical" psalms are in their original state. This Psalm is so regular and so metrical that, once we have the melody—and redundancy—, we simply follow the manuscript directions.

Psalm 96(95) is among the oldest of the Psalms. Pre-Monarchial, as is Psalm 29(28); it may be as early as the twelfth or thirteenth century BCE. Perhaps because of its age, the 96th(95th) is also one of the Psalms that most closely resembles folk music. While in the nineteenth century CE, folk song was depicted as simple, rustic, and "unspoiled," folk song tends to be fairly complex musically. Like most folk songs, this Psalm contains complexities of sound and rhythm play, but little word play. Sound play is difficult to carry across languages throughout a text; however, the lack of word play permits a *relatively* accurate denotative translation—if the parsing rhythms are similar.

Parsing rhythms have a great deal to do with the accuracy of these Old English translations. As we have already noted, unless the parsing rhythms of both source and target language are very similar, strange things happen to the songs in the target language. Further twisted by attempts to link sense with sound, these differences in parsing rhythms lead to contortions and strange grammatical structures in almost every language into which the Psalms have been translated. There is, however, one exception: Old English.

Modern English and Hebrew, along with Modern Italian, are unusual among both Indo-European and Semitic languages for their parsing rhythms. All three are very similar. If we listen to speakers of these languages and can hear only the rhythms, but not the words, we cannot immediately tell which language is being spoken.

There are obvious reasons for this rhythmic similarity: all three are stress languages. Further, the basic, everyday vocabulary in all three languages consists of short, frequently mono- or bi-syllabic words. Italian did not exist as a separate language until well into the Late Medieval period and is of little importance when examining early translations of the Bible. English and, of course, Hebrew are relevant.

Dialectic variations tend to stretch the limits of a language's rhythms. A visitor to Georgia from Maine, for instance, has to adjust to a radically different beat. An American in England needs to adapt to the local conditions. Parsing rhythms, however, are extremely stable across time. Perhaps this can be made clearer in another way. If the parsing rhythms of a language change too much, the language dies; it becomes truly a dead language. Classical Latin is a dead language; English is not. Although some scholars see discontinuity in the English language after the Norman Conquest, the continuity of basic vocabulary and parsing rhythms make it clear that this is not true. Modern Hebrew as spoken in Israel is closer to Biblical than it is to Medieval Hebrew. Both Modern English and Modern Hebrew use the same parsing rhythms today that we see in their oldest texts. The parsing rhythms have not changed: Modern English is Old English in different dress.

The similarity in parsing rhythms is visible in all the existing vernacular poetry; nevertheless, the similarities are seen most clearly in the texts of the original Psalms of the *Paris Psalter*. Although Ælfred made use of the parsing rhythms in his "Prose" translations, Psalm 96(95) is more representative of the Psalter as whole.

The majority of this Psalm is clear and unambiguous, as can be seen from the lack of known variants for these sections. In the first two verses there is only one problematic word, and it is the same one in both Old English and Hebrew. The Old English translators got it right, but we do not have an exact equivalent in Modern English. This one word is presented with its possible Modern English translations. As the translator made an effort to match sound with sense, the Hebrew has been transliterated in order to preserve the sound patterning.

Sealm 95   Tehila 96
Uox Ecclesṭʌ

1. Singaþ nu drihtne ·
    sangas neowe ·
 Singe þeos eorðe eall
    eceum drihtne ·
2. Singaþ nu drihtne ·
    and his soðne naman bealde bletsiað ·
 beornas sæcgeað fram dæg to dæg
    drihtnes hælu

                Shiru l'Adonai
                  shir hadash
                Shiru l'Adonai
                  kol haaretz
                Shiru l'Adonai
                barekhu shemo
                Basru mi yom le yom
                  yeshuato

English:
1. Sing now [to the] Lord new songs.
 Sing all the earth [to the] eternal Lord.
2. Sing now [to the] Lord and his
    true name boldly bless.
 Men tell/say from-day-to-day of the Lord's
    *hælu**
    deliverance/championship/saving

            Sing to the Lord a new song.
            Sing to the Lord all the earth.
            Sing to the Lord bless his name.

            Tell/Say from day-to-day of
              *yeshuato***
            deliverance/championship/saving

* 1) safety against attack, 2) deliverance from unfavorable conditions, 3) championship.
   The word is used with the genitive of the saver, the *u*.
** 1) deliverance, 2) championship, 3) saving. The *to* is the 3rd person pronomial ending, that is "his."

   Even a quick glance tells us that the translation into Old English is relatively accurate. The addition of *soðne* [true] in the translation of *shemo* [his name] would seem to be superfluous; although we could remember that, in antiquity, naming meant control over the named; only a very powerful being would be called by a "true" name. What is not clear is the reason for the addition of *eceum drihtne* [eternal Lord] in verse 1; why *nu* [now] is inserted after the order to "Sing"; or why the change from a bicola in Verse 1 to a tricola in Verse 2. Once we place the song into its melody, the additions make sense: they are necessary if we wish to sing the new song.

   We have the melodic formula for Psalm 96(95); it is sung to the same formula as that of Psalm 29. As we find throughout the original parts of the *Paris Psalter* translations, the translator tried to match sound with sense, which simplifies the semantic check. He also was very careful to match syllable division to syllable division (parsing rhythms) whenever possible.

   As in Psalm 23(22), the music is reconstructed by first writing down the Sephardic Hebrew melody, then entering instructions for solos, harp, and congregational singing. The Old English text is entered following the instructions in the manuscript; then the Hebrew is entered as the semantic check.

   Psalm 96(95) is very regular and rhythmic, as we could suspect from its classification as a "metrical" psalm; it is also easy to remember, as is any rhythmic work song, such as a sea chanty. The

Psalm is so regular, that these two verses are all we need, although verse 3 has been included to show the usual type of responsive singing. Once again, the printed music is presented with the Hebrew first. The tempo is brisk.

Psalm 96(95)

Psalms 96 and 29 are unusual in that they are among the very few Psalms that have precisely the same rhythms in the *first* verse and were sung to the same melody. (This is the reason that the verse from the 96th(95th) and an antiphon from the 29th(28th) appear in some of the later texts.) Psalms are sung prayers written *to* or *for* the Lord. Such songs necessarily are repetitive and make heavy use of formula; formulæ are an excellent mnemonic device. As in all the Non-Davidic Psalms, the 96th and the 29th are, understandably, quite formulaic.

While some formulæ, such as *kevod v'oz* [honor and might/strength/power], are generally repeated as is, formulaic does not necessarily mean a mechanical repeat of the exact words. Most formulæ are open, that is, the noun is static and unchanging, but the modifier changes. The formula for the imperative command *x l'Adonai* [x to the Lord], for example, turns up as *shiru l'Adonai* [Sing to the Lord] and *havu l'Adonai* [make come, that is, Bring to the Lord]. Similarly, the formula *x plus Shem* [x plus Name] shows variety, as in: *baruch hashem* [bless the name], *barakhu shemo* [bless his name]; *kevod shemo* [honor his name]; and *l'ma'an shemo* [for the sake/honor of his name].

In dealing with formulæ, a competent translator chooses carefully among the equivalents. Once he has chosen an equivalent formulaic structure base in the target language to translate a formulaic structure from the source language, the same word(s) will be used to translate the source words throughout a text whenever the formula occurs. While the *x* will obviously vary, variations in the target language in the *fixed* part of an open formula indicates one of two things. The translator used variety for the sake of variety; or, the final version is a conglomeration of more than one translation.

This schizophrenic Psalter displays all three possibilities in the translation of formula. In the purely Ælfredian part, in the Old English, we generally find variety for its own sake. Ælfred, however, was not content to rewrite only the Old English. The original Latin translation, that we can still see in the Latin Psalms 51 through 150, appears to be **Hexaplaric** (of or related to the Greek text of Origen's *Hexapla*). As we have noted, the original Latin text is so distinctive that it can be used to trace the Psalter's travels. In his new version, Ælfred ordered that the Latin text should accord with a *Romanum*. Because *Romanum* versions differ, the Latin text of the first 50 psalms shows formulæ of a conglomerate type. The first type of formula translation appears in the original part of the Psalter.

The translator of the original Psalms of the *Paris Psalter* was a competent translator; his formulaic translations are extremely consistent. He used, for example, the formula *naman* plus *bletsian* [name plus to bless] to translate *baruch hashem*. In the 96th(95th) he used an alliterating modifier, *bealde* [boldly], in order to fill out the musical phrase. His translations of *x l'Adonai*, are always of the form *x nu drihten*. The translator was so consistent that his use of formulæ has been called "mechanical," a mere plugging-in of words. While "mechanical," is an inaccurate judgement—he was merely following the original—, his extreme consistency, both rhythmically and formulaically, allows us to separate original pieces of the Psalms from the Ælfredian changes. This is just as well; Ælfred rewrote the first two verses of Psalm 29(28).

Psalm 29(28) is among the pseudepigraphic psalms. There was a strong tendency to attribute older psalms to David; the colophon at the end of Q11Ps (the "Qumran" Psalm Scroll from cave 11) credits more than 4,000 prayers, songs, and hymns to him. Although the attribution in the Masoretic version is to David (*Mizmor L'David*), the Psalm does not display his very distinctive voice. Further, it is pre-monarchial, with archaic grammatical structures and words that were already problematic as to their meaning by the second century BCE. There are variants, cruces, places that show precisely the same type of word variations that we see in any song passed down orally until it is finally written down. Because one crux is directly relevant to Ælfred and his translation of Psalm 29(28), we shall take a quick look at Verse 1 and the first colon of Verse 2. We may also begin to understand why there are so many variants among translations.

The crux originated in oral transmission: in most Hebrew dialects the words *elim* and *eilim* are pronounced the same. In Verse 1 of Psalm 29 the Masoretic text has *elim*; but a common and well documented variant is *eilim*. Nobody knows what *b'nei elim* refers to in the context of this verse, neither in Hebrew—nor in its Ugaritic cognate, for that matter—so they guess. In its other appearances in the Hebrew Bible, *b'nei elim* translates as "sons of the heavenly court" or "host of heaven" or "sons of might/power" or "angels" or "sons of God." The common and well known variant, *b'nei eilim*, translates as "sons/children of gazelles/rams," the sacrifice to be brought.

Masoretic Psalm 29

1)	Havu l'Adonai b'nei elim/eilim	Bring the Lord, sons of ???/sons of gazelles/rams
	Havu l'Adonai kevod v'oz	Bring the Lord, honor & might/strength/power
2)	Havu l'Adonai kevod shemo	Bring the Lord, honor his name

There is a grammatical problem as well; a problem that eventually caused Ælfred difficulties, too. The formula *havu l'Adonai* takes a plural accusative (direct object); it does not take a dative or a nominative. Although *elim*, as an accusative, is grammatically correct, as a direct object it makes very little sense. As the object of the colon, it turns *elim* into the sacrifice to be brought; a most unlikely state of affairs. Conversely, as a subject (nominative) it is barely grammatically possible, but violates poetic parallelism and shows abnormal diction. The Masoretes nevertheless decided on the word.

The grammatical and poetic problem presented by *elim* apparently bothered generations of translators. Centuries earlier, in Alexandria of the second century BCE, the translator faced with this crux in his texts, decided to use *both* words. He turned *elim* into a nominative, and made it the *subject* of the first colon; then he repeated the *havu* formula and used *eilim* as the direct object of the next colon.

Old Greek Psalm 28

28:1

ΕϹΕγΚΑΤΕ Τωι ΚΡιωι ϹιΟι ϑΕΟϹ	Bring to the Lord, you sons of God,
ΕϹΕγΚΑΤΕ Τωι ΚΡιωι ϹιΟϹϳΚΡιωϹ	Bring to the Lord, the sons of rams;
ΕϹΕγΚΑΤΕ Τωι ΚΡιωι δοξαϹ Και ΤιμηϹ	Bring to the Lord glory and honor.

28:2

ΕϹΕγΚΑΤΕ Τωι ΚΡιωι δοξαϹ οϹομαΤι αΤοϹ	Bring the Lord the glory due His name,

While the translator probably patted himself on the back for solving the crux, he violated the grammatical structure of the Hebrew verse. He also changed the psalm structure of Verse 1 from a bicola to a tricola. This means that, instead of singing this Psalm as bicola, tricola, as in the 96th(95th), they sang it as tricola, bicola. The Greek words (with trilling) do fit the musical phrases.

At this point, we have two versions of the Psalm being passed around; one with a bicola structure; the other with a tricola; bicola structure. The early Latin translations were from Old Greek.

Although we can see from the large Dead Sea Psalm scroll that some Hebrew Psalm texts were already being written by cola (Jerome's *cola et commata*), the early Greek texts were not written by verse; they were written by breathings, as sung. We have no evidence one way or the other that the earliest Latin translators of the Psalms even knew that there was a crux; but they apparently knew that the 29th(28th) was bicolonic in structure.

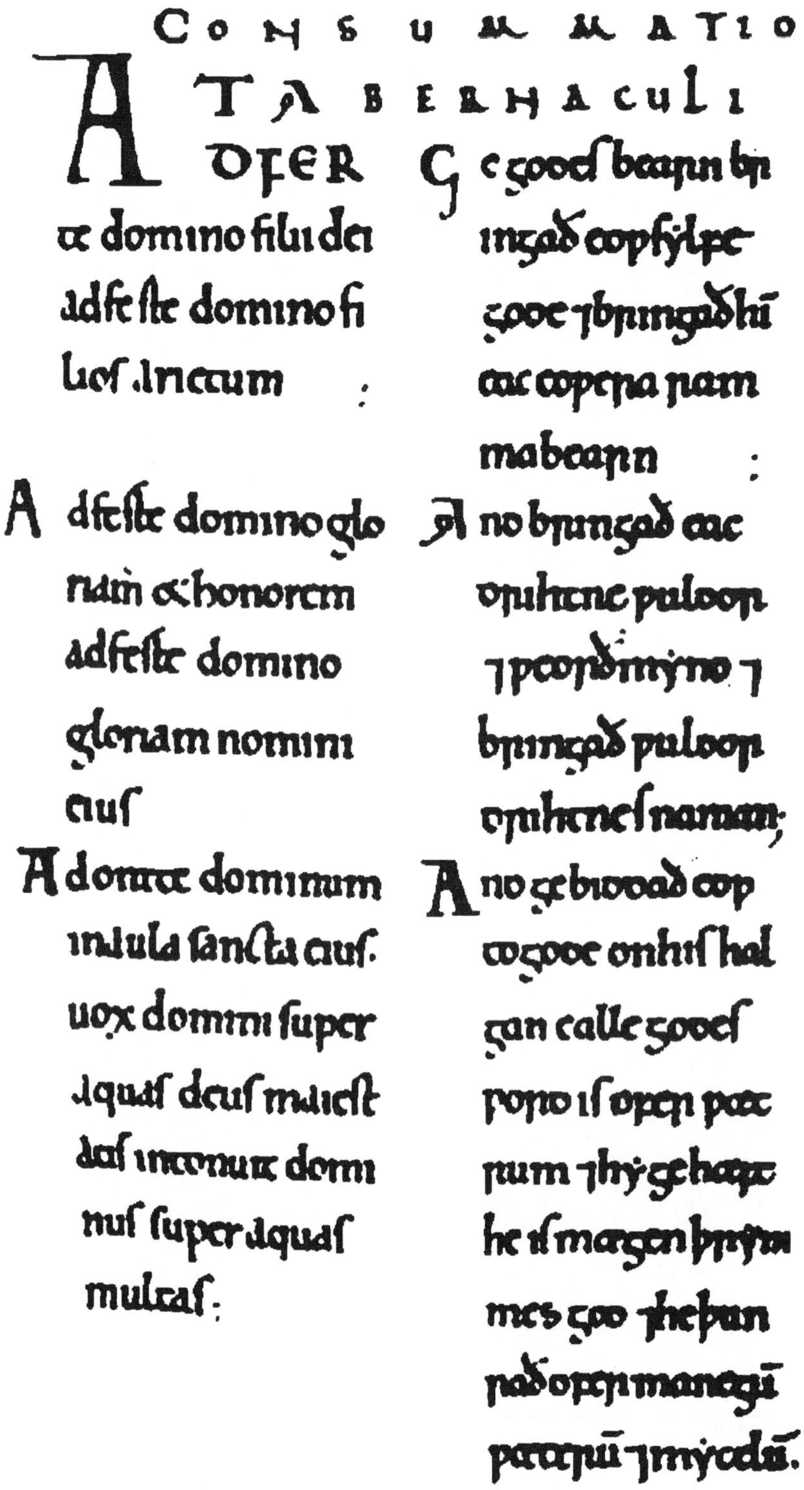

Latin

A OFER
te domino filii dei
adferte domino fi
lios . Inixtum :

A dferte domino glo
riam & honorem
adferte domino
gloriam nomini
eius

A donate dominum
intula sancta eius.
uox domini super
aquas deus maiest
das intonux domi
nus super aquas
multas :

Old English

G e godes bearn bri
ngað copsylpe
gode ⁊bringað hi
eac copepra nam
mabearn :

A no bringað eac
oþihtene puldor
⁊ peorðmynto ⁊
bringað puldor
oþihtenes naman ;

A no gebiooað cop
togode onhis hal
gan calle godes
pono is open þæt
ruim ⁊hyge hæge
he is margen hryht
mes goo ⁊heþan
nað open manegū
pæteruū ⁊mycelū .

Plate 10.1 Replica of *Paris Psalter*: f. 29r, begin Psalm 29(28) (100 percent)

Romanum/Gallican Psalm 28

Psalm 28:1

Afferte domino filii dei	Bring the Lord sons of God
Afferte domino filios arietum	Bring the Lord sons of rams

Psalm 28:2

Afferte domino gloriam et honorem	Bring the Lord fame/reknown/acclaim & honor
Afferte domino gloriam nomini eius	Bring the Lord fame/reknown/acclaim to his name

The Latin version has both *elim* [*filii Dei*, sons of God] and *eilim* [*filios arietum*, sons of rams] in the first verse—and that is it. The second colon of the Hebrew and the third colon of the Old Greek Verse 1, "Bring the Lord fame/reknown (*gloria*) and honor (*honor*)" is now the first colon of Verse 2. The first colon of the Old Greek Verse 2 [Bring the Lord fame/reknown (*gloria*) to his name] has become the second colon. The 2nd colon of Verse 2 became the first colon of Verse 3.

We now have *three* different written traditions for this Psalm. This short story about one crux in one Psalm pretty much explains why translations can vary so drastically. It also explains quite a bit about Ælfred and his revision of Psalm 29(28).

Old English Psalm 28	Hebrew Psalm 29 (Masoretic)	Hebrew Psalm 96

Verse 1

Ge godes bearn bringað eow sylfe gode	Havu l'Adonai b'nei elim	Shiru l'Adonai shir hadash
&bringað him eac eowera ramma bearn	Havu l'Adonai kevod v'oz	Shiru l'Adonai kol haaretz

Verse 2

And bringað eac drihtne wuldor [18] and wyrðmynd	Havu l'Adonai kevod shemo	Shiru l'Adonai barekhu shemo
And bringað wuldor Drihtnes naman		

Modern English

1) You sons of God bring of yourselves to God;
And bring him each of you son(s) of a ram(s)
2) And bring each to the Lord reknown/fame/acclaim & honor;
And bring reknown/fame/acclaim to the Lord's name

Although both the Old Greek and the Latin still display something of the close relationship between Psalm 29(28) and Psalm 96(95), it has disappeared from this Old English version. Ælfred brought the Old English into accord with a *Romanum* type version—more or less, that is. (The Latin side has also undergone a change; it, too, is now a *Romanum* type.) Ælfred, however, never could leave anything open to possible misinterpretation. He seems to have had an abhorrence of ambiguities; so he went about removing them, at a cost, to be sure.

When re-writing the words to popular songs, one was told to retain those parts of the original that could be integrated into the new version, presumably to retain familiar aspects and promote transference. While Ælfred's explanatory translation technique is very conspicuous, we can see where he integrated the original portions into his version.

Havu means to "make come," that is, "bring," and *Bringath nu drihtne* is precisely the same formula used to translate *Havu l'Adonai* in Psalm 96(95):7. The first half-colon of the Psalm originally must have read *Bringath nu drihtne* [Bring to the Lord]. The second half clearly did not have both "sons of god" *and* "sons of rams," for Ælfred ran himself into the same grammatical tangle that faced the translator of the Old Greek. *Bearn*, Modern Scots "bairn," is a collective; it can be either singular or plural; *bringath* is a plural imperative. Although Ælfred stuck *ge godes bearn* in front in what today is the subject position, it is still ambiguous. The words could be read as singular [You son of God] with the plural applying to the *ramma bearn* [sons of a ram]. So Ælfred added the plural dative *eow* to explain that *bringath* applied to the "sons of God." Having started off on the wrong foot, he now had to clarify the second part: "And bring him each of you son(s) of a ram." Because he was still stuck with his grammatical anomaly, in verse 2 he had to add "And" to both cola and change *nu* to *eac* [each] in the first. The original translator was so consistent in his use of formulæ, that colon 2 almost certainly went: *Bringað nu Drihtne wuldres naman.* This, however, must remain in the realm of speculation; except for these "mechanical" formulæ, we will never know what really was in the original. Similarly, we cannot once again hear this song.

Although Ælfred was always careful to fit his new words into the musical phrases, he never tried to link sound with sense or to match syllabic divisions. We have the necessary melodic formula; from Verse 3 on most of the psalm is the original seventh-century text; nevertheless, Psalm 29(28) cannot be reconstructed: Ælfred chopped off its head.

Unfortunately for Ælfred's ambitious programs, his time was running out. He became King in 871, but was involved in active warfare throughout the majority of his reign. He had no time while fighting wars for such programs. His reign of a kingdom more or less at peace, with the leisure to pursue these ends, was less than 10 years; he died in 899. *Pastoral Care* was done, so was Boethius's *Consolations of Philosophy*, as were Bede's *Historia Ecclesiastica* and Orosius's *History;* but in 899, only 50 Psalms had been revised.

It is just as well that only 50 of the Psalms had been revised, or we would never have been able to sort out the story. The Psalms, whole or in pieces, found in *Junius 121* and the *Eadwine Psalter*, would have remained tantalizing morsels in a mysterious puzzle. We should feel some pity for Ælfred and his religious re-education program. Our modern opinion of Ælfred as a songwriter clearly was a contemporary opinion as well. His adulterated Psalms did not "take." The only reason we know of their existence at all is from these first 50 Psalms in the *Paris Psalter*.

The majority of the Ælfredized Psalms cannot be reconstructed, these songs are gone forever. Nevertheless, it is just as well that these 50 had been completed. The Ælfredian introductions and re-writes saved this Psalter from selective destruction, for the Psalms of the *Paris Psalter* have yet two other major differences between them and the thirteen other Old English Psalter translations.

First, these Psalms are sung at the *original*, pre-fourth century tempi; they are not slowed down at all. The tunes are snappy and simple, and very easy for untrained people to memorize and to sing. Second, references to Christ or Christians in the original Old English texts are surprisingly sparse. In a text running more than *9,000* lines, such words occur precisely nine times: *cristene* once [106:31], and *criste* or *cristes* 8 times: 67:24; 83:8; 84:5; 88:33 and 88:45; 108:25; 118:146; 131:18; 133:2; and 134:2. The original translation was so rhythmic and so tightly structured that changes stand out. Of these nine references, six show tampering with the original rhythms; three have *criste* inserted when everywhere else the original translator used *gode*.

It is fair to say that, in the "metrical" psalms, all Christian references are confined to the *Latin* headings. The lack of Christian references was so obvious that it apparently worried Ælfred. It bothered him enough that he wrote introductions to his revised psalms. [19] These introductions are written in the purest Ælfredian explanatory voice and explain in Christian terms when David sang the psalm, and why. In the Ælfredian portion, Christ and Christians are only in his rewrites and in his introductions to the Psalms. The original Psalter texts themselves could as easily have been Jewish as Christian. In a sense, it seems almost anticlimactic to report something which the tempi and the lack of direct Christian references have already told us: the Psalms of the *Paris Psalter* are those of the extreme subordinationists, the Psalms of the "Judaizers."

The extreme subordinationists were the fiercest enemies of the Alexandrian-Roman parties. We now know that the earliest Christians among the Anglo-Saxons were converted by the "selfish" Celtic Britons, Brittonic subordinationists. Thus we now know why Bede hated the British Christians and rejoiced at the death of 1200 British monks. Clearly the hatred was mutual; but we now also know why Bede states in his final reference to them that the Britons persisted in their stubbornness and hated the English. We also have some insights into the stubbornness of the monks at Ripon who left *en masse* after Wilfrid converted from Celtic to Roman parties.

Some insights are all that we can have, a skeleton with little meat on its bones. We can see from their surviving Latin compositions that the British-Celtic society was literate and brilliant. While we also know from the *Paris Psalter*, and these odd little references in Bede and elsewhere, that the native British-Celtic peoples were anything but Alexandrian-Roman, little direct concrete evidence remains. Nevertheless, *The Paris Psalter* hands us another piece to fill in the puzzle.

It has become clear that the term Anglo-Celtic is a conflation of two different Celtic Christian peoples: the Goidelic (Irish, Manx) and the Brittonic (Welsh, Cornish, Breton). By the late seventh century, the native Brittonic influence was being edited out of the texts. The *stæfwritung* system came into being before the real battle for religious supremacy in Britain took place. Therefore, it was designed and implemented amongst an Anglo-Celtic community no later than 650, because the "Celtic" in "Anglo-Celtic" was Brittonic. While this fact puts an upper limit on the date of the original codification, it does nothing to help us date the musical notation system.

Unfortunately, none of the earliest manuscripts written by the Anglo-Saxons required musical notation. The two earliest manuscripts of Bede's *Historia* show the second stage of *stæfwritung*, but they are useless to us for dating the musical notation system. In Book 4, Chapter 18, Bede tells us that the "Englisc" were singing the chants wrong until John the Archchanter arrived in 680 to teach the chants as they were sung in Rome. Bede gives no indication that a musical notation system was devised by the time he wrote his *Historia* in 731. Still, as the system does not record melodies, Bede's statement does not really help us.

The archaisms we see in the *Paris Psalter* suggest that the notation was most probably added at the time script-by-language was instituted, but we will never know. As we saw with both the ASPA and script-by-language, it takes time for innovations to be accepted as a new standard practice. We have little direct evidence for the practice of the musical notation system before the end of the eighth century. By that time, the musical notation system had divided into Anglo-Goidelic and Anglo-Roman practices. An augmented version of the *stæfwritung* musical notation system was in use at Saint Gall monastery in what is modern Switzerland.

Saint Gall was founded by Irish missionaries. It had traditional links with various Anglo-Celtic parties, and Anglo-Celtic monks show up there with regularity. During the late eighth and early ninth centuries, however, the most influential monk at Saint Gall was Arn, a former student of Alcuin of York.

Alcuin of York played a rather important role in history—for an ecclesiastic who was never ordained as more than a deacon. He was born about 732 in or near York, England. Alcuin seems to have been quite a homebody; except for a few missions, he spent the first fifty years of his life at the York Cathedral school which, during his lifetime, was the most famous center of learning in Europe. Eventually, Alcuin became headmaster of the school and gained a reputation as the most learned man in Western Christendom of the period.

Alcuin apparently was very likeable. He inspired love in his pupils and admiration in his acquaintances. Around 300 letters of his survive. Among these letters we find correspondence with ex-pupils. One of these ex-students was Arn of Saint Gall.

Alcuin's nickname was *Albinus*. Perhaps the name referred to his origin, of Albion, the Latin name for Britain. Perhaps the nickname referred to his appearance: *Albinus* would translate as "Whitey." The existing cameo picture (technically called a **medallion**) we have of Alcuin shows that he was notably fair (Figure 10.6).

The writing at the side of the medallion states A L CVI NVS ABBA. This translates as "Alcuin, father/abbot" (Hebrew "aba" -> Greek "abbas" -> Latin "abbot"). Like all church leaders, Alcuin gained a reputation for holiness, but he was never canonized as a saint.

We should round out this picture somewhat. Alcuin may have been likeable, but he also had a magisterial cocksureness that arose from his fifty years at York Cathedral School. In 781 Alcuin traveled to Italy. There the over-confident headmaster crossed paths with the ruthless King of the Franks, Charlemagne (Charles the Great, later Emperor of the "New" Rome, 742-814). Charlemagne invited Alcuin to head the new palace school at Aachen (Modern Aix-la-Chapelle).

Although Alcuin clearly hesitated before accepting Charlemagne's offer, how could he resist such a flattering invitation? What a wonderful chance for an educator to put all his theories into practice. What a piece of political one-up-manship for York in the internal fighting among the

Fig. 10.6 Alcuin: Replica of the medallion from the Bamberg Bible, 9th century

English schools to have its headmaster chosen over that of Canterbury. Besides, he liked Charlemagne. Alcuin's letters indicate that, in spite of his certainty and overconfidence, he did have some sense of selfpreservation. His letters show that he feared Charlemagne as much as he loved him. Alcuin left the court in 796 to become abbot of the Abbey of Saint Martin at Tours.

What if Alcuin had not accepted Charlemagne's invitation? There are a surprising number of what if's, the crossroads of history, surrounding the person of this one man. Reverberations of Alcuin's role in the history of Western Europe echo to this day.

Alcuin set up new standards of education based upon English methods of learning; he systematized the curriculum. Based in the seven liberal arts, these standards endured for centuries. He instituted a system of elementary education. He encouraged the study of the liberal arts for a better understanding of the transcendent realm. He advocated the study of ancient texts; he promoted public literacy.

Alcuin was also very active in politics. He was chief propagandist for Charlemagne. It was Alcuin who referred to Charles the Great as another "David," the anointed king of the "New" Israel, preparing the stage for Empire. Who else should stand in the place of Samuel but the Bishop of Rome? In any case, the Patriarch was too far away at Constantinople; besides, he did not require the mailed fist that the Roman papa needed. The popes had realized that they may have had spiritual strength, but they needed secular armed forces to aid them. Pepin III (the short) of the House of Pepin and father of Charlemagne obliged; so did his son. Charlemagne had a pope in his pocket to back him. (Following this perhaps ill-judged acceptance of secular might, the papacy was constrained for centuries by the Emperors of the North.)

Charlemagne and Alcuin desired a conformal state religion. A conformal state religion was politically expedient for a great number of reasons, a major one being the God-given right to rule as anointed King. (Pepin III had forcibly annexed Neustria, which had been ruled by the Merovingian dynasty, and legitimized his rule by anointment.) Not all Christian groups accepted the authority of the bishop of Rome to anoint a king in David's stead; Charlemagne needed that authority. Although Alcuin wrote to Megenfird, Charlemagne's Treasurer, that faith "is a matter of will" and cannot be forced, and in a letter to Charlemagne that conversion requires "gentle teaching," Charlemagne was determined to stamp out "heresies" and bring all under his rule into the Roman fold. Charlemagne forced conversions. As conversion-by-force appears to have rendered treaties signed under these terms as non-binding in the eyes of the "forced," Charlemagne ruthlessly resorted to massacres to gain his state religion. However, to create a conformal religion, Charles and Alcuin needed a conformal service. When they sent to Rome for an official copy of the liturgy, they ran into a problem. Rome did not have a complete liturgy in Latin. Better than half of the Roman liturgy was still in Greek. Charlemagne was crowned Emperor of the "New Rome," the Holy Roman Empire, in 800 by the Pope in all the splendor of the Greek Byzantine ritual.

The lack of a complete official Latin liturgy was a bit of a setback. Alcuin promptly set about compiling and writing a temporary replacement for the missing portions. These proved to be not all that temporary. His revisions of the liturgy of the Frankish church endured for many centuries and affected Roman practices as well. Although he was careful to indicate where his writings began, over time the note stating that this was Alcuin's and not from Rome moved backwards into the books.

Alcuin was musically oriented. He introduced the Irish-Northumbrian custom of singing the creed into the liturgy of the Roman Catholic Church. His arrangement of votive masses for particular days of the week are still used to this day. He came up with his own edition of a *Gallican* version of the Bible. (It appears to have been an irresistible impulse for church writers in every period to edit the Bible.)

Stæfwritung had already passed to the continent through Anglo-Saxon missionaries. Still, each monastery retained much of its own idiosyncrasies and practices. Now Alcuin proceeded to overhaul the Frankish writing system. He standardized the punctuation system. [20] Alcuin's was the first concerted attack on the *stæfwritung* system. His classicization of *stæfwritung* shows that he emulated the first century reformers of Rome. He insisted upon one symbol-one phone and the reduction of vertical and horizontal movement within the writing limits. As scribes were required to learn the new system, official texts began to acquire the "eveness" so admired by so many nineteenth and twentieth century paleographers. Abbreviations were not permitted and ligatures were strongly frowned upon. While a new method may take time to disseminate, scribes in a royal or official *scriptorium* had no choice but to learn the new writing system immediately. There are stories that Charlemagne enforced the rule against ligatures by having the digits loped off the fingers of offending scribes. The story may or may not be apocryphal, but is very much in keeping with the well-documented ruthlessness of the man.

In line with all the other features inherent in the would-be revival of the attributes of the Roman Empire, Alcuin classicized the Latin language. We should not wonder that Medieval Latin phonology is a mare's nest. The peoples of France, Spain, and Italy all assumed that they were speaking Latin. "Not so," said Alcuin. Alcuin "knew" how classical Latin was written and spoken. The Anglo-Saxon writing system, the very system that he was tearing apart, preserved "Classical" Latin. Classical Latin, that is, as understood by Anglo-Saxon scholars of the seventh and eighth centuries. We know that Bede's Latin was anything but classical in its pronunciation; neither was Alcuin's.

There is good reason for the assertion by Roger Wright that the Romance languages did not exist until after Alcuin. [21] Although dialectic differences are recorded in Latin texts, it is also clear that the people still thought of themselves as *Romani* speaking Latin. There is no literature whatsoever in these languages until centuries after Alcuin's retroversions.

In accordance with all the Winner's standard operating techniques, Charlemagne also wanted a new official script for his kingdom. This script is the misleadingly named "Caroline" (or "Carolingian"). Caroline is a minuscule font and the ancestor of all modern "Roman" design lower case fonts.

Scholarly disputes about the origins of the Caroline official script abound. Some say that Caroline is a "development" of the fonts used at Corbie Monastery during the mid- to late-eighth century. Corbie was a daughter house of Luxeuil monastery. Luxeuil was founded by Irish missionaries. The main difficulty with this position rests on the fact that scripts and fonts do not develop, they mutate. The Luxeuil and Corbie fonts are mutations of the Irish-British-North African half-uncial, with some Syriac habits thrown in. Still others assert that the Caroline font is a result of grafting the quatrolinear ascenders and descenders of a chancery font onto half-uncial. The grafting of cursive ascenders and descenders onto the Irish half-uncial is totally unnecessary. Irish half-uncial already has quite a few ascenders and descenders. Irish minuscule fonts already existed when Luxeuil and Corbie were founded and so did Northumbrian minuscule fonts.

By Alcuin's time, York's ritual apparently was a mixture of Roman, Celtic, and Gallican. Alcuin's singing of the creed is a Celtic-Northumbrian custom. Nobody questions the relationship between Celtic scripts and fonts and some used in Anglo-Saxon England. Minuscule fonts already occur in Ireland in the mid-600's. They occur in England by the mid 600's. The fonts used at Wearmouth-Jarrow, Canterbury, and London were the Anglo-Saxon pointed minuscule, a mutation of the Greco-Roman half-unical; these fonts were late-comers on the scene. There were other fonts already around in England. The Celtic influenced fonts are called Insular scripts. We have examples of Majuscule, formal liturgical minuscule, and informal secular cursive Insular fonts.

Graphic forms in the mid- to late eighth-century models from Corbie and elsewhere that bear a resemblance to the later official Caroline script are called "Pre-Caroline." One of these Insular fonts has many of the forms considered to be "Pre-Caroline." This font antedates the official Caroline script by more than 100 years. As we already know, a font model must already exist for scribes to write its symbols in a text. The appearance of these "Pre-Caroline" forms in texts merely indicates that the scribes knew that font. Sometimes these other-script symbols are simply scribal errors; usually, though, they indicate xenographic exchange.

Although the subject of the origins of the Caroline "Official" script will undoubtedly continue to be a bone of sometimes not so genteel scholarly contention, the main two positions are not tenable. Perhaps we should pay more attention to tradition.

There is a tradition that Charlemagne so admired Alcuin's writing that he wanted his new official script modeled on Alcuin's hand. Alcuin had been writing this Anglo-Celtic Northumbrian secular font for nearly 50 years. We may have to settle for tradition: These tales frequently hold at their heart the simple truth. In this case, though, tradition has something else to support it. All we have to do is to look at the "Caroline" script used in the manuscripts during and soon after Arn's time at Saint Gall.

While scribes at an official *scriptorium* had better learn the new official script, preferably yesterday, it takes time and effort to force a new script or font on other sites. This is particularly true if the site is distant. Saint Gall is not next door to Aachen. In fact, it is hundreds of miles away and situated in difficult terrain; the Alps. Charlemagne's new official script eliminated, among other things, variant forms and ligatures; it did away with stress notation. It threw abbreviations out the window. Without exception, and this includes the *Plan of Saint Gall*, a design for the monastery (Figure 10.7), every manuscript from Saint Gall produced during this period uses the complete *stæfwritung* system: variant forms, clumping and spacing, and stress notation. In addition, abbreviations and ligatures still appear all over the place. This

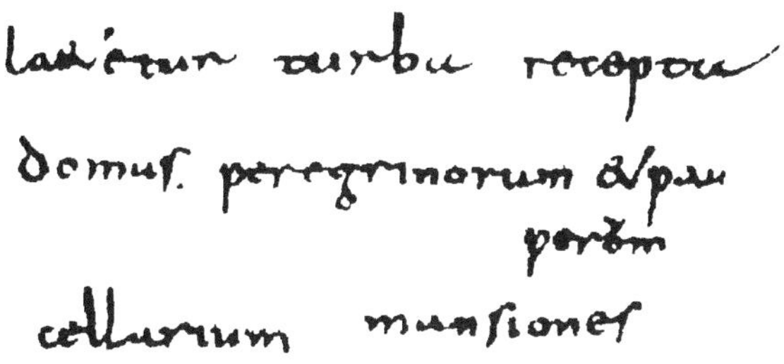

Fig. 10.7 Replicas of Examples from the *Plan of Saint Gall*. From plan for the Hospice for Pilgrims and Paupers. Duration notation, ligatures, and variant forms

strongly suggests that Arn used the script, and writing system, he learned at York under Alcuin before he went out to Saint Gall.

Not only is the complete *stæfwritung* system used in both secular and liturgical texts from Saint Gall, but an augmented version of the *stæfwritung* musical notation system is used in the musical manuscripts. This augmented system combines the *stæfwritung* musical direction notation system with a melismatic neume-based system. The combined system gave all the information both on *how* to sing a song as well as a written record of the melody.

In the *Paris Psalter*, the forms of the letters themselves are more rudimentary and not as graceful as those of Saint Gall. Further, the Psalter employs the older, mixed origin Old English-Latin graphs for xenographic exchange, whereas, being in Latin only, the Saint Gallien augmented system uses a larger variety of variant forms to indicate musical directions (Figure 10.8). We still find, for example, the aleph-*a* and the Greek-*u* among these variant forms. Two of these musical manuscripts, Saint Gall MSS 339 and 359, are the oldest known liturgical manuscripts containing neumatic notation.

The Celtic influence on the Saint Gall manuscripts is obvious; the monastery was founded by Celtic missionaries. Nobody finds it odd to see the clearly Celtic form of the decorated letter *A* in the words *Ad te levavi animam meam* [to you I turn my soul], the **Introit** (the first item in the Proper of the Mass) in both MSS 339 and 359.

As used in Gregorian chant services, an *Introit* consists of an antiphon, verse, antiphon, verse, antiphon, *Gloria Patri* (Acclaim to the Father), and antiphon. The antiphons are all parts of Psalms. If we should look up *Introit* in a dictionary, we read that the antiphon originated in a Psalm sung antiphonally, that is either one verse by half of the congregation and another verse by the other half in response, or one colon to one colon responses. The dictionary will also say that the shortening occurred by the sixth century. The story is a bit more complicated, antiphons are pieces of Psalms.

Psalmody and Hymnody are very different. The word "Psalm" comes from Greek *Psalmi*, sung to a **Psaltery** (a stringed instrument played held against the chest). Psalms, by definition, are accompanied songs; hymns, by definition, are unaccompanied. Psalms are *to* or *for* the Lord; hymns are *about* the Lord and his works. Psalms usually ask for something—forgiveness, protection, aid; hymns are pure praise songs and never ask for anything. Psalms are usually responsive, that is, solos alternating with congregational singing; hymns are congregational. Psalm melodies range from the grand hallel to the Lord of Psalm 150, to the slower beat of the Penitential Psalms, to the rhythms of works songs as in Psalm 96. Hymns are always upbeat.

Now wait just one minute; some hymns are slow. The answer is: It depends upon which tradition is followed. Along with tempi, the resolution of the accompanied versus unaccompanied religious song is yet another marker, a clue to follow, in sorting out the past. Once again, we have to step back for a moment; we are now wading in very murky waters.

In both Matthew (26.30) and Mark (14.26), when describing the Last Supper (given in both Gospels as the first night of Passover, that is, the Passover Seder), they state the distinction between Psalmody and Hymnody: "And after singing a *hymn*, they went out to the Mount of Olives." It could not be clearer that we are talking about hymnody, vocal song, not psalmody, accompanied song. These two Gospel verses were often cited by the early church writers to support their positions.

Back in the second and third centuries, many, but by no means all, of the **AnteNicene** (before the Nicene council) church writers were against the use of instruments. Even those who approved the use of instruments advocated only the psaltery. (Nobody liked the *kithara*, the

Fig. 10.8 Examples of the *stæfwritung* musical notation system. Left: The *Paris Psalter*; Right: St. Gall MSS. 339 and 359

ancestor of our modern guitar, because it was too earthy—it was played held across the "guts.") This insistence upon singing the Psalms as hymnody, vocal only, led to some remarkable explanations. They had to explain *why* a group of songs, whose very name stated that they were accompanied, should be sung unaccompanied. [22] It took several centuries and much ingenuity. In the end, the conflict between what was and what was wanted was resolved through the creation of what we call "Liturgy."

The word "liturgy" is from Greek *leitourgia* and means "public works" or "public service," that is, order of service to the state. In Modern Greece, the period of time something—a government office, a business, even a supermarket—is open to the public still lists these hours as "liturgy"; in the West, "liturgy" has come to be associated with religion. A liturgy is not religious; it is an order of service.

Liturgies are a natural result of centralized, or would be centralized, organization. Centralization eventually promotes limited audience participation, and the need for trained professionals to lead the services. Our oldest record of a "liturgy" through such centralized organization is Enheduanna and her religious songs. Even if we had no knowledge of a priestly caste, we have reason to suspect that just such a structured liturgy existed during the Monarchial period from the instructions to various choir leaders and instrumentalists in the headings of the Hebrew Psalms.

Although the following is greatly simplified (as it must be), Christian liturgies were created through the dismemberment of the Psalms. We recall that among the earliest Christians, the psalms were to be sung by everybody; further, they were to be sung all the time. As the battle to be arbiter of what was meant by "Christianity" gathered strength, opposing leaders arose and divergent structured liturgies followed.

Among some groups, the first step was to assign certain Psalms to be sung at set times *following* a reading. At this stage, the Psalms were still sung as complete Psalms. The next stage is marked by the insertion of readings *between* Psalms. It is during this period that we begin to read about parts of Psalms sung right alongside complete Psalms. We also find references to lead singers and the type of responses expected from the congregation. Slowly, but surely, we watch singing being assigned to professionally trained soloists and choirs with congregational responses being more and more limited to short phrases, Amens, and Alleluiahs. John Chrysostom (347-407), for example, in *1 Corinthios, Homily xxxvi*, 5-6, maintains that:

> . . . there must be only one voice in a church . . . the reader alone speaks . . . the singer sings psalms alone, and the response issues as if it were from one mouth, and only he who preaches gives the sermon.

The last stage in the process was the singing of only *pieces* of Psalms instead of complete Psalms. The exegetical treatments disappear from the record: pieces of Psalms no longer follow the rules of Psalmody and there is no longer any need to justify using the rules of Hymnody instead.

Not everybody, of course, went along with this dismemberment procedure. As late as the fifth century some groups, such as the desert monks, still sang the entire Psalter through once a day. Many of the subordinationist groups not only insisted upon complete Psalms, but continued responsive singing of full verses—as described by Socrates of Constantinople (circa 380-450) in his condemnation of the "Arian" services. [23] Complete verse responsive singing is what we see in the *Paris Psalter*. Many groups also insisted on using instrumental accompaniment. As late as the eleventh century, Ælfric of England (955-1020) refers to Psalms as "hearpan sang," harp song.

A liturgy, therefore, obviously varied tremendously from church to church, from monastery to monastery, and from religious affiliation to religious affiliation. We might recall that the York liturgy was not accepted by many other groups in Anglo-Saxon England, or, for that matter, even in Scotland. Alcuin was from York, as was Arn. We can already sense problems ahead.

On 25 April 1904, Pope Pius X issued a *motu proprio* that, "The melodies of the Church. called Gregorian, are to be established in their integrity and purity according to the oldest manuscripts." These two musical manuscripts from Saint Gall, numbers 339 and 359, are the oldest of the "oldest manuscripts." They form the foundation of the reconstructive efforts.

While the non-Roman character of the Saint Gall Manuscripts was recognized, nobody stopped to consider what this really meant in terms of reconstruction. In fact, in spite of the name, Gregorian Chant appears to be an amalgamation of the Roman and Frankish chants. The closest that anyone is willing to date its origin is to about 150 years after Gregory I died: between 750 and 850. [24]

The usual neumatic movement, as recorded in the melismata, is from one pitch to another. A few neumes, though, represent a repeated pitch or tone. Known as **repercussives** in Gregorian Chant terminology, they are members of the *strophicus* family. This is a family of neumes that take their form from the single *apostrophe*, more or less what we call an apostrophe in shape. A *bistropha* (or *distropha*) is a double apostrophe; a *tristropha*, logically enough, is a triple apostrophe (Figure 10.9). The *tristropha* is a combination of the simple *apostrophe* and the *bistropha*. The name for this family of neumes is based upon the form of the neume found in Saint Gall MSS 339 and 359.

Fig. 10.9 St. Gall, MSS 339 and 359: *bistropha* and *tristropha*

In the Roman Mass, the **Gradual** is the Chant of the Proper. The Proper Chant differs from the Ordinary Chant in that the texts change from day to day. It is performed as a form of responsive singing: A soloist sings a Psalm verse to which the choir responds by repeating the last line. The *bistropha* and *tristropha* are the most common of the *strophicus* family, and they appear in almost every early Gradual. While the entire *strophicus* family is named after the form found in Saint Gall MSS 339 and 359, the particular form of these neumes used in the Saint Gall manuscripts is unique.

There is little doubt that in medieval use these repercussives were meant to be sung as a fairly rapid iteration and reiteration of the same pitch. A ninth century author, Aurelianus of Réomé, is often cited on how repercussives were sung. He reports that the *tristropha* was sung as a *rapid pulsation* like a vibrating hand. It is not at all unusual to find these two neumes used in a series; the result resembles a vocal rendition of a violin *tremolo*, that is, trilling.

Among the many arguments against the reconstruction of Gregorian Chant as done by the Solesmes School, is the fact that they eliminate the repercussive neumes. According to the instructions in the manual for the Gregorian Chant as reconstructed by the Solesmes school, [25] and in the *Liber usualis* (The Book of the Ordinary), perfection in singing may be reached by a "soft, delicate repercussion on each, single, note." In practice, though, the repercussives are normally sung as very long held notes on a single tone.

Something clearly is wrong if reconstruction depends upon ignoring what is written in the manuscripts. This has been said loudly, both vocally and in print, by many Gregorian musicologists. [26] The subject of the repercussives could lead to speculations about the sites of production of many of the early Graduals, but we are concerned with the two oldest manuscripts. The two manuscripts from Saint Gall were written using the complete *stæfwritung* system.

Script differentiation by language incorporated the use of two chironomic systems; one for Latin, one for Old English. We still cannot answer the question as to which came first, chironomic notation is just as useful in poetry and prose as it is in musical texts. The *stæfwritung* chironomic notation symbol set for Old English is preserved in its entirety, all 22 symbols of it, in the *The Parker Chronicle and Laws*, the gift from Matthew Parker (1504-75), the second Archbishop of Canterbury after the Reformation of 1532-34, to Corpus Christi College, Cambridge. Among these chironomic symbols we find the forms of the *apostrophe* and *bistropha* that are supposedly unique to the Saint Gall manuscripts.

The names *apostrophe*, *bistropha*, and *tristropha* as applied to these neumes are modern; Aurelianus of Réome referred to the *tristropha* as *trinum*. These "neumes," these chironomic symbols, however, already had names assigned to them about 2,000 years ago: *geresh* (') and *gershai'im* ("). As the dual form (*ai'im*) on the latter implies, a *gershai'im* is a double *geresh*. The *geresh*/apostrophe, along with the *tifcha*/virgule, and the *e-merka* are very common; they are found in every Old English manuscript produced in Anglo-Saxon England or by scribes trained in the AngloSaxon writing system.

Fig. 10.10 The *gershai'im* over the *u* in "Brunanburh"

The *gershai'im* is rarely used, as it is, in fact, a repercussive, and it does indeed indicate a tremolo/trill. A *gershai'im* appears on folio 26a of the *Parker Chronicle* over the first *u* in "Brunanburh" (Figure 10.10).

Because the Celtic peoples on both sides of the Irish Channel and their converts, the Anglo-Saxons, were strong on missionary activities, a rather large proportion of surviving manuscripts use the *stæfwritung* system. It was used throughout the greater portion of Western Europe; it was even used at Rome. We find the unmistakable stamp of Anglo-Brittonic and Anglo-Goidelic missionary activity and training from what is today the Netherlands to North-East France, from parts of Germany to Italy, and Switzerland, including the monastery of Saint Gall.

During the nineteenth and the greater part of the twentieth centuries, a monolithic Roman church in early Ireland and England was a "given," as can be seen from comments about "The" Celtic Church and "The" Vulgate. Native British society was presented as primitive and illiterate; Anglo-Saxons were viewed as beer-guzzling, chest-pounding, barbarians; and Anglo-Saxon England as Christian only after the arrival of Augustine the lesser. Latin was assumed to have been the only foreign language known. The cheerful nineteenth and early twentieth century embrace of the desired history has had some unfortunate results. We have reason to doubt Bede could foresee that modern scholars would turn his *Historia* into a snare for his own religious party.

In spite of the doubts thrown on a monolithic Christianity in Britain by Bede; in spite of the lack of general acceptance of the York rituals in England; in spite of known contemporary complaints on the Continent that the new Alcuin rituals were so different; nobody in the early twentieth century thought to ask what it meant that the Saint Gall manuscripts were "Non-Roman."

Perhaps people should have paid more attention to the "Non-Roman" character of these manuscripts from Saint Gall. As G. B. Chambers put it, "it seems strange if such a result has arisen from a misinterpretation of history." [27] The Gregorian Chants cannot be reconstructed in "their integrity and purity" from the two oldest manuscripts. The Saint Gall manuscripts certainly are not Roman, but they are not Frankish either. They are *Englisc* and represent a completely different tradition.

How different a tradition is shown by the Psalms of the *Paris Psalter* and the Anglo-Saxon Comprehensive Writing system, *stæfwritung*. History is written by the Winners, a truism now fully accepted. The Winner's history edits out contradictory material, but the editors never manage to destroy everything; bits and pieces always remain. The story told by the manuscripts is decidedly at odds with the preferred history.

Between them, the *Paris Psalter* and the Saint Gall manuscripts throw light onto a dark area. They fill in many of the details Bede omitted. They unequivocally tell us that the reality was very different from the history as edited. They go far to explain some very peculiar aspects of later English history. They also explain how Alcuin could try to destroy what would appear to be his native writing system. Even if Alcuin were not trying to control everything in sight, from Latin to Liturgy, *stæfwritung*, too, was from a somewhat different tradition.

Alcuin's attack on the *stæfwritung* system was fairly successful on the Continent, although it took several centuries for his retroversions to spread. We look back at the Assyrian, Babylonian, and Greco-Roman reigns and see Alcuin and Charlemagne repeating an ancient pattern. Peoples touched by Alcuin and Charlemagne, and Charlemagne's descendants, eventually forgot the meaning of the variant forms, the clumping and spacing, and the stress notation. By the end of the twelfth century, even at Saint Gall, the musical notation system was forgotten.

In spite of numerous attacks and attempts at classicization at home, it took another 800 years to destroy the *stæfwritung* system in England. The manuscripts warn us to be very careful when working with Old English texts; things may not be what they appear to be. In England, they insisted upon their own way to sing, and to record, a new song.

Fig. 10.11 *The* Master Psalmist, with 4 pairs of red and yellow stripes on his harp. (Line drawing based on illustration in University Library Cambridge, MS F.f.1.23)

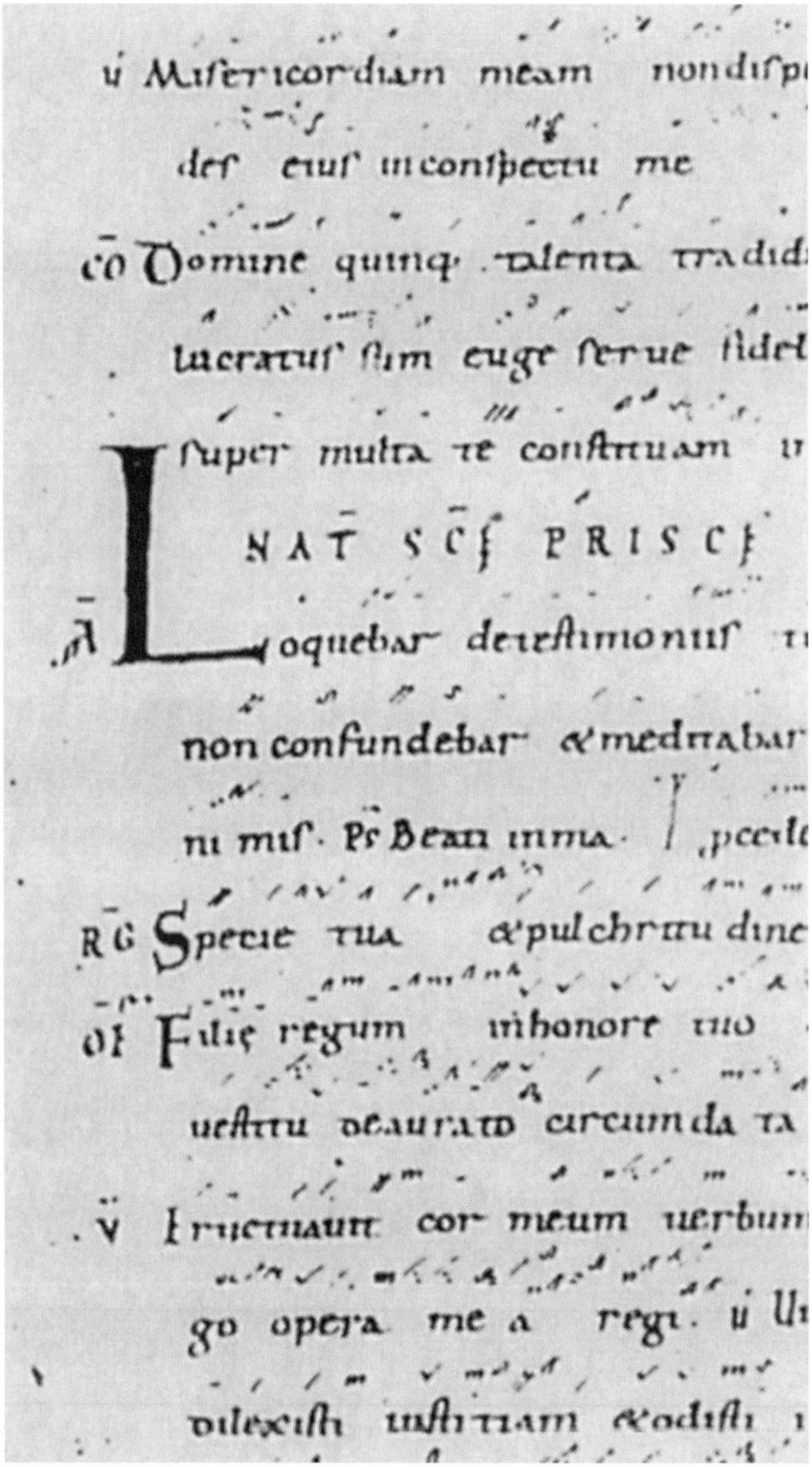

ii Misericordiam meam nondispe[r]

des eius inconspectu me

co Domine quinq̄ talenta tradidi

lucratus sum euge serue fidel

super multa te constituam u

NAT SC̄F̄ PRISCE

A Loquebar detestimoniis t

non confundebar & meditabar

ni mis. Ps Beati inma . . . peccat

RG Specie tua & pulchritudine

OF Filie regum inhonore tuo

uestitu deaurato circumda ta

V Eructauit cor meum uerbum

go opera mea regi. ii Ui

dilexisti iustitiam & odisti i

Plate 10.2 St. Gall MS 339. Lines 2-16, (*Paléographie Musicale: I. Codex 339 de la bibliothæque de Saint Gall (Xe Siècle) Antiphonale Missarum Sancta Gregorii.* France: Solesmes, 1912. 24)

Chapter Eleven

CHANGING VOICES

When we look at a Winner's Standard Operating Procedures, we find that the design and implementation of a new official script has priority. There are obvious reasons for this: by changing the voice of authority, the official script, the Winner announces a new regime.

The overwhelming majority of the existing ancient and medieval texts are standardized copies. Documents displaying a new official script in transition, the new voice of authority coming into being, are almost as rare as dictated originals. Once in a while, though, some of these unusual, and revealing, documents slip through. A few of the manuscripts produced under the iron-fisted Benedictine Reform of the mid-tenth century show monastic scribes trying to learn the new official script for *Latin* texts. Some of the scribes had a terrible time learning the new official font; they were so confused that, as one person maintains, they seemed to be designing the script as they wrote. [1] While these few manuscripts do give sociological and political information, as well as some (but not much) information on voices in transition, they are not particularly interesting—unless one be specifically interested in the Winner's techniques as enforced by yet another religious *renovatio*. Far more interesting is another group of documents showing a new official voice in the making: the manuscripts produced under Ælfred's preservation and education program.

The majority of the texts produced during Ælfred's reign were dictated originals; something that is, if we stop to think about it, explicit and logical. One must have a copy to copy from, but Ælfred could not make it clearer that these works were new translations into the vernacular or new records of existing vernacular works. In other words, any later versions of these Old English texts are copies, but the greater part of the Ælfredian "special" documents are dictated originals. As so many of the Ælfredian documents *are* dictated, they present us with a rare and unusual opportunity.

By any criterion, Ælfred's program was ambitious. The earliest of Ælfred's special documents in the vernacular dates to 890-891; his last project, the reworking of the first fifty Psalms found in the *Paris Psalter*, dates to 899. We can watch the new voice of authority come into being because translating, composing, writing, dictating, copying all take time.

With the thousands of books available today, we tend to forget that book production is a time-consuming and expensive process. Even with our modern computerized printing, originals are rarely fit for public consumption: somebody must set the copy from which all other copies are made. While substantially slower and much more costly, the process really is not that different in a hand-produced book. Someone writes or dictates the primary draft. Because the original version is only a working draft, it is more often than not anything but neat. (Although Bede's methods were a normal part of the basic education of the age, [2] he was exceptionally well organized even for the period. Bede's sentences issue forth like carefully graded pearls on a string.) Typical working drafts are messy; they contain strike-outs and insertions. Lines drawn across the surface point to auctorial and editorial addenda, and changes are written between the lines of text and scrawled in the margins. Originals contain inappropriately mixed fonts, mixed dialects, and even changes of format. Working drafts are loaded with abbreviations. Stress and durational notation are written down as spoken, hence very noticeable. Spelling often is a mixed bag of scribal habits. When production copies are made, these failings are cleaned up.

Over the centuries, old manuscripts tend to acquire marginal notes and emendations, but most surviving manuscripts began as clean copies. In these fit-for-consumption copies, the formats are regularized and the correct hierarchy of fonts are those used by the ruling power for the time and locale. Spelling is standardized in accord with the local power dialect. (This perfectly normal procedure in quality book production is not "scribal editing"; scribes are not editors. The normalization of spelling to the local dialect, however, does lead to apparent "variants.") Extreme differences among stress and durational notation are reduced to minimum guidelines, clean copies are conformed copies, but we cannot say the same for the Ælfredian manuscripts.

Many of the Ælfredian manuscripts are not, and never were, clean copies; quite a few, to put it bluntly, are a mess by any standards at any period for good book production. These Ælfredian manuscripts are among the most revealing of all the surviving documents; they are also the most fun to investigate. The manuscripts are the stage, and we, the audience, watch events acted out before us.

We can actually watch Ælfred's new voice come into being. The Anglo-Saxon Phonetic-Based Comprehensive Writing system, *stæfwritung*, is both comprehensive and versatile. Elegantly simple in conception so a novice can read it, *stæfwritung* is capable of registering fine nuances for the educated. Systematic enough to please the most inveterate pigeonholer, it is flexible enough to make allowance for change and for dialect. The codifiers designed truly and well. Their writing system works so well that documents written in *stæfwritung* preserve for us much more than the text. The key words are *comprehensive* and *phonetic*; the result is the living language, in all its diversity, recorded on the pages—even when this was not exactly what Ælfred had in mind.

We take nothing away from Ælfred's accomplishments when we acknowledge that he repeated every one of the well known ancient Winner's Standard Operating Procedures. There are important differences, though: Ælfred was first and foremost a very good shepherd.

Ælfred is the only English king to have the title "the Great." Historically, the title "The Great" was, and is, reserved for rulers who consolidate, unite. Sargon means "Great King," and Sargon I of Akkad and Sumer was a consolidator, as were Alexander the Great and Sancho the Great of Pamplona (Navarre); so was that anything but "great" ruler, Frederick of Prussia and the reputedly immoral Catherine of Russia. Ælfred is among the select company of rulers who united disparate peoples. Unlike Alexander (who was never home anyway) or Frederick (who nearly destroyed his country's economy with his wars), Ælfred, like Sargon I (but not the totally unrelated Neo-Babylonian Sargon I), is remembered with affection as the model of a Good King as well as a Great King.

Under Ælfred, for the first time the Saxon kingdoms were united under one over-ruler. For the first time, speakers of Old English from all over the island were brought together in one place: Ælfred's capital at Winchester.

With relative peace established after the submission of Northumbria in 886, Ælfred set in motion just about every Winner's technique—from a new official voice to writing histories, from classicization to editing—all, however, with a pragmatic English twist. Unlike Charlemagne, who fostered Latin at the expense of Frankish, for Ælfred, English and the English speaking people, his flock, came first.

Ælfred, who clearly was somewhat of an optimist, left the production of Latin texts, such as Bede's *Historia*, to his ecclesiastical employees. [3] In order to implement his own English translation and preservation program, he needed a battery of scribes under his own direction; so, he went about collecting the necessary staff.

According to the tale, there were very few literate people left among the Saxons; hence, Ælfred sent out a call for anybody who could write. The Ælfredian documents verify the truth of the story. The formats and fonts used by the Ælfredian scribes are from every religious party. Some Ælfredian formats follow the Roman hierarchy, some, such as the *Paris Psalter*, follow the subordinationist, and some come from various continental traditions. The fonts are even more diverse and include a large variety and mixture of formal and informal Insular and hybrid Anglo-Saxon-Insular majuscules and minuscules. The dialects in the Ælfredian manuscripts are from just about every English speaking group—Northumbrian, Mercian, Anglian, Kentish, and, of course, West Saxon. More than a few of Ælfred's manuscripts display a mixture of dialects.

Standardization is the name of the game under the Winner's Standard Operating Procedures. Along with a new voice, Ælfred wished to establish West Saxon as the Standard dialect.

In English, as in all languages, "Standard Language X" is the dialect spoken by the upper classes of a given area. In spite of numerous efforts across the centuries, freezing a living language into a desired standard never works. Even today, with compulsory public education and widespread radio and television, there are tremendous variations from dialect to dialect, from region to region, and from English-speaking country to English-speaking country. It should not surprise us that these Ælfredian voices-in-transition display a hodgepodge of dialects reflected in different spelling systems and graphic representations of phones.

Spelling and phones, however, are not the only differences among dialects; dialects do not change at the same rate. Many different elements effect changes to a language, and among these are changes in the native stress patterns.

In both Old and Modern English, stress can either be intrinsic, that is, the normal pronunciation of the word, or extrinsic, that is, modified by musical, poetic, or rhetorical requirements—of which emphasis is the most common. Similarly, close vowels (for example, long-*e*) generally receive primary stress. Open vowels (for example, short-*a*) are very flexible and may receive none, secondary, or primary stress. The English language tends towards an aversion to open endings (modern French tends towards open endings). An open vowel at the end of a word is called a weak ending; as time passes, weak endings usually disappear.

English, Old and Modern, also has a very strong tendency towards recessive accent (stress). That is, if a bisyllabic word originally has primary stress on the second syllable, over time, primary stress will move backwards to the first syllable. In Modern English, for instance, thirty-five to forty years ago, the word "contrary" had primary stress on the second syllable (conTRARy); today, primary stress is on the first syllable (CONtrary). The farther back we go in time, the more words we find with primary stress on the second syllable.

Phonological changes tend to follow repetitive and relatively predictable patterns. While such repetitive patterns are often referred to as "Laws" (for example, 'Grimm's Law', 'Verner's Law'), living languages are not quite that tidy; there are always exceptions to the "Laws." Exceptions to these tendencies aside, these repetitive patterns are what permit philologists to recover the earlier stages of a given language. These patterns are clearly visible in the manuscripts; they support most—though not all—of the phonological theories postulated by philologists. One major discrepancy between theory and practice is that more than a few of the changes we see happening before our eyes are asserted to have occurred during the pre-historic, that is, pre-written, Old English period. These Ælfredian manuscripts make it very clear that many of these changes actually occurred during the Historic Old English period. Nor do we have to theorize; we have the hard data to hand. All we have to do is to look at the manuscripts—and their comprehensive writing system.

As we have already noted, dialects do not change at the same rate. Over in Northumbria English is spoken this way, down in West Saxon land English is spoken that way, and in Kent they continue to do their own thing. Each group is firmly convinced that their way is the "correct" way—and while usually mutually intelligible, everybody else speaks "funny."

The English propensity towards recessive accent tends to speed up the process of reduction in primary stress on final syllables. Along with different spelling systems, which record differences in the quality of a phone (for example, cyning and cᵹning), one of the most obvious differences among dialects is the dialect-connected variations in stress patterns.

One dialect-connected regular pattern that shows up in these Ælfredian manuscripts is the reduction of stress on final syllables ending with an open vowel. Ælfred's manuscripts record a regular progression of the reduction in stress on final weak endings in *a* from primary stress (d́) to secondary stress (d̀) to duration (a‿) to standard (a) (and eventually to elimination).

Another regular pattern is the English recessive accent acting on vowels and vowel pairs; this pattern also varies according to dialect. In 890, some Northumbrian dialects still place primary stress on the second member of the vowel pair *ea* [eá]. In another Northumbrian dialect stress has shifted to secondary stress on the second member [eà]; but in West Saxon and Mercian dialects stress has already shifted to equal values [ea].

Clean copies are standardized, conformed to a locale, a time, and a ruling dialect. Although we may see linguistic changes in later marginal additions and emendations, we do not see dialectic distinctions in the *original* text of a standardized copy. This is most decidedly not the case with these Ælfredian voice-in-transition manuscripts; the different dialects with their variations in stress, spelling, and phones stand side-by-side for us to see.

Table 11.1 Stress Notation on Vowels and Vowel pairs in various contemporary fonts: 890-924.

| | Monographs | | | | | Digraphs | | |
	normal	medial	primary		rising	in diæresis	falling	monophthong
a	ɑ	ɖ	ɖ		eɑ	eɖ	eɑ	
	ɑ	ɑ	ɑ			eɑ	eɑ	Ɛɑ
	ɑ	ɑ	ɑ					
	ʌ	ʌ	ʌ					
	ā	ā	ā		eo	eO	eo	Ɛo	ℬ
aesc		ℰ	ℰ					
open aesc		ɷ	ɷ		ie	ɩℰ	ie	ℓe
e	e	e	ℰ		io	ɩO	io	ℓo
		ɛ	Ɛ					

The *stæfwritung* system uses the ternary base. Duration notation is shown on the x-axis; stress is shown on the y-axis. Duration notation varies according to the speaker; stress notation varies according to the design of a font. Table 11.1 gives examples of stress notation on vowels and vowel pairs in the fonts, and dialects, that we will see in these Ælfredian manuscripts.

The inclusion of a supposedly late-10th–early-11th century "late" English Caroline-*a* on the table is correct. Figure 11.1a, on page 202 shows the graph from the *Paris Psalter*'s Latin text on f.113v. The graph appears in the *Parker Chronicle and Laws* (Corpus Christi College Cambridge, MS 173) on, for example, foliis 1a, 7b (Figure 11.1b), 9a, 12b, 16a, and 19b (Figures 11.1c, 11.1d, 11.1e), both written into the text and in the abbreviations of dates in *Latin*. This font-identifying *a* graph also appears, for example, on f. 2v and f. 60r in Bodleian MS Hatton 20, one of the originals of Ælfred's translation of *Pastoral Care* (Figure 11.1f). Sometimes Ælfred's "Caroline" is squared, sometimes it is rounded; whether the square or the round font was used depended upon the type of document—and the clerk. Although one Ælfredian clerk also used the "Caroline" font for stress notation, the intention is script differentiation by language. The examples are written with different pens; the form in the *Paris Psalter* is a carefully written book hand while the other examples are rapid cursive writing, one with stress notation (11.1f). Nevertheless, there is no question that these are the same font design. "Caroline," after all, was a well known—and well used—secular insular font in Alcuin's day.

The *Parker* makes it startlingly clear that we cannot date a manuscript solely from the scripts and fonts; we can only date when a script or font became popular, not when it was first designed and used. One pertinent example of the type of problems we can run into is the dating by some scholars of the *Paris Psalter* to the 11th century on the basis of the "Late English Caroline" font used in the Latin text. The Caroline *a* that we see used in the 890's is the Caroline *a* of the *Paris Psalter*. For a scribe to have automatically used the graph in the *Parker* in 891, means that the complete script design was already around and in use in England—somewhere. This caveat with respect to the "Caroline" fonts applies equally to square and formal liturgical fonts. Some presumed "late" square scripts and fonts are very much members of Ælfred's hierarchy of fonts.

Scripts and fonts do not suffice as anchors in time; earlier authoritative scripts and fonts are regularly resurrected by the Winners to acquire power from the past. We tend to forget that, in later periods, Ælfred, as well as his fonts and his manuscripts, was an authority from the past.

Manuscripts in a given class follow set patterns, particularly before the 13th century, but the Ælfredian manuscripts differ from the majority of extant texts in many ways. Among other important differences, we should note that Ælfred's vernacular documents are *not* the products of a monastic *scriptorium*.

Although a "doesn't everybody" among professional paleographers, [4] most people automatically assume that all manuscripts were produced at monasteries; yet there is no reason for this assumption. Secular histories and codes, as secular poetry and song, are in the administrative realm, not the ecclesiastical one. Certainly many such documents were copied in a monastic *scriptorium*; similarly, many *scriptoria* were located in monasteries. Nevertheless, every administration had its own official *scriptorium*, its chancery, as well as administrative sites spotted at strategic locations around the countryside. This was as true of Ælfred's England as it was of post-Norman England.

Chancery clerks and monastic scribes may both write, but they do not have the same functions. Except for in-house requirements, such as service books (property transactions, inventories, and charters were probably handled by specialists), a monastic *scriptorium* is essentially a "print shop," that is, a copying house. In Benedictine monasteries, for instance, writing was a duty assigned to the morning hours after the office of *terce*. A chancery is a governmental business office, with the diversity of official documents to be handled, dictated, copied, sent, received, recorded, and the many different jobs this implies. Nor does a chancery clerk work only in the mornings; the tempo is accelerated, orders must be expedited. Ælfred had his own chancery and his own battery of scribes, chancery clerks, under his orders.

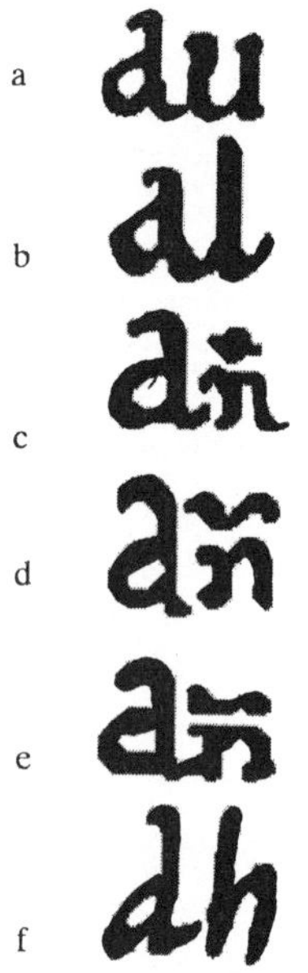

The Ælfredian Old English translations and special documents were produced in his own chancery. The manuscripts themselves tell us so—as do the same clerical ideographs that appear in more than one font and in more than one manuscript produced in Ælfred's chancery.

We should bear in mind that a writing room, whether located in a monastery or in a chancery, is a business office. Anything that disturbs the normal routine is a disruption. A prolonged disturbance will have a head of a writing room or a chief clerk pulling his hair out as urgent things fall by the way and remain unfinished. All of Ælfred's vernacular texts were "extra" work on top of the day-to-day requirements of a busy chancery. When we look at the number of non-administrative documents translated, rewritten, dictated, and copied on command, we need not guess: we know. Ælfred's translation and preservation program was not conducive to a quiet, well-ordered chancery. While we admire Ælfred for his program, and are grateful that he was able to implement part of it for posterity, it is unlikely that most of his staff were happy about either the extra work this entailed, or the noise.

Fig. 11.1 Caroline *a*: a: BN 8824; b,c,d,e: *Parker*; f: Hatton 20

We should also bear in mind that the Ælfredian unification was precarious. He was not in a position to employ direct pressure on outsiders. Ælfred could order his own employees to do something, but he could only request a monastic *scriptorium* to undertake a special or onerous task. This does not mean that he could not *nag* people to do something. Ælfred's cover letter to the Bishops, which was made an integral part of his translation of Gregory's *Pastoral Care*, is one of the politest "get off the stick already" documents in history. Ælfred's letter makes it clear that his education and preservation program had run into the snag which plagues many an administration: while the boss is doing his job, his employees are slacking off. Ælfred's letter to the bishops also makes it clear that his program was underway—sort of.

With scribes from all over the place, the "foreigners" would have to learn Ælfred's own hierarchies of scripts, fonts, and formats. They would also have to learn to record a new dialect: West Saxon.

Scribal training, as we have already noted, makes it difficult for a professional scribe to change his habits. We may recall that only senior journeymen and master scribes have ideographs; a very important point that cannot be over-emphasized and deserves reiteration.

Modern research into nerve-motor response patterns brought about by the space exploration program only verifies what the ancients already knew from empirical observation. In order to perform a physical action effortlessly, without thought, the nervous system must learn to respond automatically to that particular set of actions. Playing badminton will not help someone's tennis game; the stored, patterned nerve responses are different. Riding a bicycle will not help someone drive a truck, nor will running a drill press help someone learn to use a hand drill. Each activity has its own stored patterns and must be acquired as a separate set of nerve pattern responses. Similarly, a scribe learns a font by practice until his stored patterned nerve response is totally automatic.

A professional scribe has a large repertoire of fonts; he has to use the appropriate font for the task at hand. Depending upon his place of employment, a scribe is required to know as much as fifteen or twenty fonts. He needs cursive fonts and book fonts, as well as formal secular and liturgical fonts; if he uses the *stæfwriting* system, he needs a set of fonts for each language. If employed in a chancery, he has to know the hierarchy of chancery fonts as well. Each font has to be practiced until it is stored in the motor area of his brain; it must be practiced until the scribe reacts automatically without thought. It is during this practice process that a scribe acquires ideographs.

Ideographs are a bit more complicated than simply "that's the way I write it." Writing is hard work. As a scribe learns his font designs, he also settles on methods that will produce the correct graphs for a given font, but will shorten the time it takes to write the forms down. This shortening process depends upon the reduction of the number of pen-lifts required for each graph.

a

b

Formally, for example, Insular font designs call for 4 strokes on an *e* (back, top, bottom, hasta) and for 3 strokes on an *r* (back, upwards, downwards). In most cursive Insular fonts, however, the forms for *e* and *r* have already been reduced and technically require three strokes and two strokes respectively—with pen-lifts between strokes. These pen-lifts slow the work down; therefore, scribes "cheat."

c

One scribe finds that he can make the connecting stroke to the next graph in a continuous movement by tilting his high-*e* to the left and going back over the hasta (Figure 11.2a), another finds it quicker to have a straight back on his *e* and extend the

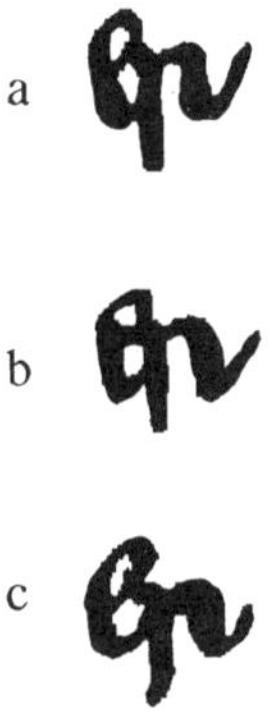

Fig. 11.2 Scribal "shortcuts" (ideographs): *er*

tongue (Figure 11.2b). and yet a third will start his *r* from the end of the top stroke on the *e* and, just as we do today when crossing a *t*, go back and insert the hasta after he has already lifted his pen at the end of the word (Figure 11.2c). In each instance, the pen is not lifted to make the first stroke of the *r*. This reduction of pen-lifts for each graph and graph cluster adds up to a significant savings in time. Once a scribe has settled on his personal "shortcuts," he has acquired identifying ideographs—and he uses these "shortcuts" in every font he writes.

Scribes are not typewriters; there are variations, particularly when writing at speed. Nevertheless, scribal ideographs do not change; the scribe literally cannot help but write these forms this way. Variations or no variations, a scribe's **angle of attack**, his approach stroke, never changes. Perhaps this may best be shown by example. The *aesc* graph amply illustrates what is meant by scribal shortcuts—and ideographs.

The formal design of an *aesc* graph contains many pen-lifts with the *a* requiring two strokes in a rounded design and three strokes in a square one; the *e* requires three strokes. In rounded designs, it is a rare scribe indeed who does not come up with a way to write an *aesc* in one motion without ever lifting the pen (Figure 11.3).

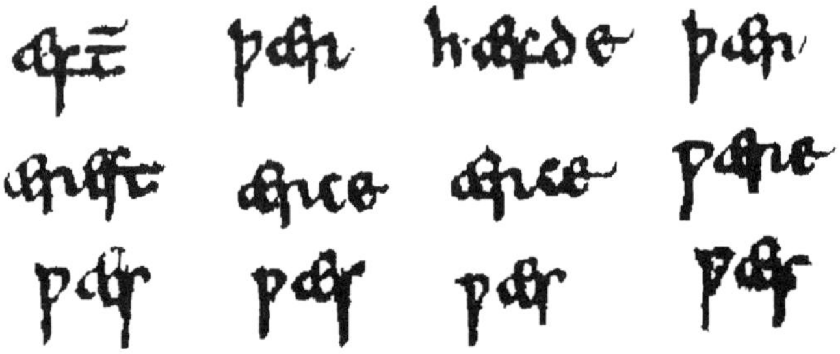

While the *aesc* graph changes depending upon the following form, for instance, *r* or *s* or *f*, and sometimes when writing very fast the lobe of the *a* will be distorted, nevertheless, the four different hands are immediately identifiable because each one has his own angle of attack. We can see that there are indeed

Fig. 11.3 The aesc graph in four hands

variations; however, we can also see that the approach stroke always begins in the same *relative* location and at the same angle.

Some graph clusters are in constant use: scribal ideographs, their shortcuts, carry across these clusters of two or three, and sometimes four graphs run together without lifting the pen. A professional scribe always writes his graph clusters the same way: it saves time, and saving time is precisely what he or she is trying to do.

A scribe's responses are so automatic that he associates a font with the feel of a pen. These virtually robotic responses allow us to isolate scribal hands—even across fonts.

Because scribes have such large repertoires, scripts and fonts by themselves are not a very accurate way to date texts. Many scripts and fonts are in use at the same time. Further, what is standard use at *scriptorium* X at one date may not become customary at *scriptorium* Y until 50 years later. Nor can we date manuscripts by comparing fonts in use at one writing center with the fonts in use at another, lest we rapidly fall into the comparing apples with oranges trap. We can know about the fonts and scripts in use at *one* writing center, when, as in the *Parker*, we have a continuous record of the mutations of a font, a register of new official fonts, and clerks who slip-up and accidentally use forms from hierarchy font A in text written in hierarchy font B (Figure 11.4).

Figure 11.4 gives three of the numerous cases of using the wrong graph for a font that turn up in these Ælfredian manuscripts. The examples appear in close proximity to each other on a leaf. In (a), the words *þy* [particle or demonstrative: the, that, because, etc.] and *feng* [took], are correctly written in Ælfred's early *record* font. In (b) one clerk has erroneously used the *y* of Ælfred's first *dictation* font in *þy* and another clerk has incorrectly used the *e* of Ælfred's *official* documentary font in *feng*. In (c), the words *se cyng* [the king] are correctly written in Ælfred's official font, and in (d), the clerk goofed and used the *y* of Ælfred's second dictation font smack in the middle of a text written in the official font.

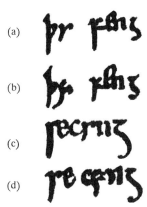

(a)

(b)

(c)

(d)

Fig. 11.4 Using the wrong graph for a font

Although this improper use of font hierarchies turns a class A book into a third class one, these slip-ups give us a great deal of information. We do not have manuscripts written in every font that was in use at a given time; these clerical goofs give us some of the graphs from other scripts and fonts—and a much needed window to peer through.

To make matters even more difficult, official fonts tend to be square. Square designs are central; they are neither too ornate nor too simple. Hence authoritative governmental (for example, Roman Capitals) and liturgical (for example, Hebrew Square Letter) scripts are generally square. One of the oldest and most frequently applied Winners' tricks is to use a version of an earlier authoritative square font to gain prestige and power. As a result, square fonts cannot be used for dating an isolated manuscript; these scripts and fonts are constantly being dusted off and put into use under a new leader.

The apparent popularity of a given font depends upon time, power structure, and locale. It also depends upon what documents have survived. In 1883, Henry Sweet tried to get these important points across with respect to the fonts of the Épinal Glossary. These points still bear repeating. [5]

Ælfred was no exception to the ancient pattern. The *Parker* tells us that he envisioned a large repertoire of his own fonts. There should be governmental and public fonts, internal documentary and external correspondence fonts, formal and informal book fonts, and square as well as round fonts. Because he always thought of his *folc* first, there would also be Latin and English fonts. Latin may have been the language of international discourse, but English was the language of his own people; the Insular scripts and fonts their national flag. All of Ælfred's voices are insular fonts.

Ælfred also wanted to classicize the language while retaining most features of the *Englisc* designed and *Englisc* implemented native writing system: *stæfwriting*. Although reversed by his heirs in *their* calls upon past authority, Ælfred's solution was typical—of Ælfred, that is. Rather than eliminating all variant forms, as in the characteristic classicization procedure, the variant forms were assigned to different fonts. He wanted a place for everything and for everything to be in its place.

Wanting and having, though, are not the same thing. A good man who believed in persuasion rather than force and example rather than coercion, Ælfred's patience must have been sorely tried.

Scribes from throughout the English-speaking world had answered Ælfred's call. Learning a complete new hierarchy of fonts, formats, sizes, and orthography takes time. A scribe is fighting ingrained patterned responses every step of the way. Some scribes obviously can treat the new hierarchies and spelling system as simply another set to learn. There are always others, though, who acquire the new methods, but "goof," revert, when working under pressure, as, for example, when taking dictation.

The Ælfredian official hierarchies took years to settle into place. When we look at the Ælfredian manuscripts, the earlier the document the greater the jumble of formats, fonts, and dialects. We can watch as the "foreigners," the scribes from all over the English-speaking world, learn Ælfred's hierarchies and spelling system while working alongside his own West Saxon men.

Ælfred's first major project, once relative peace and unity had arrived, repeated an ancient paradigm. If we look back across the millennia, we see one pattern that shows up every time diverse groups of people are brought together under one ruler: now is the time "histories" are written down. There are a number of good reasons for this. One very important reason is that, up to the point of one over-ruler, each group has its own memory men.

The memory men are those elite men and women who undergo thirty or more years of training and who are indispensable in an oral society. To kill one of these men or women is the equivalent of cultural genocide—if no replacement has been fully trained. (A point made subtly in a number of Old English texts.) While modern oral-formulaic scholarship generally has concentrated on the performers, whether we call them performers, entertainers, gleemen, jongleurs, minstrels, or guslars, they are the very lowest level of memory men. They add or subtract lines and insert variations from their memory box in response to audience feedback, but they are not the originators of their material. Ranking above these entertainers are the poets, the Irish *filid*, the Anglo-Saxon *scop*: the men and women who do write original works. At the very top of the memorizer heap we find, for example, the Irish *Ollamh* or the Anglo-Saxon *wiðbora* (or *rædbora*) whose primary job is to act as advisers, cultural guardians, historians, and record-keepers. Highly trained specialists; they are also praise singers and poets who will write songs upon demand, and can, of course, act as entertainers.

These elite memorizers are not only in a position of political power as confidential advisers to their leaders, they are also wealthy; they are constantly receiving tangible and valuable gifts. We can readily understand why it takes a direct command from a new boss to get these people to cut their economic and political throats by committing their knowledge to the written record.

On the other hand, though, we can understand why a new over-ruler would wish to merge differing—but related—traditions into an integrated whole as a means of uniting his assorted peoples. The creation of a combined tradition, one from many, is one of the primary reasons "histories" show up after the arrival of an over-ruler, be he an oligarch or a president, an emperor or a king.

Although he definitely had other motives as well, Ælfred commanded that the combined history of his own united peoples be his first preservation project. Today we call this original and its five surviving copies the *Anglo-Saxon Chronicles*.

Chronicle A, Corpus Christi College Cambridge, MS. 173, better known as *The Parker Chronicle and Laws*, is the Ælfredian original. [6] As in so many of Ælfred's productions, the *Parker* suffers from multiple personalities. We can expect changes of official fonts and scribal hands, as well as changes in the standard dialect, when looking at a record covering 180 years. After 900, the changes follow expected and normal patterns. The *Parker*, however, displays a remarkable and totally absurd number of fonts, formats, dialects, and hands on almost every leaf during, and only during, Ælfred's lifetime.

All five of the existing copied versions of the Chronicles descend from, but are not identical with, the *Parker* through the year 891. Clean copies had been made and shipped out towards the end of 891 to various sites among the now united peoples. Normally, without additional information, such as the fact that the *Moore Bede* is dictated, we cannot pin down dates too closely. We know when clean copies of the *Parker* were made: the products of Ælfred's program give us the additional information.

The entry for 892 on f. 16a is empty, although there is plenty of room to write two or three lines of text, the normal procedure elsewhere in the *Parker*. The reverse side, f. 16b, is the last leaf in **quire** B.

A leaf is one side of a piece of parchment, papyrus, or paper folded in half short-side to short-side. This yields four sides, or writing surfaces, connected at the fold (technically called **bifolia**). Because parchment is made from the skins of animals, and because there is a difference in texture or color between the hair side and the flesh side, usually care was taken to ensure that when opened flesh side faced flesh side and hair side faced hair side. [7] In a quire (also called a "gathering" or "booklet") with eight leaves numbered *a* and *b*, if flattened out, f. 1a is to the right and f. 8b is to the left. When turned over, f. 1b is to the left and f. 8a is to the right (Figure 11.5).

A quire is a group of *bifolia* inserted one into another. (A quire consisting of eight leaves equals four bifolia.) Codices (and books) are assembled in quires, which are then sewn (or glued) together along the spine, presumably (but not always) in the correct order.

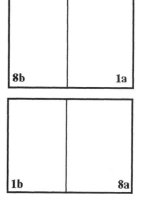

FiG. 11.5 Example *bifolia*

F. 16b, the last leaf of quire B, originally was *blank*. This blank (or empty) leaf was filled in at a later date, probably around 898-9. The script, format, and year numbering, as well as the **leading** (the space between lines) on 16b are quite different from either before or after the leaf. While very unusual to see all the techniques used at once, f. 16b displays a series of well-known copy-preparation "tricks" used to condense text and to make it fit into a restricted and predetermined space.

The text on f. 16b is written in a condensed font that is full of squared forms which were not used in the *record* documentary font until 898. The dates begin with a majuscule *A* from an insular font used for Latin texts of 100 and more years earlier. Even the punctuation used at the end of an entry (:꒓) is different from either that used on f. 16a (:–) or the end of the entry for 894 on f. 18a (·).

A short supplementary entry for 891-2 was stuffed in overlapping the normal upper margin; text was also written running well into the inner (or gutter) margin. While messy, text running into the outer margin is easily read; text in the gutter margin, however, may be sewn into the binding and be unreadable. Instead of the date standing in its own column to the left (Figure 11.6), the date is run into the text

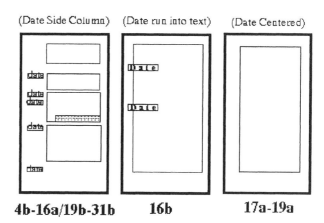

Fig. 11.6 Formats of folia 16a, 16b, and 17a

and the entry itself runs into the usual date column—as well as running into the gutter margin. Written in a condensed-font, this supplementary text for 891-2 is followed by the entry for 893.

The entry for 894 on 16b was literally packed in to make the text line up with the continuation on f. 17a—which happens to be the first leaf of the new quire C. As events are recorded *after* the completion of a year, the new quire was probably started at the beginning of 893. When f. 16b was filled in to make a continuous record, the original first *bifolium* of gathering C apparently was discarded. Because f. 16b was originally blank and filled in much later, we know that the clean copies were made in 891—although we have no idea of how many copies were made. One of the five existing copies, the *Peterborough Chronicle*, is a much later copy of one of the clean copies that had been made in 891.

The various versions differ, sometimes substantially, after 891, for the simple reason that, after the copies had been shipped out, what was entered depended upon the locale—and what was considered worth mentioning by a local recorder. Even the length of an entry depended upon locale. In addition, later scribes would go back and insert "missing" entries into the pre-891 text, particularly in the Ælfredian original.

Most chronicles (or annals) are not "histories" in our modern sense of the word; they are stories. These [hi]stories tell the story of *a* people. Other peoples are mentioned only when a group happens to impinge in some way the focus of the story: this one people. Because property rights (whether things or people) are of great importance, particularly in a patrilinear society, great care is devoted to the recording of genealogies. There is a "Genealogical Preface" to the *Parker Chronicle*.

A common purpose in writing down genealogies is to create a background, particularly if the new ruler is of humble origins. Yet another is to give a reason for the existence of a particular ruling power, to bestow the right to rule. Ælfred did not need to create a background for himself among the West Saxons; his brothers and father before him had been kings of the West Saxons. Nor did he have to be anointed in accord with the Biblical Model to validate his right to rule over his own people, that had effectively been done in 853 when the young Ælfred had visited Pope Leo. [8] Ælfred, however, now had to establish his right to rule over a united peoples—not all of whom were happy to be united.

The Ælfredian original follows the Biblical model for [hi]stories. The Biblical model includes poetry and song interspersed among the prose; so do the Chronicles. The Biblical model, as all Ancient [hi]stories, includes a "prologue." A prologue is necessary in oral societies; it tells the listeners what story they will be hearing. The Bible begins with a "prologue": Genesis 1, the outline of the story of the creation of a world. Having given aural notice, so to speak, the text then goes back to day two and fills in the details. The *Parker* begins with a prologue: the outline of the story of the house of Wessex and the creation of a kingdom.

The Ælfredian Genealogy on leaf 1a ends with his reign as king that unites, "we his kin for the first time the land of the wes[t]saxons" [9] [ƿe hiꞅ cyn æꞃeꞅꞇƿeꞅ[ꞇ]ꞅeaxend lonðjj]. The "Genealogical Preface" is the prologue: the chronicle itself begins with "sixty winters before Christ was made flesh" (60 BCE). The events recorded in the Chronicle through 891 go back and fill in the details, the causes that led up to and justify Ælfred's reign over a *united* kingdom.

We can even close in on the date when Ælfred commanded that the chronicle be started: after he had assembled his clerical cadre following the submission of Northumbria in 886, but before 891 when clean copies were distributed. For a variety of reasons, among them ingrained scribal habits, early 891 is almost certainly right on target.

As we look at these Ælfredian manuscripts, while it is sometimes difficult not to smile, we must remember that the clerks were only trying to do their job and not trying to entertain posterity. Many of the Ælfredian manuscripts tell a very amusing story; the *Parker*, for all of its serious intent, is not an exception. The *Parker Chronicle* has quite a tale to tell us—if we will open our ears.

Instead of the pristine quality of the dictated *Moore Bede*, Ælfred's first assay ended up a mess, a working draft from which clean copies were made. While an unknown number of clean copies were in fact made and sent out, nobody ever got around to making a clean copy of Ælfred's own unintentional working draft: quires A and B. His clerks were too busy with their regular duties as well as working on his other projects—and Ælfred ran out of time.

The *Parker* itself gives clear evidence that Ælfred's original was written in the royal chancery. It differs substantially from the usual run of annals and chronicles written during the Medieval period. First, it is not a clean copy. Second, although written in the large size for secular official documents in the subordinationist hierarchy, the number of format changes are quite conspicuous and definitely contrary to good *scriptorium* practice. Next, monasterial scripts and fonts have a cohesion due to scribal training at a specific monastery that is totally lacking in the *Parker* prior to 895. Finally, monasterial productions are normally written in the standard dialect prevailing in their locale; the orthography of the *Parker* is anything but standardized.

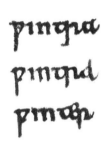

Time, time is always an important factor when dealing with written documents. It took time for trained (and some not so trained) scribes to answer Ælfred's call. Ælfred's newly assembled cadre of clerks had to be trained to his specifications, but this, too, takes time. Training clearly was well under way when Ælfred ordered the Chronicle begun. All the scribes in the earlier part of the *Parker* use the same, but not identical, hybrid insular font family (Figure 11.7). The foreign scribes, working alongside Ælfred's own West Saxons were in the process of learning Ælfred's fonts.

Fig. 11.7 *Parker Chronicle*: Learning a new font

The font family resemblance is easy to see, but it is also patent that these three clerks do not write the same font. They will eventually get there, but here, on these leaves, the foreigners are still learning. The examples are from the formula "[for] (number) wint-" on f. 1a. On top, the straight minims and rounded lobes show the West Saxon model; primary stress on the final *a* has already changed to duration in the West Saxon dialect. The middle hand, Northumbrian clerk 1, using an insular pen, writes a tilted version with the distinctive Anglo-Saxon pointed minuscule *a*. This clerk still places primary stress on the final *a*. The third hand uses a straight cross-stroke on his *wyn* and on his *n*; his spelling illustrates the archaic instrumental form: *wintEr*.

Figure 11.8 on page 210 shows some ideographs of four of the clerks. Hand 1 writes his low-*s* with a closed minum and a little flip on the top stroke (pᴁſ); Hand 2 writes his low-*s* with a split minum (pᴁſ). Hand 1 writes his *wyn* with a squared lobe having an upwards tilt and his minum starts with a small wedge; Hand 2 rounds off the top of the lobe on his *wyn* and the lobe starts precisely at the beginning of the minim. Hand 1 squares off the lobe of his *a* and tilts the *e* backwards on his *aesc* (pᴁſ). Hand 2's *aesc* has a very small round lobe on the *a* and a backwards tilt to the high rounded *e* (pᴁſ); Hand 3 writes an upright *aesc* with lobes of equal size ([h]œᵹᴅe–had; þœᴄ–that); while Hand 4 has a decided right-hand slant on both lobes (ᴁᴨᴁſᴄ–first, e.g. the superlative, -est, of "ere"). The *e* in their ligatured *e-thorn* (e-þ) also varies. Hand 1 tilts his *e* forward; Hand 2's *e* has a marked backwards tilt while the *e* of Hand 3 has a slight backwards tilt. The *e* of Hand 4 is straight. All four write their *d* somewhat differently. Three of the clerks ligature *ld* (heolᴅ-held); Hand 3 does not, and also uses a dark-*l*.

There are differences among their their *eo* ligatures and their *g* (ꝣ), *y* (ʏ), and *thorn* (þ) graphs also. Hand 1's *thorn* (cynꝣeþ) is distinguished from his *wyn* (pᴁſ—above) by the length of the upper extension on the minim and the straight stroke across the top of the lobe.

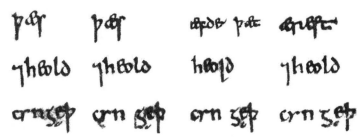

Fig. 11.8 *Parker Chronicle*: Some ideographs of four of Ælfred's clerks

The lobe on the *thorn* of Hand 2 is squared while that of Hand 3 has an upwards tilt and Hand 4 rounds his lobe. Similarly, while the *y* (ʏ) is clearly the same font, Hand 1 writes his *y* quite straight and close. Hands 2 and 3 write their *y*'s with a forward tilt, but the tilt is much greater in Hand 2. Hand 4, like Hand 1, writes an upright *y*; his *y*, however, is open.

While we can see these differences when we examine the hands individually, ordinarily they should not be too obvious *if* the hands are staggered. Sure enough, the *Parker* follows normal *scriptorium* procedures for a document that will be produced by more than one hand.

As we saw in the ninth-century scribe's handbook, the author states that a scribe should first choose his pen and then draw his guidelines. Book production for multiple hands follows the same principles, but there are differences; we are now referring to mass production techniques. Once the size of a document as determined by the content has been ascertained, the correct font of the body text is chosen from the hierarchy of scripts as well as the correct pen for the font. The chief clerk or *scriptorium* master may need to run a pen test. At this point, the number of leaves required are estimated and prepared and guidelines are marked on all the leaves in accordance with the pen. Finally, according to the correct pen, pre-cut pens, as many as is estimated will be required for the completed job, are prepared.

With parchment sized, guidelines marked, and pens pre-cut, the actual production is ready to begin. While in later periods something as large as a book might well be written by one scribe and from an exemplar, this was not the case in earlier periods. Prior to the eleventh century CE, major productions were the products of multiple hands and dictated. No matter how well trained, there are always differences among scribal hands. Writing, as we have noticed, is ultra-conservative; the procedure dates back to the days of Cuneiform writing.

The staggering technique was invented as a simple taking of turns to permit the uninterrupted dictation of large documents. The *Moore Bede* with its two scribes shows us this original use. It is only a small step from taking-turns for two scribes to staggering a dictated work for a group of scribes. The staggering technique is designed for the production of books by scribal teams taking dictation.

At the beginning of multiple-hand documents, each scribe assigned to a project writes one and one-quarter or one and one-half lines; thereafter, scribes write staggered stints. The purpose of this staggering is to reduce obvious differences among hands. These differences seem small, but if each scribe wrote a solid block, the different hands would stand out: the texture would change from block to block. One block would have all pointed *a*'s; another would have rounded *a*'s, and yet another would have a squared appearance. [10] The stints are not repeated in the same order as the beginning lines because simple rotation would create easily identifiable blocks of different textures.

The procedure is really quite easy to effect. While one clerk is working standing up at the high writing desk, the next one is stationed next to him waiting to take over. The progression is orderly and normally requires no special exertion. This cannot be said for the staggering technique in the *Parker*.

Either somebody was unduly optimistic or Ælfred was nagging his chief clerk. (Are they ready yet? Let's get started already!) The latter seems most likely; no experienced chief clerk or head of any writing room would have thought the new men ready. Indeed, the chief clerk or head trainer only prepared and marked parchment sufficient for one quire.

The new clerks were almost ready in terms of font. They had even, in general, learned the correct variant forms for this font. If Ælfred envisioned a Bede-like clean working draft and it depended upon the font, the staggering technique was passable, not good, but passable: a third class production. The fonts are so intermingled by staggering that no particular hand stands out—until one tries to read the text. From a reading distance, the staggering technique falls completely apart; staggering or no, dialectic differences in spelling and stress were not taken into account.

Senior clerks and scribes acquire many automatic responses. When taking dictation a clerk or scribe writes down what he hears as he hears it. Unless his responses have reached the automatic stage in a new system, however, he will write formulæ and common words the way he originally learned them—no matter the dialect of the speaker and no matter the font. Unfortunately for Ælfred's plans, the "foreigners" also had to learn another dialect (Figure 11.9).

The first line in majuscules and the first word on line 2 was written by the West Saxon clerk, probably to show the others what was wanted. On line 2, the clerk with the squared font took over until the first medial point; he even remembered to write *wintra*—the first time. He was replaced by Northumbrian clerk 1 (North 1) who promptly wrote *uu* instead of a *wyn* in *wintra* and gave primary stress on the final *a*. Four words later, the West Saxon took over on the same line with the words *his sunu* [his son]. He wrote a few words on line 3 and handed over to another trainee (North 2)—but not for long. Back again comes our West Saxon clerk. He wrote two words and handed over to yet another trainee, who promptly used a sigmoid-*s* from another font in his third word: *elesing*. The West Saxon wrote the last word on line 3 and the first word on line 4 and handed over to

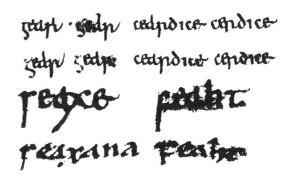

Fig. 11.9 *Parker*, f. 1a. Spelling and Stress on *a*, by dialect (The bottom words, *seaxana* [of the saxons] and *feaht* [fought] are, respectively, examples of late hands A and B from f. 7a. Note the loss of stress differentiation on *ea*.)

another trainee. This one did a little better: six words and then handed over to North 1—who wrote two words when the West Saxon stepped in again.

The poor fellow was kept very busy; his hand bobs in and out throughout the leaf showing the trainees the right way. He must have been ready to scream; North 1 came back on line 7, and again writes *uu* for *wyn*. On line 8, the clerk with the squared hand reverted to his own dialect and out comes *wintEr*. On line 16 an Eastern clerk uses a half uncial *a* for stress notation. The name *cerdice* turns up spelled *cerdice* in West Saxon, Mercian, and in an Eastern dialect, but *ceardice*—with primary stress on the *a* in the hand of North 1 and with secondary stress in the hand of North 2. Both Northumbrians and the Easterner stress the *a* in *gear* [year]. North 2 again gives secondary stress, while North 1 and the Easterner write *gear* with primary stress.

Through it all we find the poor West Saxon clerk popping in and out showing the new clerks the right way. Well, nobody has ever said that teaching is easy; however, training scribes is usually not this much of a gymnastic exercise.

Do these dialectic distinctions make a difference? An *a* is an *a*, is it not? No, it is not simply an *a*. *Stæfwritung* is a comprehensive, *phonetic*-based writing system and is easiest to understand if thought of in terms of reading modern musical notation. We can then readily see that the rhythms move up and down just as do notes in a score. As in a musical score, there are pauses, increases and decreases in volume (stress), and held sounds (duration). Instead of five lines, though, there are four; instead of musical notes, there are words written in the language of Ælfred's England: Old English.

Reading this leaf with all of its dialects and different spelling and stress patterns is the equivalent of trying to listen to a compact disc recording while someone keeps skipping back and forth between discs and between tracks. It is like hearing a preposterous mixture of Gregorian Chant, Country and Western, and Hard Rock—with a love-lorn folk ballad thrown in for good measure (Figure 11.10).

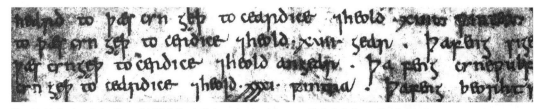

Fig. 11.10 *Parker*, f. 1a; lines 16-22. Mixed dialects *in situ* (Corpus Christi College Cambridge)

A reader is able to hear the voice of authority about as well as one can follow a television program while rapidly flicking back and forth through fifty channels. All of this seems bad enough, but it gets worse: the formats keep changing.

Ælfred himself probably decided that his chronicle would follow an annal-by-religious cycle format, the most common annal/calendar cycle then in use. Such a format usually uses prenumbered dates. As Ælfred was always careful to avoid the appearance of being innovative, we have reason to assume that this was his idea. Prenumbering is very wasteful of time and materials, but it is a common method used in liturgical calendars, hence, authoritative.

The leaves of the *Parker* are large: approximately 8 inches wide by 11-1/4 inches high. Leaf 1a contains the "Genealogical Preface." Ælfred being Ælfred, he wrote an explanatory introduction; this introduction appears at the top of leaf 1b. The introduction takes eight lines with year 1 (an i) on the left-hand side opposite the sentences that record the date of the birth (*acenned*) of Christ. Years ii and iii appear opposite the sentences that discuss Herod and his son Archilaus. Year iiii (4) is blank, as is year v (5). The Chronicle itself starts out divided into two columns, with column one prenumbered.

The numbers on the left-hand side are consecutive from year 6 through year 32. The entry for year 6 is squeezed into four lines and totally ignores the year-numbers at the side. There is no entry for year 10; there is an entry for year 11—but it is not original; this is the first of the entries by late hands A and B. Year 12 is the next original entry and, as the earlier original entry, overruns the prenumbered dates. Year 15 is blank. Year 16 fits on the one line and reports that '*her feng tiberius to rice*' [Here took (Emperor) Tiberius to kingdom]. The column is blank until year 27: this is not an original entry either, but another addition by late hand A. The next original entry is for year 30 and runs over years 31 and 32.

With the right-hand column we find a change. Perhaps in the "foreign" scribes own writing centers, entries were not supposed to run over dates because year 33 takes four lines, was written alternately by the clerk of the square hand and North 2, and does not over-run dates. Another clerk took over and wrote the entry for year 34, which also fills three lines without over-running dates. This apparently was not what was wanted. Our West Saxon friend comes back and so do prenumbered dates—until year 45, that is. At year 45 North 2 took over again and, once again, we find numbering by entry. The clerk who writes an open low-*s* comes back with the entry for year 46, which runs three lines. North 1, took over for year 47. This entry runs six and one-half lines; it ends with the word '*þeode*' [people]. This left a handy space—which was filled in 100 years later by Hand A.

There is no question that prenumbering is extravagant, but with f. 2a, prenumbering is back, which tends to confirm that this was what Ælfred had ordered. Orders are orders, and the West Saxon clerk made sure it stayed that way. F. 2a through 4a are prenumbered in the two column format. If the chief clerk wanted to make his point about the unsuitability of the format for Ælfred's chronicle (as well as the unfitness of the new clerks), the best way to convince Ælfred would be to show him. So he did.

F. 2a, with dates running from 48-112 CE has a total of ten small entries, one of which is by late Hand B. F. 2b (113-186) has one original entry and one late entry. F. 3b (262-345) has one *line* to which late Hand B added one line. F. 4a (346-417) again has two original entries and three late additions. Not only are these original entries 'lonely'; the 'square' clerk (who incidentally uses a square-*a* [ɑ] of a supposedly later type) tried to squeeze the original entry for 381 into the prenumbered line space. The result is the entry opposite the date continues *above* the line. The clerk tried to fit the entry in above, but the text ran into the right-hand prenumbered column. So, he scraped off the letters '*ten*' from the word *breten* [Britain] at the end and completed the entry "*ten londe geboren*" [bre/ten land was born] *below* the original line of text (Figure 11.11, page 214).

If the above word picture paints a description of the disorder, the reality is even more striking. Apparently the chief clerk now felt that he had enough bad examples to show Ælfred. (We can imagine Ælfred's disappointment, or perhaps chagrin is a better word, upon seeing the muddled mess.) The new clerks were not writing the West Saxon dialect and the format simply would not do. With f. 4b the format changes to a single prenumbered column.

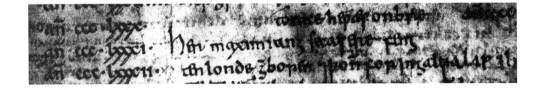

Fig. 11.11 *Parker*: f. 4a, entry for 381: above the main line *bre*; below the main line *ten* (additions by Late Hand B)

Two clerks of the "Preface" prenumbered f. 4b through the year 600 on f. 7a in a single broad column format. North 2, nevertheless, wrote the first entry on f. 4b (418-454) on the left-hand side as if it were still two columns, as did the Eastern clerk. Two later scribes (A and B), writing with two different pens, used this convenient space on the right-hand side to insert entries. Another Ælfredian clerk wrote the entry for 443 and followed the new format. (The entry was expanded by later Hand B with a different pen.) North 2 wrote the entry for 449, correctly this time, and this entry was expanded by later Hand A.

Entries by later hands appear on leaves 5a through 6b. The last entry on f. 6b, for the year 595-6 is more than a little odd and is an example of doubled dates and/or entries that occur with frequency in the *Parker*. This entry records the arrival of Augustine the lesser to bring *godes wurd engla þeoda* (God's word [to the] people of engle). The entry is not original; it is written by late Hand A, sometime around the end of the tenth century. The original entry with respect to Augustine is on f. 7a, and is worded differently.

There are *eleven* different hands on f. 7a (through 626): nine Ælfredian clerks—the West Saxon clerk and all eight trainees—and the two late tenth-century scribes, A and B. The first entry on f. 7a by clerks North 1 and North 2, is 6 lines and runs over the prenumbered dates. (Late Hand A added a line above the entry and after the end of the entry.) North 2 prenumbered 601-2: the entry takes 3 lines, thus leaving an unnumbered line. This entry was written by the Eastern clerk and North 2. At this point, the West Saxon clerk apparently came around to check—because the column is prenumbered from 603 to 626. The West Saxon clerk clearly was trying to make sure that the new format would be followed.

A slight change occurs on f. 7b. The column is prenumbered from 627 to 643, but until now, the abbreviation *an* with a bar (*anno domini*) has been written in the same font. All of a sudden, the abbreviation is written αN, with a Caroline majuscule *N*. In fact, the date for 648 is written with a Caroline *a* as well.

In spite of the decision to prenumber, from folia 8a through 11b, sometimes the entries are numbered as needed and sometimes they are prenumbered with the text over running dates. Whether the entries are prenumbered or not depends upon which clerk wrote the entry; two of them were very stubborn about overrunning dates. Sometimes the clerks write *an* in the mixed Insular/Caroline fonts; sometimes they write the abbreviation only in the insular font. Again, this depends upon which clerk is writing.

Ælfred must have resigned himself to the situation. His first project was a messy working copy, not a clean and beautiful specimen ready to be placed on a shelf to be added to each year. Apparently,

Ælfred and his chief clerk decided to go ahead with the project; they would make clean copies for distribution. The new clerks simply needed more training, and training takes time; they may just as well learn on the Chronicle. Besides, as it was already such a muddle, it would not matter if further changes were necessary: they were.

As the dates get closer to Ælfred, the entries are much longer. Apparently Ælfred finally faced reality and gave up on prenumbering. The format changes again by f. 12a (823-836). Prenumbering ceases altogether: entries are side-numbered and dates written as needed. With gathering C, we find yet another new format: dates are now centered *between* entries. Further, with the new format of centered dates, we also get the Latin dates written in Ælfred's version of the *Caroline* script (shown in Figure 11.1).

On f. 19b, following a long, almost full page entry for 897, the format changes back to prenumbering on the side. Perhaps the clerk was merely being economical; the entry for 898 was written in 899—and Ælfred's time was running out. Perhaps Ælfred had already examined his chronicle after the bridge entries on the previously blank f. 16b had been entered; perhaps he was already too ill to care or to examine his own chronicle again.

The entry for 898 overruns 899; 900 is another of those "empty" entries. On f. 20a, the completion of the entry for 898-9 was inserted *above* the prenumbered date 900. Someone inserted an *i* (1) between the 900 and the *H* of *Her* [Here, i.e. in this year]. This entry, though, records the death of Ælfred in 899.

These constant changes of format under Ælfred are about as far from good *scriptorium* practice as can be—as are the changes in script. In spite of the West Saxon clerk with his rounded forms and in spite of the fact that the font design is actually rounded, the Northumbrians and the Eastern clerk with their pointed vowel forms give Ælfred's chancery record font an overall appearance pointed enough to be called Insular pointed minuscule. The font remained a hybrid round-pointed Insular from leaf 1a and the "Genealogical Preface" through the entry for 891 on folium 16a—and the original end of quire B (Figure 11.12).

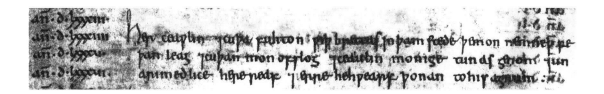

Fig.11.12 Ælfred's Voice as of 891: the Hybrid Semi-Pointed Insular font

Ælfred, as we can see from his own West Saxon clerk, preferred the more rounded insular fonts, yet he also wanted to move in the direction of an official square font. By 894, Ælfred's position had solidified enough that we find a definite change in his chancery documentary record font. The font is a hybrid with a wider *o*-base and a round overall appearance incorporating squared forms. In addition to square *a* (ɑ) and flattened lobes at the top of, for example *b*, the square effect is enhanced by the inclusion of straight Greek-*y* (γ) in place of Greek (𝖞) or Semitic (ϝ) *u*. Long-*s* (f) interferes with a square look; one solution is to "break" the back; that is, instead of a single curve from top to bottom, the top stroke is written at an angle and the upright is a second stroke. The Ælfredian solution for his chancery record font is to use only low-*s* (ſ) in all positions. Except for occasional slips by the "foreigners" (two of the clerks simply could not break their habit of writing 'east' with a long-*s*, although they managed in 'west'), the Ælfredian documentary record voice is in place (Figure 11.13).

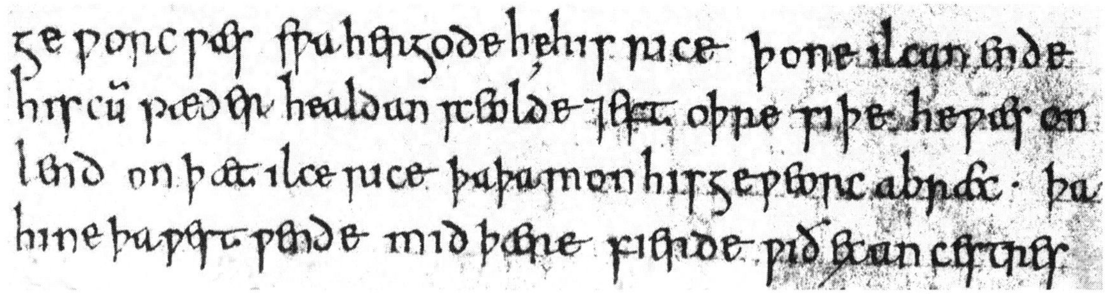

Fig. 11.13 Ælfred's voice in 894: the wide base Hybrid round-square record font

By 898-9, the font has changed again. The *o*-base has once more been narrowed. Essentially a hybrid squared-round font, it is written with a thin insular pen which has been cut at the round font angle (Figure 11.14).

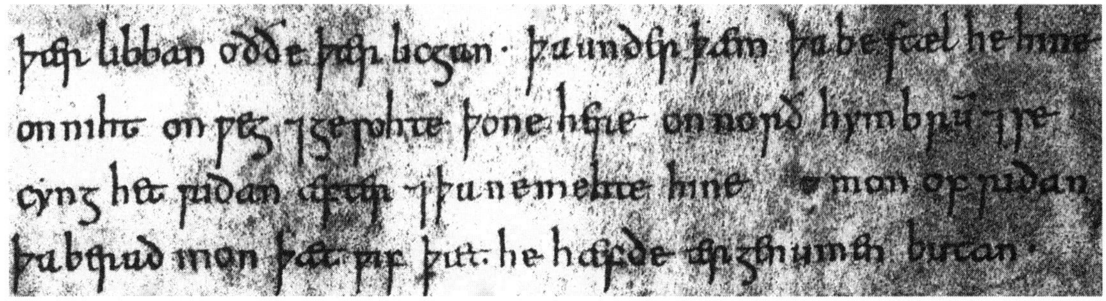

Fig. 11.14 Ælfred's voice in 898-9: the "narrow" *o*-base version of Ælfred's Hybrid record font

A change of font each time there is a change of power structure is nothing out of the ordinary. The rest of the *Parker* follows this normal pattern of change of font with change of power structure. Edward succeeded his father and Edward's record font is a very square, more liturgical, version of Ælfred's voice, and incidentally, also reinstates some of the forms of *u* and *s* that Ælfred had reserved to distinguish his other fonts. Æðelstan (925-940), Ælfred's godson and grandson, and his brothers Eadmund (940-951) and Eadred (951-55) have a totally different record font (Font Family 5); a declaration that things are going to be different now. (They were.) Theirs is an official documentary record font that incorporates the wide swinging loops on high-*e* and long-*s* of the eighth-century formal Insular fonts. [11] In another appeal to ancient authority, the font of Ælfred's three grandsons uses almost the full range of the original ASPA—including chironomic notation. We get a much simpler font under Eadred's sons Eadig and Eadgar, and so on down the centuries. Ælfred's reign did not follow the normal pattern.

Probably because Ælfred's preservation and translation program *was* ambitious, time was lacking to make clean copies of all of his working originals. More than a few of these Ælfredian working documents remain. Ælfred's name (and its use as an "ancient" authority) protected these documents from selective destruction; though centuries later negligence and a disastrous fire in 1731 were not as generous. Nevertheless, the end result is an inside look at the workings of Ælfred's chancery and the existence of documents illustrating Ælfred's official hierarchies in transition.

Ælfred wanted an identifiable voice of authority and he got it—most of the time. Ælfred also wanted to establish West Saxon as the "standard" English dialect; in this he was less successful than he was with his voice. While in general his clerks do write in West Saxon, as clean and regular as his chancery record font is by 895, a number of clerks still occasionally slip into their native dialects when taking dictation—and the text of the *Parker* is dictated. Ælfred appears to have resigned himself to making drafts and clean copies. Unfortunately for Ælfred, clean copies were not always feasible. We cannot be certain, but the insertion of the entries in a circa 898-9 font on the formerly blank leaf 16b suggests that Ælfred wanted to see the complete version of his own *Chronicle* before he died.

The *Parker* is not the only Ælfredian manuscript with improperly used multiple fonts and diverse dialects; however, it is the most important. The *Parker* gives us the ideographs of his clerks; it also gives us an anchor in time. Although unintentionally, the *Parker* allows us to track the changes to the ASPA from the Age of Ælfred to the end of the tenth century.

The Symbol set of the ASPA: from Ælfred to Ælfric

ɑ   Aleph-*a* remained in use in Old English throughout the Ælfredian period, but only by Northumbrian and Eastern clerks. The aleph-*a* was retained in liturgical texts, particularly musical or music-related manuscripts—Henry Kirkestede, a Precentor, uses the aleph-*a* in writing his late 14th-century Library Catalog. The form essentially disappears from secular texts after 900 to be replaced by the Standard West Saxon English basic-*a*.

        Although the aleph-*a* disappeared from vernacular texts, it was retained for many centuries in Latin documents. A superscripted aleph-*a* was used in Latin texts to indicate specific types of abbreviations.

α   Alpha-*a*, as aleph-*a*, dropped out in the Standard West Saxon English symbol set. By the Ælfredian period, it had fallen into disuse for secular fonts in all dialects but Northumbrian and Kentish; it disappears from the Kentish symbol set by around 950.

        The form appears in both Ælfredian and later documents under specific circumstances, for example, in Latin texts and in Biblical names. The alpha-*a* appears in Cambridge Corpus Christi College MS 183 and MS 286. The form is used for Biblical names in *The Exeter Book*

(Exeter Cathedral MS 3501). Alpha-*a* also occurs in, among others, the Ælfredian translation of Orosius's *History of the World* (British Library MS Add. 47967) and Bodleian MS Tanner 10, the Old English translation of Bede's *Historia*. In all these examples, the retention of the different phones, which the basic-*a* no longer preserves, would be required. The form remained in use in the isolated areas of Northumbria and occurs in the late 10th century *Durham Ritual*.

Aldred, the scribe of the Old English gloss to the *Lindisfarne Gospels* is the Aldred of *The Durham Ritual*, both glosses produced in the last quarter of the 10th century. He, and scribes C and D, of *The Durham Ritual* were Northumbrians, and all three use symbol graphs obsolete in the Mercian (*Vespasian Psalter*, circa first quarter ninth century), West Saxon (last quarter ninth century), and Kentish (mid-10th century) symbol sets. [12]

ᴁ The open-lobed *aesc* appears in hand four of the *Leningrad Bede*, throughout the *Moore Bede*, and in the two Northumbrian versions of "Caedmon's Hymn." The form is used throughout the OE interlinear translation of the Gospels (BL Cotton Nero D.IV). The form does not appear in the Mercian symbol set (*Vespasian Psalter*).

The graph is retained in the Northumbrian symbol set through the late tenth century (Gloss to the *Lindisfarne Gospels*, hands 1, 2, and 3). [13] Sharply slanted small-lobed open *aesc* still appears in Font 1 of *The Parker Chronicle and Laws* in Eastern and Northumbrian symbol sets (and dialects). The last remnants of the form are to be found in the ninth and early tenth century MSS written in the West Saxon dialect by Northumbrian and Eastern trained scribes. Nevertheless, the open-lobed *aesc* apparently became obsolete in some of the vernacular dialects before the end of the eighth century and finally disappears from the MSS altogether.

œ The Latin digraph a+e was assigned to the standard symbol set around 925. A somewhat modified ligatured form first appears in OE texts in Font family 5 (925-955) of *The Parker Chronicle*. During this period, the unstressed form changed to represent the central sound, and began to accept secondary stress. The distinction between the monograph (*aesc*) and the digraph (*ae ligature*) survived until at least the twelfth-century.

ᴄ The angled-*c*, which represented the soft phone (*ch* or *X*), that appears in both the *Moore* and *Leningrad* versions of Caedmon's Hymn, and in Brittonic and English names disappears from general use by circa 900, but still occasionally turns up until 955.

The *e-c* ligature, with a standard-*c* form remains in use throughout the Old English period. It shows up in, for example, B.L. Royal, MS 12D.xvii, e-ce-, e-ce-, f.25b; ce-c, f. 26a.

ʝ This is the kyrios form of the symbol *K*. ʝ is an abbreviation for "kyrië eleison"; the kyrios form differs substantially from the kappa-*k* used to signify the transcendent realm. The kappa-*K* is an open form, that is, the lobe is not closed, but reaches towards infinity (Figure 11.15 b-e). The kyrios-*k* is a finite form; the upper part is a closed lobe and the left-hand upright is serifed at both top and bottom, snipping off and containing the transcendent realm (Figure 11.15a).

The graph appears in Ælfredian texts. As with many of Ælfred's innovations, though, the kyrios-*k* only becomes a standard part of the symbol set during the mid-tenth century when Ælfred was called upon as an authority from the past to sanction the use of "English Caroline" in religious texts. The kyrios-*k* in figure 11.15a is the graph found in Bodleian MS Junius 121, a manuscript which is dated to this period.

The addition of the kyrios-*k* to the standard symbol set turned a dichotomy (transcendent versus mundane) into a trichotomy. It was used to make distinctions among the transcendent, ecclesiastical, and mundane realms. In *scriptoria* affiliated with the Benedictine Reform factions, the kyrios-*k* was assigned to the transcendent realm and was used to distinguish between a specific reference to God or Christ; the earlier *K* for *c* exchange in reference to the transcendent realm was assigned to the ecclesiastical realm (*K*).

The older transcendent-*K* could refer, for example, to anointed kings, heroes, martyred kings, or to any god. The new transcendent K (ᵬ) was reserved strictly for references to the Christian trinity. The new ecclesiastical-*K* was reserved for *any* Christian church reference. The new ecclesiastical-*K* appears in references to saints, in liturgies, on Easter tables, on liturgical calendars, and so forth. This use of ecclesiastical-*K* accounts for numerous "variant" spellings. If, for instance, the person had a *C* in his or her name, then the *c* was written with a *k*. If there was no *c* in the name, then any pertinent word in the reference would invoke the *K* for *c* exchange. The late-tenth to early-eleventh century entry for 925 of the *Parker* on f. 26a, for example, records that *Saint* Dunstan, archbishop of Canterbury, was *akænned* (instead of *acenned*, that is, born).

The form of the transcendent-*K* depends upon the font design. Figure 11.15b shows a cursive example of a late-seventh to early eighth century Anglo-Saxon pointed majuscule form. An eighth to ninth century "Caroline" form is illustrated in figure 11.15c. Figure 11.15d is the square liturgical *K* generally used by Ælfred, his son Edward, and his grandsons. Figure 11.15e, another "Caroline" form, appears under Ælfred and was also revived during the Benedictine reform.

By the twelfth century, the kyrios-*k* was used instead of simple *K* (Figure 11.16). Kyrios-*k* for *c* as a marker of the transcendent realm remained in use in Latin liturgical calendars and texts hundreds of years after the printing press came on the scene.

The *K* for *c* distinction between the transcendent and the *ecclesiastical* realms remained in use in the vernacular throughout the Old English period. On the other hand, the use of the transcendent-*K* instead of a *c* to refer to a *mundane* ruler is far more limited: its appearance is tied to the idiosyncrasies of scribes in *one* writing room. Some of their *K* for *c* exchanges appear to be more than a bit peculiar. If, however, we examine these apparent oddities in context, we can usually see why the exchange was made. This mundane use of *K* for *c* disappeared from the West-Saxon writing system by 900.

a

b

c

d

e

Fig. 11.15
a: kyrios-*K*
b–e:
Transcendent *K*

Fig. 11.16
Calendar *K/c*.
Top: 9th
century;
Bottom: 12th
century

u   The *v*-form is used by the three archaic hands of the *Durham Ritual*. Because the Northumbrians used *v* for *u* as their normal graph to distinguish *u* from aleph-*a*, they reserved the *u* form for xenographic exchange. In all English dialects and symbol sets, with the exception of the Northumbrian, the *v* form was reserved for xenographic exchange. The appearance of a *v* for *u* in any other dialect of Old English for xenographic exchange dates a document to the late eleventh century.

Examples of all of these archaic forms may be seen on f. 44r of *The Durham Ritual*. Otherwise, the three original *u*-forms, the Latin, Greek and Semitic, continue in use depending upon dialect, font, or the latest reform.

Ælfred's hierarchy of fonts assigned different versions of the Greek and Semitic forms to different fonts. What is not clear is whether he treated the Semitic and Greek-*u* forms as *y* or as *u*.

ẏ   Dotted-*y* (ẏ, ꝡ), also considered a late form, shows up in the entry for 894 of the *Parker*, and appears in a contemporary West Saxon hand (not as late insertions) in the entry for 899 on f. 20a (cynınȝᵹ, ȝſɫcynınȝ, byɲıȝ, cynȝ, cynȝᵹ, cynınȝ). All of these entries are in the hand of one clerk; the other clerks used the undotted form when writing in the documentary font. The symbol, in accord with Ælfred's variant-form-by-font hierarchies, does not belong in the documentary font. For a clerk or scribe to use a form, it must be part of his repertoire. The most important piece of information given by these clerical slips is verification that the dotted-*y* was in normal use under Ælfred.

The ẏ form appears sporadically in the documentary record font of Ælfred's son Edward. Apparently the symbol was not adopted as the documentary standard in the West Saxon symbol set until the mid-tenth century. (There was so much back and forthing going on during the last half of the tenth century that its adoption may have been part of the appeal to Ælfredian authority.)

Centuries later, the dotted-*y* became the standard graph for *y*, with the undotted-*y* representing *thorn*. The misunderstanding of this scribal convention led to the pseudo-antique use of "Ye" (as in "Ye Olde Shoppe") for the correct "the."

ea   In the Northumbrian and Eastern dialects, the vowel pair originally was a rising digraph and appears as such in Northumbrian clerks 1 and 2 and the Eastern clerk in the *Parker Chronicle*. The vowel pair appears as a rising digraph with primary stress on the *a* in one hand and with secondary stress in the other two. The vowel pair had shifted to two equally sounded phones in the West Saxon dialects by 900 and remained there until the mid-twelfth century. In the Kentish dialects, the vowel pair had already shifted to an equal−height two-phone digraph by 890 and shifted further yet to what can be called a true falling diphthong by the mid-tenth century. While we have to be on the alert for an older scribe throwing off the dating, the appearance of *ea* as a digraph in a Kentish hand places that manuscript as prior to 950.

eo   This vowel pair was not classed as a digraph at the time of codification and was written separately, that is, as two distinct graphs. Its treatment as a digraph seems to date to the early eighth century when ligatured forms begin to appear—which may indicate a shift in pronunciation. In the oldest ligatured form, *eo* is written as a rising digraph (*eO*). Although in some of the later texts written by Northumbrian scribes we still find the vowel pair written as a rising digraph, in most dialects, the vowel pair had already shifted direction to become a falling digraph (*Eo*) and later appears as a "swallowed" graph (ᛒ) indicating that it was a monophthong. In the Kentish dialect, *eo* endured as a digraph until around 950.

ᛁᛖ In Northumbrian Hand 1 of *The Parker Chronicle*, the pair appears as a rising diphthong written with the second member high (*iE*). Northumbrian Hand 2 originally wrote the pair as a rising digraph, but by around 894-5, he writes the vowel pair in diæresis, that is, two symbols of equal height. In the other dialects, the vowel pair was already two separately pronounced vowels by 890 and remained that way until the end of the Old English period.

The *Parker* acts as an anchor in time in areas other than the changes to the ASPA. Its evidence of the various fonts and symbols used in Ælfred's hierarchies allows us to place other Ælfredian manuscripts in both time and space—as do the ideographs of his clerical cadre.

While it is true that more than one scribe can end up using similar shortcuts on a given graph, the probability that, for instance, Scribe Y in 990 will use exactly the same shortcuts, graph for graph, as those of Scribe X in 890 is infinitesimal. If we are looking at the ideographs of more than one scribe, the probability that all ideographs across all scribes will coincide exactly graph for graph is zero. With Ælfred's manuscripts, we are not talking about the ideographs of only one clerk. Any document containing the conglomerate ideographs of two or more of Ælfred's clerical cadre had to have been produced during the Ælfredian period and within a very narrow time frame.

There is turnover in any place of employment; Ælfred's chancery was no exception. In 896 we find five additions (two West Saxons) to the clerical staff. As there are a total of fourteen different synchronous hands in the Ælfredian part of the *Parker*, we do not have room to follow all of Ælfred's clerks down the years; it makes more sense to track two or three.

Of the original clerical cadre, North 1 was still giving primary stress on final *a* right through f. 16a of the *Parker* and the original end of quire *B*. North 1 did finally use *wyn* instead of *uu*, although it took him until f. 12a. The ideographs of North 1 disappear from the *Parker* after 891. On the other hand, two other clerks who have been there from f. 1a are still around in 897-8: North 2 and one Easterner.

One mistake to which we are prone is to refer to scribes by number. The writing was put there by human hands with all the frailties and idiosyncrasies of humanity. These two clerks demonstrate such very human traits that it is an error to refer to them as simply numbers. Besides, as we are going to watch them carefully, they deserve names. "Wili" is a common first element in Northumbrian names, it seems appropriate to call North 2, "Wili." The Easterner may have been from Kent, the Isle of Wight, or even from some continental Anglo-Saxon enclave (his ready tendency to use Caroline graphs and liturgical forms suggests a Continental background); for convenience we shall call him "Old Joe." The name seems to suit the man; he had so many dated habits and probably was around 40 years old when he arrived at Ælfred's chancery.

Wili and Old Joe seemed to work well together as their ideographs frequently appear staggered in other Ælfredian working documents such as British Library, Cotton Vitellius A. xv, second MS (*The Nowell Codex*) and Bodleian MS Hatton 20 (*Pastoral Care*), as well as in "clean copy" Corpus Christi College Cambridge, MS. 12 (*Pastoral Care*). [14]

Wili and Old Joe were true masters. They wrote the "show-off" ending to the metrical epilogue of *Pastoral Care* on f. 98v of Hatton 20. Show-off is an appropriate description; this is a piece of scribal bravura. The epilogue in Hatton 20 is written in a descending triangle alternating between Wili (who started it) and Old Joe. Another such piece of scribal virtuosity (with flourishes) can be seen in Dublin, Trinity College Library MS 52, f.159v and is signed by master scribe Ferdomnach (circa 807). [15] Clearly the shaping technique was known, but only a top notch master scribe could aspire to execute it as the technique involves maintaining parsing structure on the fly while taking dictation.

Considering that *Pastoral Care* was the second of Ælfred's vernacular projects, produced sometime around 892-93, there is some evidence that Wili and Old Joe may have gotten fed up with being constantly corrected by a "young whippersnapper" of a West Saxon. The demonstration of scribal mastery looks very much as if it is intended to show both chief clerk and Ælfred that they know what they are doing and maybe they have a better idea of what is what with running a writing room. Though the exercise in mastery is intriguing and raises speculations, we can never know. The two of them may even have been behind the change of format to entry by date. Both of them defied orders and wrote entries by date whenever they could.

As we have already noted, one old scribe can really throw a monkey wrench into the dating works; here we have *two* old scribes. Changes of font or no, Wili and Old Joe show up in all of these Ælfredian working manuscripts. Neither master was young when he answered Ælfred's call. Indeed, Wili and Old Joe forcibly remind us of Aldred, the Northumbrian scribe of the *Lindisfarne Gospels* and the *Durham Ritual*; like Aldred, almost a century later, they were old-fashioned.

Wili and Old Joe share a number of idiosyncrasies. By 895, they must have realized that Ælfred's program was so ambitious that it was unlikely that clean copies could be made of everything; they certainly tried to write in the West Saxon dialect by then. Nevertheless, these are the two clerks who could not get used to writing "east" with a low-*s*—which is probably not too surprising as both were from Eastern areas. They also sometimes slipped up and wrote ſt instead of ɼt in words such as *stowe* (town). Both clearly were more at home with the more difficult ecclesiastical fonts: Old Joe in particular tends to use formal liturgical graph forms right in the middle of secular documents. In addition, both Wili and Old Joe employ the angled-*c* and the older use of the transcendent-mundane distinction between *K* and *c*.

As codified in 650, a word such as *cyn* or *cyning* written with a *K* referred only to the transcendent realm—whether it be foreign gods or the Christian God. As liturgical calendars are definitely in the transcendent realm, we are not surprised to see that the abbreviation for "calendar" is a barred *Kl*. Dating back to Akkad in use, the distinction in realms denoted by the exchange of *k* for *c* included mundane kings if a reference were to an anointed king or to a king in a transcendent role. Ælfred apparently did not like the conflation of the church and state by writing a reference to a mundane king with a *K* and tried to eliminate this practice from his writing system. In this endeavor he succeeded so well that the distinction between the *k* and the *c* in the *mundane* realm disappears from the West Saxon writing system after 900.

After the kyrios-*k* (ꝁ) was added to the standard symbol set during the Benedictine Reform period of the mid-tenth century, the kyrios-*k* became the transcendent-*K* and was used for direct references to the trinity. The former transcendent-*K* became a new class, the ecclesiastical-*K*, and was used to refer to transcendent representatives, such as ecclesiastics and saints. By the late tenth-century, the new, extended use of *k* for *c* in the transcendent representative realm became the norm in calendars and in references to saints or holy men. This ecclesiastical-*K* was somewhat peculiar in application, but also shows up in continental practices. If an ecclesiastic's or saint's name began with or contained a *C*, there was no problem indicating the transcendent reference; if the name did not contain a *c*, then any relevant word in the sentence referring to the person that contained a *c* was written with a *k*. The shift in application of the *K* for *C* exchange can be seen in the *Parker*. On f. 1b, Christ is *acenned* [born]; on f. 26a, the late tenth to early eleventh century entry, Saint Dunstan is *aKænned*.

Fig. 11.17 *Parker*, f. 7b Wili's "oswine kyning"

Wili and Old Joe, though, were active under Ælfred when the distinction was still only between the transcendent and the mundane realms. As we have noted, they were old-fashioned. When referring to a martyred king (that is, a slain Christian king) or a secular king in a transcendent role they wrote the word *cyning* with a *k*. On f. 7b, the entry for 651, for example, Wili wrote 'oswine *kyning* was slain' (Figure 11.17). Oswin was the "humble" king, for whom, according to Bede (Book 3, Chapter 14), Aidan (whom Bede revered) wept because such a good Christian king would necessarily die soon. Wili did it again on 6b, 8b, 10a, 11a (*kyning . . . se halgode*), and 15b (*Karl francna kyning* [Carl king of Franks, an anointed king]; *Karles sunu* [Carl's son].

An interesting example of the application of the transcendent reference of *K* for *c* occurs in the Metrical Epilogue to *Pastoral Care* in both Hatton 20 and CCCC 12. There are a number of words for a container for liquids in Old English, including *flaxe* [flask]. A *fætels* is a *vessel*; a *cylle* is a bottle made of an animal skin. Animal skin bottles were the water and wine carriers of antiquity.

In the epilogue, Ælfred was, most unusually for him, waxing poetic. He uses internal rhyme, as in *fylle* [fill] with *cylle*. Even more unusual, he used allusion through word choice. We are told to drink now of the Lord's gift . . . *fylle nu his fetels* [fill now his vessel] . . . *hider cylle brohte* [hither skin wine bottle brought]. As the reference is clearly transcendent, both Wili and Joe wrote *Kylle* instead of *cylle* (Figure 11.18).

Old Joe was rather eclectic in what he thought merited writing with a *K* (some of his *K* for *c* choices in the *Nowell Codex* are peculiar to say the least), while Wili stuck to the original use. It must be admitted, however, that some of Wili's ideas on what was or was not transcendent are odd.

Fig. 11.18 *Kylle* Top: Old Joe Bottom: Wili

Both Wili and Old Joe also have very distinctive *k*-graphs. The examples in Figure 11.19 are from fonts used during the Ælfredian period and include *The Parker Chronicle and Laws*; Hatton 20, CCCC MS 12, and both fonts of BL, Cotton Vitellius A.xv, second MS. The standard *K*'s are in the left column. At the top, we have the standard calendar *K*; below that is the standard dictation font transcendent *K*. The last example is the standard book font *K*. Old Joe is in the center column; Wili is to the right. One example each of their calendar *k*'s is given at the top. All the rest of the examples, with the exception of the very last one, are from Ælfred's first and second record fonts and his dictation fonts.

The standard square informal transcendent *K* already shows up in the *Parker* in quire *A*, that is, before 892 (Figure 11.19, second example). Wili's *K* is closer to the standard graph—but has some eccentric features. While he writes the connecting bar between the leg and the open lobe, he tends to tilt it. The top of his open lobe is always strongly curved (Figure 11.19, right). Old Joe found a short-cut; except when writing a formal book hand, he does not bother to include the connecting bar (Figure 11.19, center).

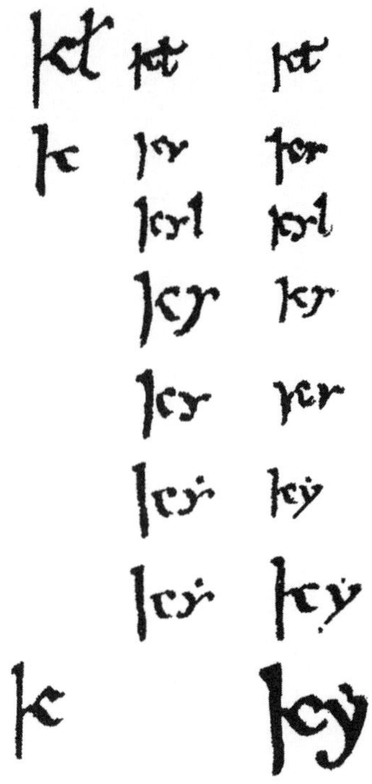

Wili seems to have idolized Ælfred; he is the only one of the chancery clerks who ever wrote *Ælfred Kyning* (Figure 11.20). Ælfred was a ruler in the old tradition; the shepherd of his flock who guarded both their physical and transcendent welfare. Yet he was neither saint nor martyr; the other surviving copies of these lines read ᛞᛚᚠᚾᛖᚩ cyninᠻ (Corpus Christi College, Cambridge, MS. 12, f. 3v; Cambridge University Library, MS. Ii.2.4, f. 6v).

Wili and his ideographs disappear from the *Parker* by 897-8. The use of the *K-c* distinction for a *mundane* ruler stops right then and there—never to return.

It may seem sad to separate the old comrades; nevertheless, Wili gives us a definite cut-off date for any manuscript containing his ideographs. His almost inseparable side-kick, Old Joe, however, lived to a ripe old age. He is with us to 925 and the very end of the original part of the *Parker Chronicle*.

Old Joe becomes quite prominent by 895. While he most certainly was a master scribe, only senior journeymen or masters took dictation, and though Old Joe was a whizz at taking dictation, he was easily flustered. When writing at speed, he used graphs from the wrong font, particularly those from liturgical and formal fonts, in his portions of the text. In Figure 11.4, the wrong *e* in *feng* is Old Joe's work.

Fig. 11.19 Left: Standard *K*'s;
Center: Old Joe's *K*'s;
Right: Wili's *K*'s;

Old Joe can be recognized through all the Ælfredian fonts and scripts; the angle of attack in his approach strokes remains the same no matter the font. He has many ideographs: we have already seen some of them. His high-*e* (Ϸ) has a very straight back. His high-*aesc* is equally distinctive. His bound forms of *aesc-s*, *aesc-r*, *er*, *ec*, *es*, and *as* are easily sorted out. In Ælfred's hierarchies, sigmoid-*s* was assigned to Latin and was used in the vernacular only at the beginning of documents, *Fits* (or *Fitts*, i.e., Chapter), or half-height to indicate new paragraph. Old Joe's sigmoid-*s*, which is always the wrong font for the text, has a decided backwards tilt.

Old Joe also quite often forgets and uses the older style *e*-merka with a curved tail (ℯ) on held sounds as opposed to the newer straight-tail *e*-merka (e–) used by Wili, and the West Saxon and the Mercian clerks. Old Joe also sporadically reverts to his native dialect when spelling common words: He has the dubious distinction of being the chancery champion at reversion. While he was more careful while

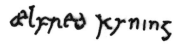

Fig. 11.20 *Hatton 20:* Wili's transcendent *K* in *ælfred Kyning*

Ælfred was still alive, his work is very easy to isolate: his habit of reverting to his own dialect when flustered contrasts quite noticeably with the other clerks. Old Joe uses *io* and *ie* where the West Saxons and Wili write *eo* and *e*; he writes *cwom* for *com* [come]. We find Old Joe's hand in words such as *sio* [plural demonstrative pronoun], *hiora* [plural genitive], *priost-* [priest], and *fiered forth* [fared forth, that is, died] contrasting with *seo, heora, preost-,* and *fered forth*.

With so many manuscripts to choose from, we have an excess of examples; however, three seem sufficient to illustrate this particular habit (Figure 11.21). The examples are in two fonts: a) and c) are in Ælfred's official document font and example b) is in Ælfred's second record font. *Heora* and *hiora* are on the same line: the change occurs as Old Joe takes over for his staggered stint. In example b), *preost* and *priost* show up on the same leaf with only one chronicle entry separating them. Even without the spelling distinction to alert us, we would know that these were written by two different clerks. The *p*, *o*, and *st* are not in the same hand. As we have already noted, Wili and Old Joe sometimes slipped up and used long-*s* instead of the low-*s* which is correct for record font 2. The word *preost* illustrates Wili's distinctive left-tilted *e*. In *prioste* we have a good example of Old Joe's straight backed-*e* as well as two of his speed-writing trademarks: the *e*-merka and the partial graphs on the *e* and on the lobe of the *p*. As in his *K*, Old Joe saved time by omitting pieces of graphs. Example c) is perhaps the most amusing: Old Joe wrote them both.

Old Joe was both a master and stubborn. We know he was a Master from more than the "Metrical Epilogue" to Hatton 20 and the very large number of fonts he knew. His graphs tell the story: his speed at taking dictation rivaled modern short-hand stenographers—only he did not use 'Pitman' or 'Gregg'. We know he was mule-headed. He was one of the clerks who repeatedly refused to run over dates, and he consistently made a distinction between the script and orthographic accuracy needed for a dictated draft and that needed for a fine copy. We can readily imagine Old Joe responding to chastisement with, "What's the problem? It's only a draft. Everything will be all right in the final copy."

Old Joe's habits undoubtedly irritated the chancery head; but it would seem that a civil service job back then was as permanent as a civil service job today. Besides, Old Joe knew so many fonts—and his speed at taking dictation made up for much.

Personality aside, Old Joe's quirks are very helpful. Although one of the junior clerks is Kentish and, perhaps influenced by proximity, sometimes imitates Old Joe's spelling, Old Joe's ideographs are so distinctive, that once we have been alerted by the spelling difference, we can tell at a glance if this is Old Joe or the young Kentish clerk.

Fig. 11.21 Old Joe and his *io*'s
a) *heora/hiora*;
b) *preost/prioste*;
c) *seo/sio*

Not counting late hands A and B, a total of fourteen clerical hands show up in the *Parker* by 900. Six of these Ælfredian hands appear in Ælfred's (and Ine's) Law code; five of these are in the *Nowell Codex*. A total of seven of Ælfred's clerical cadre are in the two manuscripts of *Pastoral Care*; among all these hands we must include both Wili and Old Joe.

As noted, scribal ideographs are shortcuts devised for personal use. If we add to shortcuts for single symbols, shortcuts to accommodate common graph clusters, scribal ideographs run into the hundreds *per scribe*. If we now add more than one font and more than one manuscript, clearly, it is not feasible to list them all. Such a list requires a good sized book in its own right.

The difficulties presented by sheer volume may be shown by examples focusing on only two cluster graphs: *e-c* and *aesc-c*. As these two graphs clusters are fairly frequent, we need a narrower focus to keep things down to a reasonable size. Table 11.2 (pages 228-229) gives examples from the *Parker Chronicle and Laws* and the *Nowell Codex* only.

This narrow focus has a two-fold purpose. First, we can see the differences between the hands of the other clerks and our two friends. Second, if there should be any doubts as to the ingrained 'can't help it' nature of scribal ideographs, these examples should make clear what is meant by "scribal ideographs." There are, however, more than 300 examples of the two graphs in just these two manuscripts; we need further reduction. Hence, in Table 11.2, while the examples were chosen at random from every leaf showing the graphs, in each case different hands are from the same leaves and the same hand is from different leaves. Table 11.2 should also make it abundantly clear why a complete list will take too much space.

There are fourteen different hands in Chronicle Font #1 (C #1); all twelve "others" are not given in all fonts either for lack of room or because, as North 1 (who disappears in 891), they do not appear at all in later manuscripts. Otherwise, the graphs on Table 11.2, both those of the other clerks and those of Willi and Old Joe, are sorted by same-hand clusters in a given font. While close examination reveals slight variations, the angle of attack never varies.

If we look carefully at the *ecg* cluster graph, for instance, in Chronicle Font #1 (C #1), even if two clerks should write their *e* with a backwards tilt, it will not be at the same angle of approach and the *c*'s are different, as are the way they write their *g*'s. We can see that Clerk 1, like Old Joe, has a straight back on his high-*e*, but Clerk 1 cuts his top stroke on his *e* short and drops down in a straight line to the hasta (the cross-stroke). Further, the hasta of this Clerk extends beyond the graph and the top stroke of his *c* is shortened, while the graph itself is rounded. Old Joe's *c* drops down from the hasta at a sharp outward angle and his top stroke always swings up and takes a sharp downwards curve. Clerks 2, 3, and 4 all have a left-ward tilt to their high-*e*, just like Wili, but the resemblance ends there.

The differences are even more striking in the five hands of Nowell Font #1 (N #1). Clerk 1 never ligatures his *e-c* graph and has a decided leftward tilt on his long-*s*. Although Clerk 2 writes his *g* like Old Joe's, his *e* in the *e-c* ligature has a left tilt and Old Joe's is straight-backed; similarly, this clerk's long-*s* (*secg-*) has a leftward tilt while Old Joe's has a rightward tilt. Clerk 3 may have a leftward tilt on his *e*, but his *c* is not the *c* written by Wili; further, this clerk's long-*s* not only tilts leftwards, but practically sits on top of *e-c* cluster.

When we examine the hands of the clerks who wrote the Laws, we see that Clerk 1 has a very distinctive *c*, whether written *aesc-c* or *e-c*, which is quite different from the others. All write their *aesc* differently, and so on throughout the Table—and the manuscripts.

The very last line on the Table was included as an example of what we can only call poetic justice. All are in close proximity on f. 25a of the *Parker Chronicle*. It was now Old Joe's turn to train two new West Saxon clerks.

The *ecg* example is only one cluster graph; every scribe comes up with his own shortcuts for each and every common cluster graph he writes. Scribal cluster graphs are as much a scribal signature as if he had signed his name to a document.

Two *ocg* graphs have been included on the Table. This is to demonstrate how automatic is a scribe's response to the formation of a cluster graph. There is also an apparent lack of *aesc-c* graphs in C #1. There is one under Wili. That is not a speck of dirt on *rec*; that is an *e*-cedille or tailed-*e* which stands for *a-e* ligature and appears most often in ligature with *thorn*. The *a-e* ligature, however, is not *Englisc*; in all the rest of Ælfred's fonts, the *e*-cedille was supposed to be used only in Latin. Nevertheless, Wili throws in an *e*-cedille in C #2 (*ecan*) and N #1 (*wrecend*) and Old Joe sometimes reverts and writes an *e*-cedille, too.

Note that Old Joe's *e*, in his *aesc* or in the middle of a low cluster-graph always has a very straight back. His *a*, in all fonts, starts at the same location relative to the cluster. Likewise, Wili's *e* always has left-ward tilt; his *a* always has the same angle of approach. Wili disappears after 898, and so do his ideographs from the Table.

The Table is chronologically ordered by font family, not by manuscript. We normally cannot arrange manuscripts this closely chronologically. These Ælfredian manuscripts, though, can be dated with a high degree of certainty. We know when Ælfred reigned over a united kingdom: 886-899. We can place Ælfred's first project, the *Parker Chronicle*, to 890-1.

As we can see from Table 11.2, Ælfred set up his hierarchy of fonts in groups of related designs. Record font 1 of the *Parker* is of the same hybrid Insular semi-pointed minuscule family as dictation font 1 of Hatton 20 (Figures 11.19 and 11.20). The same matching of font family designs can be seen in record font 2 of the *Parker*. Although some of his clerical cadre knew square fonts, we also know that some square forms were incorporated into Ælfred's hierarchy of scripts and fonts only after 894-5. The square font of Ælfred's *Laws* is a mutation of a square liturgical font which is intended for authoritative secular use; hence, the *Laws* were written down during or after 894-5. CCCC 12 is written in a heavy, formal book hand version of this same font family design. In standard use, both before and after Ælfred, as the different forms represented different phones, long-*s* appears in combination with, for example, *t* (ſt) and low-*s* is found in combinations such as *aesc-s* (ᵭſ) and *a-s* (aſ). Ælfred's classicization, that is, his standardization and levelling solution for the variant forms, helps to place the first font of the *Nowell Codex*.

Under Ælfred, different variant forms were assigned to different fonts. One example of how this worked should suffice. Except as "begin" markers, the sigmoid-*s* was supposed to be used only in Latin liturgical scripts and fonts. The design of Ælfred's second chancery record font called for the use of only low-*s* in all positions. The design of the Insular dictation font used as the first font of the *Nowell* calls for only long-*s* in all positions. *Stæfwritung*, however, uses the ternary base with movement on the y-axis to record stress. This Ælfredian restriction of variant forms is the reason why *s* graphs, in record font 2 of the *Parker* and in its parallel dictation font of the *Nowell*, keep moving up and down from the headline. In the *Nowell*, the long-*s* sits normally, as in ſt, but descends well below the baseline, as in eſ and aſ. Ælfreds solutions to the variant forms places the first font of the *Nowell* to after 894-5.

Table 11.2 The graph clusters *aesc-c* and *e-c* comparing Standard West Saxon ideographs with the ideographs of Wili and Old Joe.

	Others	Wili	Old Joe
C #1			
C #2			
N #1			

Laws

N #2

C #3

C #4

Old Joe
and
trainees

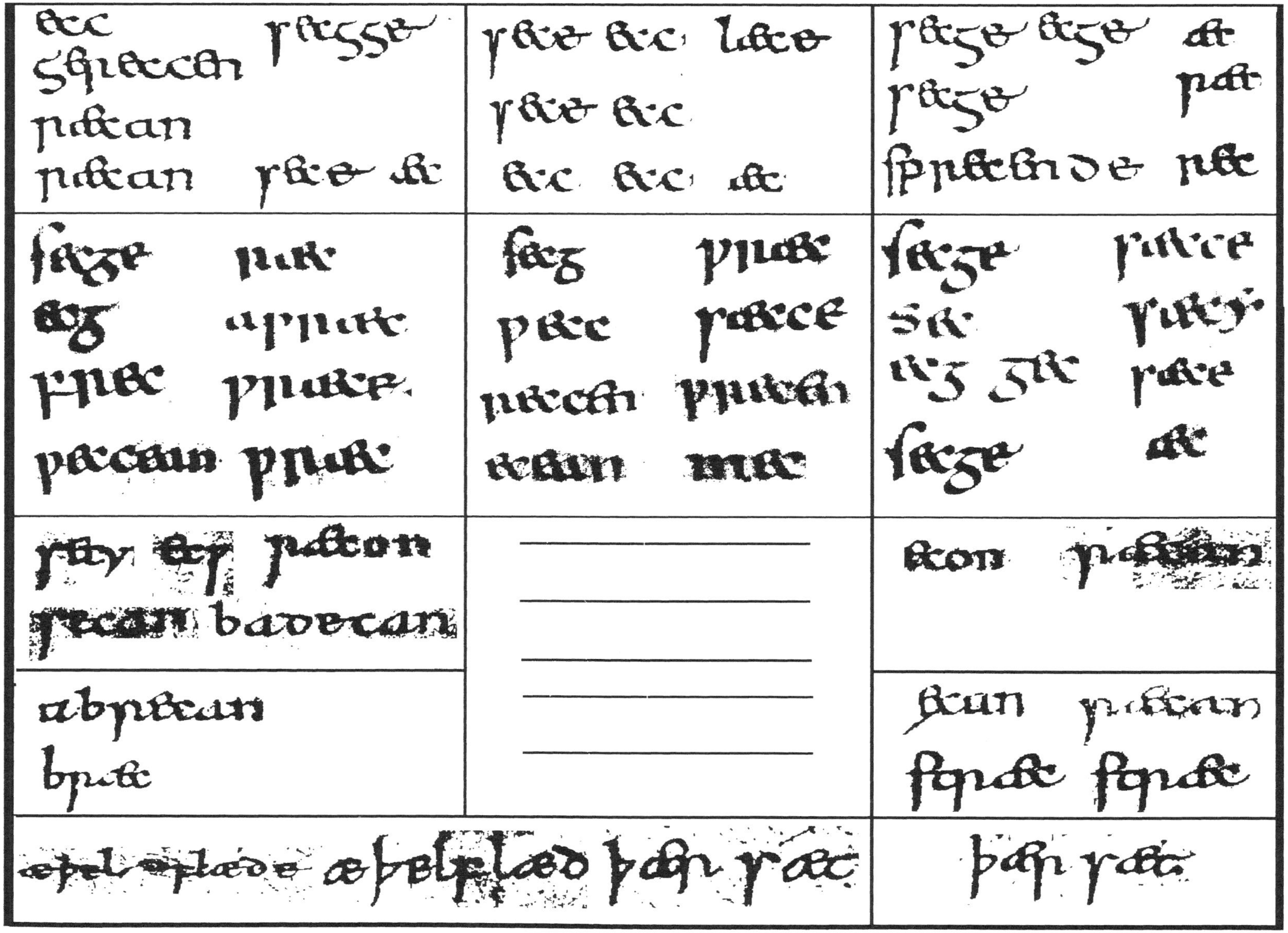

Finally, after years of a solid presence in many manuscripts, Wili's ideographs disappear in 897-8. Because Wili's ideographs appear in the *Nowell Codex*, we can place this manuscript to after 895, but no later than 897-8.

Abnormal changes of format, font, sizes, and even diction are, unfortunately for Ælfred's program, quite normal in his productions. In examining Table 11.2, the reader may have noted that the *Parker* is not the only Ælfredian manuscript subject to multiple personalities. Schizophrenia runs rampant through the Ælfredian manuscripts in one way or another; these split personalities are essentially the identifying mark of an Ælfredian provenance. The schizoid personalities are the result of a lack of time to make clean copies of every item in Ælfred's education and preservation program.

There are, after all, *five* different fonts used in the Ælfredian part of *Parker Chronicle* and *Laws*—not to mention all the liturgical font graphs thrown in by Old Joe—as well as five, no, six different formats—if we count the *Laws*. As dear to his heart as the Psalm project was, Ælfred only had time to revise the first fifty Metrical Psalms. The Psalter was divided into thirds, so an existing copy was taken apart, the original format was followed, and Ælfred's revised fifty Psalms were put in their place. Although a clean copy in terms of book production, the *Paris Psalter* ended up with two distinct auctorial styles. The *Paris Psalter* uses a correct hierarchy of fonts and script-differentiation by language: "English Caroline" for Latin and as "Italics," Rustic Capitals for *tituli*, and insular for Old English. Script-differentiation by language is so well-known in Anglo-Saxon manuscripts as to be a "doesn't everybody," yet the *Nowell Codex* shows a totally incorrect and sudden change of font in *mid-sentence*.

As both Wili and Old Joe had a lot to do with this *Nowell Codex*, we can pretty much expect some strange happenings. This seems a good place to take a look at the *Nowell*. Besides, this manuscript is probably better titled *Wili's Last Stand*.

Stæfwritung preserves speech rhythms. All of the Ælfredian part of the *Parker*, Hatton 20, and the *Nowell* are dictated originals; nevertheless, there are some major differences among them. With the exception of the "Genealogical Preface," Quire A of the *Parker*, and probably most of quire B were dictated by memory men. The memory men were accustomed to speaking and to gauging audience reaction. Likewise, the better speakers, such as Bede, used emphasis sparingly. As anybody who has ever read or told stories to an audience knows, one does not emphasize every word or the audience will quickly exhibit signs of boredom; they no longer can tell from the speaker's voice what is important and what is of secondary relevance. This even pace with appropriate emphasis is recorded in the majority of the text. Apparently Ælfred himself dictated his *Laws*. Although well paced, the text is clearly dictated by a person accustomed to public speaking rather than to ordinary dictation; the recorded speech patterns show frequent emphasis to make a point. *Hatton 20* also shows a very similar Ælfredian pattern of emphatic stress when making a point. (On the other hand, CCCC MS. 12 is normalized). In these texts, the speakers were all pacing their dictation; this is not true of the *Nowell*.

Normally when taking dictation, scribes could ask a speaker to repeat a word or a sentence. They could take pauses when needed. While ordinary dictated texts show rapid writing, they also show paced writing. What we see in the *Nowell* is something entirely different—speed at all costs and no breaks or pauses during *Fits*.

There is an important difference between recording a dictated text and recording a performance text. When dictating, the person speaking is either the author or is reading from an existing copy. (In antiquity the most common method of making multiple copies was for a Master to read the text to a group of scribes.) Interruptions are not destructive, and may be informative as well. A live performance, however, *cannot* be interrupted in the middle. One must wait for the end of a scene or the end of section.

If a scribe has robotic responses, so does a performer, whether we call him a gleeman or a jongleur or an actor. The material he is performing is not his own; the text is memorized. If interrupted, mnemonic aids become tangled, and a performer tends to lose his place. If the performer loses his place, he either has to go back to some point in the text where he can once again pick up the thread, or he can improvise.

The *Nowell* is probably unique among surviving ancient documents. The manuscript displays the staggering technique and has the very busy texture, with the extreme durational and stress notation, of dictation. Even without the staggering technique, though, the texture tells us the truth. Unlike all other known dictated manuscripts, however, the *Nowell* is a record of a live performance, or rather *three* live performances, and not simply dictation.

Although not intended to entertain posterity (but, then, so many of Ælfred's productions are unintentionally entertaining), the manuscript has quite a story to tell us. It is a funny story with mishaps and misadventures, and clerks bobbing around trying to stay out of each other's way. All this is recorded in the writing system. As they say in the theater, "let's get the show on the road."

Referring to a show is appropriate in any case. The *Nowell* contains five articles. The choices seem odd—a fairly fancif.! "Homily on Saint Christopher," a clearly fictitious account in "Marvels of the East," a purported "Letter of Alexander to Aristotle," "HWÆT WE GARDE," and part of a poem on the biblical heroine Judith—yet they are linked, not by subject matter, but by the fact that they are all fiction. That the contents are fictitious material is very clear from the size of the manuscript.

We have already seen that everything in the manuscripts holds meaning: size, format, and script tell us its status. Although there are many arguments about the exact size of the *Nowell* (it was one of the manuscripts damaged in a disastrous fire in 1731), there is no disagreement about its general dimensions. This is a small volume. The estimates of the original leaf size range from 23 x 15 cm to 19.5 x 11.5-13 cm to 19 x 12 cm. Writing space estimates range from 17.5 x 10.5 cm to 18 x 11.5 cm. [16] While the estimates of the general overall dimensions of the leaves vary, all describe a small book of approximately half of a quarto sheet folded short-side to short-side. In other words, to visualize the dimensions of the manuscript, take a sheet of ordinary 8-1/2" (21.5 cm.) x 11" (28 cm.) letterhead paper and fold it in half top to bottom. The result will be a sheet of paper consisting of four writing surfaces (*bifolia*), each 14 cm. in width x 21.5 cm. in height—the size of a *tabula*, the ancient equivalent of a paperback thriller.

The size of the *Nowell Codex* tells us that the contents were classed as "recreational" reading, not "serious" reading, such as Biblical commentaries, history, medicine, or laws. "Recreational" does not mean worthless; it does mean fanciful, or fabulous, or fictitious, or all of the above. Nor does "fiction" mean non-instructive. While articles equivalent to our modern science fiction with their bug-eyed monster stories, such as "Marvels of the East" (with its men with their heads in their stomachs), are included, so is the more serious "Judith" (Article 5) with its Old English poetic paraphrase of the apocryphal Biblical story. Article 4 may be fictitious, but it gives clear instructions on the correct behavior of a good king—including the warning that life is transitory—in terms, setting, and examples understandable in Anglo-Saxon society. [17] All five articles in the *Nowell* fall into the recreational fiction class and its size states this fact right out in front.

The size of this volume of collected fiction also answers another common question: Did the Anglo-Saxons believe in dragons and beasties and things that go bump in the night? The question itself is an example of alterity; [18] the answer is self-evident. Then, as now, there were people who believed six impossible things before breakfast and there were people who knew the difference between fact and fiction. Every society has both the gullible and the superstitious as well as the educated and the learned. (Although, admittedly, one may be learned yet still be gullible.) There is no reason to believe that those campfire songs and stories described in the story of Caedmon were regarded as other than entertainment. The main difference between then and now, with modern textbooks being printed in "pocketbook" sizes, is that the size of a document unequivocally stated what type of reading it was. The fact that this manuscript is recreational reading has other implications when we turn to the *abnormal* change in fonts.

The problem is not merely that Old Joe kept slipping into his own dialect or that he sometimes uses the wrong graphs for the body text, nor is it that Wili and Old Joe keep ringing in their *K-c* exchanges. What is out of the ordinary is the sudden change of fonts in the *middle* of writing a sentence. Although some leaves are now missing, the entire manuscript, from f. 94r through f. 209v, is written in Old English and only in Old English. Ælfred's hierarchies included script differentiation by domain and by language; yet here we have a change of font that is *not* used to identify by domain or by language.

As can be seen on Table 11.2, the *Nowell* is written in two different insular fonts. Font One is a clear, small, and legible insular design. While there are many triangular or squared forms, the overall appearance is rounded. The pen used is relatively fine and in proportion to the scale of the design. Informal in design and meant for rapid writing, it needs very few pen lifts. The *a* in this design is a hybrid standing midway between the pointed-*a* and the round-a. In its standard form, the *e* has a closed bow with no tendency towards a tongue.

Font Two is a liturgical insular minuscule book hand, a large and comparatively heavy style. The design requires the many pen-lifts that are standard in a liturgical book hand. The extra pen-lifts slow the scribes down; a technique used in formal book hands to protect the written word. Similarly, the design calls for the cuneiform wedge in a beginning stroke, another technique used to slow down the scribes. As the design uses the font-identifying square-*a*, the overall appearance is of a square design. The pen is wider and cut at a deeper angle. In this font, the bow of the *e* graph curves in slightly creating a small space between the bow and the hasta, thus incorporating a short tongue as part of the graph.

Font One is a secular, everyday dictation font meant for the vernacular; Font Two is a formal liturgical book hand meant for Latin. The font change is simply all wrong; nevertheless, there is a logical and obvious reason for this change, and it is very typical of works produced in Ælfred's chancery.

We may recall that until the late-tenth or early-eleventh centuries, large documents were produced by scribal teams. With large documents, whether copied from an exemplar or a dictated original, the standard practice was to estimate how many leaves would be needed for a given size when written with a pre-determined pen and in the appropriate script. Then all the necessary equipment was prepared in advance. The estimated number of leaves were prepared and cut to size; guidelines were marked; the estimated number of pens for the entire job were prepared and cut to the correct angle and width for the desired font. Ink had to be made up in a quantity sufficient to complete the job.

The estimation process can only be done by a very experienced scribe. Today estimation is done by specialists; back then, estimation was probably handled by the writing room master. Even today, publishers do not want to know how many pages; they want to know the word count, that is, how large is the text in number of words. A publisher normally determines the number of pages in the book-to-be from the word count in relation to the type size of the body text and the size of the pages. He then estimates the number of pages that will be needed making an allowance for front matter and taking into account the design of the book as well as possible illustrations. (The book designer, for example, determines that chapter headings should be at X number of lines [or points] down and in Y point type.) Things were done on the same basis in the age of the hand-produced book. Then, as now, the estimator had to know the word-count. With this count, he would have a very clear idea of how many words would fit on a leaf size X written with script Y using pen Z. He would also know the leaf on which a given section should occur. Like publishers today, an estimator would allow room for the inclusion of illustrations of relevant material and for mishaps.

Estimation is relatively straightforward with a copying job. A dictation job, though, depends upon the person dictating and requires that the estimator be familiar with his or her dictation style.

The estimator clearly was familiar with the style of the performer who recited Articles 1, 2 and most of Article 4 of the *Nowell*. Sketches were pre-drawn at the appropriate places to illustrate some of the "marvels." Things went according to plan at first. Articles 1 and 2 fell right into estimated place. The pre-drawn sketches are on the right leaves. (We know that the sketches were pre-drawn because the writing sometimes runs *over* the sketch outline boxes.) While stress and duration notation record the type of emphasis that we can expect from a professional story-teller, including a deliberately dead-pan, tongue-in-cheek way of describing the "Marvels," estimation and actuality ran together. With Article 3, things began to go wrong. The "Letter from Alexander to Aristotle" was performed by another performer with a very different and exaggerated style; he was, in modern terms, a ham actor. The difference in style is recorded with great clarity in the *stæfwriting* record. We can not know for certain, but it seems likely that the exaggerated style of performer 2, chock full of drawn out held sounds, used up more space per line, extending the text beyond the original estimate.

A competent estimator, though, allows for mishaps. In this case, the reverse side of f. 131 could pick up any slack. Standard practice was to leave the last leaf in a quire blank to protect the written record. (In modern *quality* book production, the last leaf is still left blank to protect the text.) If the outer leaf was needed, it could be used at the next dictation/copying session. Article 3 used up this normally blank leaf.

In the meantime, the **ductus**, that is, the direction of written strokes, tells its own tale. In Articles 1 and 2, although the ductus is rapid, it is what is to be expected from paced dictation: with Article 3, the clerks were writing at top speed, their pens fairly galloping across the leaves. Words are spread out across wide spaces; bound forms, such as, *aesc*-low-*s*, are separated into illogical, individual, widely spaced graphs (e.g. ρ ᴁ ſ instead of ρᴁſ or ρᴁſ). Old Joe got flustered, and we start finding his signature *io*'s and *cwom*'s in the text (not to mention Wili's *K*'s). Besides, after taking down 37 pages, the clerks were getting tired arms and would need a well-deserved break. [19]

We do not know how long this break was—it could have been half an hour or it could have been weeks. One thing is certain, Article 4 was not immediately bound in with the first three; the first leaf of the article shows too much wear to have been protected by being in the middle of a bound book.

While as the record of live performances the *Nowell Codex* is a unique specimen in its own right, it is best known for Article 4. Catalogued back then by the *incipit*, *HWÆT WE GARDE*, Article 4 is better known to every person who has ever passed through a survey course on English literature as *Beowulf*. The abnormal change of font occurs with the word *moste* on line 4 of f. 175v (172 old style), forty pages into the text.

The usual staggering technique was used. Every article in the *Nowell Codex* was dictated to a team of clerks. As we saw with the *Parker*, these need not be the same on any given leaf. There are a total of six hands in the *Nowell*: the first three articles and article four through the change of font were dictated to five clerks. With the change of font, one of the clerks dropped out leaving four hands in Font 2. Although there was a change of font on f. 175v, there was no further change of clerks; the clerks of Font One are the same clerks of Font Two. A sixth person, using a mutation of Font Two, emended the text of Article 4 at a much later date; hence, there are a total of six hands in the *Nowell*. Four of the five synchronous scribes appear throughout the manuscript, from Article 1 through the end of the fragmentary Article 5: one is hand 3 of Article 4, first font *and* hand 1 second font. This clerk also went back through and corrected Article 4, but none of the other articles; he apparently knew the poem quite well. We have already met this clerk before: he is our friend, Old Joe.

Article 4, *Beowulf*, is a record of two performances given by Gleemen with very different styles. Gleeman 1 was clearly a gifted performer who matched his delivery to the context; the other Gleeman was mediocre indeed. While we are concerned with the manuscript and not with the story, we will not understand what we are seeing without some idea of the context in which the following examples occur—and not everybody remembers or is familiar with the poem.

The poem opens with a prologue, so necessary in oral performances to tell people what they will be hearing about. Our prologue to the context is the necessary list of the characters referred to; some of the more important events are related as we watch the performance of Gleeman 1. There are two groups of relevant *dramatis personæ*.

The first group consists of the Danes and the Geats: Beowulf, warrior and nephew of Hygelac, King of the Geats; Hroðgar, King of the Danes and his wife, Queen Wealþeow; Hunferð, related to Hroðgar, a warrior with both words and steel; and Æschere, Hroðgar's *run wita* [wise man, comprehender of writing, e.g. literate counselor], *ræd bora* [memory man], and *eaxle ge stealla* [in modern idiom, shoulder to lean on].

The second group contains three "monsters." The first one is Grendel. As any writer of horror stories knows, true terror is raised when the familiar turns strange. Grendel is a descendant of Cain; Cain is the first born son of man. In other words, Grendel is a *human* monster and a cannibal. There is quite a bit of animal imagery in this part of the poem. Just as an animal caught in a trap will bite off its leg, Grendel, when caught in a trap, tears away, leaving behind his entire "front leg." The other two "monsters" are Grendel's mother, a bereaved mother and an avenger; and the dragon.

We should remember that both sets of monsters were minding their own business until disturbed. Hroðgar builds his great hall (Heorot) near Grendel's mere, and Grendel, annoyed by the noisy drunken song-making, no longer has to hunt for food in the woods; he has a ready supply of protein at hand. Grendel's mother (referred to affectionately as "mama" by many literary critics) is a maternal fury. The dragon is peacefully sleeping when a thief steals from the treasure hoard he is guarding, and, not too surprisingly, the dragon goes on a rampage.

After the prologue, which tells the listeners that they will be hearing about the progress and maturing of an underestimated man, the story begins in *media res*, when Beowulf, hearing of Hroðgar's woes due to Grendel, decides to go to the rescue in the best heroic tradition. Beowulf sails off with his picked crew and meets his first major challenge: Hroðgar's coast guard. His second major challenge is a *flyting* contest (verbal duel) with Hunferth; which he also successfully negotiates.

As has been pointed out, *stæfwritung* preserves more than words. The scribes recorded what they heard, including stress, lengthened sounds, and pauses between letter clusters. Unlike a determination of scribal hands, the differences between Gleeman 1 and Gleeman 2 are not subtle at all. The delivery of Gleeman 1 displays an enormous range of *tempi* and he always matches delivery to the context. When during the *flyting* contest between Beowulf and Hunferð, Hunferð maintains that Beowulf dares not stay in Heorot to face Grendel, that *dearst* [dare] is a contemptuously drawled slur on Beowulf's courage (line 4 of the MS). The long trailer on the *r* in *dearst* is very different from both the standard form of *r* or the short trailing form. Compare *dearst* [durst] with *fyrst* (Figure 11.22a). Note the long trailer on the *r* in *dearst* and the total lack of a trailer on the *r* in *fyrst*. *L* is either the normal short foot (or serif), or short trailing form (compare *eal* (line 1 of MS) and *læste* (line 2 of MS) with *fela* (line 7 of MS). The clearest example of the trailing form of *a* is visible in *fela* (Figure 11.22b).

a

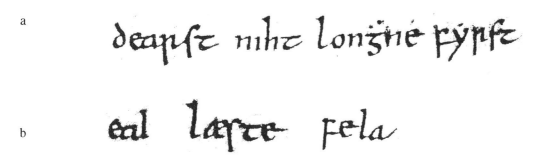

b

Fig. 11.22 f. 145: a) *Hunferð dares Beowulf*; b) variant spacing and trailers

In this font design, the normal spacing between letter clusters is the four minims of the letter *o* and varies only with emphasis. Note the differences in spacing between letter clusters in Beowulf's sarcastic response (f. 145, line 6).

hpæt þu poſın ſe-la pıne- mın hun ſeſɹ8

[What, you great muchness, my dear Hunferð]

Tempo is indicated by clumping and spacing. Notice how Gleeman 1 changes his delivery: the last line of Fit 10 on f. 149r (Figure 11.23) is quite different from the examples on f. 145.

Fig. 11.23 The end of *Fit* 10

From the spacing, the line was recited slowly, with each letter cluster bearing almost equal stress, and reflects the seriousness of Beowulf's undertaking. We can also compare the end of this *Fit* with the clumping and spacing at the beginning of the next *Fit*.

At the beginning of *Fit* eleven, Grendel comes stalking up for his nightly dinner. The tempo changes once again. This time the letter clusters and spacing indicate something else. Gleeman 1 lets us *hear* Grendel's heavy footsteps come thump, thump, thumpity-thumpity, thump thump up from the moor (Figure 11.24).

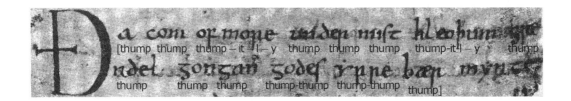

Fig. 11.24 Grendel comes thumping up from the Moor

During a twelve-year period, Grendel had not faced any real challenge to his use of Heorot as his private cattle pen. Grendel has the strength of thirty men; but so does Beowulf. Caught in a grip equal to his own, Grendel turns completely animal and tears loose from the trap of Beowulf's grip—leaving behind his *grippe* [grip] including *earme* and *eaxle* (arm and [axle], that is, shoulder).

This is followed by a celebration at Heorot, where everyone gets thoroughly drunk. Enter the next monster: Grendel's mother, who is bent on avenging the death of her son and the loss of her shoulder to lean on. Her vengeance is singularly appropriate: Grendel's mother takes only one man, but that man is Æschere, Hroðgar's memory man. It is no accident that the only thing left of Æschere is his now useless head. Nor is the eye-for-an-eye aspect an accident: Grendel lost his literal shoulder; Hroðgar, loses his figurative shoulder.

Throughout the entire first part of the tale, King Hroðgar clings to his dignity. He remains stately and gracious in his speech even when relating to Beowulf the deep distress and many griefs caused by Grendel's predations (Figure 11.25a). True, Hroðgar had every cause to be upset by the death of Æschere, and while he had rejoiced too soon in assuming that with the death of Grendel he and his people had been saved, this does not account for one fact. When back home, Beowulf reports to Hygelac that Hroðgar was *hreowa tornost* [most grievously distressed/torn] by Æschere's death. Why *most*? How did Beowulf know? Beowulf knew because Hroðgar lost all semblance of dignity. How do *we* know? Because the delivery of Gleeman 1 told clerk 1b, who recorded it for posterity. With

Hroðgar's announcement to his people *dead is æsc here-* [dead is Æschere] for the first time he shows strong emotion. For the first time, Hroðgar loses all control and wails in agony (Figure 11.25b).

a

b

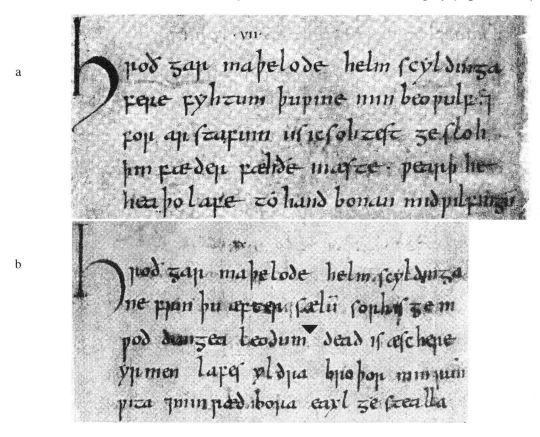

Fig. 11.25: a) Hroðgar welcomes Beowulf; b) Hroðgar wails for Æschere. Note the difference in spacing between word clusters beginning with "dead is Æschere" (marked by the arrow head)

Although in both examples the statement that *Hroðgar mapelode* [Hroðgar made a speech/orated] is recited in the same manner, the speeches themselves differ considerably. In Figure 11.25a, the letter clusters are evenly spaced, indicating a stately, dignified, controlled speech. In Figure 11.25b, the sudden appearance of many trailing letter forms and of widely varying spacing between letter clusters are indicative of a loss of control (note the extra long pause before *dead*).

On the other hand, Beowulf's report to Hygelac on this scene is quite matter of fact, a simple, straight-forward report by a lieutenant to his commander:

þ pæs hroðgare / hreopa tornost

That was Hroðgar most grievously distressed (/ = next line)

Strong emotion, a loss of control, is evinced only three times during the performance of Gleeman 1: (Wealhþeow, Hroðgar, the parting scene where Beowulf also becomes emotional.) Variation amongst the spacing between clusters, judicious use of lengthened sounds, and appropriate stress are the mark of Gleeman 1. Like any top actor today, he brings the text to life. On the other hand, Gleeman 2 is a dead bore. While he does not recite in a monotone, *intrinsic* stress is there, he never varies his delivery. We need many examples to illustrate the performance range of Gleeman 1; only one example is necessary for Gleeman 2. Gleeman 2 is a one-pace horse. It matters not whether he is telling about the theft from the treasure hoard or the fiery battle with the dragon; it makes no difference if he speaks of the desertion of Beowulf by all but one of his men or of the desolation following the death of Beowulf. In the style of Gleeman 2, all words are of equal import. The clerks tell us that this is so: with the change of performer, *extrinsic* emphasis suddenly disappears (Figure 11.26).

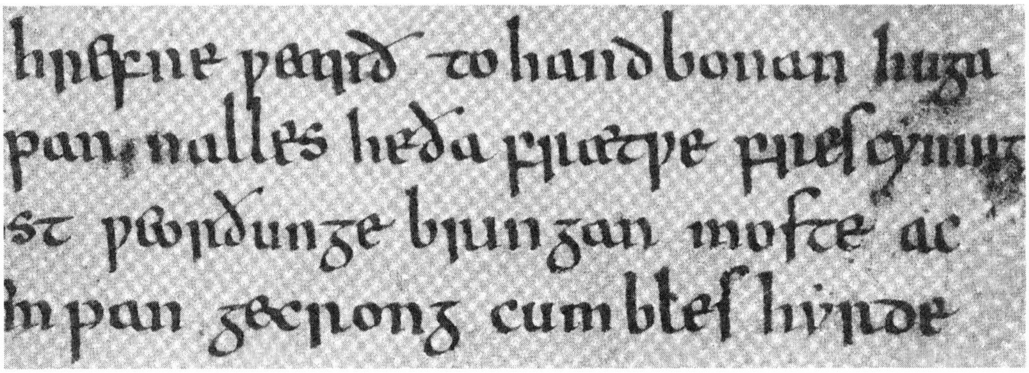

Fig. 11.26 A typical line delivered by Gleeman 2. Note the complete lack of *extrinsic* variation in stress or duration.

Gleeman 2 took over at the beginning of *Fit* 32 on f. 182 (179 old style). He must have been unbearable, the equivalent of hearing the difference between a professional performance of a Shakespeare play and a secondary school performance of the same play. While disruptive to chancery routine, the performance of Gleeman 1 need not have disturbed other clerks at work on various tasks, except perhaps for an occasional comment of appreciation. The droning performance of Gleeman 2 most certainly would have disturbed everybody. Alterity not withstanding, one can only liken it to the effect of hearing a background of Mozart suddenly change to heavy metal—the difference between variety and monotony, between interest and boredom.

The change of Gleeman explains the urgency patently evinced both by the extremely rapid ductus and the indisputably recorded account of divergence from normal practice. With the usual staggering technique, taking prepared pens from the pile, clerks took turns, phrase by phrase and sentence by sentence, overlapping to avoid making differences obvious. The skilled performance of Gleeman 1 is recorded at a swift, yet steady rate and with normal changes for staggered writing. With the advent of

Gleeman 2, as in Article 3 when compared to Articles 1 and 2, the writing flies across the pages and the staggering technique changes too: Old Joe, the chancery champion at dictation, takes on longer stints.

We can easily compare the two styles of delivery as the change of font occurs during the performance of Gleeman 1. Then why, we ask, the change of font? Well, that is really very easy to answer. With everything prepared, all leaves premarked, ink prepared, and all pens precut, the estimator goofed, and goofed badly. Although both experienced and competent, he underestimated the required number of pre-cut pens required for the job.

Wili wrote lines 2 and 3. Old Joe took over on line 4 of f. 175v. He grabbed the next pen from the pile and started to write, only *they had run out of the correct pens*. Old Joe wrote *moste* and automatically wrote the correct font for the feel of the pen. He just kept on going, wrong pen or no wrong pen (Figure 11.27). While Old Joe may have been quick-witted enough to handle the emergency—and it was an emergency: the clerks were writing in the vernacular, the new pens were for Latin, he was flustered nevertheless. We are treated to a rash of Old Joe's *io*'s and Greek-*y*'s instead of *eo* and straight-*y*.

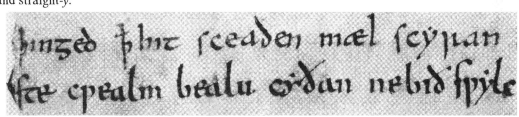

Fig. 11.27 Old Joe keeps right on going. (Note the Greek-*y* in *cyð an* and the straight-*y* in *swylc*.)

We can easily understand the problem. The clerks were writing English, the font *for the pen* was for writing Latin and used sigmoid-*s* instead of long-*s*, "horned-*y*" instead of straight-*y*, closed-*g* instead of open-*g*, and so on down the line. Needless to say, ingrained habits created a clash between the font being written with the language being heard: the pen says Latin, the words are Old English. Henceforth, confusion reigns.

The estimator had based his calculations for the entire job on 20 lines per leaf. This figure is not guesswork; that ninth-century scribe's handbook tells us how to estimate. The mathematical formula for laying out a manuscript page states:

> Suppose the page to be five units high and four units wide, it says. The height of the written space should be four such units. The inner [binding] and lower margins should be three times as wide as the outer margin and as the gutter between the columns (if it is a two column book) and a third wider than the width of the upper margin. The lines should be spaced . . . according to the size of the writing. [20]

While these proportions are easily determined geometrically using a straight edge and a piece of string, we think algebraically. These directions describe a series of simultaneous equations. Solving the equations given by the ninth century writer, where H = Height of the page, TH = Height of the writing area (Text Height), UM = upper margin, LM = Lower Margin, IM = Inner (binding)

Margin, OM = Outer Margin, TW = Width of the writing (Text Width) area, and W = width of a page, we get the dimensions given in Table 11.3.

Table 11.3 Scribe's Handbook Directions Converted to Algebraic Equations

TH	=	.80H
UM	=	.087H
LM	=	.113H
IM	=	.113H
OM	=	.0375H
TW	=	W-(IM + OM)

We can see that all margins and the height of the writing area are determined in proportion to the height of the leaf. These relative proportions with respect to the size of the top, bottom, binding, inner, and outer margins are used in the majority of the surviving manuscripts and scrolls. Writing systems are conservative: these are the same relative proportions used in, for instance, the Dead Sea Scrolls. [21]

The equations can be used in reverse. All we need is *one* reasonably accurate measurement from among preserved bottom, top, side, or inside margins to reconstruct the approximate original height of a damaged leaf or scroll. The height alone is insufficient to determine the width of the folio or writing area; width is variable. If, however, we have *one* complete line of text (that is, the inner and outer margins need not be intact—merely sufficient to show that a line is complete), then we may determine the width of the folio. We may also determine the number of lines used by the estimator as the basis for his calculations. Ælfred's estimator calculated the number of leaves, and pens, required for the *Nowell* at 20 lines per leaf.

A competent estimator (and he was, in spite of his underestimation of the required number of pens) allows for slack—or surprises. The lower margin, like the last leaf in a quire, may be used to compensate. We have reason to suspect that Gleeman 1 tended to improvise when he lost a mnemonic chain and would throw in some lines until he found the chain back. In all of quire 10 (ff. 166r-173v), during the performance of Gleeman 1, the lower margin has been truncated and we have 22 lines per leaf. A live performance can only be interrupted at a change of *Fit*; hence, these leaves coincide with beginnings of new *Fits* somewhere either on the leaf itself or on the previous leaf. *Fit* 22 starts on f. 165v and continues on f. 166r. *Fit* 26 ends and Fit 27 begins on f. 174r and is marked by a return to 20 lines per leaf. From this we can see that Gleeman 1 was running longer than estimated and that the lower margin was used to compensate for the extra length. With *Fit* 27, estimate and reality rejoined.

The chief clerk must have sighed with relief because everything was back on estimated track. His relief was premature; the change of pen, and as a result font, was a disaster in terms of estimation.

At first the clerks tried to write the correct graphs for the *language* and to stay within 20 lines per leaf, but it was a losing battle. Font 2 is substantially bigger than Font 1—and the leaves had been pre-marked for the smaller font. Now, the specter of running out of prepared leaves raised its head.

Space saving techniques went into effect immediately. On f. 176r, the numbers marking *Fit* 28 are written on the same line as the end of *Fit* 27, no space is allotted between *Fits*, and the text runs into both margins. It was not enough; further space saving techniques were called into use. With Fit 32 on f. 182r, we find 21 lines to a leaf instead of 20 lines.

The clerks put up a fight; they tried to write the correct graphs for English even though they were writing with a pen meant for Latin. The blame for what happened next can be placed squarely on Ælfred's shoulders. Ælfred's idea of assigning variant forms to different fonts was neither sensible nor realistic.

For centuries, the phone represented by long-*s* had been used with consonant clusters such as *st* and *sc*. Indeed, *st* written with a long-*s* endured until the first quarter of the *twentieth century*. Low-*s* with its *ts* or *tz* phone had been used following vowels such as *aesc* and *e*. Ælfred's peculiar solution to the variant forms was a blip in the history of symbol-to-graph systems in England and the idea died along with him. In the meantime, though, it caused his clerks a great deal of trouble and nowhere more trouble than when his clerks were faced with the clashing messages being sent while trying to take down the performances of *Beowulf*.

The wrong graphs for the *language* begin immediately with the change of pen. In spite of numerous attempts to write only long-*s*, which is correct for Font 1 and Ælfred's vernacular dictation font, low-*s* and sigmoid-*s* appear seemingly (but not really) at random. The problems were compounded when the clerks had to keep an eye on space requirements, too.

Suddenly, rather than being on automatic pilot, so to speak, and able to concentrate on the job at hand, the clerks had to pay attention to the graphs, to the dimensions of the leaf, and to the orthography. By f. 178, the clerks threw in the towel. Their job was to take down the performance and, from then on, that is precisely what they did—standard orthography and matching the graphs to the language went by the way.

Gleeman 2 only aggravated things. The clerks were writing so rapidly, jumping in and out to take their turns, that, while Old Joe had previously slipped up only occasionally, the wrong graphs for the *language* keep showing up regularly from then on (Figure 11.28). Wili also kept throwing in the wrong graphs for the *language*, but not for the *font*. Old Joe had here and there reverted to his native dialect prior to the change of pen and font; now, however, he abandoned any effort to write the West Saxon dialect. From here on, his *io*'s, *cwom*'s and other dialectic spellings populate the manuscript. Old Joe is the reason that we so frequently find, for instance, "Biowulf" instead of "Beowulf" in this part of the poem.

Although we find signs everywhere of the disarray caused by the insufficient supply of the correct pens, including totally out-of-place alpha-*a*'s and Old Joe's trademark sigmoid-*s*, the estimator had judged correctly which space-saving techniques to use. At the very end, for one moment, though, he probably quailed. While Font 1 could be squeezed into 22 lines, Font 2 was too large to write 22 lines to the leaf, thus the 21-line solution. The very last word of the poem would not fit on the 21st line. *Geornost* [the superlative of *georn*, that is, most diligent, willingest, eagerest], the last word, as in the age old practice at Akkad, sits indented on the right-hand side all by itself on line 22 of f. 201v.

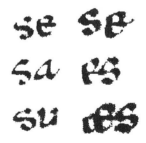

Fig. 11.28 Old Joe's sigmoid-s

Working drafts rarely survive; but no clean copy was ever made of the *Nowell*. As with so many Ælfredian manuscripts, fortune favored posterity: the manuscript is unique. This manuscript not only contains the original text of *Beowulf*, it is our only known record of a live performance, or really, three performances. The manuscript gives us inside information on the workings of Ælfred's chancery as well as facts about gleemen in action.

The change of Gleeman at *Fit* 32 is preceded by another peculiar thing about this manuscript (as if there were not already a surfeit of erratic events). Somebody, nobody knows who or exactly when, decided to emend the end of the previous *Fit* (31). Parts of the original text were scraped out and some words "freshened" here and there on the leaf. Whoever did the emendations, and for what purpose (Something not politically correct? Somebody later correcting the poem to accord with the version he knew?), it was not Old Joe. While Old Joe's ideographs still can be seen on the leaf, the emender/refresher uses very different *e*'s and *d*'s. The emendations were done long after Old Joe disappeared from the *Parker Chronicle*. Whatever the circumstances, Wili makes his last appearance with the *Nowell*; Old Joe keeps writing on.

The last entry on f. 19b (897-900) of the *Parker* and all of 20a (with the record of the death of Ælfred) through f. 22b (918-921) is the work of four clerks: two West Saxons, one Mercian, and Old Joe. Although there certainly are other hands alternating with his, Old Joe essentially takes over with the entry for 913 (f. 21a) and continues through the entry for 922 on f. 24b. *Cyng* shows up as part of the attempt at spelling reforms around 891 and again in 900 under Edward; however, when around 914 the writing of the entries was left in the hands of Old Joe, he reverted to ᴄɼnınᴣ. Two West Saxon trainees alternated with Old Joe in the entry on f. 25a. Though the new West Saxons do alternate with our friend, Old Joe more or less takes over again. He wrote most of the continuation of the entry for 924 on 25b.

When Old Joe took over in 913, he reverted completely to the spelling of his youth. Although the West Saxon clerks write *eo* and use the Greek-*y*, Old Joe never again writes *eo*, but *io*; he uses Semitic-*u* instead of Greek-*y*.

Old Joe wrote so many of the Edwardian entries, that, while it may be whimsical, one gets a very strong impression of the Chancery head being told to "let the old man write the entries; he enjoys it." A master till the end, his last entry is written firmly, and even with verve. Old Joe either retired or died in 925. He had worked at Ælfred's chancery for more than thirty-five years.

The *Parker* is the Ælfredian Age original through the entry for 924 on f. 25b. The entry for 925 on f. 26a is original, but was expanded *twice* after 990. Dunstan, Archbishop of Canterbury, and a driving force behind the Benedictine Reform, died in 988. We know that the addition to the entry for 925 was even later than 990, for the "new" entry refers to the birth of *Saint* Dunstan. The text was expanded yet again sometime around 1070.

The entry for 931 was written by one scribe, the entry for 932 by another. The original entries for 925, 934, 935 and 937 were all written by a third scribe. With f. 26a we get these new West Saxon scribes, another spelling reform, and a new official font that reinstates all three forms of *s* (ɼ, ꜱ, ſ) into the record font.

Another new official font shows up on f. 28a (955-967); entries referring to *Saint* Dunstan are inserted by a later hand. As of f. 29a, entries become sporadic. The entry for 978 reports that "Here was edward *cyning* slain. On this same year, took æðelred æðeling his brother to realm." (A rather sparse entry for the ascension of the man better known to posterity as "Æthelred the Unready.")

Cyning makes its last appearance in the *Parker* on f. 30a (1001-1006). *Cyning* turns up in its modern spelling, *king*, on f.30b (1007-29). This leaf is empty except for one laconic entry for 1017: ᵬeɼ ᴄnuᴄ ᵽeaɼ ᴣeᴄoɼan ᴄo kınᴣe– [Here Cnut comes chosen as king]. Leaf 31a (1030-54) contains five original entries. The leaf is prenumbered and the entries are terse. An entry for 1031 was inserted in 1070. On 31b we find a very terse entry indeed for the year 1066, considering the consequences: "Here forth-fared eaduuard [Edward] king. & harold earl took (*feng*) to the kingdom & held it 40 weeks & 1 day, & here comes willem. . .." The entry for 1070 in the *Parker*, by yet another hand and in another font, relates the coming of Lanfranc (*Her Landfranc*) to take over the archbishopric of Canterbury (*kantw a_reberig*).

The very last entry to the *Parker Chronicle* as a [hi]story is on f. 31b-32a. F. 32a clearly was originally blank and meant to be, but the same scribe who wrote the *second* addition to the entry for 925 and the late entry on 31a added text to the entry for 1070 and wrote on this blank leaf. He was either an apprentice or someone not accustomed to writing for he could neither hold a straight line nor control the size of his graphs. On f. 32a, immediately following this amateur effort, continuing onto the previously blank 32b, and written in a highly condensed script, we find inserted into the remaining space the icily and very professionally written Acts of Lanfranc(us) in Latin. Lanfranc's Acts are neatly fit into the blank pages between the end of the Chronicle and the next quire, which contains the *Laws of Ælfred* and *Ine*.

Ælfred plainly understood his *folc* very well. Although he was doing something new, he was very careful to avoid the appearance of being innovative. Whether creating a kingdom, translating works into the vernacular, re-writing words to popular music, or writing a [hi]story and a law code, he always claimed his authority from either Biblical or Anglo-Saxon traditions, or better yet, from both. [22] From the Genealogy—which gives him fourteen generations from founder to himself—to his Law code, the entire volume is very carefully planned as an integrated whole. Ælfred had his models, and his authorities, and he used them.

In accord with the first three books of the Bible, Ælfred's Chronicle follows the order of Genesis (prologue and [hi]story); his Laws, preceded by a Table of Contents, follow Exodus and Leviticus. Ælfred emulated his model so closely that the Preface to *his* version of the Ten Commandments on f. 36a even begins: "The Lord was speaking the word to Moses and he said." The actual list of Laws begins on f. 39b.

Ælfred's Laws read like any English translation of Leviticus; quite a few of the laws begin with *Gifmon* [If [a] man]. Law 10, for example, begins "If [a] man slays a woman with child"; Law 15 starts, "If [a] man before an archbishop fights or brings a weapon." Instead of offerings of fruit, grain, or meat, however, payment is listed in a specified number of *scillings*.

Ælfred's laws are sandwiched between the Biblical authority of the Mosaic Code and a past authority from Anglo-Saxon tradition: the *Laws of Ine*. Ine's Laws also follow the Levitical model; nevertheless, we have reason to suspect that this may be a result of Ælfred's judicious rephrasing of the earlier code.

Quires A and B were substantially less than perfect, but there apparently was no choice if Ælfred were to see the completed results of his carefully planned [hi]story and Law Code. Ælfred's [hi]story probably was bound together in one volume with both sets of Laws around the same time that the bridge entries on f. 16b were squeezed in.

The last leaves of quire F, show much wear, which suggests that the volume was not protected until after another quire (G) was added around 955. This additional quire contains a list of popes and episcopal lists to which additions were made circa 1075. The *Laws* in Old English, both Ælfred's and Ine's, were written sometime around 895 by the same chancery clerks who wrote the *Parker Chronicle*, including Wili and Old Joe.

Ælfred actually accomplished a great deal in the short time he was allotted. In addition to founding a dynasty and uniting the Saxon kingdoms, he also preserved a surprising number of records in the vernacular for posterity. The *Chronicle* was the first project, *Pastoral Care*, the second, the Laws followed. Sometime during this period Ælfred managed also to squeeze in translations of Orosius' *History*, Bede's *Ecclesiastical History*, and Boethius' *Consolation of Philosophy*. The vernacular fiction collection in the *Nowell Codex* was near the end. The re-writing of the first fifty Psalms in the *Paris Psalter* was the last.

Of all these works, the most important to us as historians of writing systems are the *Paris Psalter* and the *Parker Chronicle*. The *Paris Psalter* contains the key to the Anglo-Saxon musical encoding system; the *Parker Chronicle* gives us inside information on the organization of and proceedings at Ælfred's chancery.

The Ælfredian portion of the *Parker*, which includes one clerk who had been there from the beginning of Ælfred's program, ends with the disappearance of Old Joe. Beginnings and endings tied into a not all so neat package. As a book production, the *Parker* is a mess, as a record, it is priceless. The *Parker Chronicle and Laws* allows us to watch an official voice-in-transition. It gives us both the beginning and the end of Ælfred's program as well as anchors in time. In addition, the *Parker* gives us some new information about the character of the king.

That Ælfred preferred diplomacy to force is well known. That he was a good shepherd in the ancient tradition has become clear. That he wanted to protect his flock by preserving and guarding their heritage is also evident. The *Parker*, though, makes it clear that Ælfred understood humans and their reluctance to accept something new without an authority from the past. The volume also makes it obvious that Ælfred was inordinately optimistic. It also makes it plain that he had dreams of grandeur far beyond founding a united kingdom and a dynasty.

Ælfred saw himself leading a renaissance that would once again allow the *Englisc* to take their place as the fount of learning. Ælfred could not accomplish his end; in spite of his optimism, he was defeated by reality. Sadly enough, he had to have realized that he had not succeeded; that squeezed-in bridge job on the entries for 891-4 shows that he had given up his dreams of perfection. Unfortunately his son and his grandsons were not even interested in continuing his preservation and translation program. Ælfred nevertheless laid the foundations for the revival of the late tenth century; his great-grandchildren used him as an authority from the past to launch *their* renaissance. Perhaps this is an adequate consolation for disappointed dreams: perhaps.

Chapter Twelve

SILENCED VOICES

Alice asks why the gardeners are painting the roses red; yet paint or no paint, white roses are white. The color of a rose is an integral part of its public identity; the color can be changed only by a lengthy process of selective breeding. Paralleling the inbred identity of white roses, writing systems are an integral part of a people's public identity. [1] Every time a new power structure forces a change upon a people's writing system, something is lost; something has been chipped away. Under these circumstances, it is easy to understand why there is so much resistance to the chipping process. It is also understandable that simply "re-painting" a writing system and going around shouting "off with his head" is not enough. The chipping process, a type of selective breeding, takes time. Following the Carolinian paint-job, the chipping process took more than three hundred years on the Continent. It took close to nine hundred years in England. In the end, though, even in England the Ancient Voice was silenced.

While the selective breeding of a rose does not have major cultural implications, the selective breeding of a writing system does. Changes to a writing system always have political and religious implications. A new official script system always announces that there is a different boss—but so do alterations to *any* of the sub-systems.

Alcuin's politically motivated retroversion was the first concerted attack on *stæfwritung*. Charlemagne was founding a New Roman Empire of the North and the Carolinian overhaul took as its model Roman Imperial standards as outlined in the first century BCE. While the quattrolinear limits were kept, little else was. No movement on the x and y axes was permitted and graphs were restricted to one phone—one form. Standardization was the aim: The Carolinian *renovatio* was deliberately designed to freeze the voice of authority.

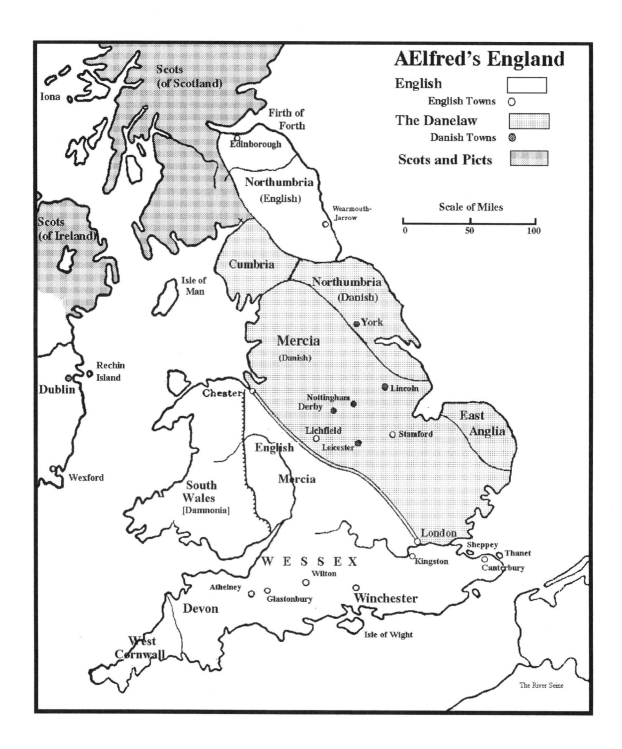

Map 3   Ælfred's England

Resistance to the Carolinian standardization was greater to the North of Western Europe than it was to the South in what was once the heart of the Old Roman Empire. To the North, diversity of liturgies and other religious customs were still common. The St. Gall manuscripts of the ninth and tenth centuries, for example, employ full *stæfwritung* generally, and both *stæfwritung* and a melisematic system in their musical texts. [2] By the late twelfth century, standardization won; [3] the St. Gall manuscripts while retaining letter-symbol differentiation between minuscule *a* and *d*, for example, no longer rely upon the other components of *stæfwritung*. [4]

By the thirteenth century, in North and Central Italy and in Provençe, for example, all that remained of *stæfwritung* was the use of xenographic exchange to distinguish the transcendent from the mundane realms. There is reason to believe that the reason for the exchange was forgotten; one simply wrote Marie—ꟿARIE, Romaniia—ROꟿANIIA, and dominus—ōn̄—like in an inscription on the Pantheon in Rome from 1270—because that is the way things were written. Handwritten texts in the Vatican Library collection attributed to authors such as Dante Alighieri (1265-1321) and Francesco Petrarch (1304-1374) are "standardized." Neither variant forms nor stress and durational notation occur. Clearly, by this time children were taught to write an "even" hand.

The English political and religious scene was very different. Resistance to Carolinian influences was both overt and determined. Religiously, England was still very much a mixture of different parties and, consequently, more tolerant of religious diversity. Politically, much of England was under Danish control—the "Danelaw" area. Ælfred was king of the *Englisc*, not of England. While Ælfred clearly borrowed ideas from Charlemagne, he was not interested in creating an imitation Roman Empire. Ælfred was trying to create a united kingdom and a homeland for his *folc*.

The Carolinian retroversion went so far as to subsume the Frankish language: Modern French consists of a Latinate vocabulary laid over Frankish and Gaelic underpinnings. As W. V. Quine points out: "The forces behind linguistic change are not wholly understood, but one conspicuous one is the change undergone by a conqueror's language when imposed as a second language upon the conquered peoples." [5] In his obsession to build a new Roman Empire of the North, right on down to the language of the vanished Imperium, Charlemagne imposed a reconstructed Latin, a language that had already undergone precisely such linguistic changes, upon both his own and his conquered peoples. The end result was the emergence of a new language; French. This was not what Charlemagne envisioned in his dreams of donning the cloak worn by the rulers out of Rome.

Unlike Charlemagne, Ælfred made no effort to replace *Englisc* with Latin; quite the contrary. For Ælfred, *Englisc* and his *Englisc* flock always came first.

Ælfred's *renovatio* of the *stæfwritung* system applied only to the variant forms and his idea of using one form to one font *throughout* the writing system died along with him. Ælfred's changes to the system were partly reversed by his son Edward (899-925). Æðelstan (925-939), Ælfred's godson and eldest grandson, was the first king of all England—and he let everyone know it. Ælfred's changes show continental influences; Æðelstan's effect on the writing system shows something completely different.

Æðelstan reinstated the full *stæfwritung* system of the early-eighth century, variant forms, chironomic notation, and all. He also reverted to a "purified" official Insular script system. We can see from his script system that Æðelstan was borrowing authority from the *Englisc* past. We can also see that he was disassociating himself from Frankish connections.

Having inherited the Danish problem, Æðelstan followed his grandfather's lead and made many efforts to assimilate Danes into his court and into English life. Nevertheless, his official script family announced out in front that he was determined to establish England as the home of the English—ten years before his decisive defeat of the Danes brought about the actuality. [6]

Eadmund (940-951) and Eadred (951-55) followed their brother's lead and strove for unity among the varied groups now under the English crown; but it was difficult. The existing records (*The Life of Oswald*, for example) are contradictory, partisan, and heavily slanted. The entire period is a muddled mess; perhaps this accounts for the reappearance of Frankish involvement under Eadred and his sons Eadwig and Eadgar. Certainly, it was during this murky period of political infighting that we find Dunstan and the Benedictine Reform. This is also the period when the Frankish "Continental" Caroline script system is introduced.

Aside from Ælfred's use of the *York* "English Caroline" font in his partially re-worked Psalter, "Caroline" is not much used in England until the ecclesiastical reforms of the mid-tenth century. The English reluctance to adopt *any* Caroline script as their ethnic font is understandable for both political and religious reasons.

Politically, the Continental Caroline fonts were tightly associated with Frankish factions. Although Ælfred used some of Charlemagne's ideas, he was clearly of the England for the English persuasion. Edward did not inherit his father's outstanding talents and was too busy holding on to what Ælfred had gained to do very much. (In fact, without substantial help from his sister, Æðelflæd, The Lady of Mercia, he would have lost ground.) Edward's son, Æðelstan, inherited his grandfather's tactical and diplomatic skills. He also hung out a sign saying "Franks not welcome."

Religiously, Continental Caroline was a *secular* font of the Insular family in use in and around York during the mid- to late-eighth century. Even if the practices at York had been generally accepted (which they were not), the use of a secular font for religious texts is difficult to enforce—on any peoples at any time. The absoluteness of script-as-authority cannot be stated often enough and is worth repeating yet again. Prior to the invention of the printing press, liturgical letter forms had religious significance and their use, shape, and script-model were prescribed, party-affiliated, and obligatory. Once a group has chosen an official script, nothing which is not written in that model "can claim to be considered as part of the sacred literature."

Although the Reform movement "Englished" their Caroline fonts to accord more with the Ælfredian model, the reformers made little headway in replacing the English "national flag" of Anglo-Celtic insular script systems with anything resembling Frankish "Caroline." "English" Caroline was used primarily for Latin texts of the Benedictine-affiliated monasteries. Exhibiting a tenacious hold, the English "national flag" continued to fly throughout the Old English period. So, incidentally, did the *Englisc*-designed and *Englisc*-implemented comprehensive writing system: *stæfwritung*.

The manuscripts tell us of the assertion of English identity and of a stubborn resistance to the chipping process. They also tell us that for roughly one hundred years the chipping process went the other way. Rather than forcing the *Englisc* to freeze their writing system, we find movement on the axes, ligatures, and variant forms in manuscripts written in "English Caroline." Cnut (circa 994-1035) attempted to follow English ways and tried to be a good shepherd in the Ælfredian tradition—including the preservation of *stæfwritung*. Nevertheless, along with Edward the Confessor (1042-1066), strong French influences reappear. By the late eleventh century, the chipping process reversed and the death knell of *stæfwritung* began to toll.

In England, *stæfwriting* lasted approximately five hundred years as a generally employed integral whole: from the 7th through the 12th centuries. The writing system did not disappear all at once. The Manuscripts display a slow, sporadic, and erratic decline in the use of various components. This decay occurs more rapidly in copied texts than in dictated texts; [7] thus, it is not very surprising that the rate of this piecemeal destruction increases and becomes more evident as writing and book production move out of monastic *scriptoria* into the secular sphere. [8]

We cannot look at every surviving document, nor do we need to. The chipping process took long enough that we can condense time and leap century by century, sampling surviving documents, until the sudden end.

We left Ælfred with his disappointed dreams; we will begin our death watch with his great-great grandsons who did indeed use their ancestor as an authority from the past. The manuscripts unequivocally tell us so.

Among the existing manuscripts we find two codices containing Old English poetry and prose. [9] These two codices, the *Exeter Book* (Exeter Cathedral MS 3501) and *The Cædmon Manuscript* (Bodleian MS Junius 11) are formal Class A, quality books; both were produced during the last half of the tenth century. The *Cædmon Manuscript* probably dates from around 950-960; the *Exeter* probably dates 20 to 30 years later. Both codices are written in Old English and both contain much more than words.

The *Cædmon Manuscript* contains religious poetry and only religious poetry. [10] The *Exeter Book* contains secular as well as sacred poetry, and riddles. (The blank leaves at the beginning were used for legal records.)

Ælfred's West Saxon hierarchy of sizes followed the Anglo-Brittonic-Goidelic system. These two codices are large books; they are the size of *secular* law codes in the Ælfred's hierarchy of sizes. The leaves of the *Exeter Book* run around 12-1/4" to 12-1/2" in height by 8-1/2" to 8-3/4" in width. The *Cædmon Manuscript* runs an average of 12-3/4" by 7-5/8". The size of these codices states out in front that *Englisc* works are not only as good as, but more important than, the works produced in Carolinian Latin.

Both codices are written in the broad column format of an authoritative secular document. They are written in what at first glance appears to be two different authoritative insular fonts. Both fonts, however, are based on Ælfred's *second* record font; both script designers used his Chronicle for their symbol-to-graph assignments.

The font of the *Cædmon Manuscript* is a carefully designed formal bookhand to be used for the vernacular. As we have noted several times, Ælfred's solution to the variant forms was eccentric. His second record font called for the use of low-*s* in all positions and the straight-limbed undotted *y* (Figure 12.1a, page 250). The font of the *Cædmon Manuscript*, in contrast with every other late manuscript from Anglo-Saxon England uses *only* low-*s* in all positions and, in spite of the date, the *y* is not dotted. Only one *aesc* is used throughout: the low-*aesc* of 894-5, which is less obtrusive and more suited to this deceptively "simple" formal design (Figure 12.1b, page 250).

The model for this script design could only have come from one place: Ælfred's chancery records—including his *Chronicle*. Further, as we have seen, with the best intentions in the world, Wili and Old Joe kept on "goofing," using *st* with long-*s* in words such as "east," *stane* [stone] and sᴘ in words such as *swithe* [very], and *swa* [so—*swa swa* equals so-so]. In spite of these "goofs," the font of the *Cædmon* uses low-*s* and *only* low-*s*. We can never know whether one of the clerks who had been a youngster during the tenure of Wili and Old Joe was still around doddering into old age or whether Ælfred's sons and grandsons were handing down family stories about the chancery clerks. One fact stands out: there was still someone around who *knew* what the Symbol-to-graph assignments in Ælfred's second record font were *supposed* to be. The *Cædmon Manuscript* had to have been produced under the orders of one of Ælfred's great- or great-great grandchildren—thus early in the second half of the tenth century.

Other than this clear use of Ælfredian authority for the font, the manuscript is written in *stæfwritung*. Nevertheless, while stress and duration are indicated, they are minimized. There is a definite attempt to follow Carolinian standards for Class A books—which also tells us that this manuscript was ordered by a "temporizer."

The font of the *Exeter Book* appears to be very different as, particularly in its majuscule graphs, it bears some resemblance to the formal, heavy, square fonts used for Biblical texts. The font was designed by a professional who managed to blend Ælfred's fonts with a formal Biblical font.

There is little doubt that the symbol-to-graph assignments of the *Exeter* font were taken directly from the *Parker Chronicle*. The symbol assignments of the *Exeter Book* pick up and use every one of Wili and Old Joe's "goofs"! Not only are the assignments from the *Parker*, but the majority of the assignments are specifically from leaves 17a-18a (894). The examples in the left hand column of Figure 12.2a are from fol. 17b. In the word *swa* (last example), to the left we can see the model for the *Exeter* font's long-*s*; on the right we have Old Joe's long-*s*.

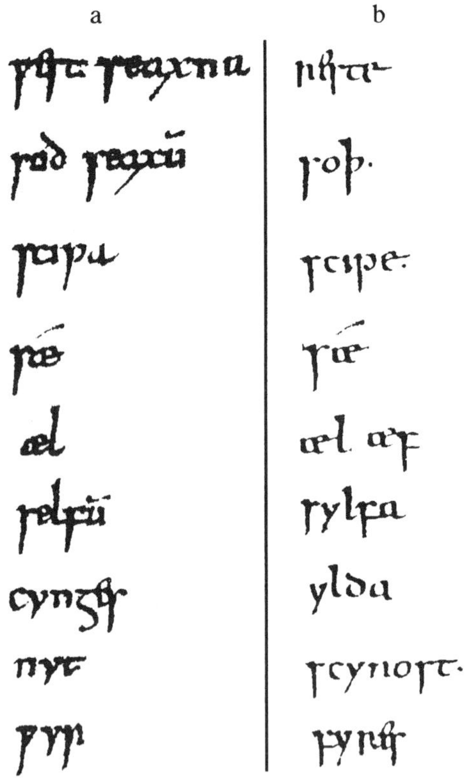

This font design calls for the complete set of variant

Fig. 12.1 a) Ælfred's second record font as written by his West Saxon clerks. b) The formal bookhand of the *Cædmon Manuscript*.

forms, including alpha-*a*. Figure 12.2b shows the three forms of *y*—among which we recognize the straight-limbed dotted *y* of Ælfred's second dictation font; the straight-limbed mutation of the Greek-*y* in his second record font, and Old Joe's *f*-form that he used exclusively from 913 on. Small-lobed *aesc* is in there as well as the low-*aesc*. The script designer clearly studied the Ælfredian part of the *Parker* very carefully. He even copied Wili and Old Joe in the way they wrote *east* and *west*.

It is obvious that the designer of the *Exeter* font had access to the records of the Royal Chancery; however, it is equally obvious that, unlike the *Cædmon* designer, the script designer of the *Exeter* did *not* know about Ælfred's peculiar solution to the variant forms. This one fact places the production of the *Exeter Book* at least a generation later than the *Cædmon*. It also tells us something about the political tug of war.

The usual practice is to assign the reappearance of literature in Old English to the effect of Dunstan and the Benedictine Reform. It is true that the so-called "Old English Renaissance" follows precisely upon the heels of the Benedictine Reform and the reintroduction of Frankish circles into the government of England. Historically, however, there are three basic patterns of "Renaissance" that emerge following a change in power structure.

The first pattern occurs when the new ruling power is a consolidator. The "consolidation" pattern is marked by a flood of literature in the old power language and by translations of the old into the new voice. Under a consolidator, the script systems show the incorporation of graphs from the old into the new as well. [11]

The second pattern is the paradigm of "defeat." This pattern shows up when a people has been successfully cowed or effectively crushed as a resisting ethnic identity. Within a remarkably short space of time after the Winners decide that victory is complete, we find a spate of literature in the *new* ruling vernacular and script system extolling the virtues of the defeated. [12]

The third pattern that shows up is the "identity" paradigm: it indicates a 'we are just as good as you are if not better' reassertion of ethnic identity in defiance of the new power structure. This third pattern is marked by the appearance of literature in the *native* language, an elevation of *native* script systems towards "official" square models, and an increase in the size of literary texts in the vernacular. [13]

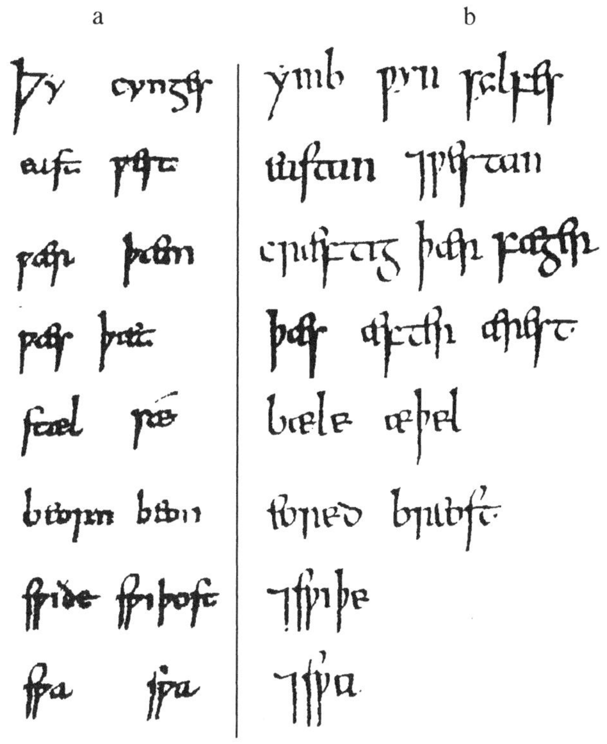

Fig. 12.2 a) Ælfred's second record font with Wili and Old Joe's "goofs." b) The Exeter Book font and its symbol-to-graph assignments.

If historical patterns are any indication, from its size to its script to its content, the *Exeter Book* is a prime example of the *third* pattern, the reassertion of equality of identity. Its full use of *stæfwriting* also places the manuscript as ordered by someone in the anti-Frankish camp. The *Exeter Book* was probably produced fairly late, right about the time that all Benedictine monasteries affiliated with the reform were required to use exactly the same Caroline font. [14]

In the meantime, the reverse chipping process was well under way during the late-tenth and early-eleventh centuries. From the same period as the *Exeter Book*, the Preface (*praefatio*) to Ælfric's Latin Grammar for the English language (*anglicam linguam*), written in Latin, is chock-a-block with variant forms and stress notation. [15]

On the Old English side, Wulfstan's Sermons and Ælfric's Homilies (both early eleventh century) are Class 3 conformal books and, as to be expected in a Class 3 book, encoded with minimum guidelines. They are, however, fully encoded with quality, quantity, and stress notation. Besides using fairly heavy punctuation, Ælfric's first series of Homilies also employs medial and ascender height majuscule letters to indicate the beginning of sentences (medial) and paragraphs (ascender).

These manuscripts confirm that *stæfwritung* was alive, well, and in use as late as the first quarter of the eleventh century. Nevertheless, if *stæfwritung* was chipping away at Caroline, scribes trained in Caroline were chipping away at the ASPA. The use of sigmoid-*s* in the middle of a word in Ælfric's Homilies is a marker. It tells us that the symbol-to-graph assignments of the ASPA were beginning to decay. Quality, in fact, was the first component of *stæfwritung* to depart.

The evidence indicates that, whereas monastic scribes trained in *stæfwritung* musical notation retained qualitative letter-symbol differentiation for a much longer period of time than secular scribes, how much was retained varied from *scriptorium* to *scriptorium* and from scribe to scribe. Then, the symbol set appears to have been simplified as the system moved out of the liturgical sphere into the secular domain. Despite this, these phonetic distinctions remained in texts written by musically trained scribes into the fourteenth-century and in handwritten documents well into the 17th century—long after many of the forms had collapsed into a "central" classicized symbol.

The *Peterborough Chronicle,* a copy of a copy of Ælfred's Chronicle from the first half of the twelfth-century, gives us a clue as to the status of quality notation. The text was written by two scribes. Scribe 2 wrote the section from 1121 to 1155. This part of the *Peterborough* retains quality differentiation. Variant forms are used throughout this later portion of the text. We have reason to suspect that Scribe 2 of the *Peterborough Chronicle* was musically trained because, with the exception of the bound forms, in the *earlier* portion—the part written by Scribe 1 that begins with Ælfred's Chronicle and runs through 1120—the scribe does not use quality differentiation. [16] This suggests that quality differentiation was no longer standard in the training of the average scribe. Further evidence that the average scribe was no longer taught to distinguish quality comes from the mid twelfth-century: the text of the "Brut" (B.M. Cotton MS. Caligula A. ix) displays neither quality nor stress notation. [17] Nonetheless, from the late twelfth-century, a musical manuscript, the *Canterbury* or *Eadwine Psalter*, is still fully encoded. [18]

Traces of quality differentiation persist long after the reason for these forms has been forgotten. While free forms indicate varied pronunciation, bound forms indicate fixed pronunciation for that form and for only that form. Bound forms, such as short-*r* after *o*, [19] tall *s* at the beginning of words, round or sigmoid-*s* at the end, and digraphs such as *St* remain in use as late as the early-twentieth century. [20] The retention of the 2-form of *r* after *o*, and the use of tall-*s*, (printer's "siwash") alongside of sigmoid-*s* are standard. Nevertheless, it is clear that, for the average scribe, by the thirteenth century the reason for the differentiation has been forgotten; these bound forms have merely become the way the graphs are written.

In the late fourteenth-century Henry of Kirkestede, a precentor (hence musically trained), still employs full *stæfwritung* in his *Catalogus Scriptorium Ecclesiae* [Catalog (of books) of Writers of the Church] from Bury St. Edmunds. [21] The late fourteenth-century Wycliffe bibles (for example, MS. Douce 370) still use two forms of *a, e,* and *y*. There are two forms each of *r* and *s*, but one is the bound form -*or* and the other is the bound -ſt.

The *l-d* ligature, another bound form, remains in use in handwriting until at least the late sixteenth century. Despite these remnants, quality is the first component to decline in use. Standardization was slowly taking its toll.

Variant forms of *a* and *r* appear sporadically through the early seventeenth century. Cambridge University Library MS Ff.2.38, for example, is assigned to the late fifteenth or early sixteenth century. The scribe uses both the Anglicana font's two-compartment *a* and the Secretary font's single-compartment *a* as well as both the Secretary short *r* and the Anglicana *r*. (In this case, it is impossible to determine whether the scribe was imitating the variations in his *exemplar* in the script chosen by the client, or merely attempting to give the work an "archaic" appearance.) Variant forms of *a* still appear in handwritten copies of theatrical texts in the first quarter of the seventeeth century. By this late date, though, these variants do not usually indicate quality, but more often are used to indicate stress.

Stress notation endured for a longer period of time than quality, yet it, too, gradually disappeared from the manuscripts. The main culprit, again, was standardization—this time, the Carolinian cum Roman ideal of book production raised its head. Roman Class A books were bilinear; Carolinian Class A books were quattrolinear without movement on either axis. As we are as concerned with beginnings as much as we are with endings, we must return to the late tenth century.

Some indications of the mechanisms involved in the loss of stress notation can be seen in the late-tenth to early-eleventh century *Old English Illustrated Hexateuch*. [22] As with so many other manuscripts, this one also gives us a great deal of interesting information.

The *Hexateuch* contains an Old English translation of the first five books of the Bible and Joshua. Preceding all, however, is Ælfric's "letter" explaining why he translated *his* portion. His portion? Yes, for a translation of Genesis, from after the binding of Isaac, already existed. Ælfric translated from Genesis 1:1 through the binding.

The examples illustrated in Figure 12.3a are from the Ælfrician part (f. 2v), Genesis 1:9-13. Those in Figure 12.3b are from the older part, specifically Jacob's return with his wives and children (f. 48v), Genesis 32:7 ff.

The fonts in both parts are similar, formal, authoritative Biblical fonts, but not the same. There is one other catch: except for the use of dotted-y, the Ælfrician part follows the phone to graph assignments of the *Cædmon Manuscript*; the older part follows the phone to graph assignments of the *Exeter Book*.

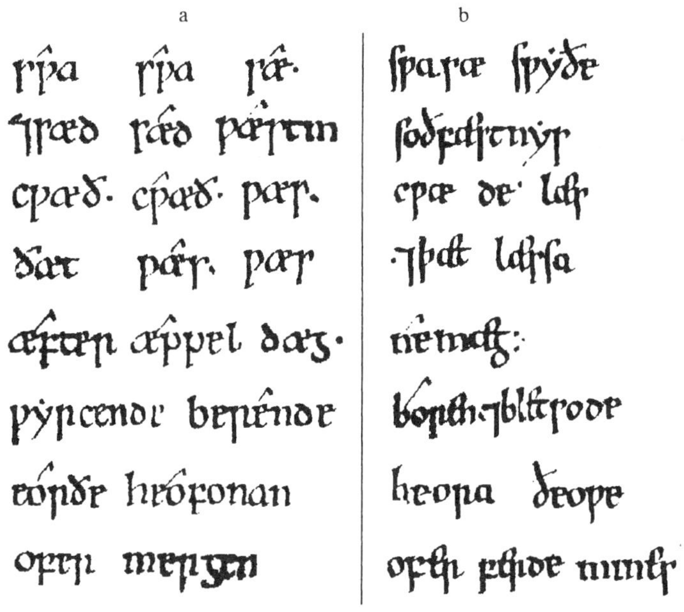

Fig. 12.3 Old English Illustrated Hexateuch. (a) fol. 2v; (b) fol. 48v

We know that Ælfric checked on copies of his work. BL Royal 7 C.XII, probably the "first edition" copy of his first series of Homilies, has a marginal footnote in Ælfric's own hand. [23] As Ælfric died around 1020, and as the *Hexateuch* manuscript displays *both* authoritative phone-to-graph assignments, the later, that is, the Ælfrician part of the *OE Hexateuch* was probably produced during the last ten years of the tenth century or the first ten years of the eleventh. (It is also more than likely that Ælfrician part was attached to an existing copy of the older part.)

As the examples in both font styles are by more than one hand, we will refer to them as Font A and Font B. In font A, what used to be written as fully-stressed high-forms are replaced with a long-stroke stress marker over vowels and digraphs. If the form receives secondary (medial) stress, there is no stress mark: compare ɼœð with ɼœð (no. 2), cpœ𝔂 with cpœ𝔂 (no. 3), or wœɼ with wœɼ in no. 4. Similarly, we can see this replacement in operation on the old high-*E*, low *n* digraphs, as in example no. 6: -cenðe versus -ɲénðe and in example no. 8: oɼeɲ and meɲȝen [morning]. (Note that, although reduced to a minimum, quantity notation is still used in pyɲcenðe, beɲénðe, and héoɼonan, as well as in meɲȝen.) In Ælfric's dialect, the digraph *eo* still receives primary stress (No. 7).

In font B this replacement of the old stressed forms is only partial. The old stressed forms of *e* and small-lobed *aesc* are retained. In this dialect, however, neither *eo* nor *ea* are usually marked for stress. In either case, though, the replacement of stressed graphs with stress markers illustrates one step in the decline of stress notation.

The main scribe of the early twelfth-century *Textus Roffensis* [24] [a copy of a late sixth or early seventh-century English law code] retains qualitative notation and language differentiation, but no longer encodes stress in the Old English parts of the text. [25] When we arrive at the the thirteenth century, the circa 1200 poem, "Vices and Virtues," retains some qualitative differences (for instance, ligatured *ld*, clear and dark *l*, two forms of *a* and *r*), yet retains stress indications only on *a* and *s*, [26] while the roughly contemporary "Poema Morale," dated to around 1225, retains neither stress nor quality. [27]

Also early in the thirteenth century, Nicholas Orme, author of the so-called *Ormulum* (Bodleian Library, Junius MS. I), designed an ingenious, though idiosyncratic, orthographic system to record current pronunciation. Orme wrote instructions that scribes were to pay particular attention to the spelling and, for example, all consonants are doubled after a short closed vowel but single after an open vowel. His system incorporates remnants of *stæfwritung*. [28] Orm retained letter form distinctions between Latin and Anglo-Norman as well as numerous variant forms in each language. He does not encode stress notation. Orme's system is a convincing confirmation that, by the thirteenth-century, stress notation has all but disappeared from the average scribe's repertoire.

By the first quarter of the fourteenth century, the *Auchinleck* Manuscript, the product of a secular bookshop, bears no traces of stress notation in any of the five hands who wrote this book. [29] Stress notation, after all, detracts from the "neat" even appearance so admired in a quality book.

Quantity (duration) was the last component to succumb to the passage of time. Although the *Auchinleck* retains some quantity notation on *e*, the late fourteenth century *Ancrene Riwle*, [30] unlike the 1225 version of this same text, [31] exhibits neither quality nor stress nor quantity notation.

Printing did not at first have much of an affect on book production—or writing systems. **Xylographic** (woodblock) printing appeared by the late fourteenth century, but carved wooden graphs are delicate and distort quickly when pressure is applied to transfer the inked text to paper. A further disadvantage, if what is wanted is standardization, is that each graph is individually carved and exact duplication of a graph depended totally upon the skill of the carver. A few small books using this technique survive from the early fifteenth century. The technique is better reserved for illustrations. **Metallographic** (relief plates, that is, raised text on a metal base) printing existed by early in the fifteenth century. Gutenburg is said to have used the technique during the late 1430's. The technique was not very satisfactory. The invention of moveable type and the printing press itself at the end of the fifteenth century changed the picture. With this invention, the desired end, durable typefaces which duplicated each graph form exactly, were available in large numbers. The press itself saw improvements. The death knell sounded even louder.

In the mid-sixteenth Century, John Day (or Daye), a master printer, produced numerous books for proponents of the English Reformation. Day designed a special Old English type-face for the publication in 1566 of the "anonymous" *A Testimonie of Antiquitie*. (Which, incidentally, is based on works by Ælfric.) The type-face is standardized. There is no evidence that he made any attempt to imitate the variant forms found in the manuscripts. In addition, words are divided by semantic units (with some amusing errors as the result of his lack of knowledge of Old English), and he does not use either stress or quantity notation. Indeed, Day seems unaware that such a system as *stæfwriting* once existed.

Hurried towards extinction by the invention of the printing press, replaced as the preferred method of book reproduction, quantity, the last remnant of the phonetic-based *stæfwriting* remains in use in handwritten letters and rough drafts [32] at least into the late sixteenth and the early seventeenth centuries.

The sixteenth century *Findern Manuscript*, "a collaborative effort involving a surprising number of amateur scribes," preserves quantity across the different hands, particularly noticeable on suffixes and in syllabic spacing. [33] Remnants of quantity notation appear in the letters of Queen Elizabeth I. This may be seen in her letter to Lord Burghley of April 11, 1572 (Fig. 12.4).

This letter is with reference to the pressed-for execution of Mary Stuart, Queen of Scotland. [34] Elizabeth writes that she considered "this exe cútion EVIL" and an "īr re uoc'ab le de de." The Queen still ligatures *ld* (from l. 1. beholdinge), separates syllables (l. 1. hin dar"), spaces suffixes, and indicates pauses, for example "determi n ation" (from l. 8), and "was co un ter maund ed" (from l. 9). We should also note that, following the tradition dating back to Sumer that an official document had to be in the voice (handwriting) of authority, the letter closes with the comment that "let this [the letter] suffice all writen with my uon [own] hand." [35]

We can see that in England, as late as the first half of the seventeenth century, handwriting was still taught to record the spacing of the spoken word. This remnant of *stæfwriting* probably accounts for the "occasional tendency to leave gaps within words" in the portion of the unique copy of *Sir Thomas More* written by Hand D—and Hand D *may* be our only example of a theatrical text written in Shakespeare's own hand. [36]

Although the printing press was an accomplice in the general destruction—the economics of production does not

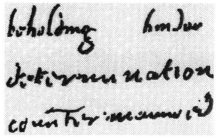

Fig. 12.4 Examples from the letter written by Elizabeth I to Lord Burghley

encourage casting separate type for variant forms or stress notation—, this does not explain what actually occurred. Elizabeth I still learned to write using quantity notation. Clearly, children were still taught to write using quantity notation. Theatrical texts (which have much in common with musical texts) still encoded quantity and stress notation as late as the closing of the playhouses under the Parliamentarians.

Was it the effect of Cromwell and company? Was it the Stuart ties with France? We shall never know what delivered the last blow. There is, however, no question: the end was as sudden as it was complete. Prior to the English Civil War, quantity notation was still alive and well; as of the Restoration, *stæfwritung* was gone. It was as if the Anglo-Saxon Phonetic-Based Comprehensive Writing System had never existed. The ancient *Englisc* voice was silenced.

EPILOGUE

Stæfwritung was a mathematically based, systematically organized, and language-independent "universal" writing system. During precisely the same period that the last vestiges of *stæfwritung* disappeared as an integral whole, intellectuals across the Western European Continent began to expend much thought and energy on the search for a mathematically based, systematically organized, and language-independent "universal" writing system. After watching so many ironic twists and turns in this story, we are not even slightly staggered. After all, how typical of humans to find a need for something after they have thrown it away. By the mid-seventeenth century, the hunt for an "ideal" writing system was on; it still is.

In England we find works such as Francis Lodowyck's, *A common writing*, issued in 1647, and *The Ground-work of a perfect new language, and an vniversal or commonwriting: and presented to the consideration of the learned by a well-willer to learning*, published in 1652. Sir Thomas Urquhart proposed a universal language: "Logopandecteision." The first book, entitled *Neaudthaumata*, and subtitled, *An introduction to the universal language*, was issued in 1653 by G. Calvert & R. Tomlins, in London. John Jones's (1645-1709) phonetic-based system, *Practical phonography* was printed for Richard Smith in 1701.

Across the channel, and demonstrating one of history's wry mockeries, Cave Beck wrote *Le charactere universel: par lequel toutes nations peuvent comprendre les conceptions l'une de l'autre en lisant par une escriture commune a toutes leur propre langage maternelle.* [The Universal Character: through which all nations may understand the conceptions of one another and write them by a common writing system each in their proper mother tongue.] This book was printed in London by Thomas Maxey for William Weekly in 1657. In Germany, philosopher and mathematician Gottfried Wilhelm Liebniz (1646-1716), demonstrating a total lack of understanding of living languages, attempted to develop a scientifically based scheme for a "Universal Linguistic calculus" designed to eliminate all ambiguity from language and writing and render argument obsolete.

In 1883, J. Heywood mistook a "universal" writing system for a "universal" language and came out with the *Origin of the western nations & languages, showing the construction and aim of Punic; recovery of the universal language; reconstruction of Phoenician geography; Asiatic source of the dialects of Britain; principal emigrations from Asia; and description of Scythian society,* (Manchester and London).

Zamenhof's artificial language, Esperanto, appeared in 1887—and still has adherents and a journal. In the computerized world of the late-twentieth century, the UNICODE Consortium was trying to create a "universal" computer character set. [1] A multitude of structures and schematic systems have been formulated in order to discuss languages. The International Phonetic Alphabet is exactly what it says: a symbol set intended to represent the quality of sounds in living languages.

Living languages change; to remain viable a writing system must be able to accommodate these changes. Writing systems are, in modern parlance, a user interface. A good user interface should be simple to use and economical of both time and resources. Above all, it must be flexible—adaptable and capable of meeting changing needs. Few user interfaces meet all these criteria.

The IPA attempts to identify the quality of individual phones, but its symbol set is not simple. Complicated linear and nonlinear systemics have been created to graphically represent phonological sequences, but are not easily accessible to the average reader. Spectrophonograms record phonological amplitude sequences as a line drawing; but contain no semantic information. None of the modern systems offers a comprehensive approach to the representation of a spoken language. None.

We are trying to reinvent the wheel. The Phoenician writing system did meet all the criteria for a good user interface. The Phoenician invention of variant forms to represent a class of phones was a major technological advance. A compact and simple technique, variant forms eliminated the need for external markings—the earlier Sumero-Akkadian solution to the problem of recording living languages. The Phoenician system became the model for so many writing systems because of its simplicity, economy, flexibility, and adaptability. Its direct descendant, the Brittonic-influenced, *Englisc* designed and *Englisc* implemented *stæfwritung* system was very popular; nearly as universal in its acceptance as the original Phoenician was. There are ample reasons for the wide-spread use of *stæfwritung*—besides Anglo-Saxon missionary activity. Unlike static systems, but like the Phoenician, *stæfwritung* is extremely flexible and accommodates to the perfectly natural changes undergone by a living language. This long-searched-for "ideal" Western writing system was a reality. More than 1300 years ago, facing the same multilingual confusion, the Anglo-Saxons designed a solution to the problem: *stæfwritung*.

Sometime during the mid-seventh century, somewhere north of the Humber in Anglo-Saxon England, a "universal" graphic symbol set was codified, and a simple to read, mathematically based, language-independent, and systematically applied writing system was designed. The system combined the rhythmic amplitude sound-wave charting of the spectrophonogram with the phonetic indications of an IPA while using a normal and easily comprehensible alpha-numeric symbol set.

Designed as an inter-ethnic, "universal" writing system to record the spoken word, *stæfwritung* solved many vexing problems. The ASPA gave a model for an "international" symbol set that could be used by any Indo-European language. As the Phoenician symbol set, one could add or subtract symbols as needed. The use of xenographic exchange throughout the system did away with the problem of ethnic identification. Peoples could still use their own scripts and fonts to identify themselves while writing in an inter-ethnic language and symbol set system. The designation of external markings only for musical and rhetorical instructions permitted the inclusion of the necessary performance information without interfering with the text.

No modern writing system or linguistic technique can approach the simplicity or comprehensiveness of this ancient system. Nonetheless, while we should not apply our modern classicized standards to the past, we should not try to reinstate phonetic-based systems as our modern writing systems. We are accustomed to standardized printed texts and we cannot turn back the clock. This does not mean that we cannot learn to understand and to listen to the past, nor does it imply that we cannot apply some of the principles of phonetic-based systems to our modern needs.

On the grim reality side, we had better learn to listen to the voices of the absent. It is vitally important to our future that we understand our past for what these documents tell us.

Despite the old proverb, history does not repeat itself; historic *patterns* repeat themselves. While these patterns never repeat exactly, the peoples and places are different, the patterns do repeat. We should try to understand the patterns. We certainly can learn to recognize them; these patterns are visible in our writing systems.

Understanding and recognition, though, are not enough; we must also correlate the data, that is, remember. The ancients were well aware that memory is the basis of all knowledge; further, they knew that the ability to correlate data is the most important function of a trained memory. [2] In an allusion to these ancient practices, one hundred years ago philosopher George Santayana (1863-1952) summed up this three-fold requirement for any knowledge in one pithy statement: "Those who cannot remember the past are condemned to repeat it." We may add to Santayana's saying that those who do not understand ancient writing systems cannot understand the past. We should once again remember how to read these ancient systems for all their distinctions still function.

Although shorn of their ternary base and the majority of their variant forms, hence their *voices*, parts of these once comprehensive phonetic-based writing systems are in use to this day. Our lowercase symbol sets in every Western language are based on the Phoenician variant forms. Our use of a variety of type-faces in a text, such as italics and bold type fonts, is directly from *stæfwritung* itself. Throughout the Western world, no matter what language or nationality, we still use the ancient hierarchies of size, script, and format—elements that date back to Sumer and Akkad. The main difference between then and now is that our many times great-ancestors knew what these distinctions meant, but we do not. Our responses are subconscious; it has become the way things are done. This lack of consciousness is a dangerous state of affairs.

Standardization has many plusses, but it has many minuses as well. When one gives up something of value, it is best to understand *why* one accepts the change and *what* is being given up. Although the *what* is obvious, individual cultural identity, the most important point to remember about the standardization of a writing system is *why* it is done.

Writing systems and politics make an uneasy marriage, but are wedded nonetheless. Whether we talk about the reformers of Augustinian Rome or the Rabbis of the Babylonian and Jerusalem schools, about Charlemagne or Samuel Johnson, the nineteenth century orthographic reformers or the "politically correct" wave of the last half of the twentieth century, there is *always* a political reason behind the standardization of a writing system.

We should know why legal papers are larger than letters. We should be conscious of the differences between, for example, Continental and Anglo-American fonts, formats, and sizes and what they mean. We should be able to differentiate between "national" type-fonts in any one language and understand why these differences appear. We should know why a reference book is larger than a text book or a work of fiction. We should understand the distinction in use between serifed and sans-serif fonts. We should be aware of the meaning of an enforced change of official script; it might possibly prevent a world war.

The absent voices are relevant to our understanding of almost every area of human social interaction and endeavor. The phonetic-based systems let us hear texts as divergent as the Bible and a Greco-Roman tax receipt, a second-century BCE treatise on political philosophy and a tenth-century CE book of vernacular poems.

On the lighter side, in antiquity there was no such thing as our modern idea of a "copy," there was only an original and everything else was an "edition." We can hear the voices of Ennandu or Kilamu. When in the ninth century BCE the King of Aram, Bar Haddad Bar Tov Rechem-Bar Hezion, wrote a thank you note to the goddess Malqodet, we can hear him talking; the tablet is in his own hand—and voice. We can listen to Bar Kochba (d. circa 135) speaking as he wrote his letters in Hebrew or dictated them in Greek to his secretary. As the scrolls of the Hebrew Torah are so scrupulously copied, we can hear the voices of antiquity talking.

Written on stele, leather, tablet, and papyrus, we can listen to the voices of late Antiquity. We can hear the Roman Governor of Thebes rebuking a subordinate. In the document known as the "Diploma of Thierry, III," written at Compiègne and dated 30 June 679 (Paris, Archives Nationales, K2, No. 13), we can hear Thierry speaking. We can listen to Bede and Ælfred and Ælfric "talk." We can see how Elizabethan upper-class English was pronounced. Elizabeth I was taught to write using durational notation; we can hear the absent voice of Elizabeth today. Tudor and Stuart theater prompts still use stress and durational notation; we can know with a fair degree of assurance how Renaissance dramatists wanted their lines performed.

The ability to listen to these absent voices brings history to life for us, and can be a great deal of fun as well. Yet *stæfwritung* has more to offer us than watching history unroll before our eyes.

If the printing press and movable type could not economically support variant forms and the ternary base, computer font production has no such limitations—as we can see from the fonts used in this book. Because both the ternary base and the variant forms are once again economical, some suggestions for modern use follow. Readers undoubtedly will think of many more.

Learning to read was a simple process with phonetic-based systems. Say as written; hear it; understand it. Phonics is only a partial success because it includes neither the parsing rhythms nor the stress and durational notations of a living language. Why not adapt these techniques to solve reading acquisition problems?

Numerous books and techniques have been devised to teach foreign languages. Learning to speak a foreign language was as simple as learning to read your native tongue with *stæfwritung*. As one of the greatest difficulties in speaking a foreign language stems from the parsing rhythms, why not add encoded texts to the repertoire of the language laboratory?

The techniques can be an aid in public speaking. Simply encode the text with stress and durational notation and even John Q. Public should be able to give a creditable speech—or a sermon.

Poetry is meant to be heard, yet reading poetry out loud is a notoriously difficult art. Encoding the text using all three components should make this task a far more enjoyable experience—not to mention open the door to poetry for a wider audience. Indeed, why not *print* poetry using a phonetic-based system. The system worked admirably in the past.

The ternary base is easy to implement on a computer. It is also far more flexible than the two-dimensional techniques invented to replace it. Why not use the ternary base in linguistic analysis? Perhaps the IPA could take a leaf from the ASPA and make their alphabet comprehensible to a wider public. Thus modified, the IPA in combination with the ternary base could record living speech.

Coming back to where we began, besides understanding history or adapting ancient techniques to our modern world, there is yet another reason why we must learn to read the phonetic-based systems. Even today a writing system is part of a culture's identity. A writing system reveals much about a culture to anyone who *can* read writing systems. Chipped away, shorn, classicized as they be—listen carefully. The whispers we hear in our writing systems are mute echoes of the ancient Absent Voices.

GLOSSARY

acoustic phonology	The branch of phonology that studies how phones sound.
aesc	One of the five monophthongs (one phone) of the English language.
agonal	A technical term in philosophy to denote a playful approach to serious contest. From Greek 'agon', a struggle or contest.
alphabet	At the most basic level, the term refers to the concrete images of a systematically ordered, finite symbol-set. Symbols stand as mnemonics for the transductions of the sounds in a given language. The Western symbol set is called by the Greek name for the first two symbols of the North-West Semitic consonantal symbol set, Aleph-Bet, that is, Alpha-Beta.
angle of attack	A technical term for the approach or starting stroke of a hand-written graph. The term also applies to the approach stroke of a painter. The angle of attack is a personal idiosyncrasy that identifies a given artist or scribe.
AnteNicene	Before the Nicene council, that is, the Council of Nicaea in 325.
antiphon	The technical term for a liturgical chant used in the Roman liturgy. Antiphons are the bits and pieces of Psalms, usually a refrain, set off against prose texts and sung in alternation by two choirs.
articulative phonology	The branch of phonology that studies where and how a phone sound is produced.
ascender	The paleographic term for the area between the upper limit and the headline in quattrolinear limit systems.
ASPA	The Anglo-Saxon Phonetic Alphabet, that is, the phone-to-symbol assignments of the symbol-set of the Anglo-Saxon writing system.
baseline	The paleographic term for the area between the lower interior limit and the descender line in quattrolinear limit systems.
bicola	The technical term in Classical Hebrew poetry for a two-line phrase. A bicola consists of two cola each with a central pause or caesura. (See, 'colon'.)
bilinear	The upper and lower writing limits, that is, the external skeleton of all writing limit systems. Bilinear scripts and fonts fill the entire space between the upper and lower limits.
bilingual	More accurately termed bi-ethnos, a bilingual is a text written or inscribed in two ethnic languages and two ethnic scripts.
bound form	A group of symbols that is the normal way to state a particular expression.
boustrophedon	A Greek term meaning back and forth like an ox plowing a field. Boustrophedon writing changes direction on every other line. As the technique requires almost a complete double graphic-set (scripts), except for

	its apparent use to record incantations and charms, boustrophedon writing was quickly abandoned in every writing system where it was tried.
bow	In paleography, the round part of a 'p' or 'b'.
breathings	The number of syllables that can be uttered in one breath. (See 'utterances'; 'expressions'; *scripto continuo*'.)
caesura	A pause, usually central, in a line of poetry.
cartonage	The technical turn for the materials wrapped around a mummy.
case	An early form of punctuation; the incised box in which a word was written around the 25th century BCE.
catch line	The final line on a tablet, column, or leaf, repeated to order and assemble books.
catch words	The last word on a page, repeated to order a manuscript or a printed page.
causative	A verb that causes or makes a person or an abstraction do something. Causatives derive from existing verbs and change the type of action, e.g. "to set" means to "cause to make sit"; "to drench," means "cause to make drink."
cephalicus	A neume used in the *stæfwritung* musical notation system to indicate how many and which of the 'heads', that is, lead singers, lead a congregation in song or psalm. The name comes from *Kephalikos*, Greek, "of or for the head."
Celtiberians	A mixture of Celtic and Iberian stocks who lived in what is modern Portugal. They spoke a language called "Celto-Iberian" and were the inventors of the two-edged "Spanish" sword.
central space	In trilinear limit systems, the internal area between the lower upper limit and the bottom of the central space. In quattrolinear systems, the area between the headline and the baseline.
chironomic	A notational system that graphically imitates the hand movements of a chorale leader and is equally useful as recitation guides. (Also spelled cheironomic)
classicization	The retroversion of a writing system to what was thought to be "Classical" standards, Roman or Greek, at a given point in time. (See *renovatio*'.)
clubbed, clubbing	A widening of the ascenders, by going back over an already written line or turning the pen.
coherence strategies	The technical term for the various strategies used in composition to bind parts of a work together.
colon	In Classical Hebrew Poetry, the technical term for a one-line phrase separated by a central pause or caesura.
colophon	A paragraph that appears at the end of a work and contains some information that is apart from the text, for example, about the scribes, the place of writing, or the authors.
Componential Analysis Matrix	A technique used by professional translators and in the study of semantics to analyze the components and structure of a text. THe components are then placed on a table called a matrix.

comprehension units	Cognitive "sound-bites"; the segments that divide and combine according to the natural speech rhythms of a spoken language and enable a speaker to comprehend the language.
concatenations	Clusters of finite collections of a language's symbols. In a syllabogramic writing system, such as Sumerian, concatenations of symbols are what today we call rebuses. In semantic-based writing systems concatenations are called words. (See 'semantic units'.) In phonetic-based writing systems concatenations are called expressions. (See 'expressions'.)
conceptual domain	The technical term in the study of semantics for the sphere or image that carries the idea of a work
conformal	Texts that are standardized, conformed to meet specifications at a given time and location.
conglomerate script	A script that displays the indiscriminate use of graphs from different ethnic designs in one document. The use of a conglomerate script is not to be confused with the xenographic exchange technique. In xenographic exchange, a word or words will be written entirely in another font; the exchange technique, in fact, depends upon the strict observance of script differentiation by ethnos. In a conglomerate script, it is not unusual to find a mixed up mass of different ethnic scripts used in one word. Prior to the twentieth century, the appearance of a conglomerate script in a document is *prima facia* evidence that the document is a forgery.
consolidated script	A consolidated script is a design that combines elements from two (or more) different ethnic fonts to create a new, combined official voice of authority. The purpose of a consolidated script is to merge the voices of different groups under one authority.
constant	The unvarying part of a writing system. By definition, a constant is a symbol that keeps the same meaning across contexts. (See 'variable'.)
corn	The generic name for grain.
cube	A three-dimensional form intrinsically orthogonal in properties. (See 'orthogonal'.)
cuneiform	Literally, "nail-head." A wet surface inscribing technique using a stylus and wet clay to record the spoken word. The stylus was poked into the wet clay, creating a starting wedge which was followed by the completion of the graph as a thin line.
cuneiform wedge	The starting wedge produced by the cuneiform wet surface writing technique. As the cuneiform wedge was the mark of an authoritative or official script, it was incorporated into all Western official or authoritative script designs. The cuneiform wedge is still used today, only now we call it a "serif." (See 'serif'.)
DSS	The Dead Sea Scrolls, that is, the written records found in numerous caves in the desert of the Judean Hills.
decatetartos	A Greek term meaning "fourteenthers," that is, people who celebrated Easter on the fourteenth of Nissan, the Jewish Passover.

dental phones	Sounds made when the tongue presses against the teeth.
descender	The paleographic term for the area between the baseline and the outside (lower) limit in quattrolinear limit systems.
diacriticals	The external markings used to indicate distinctions among otherwise undistinguished forms. In modern symbol sets, for example, that of French, the accents added to distinguish an 'e' from an 'é' or an 'è' are diacriticals.
diaspora	Outside the land; literally lands of dispersion.
digraph	A digraph is graphic symbol composed of two graphs representing a diphthong, that is, two phones pronounced with a glide.
diplomatic	A format technique used for study and research. Multiple versions of a single text are displayed in a manner so as to permit comparison of the variations among texts. A diplomatic edition uses one version as the base text and sets other versions in parallel or assigns sigla, that is, identifying symbols, to each component text and lists differences in footnotes.
ductus	The direction of a stroke as written by a scribe. Ductus can be used to identify a scribal hand, but only when documents are from different *scriptoria*. If a document is written by a team of scribes, all of whom have been trained at the same *scriptorium*, then all the scribes will have the same ductus.
edit technique	A technique used when the selective destruction technique would be counter-productive, as when someone (e.g. Origen) is too well known to simply hide. In these cases, his or her work will be emended (edited) to conform to the desired line.
ektephonic	A complicated Greek musical notation system involving an external notation system that evolved from chironomy. Also called ekphonetic.
Estrangela	The original official script of the Syriac Christian parties. (See 'Garshuni'.)
expressions	In phonetic-based writing systems, the term refers to writing by utterance, that is, as spoken—inclusive of the clumping and spacing of spoken parsing rhythms. (See 'parsing rhythms'; 'utterances'; 'breathings'.)
flourish	The upwards tilt or "flip" at the end of a hasta or finishing stroke. (See 'hasta'.)
fonts	The mutation of a script: Scripts are the class. There are thousands of fonts, but only four scripts in Latin and two in Hebrew.
Fourier transform	A mathematical technique devised by Baron Jean-Baptiste Fourier and used to solve boundary-value problems. Fourier transforms are used to convert wave forms to or from frequency and time domains. The results of orthonormalized Fourier coefficients are invariants. (See 'invariants'; 'orthonormalized'.)
frame	The minimum amount of white space surrounding a graphic symbol in order to separate one graph from another.
free	In formal or informal languages, combinations of symbols that occur separately, e.g. -er and -re are free expressions. (See 'bound expressions')

fricatives	Sounds made when the tongue, pressing against the hard palate or teeth, relaxes to permit some air to flow causing friction, that is, vibration, rubbing.
Futhark	The ethnic script held in common by the Germanic tribes.
Futhorc	The Anglo-Saxon expansion of the Common Germanic Futhark.
Garshuni	The official script of the Syriac Christian parties after the Moslem Conquest.
gloss	A word or words inserted between lines of a text or in the margins to explain a foreign, difficult, or uncommon word.
Gnostic	Refers to the early Christian parties who claimed special knowledge of the transcendental or spiritual realms; found mostly in Egypt. The name comes from Greek "gnosis," meaning "investigation" or "knowledge."
Gradual	In the Roman Mass, the Chant of the Proper, that is, texts that change from day to day.
gutturals	Phones sounded in the throat.
hasta	In paleography, the technical term used to refer to the cross-bar on, for example, an 'e'.
headline	In quattrolinear limit systems, the technical term for the *interior* upper limit of the writing space, that is, the height of an 'o'.
heteroousians	A Greek term meaning "different essences"; applies to early Christian parties who ascribed to this point of view.
Hexaplaric	A text that is translated from or related to the Greek text of Origen's *Hexapla*.
holster book	A narrow manuscript format used for books meant to fit into a pouch or sack for ease of transport.
homoousians	A Greek term meaning "same essence"; applies to early Christian parties who ascribed to this point of view.
homooiousians	A Greek term meaning "similar essence"; applies to early Christian parties who ascribed to this point of view.
ideographs	The systematically and automatically formed differences in the way a scribe writes a graph; the "signature" of a scribe.
incipit	The first line of an early text, usually written in a different font from the body of the text. Works were catalogued by incipits for nearly 4,000 years.
intervocalic	The technical term for a consonant sandwiched between two vowels.
in-text encoding	The technique of writing, for example, pronunciational or musical directions, into the text itself.
invariants	The unfluctuating portion of a written text. Invariants include the auctorial content and the relative amplitude, duration, and the frequency of the content as said by the author. (See also 'constant'.)
Introit	The first item in the proper of a mass. In Gregorian Chant services, and introit consists of an antiphon, verse, antiphon, verse, antiphon, *Gloria Patri* (Acclaim to the Father), and antiphon.
IPA	The International Phonetic Alphabet. The symbol-set used in articulative phonology and derived from study of the Old English alphabet.

kerning	In printing, kerning refers to the amount of overhang on a given graphic symbol. In handwritten documents, kerning refers to the amount of white space between graphic symbols beyond that of the normal frame. (See 'frame'.)
koine	A Greek term meaning "common tongue." Originally applied to the "vulgar" Greek used in the Ptolemaic Empire, the word extended to mean the common or inter-ethnic language used in a given area.
Law of Parsimony	A rule originally formulated based on scientific research, the Law of Parsimony states that a system or organism uses what is needed and no more. The Law of Parsimony has turned out to apply to all systems.
leading	Although somewhat of a misnomer for a handwritten document, the amount of space between the descender and ascender lines of text. In printing, the extra space beyond that of the shoulders in metal type produced by inserting thin strips of lead into the space, hence, the name leading (pronounced 'leding').
lenition	The technical term for the softening of a sound. The letter 'h' is frequently used to indicate this softening, as in 'Ogham', where the "h" is not sounded, but tells the speaker to soften the preceding 'g'.
letters	Letters are graphic mnemonics standing for the symbol-set of a writing system. (See 'symbol-set'; 'script'.)
ligatured	The technical term for symbols that are tied together.
limits	The framework, that is, the skeletal structure, of a writing system.
lobe	The technical term in paleography for the rounded part of an 'a'.
logograms	The technical term for abstracted images of, for example, a foot, to represent walking or standing.
lower limit	The outer bottom limit of the limit system used in a writing system.
majuscule	Bilinear scripts and fonts, that is, all capitals or upper case.
medallion	The technical term for a cameo picture or portrait; a type of illustration used in manuscripts.
medially	The technical term for a graph that appears in the middle of a word.
mensural base	In script design, the scale of a design as determined by the width of a given writing instrument and the graph 'o' ('ayin' in Semitic design) is the mensural base. (See 'minim'; 'o-base'.)
metaphorical categories	The technical term in the study of semantics for the class, or family, of a metaphor.
metaphoric trigger	The technical term in the study of semantics for a word that signals a change of conceptual domain. (See 'conceptual domain')
metallographic printing	A method of creating a relief (raised) plate from which to print a text. A set of dies, each a letter of the alphabet, is engraved in brass or bronze. Then the text is set by striking the dies, one by one, into a soft matrix. Finally, lead is poured over the surface of the prepared matrix and allowed to harden. The resulting relief plate is then used to print the page.

minim	The mensural base of all script design. A minim is the width of the upright stroke, whether long or short, as produced by a pen, stylus, quill, or for that matter, pixels on a monitor screen or as sent by a computer to a printer.
minuscule	Lower case graphic symbols. In antiquity, cursive scripts and fonts were written in all lower case, that is, all minuscule.
monograph	A monograph is graphic symbol that represents one phone.
monoline	Scripts written in a single line, that is, the thickness does not fluctuate as graphs are formed as opposed to scripts written in thick and thin lines.
monophysites	A Greek term meaning "single nature"; applies to early Christian parties who ascribed to this point of view.
monothelites	A Greek term meaning "dual nature-single will"; applies to early Christian parties who ascribed to this point of view.
monumentary script	An engraved or incised formal official script or font used on monuments.
morphologically determinate	Whether a phone is voiced or not, depends upon the *shape* of the utterance. This means that some phones are voiced when intervocalic, that is, between vowels, e.g. the vowels surrounding the 'f' in *ofer* determines from its morphology that the 'f' is voiced, that is pronounced as 'v'. (See 'voiced'.)
neume	A form of musical notation that derives from chironomy. The pre-cursors of modern notes.
o-base	The height and width of the minuscule graph 'o' in Latin and 'ayin' in Semitic scripts and fonts. The o-base determines the height of the upper limit of the central space in quattrolinear limit systems. The o-base also determines the standard amount of white space between expressions in phonetic based-systems and between words in semantic-based writing systems. (See 'mensural base.')
Ogham	The Old Irish writing system. Sometimes written as 'Ogam' or 'Og'am'.
oral cavity	The technical term for the mouth.
orthography	Spelling, how a word is spelled.
orthographic system	Of or pertaining to the spelling sub-system employed in a writing system.
orthogonal dimensions	Orthogonal dimensions lie at ninety degrees to one another. This means that any or all dimensions in an orthogonal system may act in concert, in partial conjunction, or individually. No single dimension is dependent upon the others.
orthonormalize	To straighten data to present relevant material at 90 $^{\circ}$ to each other. Orthonormalized data is independent, that is, each component can work together, in partial conjunction, or independently.
ostraca	The plural of ostracon; pieces of broken pottery used for writing just about everything from "refrigerator" notes to the death sentence in Athens of the 4th-century BCE. Although technically incorrect, the term has also been applied to any broken piece—stone or man made—containing some type of written record, e.g. the "Qumran ostracon" is a fill-in-the-blanks legal form written in ink on stone with part of the left-hand side broken off.

palatal phones	Sounds made when the tongue presses against the upper palate or roof of the oral cavity (mouth).
parsing rhythms	The basic speech rhythms of a language which permit a hearer to parse speech, that is, to separate and distinguish grammatical elements and semantic segments when words are spoken. Sometimes referred to as speech rhythm, tone of voice, or paralanguage, parsing rhythms are actually the music of a language.
parties	The different religious groups existing during the Early Christian period did not refer to themselves as "sects"; they called themselves "parties"—with the same meaning as modern political parties.
phonemic	A sound that is an integral part of the phonetic structure of a language is called phonemic. In quantitative languages, quantity, that is, the length of a phone is phonemic. In stress languages, the correct amount of stress or accent on a given syllable is phonemic.
phonetic-based	A writing system designed to communicate the spoken word. The product of phonetic-based writing systems is the equivalent of a visual tape-recording.
phonology	The study of vocal sounds, that is, how phones are sounded in a language.
pictographs	Pictographs are simple outline pictures reputed to represent "words."
pith	The inner layers of the papyrus plant. The plant is a water reed with stalks or stems that can be as much as 8 to 10 feet in height. Papyrus leaves are made by peeling off layers of the pith.
psaltery	A stringed instrument played by being held against the chest.
pseudepigraphy	Works written by others in the name of a known authority.
quality	Quality is the individual and distinctive sound of a phone.
Qumran	One of the numerous sites in the Judean Hills where scrolls and other records from around the 6th-century BCE to the 2nd-Century CE were found.
quantitative language	A quantitative language is one in which quantity, the length of a sound, is phonemic, that is, an integral part of the language. Modern French is classified as a quantitative language.
quantity	Quantity is the amount of time a sound is held.
quattrolinear	Writing limits consisting of four lines. Quattrolinear limits are trilinear limits moved downwards to the central space to accommodate ascenders, that is, the upper extension on, for example, a 'd'.
quire	A gathering (or booklet) of folded leaves to make a section of a book. Today the technical term for a quire is a signature.
redundancy	Constructive repetition in fields a known source to compare with the unknown, a necessary check on the unknown. The Rosetta Stone is trilingual with the same text inscribed in Hieroglyphics, Hieratic, and Demotic, thus the constructive repetition that supplied a key to deciphering hieroglyphics.
renovatio	The term used for the retroversion of a writing system to some presumed ancient standard. (See 'classicization'.)

repercussives	In Gregorian Chant studies, the technical term for members of the *strophicus* family.
Saints' Lives	A literary genre, specifically the stereotyped hagiographical stories about Christian Saints.
sans serif	French for "without serif," that is, without the little finishing strokes on, for example, an 'm' or a 'l'.
schwa	The amount of "blur" on a vowel. The central vowel sound; that is, the vowel in question is neither clear nor muddy.
script	A script is the graphic representation of the symbol-set of a writing system. These graphic representations are commonly referred to as 'letters'. Script is the class from which all fonts, that is, mutations of the class, are derived. Latin fonts descend from four and only four scripts: Roman Capitals, African Rustic Capitals, Roman half-uncial, and African half-uncial. All Hebrew fonts are descendants of two scripts: Paleo-Hebraic and "Aramaic" business scripts.
script design	The art of constructing and balancing a font to work in concert with the components of a complete writing system.
script system	The sub-system consisting of the graphic representations of the symbol set sub-system. Script systems are variables.
selective destruction	A procedure that involves picking among works and destroying those that contradict this desired history.
semantic-based	A writing system designed to communicate data.
semantic units	Individual words. Semantic units are the segments that contain the sense or meaning of the graphic symbols. (See 'semantic-based'.)
serif	Technically, the finishing stroke on a graph, such as the line across the bottom of an 'l'. All serifs descend from the Cuneiform wedge and identify a script or font as having official or authoritative status.
scripto continuo	Text written in a continuous stream. (See 'breathings'.)
sound	The differences among vocalizations of an author's text when read aloud. Sound is the variable part of speech that cannot be recorded in a written record.
source language	The technical term used in translation studies to refer to the language in which a text is originally written.
space curve	The technical term for the multidimensional aspects of spoken language. Speech is three dimensional. Sounds may recede or advance, may be short, or long, voiced or unvoiced or mute, and each sound has a distinct quality. (See 'quality'.)
staggering technique	A technique designed for the production of a work by scribal teams taking dictation meant to blur the slight differences between scribal hands. At the beginning of a new job, each scribe takes a turn writing one and a quarter to one and half lines creating an overlap. After this, the scribes take turns writing short stints in an order different from the openers.

stops	Sounds made when the tongue cuts off the air stream, stopping the sound.
stress	The amount of volume allotted to a given sound as spoken.
stress language	A language in which the stress on a given syllable is phonemic, that is, an integral part of the language. English is a stress language.
syllabary	A writing system whose symbol-set consists of syllables, that is, each symbol stands for one consonant plus an associated vowel phone.
syllabograms	A single syllable graphic symbol, syllabograms are the consonant plus vowel mnemonic system used as the symbol-set of a syllabary.
symbol-set system	A finite set of constants: the set of symbols used in a writing system. Symbol-set systems are commonly referred to as letters.
symbol-style	Symbol style is a variable; it is the form of a given symbol as determined by a font design.
system design	The deliberate construction of a framework within which the listed components function.
system performance	The application of a system design as accomplished by the appropriate trained personnel.
target language	The technical term used in translation studies to refer to the language into which a text is being translated.
tetragrammaton	The Greek term for the four symbols used in Hebrew to refer to God (YHVH).
The technique	A technique that is used to create an illusion or aura of single or monolithic identity.
titulus	This is the technical term in Latin liturgical studies for the explanatory remark that appears at the head of a psalm describing what is occurring and why the psalm is written.
tokens	The oldest known form of bookkeeping and fraud prevention, 'tokens' are flattened clay pieces shaped so as to represent items of trade.
trilinear	Trilinear writing limits have three positions: upper limit, central space, and lower limit. (See also bilinear and quattrolinear)
triliterals	Languages in which the roots of words are represented by three consonants. Vowels are not part of the root word.
uni-colon	A line with a central caesura, or pause.
unvoiced	The sounds made when the vocal cords in the throat do not vibrate.
upper limit	The outer top limit of the limit system used in a writing system.
utterances	The terms refers to words as 'uttered', that is, as spoken. (See 'expressions'.)
variables	A variable, by definition, keeps the same meaning throughout any one context.
variants	In writing systems, the sub-sets of a set of a symbol, for example, ɑ, ɑ, ɑ. In textual studies, the alternate words or orthographic differences that vary from copy to copy of a text.
voice	The spoken words as dictated or written by the author. Voice is the invariant part of a text that can be captured in a written record. (See 'invariants'.)

voiced	The sound made when the vocal cords in the throat vibrate.
volume	Volume is the loudness of a given phone as spoken. Volume may also be referred to as stress. (See 'stress'.)
vowel pair	A diphthong, that is, a pair of vowels said as a glide where one of the pair is more stressed then the other. Vowel pairs may have stress on first member or second member.
WSOP	Winner's Standard Operating Procedures, the techniques developed and used to censor and control the written word.
writing	The technology invented to record the spoken word.
writing cube	The ternary base of all phonetic-based writing systems. Speech is represented as separate segments as if on the faces of a cube. Stress is represented on the x-axis; duration on the y-axis, and the quality of the phone by its shape.
Writing system	"A set or assemblage of things connected, associated, or interdependent, so as to form a complex unity; a whole composed of parts in an orderly arrangement according to some scheme or plan." A complex unity composed of a finite number of sub-systems that work together to form the complete writing system. These sub-systems are: a finite symbol set; a prescribed graphic symbol set; writing limits, direction of writing, format, punctuation, orthographic, comprehension, and content systems.
xenographic exchange	The term means foreign graph exchange, that is, the use of Script B in a text written in Script A to indicate a distinction. The modern use of italics is an example of xenographic exchange.
Xylography	The art of printing from carved wood. e.g. a woodcut.
writing zone	The writing space, that is, the area within which one places the graphic representatives of a symbol-set.

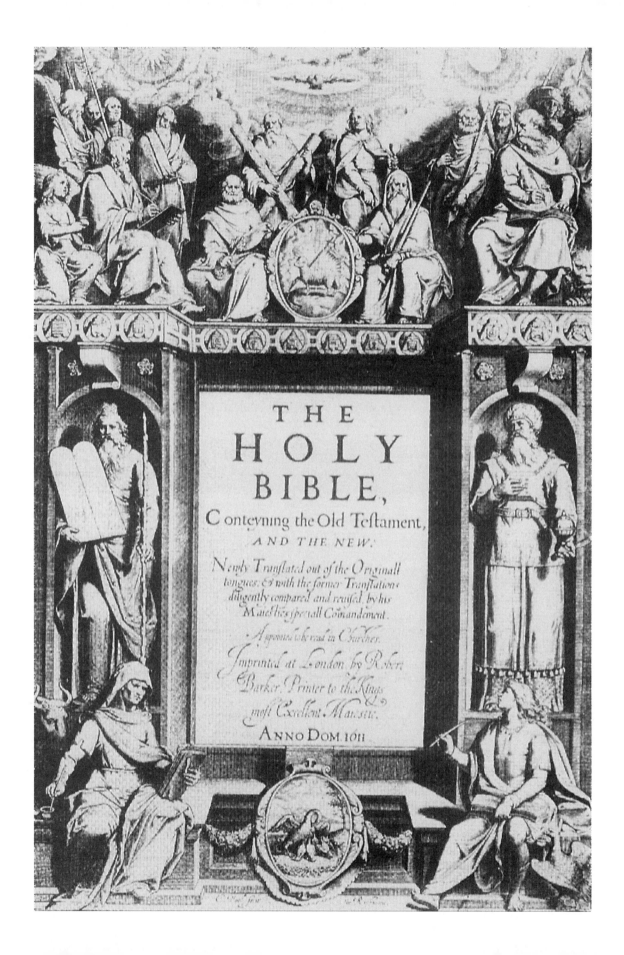

NOTES

Notes to the Introduction

1   The size of law codes for public display remained within these tight parameters. By the mid-second millennium, however, "double" clay tablets meant solely for internal use, such as tax records, appear. These double archival tablets are thick, very large, and written on both sides. they are also a two-man job to move around.

2   The familiar "block" structure, what today we call "justified text," descends from this ancient practice of filling a tablet from side-to-side. The purpose, though, is not merely to create a neat appearance. The complete filling of a tablet (or "justified" text), performs two functions. First and foremost, the block structure is designed to protect the integrity of an author's words. Any forgeries or other illegal insertions into a text are immediately obvious. The baking of tablets was both a preservative and a further anti-fraud technique; one cannot insert forged words into a baked tablet. The block technique was used on inscriptions as well. For rather obvious reasons, the fraud-prevention technique of the block structure was retained when clay was replaced by leather, parchment, papyrus, and paper. While in recent practice we find an increase in "ragged right-edge" documents, particularly in low quality books, until this century, such a ragged edge on a formal document (for example, a Medieval charter) is a dead-give away that the document is a forgery. To this day ragged edges are not permissible on a cash register tape, in any form of bookkeeping, in a covenant, or in any legal or official document; block text still functions as a fraud deterrent. Second, as a serendipitous side-effect, the block structure acts as the equivalent of a picture frame and helps the reader to keep his eyes within the reading area.

3   Leonard Bloomfield, *Language*. New York: Holt, Rinehart and Winston, 1933. 21. Nothing has changed across the past 70 years. In the *Blackwell Encyclopedia of Writing*, edited by Florian Coulmas (Oxford: Blackwell, 1996), writing is said to be "a set of visible or tactile signs used to represent language in a systematic way."

4   As John DeFrancis writes in the preface to his book, *Visible Speech: The Diverse Oneness of Writing Systems* (Honolulu: University of Hawaii Press, 1989), it is "simply intolerable that Chinese writing continues to be misrepresented as 'pictographic' . . .. It is also intolerable that the nature of writing—of all writing—continues to be misunderstood in large part because of the misrepresentation of Chinese" (xi).

5   Metrical scansion systems are linear; some are dreadfully complicated and tend, writes Bernard HuppÇ, "to suffer as hypotheses in being more complex than the material to be explained." (*The Web of Words: structural analyses of the old english poems vainglory, the wonder of creation, the dream of the rood, and judith*. Albany, NY: State University of New York Press, 1970). cf 1, xiv.

6   F. Katamba discusses the concept of nonlinear phonology in chapters 9-11 of his *An introduction to phonology*. (London: Longman, 1989). Roger Lass offers a concise discussion of the subject in Chapter 4, "Suprasegmentals," of his *Old English: A historical linguistic companion*. (Cambridge: Cambridge University Press, 1994.)

7.   John Julian lists 326 attempts between 1414 and 1889, either partial or whole, to translate the Psalter into metrical English. See *A Dictionary of Hymnology*. Vol. II. New York: Dover, 2nd Edition, Revised, 1987. This list, of course, excludes the Old English translation, but does include the early fourteenth-century translation by Rolle. See also, Henry Glass *The story of the Psalters; a history of the metrical versions of Great Britain and America from 1549 to 1885*. London, K. Paul, Trench, 1888.

Notes to Chapter 1

1 Speech is necessarily metaphorical and never the "thing" itself. Metaphor is not just for poets. For a good introduction to the importance of metaphor in everyday life, see George Lakoff and Mark Johnson, *Metaphors We Live By*. Chicago and London: University of Chicago Press, 1980.

2 For an accessible translation of Aristotle on memory, see, *De Memoria*, Translated and with notes by Richard Sorabji. London: Duckworth, 1972. Chapter I, 450b 11-20. 50-51.

3 *Quid enim aliud litterae scriptae quam se ipsas oculis et praeter se voces animo ostendunt?* Augustine, *De dialectica*, v. 11.

4 *Litterae autem sunt indices rerum, signa verborum, quibus tanta vis est, ut nobis dicta absentium sine voce loquantur.* (W[illiam] M. Lindsay, ed. Isidore of Seville, *Etymologiae*. 2 vols, Oxford: Clarendon, 1911) Book i, Chapter 3, lines 6-8.

5 *Littere autem, id est figure, primo vocum indices sunt . . . et frequenter absentium dicta sine voce loquuntur.* John of Salisbury, *Metalogicon*. Editor, Clement C. J. Webb, Oxford: Oxford University Press, 1929. Book I, Chapter 13.

6 ñlfric. *Grammatica Latino-Saxonica*, ed. William Somners. Oxford, 1659. Reprt. Menston: Scolar Press, 1970. 2-3. ñlfric also wrote a *Colloquy*, a question and answer text between a master and students, as a guide to learning how to pronounce Latin.

7 Albertus Magnus, *Opera Omnia* [Complete Works]. August Borgnet, ed. Paris: Ludovicum Vives, 1890. Vol. 9. tract II, cap. I. 107-108.

8 *Nisi enim ab homine memoria teneantur soni, pereunt, quia scribi non possum.* Isidore, *Etymologiae* III, xv.

Notes to Chapter 2

1 For literacy mandated by law, see *The Anchor Bible Dictionary* (ABD), New York: Doubleday, 1992, under "Hammurabi," or David Diringer, *The Hand-Produced Book* (New York, 1948).

2 For Knuth's work on designing a computer font creation application, see Donald Ervin. Knuth, *METAFONT: the program*. Reading, Mass.: Addison Wesley, 1986. For a description of the complexities of scripts and their design, as well as the difficulties one faces when attempting to develop a computerized universal font creation application, see, Douglas R. Hofstadter, "Metafont, Metathematics, and Metaphysics," in *Metamagical Themas: Questing for the Essence of Mind and Pattern*. New York: Basic Books, Inc. 1985.

3 For a concise description of the Ugaritic Language, see the *ABD* under "Languages," Vol. 4, 227 ff.

4 For a basic introduction to the characteristics of the Phoenician language, see the *ABD*, Vol. 4, 222 ff.

5 See Christopher De Hamel, *Scribes and Illuminators*. London: British Museum Press, 1992. 21.

6 Early churches are long and narrow with an "arched" roof, or tunnel arch, running the length of the building. The ancient Church of the "Scintillating One" in Halandri, Greece, (located behind the new, Byzantine style church) is a fine example of such a church. This type of construction is typical of the Cyclades style churches. As the construction emulates ancient Mesopotamian standard architecture, architecural archaeologists surmise that the ancient house of god type buildings also were roofed with a tunnel-arch, that is, a long dome roof. As none of the existing structures have retained their roofs, however, this will have to remain in the realm of reasonable conjecture.

7 The stele of Naram-Sin is in the Louvre Museum, Paris, France.

8 The stylized "cloud" arch can be seen on, for example, Laurentian Library, Florence, Cod Plu. I.56 and MS 16, in the Chester Beatty Library.

9 British Library Inscription 441. (BL I.441)

10 This stele is in the courtyard of the Museum at Manisa, Italy.

11   Saint Mary's, the Anglo-Norman church at Iffley near Oxford, England is a classic example of this type of arch-within-an-arch design.

12   The main entry to Notre Dame de Paris is a classic example of the round-topped Gothic entry arches.

13   The Persian arch combines the "cloud" arch with the "pointed" arch. A minaret is a "high place" with an in-the-round Persian-style "cloud" arch on topjzja stylized adaptation of the stele of Naram-Sin. The mosques themselves are the shape of "The" Law. As has been noted, writing systems are unbelievably conservative.

Notes to Chapter 3:

1   See Larissa Bonfante, ed., *Etruscan Life and Afterlife*, Detroit: 1986 for details on the Etruscans. For a discussion of the language, see Giuliano Bonfante and Larissa Bonfante, *The Etruscan Language*, Manchester: Manchester University Press: 1983.

2   Greek "suspended" symbols are so well known among Greek paleographers as to be mentioned in passing in articles written for encyclopedias. For an overview of Greek palaeography, see Eric G. Turner. *Greek Manuscripts of the Ancient World* (Oxford: OUP, 1971).

3   For the use of red Ink points as word dividers and as titles in Akkadian and Egyptian Literary Texts, see Anne F. Robertson, *Word Dividers, Spot Markers and Clause Markers in Old Assyrian, Ugaritic, and Egyptian Texts*. Dissertation, New York University, November 1993. (University Microfilms, No. 9422934). Robertson also has an illustrated web site discussing the subject. This may be found at http://soho.ios.com/~arobe/grphterm.html

4   The fight on customs and observance among the assorted factions was (and is) an ongoing affair. Cambridge University Library, T-S NS 275.27 [Taylor-Schechter Cairo Genizah, 9th century], is a propaganda sheet from the Yeshiva [Rabbinical Institute] at Sura to the people in Maghreb attempting to persuade the Maghrebis to adopt the Bavli [Sura and Pumbedita], or Sephardic traditions, rather than the Yerushalmi [Jerusalem], or essentially Ashkenazic [European], traditions. Each faction, of course, used its own Font of the "official" script.

5   The cuneiform wedge is the starting stroke of the wet surface writing technique used in cuneiform writing. As the cuneiform wedge was the mark of an official or authoritative script or font, it was incorporated into all Western Official script and font designs. (See also p.38, and Glossary.)

6   The format shows that the fragments of the MT in Paleo-Hebraic, the five books of the Pentateuch and the Book of Job, were written down from inscriptions [for example, 11Q1[PaleoLev], most likely from tablets affixed to a wall. [In the courtyard of the Temple? At the Sanhedrin [Judicial court]? The "antique" font may also point to an early date. There is a distinct possibility that these fragments may even be pre-exilic, i.e. 7th century BCE. [The scrolls Jeremiah took with him?]

Notes to Chapter 4

1   Early Christian history is the subject of an immense body of literature, both exegetical and hermeneutical. For a more recent survey, see David Noel Freedman, Editor-in-chief. *The Anchor Bible Dictionary*. (6 vols.) New York: Doubleday, 1992.

2   Perhaps the best biography on Origen is Henri Crouzel's *Origen,*; translated by A. S. Worrall. Edinburgh: T. & T. Clark, 1989. For a comparison of the different approaches, see Peter Gorday, "Principles of patristic exegesis: Romans 9-11," *in Origen, John Chrysostom, and Augustine*. New York: E. Mellen Press, 1983.

3   See Stanley Morison, *Politics and Script: Aspects of authority and freedom in the development of Greco-Latin script from the sixth century B.C. to the twentieth century A.D. The Lyell Lectures 1957. Edited and completed by Nicolas Barker* (Oxford: Clarendon Press, 1972). Italo Gallo, in his introduction to the study of papyri, sounds very wistful

when he remarks on the diversity of sizes even among formulaic documents. See, Maria Rosaria Falivene, Jennifer R. March trs., Italo Gallo. *Greek and Latin Papyrology* (London: 1986) for further information on the subject. Note that in areas where the profession of scribe and the art of calligraphy has never been conflated, people are aware of the use of script as power. See Richard Curt Kraus, *Brushes with power: modern politics and the Chinese art of calligraphy.* (Berkeley, University of California Press, 1991.)

4   See the *Discoveries in the Judean Desert* series (Oxford: Clarendon Press, 1962- forward).

5   Diplomatic editions were not only discouraged. Between the 12th and 16th centuries, along with translations into the vernaculars, multiple-editions were considered heretical.

6   A short discussion of these scripts, sub-scripts, and symbol sets may be found in David Diringer, *The Alphabet: A Key to the History of Mankind.* London: Hutchinson. 3rd ed.1968. 2 Vols. Vol. 1, 218-229.

7   For a discussion of the literally concrete evidence about the languages and scripts of Syria, see: Michael H. Dodgeon and Samuel N. C. Lieu, eds. *The Roman Eastern Frontier and the Persian Wars (A.D. 226-363): A Documentary History.* London: Routledge, 1991.

8   See *The Jewish War, and other Selections from Flavius Josephus.* Trans. H. St. J. Thackeray and Ralph Marcus. New York: Washington Square, 1965. Book 1:3.

9   It has usually been accepted that the vernacular of the African Jews was Latin. The Alexandrian community clearly spoke Greek, but evidence that the African community used either Greek or Latin is sparse. The monolithic approach is under dispute, a common situation in Religious studies—and one which need not be gone into here.

10   At least four isotopic studies have been done on tin. Three of these studies came to the conclusion that tin isoptopes can be distinguished as to place of origin. One study cautiously stated that, while it can be difficult to distinguish the isotopic profiles of Iberian and Cornish tin, the profiles of tin from Eastern sources do not coincide with either. Another study, the English one, is currently under dispute.

Modern extraction techniques permit relatively low grade ore to be processed; the Iberian deposit on the coast of Portugal is once again in operation. The Cornish tin deposit, however, was very big; it finally was depleted during the 19th century CE. For nearly 4500 years, whoever held Cornwall, held a near monopoly on an essential ore.

11   The ancient town of Akrotiri on Thera (Santorini) was buried under volcanic ash in 1500 BCE. Many of the well preserved materials from the excavations may be seen at the Archaeological Museum in Athens—including the wall paintings. The war vessels do not have a reinforced prow and do not have what a millenium later became normal on war craft: a ram. Incidentally, the volcano is still active.

12   The name of the vessel indicates its association with ore cargoes. The name comes from a root (Tav-Shin-Shin) which in Akkadian meant "to melt" or "to smelt," and in Hebrew, "clods or heaps of earth." For further information, see, the *Anchor Bible Dictionary*, under "Tarshish."

13   Iberian is not fully understood; it appears to have been related to Basque. Punic is a Semitic language and a very close relative of Hebrew, Moabite, and Aramean.

14   For an overview of Montanism, see the *Anchor Bible Dictionary*, "Montanus, Montanism," Vol. 4, 898-902.

15   The implication of the size of the *Vaticanus* is that the words are inscribed in stone. For further information on the format of the *Vaticanus*, see R. I. Altman, "Report on the Zoilos Votive Inscription from Tel-Dan." *Abstracts and Papers.* 2001. < http://ORION@mscc.huji.ac.il/orion/programs/Altman/Altman00.shtml >

16   Each graphic symbol has a "frame," the white space around it. What we are looking at, however, is the white space *between* symbols. There is no paleographic term to describe this area. In printing, the term "kerning" means the amount of overhang of a graphic symbol; by definition, this overhang intrudes upon the frame of the next graph. "Kerning" accurately describes this area between frames. The technical term existed long before the field of modern paleography came into being; we need not invent a new term.

17   A consolidated font is a script design that merges elements from different official ethnic scripts into a combined official voice. The merger of Hebrew Square Script with Paleo-Hebraic that appears in 11QPs, the Psalm scroll from Cave 11 among the DSS, is one example of a consolidated font; another is the Constantine uncial.

The exact opposite of a consolidated font is a conglomerate font. In a conglomerate font, we find graphs from different ethnic fonts used *indiscriminately* in one document, even in one word. This is the equivalent of writing, for example, ∏Ruℰ instead of "true." While today graphic artists sometimes use conglomerates to create special effects, prior to the twentieth century the appearance of a conglomerate font in a document is *prima facia* evidence that the document is a forgery.

18   E[ric] G. Turner. *Greek Manuscripts of the Ancient World.* (Oxford: OUP, 1971). 20. Every one of Turner's examples includes the statement "essentially bilinear" followed by a list of the exceptions to the "bilinear rule."

19   By late in the 4th century, Latin documents of the Alexandrian-Roman parties use the Imperial broad column format for official Biblical texts.

20   Timothy John Finney reported to the tc (text critical) list on the work he has been doing with computers, manuscripts, and data matrices. He transcribed all of the papyrus and uncial manuscripts of the Letter to the Hebrews. Then he wrote a program that collated them all with each other to create a data matrix. He then separated textual from spelling variants. This separation produced two matrices per document: one of spelling variants and one of textual variants. Finney next ran them through a procedure known as classical scaling (a multivariate analysis procedure) that plots each document as a single point on a two-dimensional map. As he stated, "In my opinion, the groups observed in the spelling variation maps (and they are definite groups—not just a random spread) are related to localitites." He concluded that the mapping displays three main groups which he *tentatively* associates with Egypt, Palestine, and Constantinople/Antioch. He also stated the maps indicate that Sinaiticus, Alexandrinus, Vaticanus, and Claromontanus all are neighbours of P46 and P13 (these latter are non-codex papyri); "that is, they were all written in Egypt." <tc-list@shemesh.scholar.emory.edu>, Thu, 4 Feb 1999.

21   An attempt has been made to give the more accessible source or sources for the reader who wants to see the material. The C. Antonius Rufus inscription may be found in Diringer, *Alphabet*, 22.8a, Vol. 2.

22   The Election notice from Pompeii may be seen in Morison, *Politics*, Fig. 35.

23   Constantine's Arch, a massive construction, may be seen in Morison, *Politics*, Fig. 37.

24   A photograph of Vatican, MS. lat. 3256 may be seen in Morison, *Politics*, Fig. 38.

25   A portion of a leaf from the Codex Sangellensis is given in Morison, *Politics*, Fig. 39.

26   BL, Papyrus 229. See, Michelle P. Brown. *A Guide to Western Historical Scripts from Antiquity to 1600.* Toronto: University of Toronto Press, 1990, Pl. 3.

27   For photographs, see, Diringer, *Alphabet*, Pl. 22.15.

28   Diringer, *Alphabet*, Vol. 2, Number 22.9b, gives a variety of 1st-century Roman cursive scripts from Pompeii and Alburnus.

29   The oldest dated example of the use of epsilon-*e* is the Elephantine Skolia, dated to 284/3 BCE (Berlin, Staatliches Museum, P. Berol. 13270, Morison, *Politics*, Fig. 14). As Morison comments, the book script used on the 88 CE papryus from Fayoum containing "a cessation of land" is formal, "but not official" (Morison, *Politics*, 13-14, Pl. 11).

30   The Hawara fragment is at the British Library, numbered Oxy. i. 20. A photograph appears in Morison, *Politics*, Pl. 12.

31   For an example of the spacing in documentary cursive texts, see Morison, *Politics*, Fig. 13, Oxford, Bodleian, Gr[eek]. class C 21 [P], an Official letter with regard to the sale of oil.

32   For examples of the "everyday script," see Morison, *Politics*, Pl. 45.

33   See, Brown, *Guide*, Pl. 8.

34   See Brown, *Guide*, Pl. 30.

35   For examples of the rounded forms, see Morison, *Politics*, Chapter 2, Figures 44, 45 and 46.

36   Morison's Figure 47 is an illustration of the *Vocontio* Stele symbols (Timgad, Algeria, circa iii 2). Photographs of the Vocontio may be seen also in C.I.L. (viii, 17910) or in C.L.A. No. XI, viii.

37   See Morison, *Politics*, page 58 and forward, for a discussion of the political aspects of the new official script.

38   For a thorough discussion on the elements of the new Uncial script, see above, Morison, *Politics*.

39   By the late fourth century, a system of punctuation begins to appear in secular texts. The fifth century Biblioteca Medicea-Laurenziana, MS 39. 1, a copy of Virgil's *Aeneid*, is written in Book Rustic and employs high, medial,

and low points. The system of punctuation appears to be a mixture of the *distinctiones* described in Donatus's 4th century Latin grammar and the old Phoenician three point system (high, medial, and low points). A photograph of this MS may be found in Pl. 2 of M[alcolm] B. Parkes's *Pause and Effect: An Introduction to the History of Punctuation in the West.* Aldershot, Hants: Scolar, 1992.

40   E. A. Lowe, *Codices Latini Antiquiores: A Palaeographical Guide to Latin Manuscripts prior to the Ninth Century. Supplement.* Oxford: Clarendon, 1971, p. viii.

41   See C. A. Ralegh Radford, "The Archaeological Background on the Continent," in *Christianity in Britain, 300-700: Papers presented to the Conference in Roman and Sub-Roman Britain held at the University of Nottingham 17-20 April 1967.* Edited M. W. Barley and R. P. C. Hanson. (Leicester: Leicester University Press, 1968). 19-36. For the Syriac influence on the clubbing in the Luxeuil script, see Morison, *Politics,* 1972. 116.

42   For a discussion of the Carian syllabaries of the Iberian Peninsula, see Chapter 4 of Martin Bernal's *Cadmean Letters: The Transmission of the Alphabet to the Aegean and Further West before 1400 BC.* Winona Lake: Eisenbrauns, 1990. Bernal reviews scholarly discussions on the topic, as well as providing illustrations and tables.

43   The older script systems on the Iberian Peninsula divided into eastern and southern; the new Christian script systems show an east-west division. See, Bernal, *Cadmean,* Chapter 4.

44   The older form of musical notation employed only the ancient Semitic hand-signal neumes and appeared throughout the Anglo-Saxon sphere of influence. The enhanced form included external notation and incorporated neumes into the graphic symbols themselves. See Chapter 10, "To Sing A New Song," for further information.

Notes to Chapter 5

1   See Dodgeon and Lieu, *Roman Eastern Frontier.*

2   For more information on clubbing, see Morison, *Politics,* 116. "Clubbing," a term coined by Maunde Thompson, accurately describes the shape of the "candlestick" *lamed* used in the Dead Sea Scrolls.

3   For more information on the Syrian presence in and around Orleans, see Morison, *Politics,* 117 and forward. The major source for information on the Syriac parties and the Syrian presence in Western Europe can be found in the works of Louis Brehier

4   See Morison, *Politics,* 217 for a discussion of the Palmyrene-Latin inscription at South Shields. For an illustration of the stele, see David Diringer, *Alphabet,* Vol. 2.

5   Johann Blumenbach (1752-1840) came up with the name "Caucasian" to refer to the "white" race—as the "finest skull," and hence "the most superior species," in his collection came from the area between the Caspian and Black Seas. Although still used as a "popular" term, anthropologists during the 1930's and 1940's divided the human species into three races: white (Mediterranean, Alpine, Nordic), yellow-bronze (Mongoloid, Malay, and American Indian), and Black (Negrito, Negrillo, Bushman, Melanesian Negro, Australian and African negro).

6   The evidence on the extremely high cultural level of the British is turning up on stones inscribed in Inscriptional Old Celtic (IOC) and in surviving letters and compositions. For just a fraction of this information, see: David R. Howlett, *Liber Epistolarum Sancti Patricii Episcopi: The book of Letters of Saint Patrick the Bishop,* 1994; *The Celtic Latin Tradition of Biblical Style,* 1995; *British Books in Biblical Style,* 1997; *Cambro-Latin Compositions: Their Competence and Craftsmanship,* 1998, all from Four Courts Press, Dublin, Ireland. For their knowledge of Hebrew, see Howlett, "Israelite Learning in Insular Latin," *Peritia: The Journal of the Medieval Academy of Ireland,* No. 11 (1997), pages 117-152. For their knowledge of Greek, see Howlett, "Hellenic Learning in Insular Latin," *Peritia,* No. 12, 1998; "Seven Studies in Seventh-Century Texts," *Peritia,* No. 10, pages 1-70; and "Five Experiments in Textual Reconstruction and Analysis," *Peritia,* No. 9, 1995, pages 1-50. For inscriptions, see, Charles Thomas, *Christian Celts: Messages and Images.* Stroud, Gloucester: Tempus, 1998. Arguments that Brittonic was a written language before the 6th century appears in works by John T. Koch; more by Howlett and Thomas was scheduled for release in 1999-2001.

7   For proof, from another direction, that the British shared their knowledge with their neighbors, see Chapter 10, "To Sing A New Song."

8   Robert Alexander Stewart Macalister's, *Corpus Inscriptionum Insularum Celticarum* (Dublin, Ireland: Four Courts Press, reprinted, 1996) contains a collection of over 1,000 Celtic related inscriptions to be found in Ireland and Britain. Among these are hundreds of Ogham stones from Ireland.

9   For Patrick's own statements, see Howlett, *Liber Epistolarum Sancti Patricii Episcopi: The book of Letters of Saint Patrick the Bishop,* 1994. For further reference, see the Foreword by Thomas A. Finnegan, Bishop of Killala in, *Patrick the Pilgrim Apostle of Ireland, St. Patrick's Confessio and Epistola.* Edited and Translated with Analysis and Commentary by Ma'ire B. de Paor PBVM. Dublin: Veritas, 1998. 1-2.

10   See Wendy Davies, "The Myth of the Celtic Church," in *The Early Church in Wales and the West: Recent work in Early Christian Archaeology, History and Place-Names,* (Oxford: Oxbow Monograph 16, 1992).

11   See R. G. Collingwood and R. P. Wright, *Roman Inscriptions of Britain.* (Oxford: Clarendon, 1965).

12   For further information about tin and ñlfred, see J. R. Maddicot, "Trade, Industry and the Wealth of King Alfred," in *Past and Present: Journal of Historical Studies.* May 1, 1989, no. 123, 3-44.

13   For recent discussions of the Anglo-Saxon foundations underlying the Anglo-Norman Cathedral at Canterbury, England, see, Kevin Blockley's article in *Current Archaeology,* No. 136, Nov. 1993.

14   See, Bede, *Historia,* Book I, Ch. 27: Gregory's answer to Augustine's 7th question about what to do about the British bishops.

15   For Augustine's inept handling of the British Christians, see Bede, *Historia,* Book II, Chapters, 2 and 3.

16   For a good discussion of the Germanic and English Runic writing system, see R. I. Page, *Introduction to English Runes.* London: Metheun & Co., Ltd., 1973.

17   For the specific meaning of *charaxare,* see M. Herren, "Insular Latin C(h)araxare (Craxare) and its derivatives," *Peritia* 1, 1982, 273-77. For a discussion of the distinction between the physical act of writing and the mental act of writing (composition), see M. Richter, *The Formation of the Medieval West: Studies in the Oral cultures of the Barbarians,* (Dublin: Four Courts, 1994). 50 ff.; or Michael Clanchy, *From Memory to Written Record: England, 1066-1307.* (Cambridge, MA: Harvard University Press, 1979). 97 ff.

18   Clanchy devotes all of Chapter 8 of his *From Memory to Written Record* to the oral aspect of English Law and to the need to both hear and see legal documents (1979). See also Stanley B. Greenfield and Daniel G. Calder, *A New Critical History of Old English Literature* (New York" NYU Press, 1986), Chapter 4 for a discussion of the oral law.

19   See Roscoe Pound *The History and the System of the Common Law* (Volume I of the National Law Library) for a discussion of the basis of common law.

20   For illustrations of such "nonlinear" hierarchical trees, see Roger Lass, *Old English: A historical linguistic companion,* (Cambridge: Cambridge University Press, 1994); or F. Katamba, *An introduction to phonology,* (London: Longman, 1989).

21   For Isidore's comment on the distinction between voice and sound, see Chapter 1, p. 3.

Notes to Chapter 6

1   For a discussion of the sphere of influence of *scriptoria* (writing rooms) in general, see Hanoch Avenary, *Studies in the Hebrew, Syrian and Greek Liturgical Recitative,* (Tel-Aviv: Israel Institute of Music, 1963).

2   For a discussion of the sphere of influence of monastic *scriptoria,* see, Solange Corbin. "Die Neumen," in *Palaeographie der Musik,* (Köln: Arno Volk, 1979). No. 3.

3   For a discussion of the sphere of influence of a *scriptorium* as well as its decline, see R[osamund] McKitterick, *The Carolingians and the Written Word,* (Cambridge: Cambridge University Press, 1989).

4   Jerome translated the Psalter three times. The first translation is known as the *Vulgate* (*Gallican*), the second as the *Romanum*, and the third, because it was translated from Hebrew, as the *Hebraicum*.

5   For a concise summary of the arguments with respect to *The Cathach* as an autograph copy, see Morison, *Politics*, 152-4.

6   For a thorough discussion of Psalter *Tituli*, see Dom Pierre Salmon, *Les "Tituli Psalmorum" des Manuscrits Latins*, (Roma: Libreria Vaticana, 1959).

7   The *practice* of abbreviation follows the Hebrew tradition. However, the *origin* of the Greek *Kurios* is a hotly debated question among scholars.

8   A photograph of the large Psalm scroll (DSS [Qumran], Cave 11, Psalms—Q11Ps) is included in J. A. Sanders, *The Dead Sea Psalms Scroll,* (Ithaca, NY: Cornell University Press, 1967).

9   Due to the problems of translation, the Latin collapses two verses into one here. *Pacem* is the beginning of another colon when sung.

10   A complete facsimile of the *Bangor Collectarium* is available, but not readily accessible. For a complete photograph of folio 8v of the *Bangor Collectarium*, see William M. Lindsay, *Early Irish Minuscule Script*, (Oxford: James Parker and Co. 1910) (Rprt. Hildesheim: Georg Olms, 1971. No. 1.)

11   Adamnan's reforms, enacted at the Council of Birr in County Offaly, included provisions that women were to be exempted from serving in wars and that women, children, and clerics were not to be taken prisoners or slaughtered.

12   See Lindsay, *Early Irish*, No. 3, for a photograph of folio 108 of the *Schaffhausen Adamnan*. A much smaller photograph of a leaf can be seen in Morison, *Politics*, 167. Unfortunately, the latter does not include an example of Dorbbene's unusual *ae*-ligature.

13   For a summation of the evidence as to York's importance as a center of learning in the 8th century, see Dorothy Whitelock, *The Audience of Beowulf*, (Oxford: Clarendon Press, 1951). 100-101.

14   ᚠᚱᚫᚷᚾᚪᛚᚪᛖᚻ is the way the place name is written in The *Moore* manuscript of Bede's *Historia*.

15   See. Dӧibhi O Croinin, "Is the Augsburg Gospel Codex a Northumbrian Manuscript?", in *St. Cuthbert, His Cult and His Community to AD 1200*, edited by Gerald Bonner and others (Woodbridge: Boydell, 1989), 189-201.

16   For a photograph of the complete folio 39b of the *Willibrord Kalendar*, see James Campbell, Eric John, and Patrick Wormald. *The Anglo-Saxons*, (Ithaca, NY: Cornell University Press, 1982).

17   See Avenary, *Liturgical Recitative,* for a discussion of the "individual solutions" found by each church and each synagogue.

Notes to Chapter 7

1   As the ancients were aware of the origin of the collection of letter symbols moderns call an alphabet, the question would not have arisen at the time. Herodotus specifically relates the Phoenician origin of the Greek alphabet in Book 5, 58-59 of his *Histories*. English: see, *Herodotus: The Histories*. Aubrey de Sîlincourt, trans. Rev. Ed. (Harmondsworth, Middlesex: Penguin, 1978).

2   Bloomfield, *Language*, 1933. 21. see, Note 1, Introduction.

3   See David Diringer, *Alphabet*, Vol. 1, 12.

4   For a discussion of the symbols of a writing system, see, Joseph R. Schoenfeld. *Mathematical Logic*, (Reading, MA: Addison-Wesley, 1967). 3.

5   See Chapter 2 under "A-ness."

6   For a photograph of the original document, see *The Pastoral Care: King Ælfred's Translation of St. Gregory's Regula Pastoralis*. MS. Hatton 20 in the Bodleian Library at Oxford. N. R. Ker, ed. (Copenhagen: Rosenkilde and Bagger, EEMF, 1956). Vol. 6.

7   The idea for using something as well known as the opening line of "The Gettysburg Address" has been borrowed from John DeFrancis's, *Visible Speech*.

8   Ælfric, *Grammatica, folios 2-3*. (See Note 5, Chapter 1).

9   While there is continued disagreement about the way Greek and Hebrew were pronounced in antiquity, the phone-by-language division used in the ASPA has some interesting implications with regard to their perceived pronunciation. It should be noted that even today Greek vowels are still muddy in comparison to English ones, and Hebrew vowels are still very clear.

10   Isidore's remark on the distinction between "sound" and "voice" is quoted in full in Note 3 to Chapter 1; an English translation appears on page 10.

11   For an idea as to the enormous variety of *a*-phone symbols used across the centuries and among the various symbol-assignment systems and scripts, see A. Cappelli's *Dizionario de Abbreviature latine ed italiane*, (Milan: Ulrico Hoepli, Re-issued, 1967).

12   The Palmyrene alpha-symbol set contains five distinct *a*-graphemes. The Palmyrene Alphabet is illustrated in Diringer, *Alphabet,* Pl. 15.34, Vol. 2, 218. Please note that Diringer merely lists symbols. He gives no indication as to which symbols occur in which sets. The symbols must be seen *in situ* to understand their use, or to place them in their political settings.

13   The DSS scripts were first classified by Frank Moore Cross and David Noel Freedman in 1952 in their *Early Hebrew Orthography: A Study of the Epigraphic Evidence*. American Oriental Society Monograph 36. (New Haven, CT: American Oriental Society). Cross has published a number of articles on the subject. The most accessible of these articles is his "The Development of Jewish Scripts," in *Essays in Honor of William F. Albright*, G. E. Wright, ed, 133-202. (New York: Anchor Book edition, 1965). 170-264.

14   The use of "Herodian" forms has important implications as to the status of the DSS fonts. Examples may be found in Diringer, *Alphabet*; Cross, "Development of Jewish Scripts"; or Eileen M. Schuller, *Non-Canonical Psalms from Qumran: A Pseudepigraphic Collection*. Harvard Semitic Studies No. 28. (Atlanta: Scholars Press, 1986).

15   Henry Sweet refers to the aleph-*a* symbol by this name on page xii in his introduction to *The Épinal Glossary: Latin and Old English of the Eighth Century*. (London: Humphrey Milford, 1883). Sweet also makes it clear that he thinks the *Épinal* is 7th century. (It is)

16   "Chicken" was spelled *cicen* in OE. One interesting point on spelling reforms should be noted. These reforms usually tried to maintain correct sounds. Our modern "chicken" results from the *h* added later to show that the first *c* was soft and the *k* added to keep the second *c* hard.

17   For further details on the round-*d*, see A[listair] Campbell, *Old English Grammar*, (Oxford: Clarendon, 1962). No. 57:5.

             Campbell's *Grammar* is an indispensable tool for anyone interested in the phonology and grammar of English—Old or Modern. It brings together information that the reader would otherwise have to search for among numerous sources. However, the reader should be warned that it is also one of the most oddly organized books ever written and difficult to use. It is, nevertheless, worth the effort.

18   Examples of all these different forms may be found in Diringer, *Alphabet*, Vol. 2. The illustrations and collected data are immensely useful; however, his conclusions must be used with caution as a great deal of ancillary information has surfaced since the publication of his book.

19   In N. R. Ker's introductory "Notes" to the *Catalogue of Manuscripts Containing Anglo-Saxon* (Oxford: Clarendon, 1957), he comments that *l* is "often written partly below the line in early manuscripts and occasionally later." xxx.

20   Good examples of the distinction between the *o*-forms used in Latin and those used in OE, as well as those between *c, d, e, g, h,* and long-*s*, may be seen on Plates II, III, and V of Ker's *Catalogue*.

21   Campbell does not make this error in classification. For more information, see Campbell, *Grammar*, No. 67.

22   *Incipit Interpretatio Psalmi CXVIII Per singulas Litteras*.

23   A facsimile edition of the *Vespasian Psalter* is available in Volume XIV in the Early English Manuscripts in Facsimile (EEMF) series published by Rosenkilde and Bagger of Copenhagen in 1967.

24   See Campbell, *Grammar*, No. 199.

25   See Campbell, *Grammar*, No. 199.

26   For example, F. G. Cassidy and Richard N, Ringler. *Bright's Old English Grammar & Reader*. 3rd Ed. (New York: Holt, Rinehart and Winston, Inc. 1891, 1894, 1917, 1935, 1961, 1971). p. 10.

27   See Ker's *Catalogue,* page xxxi, for a discussion of the voiced and unvoiced dental fricatives.

28   The phonological change from rising diphthong > diphthong > falling diphthong is documented in Anglo-Saxon Chronicle A (*The Parker Chronicle and Laws*). In Chapter 11, "Changing Voices," we see the changes occur.

Notes to Chapter 8

1.   Although the conflation of calligraphers with scribes is known, it is still taught. Lowe in 1971 refers to "calligraphic excellence"; O Croinin in 1989 refers to bringing a script "to perfection"—as if we have the slightest idea of what people back then thought of as perfection. Both statements are from the point of view of modern ideas of the art of calligraphy. Most of the introductory textbooks date to more than 50 years ago. It takes a very long time for new information to make its way into textbooks.

2.   Correspondence falls between copied and dictated texts. On one hand, formulas of greeting, for example, must be followed; but on the other, the personal voice of the writer must come through to authenticate the document as having come from the originator. Autograph letters generally have the busy texture of dictated texts.

3   Many examples of the staggering technique show up among the Dead Sea Scrolls; the majority are the non-authoritative products of bookshops. Bookshops were the "publishing houses" of antiquity. Among these bookshop products are the so-called "Manual of Discipline" (1Qs) and the "War Scroll" (1QM). The latter is set in the future; an example of future-fantasy fiction, first-century BCE style.

Notes to Chapter 9

1   Jerome, Epistle XLVI, 12.

2   Basil, *Homilia in psalmum* 1.

3   Ambrose, *Explantio psalmi* i, 9.

4   For more information on Enheduanna and early religious music, see Gerald Henry Wilson, *The Editing of the Hebrew Psalter*, (Chico, CA: Scholars Press, 1985); Samuel Noah Kramer. "A Hymnal Prayer of Enheduana: the adoration of Inanna in Ur", *Ancient Near Eastern Texts*, 1969. 579-82; or William W. Hallo and J.J. Van Dijk. *The Exaltation of Inanna*. (New Haven: Yale University Press. 1968)

5   Only one other such embedded colophon is known; it appears in the Psalter after Psalm 72. This embedded colophon follows the collection formula set by Enheuanna:

        Amen Amen

        Completed are the prayers of David,

        son of Jesse.

Like Enheduanna's collection, there are pseudepigraphic psalms among the first 72; also like Enheduanna, the Davidic Psalms are identifiable by their distinctive style.

6   The names of the Five books in Hebrew are as follows:

Berashit [at first]–Genesis

veleh shmot [and these are the names]–Exodus

vayikra [and called]–Leviticus

videber YHVH al Moshe bamidbar, [and spoke Adonai (the Lord) to Moses

        in the *waste*]–Numbers

eleh hadverim [these are the spoken words]–Deuteronomy

7　To this day, except for musicologists specializing in this area, most people do not know that the Tiberian vowel and cantillation notations are derived from the ancient Hebrew chironomic notation.

8　For a concise discussion of Platonist thought in the period, see Joseph Wilson Trigg, *Origen: the Bible and philosophy in the third-century church,* (Atlanta, Ga.: J. Knox, 1983).

9　Jerome's last translation of the Psalms was from Hebrew (*Hebraicum*). Random sampling among the Psalms indicates that, whenever a word has been changed, it is shorter in a Hebraicum than in either a Romanum or a Vulgate translation.

10　The name of the *cephalicus* neume, for example, is from Greek "kephali," head.

11　See Raphael Taubenschlag, *The Law of Greco-Roman Egypt in the Light of the Papyri: 332 B.C. - 640 A.D.* 2nd. Edition. (Milano: Cisalpino-Goliardico, 1972).

12　Numerous experts examined the manuscript; most saw the notation as a real-time notation and the music was reconstructed according to the directions in the manuscript. One of the experts, however, assumed that this color-coding technique could never have had a practical application. Clearly, a professional musician would never buy "toy" instruments and would not know what manufacturers of toys know. Color-coding is a common modern technique used to teach small children their scales and to play simple tunes. Toy xylophones, for example, have brightly colored keys for good reasons. In these toys, each key is assigned a color. The little books of simple tunes that come with these toys present the music color-coded to match the keys. The technique permits the child to learn his scales and to immediately "make music." He was correct, however, that color-coding is not practical as a general musical notation system.

13　For a thorough discussion of the use of colored inks as punctuation see, Robertson, Word Dividers, Spot Markers and Clause Markers.

14　In both Western and Eastern musical notation systems, yellow to indicate the base note seems to be very old. In Chinese systems, said to date back to 3,000 BCE, the "Golden Bell," (yellow) was the base note. As we have seen, stripes indicate rank. Three stripes denotes a Master; 4 stripes indicates "The" Master. In 3rd- and 4th-century Syriac MSS as well as later Anglo-Saxon Psalters, David in his role as "The" Psalmist is drawn holding his harp. David's harp has eight stripes, that is, four pairs of yellow and red. (See Figure 10.11, page 195) When staff notation finally shows up in Western systems during the renaissance, two lines were used: yellow indicated C; red indicated F.

Notes to Chapter 10

1　Ælfric called a choir a *singende heap*, a "singing pile" or "heap" (unordered, not dis-ordered). Anyone who has ever heard a congregation singing at a village church in England will agree that "singing heap" is a very accurate description. Some people will be a note behind and some a note ahead of the main part of the group, while yet others will be singing a different hymn or Psalm because they opened to the wrong page.

2　See Hope Emily Allen, *English Writings of Richard Rolle: Hermit of Hampole*, (Oxford: Clarendon Press, 1931). (Repr. 1963).

3　Among Biblical scholars, direct translations from the Hebrew for the Masoretic Text and Greek for the Old Greek are considered primary sources. Primary sources shed light on cruces, those places where meaning is unclear. Translations of translations, such as a translation of a Latin Psalter into a vernacular, are considered secondary sources. While secondary sources have their place, they are of little aid in Biblical studies.

4　Not too surprisingly, the *Vespasian* translation bears some similarities to the *Paris Psalter* translation. For a partial analysis of the different translation traditions, see Sarah Larrat Keefer, *The Old English Metrical Psalter, An Annotated Set of Collation Lists*, (New York: London: Garland, 1979).

5　The *Paris Psalter* was whole when used by Richard Rolle around 1340 to make *his* translation of the Psalms. It was still complete in 1402 when it shows up as an entry in the inventory of John Duc du Berry's book collection. Du Berry gave it to Sainte Chappelle de Bourges around 1406. By 1689 Thaumas de la Thaumassière reports that the de Bourges library was in a very bad state. Dom Martène reported finding the MS on the floor of a poultry house there in 1708. The MS finally found refuge when the house at de Bourges gave it to the library of the King on August 8th of 1752—already missing the 14 leaves containing its 14 illuminations and its original binding.

6   Just an amusing sidelight. During the 19th century, many suggestions as to the reason for the size and shape of the *Paris Psalter* were proposed. One scholar decided that this hefty book, almost 2 feet high, was a "lady's pocketbook" (*taschenbuch*). The gentleman clearly was unfamiliar with women's clothing and its construction. Perhaps he assumed women carried portmanteaus around with them to lug such a heavy oversize book.

7   Rolle was not the only one to claim an "official" source for his work. Wycliffe also stated that he used the Latin Bible as his source for his translation, and he probably did—for most of the work. He then made the curious statement that the Psalms could not be translated into English from the Latin text. The Wycliffe Bible contains the Psalter, but Wycliffe is totally silent on the source text for his Psalms.

8   See *Richard Rolle, Psalms from the English Psalter. Commentary. Edited from the MS Huntington 148 with notes and glossary*, by Marjorie Orchard Collins. Collins specifically mentions that nobody knows the source of Rolle's Psalm 96(95).

9   As almost all strong intransitive verbs had a causative, Old English left Modern English quite a few causatives. "Lie," for example, means to "make lay"; "set" means to "make sit"; "drench" means to "make drink"; "stench" means to "make stink."

10   King Ælfred, *Hierde-boc*. [Pastoral Care]. Folio 2 recto. Facsimile available from Early English Manuscripts in Facsimile, (Copenhagen: Rosenkilde and Bagger, 1956).

11   See Janet Bately, *The Literary Prose of King Alfred's Reign: Translation or Transformation?* (London King's College: University of London, 1980). See also Bately's "Lexical Evidence for the Authorship of the Prose Psalms in the Paris Psalter." *Anglo-Saxon England* 10, 1982. 69-95; J. Bromwich, "Who was the Translator of the Prose Portions of the Paris Psalter?" Fox and Dickins 1950. 289-303; J. Wichmann, "König Aelfred's angelsächsische Obertragung der Psalmen I-LI," *Anglia* XI, 1889.

12   Michael D. Goulder, while appreciating previous scholarship of the 19th and early 20th centuries Old Testament research, sums up the relevant point: "I reached the common conclusion that most of the historical notes were late and worthless for the psalms' original meanings . . .". For further discussions, see Michael D. Goulder, *The Prayers of David (Psalms 51-72): Studies in the Psalter, II.* JSOT, Supplement Series 102. (Sheffield: Sheffield Academic Press, 1990).

13   For discussions of metaphorical categories and conceptual domains, see George Lakoff and Mark Turner, *More Than Cool Reason: A Field Guide to Poetic Metaphor,* (Chicago and London: University of Chicago Press, 1989).

14   The fullest discussions of the agonal sense is found in Johan Huizinga, *Homo Ludens,* (English translation, Boston: Beacon Press, 1955); and Walter Kaufmann, *Critique of Religion and Philosophy,* (New York: Harper & Brothers, 1958). 163-197.

15   See *A. Z. Idelsohn Archives at the Jewish National and University Library: Catalogue.* Edited by Israel Adler and Judith Cohen, (Jerusalem: Magnes, 1976).

16   The "Riddle Song," the folk song that begins "I gave my love a cherry that had no stone," for example, began its long life as the Middle English "I have a Swester [sister]." The original words are mostly one-syllable-to-one-note, with few extended or held notes, and suit the melody far better than our modern version. (For an arrangement of "The Riddle Song," see *The Burl Ives Songbook: American Song in Historical Perspective.* (New York: Ballantine, 1953, 36-37.) Similarly, the children's charm chant against rain spoiling their play ("Rain, rain go away") is the same chant tune used for the Old English "Charm against a Wen" (Wen-ne wen-ne wen-chi chen-ne"). Once again, the original charm is sung one-syllable-to-one-note; the modern charm chant must extend, for instance, the words "rain" [ra-in] and "away" [a-wa-ay] across two or more notes to fit the melody.

17   See W. Thomas Marrocco and Nicholas Sandon, eds., *Medieval Music,* (London: Oxford University Press, 1977). 105-6.

18   Latin *Gloria* does not mean "glory" in our modern sense; it means fame/reknown/acclaim. The Old English *wuldor* was an accurate translation. The misunderstanding of the word is a result of a side-slip in meaning across the

centuries. The only remnant in modern English of the original meaning is in the word "vainglory": an ill-advised or futile pursuit of fame or renown. Our association of light with *glory*, and therefore with *wuldor*, is anachronistic. It is far better to translate *wuldor* as fame or renown.

19   The best work on the Ælfredian introductions and their Celtic format remains Patrick Paul O'Neill's, "The Old English Introductions to the Prose Psalms and the Paris Psalter: Sources, Structure, and Composition." *Studies in Philology* 1981, Early Winter v 78(5), 20-38.

20   See Malcolm Parkes, *Pause and Effect: an Introduction to the History of Punctuation in the West*. (Aldershot, Hants: Scolar, 1992) for a discussion of Alcuin and the "Insular system of punctuation . . . in manuscripts attributed to the 'Palace School'" 32-3.

21   See Roger P. Wright, *Late Latin and Early Romance in Spain and Carolingian France*, (Liverpool: Francis Cairns, 1982).

22   For a collation of references to both exegesis and references to music, see James McKinnon, *Music in early Christian literature*, (Cambridge: Cambridge University Press, 1987).

23   Socrates, *Ecclesiastical History*, vi, 8. PG

24   For a concise summary of the situation and the antecedents, see Willi Apel, *Gregorian Chant*, (Bloomington: Indiana University Press, 1990).

25   See Dom Joseph Gajard, *The Rhythm of Plainsong*. Trans. Aldhelm Dean. (New York: J. Fischer, 1943).

26   For a succinct discussion of these arguments against the reconstruction as done by the Solesmes School, See Apel, *Gregorian Chant*, pages 106-108. For an example of some of the other arguments against the Solesmes reconstruction, see G. B. Chambers, *Folksong-Plainsong: A Study in Origins and Musical Relationships*, (London: Merlin Press, 1956).

27   Chambers, *Folksong-Plainsong*, 54.

Notes to Chapter 11

1   T. A. M. Bishop, *English Caroline Minuscule*, (Oxford: Clarendon Press, 1971).

2   See Mary J. Carruthers, *The Book of Memory: A Study of Memory in Medieval Culture* (Cambridge: Cambridge University Press, 1990) for memorization and organizational techniques; Howlett for the standard education and training in composition techniques.

3   "Ælfred's Scholars"—Plegmund (later Archbishop of Canterbury), Werferth (Bishop of Worcester), Asser of Saint David's in Wales, Grimbald of Saint Omer, and Werwulf and Æthelstan—came at Ælfred's request. We may like to pretend that nothing so crass as money was part of the arrangement, but these men were supported by Ælfred's money. Unlike Charlemagne and his heirs, Ælfred (state) was not about to tell his transcendent employees (church) what to do; nevertheless, the letter makes it clear that he obviously felt he had, at the very least, the right to nudge them.

4   As N. Denholm-Young points out in his book intended for students of paleography, *Handwriting in England and Wales* (Cardiff: University of Wales Press, 1964); "Even in the hey-day of English monastic life the monks can never have produced all the books required." 55

5   Sweet, *Épinal*, 1883. xi.

6   *The Parker Chronicle and Laws* is available in a facsimile edited by Robin Flower and Hugh Smith, London: Humphrey Milford, 1941. Due to war-time exigencies, the facsimile lacks any editorial or explanatory material other than a short preface by Flower.

7   Some things never change. Today we may use wood or fabric fibers instead of animal skins, but it should be noted that paper has a grain. When using a modern laser printer, care should be taken to assure that the paper is all in the same direction when placed in the printer feed tray.

8   The practice of handing a blessed sword to newly crowned emperors or kings was initiated by Pope Paschal (817-824) in 823 as part of his ongoing attempts to keep some control over the Emperors of the North. The sword was

the symbol of temporal power to fight evil; the act was meant to emphasize the distinction between ecclesiastical and temporal domains. Like anointment, the ceremony soon was seen as including heirs to a succession as well.

9   The [T] was added by another scribe. Whether "west" was written "wes" or "west" depended upon the official orthography at a given time and place, and, of course, dialect.

10   The technical term for "appearance" in Latin and Insular paleography is "aspect."

11   The *s* of Æðelstan's official record font shows up on f. 25a (924) in the hand of a chancery clerk in training. This tells us that the font was around, but not used for chancery records until after the death of Edward.

12   For the conservatism of the Northumbrian writing system and scribes, see T. Julian Brown's Introduction to *The Durham Ritual: A Southern English Collectar of the Tenth Century with Northumbrian Additions*, Durham Cathedral Library A.IV. 19 (Copenhagen: Rosenkilde and Bagger, 1969). EEMF XVI. With regard to the Northumbrian scribes, Brown states that their writing looks "like the products of an ancient and unbroken Northumbrian tradition, preserved in isolation from developments elsewhere in England" (col. b. 41). "For all [Aldred's] skill, he was living in the past" (col. a 41).

13   A complete facsimile of the *Lindisfarne* manuscript was published in Lausanne in 1956; however, this was a limited edition and is quite difficult to access. *The Lindisfarne Gospels*, with an introduction by E. G. Millar, contains three color and thirty-six monochrome plates, (London: British Museum, 1923). A facsimile of f. 258 may be found in CLA, plate number 187.

14   British Library, MS Cotton Otho A. vi, Ælfred's translation of Boethius's *The Consolation of Philosophy* (*De consolatione philosophae*), prose and meters, was badly damaged in the fire of 1731. The leaves are too warped to be able to check ideographs with any precision.

15   A photograph of f. 159v from Trinity College, Dublin, MS 52 can be seen in M. Brown, *Guide*, Plate 19. As Brown notes, "the virtuoso technique hides the fact that the text was written very rapidly."

16   Outer dimensions, respectively: Dobbie 1942, xiv;, Ker 1957, 282; Førster 1919, 4. Writing space dimensions: Ker 1957, 281; Dobbie, 1942, xiv.

17   David R. Howlett asserts that the fourth article in this manuscript was composed, at Ælfred's request, by Æðelstan, one of Ælfred's scholars and an ecclesiastical *wiðbora*, for Æðelstan, Ælfred's grandson and godson. The manuscript itself lends support to Howlett's evidence about the author, date, and purpose of the poem. See David R. Howlett, *British Books in Biblical Style*. (Dublin: Four Courts Press, 1995).

18   Alterity simply means "otherness" and it is a very real problem. The concept, however, can easily be taken to an extreme and imply that modern society has altered to the extent that we cannot understand the past. The concept of alterity should not be dismissed, in spite of the extremist view. It is a useful reminder that twenty-first century perspectives and customs should not be foisted upon earlier periods. The importance of alterity lies in our comprehension that at any given point in time contemporary customs become the aesthetic measure. Much of the apparent alterity problem stems from the conflation of aesthetics with purpose, whether the reference be to language, mores, architecture, social programs, or the purpose and modes of written communication. Our understanding of past procedures requires recognition that aesthetic preference based on contemporary norms has no relevance whatsoever outside of the study of contemporary aesthetics.

19   Just a note: When writing with a reed pen, one writes from the elbow; when writing with a quill, one writes from the wrist. With a reed, one does not change the angle at which the pen is held; with a quill, one changes the angle of the pen hold. These Ælfredian manuscripts are written with reeds.

20   DeHamel, *Scribes and Illuminators* 1992, 21.

21   These are the same proportions used in fourth-century Greek Bibles as well as the printed Gutenberg Bible. After studying numerous medieval manuscripts, Jan Tschichold, the book designer, worked out formulae for quality book design. He came up with the same proportions. See Tschichold, *The form of the book: essays on the morality of good design*. Translated from the German by Hajo Hadeler; edited, with an introduction, by Robert Bringhurst. (London: Lund Humphries, 1991.)

22.   Ælfred's tendency to wear both braces and a belt permeates his works. Whenever he could, he would call on authorities from both the Bible and the Anglo-Saxon past. We should note in passing that Aldhelm, who was

considered the greatest of the early English poets, was known to stand around on bridges rewriting the words to popular songs. We could also note that this technique for making converts among the ordinary people was referred to by Athansius as "Thalia." The gifted poet who used the technique was Arius. For a description of, and lengthy excerpts from, Arius's "Thalia," see: Athanasius, *De Synodis*, 15. PG. A translation is available in James Stevenson, *A new Eusebius: documents illustrative of the history of the church to A.D. 337*. London: 1957.

Notes to Chapter 12

1   Jack Goody succintly sums this up in his *The Interface between the written and the Oral*. "In any case, the act of changing the script, like changing one's language, carries much emotive and cultural significance." (Cambridge: Cambridge University Press, 1986. 56.)

2   See Chapter 10, "To Sing a New Song," for some of the notations inserted in appropriate spaces on the *Plan of St. Gall*. The entire Plan is encoded in *stæfwritung*. On page 33, Chapter 10, of the facsimile edition of the Plan, for example, maneflo me-ɔɪsɪ ɪpfluf is written in the "building" above the "Medicinal Herb Garden." For further information, see *The Plan of St. Gall in Brief*, introduction and commentary by Lorna Price, 1982.

3   See Chapter 10, "To Sing a New Song." This mixture of *stæfwritung* and melisematic notation may be found in Saint Gall Codex 339, *Paléographie Musicale* I, 1912, and St Gall Codex 359 *Paléographie Musicale* II, 1914.

4   For an example of this qualitative remnant, see, BL. Add. 11669, written in early Textura.

5   W. V. Quine. *Quiddities: An Intermittently Philosophical Dictionary*. Cambridge, MA: Harvard UP, 1987. 112.

6   Please note that such reversions to an older authoritative script family *always* advertises intent. When the Neo-Babylonians, for example, adopted the ancient complex cuneiform system, they announced their intent to re-create the Old Babylonian Empire. Similarly, when Adolph Hitler replaced the centuries old Fraktur script of identity for German with the Roman script family, he announced that he had dreams of empire.

7   Aside from the staggering technique, which unequivocally states that a text is dictated, there are a number of striking differences between conformed (copied) and dictated texts. These differences are clearly visible and make it extremely easy to identify whether a text was copied from an *exemplar* or whether it was dictated. Conspicuous variations in quantity—both internally and externally, extremely long trailers, extensive variation in the length of tongues, and obvious irregularity in spacing and clumping are clear indications of a dictated text. Copied texts are regularized, conform to norms, and eliminate exaggerated variations. See Chapters 8 and 11 for detailed and illustrated discussions of these differences.

8   See Chapter 6, note 3, McKitterick. Part 3 of McKitterick's book, sections VIII and IX in particular, contain a detailed discussion tracing the decline of a monastic *scriptorium*.

9   There is a third "poetic" codex, the *Vercelli Book* (Vercelli Biblioteca Capitolare CXVII), containing 23 Homilies and 6 poems in Old English. A third class copy, possibly from a Continental bookshop/*scriptorium*, the codex cannot be dated closer than sometime during the eleventh century. The book was copied from various existing *exemplaria* by a scribe who was probably not an Anglo-Saxon. This scribe appears to have carefully copied what he saw in each *exemplar*, but made errors distinguishing between *wyn* and *thorn*, a point confirmed by Celia Sisam in her introduction to the Facsimile edition of the *Vercelli Book* (Copenhagen: Rosenkilde and Bagger, 1976). Sisam also accurately notes that the scribe did not use script differentiation by language: Latin and Old English are written in the same font. In addition, although he copies the movement on the axes, the scribe does not always follow the phone-to-graph assignments of the ASPA. These last two points, however, may have been in his *exemplaria*; some of the poems date from the late-seventh and early-eighth centuries.

10   The *Cædmon Manuscript* may not be "poetry" in the usual sense of the term. The manuscript is encoded to include "cues" marking changes of speaker. There is a possibility that the "poems" could be Anglo-Saxon religious plays, fore-runners of the Medieval "Mystery Plays."

11   Ælfred, for example, incorporated Northumbrian graph forms into his first record and dictation fonts; Sargon I retained the Sumerian symbols for xenographic exchange. Constantine's consolidated uncial is a blend of Roman and Greek graph forms.

12 Examples of the pattern of defeat can be seen in the proliferation of the "Arthurian" literature in English and in English script systems following the erection of the "castles" on the border between Wales and England in the late 14th century. Arthur, we may recall, was Welsh. In the twentieth century We have the recent spate of English literature extolling the virtues of the North American Indians; the same pattern shows up earlier in British literature on India and in Australian works on the aborigines.

13 Clear examples of the identity pattern are the Hebrew literature produced during the post-exilic and Hellenistic periods (later books of the Bible—for example, Esther and Daniel, plus commentaries, works of fiction, and so on found in the DSS), and the proliferation of copies of ancient Greek literature, such as poetry and "consitutions," following the Roman conquest of Greece. In both cases, we also find attempts to reassert identity through scripts.

14 The script used by monasteries affiliated with the Benedictine Reform was prescribed, but the affiliates still managed to assert some independence. David Dumville discovered that the choice of texts produced in their scriptoria differed, See David N. Dumville, *English Caroline Script and Monastic History: Studies in Benedictinism, A.D. 950-1030*, (Woodbridge, Suffolk: Boydell Press, 1993).

15 Ælfric's Latin Grammar, Oxford, St. John's College, MS. 154, f. 1r.

16 Bodleian MS. Laud Misc. 636. The *Peterborough* is an important witness with regard to tracing the decline of *stæfwritung*. At first Scribe 1 tried to follow the exemplar letter forms; however, he very quickly gave up. As Dorothy Whitelock comments, "the first scribe seems to have started with the intention of using different forms of certain letters in the Latin part of his text . . . he is not consistent, and he soon desists from the practice" (14). It should be remembered that a scribe writes as he or she is trained, and a long-lived scribe will create what seem to be anachronisms. Generational overlap would appear to account for the apparently puzzling survival of forms in a later portion of a text which do not appear in an earlier section. Wright, Pl. 1, has an example of Scribe 2's writing. Scribe 2 still differentiates among high, medial, and low *a*; Insular and Caroline *d*; and, of course, retains the bound forms. The loss of script-ethnos differentiation, another part of *stæfwritung*, appears in Scribe 2's use of "Caroline" *a*. A facsimile is available. *The Peterborough Chronicle (The Bodleian Manuscript Laud Misc. 636)*. Dorothy Whitelock, ed. (Copenhagen: Rosenkilde and Bagger, 1954). EEMF, Vol. 4.

18 Wright, Pl. 6. The "Brut" retains some quantity notation, but not a great deal. Phonetic division, though, remains in use: Lines 2b-4b, for example, "sie/de" and "set/te"; lines 7b-8b "ru/nan" and "seg/ge," etc.

18 A facsimile edition of *The Canterbury Psalter* was published in 1935 with and introduction by M. R. James (London: Lund, Humphries). See also Chapter 10.

19 As has already been noted, this bound form is quite old. Ligatured "*o* short-*r*" appears in the *Épinal*, see Chapter 6. *O* followed and ligatured to a short *r* occurs, for example, in "ald*or*" (l. 3, year 755) of the *Parker Chronicle* (f. 10a).

20 C. E. Wright's *English Vernacular Hands From the Twelfth to the Fifteenth Centuries* (Cardiff: University of Wales Press, 1964), contains a good cross-section of plates showing the decline of *stæfwritung*. To enable the reader to follow this decline, as many examples as possible have been given from Wright.

21 Specimen facsimile pages of Kirkestede's handwriting are available in *Speculum*, Vol. XLI, No. 3, July 1966. However, Richard H. Rouse's description covers the main points.

> It is an upright hand with strokes somewhat heavily drawn, and does not hold an even line; the size of certain letter forms is frequently out of proportion to those of others in the same word [Pl. number omitted]. Two different forms for the same letter are often used—for example, a headless *a* and a two-compartment *a* [Pl. number omitted]. . . Frequently he uses the small capital *s* form initially and in ligatures . . .. (475)

22 BM Cotton Claudius B. IV. Facsimile available, EEMF 18. C. R. Dodwell and Peter Clemoes, ed. (Copenhagen: Rosenkilde and Bagger, 1974).

23 See f. 105r in the facsimile edition, EEMF 13, Clemoes, (Copenhagen: Rosenkilde and Bagger, 1966).

24 Rochester Cathedral Library, MS. A. 3.5. Facsimile published in Volumes VII and XI of the EEMF series. Peter Sawyer, ed. (Copenhagen: Rosenkilde and Bagger, 1957, Pt. 1).

25   Vol. 2 (EEMF XI), of Rochester MS. A. 3.5, f. 179r exhibits particularly good illustrations of both the retention of language differentiation and the use of medial and primary stresses on *a* in Latin. For example, l. 3. the abbreviation for Saint uses medial *a*, while "SciAtis" shows primary stress. "Lanfranco," (l. 6) where the first *a* is medial and the second is unstressed; "unquAm" (l. 9) is a particularly clear example of stressed *a*.

26   B.L., Stowe MS. 34. Wright, Pl. 3.

27   B.L., Egerton MS. 613. Wright, Pl. 4.

28   No facsimile edition of *The Ormulum* has been published. Two "fac-simile" pages are available for study in the AMS 1974 reprint of the new 1878 edition. A sample of Orm's writing may be found on Wright, Pl. 2.

29   The MS preserves an attempt to "archaize" a text. The "Battle List of Barons" is written in an "antique" style by Scribe 1; this scribe's very distinctive "modern" bitten form of *de* incongruously appears on page 3, column 4 in the list. Derek Pearsall and I. C. Cunningham. *The Auchinleck Manuscript: National Library of Scotland, Advocates' MS. 19.2.1.* (London: Scolar Press, 1977).

30   MS. Pepys 2498. Two pages are reproduced in EETS No. 274, 1976.

31   BL Cotton MS. Titus D. xviii. Wright, Pl. 5. While both quality and stress are missing in the older version of the "Riwle" and semantic unit separation is more marked, quantity is still employed. For example, hitwile for_þi [hit wile for thi] (l. 2), or þiseide" [that I seide] (l. 7).

32   In the fifteenth century, Sir John Paston still used variant forms and quantity notation. (See Sir John's letter to Margaret Paston, 17 January 1476 on the endpapers of *Illustrated Letters of the Paston Family: Private Life in the Fifteenth Century*. Ed. Roger Virgoe. New York: Widenfield & Nicolson, 1989.) Late 16th and early 17th century "foule" copies, that is, theater prompts, still use quantity notation.

33   The last Findern died in 1558. Richard Beadle & A. E. B. Owen, ed. *The Findern Manuscript: Cambridge University Library MS. Ff.1.6.* (London: Scolar Press, 1977). xii.

34   Bodleian Library, MS. Ashmole 1729, f. 13r.

35   The need for a document to be "In my own hand" dates back to Antiquity. During the Biblical period, for example, there was no such thing as a "copy" in our modern sense. There could only be one original; anything else, no matter how accurate, was an "edition." See also Chapter 8, Note 2.

36   MacD. P. Jackson. "The transmission of Shakespeare's text" in *The Cambridge Companion to Shakespeare Studies*. Stanley Wells, ed. Cambridge: CUP, 1986. 170.

Notes to the Epilogue

1   The search for a "universal" writing system shows up even in the Congressional record of the United States—as can be seen in the bibliography.

2   See Carruthers, *Memory*.

Abbreviations

ABD	Anchor Bible Dictionary
ANTS	Anglo-Norman Text Society
ASE	Anglo Saxon England
ASPR	Anglo-Saxon Poetic Records
BAR	British Archaelogical Reports
BL	British Library, London
BM	British Museum, London
BN	Bibliothèque Nationale, Paris
CLA	Codices Latini Antiquiores
CUP	Cambridge University Press
DJD	Discoveries in the Judean Desert
DSS	Dead Sea Scrolls
EETS	Early English Text Society
EEMF	Early English Manuscripts in Facsimile
HMSO	Her/His Majesty's Stationery Office
LCL	The Loeb Classical Library
JSOT	Journal for the Study of the Old Testament
OUP	Oxford University Press
PBA	Proceeedings of the British Academy
PG	Patrologiae cursus completus. Series graeca.
PL	Patrologiae cursus completus. Series secunda [Latin]
SUNY	State University of New York
UP	University Press

A PRACTICAL BIBLIOGRAPHY

At last count, the bibliography on the *Paris Psalter*, discussed in Chapter 10, ran 295 items. The secondary literature on the *Paris Psalter*, however, is lilliputian in comparison to the secondary literature in other areas. A bibliography of works consulted would be far too large; nor would it serve any useful purpose. Instead, this is a *practical* bibliography. Listed are works referred to in the text, sources both introductory and specialized that expand on a specific subject area, sources that illustrate a concept, and sources of primary material.

Scholarly works are secondary sources and contain bibliographies; the reader has a choice among the works listed and may follow up on a subject there. Artisan works are meant as primary sources and few have bibliographies; hence, the inclusion for the reader of a fairly broad choice among publications on the various components of writing systems.

Writing systems are a user-interface; they make no distinctions among sources. All items are in alphabetic order in the list. Items that indicate [Plates] or [ill.] or [Facs.] identify works that contain primary sources. Works that address the various components of a writing system are indicated within square brackets. The number or numbers in parenthesis following an entry refer to the relevant Chapter or Chapters in the text. Translations of sources into English are given where available.

Aarne, Antti Amatus, 1867-1925. *The Types of the Folk-Tale: A Classification and Bibliography*. Trans. Stith Thompson. New York: Burt Franklin, 1928. (2, 4, 9, 10, 11, 12)

Aaron, P. G. and R. Malatesha Joshi eds. *Reading and writing disorders in different orthographic systems. (NATO Conference on Advanced Study Institute on Developmental and Acquired Disorders of Reading and Writing Systems in Different Languages: a Cognitive Neuropsychological Perspective, 1987: Il, Ciocco, Italy.)* Dordrecht; Boston: Kluwer Academic Publishers, 1989. [Orthographic Systems] (Intro., 4, 6, 11, Epilogue)

Abasolo Alvarez, Jose A. *Epigrafia romana de la region de Lara de los Infantes*. Prologo de Pedro De Palol. Burgos: Diputacion Provincial de Burgos, 1974. [Script Systems; 108 plates: ill.] (3, 4)

Abbot Aelfric: *A Testimonie of Antiquitie*. London: Iohn Day, dwelling ouer Aldersgate. [Rprt. New York: Da Capo, 1970]. (12)

Abbott, Kenneth. "The Grammarians and the Latin Accent." In *Classical Studies In Honor of William Abbott Oldfather*. Urbana: Illinois UP, 1943. (3, 10)

Adams, Corinne. *English Speech Rhythm and the Foreign Learner*. The Hague; New York: Mouton, 1979. [Parsing Rhythms] (Intro., 5, 10, 11, Epilogue)

Adams, Eleanor N. *OE Scholarship In England from 1566-1800*. New Haven 1917. Rprt. Hamden, Conn.: Archon, 1970. (12)

Adler, Israel and Judith Cohen, *A. Z. Idelsohn Archives at the Jewish National and University Library: Catalogue*. Jerusalem: Magnes, 1976. [Scores] (10)

Ahlquist, Anders. "Latin Grammar and native Learning," *Sages, Saints and Storytellers: Celtic Studies in Honour of Professor James Carney*. Donnchadh O' Corrain, Liam Breatnach, and Kim McCone, eds. Kildare, Ireland: An Sagart, 1989. 1-6. (5, 11)

Aland, K. and B. *The Text of the New Testament*. Trans. E. F. Rhodes. Leiden: Brill, 1987. (4)

Albertus Magnus, *Opera Omnia* [Complete Works]. August Borgnet, ed. Paris: Ludovicum Vives, 1890. (1)

Albright, Robert W. *The international phonetic alphabet: its backgrounds and development*. Bloomington, Ind.: Publication of the Indiana University Research Center in Anthropology, Folklore, and Linguistics, 1958. [Symbol-set Systems; Script Systems] (2, 7, 8, Epilogue)

Albright, William Foxwell. *From the Stone Age to Christianity: Monotheism and the Historical Process*. Rev. ed. New York: Anchor Books, 1957. (4)

Alcuin, 735-804. *Two Alcuin letter-books*. Edited by Colin Chase from the British Museum ms. Cotton Vespasian A XIV. Toronto: published for the Centre for Medieval Studies by the Pontifical Institute of Mediaeval Studies, 1975. (10)

Aldhelm, Bishop of Sherborne, 640?-709. *De laudibus virginitatis; with Latin and Old English glosses. Manuscript 1650 of the Royal Library of Brussels*, with intro. by George van Langenhove. Bruges: Saint Catherine Press, 1941. [Facs.] (10)

Ælfric. *Latin Grammar*. Oxford: St. John's College, MS. 154. [Plates on-line from the St. John's College web-site.] (1, 7, 12)

- - -. *Grammatica Latino-Saxonica*. William Somners. Oxford, 1659. Rprt. Menston: Scolar, 1970. (1, 7, 12)

Aller, Fernandez y Maria del Carmen, *Epigrafia y numismatica romanas en el Museo Arqueologico de Leon*. Leon: Colegio Universitario de Leon, 1978. [Script Systems; Plates] (3, 4, 5, 10)

Allen, Hope Emily. *English Writings of Richard Rolle: Hermit of Hampole*. Oxford: Clarendon Press, 1931. Rprt., 1963. (10, 12)

Almagro Basch, Martin. *Segobriga II: inscripciones ibericas, latinas paganas y latinas cristianas*. Madrid: Ministerio de Cultura, Direccion General de Bellas Artes y Archivos, Subcireccion General de Arqueologia y Etnografia, 1984. [Script Systems; Plates] (3, 4, 5, 10)

Alonso Schokel, Luis. *A manual of Hebrew poetics*. Roma: Editrice pontificio Istituto biblico, 1988. (10)

Alster, Bendt. *Proverbs of ancient Sumer: the world's earliest proverb collection*. Bethesda, Md.: CDL Press, 1997. (2, 10)

Altick, Richard D. *The Scholar Adventurers*. New York: The Free Press; London: Collier-Macmillan Ltd, 1966, 1959. Robert Burns, 240-43; 257-59. (8)

Alter, Robert. *The Art of Biblical Poetry*. New York: Basic Books, Inc. 1985. (10)

Altman, Rochelle I. S. "The Size of the Law: Document Dimensions and their significance in the Imperial Administration," in Linda Jones Hall, ed., *Confrontation in Late Antiquity: Imperial Presentation and Regional Adaptation*. Cambridge, Cambridgshire: Orchard Academic, 2003 [Format Systems; Size Systems] (Intro.)

- - - . "Report on the Temple Tablet." Bible and Interpretation, 2003. www.bibleinterp.com [Writing systems] (Intro. 2, 4, 6, 10)

- - - . Official Report on the James Ossuary. Bible and Interpretation, 2002. www.bibleinterp.com [writing systems] (Intro. 2, 4)

- - - . "The Writing World of the Dead Sea Scrolls." *Lecture*: St. Mary's School of Divinity, University of St. Andrews, Fife, Scotland, 2001. <http://www.st-andrews.ac.uk /~www_sd/altman_dss.html>. [Writing Systems; Facs.] (2, 4, 11)

- - - . "Report on the Zoilos Votive Inscription from Tel-Dan." Orion Center for the Study of the Dead Sea Scrolls. Jerusalem: *Abstracts and Papers*. 2001. <http://ORION@mscc.huji.ac.il/orion/programs/Altman/Altman00.shtml>. [Writing Systems; Facs.] (2, 4)

- - - . "Some Aspects of Older Writing Systems: With Focus on the DSS." Orion Center for the Study of the Dead Sea Scrolls. Jerusalem: *Abstracts and Papers*, 1999. <http://ORION@mscc.huji.ac.il/orion/programs/Altman/Altman99.shtml>. [Writing Systems; Facs.] (2, 4, 7)

- - - . "Writing Systems and Manuscripts." *Lecture*: St. Mary's School of Divinity, University of St. Andrews, Fife, Scotland, 1999. <http://www.st-andrews.ac.uk/~www_sd/Altman_writing.html>. [Writing Systems; Facs.] (2, 4, 7, 11, Epilogue)

- - - . An Application and a Text: Electronic Research Diplomatic Editions for Computers in the Humanities. Diss. Arizona State University, 1995. [Script Systems; Format Systems; Ill.] (7, 10, 11, Epilogue)

Ambrose 339(?)-397. *Epistolae*. PL, 16. (10)

- - - . [English] *The letters of S. Ambrose, Bishop of Milan*. E. B. Pusey, 1800-1882, ed. Rev. Henry Walford, 1824-1893. Oxford: J. Parker, 1881. (10)

- - - . *Explantio psalmi*. PL, 16. i, 9. (10)

Ames, Ruth Margaret. "The Debate between Christians and the Synagogue in the Literature of Anglo-Saxon and Medieval England." Diss. Columbia U. 1950. [Plates, ill.] (5, 7, 11, 12)

Ancrene riwle. *The English text of the Ancrene Riwle, edited from Magdalene College, Cambridge Ms. Pepys 2498 by A. Zettersten*. London; New York: EETS, by OUP, 1976. [2 plates: facs.] (12)

- - - . *The English text of the Ancrene riwle, edited from Gonville and Caius College ms. 234/120 by R. M. Wilson*. With an introd. by N. R. Ker. London; New York: EETS by OUP, 1954, Rprt. 1957. [Facs.] (12)

Anderson, A. A. *The Book of Psalms*. New Century Bible. London: Oliphants, 1972. (10)

Anderson, John M. and Charles Jones. *Phonological structure and the history of English*. Amsterdam; New York: North-Holland Pub. Co.; Elsevier North-Holland, 1977. [Parsing Rhythms] (7, Epilogue)

Anderson, L. The Anglo-Saxon Scop. Diss. Ann Arbor, Mich: 1976. (11)

Apel, Willi. *Gregorian Chant*. Bloomington: Indiana UP, 1990. [Plates] (10)

Apostolic Fathers, with an English Translation. Trans. Kirsopp Lake. London: W. Heinemann, 1912-1913; Rprt. New York: Macmillan Co. London: 1949; LCL No. 82. Cambridge, Mass.: Harvard UP, 1965, 1949. (1, 4, 10)

Archi, Alfonso and Francesco Pomponio. *Testi cuneiformi Neo-sumerici da Drehem, N. 0001-0412*. Milano: Cisalpino, Istituto Editoriale Universitario, 1990. [Script Systems; Plates: ill.] (2)

Aristotle. *De Memoria*. English: in *Aristotle on Memory*, Trans. with notes by Richard Sorabji. London: Duckworth, 1972. (1)

Arngart, O. ed. *The Leningrad Bede: An Eighth Century Manuscript of the Venerable Bede's Historia Ecclesiastica Gentis Anglorum in the Public Library, Leningrad*. EEMF. v. 2. Copenhagen: Rosenkilde & Bagger, 1952. [Facs.] (5, 6, 11)

Arrighi, Ludovico degli. *The first writing book; an English translation & facsimile text of Arrighi's Operina, the first manual of the chancery hand*. [1522] With introd. and notes by John Howard Benson. New Haven: Yale UP, 1955. [Script Systems, Facs.] (2, 4, 7, 11, 12)

Athanasius ca. 297-373. *De Synodis. A select library of the Nicene and post-Nicene fathers of the Christian church*. Ed. Philip Schaff, with a number of patristic scholars of Europe and America. Edinburgh: T. & T. Clark; Grand Rapids, Mich.: Wm. B. Erdmanns, 1989-94. v. 4. (10)

Augustine. *De dialectica*, PL, v. 11. (1)

Avenary, Hanoch. *Encounters of east and west in music: selected writings*. Tel-Aviv: Faculty of Visual and Performing Arts, Dept. of Musicology, Tel-Aviv University, 1979. [Script Systems; Musical Notation Systems; ill.] (9, 10)

- - - . *Studies in the Hebrew, Syrian, and Greek liturgical recitative*. Tel-Aviv: Israel Music Institute, 1963. [Script Systems; Musical Notation Systems; ill.] (9, 10)

Avery, Robert Stanton. *Avery's phonetic alphabet: for teaching children and all who wish to learn how to spell the words of the English language as they are spoken, and as they are written by short-hand writers. It is especially designed to aid beginners in phonography and foreigners in learning our language*. Washington, D.C., The Author, 1893. (Epilogue)

Avrin, Leila. *Scribes, Script and Book: The book Arts from Antiquity to the Renaissance*. Chicago: American Library Association, 1991. [Codicology; Format Systems; Script Systems; Plates; ill.] (Intro, 2, 11)

Bagnall, Roger S. *Reading Papyri, Writing Ancient History*. London, New York: Routledge, 1995. (4)

Baker, Donald C. and J. L. Murphy, eds. *The Digby plays: facsimiles of the plays in Bodley MSS Digby 133 and e Museo 160*. Leeds: University of Leeds, School of English, 1976. [Facs.] (12)

Balogh, Josef. "Voces paginarium," *Philologus* 82. (1926) 84-109. (Intro., 1)

Baltzer, Rebbeca A., Thomas Cable, and James I. Wimsatt. *The Union of Words and Music in Medieval Poetry*. Austin: U of Texas P, 1991. (10, 12)

Bangor Collectarium. *The antiphonary of Bangor; an early Irish manuscript in the Ambrosian library at Milan; edited by F. E. Warren.* [Biblioteca Ambrosiana. Ms. C. 5.] London: Harrison and sons, printers, 1893-95. 2 vols. v. I: A complete facsimile in collotype by W. Griggs, transcription by F. E. Warren. [Facs.] (4, 6, 10)

Barber, Russell J. and Frances F. Berdan. *The emperor's mirror: understanding cultures through primary sources.* Tucson: U of Arizona P, 1998. (2, 3, 4, 6, 8, 10, 11, 12)

Barbour, Ruth. *Greek literary hands, A.D. 400-1600.* Oxford: Clarendon Press, 1981. [Script Systems; Plates: facs.] (4, 5, 7, 11, 12)

Barley, M. W. and R. P. C. Hanson, eds. *Christianity in Britain, 300-700: Papers presented to the Conference on Christianity in Roman and Sub-Roman Britain, held at the University of Nottingham, 17-20 April 1967.* Leicester: Leicester UP, 1968. (4, 5)

Barton, George A[aron], 1859-1942. *The royal inscriptions of Sumer and Akkad.* New Haven, Pub. for the American oriental society by the Yale UP; London: Humphrey. Milford, UP, 1929. [Script Systems; Facs.] (2)

Bascom, William R. "Four Functions of Folklore," in *The Study of Folklore.* Alan Dundes, ed. Englewood Cliffs, NJ: Prentice-Hall, 1965. 279-298. (6, 11)

Basil (329-79). *Homilia in Psalmum, 1.* [In, *Exegetic homilies.* Trans. Agnes Clare Way. SERIES: Fathers of the Church, v. 46. Washington, DC: Catholica University of America P, 1963.] (10)

Bassett, S. .R. "Church and diocese in the West Midlands: the transition from British to Anglo-Saxon control," in J. Blair and R. Sharpe, eds. *Pastoral care before the parish.* Leicester: Leicester UP, 1992. 13-40. (5)

Bately, Janet M. "Lexical Evidence for the Authorship of the Prose Psalms in the Paris Psalter." *ASE* 10, 1982. 69-95. (10)

- - -. *The Literary Prose of King Alfred's Reign: Translation or Transformation?* London King's College: U of London, 1980. (10)

Beadle, Richard and A. E. B. Owen, intro. *The Findern Manuscript: Cambridge University Library MS. Ff.1.6.* London: Scolar Press, 1977. [Facs.] (2, 7, 12)

Beck, Cave. *Le charactere universel: par lequel toutes nations peuvent comprendre les conceptions l'une de l'autre en lisant par une escriture commune a toutes leur propre langage maternelle.* Printed for William Weekly. London: Thomas Maxey, 1657. [Epilogue]

Bede. *The Tanner Bede: the Old English version of Bede's Historia ecclesiastica, Oxford Bodleian library Tanner 10, together with the mediaeval binding leaves.* EEMF v. 24. Copenhagen: Rosenkilde & Bagger, 1992. [Facs.] (11)

Begg, John. *Form and format; abstract design and its relation to book format.* Brooklyn, New York: G. McKibbin, 1949. [Format Systems; Codicology; Book Design; ill.] (11, 12)

Bell, Alexander, ed. *An Anglo-Norman 'Brut' (BM MS, Royal 13.A.xxi).* Oxford: Published for the Anglo-Norman Text Society by Blackwell, 1969. [Plate, facs.] (12)

Benedictine of Stanbrook. *A Grammar ofPlainsong.* Liverpool: Rushworth & Dreaper, 1934. (10)

Benton, Megan. *Beauty and the book: fine editions and cultural distinction in America.* New Haven: Yale UP, 2000. [Book Design; Format Systems; Codicology; ill.] (Intro, 11, 12, Epilogue)

Bergen, Robert D., ed. *Biblical Hebrew and discourse linguistics*. Dallas, TX: Summer Institute of Linguistics; Winona Lake, IN: Distr. Eisenbrauns, 1994. (10)

Berlinerblau, Jacques. *The vow and the "popular religious groups" of ancient Israel: a philological and sociological inquiry*. Sheffield, England: Sheffield Press, 1996. (2, 4, 9)

Bernal, Martin. *Cadmean Letters: The Transmission of the Alphabet to the Aegean and Further West before 1400 BC*. Winona Lake, IN: Eisenbrauns, 1990. [Script Systems; Plates, ill.] (3)

Berry, W. Turner. *Catalogue of specimens of printing types by English and Scottish printers and founders, 1665-1830,* compiled by W. Turner Berry & A. F. Johnson. With an introduction by Stanley Morison. London: OUP, 1935. [Script Systems; ill.] (12)

Best, Jan and Fred Woudhuizen, eds. *Ancient scripts from Crete and Cyprus*. Leiden; New York: E.J. Brill, 1988. [Script Systems; ill.] (2, 3)

Best, R[ichard] I[rvine] and Eoin MacNeill, intros. *The Annals of Inisfallen, reproduced in facsimile from the original manuscript (Rawlinson B 503) in the Bodleian library*. Pub. by the Royal Irish Academy. Dublin: Hodges, Figgis & co.; London: Williams & Norgate, 1933. [Facs.] (5, 6)

[Bible] The Holy Bible Containing the Old Testament and the New, Newly Translated out of the Originall tongues: & with the former translation ~ diligently compared and reuised by His Maiesties Com(m)andement. Appointed to be read in Churches. London: Robert Barker, Printer to the King, 1611. (10, 12)

[Bible] *The Holy Bible, containing The Old and New Testaments, with the Apocryphal Books, in the Earliest English Versions Made from the Latin Vulgate by John Wycliffe and His Followers*. Ed. by Josiah Forshall and Frederic Madden. Oxford: At the UP, 1850. Rprt. New York: AMS Press, 1982. 3 vol. (10, 12)

Biblia Hebraica Stuttgartensia: Torah, Nevi'im, u-Khetuvim. 2nd ed. Ed. K. Elliger and W. Rudolph, et al. Stuttgart: Deutsche Bibelgesellschaft, 1984. (4, 10)

[Biblia] Novum Testamentum e Codice Vaticano Graeco 1209 (codex B) tertia vice phototypice expressum. In Civitate Vaticana: Ex Bibliotheca Apostolica Vaticana, 1968. SERIES: Vaticanus: v. 30 [Facs.] (4, 10)

Biblia Sacra Iuxta Latinam Vulgatam Versionem. I GENESIS-PSALMI. Stuttgart: Württembergische Bibelanstalt, 1975. (10)

Biblia Sacra Iuxta Latinam Vulgatam Versionem. v. X PSALMI. Rome: Typis Polyglottis Vaticanis, 1953. (10)

Biblia Sacra Iuxta Vulgatam Versionem. Ed. Bonifatio Fischer, et al. Vol. I. Stuttgart: Wurtembergische, 1945. (10)

Biblia Sacrorum graecus Codex vaticanus auspice Pio IX. Romae: typis et impensis S. Congregationis de propaganda fide, 1868-81. 6 vol. [Facs.] (4)

[Biblia] Septuaginta; id est, Vetus Testamentum Graece iuxta lxx interpretes, edidit Alfred Rahlfs. Editio quinta. Stuttgart, Privilegierte Württembergische Bibelanstalt, 1952. (4, 10)

Biegeleisen, J.I. *Art directors' workbook of type faces, for artists, typographers, letterers, teachers & students*. Intro. R. L. Leslie. New York: Arco Pub. Co. 1963. [Script Systems; ill.] (2, 4, 7, 11, 12)

Bieler, Ludwig. *Psalterium Graeco-Latinum: Codex Basiliensis A. VII. 3*. (Greek with Latin interlinear translation). Sir Roger Aubrey Baskerville. Rprt. Amsterdam: North-Holland Publishing Co., 1960. [Facs.] (4, 9, 10)

Bierut, Michael, Elinor Pettit, and Theodore Gachot, eds. *Looking closer: critical writings on graphic design*. Intro. by Steven Heller. New York: Allworth Press: American Institute of Graphic Arts; Saint Paul, Minn., 1994. [Script Systems; Format Systems; Book Design] (4, 11, 12)

Billeter, Jean Franβois. *Art chinois de l'Écriture*. [The Chinese art of writing]. New York: Skira/Rizzoli, 1990. [Script Systems; ill.] (Intro., 8)

Bischoff, Bernhard. *Manuscripts and Libraries in the age of Charlemagne*. Trans. Michael Gorman. Cambridge; New York: CUP, 1994. [ill.] (10)

- - - , ed. *The Épinal, Erfurt, Werden, and Corpus glossaries: Épinal Bibliothèque municipale 72(2), Erfurt Wissenschaftliche Bibliothek Amplonianus 2{ 42, Dusseldorf Universitatsbibliothek Fragm. K 19: Z 9/1, Munich Bayerische Staatsbibliothek Cgm. 187 III (e.4), Cambridge Corpus Christi College 144*. EEMF v.22. Copenhagen : Rosenkilde & Bagger, 1988. (5, 6)

Bishop, T[errence] A[lan] M[artyn]. *English Caroline Miniscule*. Oxford: Clarendon Press, 1971. [Script systems; Plates] (4, 5, 10, 11, 12)

- - - . *Scriptores regis: facsimiles to identify and illustrate the hands of royal scribes in original charters of Henry I, Stephen, and Henry II*. Oxford: Clarendon, 1961. [Script Systems; Plates, facs.] (11, 12)

Blair, Peter Hunter. *Roman Britain and Early England: 55 B.C.-A.D. 871*. Edinburgh: Thomas Nelson & Sons, 1963. (5)

- - - and R. A. B. Mynors. Bede: *Historia ecclesiastica gentis Anglorum. The Moore Bede. Cambridge University Library (Kk.5.16)*. EEMF v 9. Copenhagen: Rosenkilde & Bagger, 1959. [Facs.] (2, 6, 8, 10, 11)

Bloomfield, Leonard. *Language*. New York: Holt, Rinehart and Winston, 1933. (Intro, 1)

Blumenthal, Uta-Renate. ed. *Carolingian essays: Andrew W. Mellon lectures in early Christian studies*. Washington, D.C.: Catholic U of America P. 1983. (10)

Bodoni celebrato a Parma. A centocinquanta anni dalla morte nasce un museo dedicato al grande tipografo nella Biblioteca palatina di Parma. 2. ed. Biblioteca palatina, novembre 1963. Parma: La Nazionale, 1964. [Script Systems; Script design; Plates, ill.] (Intro., 7, 11, 12)

Boethius. BM MS Cotton Otho A vi. Ælfred's translation of *De consolatione philosophae*]. Robinson and Stanley, EEMF, v. 23 [Plates]. (11)

Bolinger, Dwight L. *Two Kinds of vowels, two kinds of rhythms*. Bloomington, IN: Indiana Univerity Linguistics Club, 1981. [Parsing Rhthyms] (5, 10, 11, Epilogue)

- - - . "Visual Morphemes." *Language* 22, 1946. 333-350.

Bolter, J. David. *Writing space: the computer, hypertext, and the history of writing*. Hillsdale, N.J.: L. Erlbaum Associates, 1991. [Script Systems; Format Systems] (Epilogue)

Bonfante, Larissa, ed. *Etruscan Life and Afterlife: a handbook of Etruscan studies*. Detroit: Wayne State UP, 1986. (3)

Bonfante, Guiliano and Larissa Bonfante, *The Etruscan Language*. Manchester: Manchester UP: 1983. (3, 5)

Bonfante, Julian Hugo, 1904-?. *Some new Latin inscriptions from Spain* [by] G. Bonfante. Princeton University, the Archaeological Institute of America, 1941. [SCript Systems; ill..] (3, 4, 5)

Bordreuil, Pierre et Dennis Pardee. *La trouvaille épigraphique de l'Ougarit*. Avec la collaboration de Brigitte Arzens. Bibliographie par Jesüs-Luis Cunchillos. Paris: Éditions Recherche sur les civilisations, 1989-1990. [Script Systems; Plates, ill.] (2)

Boswinkel, E. and P. J. Sijpesteijn. *Greek Papyri, Ostraca and Mummy Labels*. Amsterdam: Adolf M. Kakkert, 1968. [Script Systems; Plates] (3)

Bowman, Alan K. and J. David Thomas, with contributions by J.N. Adams and Richard Tapper. *Vindolanda: the Latin writing-tablets*. Gloucester: A. Sutton; London: Society of the Promotion of Roman Studies, 1984, 1983. [Script Systems; Plates: ill..] (5)

Boyle, Leonard E. *Medieval Latin Palaeography, A Bibliographical Introduction*. Toronto: Toronto UP, 1984. (4)

- - -. "Optimist & Recensionist: 'Common Errors' or 'Common Variations'?" *Latin Script and Letters: AD 400-900*. John J. O'Meara & Bernd Naumann, eds. Leiden: E. J. Brill, 1976. (4, 5, 10)

Bradshaw, Paul. *The Search for the Origins of Christian Worship: Sources and Methods for the Study of Early Liturgy*. New York: OUP, 1992. (4, 10)

- - -. and Lawrence A. Hoffman, eds. *The Making of Jewish and Christian worship*. Notre Dame: UP of Notre Dame, 1991. (10)

Braswell, Laurel Nichols. *Western Manuscripts from Classical Antiquity to the Renaissance: A Handbook*. Garland Reference Library of the Humanities, 139. New York: Garland, 1981. [Script Systems: ill.] (2, 4, 7, 11, 12)

Bray, Dorothy Ann. *A list of motifs in the lives of the early Irish saints*. Helsinki: Suomalainen: Tiedeakatemia, 1992. (6)

Bright, James Wilson. "Notes on the 'Introductions' of the West Saxon Psalms." *Journal of Theological Studies* xiii, 1912. 520 ff. (10)

Bright, William and Peter T. Daniels. *The World's Writing Systems*. New York; Oxford: OUP, 1996. [Script Systems; Symbol-Set Systems; ill.] (2, 4, 7, 11, 12)

Bringhurst, Robert. *The elements of typographic style*. Point Roberts, WA: Hartley & Marks, 1992. [Script Systems; Script Design] (2, 4, 7, 11, 12)

Brock, S. P., C. T. Fritsch, and S. A. Jellicoe. *A Classified Bibliography of the Septuagint*. Leiden: Brill, 1973. (10)

Bromwich, J. "Who was the Translator of the Prose Portions of the Paris Psalter?" In *Fox and Dickins*, 1950. 289-303. (10)

Brook, G. L., ed. *The Harley lyrics: the Middle English lyrics of Ms. Harley 2253*. 2nd ed., with minor corrections and rev. Manchester, Eng.: Manchester UP, 1956. [Facs.] (9, 10, 12)

- - - and R. F. Leslie, eds. *Laȝamon: Brut. BM MS. Cotton Caligula A.ix and BM MS. Cotton Otho C.xiii*. EETS 277. London: OUP, 1978. 2 vols. [2 Plates] (12)

Brown, Francis, S. R. Driver, and Charles A. Briggs, eds. *A Hebrew and English Lexicon of the Old Testament* (Oxford: 1907). (10)

Brown, Michelle P. *A Guide to Western Historical Scripts from Antiquity to 1600*. Toronto: University of Toronto Press, 1990. [Script Systems; Plates] (Intro, 2, 3, 4, 7, 11, 12)

Brown, Peter Robert Lamont. *The rise of Western Christendom: triumph and diversity, 200-1000 A.D.* Cambridge, Mass.: Blackwell, 1995. (4, 5, 10, 11)

Brown, T. Julian, ed. *The Durham Ritual: A Southern English Collectar of the Tenth Century with Northumbrian Additions*, Durham Cathedral Library A.IV. 19. Contributions by F. Wormald, A. S. C. Ross and E. G. Stanley. Early English Manuscripts in Facsimile. v. 16. Copenhagen: Rosenkilde & Bagger, 1969. [Facs.] (11, 12)

Bruce, J. D. "Immediate and Ultimate Source of the Rubrics and Introductions to the Psalms of the Paris Psalter." *Modern Language Notes* 8, 1893. 72-82. (10)

Brüning, Elisabeth. Die altenglischen metrischen Psalmen in ihrent Verhältnis zur lateinischen Vorlage. Diss. Kànigsberg, 1921. (10)

Bullough, D. A. "The Educational Tradition in England from Alfred to Ælfric: Teaching Ultrusque Linguae." *La Scuolanell' Occidente Latino dell' Alto Medieovo*. Seltinone di Studio del Centro Italiano di studi sull' alto Medieovo 19, 1972. 453-94, 547-54. (11, 12)

Burke, Christopher. *Paul Renner: the art of typography*. New York: Princeton Architectural Press. 1998. [Script Design; Plates, ill.] (2, 4, 7, 11, 12)

Burn, A[ndrew] R[obert]. *The Romans in Britain; an anthology of inscriptions*. With translations and a running commentary by A. R. Burn. 2nd ed. Columbia: South Carolina UP, 1969. [Script Systems; ill.] (5)

Camden, William, 1551-1623. *Remains Concerning Britain*. Rprt. R. D. Dunn, ed. Toronto: U of Toronto Press, 1984. (12)

Campbell, Alastair. *The Graphic Designer's Handbook*. Philadelphia: Running Press, Reprt. 1991. [Script Systems; Format Systems; Script Design; Book Design] (2, 4, 7, 11, 12)

Campbell, A[listair]. *Old English Grammar*. Oxford: Clarendon Press, 1962. (7)

Campbell, James. *Essays in Anglo-Saxon Hstory*. London; Ronceverte, WV, USA: Hambledon Press, 1986. (5, 10, 11, 12).

- - -, Eric John, & Patrick Wormald. *The Anglo-Saxons*. Ithaca: Cornell UP, 1982. [Plates,] (5, 10, 11, 12)

Capelli, Adriano. *Manuali Hoepli Lexicon Abbreviaturum Dizionario di Abbreviature Latine ed Italiane: usate nelle carte e codica specialmente del Medio-Evo riprodotte con oltre 14000 segni incisi. com l'aggiunta di uno studio sulla brachigrafia medioevale, un prontuario di Sigle Epigrafiche, l'antica numerazione romana ed arabica ed i segni indicanti monete, pesi, misure, etc.* 6th Ed. Milano: Hoepli, 1967. [Script Systems, ill.] (3, 4, 6, 10)

Cardamone, Tom. *Advertising agency and studio skills; a guide to the preparation of art and mechanicals for reproduction*. New York: Watson-Guptill Publications, 1970. [Format Systems] (11)

Carnoy, Albert Joseph, 1878-? *Le latin d'Espagne d'apres les inscriptions; etude linguistique*. [2. ed. revue et augm.] Hildesheim; New York: G. Olms, 1971. [Script Systems; Orthographic Systems] (4, 6)

Carozzi, Claude et Huguette Taviani-Carozzi, eds. *Peuples du Moyen Age: problèmes d'identification*: séminaire Sociétés, idéologies et croyances au Moyen Age. Aix-en-Provence: Publications de l'Université de Provence, 1996. [Papers presented at a seminar given during 1993 and 1994.] (1, 4)

Carcopino, Jéröme, 1881-1970. *Daily life in ancient Rome; The People and the City at the Height of the Empire*. Edited with bibliography and notes by Henry T. Rowell. Trans.from French by E. O. Lorimer. New Haven; London: Yale UP, 1963; 1940. (4)

Carruthers, Mary J. *The Book of Memory: A Study of Memory in Medieval Culture*. Cambridge: CUP, 1990. [Mnemonic Systems; Facs.] (3, 4, 11)

Cartledge, Tony W. *Vows in the Hebrew Bible and the ancient Near East*. Sheffield, England: JSOT Press, 1992. (2, 4)

Carver, M[artin] O. H., ed. *The Age of Sutton Hoo*. Woodbridge: Boydell, 1992. (11)

Cassidy, F. G. and Richard Ringler. *Bright's Old English Grammar & Reader.* 3rd ed. New York: Holt, Rinehart and Winston, 1971. [Script Systems; Orthographic Systems; Plates] (7, 11)

Cattin, Giulio. *Music of the Middle ages I.* Trans. Steven Botterill. Newcastle-on-Tyne; New York; Melbourne: CUP. Rprt. 1993. [Musical Notation Systems; ill.] (10)

Cavallo, G. and H. Maehler. *Greek Bookhands of the Early Byzantine Period.* London: U of London, Institute of Classical Studies, 1987. [Script Systems; Facs.] (4, 7, 11)

Cavanagh, J. Albert. *Lettering and Alphabets: 85 complete alphabets designed and rendered by one of America's great letterers.* New York: Dover, 1946. [Script Systems/Design; ill.] (2, 4, 7, 11, 12)

Cepas, Adela. *The north of Britannia and the north-west of Hispania: an epigraphic comparison.* Oxford, England: B.A.R., 1989. [Script Systems; Orthographic Systems; ill.] (3, 4, 5)

Chambers, G. B. *Folksong-Plainsong: A study in Origins and Musical Relationships.* London: Merlin Press, 1956. (10)

Chambers, Raymond W. *On the Continuity of English Prose from Alfred to More and his School.* EETS, 191A. London: NN, 1932. (11, 12)

- - -, Max Forster, and Robin Flower, intros. *The Exeter book of Old English poetry.* London: Printed and pub. for the dean and chapter of Exeter cathedral by P. Lund, Humphries & co., ltd., 1933. [Facs]. (7, 11, 12)

[La] Chanson de Roland. 2 Vol. Ed. Guillame Picot. Paris: Larousse, 1972 [1933]. (10)

Chao, Yuen Ren. *Language and symbolic systems.* Cambridge: Cambridge U.P., 1968. [Symbol-set Systems] (6, 8, 10)

Chase, Wayland Johnson. *The Ars minor of Donatus, for one thousand years the leading textbook of grammar.* Madison, WI; NN, 1926. [Punctuation Systems] (2, 3, 4)

Chassant, L-Alph. *Dictionnaire des Abbréviations Latines et Françaises usitées dans les inscriptions Lapidaires et Métalliques les Manuscrits et les Chartes du Moyen Age.* 1884. 5th Ed. Rprt. New York: Burt Franklin, 1973. [Script systems, ill.] (7, 11)

Chaytor, H[enry] J[ohn]. *From Script to Print: an introduction to medieval vernacular literature.* Cambridge, Eng.: Heffer, 1945. [Script Systems; ill.] (10, 11, 12)

Child, Francis James. *The English and Scottish Popular Ballads.*, 1st ed. 1882-98. (Reprt. New York: Dover Publications, 1965. 5 vol. (10, 12)

Chittenden, John, ed. *Donatus Ortigraphus, Ars grammatica.* Turnholt: Brepols, 1982. [Punctuation Systems] (2, 3, 4)

Christie, Neil. *The Lombards. The Ancient Longobards.* Oxford: Blackwell, 1995. (4)

Christin, Anne Marie. *L'Image écrite, ou, La déraison graphique.* Paris: Flammarion, 1994. [Script Systems; ill] (2, 4, 7, 11, 12)

Clanchy, Michael T. *From Memory to Written Record: England, 1066-1307.* Cambridge, MA: Harvard UP, 1979. (11, 12)

Clapperton, Robert H. *Paper; an Historical Account of Its Making by Hand from the Earliest Times Down to the Present Day.* Oxford: Shakespeare Head Press, 1934. (Intro.; 2)

Clay, Albert Tobias, 1866-1925. *Documents from the Temple archives of Nippur dated in the reigns of Cassite rulers.* Philadelphia: Published by the Dept. of Archaeology, of the University of Pennsylvania, 1906. 2 vol. [Script Systems; Orthographic Systems; Facs.; Plates; ill.] (2)

- - -. *Business documents of Murashu sons of Nippur dated in the reign of Darius II (424-404 B.C.)*

Philadelphia: Published by the Dept. of Archaeology and Palaeontology of the University of Pennsylvania, 1904. [Script Systems; Orthographic Systems; Facs.; Plates] (2)

Clement, Richard W. "The Production of Pastoral Care: King Alfred and His Helpers." In Paul E. Szarmach, ed., *Studies in earlier Old English prose: sixteen original contributions*. Albany: SUNY Press, 1986. 129-52. (11, 12)

Clemoes, Peter. *Liturgical influence on punctuation in late OE and Early Middle English manuscripts*. Binghampton: SUNY, 1980. (2, 10, 11, 12)

Closson, Ernest, introd. et transcription. *Le manuscrit dit des Basses danses de la Bibliothèque de Bourgogne*. Genéve: Minkoff Rprt, 1976. [Musical Notation Systems; ill.] (9, 10)

Cobden-Sanderson, T[homas] J[ames], 1840-1922. *The ideal book, or, Book beautiful: a tract on calligraphy, printing & illustration and on the book beautiful as a whole, by T.J. Cobden-Sanderson of the Doves Press*. San Francisco: Printed by J.H. Nash for the Zellerbach Paper Co., 1919. [Script Systems; ill.] (11)

CLA. *A Palaeographical Guide to Latin Manuscripts prior to the Ninth Century*. Oxford: Clarendon, 1934-66. SERIES: Part I. The Vatican City. Part II. Great Britain and Ireland. (4, 5, 11, 12). Part III. Italy: Ancona-Novara. Part IV. Italy: Perugia-Verona. Part V. France: Paris. Part VI. France: Abbeville-Valenciennes. Part VII. Switzerland. Part VIII. Germany: Altenburg-Leipzig. Part IX. Germany: Maria Laach-Wurzburg. Part X. Austria, Belgium, Chechoslovakia, Denmark, Egypt, and Holland. Supplement. Russia, United States, Egypt, misc. Oxford: Clarendon, 1966. [Script Systems] (2, 4, 5, 7, 11, 12)

Colgrave, Bertram and R. A. B. Mynors, Ed. *Bede's Ecclesiatical History of the English People*. Oxford: Clarendon Press (1969). (5, 6)

- - -., gen. ed. *The Paris psalter: Ms. Bibliothèque Nationale Fonds Latin 8824*. EEMF v. 8. Copenhagen: Rosenkilde & Bagger, 1958. [Facs.] (2, 4, 5, 10, 11)

Collingwood, R. G. & R. Wright. *Roman Inscriptions of Britain*. Oxford: Clarendon, 1965. [Script systems; Orthographic Systems] (5)

- - -. *Roman Inscriptions of Britain*. Gloucester, UK: A. Sutton, 1990- . [Script systems; Orthographic Systems] (5)

Collins, Marjorie Orchard, ed. Richard Rolle of Hampole, Psalms from the English Psalter. Edited from MS Huntington 148 with notes and glossary. Diss. U. Michigan, 1966. (10)

Collins, Roger. *Early Medieval Spain. Unity in Diversity. 400-1000*. 2nd ed. NY: Macmillan, 1995. (4)

Colwell, Ernest Cadman. *Studies in methodology in textual criticism of the New Testament*. Leiden: E. J. Brill, 1969. Vo. 9 (4)

Concordant Greek text, designed to be used with the Concordant literal New Testament, its keyword concordance and the Greek elements, and consisting of a Greek text restored from uncial manuscripts (Sinaiticus, Vaticanus, Alexandrinus) and their ancient editors with the variant readings in the superlinear, and an ultraliteral English translation in the sublinear. 4th ed. Canyon Country, Calif.: Concordant Pub. Concern, 1975. [Script Systems; Orthographic systems; Facs.] (4)

Conner, Patrick W. *Anglo-Saxon Exeter: A Tenth-century Cultural History*. Woodbridge: Boydell, 1993. [Script Systems; Script Design; Facs., ill.] (12)

Conomos, Dimitri E. *Byzantine Hymnography and Byzantine Chant*. Brookline MA: Holy Cross Orthodox Press, 1984. [Musical Notation Systems] (9)

Conybeare, John Josias, 1779-1824. *Illustrations of Anglo-Saxon poetry*. Ed. by Wm. Daniel Conybeare. 1826. Rprt. New York: Haskell House, 1964. (12, Epilogue)

Cook, Albert S. *Biblical quotations in Old English Prose Writers: edited with the Vulgate and Other Latin Originals; Introduction on Old English Biblical Versions; Index of Biblical Passages, and Index of Principal Words*. London: Macmillan and Company, 1898. (Rprt. 1977). (5, 10, 11, 12)

Cook, William R. and Ronald B. Herzman. *The Medieval World View*. Oxford: UP, 1983. (10, 11, 12)

Cooley, Alison E., ed. *The afterlife of inscriptions: reusing, rediscovering, reinventing & revitalizing ancient inscriptions*. London: Institute of Classical Studies, School of Advanced Study, University of London, 2000. [Script Systems] (7, 11, 12)

Copeland, L'Harl. *Design of the Roman letters*. New York: Philosophical Library, 1966. [Script Design, Ill.] (2, 4, 7, 11, 12)

Corbin, Solange. "Die Neumen." *Palaeographie der Musik*. Koln: Arno Volk, 1979. [Musical Notation Systems; Plates]. (9, 10)

Corpus inscriptionum latinarum (CIL), SERIES: "consilio et auctoritate Academiae Litterarum Regiae Borussicae." 14 vols: v. 3, 4 pts; v. 5, 2 pts; v. 8, 7 pts; v. 10, 2 pts.; v. 13, 5 pts.; v 14, 2 pts. [Most] Rprt. Berlin: W. de Gruyter, 1930-1974. [Script Systems; Plates, facs.] (3, 4)

Coussemaker, Edmond de, 1805-1876. *Histoire de l'harmonie au moyen age*. Nachdruck der Ausgabe Paris 1852. Rprt. Hildesheim: Olms, 1966. [Musical Notation Systems; ill.] (10)

Coverdale, Miles. *The book of Psalms from the version of Miles Coverdale as published in the "Great Bible" of 1539*. Intro. Francis Wormald; includes 8 reproductions from the fourteenth century manuscript known as Queen Mary's Psalter. London: The Haymarket press, 1930. [Plates] (10, 12)

Cox, Alfred J[ohn], 1835-1909. *The making of the book : a sketch of the book-binding art; edited with an introduction by Paul S. Koda*. New Castle, Del.: Oak Knoll Books, 1986. [Codicology; ill.] (Intro., 4, 10, 11)

Craig, James and Bruce Barton. *Thirty Centuries of graphic design: an illustrated survey*. New York: Watson-Gutill Pulications, 1987. [Book Design; Script systems; ill.] (2, 3, 4, 5, 11, 12)

Crandall, Ashley Amos. *Linguistic means of determining the dates of Old English literary texts*. Cambridge: Medieval Academy of America, 1980. (7, 11)

Crawford, Harriet. *Sumer and the Sumerians*. Cambridge; New York: CUP, 1991. (2)

Creasy, William C. and Vinton A. Dearing. *Microcomputers & literary scholarship: papers read at a Clark Library conference, 30 December 1982*. Intro.George R. Guffey. Los Angeles, Calif.: William Andrews Clark Memorial Library, University of California, Los Angeles, 1986. (Epilogue)

Crocker, Richard. *The Early Medieval Sequence*. Berkeley: U of California P, 1977. [Musical Notation Systems; ill.] (6, 10)

Crosby, Ruth. "Oral Delivery in the Middle Ages." *Speculum*, XI, 1936. 88-110. (10, 11)

Cross, Frank Moore. "The Development of Jewish Scripts." In *Essays in Honor of William F. Albright*, G. E. Wright, ed, 133-202. NY: Anchor Book edition, 1965. 170-264.] [Script Systems; ill.] (3, 7)

- - - . "The Oldest Manuscripts at Qumran." In *Journal of Biblical Literature*. 74, 1955. 147-172. [Script Systems] (3, 7)

- - - and David Noel Freedman. *Early Hebrew Orthography: A Study of the Epigraphic Evidence*. American Oriental Society Monograph 36. New Haven, CT: American Oriental Society, 1952. [Script Systems; Orthographic Systems; ill.] (3, 7)

Cross, James. "The Literate Anglo-Saxon—On Sources and Disseminations." *PBA* 58, 1972. 67-100. (5)

- - -. "The Metrical Epilogue to the OE Version of Gregory's Cura Pastoralis." *Neuphilologische Mitteilungen* 70, 1969. 381-386. (11)

Crouzel, Henri. *Bibliographie critique d'Origène, Supplement.* Hagae Comitis: M. Nijhoff; Steenbrugis: In Abbatia Sancti Petri, 1982. (4)

Crouzel, Henri. *Origen.* trans. by A.S. Worrall. San Francisco: Harper & Row. 1989. (4)

Crystal, David. *The English Tone of Voice: Essays in Intonation, Prosody and Paralanguage.* New York: St. Martin's Press, 1976, 1975. [Parsing Rhythms] (5, 10, 11, Epilogue)

Coulmas, Florian. *The writing systems of the world.* Oxford, UK; New York, New York: B. Blackwell, 1989. [Script Systems; ill.] (1, 3)

Cuneiform texts from Babylonian tablets in the British Museum. SERIES. London: The Trustees, 1896-58 vols. [Script systems; Orthographic Systems; "Each part, as a rule, consists of 50 plates."] (2, 4)

Dagenais, John. *The Ethics of Reading in Manuscript Culture: glossing the Libro de Buen Amor.* Princeton: Princeton UP, 1994. (Intro., 2, 12, Epilogue)

Daiches, David. *The King James Version of the English Bible. An account of the Development & Sources of the English Bible of 1611 with Special Reference to the Hebrew Tradition.* New York: Archon, 1968. (10, 12)

Dallin, Leon. *Foundations in Music Theory.* Belmont, CA: Wadsworth, 1962. [Musical Notation Systems; ill.] (10)

Dalley, Stephanie and Norman Yoffee. *Old Babylonian texts in the Ashmolean Museum: texts from Kish and elsewhere.* Oxford: Clarendon Press, 1991. [Script Systems; Orthographic Systems; ill.] (2)

Dante Alighieri, *Traite de l'eloquence vulgaire; manuscrit de Grenoble.* Venise: Olschki, 1892. [Facs.] (12)

Daunt, Marjorie. "Old English Verse and English Speech Rhythms." *Transactions of the Philological Society,* 1946. 56-72. [Parsing Rhythms] (2, 5, 10, 11, 12)

Davies, Wendy. "The Myth of the Celtic Church," in *The Early Church in Wales and the West: Recent work in Early Christian Archaeology, History and Place-Names,* Oxford: Oxbow Monograph 16, 1992. (5)

Deansley, Margaret. *Sidelights on the Anglo-Saxon Church.* London: Adam & Charles Black, 1962. (5, 10, 11)

DeFrancis, John. *Visible Speech: The Diverse Oneness of Writing Systems.* Honolulu: Hawaii UP, 1989. [Script Systems; Kerning Systems: ill.] (1, 3)

De Hamel, Christopher. *Scribes and Illuminators. Medieval Craftsmen.* London: Publications of the British Museum. 1992. [Script Systems; Format Systems; Plates, ill.] (Intro, 6, 8. 11, 12)

de Moor, Johannes C. and Wilfred G. E. Watson, eds. *Verse in ancient Near Eastern prose edited.* Kevelaer [Germany]: Verlag Butzon & Bercker; Neukirchen-Vluyn: Neukirchener Verlag, 1993. (2, 10, 11)

Denholm-Young, N. *Handwriting in England and Wales.* Cardiff: University of Wales Press, 1964. [Script Systems; Plates] (5, 6, 8, 11, 12)

De Poli, Giovanni, Aldo Piccialli, and Curtis Roads. *Representations of Musical Signals.* Cambridge, Mass.: MIT Press, 1991. [Musical Notation Systems] (Intro, 1, 10, Epilogue)

Dessauer, John P. *Book Publishing: What it is, What it does.* New York & London: R. R. Bowker Company. 3rd Printing, 1977. (11)

d'Étaples, Jacques Lefevre. *Quincuplex Psalterium*. Facsimile de l'édition de 1513. Paris: Librairie Droz, 1979. (10)

Dietrich, F. "Hycgan und Hopian." *Zeitschrift fur deutsches Alterum* IX, 1852. 214-222. (10)

Diplomata Karolinorum; recueil de reproductions en facsimile des actes originaux des souverains carolingiens conserves dans les archives et bibliothèques de France. Publie sous la direction de Ferdinand Lot et Philippe Lauer. Toulouse, E. Privat; Paris, H. Didier, 1936-. [Facs.] (10)

Diringer, David. *The Alphabet, A Key to the History of Mankind*. 2 v. 3rd ed. New York; London: Hutchinson, 1968. [Script Systems; v. 2: Plates, Facs., ill.] (2, 3, 4, 6, 7, 11)

- - -. *The Hand Produced Book*. New York: Philosophical Library, 1953. [Codicology; Scribal Techniques] (11)

Dodds, Eric Robertson. *Pagan and Christian in an Age of Anxiety: some aspects of religious experience from Marcus Aurelius to Constantine*. Cambridge; New York: CUP, 1990. (4)

Dodgeon, Michael H. and Samuel N. C. Lieu, eds. *The Roman Eastern Frontier and the Persian Wars (A.D. 226-363): A Documentary History*. London: Routledge, 1991. (4)

Dodwell, C. R. and Peter Clemoes, ed. *The Old English ill.trated Hexateuch: British Museum Cotton Claudius B. IV*. EEMF. 18. Copenhagen: Rosenkilde & Bagger, 1974. [Plates; Facs.] (4, 5, 12)

Donovan, Claire. *The Winchester Bible*. Toronto: University of Toronto Press, 1993. [Plates] (12)

Douglas, David C. *The Domesday Monachorum of Christ Church Canterbury*. [Cathedral Library. MS. (E 28)] London: Royal Historical Society, 1944. [Plates] (11, 12)

Drogin, Marc. *Calligraphy of the Middle Ages and how to do it*. Mineola, New York: Dover Publications, 1998. [Script Systems; ill.] (6, 10, 11, 12)

- - -. *Medieval Calligraphy. Its History and Technique*. Montclair, NJ, 1980. [Script Systems; ill.] (6, 10, 11, 12)

Drucker, Johanna. *The Alphabetic Labyrinth: The Letters in History and Imagination*. London; Thames & Hudson, 1999. [Script Systems; Symbol-set systems; Facs.; ill.] (2, 3, 4, 7, 12, Epilogue)

Duckett, Eleanor Shipley. *Alcuin, friend of Charlemagne, his world and his work*. New York, Macmillan, 1951. (10)

Dumville, David N. *English Caroline Script and Monastic History: Studies in Benedictinism, A.D. 950-1030*. Woodbridge, Suff.: Boydell, 1993. [Script Systems] (11, 12)

- - -, ed. and Trans. *The Historia Brittonum*. vol. 3, The "Vatican" Recension. Cambridge; Dover, NH: D.S. Brewer, 1985. [ill.] (5)

Dyer, Joseph. "The Singing of Psalms in the Early-Medieval Office." *Speculum*. July 1, 1989, v. 64(3); 535 ff. (10)

Eckerstrom, Ralph E. *Contemporary book design*. Urbana, Ill.: Beta Phi Mu, 1953. [Format systems; Codicology; Book Design; ill.] (11, 12)

Edmonds, George, 1788-1868. *The philosophic alphabet: with an explanation of its principles, and a variety of extracts, illustrating its adaptation to the sounds of the English language.. to which is added, a philosophic system of punctuation*. London: Simpkin and Marshall, 1832. (Epilogue)

Edwards, Nancy and Alan Lane, eds. *The Early Church in Wales and the West: Recent Work in Early Christian Archaeology, History and Place-Names*. Oxford: 1992. (5)

Ehrman, Bart. *The New Testament: A Historical Introduction to the Early Christian Writings*. Oxford: OUP, 1996. (4, 10)

Eliason, Norman and Peter Clemoes, eds. *Ælfric's First Series of Catholic Homilies: British Library Royal 7 C. xii*. EEMF v. 13. Copenhagen: Rosenkilde & Bagger, 1966. [Facs.] (12)

Eliot, T[homas] S[tearns]. *The Wasteland: Fascimile and Transcript*. Faber & Faber, NY, 1971. [Typical Working Drafts; Facs.] (11)

Ellard, Gerald. *Master Alcuin, Liturgist: A Partner of Our Piety*. Chicago: Loyola UP, 1956. 2nd ed. Manchester: Manchester UP; New York, New York: St. Martin's Press, 1989. (10)

Elliott, Ralph Warren Victor. *Runes, an introduction*. [ill.] (5)

Eusebius, of Caesarea, Bishop of Caesarea, ca. 260-340. *The ecclesiastical history*. English & Greek. English trans. by Kirsopp Lake. 2v. LCL; 153 and 265. London: Heinemann, 1926; 1932. (4, 5)

The Épinal glossary. Latin and Old-English of the eighth century. Photo-lithographed from the original ms. by W. Griggs and edited, with transliteration, introduction and notes, by Henry Sweet. London: Published for the Philological and Early English Text societies, 1883. [Script Systems; Orthograpghic Systems; facs.] (4, 8)

Even-Shoshan, Abraham. *Concordance to the Bible*. IV Vols. Jerusalem: Kiryath Sepher Ltd., 1980, 2nd printing. [Hebrew] (10)

Fairbank, Alfred J. and Berthold Wolpe. *Renaissance handwriting; an anthology of italic scripts*. Cleveland: World Pub. Co., 1960. [Script Systems; 96 plates] (Intro., 12)

Farmer, D. H., ed. *Regula: The rule of St. Benedict. Oxford, Bodleian Library, Hatton 48*. EEMF v. 15, Copenhagen: Rosenkilde & Bagger, 1968. [Facs.] (4, 5, 12)

Fausboll, Else. *Fifty-Six Ælfric Fragments: The newly found Copenhagen fragments of Ælfric's "Catholic Homilies" with facsimiles*. Copenhagen: Copenhagen UP, 1986. [Facs.] (12)

Feiler, Emil Von. *Das Benedictine-Officium, ein altenglisches Brevier aus dem II. Farhundert. Ein Beitrag zur Wulfstanfrage*. Heidelberg: Winter, 1901. (6, 12)

Felici, James and Ted Nace. *Desktop publishing skills: a primer for typesetting with computers and laser printers*. Reading, Mass.: Addison-Wesley, 1987. (Epilogue)

Fernandez Aller, Maria del Carmen. *Epigrafia y numismatica romanas en el Museo Arqueologico de Leon*. Leon: Colegio Universitario de Leon, 1978. [Script Systems; Plates: ill.] (3, 4, 5)

Février, James Germain. *Histoire de l'écriture, avec 135 figures dans le texte et 16 planches hors-texte*. Paris, Payot, 1948. [Script-systems; Plates, ill.] (2, 3, 4, 7, 10, 11, 12)

Finegan, J. *Encountering New Testament Manuscripts*. Grand Rapids: Eerdmans, 1974. (4)

Finnegan, Ruth H. *"Short time to stay": comments on time, literature, and oral performance*. Bloomington, Ind.: Indiana University, 1981. (11)

- - . *Oral Poetry*. Cambridge, Cambridgeshire: CUP, 1977. (10, 11)

Finnegan, Thomas A., Bishop of Killala, Intro. to, *Patrick the Pilgrim Apostle of Ireland, St. Patrick's Confessio and Epistola*. Edited and Translated with Analysis and Commentary by Ma'ire B. de Paor PBVM. Dublin: Veritas, 1998. 1-2. (5)

Finney, Timothy John. Subject: *Provenance of MSS*. <tc-list@shemesh.scholar.emory.edu>, Thu, 4 Feb 1999. (4)

Fishman, Joshua A., ed. *Advances in the creation and revision of writing systems*. The Hague: Mouton, 1977. [Orthographic Systems] (Intro, 2, Epilogue)

Flesch, Rudolf Franz. *Why Johnny still can't read: a new look at the scandal of our schools*. Frwd by Mary L. Burkhardt. New York: Harper & Row, 1983, 1981. (Intro., Epilogue)

Flower, Robin and Hugh Smith. *The Parker Chronicle and Laws: Corpus Christi College, Cambridge MS 173: A Facsimile*. London: Humphrey Milford, 1941. [Facs.] (6, 11, 12)

Flowers, Stephen E. *Runes and magic: magical formulaic elements in the older runic tradition*. New York: P. Lang, 1986. (5)

Fàrster, Max. "Die altenenglischen Texte der Pariser Nationalbibliothek." *Englische Studien* LXII, 1927. 113-131. (10)

- - -. *Die Beowulf-Handschrift*. Beriche über die Verhandlungen der Sächsischen. Akademie der Wissenschaften zu Leipzig. Philologische-historiche Klasse 71: 4, 1919. (11)

Foley, John Miles. *The Theory of Oral Composition: history and methodology*. Bloomington: Indiana UP, 1988. (10, 11)

- - -, ed. *Oral Tradition in Literature*. Columbia: U of Missouri Press, 1986. (4, 10, 11)

Folkingham, William. *Brachygraphie, post-writt; or, The art of short-writing, where most letters consist of single stroakes or motions of the pen, in best forms of penship...* London, T. Snodham, 1622. 2nd ed. A[lexander] T[remaine] Wright, ed. Typographic reproduction from the Duke of Devonshire's unique copy in Chatsworth library. London, 1898. (Epilogue)

Fowler, David. *The Bible in Early English Literature*. Seattle: WA; WUP, 1985. (10, 11, 12)

Fox, Cyril, Sir [1882-1967] and Bruce Dickins, eds. *The early cultures of north-west Europe* (H. M. Chadwick memorial studies). Cambridge, Eng.: CUP, 1950. (5)

Fraenkel, Gerd. *Writing systems*. Boston, Ginn. 1965. [Orthographic systems] (Intro, 2, 3)

Freedman, David Noel. "Another Look at Biblical Hebrew Poetry." *Directions in Biblical Poetry*. Ed. Elaine R.Follis. Sheffield: University of Sheffield, 1987. (10)

Frei, Hans W. *The Eclipse of Biblical Narrative: A Study in Eighteenth and Nineteenth Century Hermeneutics*. New Haven and London: Yale UP, 1974. (10, 12, Epilogue)

Frend, W. C. H. "The Christanization of Roman Britain." In M. W. Barley and R. P. C. Hanson, eds. *Christianity in Britain, 300-700*. Leicester: Leicester UP, 1968. 37-50. (5)

Frere, Walter Howard. *Antiphonale Sarisburiense* [Salisbury]*: a reproduction in facsimile of a manuscript of the 13th century, with a dissertation and analytical index*. Prepared for members of the Plainsong and Mediaeval Music Society. Farnborough, Hants., Eng.: Gregg Press, 1966. 6 v. [Musical Notation systems; Facs.] (10)

Frey, Jean Baptiste 1878-1939. *Corpus of Jewish inscriptions: Jewish inscriptions from the third century B.C. to the seventh century A.D.* Prolegomenon by Baruch Lifshitz. Volume 1, Europe. New York: Ktav Pub. House, 1975. Rprt of the 1936 ed. published under title: *Corpus inscriptionum judaicarum*, by Pontificio instituto di archeologia cristiana, Rome. [Script Systems; ill.] (4, 7, 9)

Gadd, C[yril] J[ohn]. *The early dynasties of Sumer and Akkad*. London: Luzac & co., 1921. (2)

Gaeng, Paul A. *An inquiry into local variations in vulgar Latin; as reflected in the vocalism of Christian inscriptions*. Chapel Hill: University of North Carolina Press, 1968. [Script Systems; Orthographic Systems] (4, 5, 6, 10)

Gajard, Dom Joseph. *The Rhythm of Plainsong*. Trans. Aldhelm Dean. New York: J. Fischer, 1943. (10)

Gallo, Italo. *Greek and Latin Papyrology*. Maria Rosaria Falivene and Jennifer R. March trns. London: University of London, 1986. [Script Systems; ill.] (3, 4)

Galpin, F[rancis] W[illiam], 1858-1945. *The music of the Sumerians and their immediate successors, the Babylonians & Assyrians. Described and illustrated from original sources*. NEw York: Da Capo Press, 1970. (1937) [Musical Notation Systems; Ill., music, plates] (9)

Ganz, David. *Corbie in the Carolingian Renaissance.* Sigmaringen: Jan Thorbecke, 1990. [Script Systems; Plates] (10)

Garamond: a note on the transmission of the design of the Roman typeface cut by Claude Garamond in the sixteenth century, with a discussion regarding the ultimate desposition of the punches cut by the celebrated typefounder. Chicago: Ludlow Typograph Co., 1930. [Script Design; ill.] (4, 10, 12)

Garcia Lobo, Vicente. *Las inscripciones de San Miguel de Escalada: estudio critico.* Barcelona: El Albir, 1982. [Script Systems; Orthographic Systems; Plates, facsims.] (4, 5)

Gascou, Jacques et Michel Janon. *Inscriptions latines de Narbonnaise (I.L.N.): Frejus.* Paris: Éditions du Centre national de la récherche scientifique, 1985. [Script Systems; ill] (4)

Gastoue, Amedee, 1873-1943. *Les origines du chant romain: l'Antiphonaire gregorien.* Rprt of the 1907 ed. published by A. Picard, Paris, which was issued as v. 1 of Bibliothèque musicologique. New York: AMS Press, 1975. [Musical Notation Systems; ill.] (10)

Gaur, Albertine. *A history of writing.* London: BL, 1987. [Script Systems; Plates, ill.] (Intro, 2, 3)

Geller, Stephen A. *Parallelism in early biblical poetry.* Missoula, Mont.: Scholars, 1979. (10)

Gem, Samuel H. *An Anglo-Saxon Abbott: Ælfric of Eynsham. A Study.* Edinburough: T and T Clark, 1912. (1, 6, 12)

Gentry, Helen and David Greenhood. *Chronology of books & printing.* Rev. ed. New York: Macmillan company, 1936. (2, 4, 6, 11, 12)

Georgiou, K. "Seafaring, Trade Routes, and the Emergence of the Bronze Age." *Res maritimae: Cyprus and the eastern Mediterranean from prehistory to late antiquity: proceedings of the Second International Symposium "Cities on the Sea", Nicosia, Cyprus, October 18-22, 1994.* Stuart Swiny, Robert L. Hohlfelder, Helena W. Swiny, eds. Atlanta, Ga.: Scholars Press, 1997. 117-124. (2, 3, 5)

Gerson-Kiwi, Edith. *Migrations and mutations of the music in East and West: selected writings.* Tel-Aviv: Tel-Aviv University, Faculty of Visual and Performing Arts, Department of Musicology, 1980. [Musical Notation Systems; ill.] (4, 9, 10)

Geveryahu, H. M. I. "Biblical Colophons: A Source for the Biography of Authors, Texts and Books," *Vetus Testamentum*, Sup. 28, 1975. 42-59 (9, 10).

- - - . "On the Method of Giving Names to Biblical Books," *Beth Mikra* 45, 1971. 146-51. (10)

- - - . "Notes on Authors and Books in the Days of the Bible." *Beth Mikra* 43, 1970. 368-74. (4, 10)

Gibson, Margaret, T.A. Heslop, and Richard W. Pfaff, eds. *The Eadwine psalter: text, image, and monastic culture in twelfth-century Canterbury.* London: Modern Humanities Research Association; University Park: Pennsylvania State UP, 1992. [Script Systems; Illuminations; Plates: ill.] (10, 12)

Giegerich, Heinz J. *English phonology: an introduction.* Cambridge [England]; New York: CUP, 1992. [ill.] (7)

- - - . *Metrical Phonology and Phonological Structure: German and English.* Cambridge: CUP, 1985. (7)

Gildas. *De excidio Britanniae*, ed. Joseph Stevenson. 1838. Rprt. Vaduz: Kraus Rprt, 1964. (5)

Gilgamesh, The Epic of. N. K. Sanders, Trans. and Intro. Harmondsworth; Penguin, 1976. (8)

Gillingham, S[usan]. *The poems and psalms of the Hebrew Bible.* Oxford; New York: OUP, 1994. (10)

Glaister, Geoffrey Ashall. *Glaister's Glossary of the Book.* Berkeley: U of California P, 1979. (11)

Glass, Henry Alexander. *The story of the Psalters; a history of the metrical versions of Great Britain and America from 1549 to 1885.* London, K. Paul, Trench, 1888.

Glassner, Jean-Jacques *Ecrire à Sumer: l'invention du cunéiforme.* Paris: Seuil, 2000. [Script Sys.] (2)

Goffart, Walter. *Barbarians and Romans A.D. 418-584: The Techniques of Accommodation.* Princeton: Princeton UP. 1980. (4, 5)

Goines, David Lance. *A constructed Roman alphabet: a geometric analysis of the Greek and Roman capitals and of the Arabic numerals.* Boston: D. R. Godine, 1982. [Script Design; Script Systems; ill.] (3, 5, 11, 12)

Gollancz, Sir Israel, intro. *Pearl, Cleanness, Patience and Sir Gawain, reproduced in facsimile from the unique MS. Cotton Nero A.x in the British Museum.* London, 1923. Rprt. London: EETS by OUP, 1955. [Facs.] (12)

- - - . *The Cædmon Manuscript of Anglo-Saxon Biblical Poetry: Junius XI in the Bodleian Library.* Oxford: Humphrey Milford, 1927. [Facs.] (11, 12)

Goodenough, Erwin R[amsdell], 1893-1965. *Jewish Symbols in the Greco-Roman Period.* 1953-1965. Rprt. Abridged; ed, Foreword, Jacob Neusner. Princeton, NJ: Princeton UP, 1988. [Script Systems; Symbol-set Systems; Plates; ill.] (4, 7)

Goody, Jack. *The logic of writing and the organization of society.* Cambridge; New York: CUP, 1986. (1)

- - - . *The interface between the written and the oral.* Cambridge: CUP, 1987 (1982). (1, 12)

Gorday, Peter. "Principles of patristic exegesis: Romans 9-11." In *Origen, John Chrysostom, and Augustine.* New York: E. Mellen Press, 1983. (4)

Gordon, Arthur Ernest. *illustrated introduction to Latin epigraphy.* Berkeley: California UP, 1983. [Script Systems; Plates, ill.] (3, 4)

Gordon, Joyce S. and Arthur E. Gordon. *Contributions to the palaeography of Latin inscriptions.* Berkeley: California UP, 1957. [Script Systems; ill.] (3, 4)

Gordon, Cyrus Herzel 1908-2001. *Forgotten scripts: their ongoing discovery and decipherment.* Rev. and enlarged ed. New York: Dorset Press, 1987. [Script Systems; ill.] (2, 12)

- - - . *Ugarit and Minoan Crete; the bearing of their texts on the origins of Western culture.* New York: W. W. Norton, 1966. (2, 3)

Goudy, Frederic W[illiam], 1865-1947. *The capitals from the Trajan column at Rome.* With xxv plates drawn & engraved by the author. New York: OUP, 1936. [Script Systems; ill.] (3, 5, 11, 12)

Goulder, Michael D. *The Prayers of David (Psalms 51-72): Studies in the Psalter, II.* JSOT, Suppl. 102. Sheffield: Sheffield Academic Press, 1990. (10)

- - - . *The Psalms of the Sons of Korah.* JSOT. Suppl. 20. Sheffield: JSOT Press, 1982. (10)

Gradon, Pamela. *Form and Style in Early English Literature.* London: Methuen & Co. Ltd., 1971. (8, 10, 11)

Graham, William A[lbert]. *Beyond the written word: oral aspects of scripture in the history of religion.* Cambridge [Cambridgeshire]; New York: CUP, 1987. [ill.] (4, 10, 11)

Gransden, Antonia. "Traditionalism and continuity during the last century of Anglo-Saxon monasticism." *The Journal of Ecclesiastical History.* v. 40, Apr. 1989. 159-207. (12)

- - - . *Historical Writing in England c. 550 to c. 1307.* London: 1974. (11, 12)

Graduale Triplex seu Graduale Romanum Pauli PP.VI cura recognitum & Rhythmicis signis a Solesmensibus Monachis ornatum Neumis Laudunensibus (Cod.239) et Sangallensibus (Codicum Sangallensibus 359 et Einsidlensis 121) nunc auctum. Tournai, Belgium: Thomas, 1973. (10)

Grattan, J. H. R. "On the Text of the Prose Portion of the Paris Psalter." *Modern Language Review* IV, 1908-9. 185-9. (10)

Grayson, Albert Kirk. *Assyrian rulers of the third and second millennia BC: to 1115 BC*. With Grant Frame, Douglas Frayne, and contr. on Nuzi by Maynard Maidman. Toronto; Buffalo: University of Toronto Press, 1987. [Facs. Microfiche] (2)

Greenfield, Kathleen Bolster. "Social and Political Ideas in English Vernacular Homiletic Literature c. 960-c. 1225: Church Doctrine as Ideology." Diss. Brandeis U, 1979. (11, 12)

Greenfield, Stanley B. and Daniel G. Calder. *A New Critical History of Old English Literature*. New York: New York UP, 1986. (11, 12)

Grein, C. W. M. *The Anglian Psalms, including the "Fragments."* Leipzig: Wigand, 1898. 83-230. (10)

- - - . *Kurzgefasste Angelsächsische Grammatik*. Cassel 1880. 9. (10)

- - - . *The Anglian Psalms, exclusive of the "Fragments."* Goettingen: Wigand, 1858. 83-230. (10)

Greenspoon, Leonard J. "The Use and Abuse of the term "LXX" and related terminology in Recent Scholarship," in *Bulletin of the International Organization for Septuagint and Cognate Studies*, No. 20, 1987. 21-29 (4)

Gress, Walter Banzet. *Advanced typography*. Washington, D.C.: United Typothetae of America, 1931. [Script Systems; Script Design; ill.] (12)

Gretsch, Mechthild. "Æthelwold's translation of the "Regula Sancti Benedicti," in *ASE* 3, 1974. 125-162. (12)

Grierson, P. "Relations between England and Flanders before the Norman Conquest." *Transactions of the Royal Historical Society*, 4th Ser. 32, 1941. 71-112. (12)

Griffith, M. S. The Method of Composition of Old English Verse Translation, with Particular Reference to the Metres of Boethius, The Paris Psalter and Judgment Day II. Diss. Oxford, 1985. (4, 10)

Gwynn, Edward, intro. *Book of Armagh, the Patrician documents*. [Trinity College, MS] Dublin: Stationery office, 1937. SERIES: Coimisiun laimhscribhinni na Heireann [The Irish manuscripts commission]. Facs. of Irish manuscripts. III. [Facs.] (5, 11, 12)

Haas, William. *Phono-graphic Translation*. Manchester: Manchester UP, 1970. (Epilogue)

Hallo, William W. and J.J. Van Dijk. *The Exaltation of Inanna*. New Haven: Yale University Press. 1968 (9)

Hamer, Enid. *The Metres of English Poetry*. London: Metheun, 1951. (5, 10)

Hamlin, Talbot. *Architecture Through the Ages*. New York: G. P. Putnam's Sons, 1953. [Plates; ill.] (2, 4, 5)

Hammond, Gerald. *The Making of the English Bible*. NY: Philosophical Library, 1983. (10)

Hammurabi, King of Babylonia. *The letters and inscriptions of Hammurabi, King of Babylon, about B.C. 2200: to which are added a series of letters of other kings of the first dynasty of Babylon; the original Babylonian texts, edited from tablets in the British Museum, with English translations, summaries of contents, etc., by L. W. King*. London: Luzac, 1898-1900; Rprt. New York: AMS Press, 1976. 3 v. in 2 [ill.] (2)

Harmon, James A., *Codicology of the court school of Charlemagne: Gospel book production, illumination, and emphasized script*. Frankfurt am Main; New York: P. Lang, 1984. [Codicology; Format systems; Book Design] (10)

Harper, John. *The forms and orders of western liturgy from the tenth to the eighteenth century.* Oxford: Clarendon, 1991. (10, 12)

Harper, Nicki D. C. and Tom Rindflesch. "A Computer-Aided Study in Graphemic Analysis." *Computing in the Humanities.* Peter C. Patton and Renee A. Holden, eds. Lexington, Mass: Lexington Books, 1981. 135-43. 135-43. (Epilogue)

Harris, John. *English sound structure.* Oxford, UK; Cambridge, Mass.: Blackwell, 1994. (7, 10, 11, Epilogue)

Harris, Roy. *The origin of writing.* LaSalle, IL: Open Court, 1986. [Script Systems; ill.] (2, 3)

Harris, William V. *Ancient Literacy.* Cambridge, Ma; London: Harvard UP. 1989. (Intro., 3, 4)

Hartog, François. *The Mirror of Herodotus: The Representing of the Other in the Writing of History.* Trans. Janet Lloyd. Berkeley: U of California P, 1988. (11)

Harvey, Anthony. "Some significant points of early Insular Orthography." In O' Corrain, 1989. 56-66. [Orthographic Systems] (5)

Harrison, Michael A. *Introduction to Formal Language Theory.* Reading, Mass.: Addison-Wesley, 1978. [Symbol-set Systems] (6, 8)

Hatch, W. H. P. *The Principal Uncial Manuscripts of the New Testament.* Chicago: Chicago UP, 1939 [Script Systems; Facs.] (4)

Hassall, W. O., intro. *The Macregol or Rushworth Gospels.* [Latin text ca. 800; Old English interlinear 900's] Bicester, Eng.: Oxford Microform Publications, 1978. [ill.] (6, 10, 11)

Hayakawa, S. I. *Language in Action.* New York: Harcourt, 1941. [Acoustic Phonology] (7)

Hayward, C. T. R. *Jerome's Hebrew Questions on Genesis.* Oxford: Clarendon, 1995. (4)

Healey, John F. *The early alphabet.* London: Published for the Trustees of the British Museum by British Museum Publication's, 1990. [Script systems; ill.] (2, 3, 4)

Heather, Peter. *The Goths.* Oxford: Blackwell Publishers, 1996. (4, 5)

- - - . *Goths and Romans.* Oxford: Blackwell, 1991. (4, 5)

Hector, Leonard Charles. *The Handwriting of English Documents.* London: Edward Arnold, 1966. [Script Systems; Plates] (12)

Henderson, George. *From Durrow to Kells: the insular gospel-books, 650-800.* London: Thames and Hudson, 1987. [Script Systems; Facs.] (5, 10)

Henry, Avril, trans. *The Eton roundels: Eton College MS 177 ("Figurae bibliorum"): a colour facsimile.* Aldershot, Hants, Eng.: Scolar Press; Brookfield, VT.: Gower Publishing Co., 1990. [Musical Notation systems; Facs.] (9, 10, 12)

Henry, Charles. "The Image of A Word." In *Humanities and the computer: new directions.* David S. Miall, ed. Oxford, Eng.: Clarendon; New York: OUP, 1990. 93-101. [Script Systems; ill.] (Epilogue)

Herodotus of Halicarnassus. *Herodotus: The Histories.* Trans. Aubrey de Sélincourt. Rev., intro. and notes, A. R. Burn. (Harmondsworth, Middlesex: Penguin, 1978). (10)

Herren, M. "Insular Latin C(h)araxare (Craxare) and its derivatives," *Peritia* 1. 273-77. (5)

Hessen, Otto von. *Il materiale altomedievale nelle collezioni Stibbert di Firenze*. Florence: All'insegna del giglio, 1983. [SCript Systems; Plates] (2, 4, 5, 11, 12)

Heywood, J. *Origin of the western nations & languages, showing the construction and aim of Punic; recovery of the universal language; reconstruction of Phoenician geography; Asiatic source of the dialects of Britain; principal emigrations from Asia; and description of Scythian society*. Manchester and London: NN, 1883. [Epilogue]

Higham, N. J. *The Convert Kings: power and religious affiliation in early Anglo-Saxon England*. Manchester; New York: Manchester U. Press, 1997. (5, 6, 10, 11)

- - - . *The English Conquest: Gildas and Britain in the Fifth Century*. Manchester; New York: Manchester UP, 1994. (5)

Hobson, G. D. *English Binding Before 1500*. Sandars lectures; 1927. Cambridge, At the University Press, 1929. [Codicology; ill.] (11)

Hochuli, Jost and Robin Kinross. *Designing books: practice and theory*. London: Hyphen, 1996. [Format Systems; Book Design; ill.] (11)

Hodge, Carleton Taylor. *Ritual and writing: an inquiry into the origin of Egyptian script*. Lisse, The Netherlands: Peter de Ridder, 1975. [Script systems; ill.] (2)

Holtz, Louis. *Donat et la tradition de l'enseignement grammatical: étude sur l'Ars Donati et sa diffusion (IVe-IXe siècle) et édition critique*. Paris: Centre national de la recherche scientifique, 1981. [Punctuation Systems; Plates; ill.] (2, 3, 4)

Hofstadter, Douglas R. "Metafont, Metathematics, and Metaphysics," *Metamagical Themas: Questing for the Essence of Mind and Pattern*. New York: Basic Books, Inc. 1985. [Script Systems; Script Design; ill.] (2, 4, 5, 7, 11, 12)

Hollahan, Patricia. "The Anglo-Saxon use of the Psalms: Liturgical Background and Poetic Use." Diss. U of Illinois at Urbana, 1977. (10)

Hollister, Paul M., ed. *American alphabets*. New York: Harper & Brothers, 1930. [Script systems] (7, 11, 12)

Holt, Robert. *The Ormulum with Notes and Glossary of Dr. R. M. White*. Oxford: Clarendon, 1878. Reprt. 1974. [2 plates] (12)

Hooker, J. T., intro. *Reading the Past: ancient writing from cuneiform to the alphabet*. Berkeley, California UP,; London: British Museum, 1990. [Script Systems; ill.] (2, 3)

Howard, Michael. *Angels & goddesses: Celtic Christianity & paganism in ancient Britain*. Chieveley, Berks [England]: Capall Bann Pub., 1994. (5, 10)

Howlett, D[avid] R. *Cambro-Latin Compositions: Their Competence and Craftsmanship*. Dublin: Four Courts Press, 1998. (5)

- - - . *British Books in Biblical Style*. Dublin: Four Courts Press, 1997. (5)

- - - . "Israelite Learning in Insular Latin," *Peritia: The Journal of the Medieval Academy of Ireland*, No. 11 (1997). 117-152. (5, 10)

- - - . *The Celtic Latin Tradition of Biblical Style*. Dublin: Four Courts Press, 1995. (5)

- - - . *Liber Epistolarum Sancti Patricii Episcopi: The book of Letters of Saint Patrick the Bishop*. Dublin: Four Courts Press, 1994. (5)

Hubner, Emil, 1834-1901. *Inscriptiones Hispaniae latinae*. CIL. Rprt. Berolini: W. de Gruyter, 1962-1974. 2 vol., v.2 [Script Systems; ill.; maps] (3, 4, 5)

- - - . *Inscriptiones Britanniae latinae*. Rprt. Berolini: W. de Gruyter, 1959. CIL, v.7 [Script Systems; ill.] (4, 5)

Hughes, Andrew. *Medieval Manuscripts for Mass and Office: A guide to Their Organization and Terminology*. Toronto: Toronto UP, 1982. [ill.] (10)

Huizinga, Johan. *Homo Ludens: Vom Ursprung der Kultur im Spiel*. Rprt. Hamburg: Rowohlt, 1956. English: *Homo Ludens*. Rprt. Boston: Beacon Press, 1955. (10)

Humphreys, Henry Noel, 1810-1879. *The origin and progress of the art of writing: a connected narrative of the development of the art in its primeval phases in Egypt, China, and Mexico; its middle state in the cuneatic systems of Nineveh and Persepolis; its introduction to Europe through the medium of the Hebrew, Phoenician, and Greek systems; and its subsequent progress to the present day*. 2d ed. London: Day and Son, Gate Street, Lincoln's Inn, 1855. [Script Systems; Plates; ill.] (2, 4, 5, 11, 12, Epilogue)

Hunt, Tony. *Teaching and Learning Latin in Thirteenth-Century England*. Cambridge: Brewer, 1991. (8, 12)

Huppé, Bernard F. *The Web of Words: structural analyses of the old english poems vainglory, the wonder of creation, the dream of the rood, and judith*. Albany, New York: SUNY Press, 1970. (Intro., 10, 11, 12)

Hutton, Ronald. *The Pagan Religions of the Ancient British Isles: their Nature and Their Legacy*. Oxford: Blackwell, 1991. (5)

Iberian Fathers. Claude W. Barlow, comm. and trans. Washington, D. C.: Catholic U of America P, 1969. vol. 62-63. (4)

Idelsohn, A. Z. *Jewish Music in its Historical Development*. New York: Schocken Books, 1967, 1929. [Musical Notation Systems; ill.] (9, 10)

Isidore of Seville. *Etymologiae*. W[illiam] M. Lindsay, ed. 2 vols, Oxford: Clarendon, 1911. (1)

Ives, Burl. *The Burl Ives Songbook: American Song in Historical Perspective*. New York: Ballantine, 1953. 36-37. (10)

Jackson, Donald. *The story of writing*. London: Studio Vista, 1981. [Script Systems; Kerning Systems; ill.] (Intro, 2, 3)

Jackson, Holbrook, 1874-1948. *The printing of books*. London: Cassell, 1938. (2, 11, 12)

Jackson, Hartley E. *26 lead soldiers: a textbook of printing types, methods, and processes for journalism students, and a convenient reference work for juniors in advertising offices and all others who have to do with the printed word*. Stanford University, Calif.: Stanford UP, 1937. [Script Systems; Script Design; ill.] (12)

Jacoby, Henry Sylvester, 1857-1955. *A text-book on plain lettering*. New York: The Engineering News Publishing Company, 1895. [Script Systems; ill.] (2, 12)

Jackson, MacD. P. "The transmission of Shakespeare's text." In *The Cambridge Companion to Shakespeare Studies*. Stanley Wells, ed. Cambridge: CUP, 1986. 163-85. (12)

Jaeger, W. *Early Christianity and Greek Paediea*. Cambridge, MA: Harvard UP, 1961. (4, 10)

Jain, Lakhmi C. and Beatrice Lazzerini. *Knowledge-based intelligent techniques in character recognition*. Boca Raton, Fla.: CRC Press, 1999. [Script Systems; symbol-set Systems] (Epilogue)

James, Allan. *Suprasegmental phonology and segmental form: segmental variation in the English of Dutch speakers*. Tubingen: M. Niemeyer, 1986. (5, 10, 11, Epilogue)

James, M[ontague] R[hodes]. *The Canterbury Psalter*. London: Lund, Humphries, 1935. [Facs.] (10, 12)

Jammers, Ewald. "Aufzeichnungsweisen der einstimmigen ausserliturgischen musik des Mittelalters." *Palaeographie der Musik*. Koln: Arno Volk, 1979. [Plates, ill.] (9, 10)

- - -. *Tafeln zur Neumenschrift*. Munich: Schneider, 1965. [Plates, ill.] (9, 10)

Jeffery, L[ilian] H[amilton]. *The local scripts of archaic Greece: a study of the origin of the Greek alphabet and its development from the eighth to the fifth centuries B.C.* Rev. ed., supplement by A. W. Johnston. Oxford: Clarendon Press, 1990. [Script Systems; 82 p. of plates: ill.] (2, 4)

Jeffery, Peter. *Re-Envisioning Past Musical Cultures: Ethnomusicology in the Study of Gregorian Chant*. Chicago: Chicago UP, 1992. (9, 10)

Jensen, Hans, 1884-? *Sign, symbol, and script; an account of man's efforts to write*. [Geschichte der Schrift.] George Unwin, trans. New York: Putnam, 1969. 3d ed., rev. and enl. [Symbol-set Systems, Script Systems] (2, 4, 5, 7, 11, 12)

Jensen, J[ohn] T[illotson]. *English phonology*. Amsterdam; Philadelphia: J. Benjamins, 1993. [Articulative Phonology] (5, 10, 11, Epilogue)

Jerome [Eusebius Hieronymus Sophronis] 342?-420. *Epistle* xlvi, 12. PL v. 22. (9)

John of Salisbury. *Metalogicon*. Clement C. J. Webb, ed. Oxford: OUP, 1929. Book I. (1)

Johnston, Paul. *Biblio-typographica, a survey of contemporary fine printing style*. New York: Covici, Friede, 1930. [Script Systems; Facs.] (2, 12)

Jones, Charles. *A history of English phonology*. London; New York: Longman, 1989. (5, 10, 11, Epilogue)

Jones, John (1645-1709). *Practical phonography*. Printed for Richard Smith. London: 1701. (Epilogue)

Jonsson, Bengt R. "Oral Literature: Written Literature." In *The Ballad and Oral Literature*. Joseph Harris, ed. Cambridge, MA: Harvard UP, 1991. 139-170. (10, 11)

Jousse, Marcel. *The oral style*. Trans. of *Style oral rythmique et mnemotechnique chez les verbo-moteurs*. Edgard Sienaert and Richard Whitaker. New York: Garland, 1990. (4, 10, 11)

Julian, John. "Psalms; Metrical Translations," in *A Dictionary of Hymnology*. Vol. II. New York: Dover, 2nd Edition, rev., 1907 (Intro, 10)

Kabell, Inge, Hanne Lauridsen, and Arne Zettersten. *Studies in early modern English pronunciation: a DEMEP publication*. Copenhagen: Dept. of English, University of Copenhagen: Atheneum Booksellers, 1984. (5, 10, 11, Epilogue)

Kahn, Daniel. *Syllable-based generalizations in English phonology*. Bloomington: Indiana University Linguistics Club, 1976. (5, 10, 11, Epilogue)

Kamesar, A. *Jerome, Greek Scholarship, and the Hebrew Bible*. Oxford Classical Monographs: Clarendon, 1993. (4, 10)

Katamba, F. *An introduction to phonology*. London: Longman, 1989. [Articulative Phonology] (Intro., 7, Epilogue)

Kaufmann, Walter. *Critique of Religion and Philosophy*. New York: Harper & Brothers, 1958. (4, 9, 10)

Keefer, Sarah Larratt. *Psalm-Poem and Psalter Glosses: The Latin and Old English Psalter-Text Background to "Kentish Psalm 50."* New York: Peter Lang, 1991. (10)

- - -. *The Old English Metrical Psalter, An Annotated Set of Collation Lists*. New York: London: Garland, 1979. (10)

- - - and David R. Burrows, "Hebrew and the "Hebraicum' in Late Anglo-Saxon England." *ASE* 19. (1990). 67-80. (10, 11)

Kelly, Rev. Columba, O.S.B. *The Cursive Torculus Design in the Codex St. Gall 359 and its Rhythmical Significance: A Paleographical and Semiological Study*. St. Meinrad, Indiana: Abbey, 1964. [Script Systems; Kerning Systems, Facs.] (10)

Kenney, E. J., ed. "Books and Readers in the Roman World." *Cambridge History of Classical Literature*, v. 2. Latin Literature. Cambridge: CUP, 1982. 3-32. (4)

Kenyon, Frederic G[eorge], Sir, 1863-1952. *Our Bible and the Ancient Manuscripts*. Rev. by A. W. Adams. New York: Harper, 1958. [Script systems; Plates; ill.] (4, 10, 12)

- - - , ed. *Facsimiles of Biblical manuscripts in the British Museum*. London: Printed by order of the Trustees, 1900. [Facs.] (4, 10, 12)

Keppie, L. J. F. *Understanding Roman inscriptions*. London: B. T. Batsford, 1991. [Script Systems; Plates; ill.] (4, 5, 11, 12)

Ker, Neil Ripley. *English manuscripts in the century after the Norman Conquest. The Lyell lectures, 1952-3*. Oxford, Clarendon Press, 1960. [Script Systems; 29 plates.] (2, 12)

- - -. *Catalogue of Manuscripts containing Anglo-Saxon*. Oxford: Clarendon, 1957. [Script Systems; Orthographic Systems; Punctuation systems; Plates] (4, 5, 11, 12)

- - - , gen. ed. *The pastoral care; King Alfred's translation of St. Gregory's Regula pastoralis. Ms. Hatton 20 in the Bodleian Library at Oxford, Ms. Cotton Tiberius B.XI in the British Museum, Ms. Anhang 19 in the Landesbibliothek at Kassel*. EEMF v. 6. Copenhagen: Rosenkilde & Bagger, 1956. [Facs.] (2, 5, 11, 12)

Keynes, Simon, ed. *Facsimiles of Anglo-Saxon charters*. Oxford; New York: Published for British Academy by OUP, 1991. *Anglo-Saxon charters*. Suppl. v. 1. [Script Systems; Orthographic systems; Facs.] (6, 7, 11, 12)

Keyser, Samuel Jay and Wayne O'Neil. *Rule generalization and optionality in language change*. Dordrecht, Holland; Cinnaminson, N.J., U.S.A.: Foris, 1985. (8, 10, 11, Epilogue)

Kiernan, Kevin S[tephen]. *Beowulf and the Beowulf Manuscript*. New Brunswick: Rutgers UP, 1981. [Script Systems; ill.] (11)

King, Margot H. and Wesley M. Stevens, eds. *Saints, scholars, and heroes : studies in medieval culture in honor of Charles W. Jones*. Collegeville, Minn.: Hill Monastic Manuscript Library, Saint John's Abbey and University, 1979. (6, 10, 11)

King, P. D. *Law and Society in the Visigothic Kingdom*. Cambridge: CUP, 1972. (4, 5)

Kirchner, Ioachimi. *Scriptura Latina Libraria: A Saeculo Primo usque ad finem medii aevi LXXVII imaginibus illustrata*. Monachii: R. Oldenbourg, 1970. [Script Systems; Plates] (4, 5, 11, 12)

Kittel, Bonnie Pedrotti. *The Hymns of Qumran: Translation and Commentary*. Society of Biblical Literature: Dissertation Series. 1981. (8, 9, 10)

Kleist, James A. *Clemens Romanus: The epistles of St. Clement of Rome and St. Ignatius of Antioch*. New York: Newman Press. 1946. (4)

Knapp, Robert C. *Latin inscriptions from central Spain*. Berkeley: University of California Press, 1992. [Script Systems; Orthographic systems; Plates] (4)

Kopecek, Thomas A. *A history of Neo-Arianism.* Cambridge, MA: Philadelphia Patristic Foundation; Winchendon, MA, 1979. 2 v. (4, 5)

Korhammer, Michael, ed. *Words, Texts, and Manuscripts.* Cambridge: Brewer, 1992. [Script systems; Format Systems; ill.] (4, 12)

Korpel, Marjo C. A and Johannes C. de Moor. "Fundamentals of Ugaritic and Hebrew Poetry." In *The Structural Analysis of Biblical and Canaanite Poetry.* Willem van der Meer & Johannes C. de Moor, eds. JSOT. Supp. Ser. No. 74. Sheffield: UP, 1988. (2, 9, 10)

- - - and Johannes Calvijnstichting de Moor. *A rift in the clouds: Ugaritic and Hebrew descriptions of the divine.* Munster: Ugarit-Verlag, 1990. (2, 9, 10)

Knuth, Donald E[rvin]. *The METAFONTbook.* Reading, MA: Addison Wesley, 1986. [Script Design] (2, Epilogue)

- - - . *METAFONT: the program.* Reading, Mass.: Addison Wesley, 1986. (2, Epilogue)

- - - . *Computer modern typefaces.* Reading, MA: Addison-Wesley, 1986. [Script Design] (2, Epilogue)

Kramer, Samuel Noah. "A Hymnal Prayer of Enheduana: the adoration of Inanna in Ur", Ancient Near Eastern Texts, 1969. 579-82 (9)

- - - . *From the tablets of Sumer; twenty-five firsts in man's recorded history.* Indian Hills, Colo., Falcon's Wing Press [1956] (2)

Kraus, Richard Curt. *Brushes with power: modern politics and the Chinese art of calligraphy.* Berkeley: California UP, 1991. [Script Systems; Facs.] (Intro., 2, Epilogue)

Kugel, James L. *The Idea of Biblical Poetry.* New Haven: Yale UP, 1981. (10)

Lakoff, George and Mark Turner, *More Than Cool Reason: A Field Guide to Poetic Metaphor.* Chicago and London: U of Chicago P, 1989. (Intro, 1, 10)

- - - and Mark Johnson. *Metaphors We Live By.* Chicago and London: U of Chicago P, 1980. (Intro, 1, 10)

Labande, Edmond-Rene, dir. SERIES: *Corpus des inscriptions de la France medievale.* 15 vols (CIFM). Textes etablis et presentes par Robert Favreau, Jean Michaud. Paris: Centre national de la recherche scientifique, 1974-. 15 vols. V. 6 with the collaboration of Bernadette Leplant. V. 9: Centre d'études superieures de civilisation medievale, Universite de Poitiers. [Script Systems; Plates; ill.] (2, 5, 11, 12).

Laister, M. L. W. "The Library of the Venerable Bede," In Alexander H. Thompson, ed. *Bede, his Life, Times and Writings.* Oxford: Clarendon, 1935. (8)

La Molette, Phillipe 1737-1793. *Traite sur la poesie et la musique des Hebreux, pour servir d'introductionaux Psaumes explique.* Paris: Moutard, 1781. (10)

Lane Fox, Robin. *Pagans and Christians.* New York: Knopf, 1987. (4, 5)

Lapidge, Michael. "Surviving Book Lists from A-S England," In Michael Lapidge and H. Gneuss. *Learning and Literature in A-S England.* Cambridge: CUP, 1985. 33-89. (5, 8, 11, 12)

Lass, Roger. *Old English: A historical linguistic companion.* Cambridge: CUP, 1994. [Articulative Phonology] (7)

Lassus, Orland de. *Psalmi Davidis poenitentiales Septem Psalmi Davidis.* [Recording] (10)

Laurian, Anne-Marie. "Humour et traduction au contact des cultures." *META*, 34:1. (Mars/March 1989): 5-14. (10)

Laurent, Dominican, fl. 1279. *The book of vices and virtues; a fourteenth century English translation of the Somme le roi of Lorens d'Orleans, edited from the three extant manuscripts by W. Nelson Francis*. Rprt. London; New York: EETS by OUP, 1968. [Plate] (12)

Lawson, Alexander S. *Anatomy of a typeface*. Rprt. Boston: Godine, 1990. [Script Design; ill.] (2, 12)

Layamon: *Brut. Edited from British Museum ms. Cotton Caligula A. IX and British Museum ms. Cotton Otho C. XIII, by G. L. Brook and R. F. Leslie*. London; New York: Published for the EETS, by OUP, 1963. [Facs.] (12)

Lee, John A. N. *Computer semantics; studies of algorithms, processors, and languages*. New York: Van Nostrand Reinhold, 1972. (7, Epilogue)

Lefferts, Peter M. *Robertus de Handlo The Rules and Johannes Hanboys The Summa: A new critical text and translation on facing pages, with an introduction, annotations, and indices verborum and nominum et rerum*. Lincoln and London: Nebraska UP, 1991. [Greek and Latin Music Theory] (9, 10)

Lehmann-Haupt, Hellmut, ed. *Gottingen: Niedersächsische Staats- und Universitatsbibliothek. Manuscript. Cod. Ms. Uffenb. 51*. [English and German: The Gottingen model book: a facsimile edition and translations of a fifteenth-century illuminators' manual.] Columbia: Missouri UP, 1978, 1972. [Facs.] (Intro, 11, 12)

Leo, Heinrich. *Altsächsische und angelsäschische Sprachproben*. Halle: NN, 1838. (5, 10, 11, Epilogue)

Lepsius, Richard, 1810-1884. *Standard alphabet for reducing unwritten languages and foreign graphic systems to a uniform orthography in European letters. Recommended for adoption by the Church missionary society*. London: Williams & Norgate, 1863. (Epilogue)

Levine, Samuel R. *The Semantics of Metaphor*. Baltimore & London: Johns Hopkins UP, 1977. (Intro., 2, 10)

Lewis, John Noel Claude. *The 20th century book: its illustration and design*. London: Herbert Press, 1984. 2d ed. [Book Design; ill.] (2, 4, 5, 11, 12)

Lewis, Naphtali ed. *Papyrology*. Department of Classics. Cambridge, Eng.; New York: CUP, 1985. [Script Systems; ill.] (3, 4)

Liber Usualis with Introduction and Rubrics in English. Ed. by Benedictines of Solesmes. Tournai, Belgium: Desclée & Co. 1950. [Musical Notation systems] (9, 10)

Lieberman, Saul. *Hellenism in Jewish Palestine: Studies in the Literary Transmission of Beliefs and Manners of Palestine in the I Century BCE-IV Century CE*. New York: Jewish Theological Seminary, 1950. (4)

- - - . *Greek in Jewish Palestine: Studies in the Life and Manners of Jewish Palestine in the II-IV Centuries CE*. New York: Jewish Theological Seminary, 1942. (4)

Lieu, Samuel N. C. *Manichaeism in Mesopotamia and the Roman East*. Leiden; New York: E.J. Brill, 1994. (4)

- - - . *Manichaeism in the later Roman Empire and medieval China: a historical survey*. Manchester: Manchester UP, 1985. (4)

Lindsay, Wallace Martin, ed. *Palaeographia Latina*. Hildesheim and New York: Olms, 1974. [Script Systems; Plates] (3, 4, 5)

- - - . *Early Irish Minuscule Script*. Oxford: James Parker and Co., 1910 (Rprt. Hildesheim: Georg Olms, 1971. [Script Systems; Plates] (4, 5, 11, 12)

Lipman, Michael, 1878-? *A history of the alphabet; illustrated by the author.* [New York] Royal Typewriter Company, Bureau of Research, 1930. [Script systems; ill.] (2, 10, 11, 12)

Lipp, Frances R. "Ælfric's Old English Prose Style." *SP* 66 (1969) 689-718. (1, 6, 12)

Lodowyck, Francis. A common writing. London: NN, 1647. (Epilogue)

- - - . *The Ground-work of a perfect new language, and an vniversal or commonwriting: and presented to the consideration of the learned by a well-willer to learning.* London: NN, 1652.

Logan, Robert K. *The alphabet effect: the impact of the phonetic alphabet on the development of Western Civilization.* NY: Morrow, 1986. [Symbol-set Systems; ill.] (2, 4, 5, 11, 12)

Lord, Albert Bates. "The Merging of Two Worlds: Oral and Written Poetry as Carriers of Ancient Values." In Foley, 1986. 19-64. (4, 10)

Loretz, Oswald. *Colometry in Ugaritic and Biblical poetry: introduction, illustrations and topical bibliography.* Altenberge: CIS-Verlag. 1987. (10)

Lot, Ferdinand. *The End of the Ancient World and the Beginnings of the Middle Ages.* Trans. Philip and Mariette Leon. New York: Harper, 1961. (4)

- - - et Philippe Lauer, dir. *Diplomata Karolinorum; recueil de reproductions en facsimile des actes originaux des souverains carolingiens conserves dans les archives et bibliothèques de France.* Toulouse: E. Privat; Paris: H. Didier, 1936- [Facs.] (4, 5, 11, 12)

Lowe, E. A., 1879-1969. *English Uncial.* Oxford: Clarendon, 1960. [Script Systems; Plates] (4, 5, 11, 12)

- - - and E.K. Rand. *A sixth-century fragment of the letters of Pliny the Younger; a study of six leaves of an uncial manuscript preserved in the Pierpont Morgan library, New York.* Washington: Carnegie Institution of Washington, 1922. [Script Systems; Plates, ill.] (4, 5)

- - - . *The Beneventan script : a history of the South Italian minuscule.* 1st ed. 1914; 2nd ed. prepared and enl. by Virginia Brown. Roma: Edizioni di storia e letteratura, 1980. 2 vol. [Script Systems; ill.] (2, 4).

Loyn, Henry R., ed. *A Wulfstan manuscript containing institutes, laws and homilies. British Museum Cotton Nero A.I.* EEMF. Copenhagen: Rosenkilde & Bagger, 1971. [Facs] (6, 12)

Ludovico degli Arrighi, Vicentino, fl. 1522. *The first writing book; an English translation & facsimile text of Arrighi's Operina, the first manual of the chancery hand.* With introd. and notes by John Howard Benson. New Haven: Yale UP, 1954;1955. SERIES: Studies in the history of calligraphy, 2. [Script Systems; Facs.] (12)

Lutz, C. E. *Schoolmasters of the Tenth Century.* Hamden, Conn: Archon, 1977. (11, 12)

Lynch, Joseph H. *The medieval church. A brief history.* London; New York: 1992. (11, 12)

Macalister, Robert Alexander Stewart. *Corpus Inscriptorium Insularum Celticarum.* Rprt. Dublin: Four Courts Press, 1996. (4, 5, 11, 12)

Mac Cana, Proinsias. "Notes on the Combination of Prose and Verse in Early Irish Narrative," *Early Irish LiteraturejẓjMedia and Communication.* Stephen N. Tranter and Hildegard L. C. Tristram, eds. Tübingen: Gunter Narr, 1989. 125-147. (5, 11)

- - - . *The learned Tales of Medieval Ireland.* Dublin Institute for Advanced Studies. Dublin: W. & S. Magowan, 1980. (5, 11)

Mac Eoin, Gearóid. "Orality and Literacy in Some Middle-Irish King-Tales." In Tranter and Tristram, 1989. 149-183. (5, 11)

Maddicot, J. R. "Trade, industry and the Wealth of King Alfred," *Past and present; Journal of Historical Studies*, May 1, 1989, no. 123. 3 ff. (4, 5, 11)

Mahoney, Dorothy. *The craft of calligraphy*. New York: Taplinger Pub. Co., 1982. [Script Systems; ill.] (2, 4, 5, 11, 12)

Mallon, Jean. *De l'ecriture: recueil d'etudes publiees de 1937 a 1981*. Paris: Editions de Centre National de la Recherche Scientifique, 1982. [Script Systems; ill.] (4, 6, 7, 10, 11)

- - - , R. Marichal, and C. Perrat. *L'Écriture latine de la capitale romaine à la minuscule*. Paris: Arts et Métiers Graphiques, 1939. [Script Systems; ill.] (4, 6, 7, 10, 11)

Malone, Kemp, ed. *The Nowell Codex: British Museum Cotton Vitellius A. xv, 2nd MS*. EEMF. v. 12. Copenhagen: Rosenkilde & Bagger, 1963. [Facs.] (11, 12)

- - - . *The Thorkelin Transcripts of BEOWULF*. EEMF. v. 1. Copenhagen: Rosenkilde & Bagger, 1951. (11, 12)

Mansoor, Menahem. *The Thanksgiving Hymns: Translated and Annotated with an Introduction*. Leiden: E. J. Brill, 1961. (8, 9, 10)

March, Francis A. *A Comparative Grammar of the Anglo-Saxon Language in which its forms are illustrated by those of the Sanscrit, Greek, Latin, Old Saxon, Old Friesic, Old Norse, and Old High-German*. New York: Harper, 1877. (4, Epilogue)

Marchand, James W. *The Sounds and Phonemes of Wulfila's Gothic*. The Hague: Mouton, 1973. [Script systems; Symbol-set Systems; Ill.] (4, 6)

Marenbon, John. *From the circle of Alcuin to the school of Auxerre: logic, theology, and philosophy in the early Middle Ages*. Cambridge, Eng.; New York: CUP, 1981. (11, 12)

Marrocco, W. Thomas & Nicholas Sandon, eds. *Medieval Music*. London: OUP, 1977. [Scores] (10, 12)

Martin, Douglas. *Book design: a practical introduction*. New York: Van Nostrand Reinhold, 1991. (2, 4, 11, 12)

Martin, Henri Jean et J. Vezin, eds. *Mise en page et mise en texte du livre manuscrit*. Paris: 1990. [Format Systems; Plates; Facs.] (2, 4, 11, 12, Epilogue)

- - - . *Histoire et pouvoirs de l'écrit*. Avec la collaboration de Bruno Delmas; prèface de Pierre Chaunu. Paris: Libr. académique Perrin, 1988. English: *The history and power of writing*. Trans. Lydia G. Cochrane. Chicago: UC Press, 1994. [Script Systems; ill.] (2, 4, 11, 12, Epilogue)

Mathieson, Robert. *The Great Polyglot Bibles: The Impact of Printing on Religion in the Sixteenth and Seventeenth Centuries*. Providence, RI: Brown Library, 1985. [Facs.] (12)

Mayr-Harting, Henry. *The Coming of Christianity to England*. New York: Schocken Books, 1972. (5)

Mazar, Benjamin. *The excavations in the Old City of Jerusalem; preliminary report of the first season, 1968; The Latin inscription from the excavations in Jerusalem*, by M. Avi-Yonah. [English translated by R. Grafman]. Jerusalem: Israel Exploration Society, 1969. [Plates; ill.] (4)

McCarter, P[eter] Kyle. *The antiquity of the Greek alphabet and the early Phoenician scripts*. Missoula, Mont.: Scholars Press for Harvard Semitic Museum, 1975. [Script Systems; ill.] (2, 4, 11, 12)

McCreesh, Thomas P. *Biblical Sound and Sense: Poetic Sound Patterns in Proverbs 10-29*. Sheffield: JSOT, 1991. (10)

McDonald, Lee Martin. *The Formation of the Christian Biblical Canon*. Nashville: Abingdon Press, 1988. (4)

McGann, Jerome J. *The textual condition*. Princeton studies in culture; power; history. Princeton, N.J.: Princeton UP, 1991. (12, Epilogue)

- - - . *A Critique of Modern Textual Criticism*. Chicago: University of Chicago Press, 1983. (12, Epilogue)

McGurk et al, eds. *An Eleventh-Century Anglo-Saxon illustrated Miscellany: British Library Cotton Tiberius B. V Part I with leaves from British Library Cotton Nero D. II*. EEMF. v. 21. Copenhagen: Rosenkilde & Bagger, 1983. [Facs.] (5, 11, 12)

McKinnon, James. *Music in early Christian literature*. Cambridge: CUP, 1987. (9, 10)

- - - , ed. *Antiquity and the Middle Ages: From Ancient Greece to the 15th Century*. Music and Society Series, Vol 1. Englewood Cliffs NJ: Prentice Hall, 1990. (4, 9, 10)

McKitterick, Rosamond. *Books, scribes, and learning in the Frankish Kingdoms, 6th-9th centuries*. Aldershot, Hampshire, Great Britain; Brookfield, Vt., USA: Variorum, 1994. (5, 10)

- - - , ed. *Carolingian culture: emulation and innovation*. Cambridge [England]; New York, N.Y., USA: CUP, 1994. (10)

- - - . *The Carolingians and the Written Word*. Cambridge: CUP, 1989. (10)

- - - . *The Frankish church and the Carolingian reforms, 789-895*. London: Royal Historical Society, 1977. (10)

McLean, Ruari. *Victorian book design & colour printing*. London: Faber & Faber, 1963. [Plates,] (12)

- - - . *Modern book design: from William Morris to the present day*. London: Faber, 1958. [ill.] (11)

McNamara, M. *Glossa in Psalmos. The Hiberno-Latin Gloss on the Psalms & Codex Palatinus Latinus 68 (Psalms 39:11-151:7)*. Studi e Testi 310. Roma: Vatican City, 1986. (4, 5, 10)

McSparran, Frances and P[amela] R. Robinson, intro. *Cambridge University Library MS Ff.2.38*. London: Scolar Press, 1976. [Facs.] (2, 12)

Meeks, Wayne A. *Jews & Christians in Antioch in the first four centuries of the common era*. Missoula, Mont. Scholars Press. 1978. (4)

Mellersh, H. E. L. *Sumer and Babylon*. New York: Crowell 1965, 1964. (2)

Mercati, G. *Psalterii Hexapli Reliquiae. Pars prima. Codex rescriptus Bybliothecae Ambrosianae o.39*. Roma: Vatican City, 1958. [Plates] (2, 4, 5, 10, 12)

Meredith, Peter and Stanley J. Kahrl, intro. *The N-town plays: a facsimile of British Library MS Cotton Vespasian D VIII*. Leeds: University of Leeds, 1977. [Plates] (11, 12)

Metzger, Bruce M[anning]. *Manuscripts of the Greek Bible: an introduction to palaeography*. New York: OUP, 1981. [Script Systems; Plates]. (2, 4, 5, 7, 11, 12)

Millar, Eric George, ed. *Lindisfarne Gospels: three plates in colour and thirty-six in monochrome from Cotton ms. Nero D.IV in the British Museum with pages from two related manuscripts*. London: British Museum, 1923. [Plates] (5, 11, 12)

- - - . *The Luttrell psalter; two plates in colour and one hundred and eighty-three in monochrome from the Additional manuscript 42130 in the British Museum*. London: British Museum, 1932. [Plates] (10)

Millar, Fergus. *The Roman Near East, 31 B.C.-A.D. 337*. Cambridge: Harvard UP, 1993. (4)

Millares Carlo, Agustin, 1893-? *Consideraciones sobre la escritura visigotica cursiva*. Leon: Centro de Estudios e Investigacion San Isidoro, Archivo Historico Diocesano, 1973. [Script Systems, ill.] (4, 5, 7)

Milne, H. J. M. and T. C. Skeat, *Scribes and Correctors of the Codex Sinaiticus*. London: British Museum, 1938. [Plates, facs.]. (4)

- - - , eds. *The Codex Sinaiticus and the Codex Alexandrinus*. 2d ed. London: British Museum, 1955 [ill., plates] (4)

Mirande, Dominique, 1835-? *Le code de Hammourabi et ses origines, aperçu sommaire du droit chaldéen*. Paris, E. Leroux, 1913. (2)

Mitchell, Bruce. "The Dangers of Disguise: Old English Texts in Modern Punctuation." *RES*, Vol. XXXI, 124, Nov. 1980. 385-413. (Intro., Epilogue)

Mommsen, Theodor 1817-1903. *Inscriptiones Bruttiorum, Lucaniae, Campaniae, Sicilae, Sardiniae latinae*, Berolini: W. de Gruyter, 1963. 2 vols. CIL. v. 10 [ill., plates, maps.] (3, 4, 5, 7)

- - - . *Inscriptiones Asiae, provinciarum Europae graecarum, Illyrici latinae*, consilio et auctoritate Academiae Litterarum Regiae Borussicae. Rprt. Berolini: W. de Gruyter, 1958-1967. 4 v. [ill., maps] (3, 4)

Morn, Hugh Anderson. *The alphabet and the ancient calendar signs: astrological elements in the origin of the alphabet*. Palo Alto, Calif.; Pacific Books, 1953. [Symbol-set Systems; Script Systems; ill.] (2, 3)

Morison, Stanley, 1889-1967. *Politics and Script: Aspects of authority and freedom in the development of Graeco-Latin script from the sixth century B. C. to the twentieth century A.D. The Lyell Lectures 1957*. Nicolas Barker, ed. Oxford: Clarendon Press, 1972. [Script Systems; Plates] (Intro., 2, 4, 5, 11, 12)

- - - . *Letter forms, typographic and scriptorial: two essays on their classification, history, and bibliography*. London: Nattali & Maurice, 1968. [Script Systems; Facs.; ill.] (Intro., 2, 4, 5, 11, 12)

- - - . *Calligraphy, 1535-1885; a collection of seventy-two writing-books and specimens from the Italian, French, Low Countries and Spanish schools, catalogued and described*. Milano: La Bibliofila, 1962. [Script Systems; ill.] (Intro., 12)

Morrell, Minnie Cate. *A Manual of Old English Biblical Materials*. Knoxville: U of Tennesse P, 1965. (10, 11, 12)

Morris, Richard Lee, *Runic and Mediterranean epigraphy*. Odense: Odense UP, 1988. [Script Systems, Facs.] (2, 4, 5, 11, 12)

Mozley, F. W. *The Psalter of the Church. The Septuagint Psalms Compared with the Hebrew*. Cambridge: CUP, 1905. (4, 10)

Mulhern, John F., Steven R. Sparley, and Peter C. Patton. "Computer Aids to Sumerian Lexicography." *Computing in the Humanities*. Peter C. Patton and Renee A. Holden, eds. 5383. Lexington, Mass: Lexington Books, 1981. (Epilogue)

Mumby, Frank Arthur, 1872-1954. *Publishing and bookselling: a history from the earliest times to the present day*. Bib. by W. H. Peet. London: Jonathan Cape, 1930. (2, 4, 5, 11, 12)

Munch, Klaus Heje. *Computational Language ComprehensionjzjA Knowledge-Based Process*. Dept. of Computer Science. Lyngby: Technical University of Denmark, 1987. (Epilogue)

Murphy, Michael Anthony. *The Contribution of Polemics to Old English Studies in the Sixteenth and Seventeenth Centuries*. Diss. University of Pittsburgh, 1965. (12)

The Musical notation of the middle ages exemplified by facsimiles of manuscripts written between the tenth and sixteenth centuries inclusive, dedicated (by permission) to H.R.H. the Duke of Edinburgh.

Produced for the members of the Plainsong and mediaeval music society. London: J. Masters & co., 1890. [Facs.] (9, 10, 12)

Myers, Robin and Michael Harris, eds. *A millennium of the book: production, design & illustration in manuscript & print, 900-1900.* Winchester, Hampshire: St. Paul's Bibliographies; New Castle, Delaware: Oak Knoll Press, 1994. [Facs., ill.] (10, 11, 12)

Mynors, A. B., ed. *The Moore Bede: an eighth century ms of the Venerable Bede's Historia Ecclesiastica: MS Kk.v.16 in the University Library, Cambridge.* Copenhagen: Rosenkilde & Bagger, 1959. [Facs.] (8, 11, 12)

Nakanishi, Akira. *Writing systems of the world: alphabets, syllabaries, pictograms.* [Sekai no monji]. English: Rutland, Vt.: Tuttle, 1980. [Script Systems] (2, 4, 5, 11, 12)

Naveh, Joseph. *Early History of the Alphabet: An Introduction to West Semitic Epigraphy and Palaeography.* Jerusalem: Magnes, 1982. [Script Systems; Plates, ill.) (2, 4, 7)

Napier, A[rthur] S. *History of the Holy Rood-Tree, a twelfth century version of the cross legend, with Notes on the Orthography of the Ormulum (facs.) and a Middle English Compassion Mariae.* London: EETS, K. Paul Trench, Trubner & Co., 1894. [Orthographic systems, Facs.] (12)

Neale, J[ohn] M[ason], and R[ichard] F[rederick] Littledale. *A Commentary on the Psalms from Primitive and Medieval Writers: and from the various office-books and Hymns of the Roman, Mozarabic, Ambrosian, Gallican, Greek, Coptic, Armenian, and Syriac Rites.* 1884. Rprt. New York: AMS Press, 1976. (10)

Needham, P. *Twelve Centuries of Book-Binding. 400-1600.* New York: Pierpont Morgan Library: OUP, 1979. [Ill.] (3, 4, 10, 11)

Neusner, Jacob. *Oral tradition in Judaism : the case of the Mishnah.* New York: Garland, 1987. The Albert Bates Lord studies in oral tradition ; vol. 1 (10, 11)

- - - . *The oral Torah: the sacred books of Judaism: an introduction.* San Francisco: Harper & Row, 1986. (4, 10, 11)

Newmark, Peter. "The Translation of Metaphor." Paprotté and Dirven, *Ubiquity.* 295-326. (Intro, 1, 10)

Nevanlinna, Saara. "Simile in the Old English Paris Psalter: Syntax and Variation." Modern Language Society 100 Years: Helsinki: *Soc. Neophilol.,* 1987. 317-334. (10)

Nickelsburg, George W. E. *Jewish literature between the Bible and the Mishnah: a historical and literary introduction.* Minneapolis: Fortress, 1981. (4, 9, 10)

Nielsen, Hans Frede. *Old English and the continental Germanic languages: a survey of morphological and phonological interrelations.* 2nd, rev. ed. Innsbruck: Institut fur Sprachwissenschaft der Universitat Innsbruck, 1985. (5, 10, 11, Epilogue)

Nietzsche, Friedrich. *On the Genealogy of Morals.* Walter Kaufmann, Trans. and ed. New York: Vintage, Rprt. 1989. (Intro, 1, 4, 10)

Nilsen, Don Lee Fred and Alleen Pace Nilsen. *Language play: an introduction to linguistics.* Rowley, MA.: Newbury House Publishers, 1978. (7, 10)

Nissen, Hans J., Robert K. Englund, Peter Damerow. *Archaic Bookkeeping: Early Writing and Techniques of Economic Administration in the Ancient Near East.* Trans. by Paul Larsen. Chicago: Chicago UP, 1993. [Illus.] (2)

Nist, John A. *Textual Elements in the Beowulf Manuscript*. Paper of the Michigan Academy of Science, Arts, and Letters, vol. xlii, 1957. 331-338. (11)

Nunberg, Geoffrey. *The linguistics of punctuation*. Stanford, CA.: Center for the Study of Language and Information. 1990. (2, 3, 10, 11)

Norman, James. *Ancestral voices: decoding ancient languages*. New York: Four Winds Press, 1975. [Script Systems, ill.] (2, 3)

O'Connor, Michael Patrick.'The Pseudosorites: A Type of Paradox in Hebrew Verse,' in *Direction in Biblical Hebrew Poetry*. Sheffield: JSOT, 1987. (10)

- - - . *Hebrew verse structure*. Winona Lake, Ind.: Eisenbrauns, 1980. (10)

O Cuiv, Brian. *The Linguistic Training of the Mediaeval Irish Poet*. Statuatory Lecture 1969. School of Celtic Studies. Dublin. Hertford: Stephen Austin and Sons, Ltd., 1973. (5, 10)

O'Curry, Eugene, 1796-1862. *Lectures on the manuscript materials of ancient Irish history*. Delivered at the Catholic University of Ireland, during the sessions of 1855 and 1856. Dublin: W. A. Hinch [etc.] 1878. [Plates] (5, 10, 11)

O Croinin, Dàibhi."Is the Augsburg Gospel Codex a Northumbrian Manuscript?" In *St. Cuthbert, His Cult and His Community to AD 1200*, edited by Gerald Bonner and others. Woodbridge: Boydell, 1989. 189-201. (6)

Odenstedt, Bengt. *On the origin and early history of the runic script: typology and graphic variation in the older futhark*. Uppsala: Gustav Adolfs akademien; Stockholm, Sweden: Distributor, Almqvist & Wiksell International, 1990. [Script Systems; ill.] (5)

Ogg, Oscar. *The 26 letters*. Rev. ed. New York: Crowell, 1971. [Script Systems; ill.] (2, 4, 5, 11, 12)

Ohba, Keizo. "The Dangers of Emendation and Modern Punctuation in Beowulf." In *Annual Reports of Studies: Doshisha Women's College*, 32.1, 1981. 1-27. (Intro., 11, Epilogue)

O'Keeffe, Katherine O'Brien. *Visible Song: Transitional Literacy in Old English Verse*. Cambridge: CUP, 1990. [Script Systems; Facs.] (5, 10, 11, Epilogue)

Omeltchenko, Stephen William. *A quantitative and comparative study of the vocalism of the Latin inscriptions of North Africa, Britain, Dalmatia, and the Balkans*. Chapel Hill: NC, UNC. Dept. of Romance Languages: [Orthographic systems; ill.]. (4, 5, 10)

O'Neill, Patrick P. "The Old English Introductions to the Prose Psalms and the Paris Psalter: Sources, Structure, and Composition." *Studies in Philology 1981*, vol. 78(5). 20-38. (10)

O'Neill, Timothy, ed.; Francis John Byrne, intros. *The Irish hand: scribes and their manuscripts from the earliest times to the seventeenth century : with an exemplar of Irish scripts*. Mountrath, Portlaoise, Ireland: Dolmen Press, 1984. [Script Systems, ill.] (5, 6, 11, 12).

Ong, Walter J. "Text as Interpretation: Mark and After." In Foley, 1986. 147-169. (4, Epilogue)

- - - . *Orality and literacy : the technologizing of the word*. London; New York: Methuen, 1982. [Script Systems; Orthographic Systems] (Intro., 1, Epilogue)

Opland, Jeff. *Anglo-Saxon Oral Poetry: A Study of the Traditions*. New Haven: Yale UP, 1980. (11)

Oring, Elliott, ed. *Folk Groups and Folklore Genres*. Logan, UT: Utah State UP, 1986. (10)

Orosius, Paulus. *The Tollemache Orosius (British Museum Additional manuscript 47967)*, ed. Alistair Campbell. EEMF. v. 3. Copenhagen: Rosenkilde & Bagger, 1953. [Facs.] (11, 12)

Osley, A. S., ed. *Caligraphy and Paleography: essays presented to Alfred Fairbank on his 70th birthday.* New York: October House, 1966 [Script Systems; ill. Facs.] (2, 4, 7, 11, 12)

Owen, Robert Latham, 1856-1947. *The global alphabet.* Washington, U.S. Govt. print. off., 1943. Congressional Record: 78th Cong., 1st sess. Senate. Doc. 49 (Epilogue)

Owens, Henry Lee. *Fonetik English.* Tacoma Park, Washington, D.C.: Washington College Press, 1935. (Epilogue)

Page, R[Raymond] I[an]. *Runes.* London: British Museum Publications, 1987. [Script Systems; ill.] (5)

Palol, Pedro de y Jose Vilella. eds. *Clunia II: la epigrafia de Clunia.* Madrid: Ministerio de Cultura, Direccion General de Bellas Artes y Archivos, Subdireccion General de Arqueologia y Etnografia, 1987. [Script Systems; Plates] (4)

Palmer, F. R. *Semantics.* Cambridge: CUP, 1976, 1981. (10)

Paprotté, Wolf, and René Dirven, eds. *The Ubiquity of Metaphor: Metaphor in Language and Thought.* Amsterdam & Philadelphia: John Benjamins, 1985. (Intro, 1, 10)

Pardee, Dennis, *Ugaritic and Hebrew poetic parallelism: a trial cut (NT I and Proverbs 2).* Leiden; New York: E.J. Brill, 1988. (10)

Paris, Gaston Bruno Paulin, 1839-1903, ed. *Les plus anciens monuments de la langue francaise (IXe, Xe siecle).* Societe des anciens textes francais. Paris: Firmin-Didot, 1875; Rprt. New York: Johnson, 1965. [Script Systems; Facs.; ill.] (4, 10)

Parker, D[avid] C. *Codex Bezae: an early Christian manuscript and its text.* Cambridge; New York: CUP, 1992. [Ill.] (4)

Parkes, Malcolm B. *Pause and Effect: An Introduction to the History of Punctuation in the West.* Aldershot, Hants.: Scolar Press, 1992. [Script Systems; Punctuation Systems; Plates] (2, 3, 10)

- - - . *Scribes, Scripts and Readers: Studies in the Communication, Presentation and Dissemination of Medieval Texts.* London: Hambledon Press, 1991. (12)

- - - and Andrew G. Watson. *Medieval Scribes, Manuscripts and Libraries: Essays Presented to N. R. Ker.* London: Scolar Press, 1978. (12)

Parrish, Carl. *The Notation of Medieval Music.* New York: Pendragon Press, 1978. [Ill.] (9, 10)

Parsell, Jack Rogers. *World fonetic alfabet.* New York, 1946. 3rd ed. 1st ed., December 1942. (Epilogue)

Parsons, David, ed. *Tenth-Century Studies.* London: Phillimore, 1975. (12)

Partridge, A. C. *English Biblical Translations.* New York: Andre Deutsch, 1973. (10, 12)

Patrologia Graeca [Fathers of the Church: Greek] Ed. Jacques-Paul Migne. 157 vols. Paris: Migne, 1857-66.

Patrologia [Fathers of the Church: Latin.] 221 vols.; 218-221, Indices. Paris: Migne, 1841-64.

Patrologia Syriaca: [Fathers of the Church: Syriac] with Latin translations. Paris: Firmin-Didot, 1894-1926. (4)

Pearce, Charles. *The anatomy of letters: a guide to the art of calligraphy.* New York: Taplinger Pub. Co., 1987. [Script Systems; Script Design; ill.] (2, 4, 7, 11, 12)

Pearsall, Derek and I. C. Cunningham, eds. *The Auchinleck Manuscript: National Library of Scotland, Advocates' MS. 19.2.1.* London: Scolar Press, 1977. [Facs.] (8, 11, 12)

Pearson, Birger, ed. *The Roots of Egyptian Christianity*. Minneapolis: Fortress Press, 1986. (4, 9)

Peckham, John Brian. *The development of the late Phoenician scripts*. Cambridge, MA: Harvard UP, 1968. Harvard Semitic series, v. 20. [Script Systems; 17 plates] (Intro. 2, 4, 5, 7)

Pelzer, Auguste. *Abreviations latines medievales. Supplement au Dizionario di abbreviature latine ed. italiane, de Adriano Cappelli*. Louvain: Publications universitaires; Paris: Beatrice-Nauwelaerts, 1964. [Script Systems; ill.] (4, 5, 8)

Petrucci, Armando. *Public Lettering: Script, Power, and Culture*. Trans. Linda Lappin. Chicago; London: University of Chicago Press, 1993. [Script Systems; Plates] (Intro., 1, 2, 4, 5, 11, 12, Epilogue)

Petti, Anthony G. *English literary hands from Chaucer to Dryden*. Cambridge, Mass.: Harvard UP, 1977. [Script Systems; facs.] (12)

Pietersma, A[lbert]. "New Greek Fragments of Biblical Manuscripts in the Chester Beatty Library." *Bulletin of the Society of Papyrologists* 24 (1987). 37-61. (4, 10)

- - - . "David in the Greek Psalms." *Vetus Testamentum* 30 (1980), 213-26. (10)

- - - , ed. *Two Manuscripts of the Greek Psalter in the Chester Beatty Library, Dublin*. Rome: Biblical Institute Press, 1978. [facs.] (10)

- - - . "The Greek Psalter: A Question of Methodology and Syntax," *Vetus Testamentum* 25, 1975. 60-69. (10)

Pirenne, Henri. *Mohammed and Charlemagne*. Trans. Bernard Miall. Totowa, NJ: Barnes, 1980. (10)

Pitman, Isaac, Sir, 1813-1897. *A manual of phonography, or, writing by sound: a natural method of writing by signs that represent spoken sounds; adapted to the English language as a complete system of phonetic shorthand*. London: F. Pitman, 1878. (Epilogue)

Plainsong & Medieval Music Society. *The Elements of Plainsong compiled from a Series of Lectures*. London: Wantage, 1909. (10)

Plantin, Christophe, ca. 1520-1589, (presumed author). *An account of calligraphy & printing in the sixteenth century from dialogues attributed to Christopher Plantin, printed and published by him at Antwerp, in 1567*. French and Flemish text in facs., English trans. and notes Ray Nash; foreword Stanley Morison. Cambridge, Mass.: Department of Printing and Graphic Arts, Harvard College Library, 1940. [Script Systems; Facs.] (12)

Posner, Raphael and Israel Ta-Shema. *The Hebrew Book: An Historical Survey*. New York: Amiel, 1975. (4, 12)

Pound, Roscoe. *The History and the System of the Common Law*. Vol. 1. National Law Library. New York: P. F. Collier & Son, 1939. (5)

Preston, Jean F. and Laetitia Yeandle. *English handwriting, 1400-1650: an introductory manual*. Binghamton, N.Y.: Pegasus Paperbooks, Medieval & Renaissance Texts & Studies, 1992. [Script Systems; Plates] (12)

Price, Lorna. *The Plan of St. Gall in Brief*. Berkeley: University of California Press, 1982. [Facs.] (5, 7, 10, 12)

Propp, Vladimir. "Morphology of the Folktale." *International Journal of Linguistics*. Vol. 24, No. 4, October 1958. (8, 10, 11)

Pryor, John H. *Geography, technology, and war : studies in the maritime history of the Mediterranean, 649-1571*. Cambridge: New York: CUP, 1992. (2, 3, 5, 10)

Pseudo-Turpin. *Historia Karoli Magni et Rotholandi. The Anglo-Norman Pseudo-Turpin chronicle of William de Briane*. Ian Short, ed. Oxford: Blackwell for the Anglo-Norman Text Society, 1973. [Text: Anglo-French; commentary and notes: English] [Plate; facs.] (10)

Quine, W. V. *Quiddities: An Intermittently Philosophical Dictionary*. Cambridge, MA: Harvard UP, 1987.

Quinn, William A. and Audley S. Hall. *Jongleur: A Modified Theory of Oral Improvisation and Its Effects on the Performance and Transmission of Middle English Romance*. Washington, DC: University Press of America, 1982. (10, 11)

Qumran Cave 4, VIII: Parabiblical Texts, Part 1. Harold Attridge, Torlif Elgvin, Jozef Milik, Saul Olyan, John Strugnell, Emanunel Tov, James Vanderkam, and Sidnie White. DJD, 1962- . Vol. XIII. Oxford: Clarendon Press, 1994. [Script Systems; Plates] (Intro, 2, 4, 5, 7, 10, 11)

Raabe, Paul R. *Psalm Structures: A Study of Psalms with Refrains*. JSOT. Supplement Series 104. Sheffield: Sheffield Academic Press, 1990. (10)

Raasted, Jorgen. *Intonation Formulas and Modal Signatures in Byzantine Musical Manuscripts*. Copenhagen: Munksgaard, 1966. (9)

Rabanal, Alonso y Manuel Abilio. *Fuentes literarias y epigraficas de Leon en la antiguedad*. Leon: Institucion "Fray Bernardino de Sahagun" de la Excma. Diputacion Provincial: Consejo Superior de Investigaciones Cientificas (CECEL), 1982. 2 vol. V. 2 Plates. [Script Systems; Plates] (4, 5, 7)

Radford, C. A. Ralegh. "The Archaeological Background on the Continent." In Barley and Hanson, 1968. 19-36 (5)

Raeburn, Michael, ed. *Architecture of the Western World* edited and with an introduction by Michael Raeburn; foreword by Sir Hugh Casson; chapters by J.J. Coulton, et al. New York: Crescent Books: Distributed by Crown Books, 1984. [ill.] (5)

Ramsay, Robert L. "The Latin Text of the Paris Psalter: A Collation and some Conclusions." *American Journal of Philology* 41 (1920). 147-176. (10)

Rankin, Susan. "Neumatic Notations in Anglo-Saxon England." *Musicologie Medievale, Notations et Sequences*. Paris: Librarie Honore Champion, 1987. 129-144. (10)

Rapp, Albert. *The Origins of Wit and Humor*. New York: Dutton, 1951. (10)

Raskin, Victor. *Semantic Mechanisms of Humor*. Dordrecht and Boston: D. Reidel, 1985. (10)

Ray, Eric, Joel Lurie Grishaver. *Sofer: the story of a Torah scroll*. Los Angeles: Torah Aura Productions, 1986. [ill.] (4)

Rees, B. R. *Pelagius: A Reluctant Heretic*. Woodbridge: Boydell, 1988. (5)

Renoir, Alain. "Oral Formulaic Rhetoric and the Interpretation of Literary Texts." In Foley, 1986. 103-135. (10, 11)

- - - . *A key to old poems: the oral-formulaic approach to the interpretation of West-Germanic verse*. Frwd. by Albert B. Lord. University Park: Pennsylvania State UP, 1988. (10, 11, 12)

Riethmueller, A. and F. Zaminer. *Musik des Altertums*. Laaber: Laaber-Verlag, 1989. (10)

Rice, Stanley. *Book design systematic aspects*. New York: R. R. Bowker, 1978. [Ill.] (8, 11, 12)

Richter, Michael. *The Formation of the Medieval West: Studies in the Oral cultures of the Barbarians*. Dublin: Four Courts, 1994. (4, 5)

Ritson, Joseph, 1752-1803, ed. *Ancient songs and ballads : from the reign of King Henry the Second to the Revolution collected by Joseph Ritson*. London: For Payne and Foss, by T. Davison, 1829. (12)

- - - , editor. *Ancient Engleish metrical romancees, selected and publish'd by Joseph Ritson*. London, Printed by W. Bulmer and Company, for G. and W. Nicol, 1802. (12)

Rives, J. B. *Religion and authority in Roman Carthage from Augustus to Constantine*. Oxford: Clarendon Press; New York: OUP, 1995. (4, 5)

Roberts, the Rev. Alexander and James Donaldson, eds. *The Ante-Nicene Fathers: translations of the writings of the Fathers down to AD 325*. 10 vol. Tertullian, v. 3 & 4; Clement of Alexandria, v. 3; Origen, pts. 1 & 2, v. 5. Rprt. Grand Rapids: Eerdmans, 1969-73. (4)

Roberts, Colin Henderson. *Greek literary hands, 350 B. C.-400*. Oxford: Clarendon, 1955. [Script Systems; ill.] (4, 5, 11, 12)

- - - and T[heodore] C[ressy]. Skeat. *The Birth of the Codex*. London: OUP, 1983. [Ill.] (2, 4, 5, 11, 12)

Robertson, Anne F. *Word Dividers, Spot Markers and Clause Markers in Old Assyrian, Ugaritic, and Egyptian Texts*. Diss. New York University, November 1993. [Punctuation Systems; Color coding systems; ill.] (2, 4, 5, 9, 10, 11, 12)

Robinson, Fred C. and E.G. Stanley, eds. *Old English verse texts from many sources: a comprehensive collection*. EEMF v. 23. Copenhagen: Rosenkilde & Bagger, 1991. [Facs.] (6, 7, 8, 10, 11, 12)

Robinson, J. M., intro. *Facsimile Edition of the Nag Hammadi Codices*. Leiden: Brill, 1972-1984. 11 + 1 vols. [Facs.] (2, 4, 9)

Robinson, Pamela, R., intro. *Manuscript Bodley 638, Bodleian Library, Oxford University: a facsimile*. Norman, OK: Pilgrim, 1982. The Facsimile series of the works of Geoffrey Chaucer; v. 2. (12)

- - - , intro. *Manuscript Tanner 346: a facsimile: Bodleian Library, Oxford University*. Norman, Okla.: Pilgrim Books; Suffolk, England: Boydell-Brewer, 1980. The Facsimile series of the works of Geoffrey Chaucer; v. 1 (12)

- - - . "Self-Contained units in composite manuscripts of the Anglo-Saxon period." In *Anglo-Saxon England*, No. 7. 1978. 231-8. (2, 5, 8. 11)

Robinson, Peter M. W. "Manuscript Politics." In *The Politics of the Electronic Text*. Warren Chernaik, Caroline Davis, and Marylin Deegan, ed. 9-15. Oxford: Office for Humanities Communication, 1993a. (Epilogue)

- - - . "Redefining Critical Editions." In *The Digital Word: Text-Based Computing in the Humanities*, George P. Landow and Paul Delany, ed. Cambridge, MA: MIT Press, 1993b. 271-91. (Epilogue)

Rolle, Richard. *Prose and Verse*. Ed. S. J. Ogilvie-Thomson. EETS. No. 293. Oxford: UP, 1988. (12)

Rolle, Richard. *Psalms from the English Psalter*. Commentary. Microform Edited from the MS Huntington 148 with notes and glossary, by Marjorie Orchard Collins. (10, 12)

Romano, Tim. "The Wanderer." www.aimsdata.com/tim/anhaga. 1999. [Plates] (12)

Rosenberg, Bruce A. *Folklore and literature: rival siblings*. Knoxville: University of Tennessee Press, c1991. (6, 8, 10, 11, 12)

Rosenow Company. *Book of type faces and interesting highlights on the graphic arts*. Chicago: Rosenow company, 1930. [Script Systems; Plates] (2, 4, 5, 11, 12)

Rosier, James L., ed. *The Vitellius Psalter: Edited from British Museum MS Cotton Vitellius E. xxvii*. Ithaca: Cornell UP, 1962. [2 Plates] (10, 12)

Rouse, Richard H. "Bostonus Buriensis and the Author of the *Catalogus Scriptorium Ecclesiae*," *Speculum*, XLI, No. 3, July 1966. 471-99. [Plates] (Intro., 2, 6, 11)

Rubinstein, Richard. *Digital typography: an introduction to type and composition for computer system design*. Reading, MA: Addison-Wesley Pub. Co., 1988. [Script Design; System Design] (Epilogue)

Russom, Geoffrey. *Old English Meter and Linguistic Theory*. Cambridge: CUP, 1987. (Intro., 10, Epilogue)

Russell, James C. *The Germanization of Early Medieval Christianity: A Sociohistorical approach to Religious Transformation*. New York: OUP 1994. (5, 6, 7, 10, 11, 12))

Saint Gall [The Handwriting of the Catalogs of Saint Gall.] *Die Handschriften der Stiftsbibliothek St. Gallen: Codices 1726-1984 (14.-19. Jahrhundert)* bearbeitet von Beat Matthias von Scarpatetti; mit einer Einleitung zur Geschichte der Katalogisierung von Johannes Duft. St. Gallen: Stiftsbibliothek, 1983. [Script Systems; 4 p. of plates; ill.] (4, 5, 10, 11)

Salmon, Dom Pierre. *Les "Tituli Psalmorum" des Manuscrits Latins*. Roma: Libreria Vaticana, 1959. I-80. (10)

Salter, Stefan. *From cover to cover: The occasional papers of a book designer*. Englewood Cliffs, N.J.: Prentice-Hall, 1969. [Book Design; ill.] (11, 12)

Sampson, Geoffrey. *Writing systems: a linguistic introduction*. Stanford, Calif.: Stanford UP, 1985. [Script systems; see also DeFrancis, *Visible*; ill.] (2, 4, 5, 11, 12)

Sanders, Henry A., intro. *Facsimile of the Washington manuscript of the four Gospels in the Freer collection*. Ann Arbor, Mich.: University of Michigan, 1912. [Facs.] (2, 4, 5, 11, 12)

Sanders, J. A. *The Dead Sea Psalms Scroll* [Q11Ps]. Ithaca, New York: Cornell UP, 1967. [Plate] (4, 10)

Santayana, George [Jorge Augustin Nicolas Ruiz de Santayana] 1863-1952. *The Life of Reason or The Phases of Human Progress*. 5 v. New York: C. Scribner's Sons, 1905-1906. (Epilogue)

Sawyer, P. H. *From Roman Britain to Norman England*. London: Metheun, 1978. (5, 11, 12)

- - -, ed. *Ernulf, Bishop of Rochester, 1040-1124. Textus Roffensis: Rochester Cathedral Library, MS. A. 3.5*. EEMF, v. 7 & 11. Copenhagen: Rosenkilde & Bagger, Pt. 1, 1957. [Facs.] (5, 11, 12)

Schaeffer, Claude F[rédéric]-A[rmand], 1898-1982. *The cuneiform texts of Ras Shamra-Ugarit*. London, Pub. for the British Academy, by H. Milford, OUP, 1939. [Script Systems; ill.] (2)

Schenker, Adrian. *Hexaplarische Psalmenbruchstücke: die hexaplarischen Psalmenfragmente der Handschriften Vaticanus graecus 752 und Canonicianus graecus 62*. Freiburg/Schweiz: Universitatsverlag; Gàttingen: Vandenhoeck & Ruprecht, 1975. (4, 10)

Schimmel, Annemarie. *Calligraphy and Islamic culture*. New York: New York UP, 1984. [Script Systems; ill.] (8)

Scholz, Bernhard Walter and Barbara Rogers, trs. *Carolingian chronicles: Royal Frankish annals and Nithard's Histories*. Ann Arbor, University of Michigan Press. 1970. (10, 11, 12)

Schuller, Eileen M. *Non-Canonical Psalms from Qumran: A Pseudepigraphic Collection*. Harvard Semitic Studies No. 28. Atlanta: Scholars Press, 1986. [Facs.] (4, 10)

Schmandt-Besserat, Denise. *How Writing came about*. Austin, TX: Texas UP, 1996. [Script Systems; Ill.] (2)

- - -, ed. *The Legacy of Sumer: invited lectures on the Middle East at the University of Texas at Austin*. Malibu, Ca.: Undena Publications, 1976. [Script Systems] (2)

Schwartz, Seth, "Language, Power and Identity in Ancient Palestine," in *Past and Present*, 148. August 1995. 3-47. (Intro., 2, 4, 11, 12, Epilogue)

Scragg, Donald G. "Accent Marks in the Old English Vercelli Book." *Neuphilologische Mitteilungen*, Vol. 72 - 1971. 699-710. [Musical Notation Systems] (4, 10, 12)

Segert, S[tanislav]. *A Basic grammar of the Ugaritic Language: with selected texts and glossary*. Berkeley: California UP, 1984. (2)

Serralda, Vincent. *La philosophie de la personne chez Alcuin*. Paris: Nouvelles éditions Latines, 1978. (10)

Seton, Lloyd and Hans Wolfgang Muller. *Ancient architecture*. New York: Electa/Rizzoli, 1986. [Ill., plates, figs] (2)

Setzer, Claudia, "Jews, Jewish Christians, and Judaizers in North Africa." In: V. Wiles [et al], eds. *Putting body & soul together: essays in honor of Robin Scroggs*. Valley Forge Pa.: 1997. 185-200. (4, 10)

Sharpe, Richard. *Medieval Irish saints' lives: an introduction to vitae sanctorum Hiberniae*. Oxford: Clarendon; New York: OUP, 1991. (6)

Shaw, Paul. *Letterforms: an introductory manual of calligraphy, lettering & type*. New York: Paul Shaw; Letter Design, 1986. [Script Systems; Plates; ill.] (4, 5, 7, 11, 12)

Shepherd, Margaret. *Learning calligraphy: a book of lettering, design and history*. New York: Collier Books, 1978. [Script Systems; ill.] (2, 4, 5, 11, 12)

Shoenfield, Joseph R. *Mathematical Logic*. Reading, Mass: Addison-Wesley, 1967. [Symbol-set Systems] (7, 8, 11)

Short, Ian, ed. *The Anglo-Norman Pseudo-Turpin chronicle of William de Briane*. [Historia Karoli Magni et Rotholandi.] Oxford: Blackwell for the ANTS, 1973. [Plate, facs.] (12)

Silva Neto, Serafim, 1917-1960, ed. *Textos medievais portugueses e seus problemas* [por] Serafim da Silva Neto. Rio de Janeiro: Ministerio da Educacao e Cultura, Casa de Rui Barbosa, 1956. [Plates, facs.] (4, 5, 11)

Simms, George Otto, notes & descr. *The Book of Kells; a selection of pages*. Dublin: Printed at the Dolmen Press for the Library of Trinity College, 1961. [20 facs.] (5, 11)

Simms, K. "The poet as chieftain's widow: bardic elegies." In *Sages*, 1989. 400-11. (5, 11)

Simms, Norman, ed. *The Word-singers: the makers and the making of traditional literatures*. Hamilton, N.Z.: Outrigger Publishers, 1984. (5, 10, 11)

Simon, Uriel. *Four approaches to the Book of Psalms: from Saadiah Gaon to Abraham Ibn Ezra*. [Arba gishot le-Sefer Tehilim]. Trans. from Hebrew Lenn J. Schramm. Albany: SUNY Press, 1991. (10)

Sims-Williams, Patrick. *Britain and early Christian Europe: studies in early medieval history and culture*. Aldershot, Great Britain; Brookfield, Vt., USA : Variorum, 1995. (4, 5)

- - - . *The Early Church in Wales and the West: Recent work in Early Christian Archaeology, History and Place-Names*. Oxbow Monograph 16, 1992. (5)

- - - . *Religion and literature in western England, 600-800*. Cambridge, [England]; New York : CUP, 1990. (5)

Sisam, Celia, ed. *The Vercelli Book: a late tenth-century manuscript containing prose and verse, Vercelli Biblioteca Capitolare CXVII*. EEMF v. 19. Copenhagen: Rosenkilde & Bagger, 1976. (11, 12)

- - - and Kenneth Sisam. *The Salisbury Psalter*. EETS. London: OUP, 1959. [Plate] (10)

Skeat, Theodore Cressy. "Early Christian Book-Production: Papyri and Manuscripts." *Cambridge History of the Bible,* vol. 2. Cambridge: CUP, 1969. 54-79. [Format Systems; Book Design] (4, 5, 11, 12)

Skeat, Walter William. *Twelve Facsimiles of OE Manuscripts.* Oxford: Clarendon, 1892. [Facs.] (5, 8, 11, 12)

Skehan, P. W. "The Divine Name at Qumran, in the Masada Scroll, and in the Septuagint," *Bulletin of International Organization for Septuagint and Cognate Studies,* No. 13, Fall. 1980. 28-44. (4, 6, 10)

Smalley, William Allen, ed. *Orthography studies, articles on new writing systems.* London: Published by the United Bible Societies in co-operation with the North-Holland Pub. Co., Amsterdam, 1964, [c1963]. [Orthographic systems] (Intro., Epilogue)

Smith, Hermann. *The world's earliest music: traced to its beginnings in ancient lands, by collected evidence of relics, records, history, and musical instruments from Greece, Etruria, Egypt, China, through Asyria and Babylonia, to the primitive home, the land of Akkad and Sumer.* Sixty-five illustrations. London: W. Reeves, 1904. [Ill.] (9, Epilogue)

Smith, Keith A. *Structure of the visual book.* Rochester, New York Visual Studies Workshop Press, 1984. [Book Design; Format Systems] (11, 12)

Smith, Morton. "Palestinian Judaism in the First Century," in *Israel: Its Role in Civilization.* M. Davis, ed. New York: Israel Institute of the Jewish Theological Seminary, 1956. 67-81 (4)

Socrates, *Ecclesiastical History.* PG. vol. vi, 8. (9, 10)

Solesmes, Monks of. *Le Graduel Romain: Édition Critique par les Moines de Solsmes, IV.* Le Texte Neumatique. Solesmes: par l'Abbaye, 1962. (10)

Solesmes, Monks of. "Codex 339 de la bibliothèque de Saint Gall (Xe Siècle): Antiphonale Missarum Sancti Gregorii." Solesmes: *Paléographie Musicale I,* 1912. [Facs.] (11)

- - -. "Codex 359 de la bibliothèque de Saint Gall (Xe Siècle): Antiphonale Missarum Sancti Gregorii." Solesmes: *Paléographie Musicale II,* 1914. [Facs.] (11)

South, Helen Pennock. *The Dating and Localization of "The Proverbs of Alfred."* Bryn Mawr, PA: Bryn Mawr Press, 1929. 1931. 104. (10, 11)

Southworth, James, G. *Verses of Cadence: An Introduction to the Prosody of Chaucer and his followers.* Oxford: Blackwell, 1954. (5, 10, 11, Epilogue)

Spadaccini, Nicholas and Jenaro Talens, ed. *The Politics of editing.* Minneapolis: University of Minnesota Press, 1992. (4, 10, 11, 12)

Spronk, Klaas. "The Legend of Kirtu (KTU 1.14-16). in Van de Meer and de Moor. 62-82. (2, 4, 10)

Stanley, E[ric]. G. *Unideal Principles of Editing Old English Verse.* London: Proceedings of the British Academy, 1984. 231-273. (Intro., 11)

- - - . "Translation from Old English: 'The Garbaging War-Hawk' or, the Literal Materials from which the Reader Can Re-Create the Poem," in *Acts of Interpretation: the Text and its Contexts, 700-1600: Essays in Medieval and Renaissance Literature in Honor of E. Talbot Donaldson.* Mary J Carruthers and Elizabeth D. Kirk, eds. Norman, OK: Pilgrim Press, 1982. 67-101 (Intro., 11)

Stevens, John. *Words and Music in the Middle Ages: Song, Narrative, Dance and Drama, 1050-1350.* Cambridge: CUP, 1986. 204-267. [Plates] (9, 10, 12)

Stevenson, James, 1901-, ed. *A new Eusebius; documents illustrative of the history of the church to A.D. 337.* Based upon the collection edited by B. J. Kidd. London: S.P.C.K., 1957. (10)

Stevick, Robert D. *Suprasegmentals, Meter and the Manuscript of Beowulf.* The Hague: Mouton (1968). (11)

Story, Charles Augustus, 1837-1907. *The fonetic primer, offering the universal alfabet and the science of spelling.* New York: Blanchard, 1907. (Epilogue)

Stratton, Charles Robert. Linguistics, rhetoric, and discourse structure. Thesis, University of Wisconsin. 1971. (10)

Sunyol, Gregori M. *Introducció a la Paleografia Musical Gregoriana.* Montserrat: Abadia, 1925. [Plates] (4, 5, 9, 10)

Susini, G[ian] C[arlo] [*Il lapicida romano*]. *The Roman stonecutter: an introduction to Latin epigraphy.* Intro. E. Badian; trs. A. M. Dabrowski. Totowa, N.J.: Rowman and Littlefield, 1973. [Script Systems; ill.] (2, 4, 5, 11, 12)

Svaren, Jacqueline. *Written letters: 22 alphabets for calligraphers; written out by Jacqueline Svaren.* Freeport, ME.: Bond Wheelwright Co., 1975. [Script Systems; ill.] (2, 12)

Swanson, Gunnar, ed. *Graphic design & reading: explorations of an uneasy relationship.* New York: Allworth Press, 2000. (Intro, 2, 4, 5, 11, Epilogue)

Sweet, Henry, ed. *The Épinal Glossary: Latin and Old English of the Eighth Century.* London: Humphrey Milford, 1883. [Facs.] (6, 11)

Swerdlow, N[oel] M. *Ancient astronomy and celestial divination.* Cambridge, Ma.: MIT Press, 1999. [ill.] 9

- - - . *The Babylonian theory of the planets.* Princeton, N.J.: Princeton UP, 1998. [ill.] (9)

Tanger, Gustav. "Collation des Pariser Altenglischen Psalters mit Thorpe's Ausgabe." *Anglia* VI, 1883, Anzeiger. 125-141. (10)

Tanselle, Thomas. "Classical, Biblical, and Medieval Text Criticism and Modern Editing," in *Studies in Bibliography* 36, 1983. 21-68. (Intro., 4, 10, Epilogue)

Tarragon, Jean-Michel de, O.P. *Le Culte à Ugarit: d'aprés les textes de la pratique en cunéiformes alphabétiques.* Paris : J. Gabalda, 1980. (2, 4)

Taubenschlag, Raphael. *The Law of Greco-Roman Egypt in the Light of the Papyri: 332 B.C. - 640 A.D.* 2nd. Ed. Milano: Cisalpino-Goliardico, 1972. (4)

Taylor, C. *Hebrew-Greek Cairo Genizah Palimpsests from the Taylor-Schechter collection: including a fragment of the twenty-second Psalm according to Origen's Hexapla.* Cambridge, Eng.: CUP, 1900. [Plates] (4)

Thackeray, H. St. J. and Ralph Marcus, trans. *The Jewish War, and other Selections from Flavius Josephus.* New York: Washington Square, 1965. (4)

Thibaut, Jean-Baptiste. *Monuments de la Notation Ekphonétique et Neumatique de l'Église Latine.* Rprt. Hildesheim; New York: Olms, 1984. [Plates] (9)

- - - . *Origine Byzantine de la Notation Neumatique de l'Église latine.* Rprt. Hildesheim; New York: Olms, 1975. [Plates] (9)

Thomas, Charles. *Christian Celts: Messages and Images.* Stroud, Gloucester: Tempus, 1998. (5)

Thompson, E. "The Benedictine Office." In *Godcunde Lar 7 þeodom. Select Monuments of the Doctrine and Worship of the Catholic Church in England before the Norman Conquest.* London: Lumley, 1849. 113-211, (12)

Thompson, E. Maunde, ed. *Facsimile of the Codex Alexandrinus, Codex Royal I. D. V-VIII.* 4 vols. London: British Museum, 1879-1883. [Facs.] (4)

Thomson, Samuel Harrison. *Latin bookhands of the later Middle ages, 1100-1500.* London: CUP, 1969. [Script Systems, plates; ill.] (12)

Thompson, Stith. *Motif-index of folk-literature: a classification of narrative elements in folktales, ballads, myths, fables, mediaeval romances, exempla, fabliaux, jestbooks, and local legends.* Rev. and enl. ed. Bloomington, IN: Indiana UP, 1989. (6, 8, 11, 12)

Thornley, G. C. "The Accents and Points of MS Junius 11." London: *Transactions of the Philological Society*, 1954. [Musical Notation systems; punctuation systems] (11)

Thorpe, Benjamin, ed. *Libri Psalmorum versio antiqua Latina: cum Paraphrasi Anglo-Saxonica, partim soluta oratione, partimmetrice composita.* Oxford: OUP, 1835. (10)

Tillyard, Henry Julius Wetenhall. *Byzantine Music and Hymnography.* London: The Faith Press, 1923. Rprt. AMS Press, 1976. (9)

Tinkler, John Douglas. *Vocabulary and Syntax of the Old English Version in the Paris Psalter.* Janua Linguarum series practica 67. The Hague: Mouton, 1972 [1971]. (10)

Tischendorf, Constantin von, 1815-1874. *Codex sinaiticus, the ancient Biblical manuscript now in the British museum; Tischendorf's story and argument related by himself.* 3rd imp.of 8th ed. London: The Lutterworth Press, 1934. (4)

Toon, Thomas E. *The politics of early Old English sound change.* New York, N.Y.: Academic Press, 1983. (5, 10, 11, Epilogue)

Tov, Emanuel. *Textual criticism of the Hebrew Bible.* [Trans. of Bikoret nusah ha-Mikra.] Minneapolis: Fortress Press, 1992. (4)

- - - . *The Greek Minor Prophets scroll from Nahal Hever: (8HevXIIgr).* With the collaboration of Robert A. Kraft; contribution by P.J. Parsons. DJD, v. 8 Oxford: Clarendon Press; New York: OUP, 1989, 1988. (4)

Treitler, Leo. "Oral, Written, and Literate Process in the Transmission of Medieval Music." *Speculum* 56.3 (1981), 471-491. (9, 10)

Trigg, Joseph Wilson. *Origen.* London; New York: Routledge, 1998. (4)

- - - . *Origen: the Bible and philosophy in the third-century church.* Atlanta: J. Knox, 1983. (4)

Tschichold, Jan, 1902-1974. *The form of the book: esssays on the morality of good design.* Translated from the German by Hajo Hadeler; edited, with an introduction, by Robert Bringhurst. London: Lund Humphries, 1991. [Book design] (4, 5, 11, 12)

- - - . *Designing books; planning a book; a typographer's composition rules; fifty-eight examples by the author.* [Authorized translation by Joyce Wittenborn] New York: Wittenborn, Schultz, 1951. [Book Design] (4, 5, 11, 12)

- - - . *An illustrated history of writing and lettering.* London, A. Zwemmer, 1946. [Script systems] (2, 4, 5, 11, 12)

Tschischiwitz, Benno. *Die Metrik der angelsächsischen Psalmenübersetzung.* Diss. Breslau, 1908. (10)

Turner, Eric G. *The Typology of the Early Codex.* Philadelphia: U of Pennsylvania Press, 1977. (2, 4, 5, 11, 12)

- - -. *Greek Manuscripts of the Ancient World* Oxford: OUP, 1971. [Script Systems; Facs.; ill.] (3, 4, 10)

Ullman, Berthold Louis. *Ancient Writing and Its Influence*. Julian Brown, ed. 2d ed. Cambridge, Mass., 1969 (1st ed. 1932). Medieval Academy Reprints for Teaching (Toronto, 1980). Cambridge, MA: MIT Press, 1969. [Script Systems] (2, 4, 5, 11, 12)

Ullmann, Walter. *The Carolingian Renaissance and the idea of kingship*. London, Methuen, 1969. (10, 11)

Upington, Henry. *An easy, rapid and compendious method of writing, perspicuous in the extreme, and adapted to the muscular capability of all*. London: Longman, Hurst, Rees, Orme, Brown, and Green, 1825. (Epilogue)

Ure, James M. *The Benedictine Office*. Edinburgh: Edinburgh UP, 1957. (12)

Urquhart, (Sir) Thomas. *Neaudthaumata*: *An introduction to the universal language*. Londn: G. Calvert & R. Tomlins, 1653. (Epilogue)

Van der Meer, Willem and Johannes C. de Moor, eds. *The Structural analysis of Biblical and Canaanite Poetry*. Sheffield: JSOT, 1988. (4, 6, 10)

van Deusen, Nancy. *The Harp and the Soul: Essays in Medieval Music*. Studies in the History & interpretation of Music, Vol. 3. Lewiston: Edwin Mellen. 1989. [Musical notation systems; ill.] (9, 10)

Van Dijk, Teun A. *Some Aspects of Text Grammars*: *A Study in Theoretical Linguistics and Poetics*. The Hague: Mouton, 1972. (10)

Van Kirk Dobbie, Elliott. *The Manuscripts of Cᴈdmon's Hymn and Bede's Death Song: with a critical text of the Epistola Cuthberti de obitu Bede*. New York: Columbia UP, 1937. (6)

- - - . *Beowulf and Judith*. ASPR, No. 4. New York: Columbia UP, 1953. (11)

. *The Anglo-Saxon Minor Poems*. ASPR, New York: Columbia UP, 1942 (11, 12)

Vansina, Jan. *Oral tradition as history*. Madison, Wis.: Wisconsin UP, 1985. (11)

Vervliet, H. D. L., ed. *The Book through Five Thousand Years*. New York and London: Phaidon, 1972. [ill.] (2, 4, 5, 11, 12)

Virgoe, Roger, ed. *illustrated Letters of the Paston Family: Private Life in the Fifteenth Century*. New York: Widenfield & Nicolson, 1989. [Facs.; ill.] (12)

Virolleaud, Charles, 1879-? *La légende phéenicienne de Danel*. Paris: P. Geuthner, 1936. (4, 12)

von Gleich, Utta and Ekkehard Wolff, eds. *Symposium on Language Standardization, 2-3 February 1991. Hamburg, Germany*: Unesco Institute for Education, 1991. (Epilogue)

Von Wulf, Arlt. "Aspekte der musikalischen Palaeographie," in *Palaeographie der Musik*, 1979. (9)

Wallach, Luitpold. *Diplomatic studies in Latin and Greek documents from the Carolingian Age*. Ithaca, N.Y.: Cornell UP, 1977. (10, 11)

- - - . *Alcuin and Charlemagne: studies in Carolingian history and literature*. Ithaca, N. Y., Cornell UP, 1959. (10)

Wales, Hugh G., Max Wales, and Dwight L. Gentry. *Advertising copy, layout, and typography*. Ronald Press Co., 1958. [Book Design; Format Systems; Script Systems; ill.] (2, 4, 5, 11, 12)

Walker, C. B. F. *Cuneiform*. London: Published for the Trustees of the British Museum by British Museum Publications, 1987. [ill.] (2)

Walter, Rev. Henry. *Doctrinal Treatises and Introductions to Different Portions of The Holy Scriptures by William Tyndale, Martyr, 1536*. Parker Society, Cambridge: CUP, 1858. (12)

Walton, Brian. *Biblia sacra polyglotta, complectentia textus originales, Hebraicum cum Pentateuch Samaritano, Chaldaicum, Graecum, versionumque antiquarum, Samaritanae, Graecae LXXII interpretum, Chaldaicae, Syriacae, Arabicae, Aethiopicae, Persicae, Vulgatae Latinae.* 1657. Facsimile: Graz, Austria: Druck, 1964. (10)

Warmington, E. H. *Remains of old Latin: newly edited and translated by E.H. Warmington.* Cambridge, Mass.: Harvard UP, 1959-1961. 4 v. [Facs.; plates] (3, 4)

Watson, Wilfred G. E. *Classical Hebrew Poetry: A Guide to its Techniques.* Sheffield: JSOT Press, 1984. (4, 10)

- - - and Nicolas Wyatt, eds. *Handbook of Ugaritic studies.* Boston: Brill, 1999. (2)

Watt, David L. E. *The phonology and semology of intonation in English: an instrumental and systematic perspective.* Bloomington, Ind.: Indiana University Linguistics Club Publications, 1994. (5, 10, 11, Epilogue)

Watt, W. C. *Writing systems and cognition: perspectives from psychology, physiology, linguistics, and semiotics.* Dordrecht; Boston: Kluwer, 1994. [Script systems; orthographic systems] (2, 5, 11, Epilogue)

Watts, Ann Chalmers. *The lyre and the harp; a comparative reconsideration of oral tradition in Homer and Old English epic poetry.* New Haven, Yale UP, 1969. (10, 12)

Weil, Daniel Meir. *The masoretic chant of the Bible.* Jerusalem: R. Mass, 1995. (10)

Weitzman, M. P. "The Peshitta Psalter and its Hebrew Vorlage." *Vetus Testamentum* 35, 1985. 341-54. (4, 10)

Wellesz, Egon. 1885-1974. *Eastern elements in Western chant. Studies in the early history of ecclesiastical music.* 2nd prt. Copenhagen: Munksgaard, 1967. [11 plates] (9, 10).

- - - . *Ancient and Oriental Music*, New Oxford History of Music, Vol.1. London: OUP, rprt. 1979; 1957. (9)

Werlich, Egon. Der westgermanische Skop: der Aufbau seiner Dichtung und sein Vortrag. Diss. Duisburg: Universitat zu Munster, 1964. (11)

Werner, Eric, *The sacred bridge; the interdependence of liturgy and music in synagogue and church during the first millennium.* London, D. Dobson; New York, Columbia UP, 1959-1984. (9, 10)

- - - , ed. *Contributions to a historical study of Jewish Music.* New York, Ktav, 1976. (9, 10)

West, M. L. *Ancient Greek Music.* Oxford: Clarendon, 1992. (4, 9)

Whalley, Joyce Irene. *English handwriting, 1540-1853: an illustrated survey based on material in the National Art Library, Victoria and Albert Museum.* London: HMSO, 1969. [Script Systems; Plates; Facs.] (11, 12)

Wheless, Joseph. *Forgery in Christianity: a documented record of the foundations of the Christian religion.* New York: Knopf, 1930; Rprt. Gordon Press, 1976. (4, 6, 10)

White, R. M., notes, and Robert Holt, ed. *The Ormulum.* Oxford: Clarendon, 1878. Rprt. New York: AMS, 1974. [Orthographic Systems; 2 facs.] (12)

Whitelock, Dorothy, ed. *The Peterborough Chronicle: (Bodleian MS Laud Misc. 636).* Appendix by Cecily Clark. EEMF v. 4. Copenhagen: Rosenkilde & Bagger, 1954. [Facs.] (11, 12)

- - -. *The Audience of Beowulf.* Oxford: Clarendon Press, 1951. (11)

Wichmann, J. "König Aelfred's angelsächsische übertragung der Psalmen I-LI" excl., *Anglia* XI, 1889; Halle, 1888. (10)

Wickham, Chris. *Early medieval Italy: central power and local society 400-1000.* London; New York: MacMillan Ltd., 1981 (3, 5, Epilogue)

Wieder, Naphtali *The Judean Scrolls and Karaism.* London: East & West Library, 1962. [Facs.] (5, 10)

Wiener, Joel H., ed. *Innovators and preachers: the role of the editor in Victorian England.* Based on the proceedings of the fifth CUNY Conference on History and Politics. . . held at the Graduate Center of the City University of New York on October 29-30, 1982. Westport, Conn.: Greenwood Press, 1985. [Plates; ill.; facs.] (12)

Wildhagen, K. "Das Psalterium Gallicanum in England." *Englische Studien* 54 (1920), p.35 ff. (10)

Willard, Rudolph, ed. *The Blickling Homilies, the John H. Scheide library, Titusville, Pennsylvania.* EEMF. v. 10. Copenhagen: Rosenkilde & Bagger. 1960. [Facs.] (11, 12)

Williams, John Ellis Caerwyn. *The court poet in Medieval Ireland.* London: British Academy by OUP, 1973. (5, 10)

Williams, Rowan. *Arius: heresy and tradition.* London: Darton, Longman and Todd, 1987. (4, 5, 10)

Williamson, Hugh Albert Fordyce. *Methods of book design: the practice of an industrial craft.* New Haven: Yale UP, 1983. 3rd ed. [Book Design; Format Systems] (2, 4, 8, 11)

Wilmanns, Gustav, 1845-1878. *Inscriptiones Africae latinae.* Berolini: G. Reimerum, 1881-1959. CIL v. 8. Pt. 1, 2 & Suppl., pts 1-4, 5: Rprt. de Gruyter, 1942-1959; 1960-1974 [Script Systems; ill., maps.] (3, 4, 5, 10)

Wilson, Adrian. *The design of books.* New York: Reinhold Pub. Corp. 1967. [Book Design; Format Systems; ill.] (2, 4, 5, 8, 11, 12)

Wilson, Edward, intro. and Iain Fenlon, music. *The Winchester anthology: a facsimile of British Library additional manuscript 60577.* Woodbridge, Suffolk: D.S. Brewer; Totowa, N.J.: Distr. in USA by Biblio Distribution Services, 1981. [Plates, Facs. illus] (12)

Wilson, Gerald Henry, *The Editing of the Hebrew Psalter.* Chico, CA: Scholars Press, 1985. (9, 10)

Wilson, H[enry] A[ustin], 1854-1927. *Calendar of St. Willibrord: from MS. Paris. Lat. 10837: a facsimile with transcription, introduction, and notes.* 1918. Note: Rprtd. for the Henry Bradshaw Society, Woodbridge, Suffolk; Rochester, New York: Boydell Press, 1998. [Facs.] (6, 11)

Wilson, Richard M. "On the Continuity of English Prose." In *Mélanges de Linguistiques et de Philologiques: Ferdinand Mossé in Memoriam.* Paris: Didier, 1959. 486-494. (7, 11, 12)

Wilson, R. M. *The Lost Literature of Medieval England.* London: Metheun, 1952. (10, 11, 12)

Wittgenstein, L[udwig]. *Philosophical Investigations.* Oxford: Blackwell, 1969. (Intro, 1, 4, 10)

Wiseman, Donald John. "Books in the Ancient Near East and in the Old Testament." *Cambridge History of the Bible,* v. 1. Cambridge: CUP, 1970. 30-47. (2)

Wolkstein, Diane and Samuel Noah Kramer. *Inanna, queen of heaven and earth: her stories and hymns from Sumer;* art com. by Elizabeth Williams-Forte. New York: Harper & Row, 1983. [ill.] (2, 9)

Wooley, C. L. *Ur Excavations: The Royal Cemetery.* Oxford: Oxford UP, 1934. [Plates; ill] (2, 9)

Woolley, Leonard. *The Sumerians.* Norton & Company: New York, 1965. [ill.] (2, 9)

Worp, K. A. *Greek Papyri from Kellis: I.* Oxford: OUP, 1995. [Plates] (2, 4, 7, 11, 12)

Wrenn, Charles L. "On the Continuity of English Poetry." *Anglia* 76, 1958. 41-59. (7, 10, 12)

Wright, Charles Darwin, *The Irish tradition in Old English literature.* New York: CUP, 1993. (5, 10)

Wright, C. E., *English Vernacular Hands from the Twelfth to the Fifteenth Centuries.* Oxford: Clarendon, 1960. [Script Systems; Plates] (12)

Wright, C. E., ed. *Bald's Leechbook: British Library Royal Manuscript 12 D.xvii*. With an appendix by Randolph Quirk. EEMF. v. 5. Copenhagen: Rosenkilde & Bagger, 1955. [Facs.] (5, 11, 12)

Wright, David H., ed. *The Vespasian Psalter: British Museum [Library] Cotton Vespasian A. I. Contribution on the Gloss by Alistair Campbell*. EEMF. v. 14. Copenhagen: Rosenkilde & Bagger, 1967. [Fasc.] (4, 5, 10)

Wright, H. C. *Ancient burials of metallic foundation documents in stone boxes*. Champaign, IL: University of Illinois, Graduate School of Library and Information Science, 1983. (2, 4)

Wright, Roger P. *Late Latin and Early Romance in Spain and Carolingian France*. Liverpool: Francis Cairns, 1982. (10)

Wulfstan, Archbishop of York, d. 1023. *Canons of Edgar*. Edited by Roger Fowler. London; New York: EETS by the OUP, 1972. [Facs.] (6, 11, 12)

Yorke, Barbara, ed. *Bishop Aethelwold*. Woodbridge: Boydell, 1988. (11, 12)

Zapf, Hermann. *About Alphabets: some marginal notes on type design*. Cambridge, MA: MIT Press, 1970. [Script Systems; ill.] (7, 11)

- - - . *Typographic variations: on themes in contemporary book design and typography in 78 book- and title-pages, designed by Hermann Zapf*; with prefaces written by Paul Standard, G. K. Schauer, and Charles Peignot, together with commentary notes and specifications. New York: Museum Books, 1964, 1963. [Script Systems; Book Design] (2, 4, 11, 12)

- - - and John Dreyfus. *Classical typography in the computer age: papers presented at a Clark Library seminar, 27 February 1988*. Introduction by John Bidwell. Los Angeles, Calif.: William Andrews Clark Memorial Library, U of California, Los Angeles, 1991. [Script Systems] (2, 4, 5, 11, 12)

Zeller, Otto. *Der Ursprung der Buchstabenschrift und das Runenalphabet: mit Faksimile-Wiedergabe der ältesten Runenalphabete und Runennamen*. Osnabrück: Biblio-Verlag, 1977. [Plates] (5, 7, 11)

Zettersten, A. ed. *The English Text of the Ancrene Riwle: Magdalene College, Cambridge, MS. Pepys 2498*. EETS 274. London: OUP, 1976. [2 plates] (12)

Zumthor, Paul. [*Introduction a la poesie orale.*] *Oral poetry: an introduction*. Trans., Kathryn Murphy-Judy; foreword, Walter J. Ong. Minneapolis: University of Minnesota Press, 1990. (10, 11)

Zupitza, Julius, ed. *Beowulf: Reproduced in Facsimile from the unique Manuscript, British Museum MS. Cotton Vitellius A. xv, with a Transliteration and Notes. 2nd Ed. containing a new reproduction of the manuscript, with an introductory note by Norman Davis*. EETS 245. London: OUP, 1959. [Facs.] (2, 4, 5, 11, 12)

Original Documents Cited

Académie George Tseret'eli
    Armazi Stele
Archives Nationales, Paris
    K2, no. 13
Baghdad, Iraq Museum
    Dudu, the Sumerian Scribe
Bardo Museum, Tunsia
    Phoenician Inscriptions
Beirut, Museum
    Yehaw-milk stele
Berlin, Staatliches Museum, [Berol.]
    P. 9875
    P. 13270
Biblioteca Apostolica Vaticana
    Gr. 1209
    Lat. 317
    Lat. 3225
    Lat. 3226
    Lat. 3256
    Lat. 3835
Biblioteca Ambrosiana, Milano
    Ms C. 5.
Biblioteca Medicea Laurenziana,
    Firenze
    MS 39.1
    P.SI 743, xi.1695
Bibliothèque Nationale, Paris
    Lat. 8824
    Lat. 10837
    Lat. 10857
Bibliothèque de Saint Gall
    Codex 339
    Codex 359
    Plan of St. Gall

Bodleian Library, Oxford
    MS Greek Class. a.I (P)
    MS Greek Class. C 21 (P)
    MS Greek Class. C 75 (P)
    MS Ashmole 1729
    MS Bodley 638
    MS Digby 133
    MS Hatton 20
    MS Hatton 48
    MS Junius XI
    MS Junius 121
    MS Laud Misc. 636
    MS Rawlinson B 503
    MS Tanner 10
    MS Tanner 346
British Library, London
    MS Add. 11669
    MS Add. 43723
    MS Add. 47967
    MS Add. 60577
    MS Cotton Caligula A.ix
    MS Cotton Claudius B. IV
    MS Cotton Nero A.I
    MS Cotton Nero D.IV
    MS Cotton Otho A. vi,
    MS Cotton Otho C.xiii
    MS Cotton Royal 12D.xvii
    MS Cotton Tiberius B.XI
    MS Cotton Titus D.xviii
    MS Cotton Vespasian A.I
    MS Cotton Vitellius A.xv
    MS Cotton Vitellius E.xxvii
    MS Egerton 613
    MS Royal V-VIII

British Library, London
    MS Royal 7 C.xii
    MS Royal 12 D.xvii
    MS Stowe 34
    P. Oxy. i.20
    P. Oxy. xvii 2075
    Pap. 131
    Pap. 229
    Pap. 733
    Pap. 825
    Pap. 1523
    Pap. 1527
    Pap. I.441
    BL Insc. I.441
    Rosetta Stone
    Siloam Inscription
Cambridge University Library
    MS Ii.2.4
    MS II.41
    MS Ff.1.6.
    MS Ff.2.38
    MS Kk.5.16
    MS Kk.v.16
    MS Pepys 2498
    T-S NS 275.27
Canterbury Cathedral Library
    Eadwine (Canterbury Psalter)
Chester Beatty Library
    MS 16
Corpus Christi College Cambridge
    MS 12
    MS 173
    MS 183
    MS 286
Durham Cathedral Library
    MS A.IV.19
Dead Sea Scrolls
    1QH [Thanksgiving Hymns]
    1QM [War Scroll]
    1QS [Community Rule]
    11QPs.[Psalms Scroll]
    11Q1 [PaeloLev]

    Mur. Ex: 4, 5 (DJD II, Pl. 1)
    Mur. Hymns
Edmund St. Bury's
    Catalogus Scriptorium Ecclesiae
Egyptian Exploration Society, London
    Oxy. P. 2103
Épinal Bibliothèque municipale
    MS 72(2)
Exeter Cathedral Library
    MS 3501
Freer Art Gallery (Smithsonian)
    Codex Washingtonianus
Fulda Landesbiblkiothek
    Cod. Boniface I
Giessen, Universitätsbibliothek
    Pap. Ianda, 90
Gonville and Caius College, Cambridge
    MS 234/120
Hayden Libray, Tempe Arizona
    MS Coptic Music
Huntington Library
    MS 148
Kellis Inv. P. 61.R + P. 65.D (6.i.321)
Landesbibliothek, Kassel
    MS Anhang 19
Laurentian Library, Florence
    Cod Plu. I.56
Leiden University Library
    Pap. 118 R
    Pap. I.400
    Pap. I.406
    Pap. I.411
    Pap. I.413
    Pap. I.414
Louvre, Paris
    Victory Stele of Naram-Sin
Magdalene College, Cambridge
    MS Pepys 2498
Manissa Museum
    Stele 101
National Library of Scotland
    Advocates' MS 19.2.1.

Rochester Cathedral Library
  MS A. 3.5
Royal Irish Academy, Dublin
  MS 12R33
Royal Library of Brussels
  MS 1650
Russian National Library St. Petersburg
  Bede Venerabalis [The Leningrad Bede]
Rylands Library, Manchester, England
  Pap. III. 458
Sardinia, La Mormara
  Phoenician Stelae
St. John's College, Oxford
  MS 154
Schaffhausen, Library
  Adamnan Vita S. Columba
Scheide Library, Titusville, PA
  The Blickling Homilies
Sociéte égypt de Papyrologie, Cairo
  I. 266
  I. 47446
Timgad, Algeria
  Vocontio Stele
Trinity College, Dublin
  MS 52
University of California
  Pap. 2390
University of Michigan
  P. 429, xi.212
  P. 430; frag.8
  P. 622

University of Washington
  Pap. Inv. No. 445 (+ Vindob 2)
  Pap. Inv. No. 14
  Pap. Inv. No. 317r
  Pap. Inv. No. 438
University of Wisconsin
  Pap. Inv. No. 5
  Pap. Inv. No. 8
  Pap. Inv. No. 19
  Pap. Inv. No. 24
  Pap. Inv. No. 26
  Pap. Inv. No. 32
  Pap. Inv. No. 37
  Pap. Inv. No. 38
  Pap. Inv. No. 42
  Pap. Inv. No. 46
  Pap. Inv. No. 58
  Pap. Inv. No. 68
  Pap. Inv. No. 69
  Pap. Inv. No. 79
Vercelli Biblioteca Capitolare
  MS CXVII
Verona Biblioteca Capitolare
  MS xxxvii
Vienna, Austrian National Library
  Pap. G.12.558
Warren Library
  P. Inv. No. 5
  P. Inv. No. 7
  P. Inv. No. 11

INDEX

Absent Voices

Ælfred's clerks cont.
221-230 ; use of wrong font 205, 224, 232,
239, 241; (*see also Old Joe Clerk, Wili*)

Ælfred's [Hi]story (*see Parker Chronicle and Laws*)

Ælfred's Laws sandwiched between Mosaic Code and
the Laws of Ine 243; (*see also Ælfred's clerks,
Parker Chronicle and Laws*)

Ælfric the Grammarian, and class three conformal
texts 134; as source for John Day(e) 254;
classification of vowels 112; Grammar as
model for semantics 170; *Grammatica* 275 n.
6, 281 n. 8, 289 n. 15; homilies 251; letter in
Hexateuch 252; name for a singing
congregation 284 n. 1; name for Psalms 191;
preface to his Latin Grammar 251; sigmoid-*s*
as marker of decay 251; *stæf* as pronunciation
12; symbol set from Ælfred to 217-221; use of
popular songs for Saint's Lives 165

Æschere, Hroðgar's figurative shoulder to lean on
234, 236 (*see also Beowulf, Hroðgar,
Wealþeow*)

Æðelflæd, Lady of Mercia, daughter of Ælfred 248

Æðelstan, Ælfred's grandson and godson, 216; 247;
first king of all England 247; *spraec* in Law
code 87; official voice 216-217; symbol-set
247, 248, 286 n. 11

Æðelstan, Ælfred's Scholar, 286 n. 3, as
author/compiler of "Beowulf" 287 n. 17

ae-ligature bigraph 116, 218; Dorbenne's distinctive
open-a + high-e in Schaffhausen Adamnan
101; for aesc in Willibrord Kalendar 102, 104;
in *Bangor Collectarium* 99-100; rare in early
texts 126

aesc Aramaic/Syriac model 126; as marker of aesc
scribal ideographs 204-; in ASPA 113; in
Caedmon's Hymn 137, 143; in *Épinal* Glossary
130, 131; in Futhorc 126; in Hildae
Abbess 102, 104; one of five monophthongs of
English language 99, 113; open-lobed 117;
open-lobe in *Leningrad Bede* 143, 145; small-
lobed 116; small-lobed in *Moore Bede* 136;
small-lobed reserved for only Old English after
stage 2 of codification 139

African half-uncial 71, official voice of
subordinationist parties 71 (*see also Insular
script family, Official voice of, Uncial script
family*)

African Rustic Book Rustic 278 n. 39; Capitals for
tituli 230; cursive Rustic-*A* 68; *cephalicus*
neume as left-hand leg 167; cursive in
Michigan Papyrus 430 68; cuneiform wedge
added as thick finishing stroke 4; elevated to
an authoritative script 55, 69-70; one of four
Latin script classes 67, 71; Public Rustic
Capitals 67; third problem with uncial from
69; triangular form as essence of *A* 25 (*see
also musical notation systems, scripts*)

Alcfrid of Deira 102

Agonal sense 169

Agricultural revolution 16; in Ancient Near East
16; in Northern climates 16; recorded in Bible
16

Aidan of Lindisfarne, 100; Bede's admiration of 85;
founder of Lindisfarne 100; wept for Oswine
223

Akiba ben Josef 48

Akkad, Akkadian colophon on tablets 148; deeds
of sale 50, 51; equivalent of a *scriptorium*
148; indentation of run-over line on right-hand
side 24, 241; location of 26, 27; modification
of Sumerian symbol set 28; hymn set 148;
Naram-Sin stele 34; punctuation by space 28;
religion as province of women 120; religious
music as control 147, 151; script differentiation
by domain 127; syllabic cuneiform 24;
use of xenographic exchange to distinguish
realms 92, 119, 158, 222; writing system 2-3
(*see also Enheduanna, punctuation systems,
Sargon I, script differentiation, xenographic
exchange*)

Albertus Magnus, letters as voices 12, 275 n. 7

Alcuin 186-194; classicization of Latin language
188; conformal state religion 187, destroy
native writing system 194; introduced singing
of the creed 187; letters 186, 187; meeting
with Charlemagne 186; new official script
188-190; overhaul of Frankish writing system
187-188; temporary replacement for missing
portions of the Latin liturgy 187 (*see also
Caroline script, classicization*)

Aldhelm, Bishop of Sherborne, 165; re-wrote songs
287 n. 22

Aldred a scribe of the Lindisfarne Gospels and the
Durham Ritual 218, 222, 285-6 n. 12

Absent Voices